Heat, Power and Light

To Tanya and Ruben

Heat, Power and Light

Revolutions in Energy Services

Roger Fouquet

Senior Lecturer, School of Economics, University of the South Pacific, Fiji and Honorary Research Fellow, Centre for Energy Policy and Technology, Imperial College London, UK

Edward Elgar
Cheltenham, UK • Northampton, MA, USA

Published by
Edward Elgar Publishing Limited
Glensanda House
Montpellier Parade
Cheltenham
Glos GL50 1UA
UK

Edward Elgar Publishing, Inc.
William Pratt House
9 Dewey Court
Northampton
Massachusetts 01060
USA

A catalogue record for this book
is available from the British Library

ISBN 978 1 84542 660 6 (cased)

Printed and bound in Great Britain by MPG Books Ltd, Bodmin, Cornwall

Contents

Preface   *vii*

PART ONE: INTRODUCTION

1. The Past, Present and Future of Energy Services   3
2. Energy Demand, Technological Change and Economic Development 11
3. Historical Data and Methods   28

PART TWO: THE PAST

4. Heating   45
5. Stationary Power   100
6. Transport   139
7. Lighting   191

PART THREE: ANALYSIS

8.   Producing Cheaper Services   219
9.   Consuming More Services   260
10. External Costs of Cheaper and More Energy Services   301
11. Policies Influencing the Trends in Energy Services   332

PART FOUR: THE FUTURE

12. Future Trends in Energy Services   349
13. Policy Discussion Related to Long-Run Energy Services   364
14. Conclusion   376

Data Appendix   *389*
References   *439*
Authors' Index   *459*
Subject Index   *465*

Preface

THE SEED

In the summer of 1995, Peter Pearson and I visited the BP headquarters in Finsbury Circus, London, to attend the launch of their Statistical Review of World Energy. Peter Davies was discussing future oil production scenarios. He then presented a now-famous graph of crude petroleum prices back to the days when Colonel Drake drilled into the Pennsylvanian mud.

The graph fascinated us. It mirrored one hundred and fifty years of the story of petroleum, which was revived in Daniel Yergin's (1991) book *The Prize*. It also told us that those peaks and troughs represented experiences of energy markets that had much to teach us about today, and that were relevant for the future. It suggested that the Oil Shocks of the 1970s were not so dramatic: perhaps the period was not such a major structural break, there had been other equally significant events in the past and it could be compared with other major shocks in the history of energy markets.

That graph catalysed us into searching for other statistics on the United Kingdom's past energy markets and showing their relevance for the present. Blowing away a little dust made us discover that a wealth of data lay in the bookshelves of British libraries and that we were not the first to unearth them for the benefits of energy economists.

We persevered, nevertheless, knowing there was more to learn, and in 1998 produced, under the benediction of the late Campbell Watkins, our paper on 'A thousand years of energy use in the United Kingdom' in *The Energy Journal*. It recounted the story of how the British economy made the transition from a biomass energy system to one reliant on fossil fuels. It also provided evidence of the long run trend in the nominal price of fuels, shown beside an index of the average price of consumables. One could discern, for instance, a phase of rising real woodfuel prices in the seventeenth century that made the Oil Shocks of the 1970s seem a series of minor events.

Almost immediately after the article was published, Denny Ellerman invited us to Boston to present the data on long run energy prices to the staff and sponsors of MIT's Center for Energy and Environmental Policy Research. He proposed combining the nominal energy price series with the average retail price series. The graph gave us a feel for the cost of fuels in the past compared with the present. Our ancestors had it hard. The discussion stimulated by the likes of Bob Pindyck, Richard Schmalensee, Paul Joskow and Hank Jacoby at MIT was inspiring.

Others also encouraged us to pursue. In the front row, as director of Imperial College's Centre of Energy Policy and Technology (ICCEPT), Dennis Anderson was a keen follower of our work, but quizzical about the direction. The research team there, including Tim Foxon, Robert Gross, Matthew Leach, Malcolm Grimston, Julio Pena-Torres, David Hart, Ausilio Bauen, Jeremy Woods and Adam Hawkes, were also excited by the results. In the same building at Imperial College, the environmental lawyers, Ray Purdy, Martin Hession, Richard Macrory, Stella Diamantidi and Kaveh Guilanpour, as well as Bill Sheate, were bemused by what some economists research.

Outside, more scholars stimulated debate and offered suggestions: Reinhard Madlener, Stanley Lebergott, Jean-Marie Martin, David Fisk, David King, Knick Hartley, Robert Ayres, Cutler Cleveland, David Stern, Richard Tol, William Nordhaus, Jess Tsao, Astrid Kander, Hannah Devine-Wright, Patrick Devine-Wright and Alan Morton. The British Institute of Energy Economists (BIEE) conferences and seminars were the main testing ground for the research – and benefited from the sharp minds of Gordon MacKerron, John Cheshire and Paul Stevens. The late David Pearce, another strong supporter of our work, convinced us to refine our MIT paper for the journal *World Economics*.

AN INDUCTIVE PROCESS

The research that went into this book followed in three phases. Up until 1998, Peter Pearson had managed to procure funding for my research assistance with university funds. It was to study energy transitions, which he had investigated in depth for developing countries.

My Ph.D. had been on modelling and forecasting energy demand in the United Kingdom. It was supervised by Peter Pearson and David Hawdon in the Surrey Energy Economics Centre (SEEC) at the University of Surrey. I learnt greatly from my supervisors, the members of the centre, especially Colin Robinson, Paul Stevens, Lester Hunt and the late George Ray, through his library on energy, and the visitors to the centre, such as Leonard Brookes.

When, in 1995, I came to Imperial College London, where Peter Pearson was then working, we combined our two fields and ended up exploring energy transitions in the United Kingdom – studying it as a developing country. My data collection and our efforts to understand what it explained produced fascinating results. The first phase ended with the publication of the paper in *The Energy Journal* in 1998.

The return from MIT marked the beginning of phase two. It was a bleaker time for our research. We were encouraged but faced the reality of needing funding. From the beginning, we had been preparing research proposals for funding from the usual suspects. The letters back almost invariably explained that the referees deemed the research worthy of funding but that the committees decided that due to limited resources the project was not prioritised.

The research project suffered a central flaw, in the eyes of the committees. Despite our efforts to argue for a direction, a question and a hypothesis, it was 'blue sky' research. It sought to look and see what would be found.

Much of twentieth century economic analysis has been based on a deductive approach – that is, we start with a hypothesis, gather evidence and test to refute (or, more frequently, support) our pet theory. At times, however, we can learn lessons about economic behaviour by first observing, then drawing conclusions – an inductive approach. After all, we are indebted to scholars, like Thorold Rogers and William Beveridge, who collected extraordinary collections of data about the past, without knowing what the research would unearth.

Without trying to put ourselves in their shoes, we humbly wanted to go against the grain by presenting first the facts, then the lessons. The main reason was that our analysis followed this order – we started by being curious and fascinated by the story of energy markets, afterwards we discovered how much understanding came out of the process.

Research is an inevitably risky and uncertain business. Yet, the 'knowledge industry' works against the inductive method so revered by gentleman-scientists and scholars of the past. At the beginning of the twenty-first century, the laudable desire to be accountable and efficient in the funding process has led to a bias towards supporting deductive reasoning.

The upshot was that despite wanting to continue this project, I had to accept research funding that focused on other interesting and valuable topics, and start lecturing. Peter Pearson's duties as director of the Environmental Policy and Management Group at Imperial College London were a more than full-time occupation. Our efforts on the project shrank. Slowly, we managed to put together the article for *World Economics*, which appeared in 2003.

ENERGY SERVICES

The article showed that, over the last five hundred years, the trend in real energy prices was not upwards; that is, in the long run, the economy was not faced with increasing scarcity. Another feature stood out – from the end of the nineteenth century, prices did initially shift to a higher level, before declining again.

Peter Pearson directed me to William Nordhaus' (1997) article on energy services. This offered a fascinating direction. His article showed how important it was to consider technological improvements when analysing a trend in prices. Over the long run, not factoring-in the role of technology would severely underestimate the reductions in prices to the consumer.

This could explain the leap in prices presented in our *World Economics* paper, not as increased scarcity but greater value. The consumer might be willing to pay more for energy, if it means getting a lot more from a new fuel or technology.

Invigorated, but not funded, we followed William Nordhaus' tracks by also looking at the price of lighting. We used our more detailed data to identify the dramatic decline in the price of illumination in England and then the United Kingdom. We were also interested to observe the consumer reaction to such a dramatic price fall.

In 2006, the resulting paper was published in *The Energy Journal*, again with great support from the late Campbell Watkins. It was awarded the *Campbell Watkins Award for Best Paper* in the journal that year. It is with great appreciation that Peter and *The Energy Journal* have allowed me to use a revised version of the article (as Chapter 7 in this book). This chapter should be seen as joint authorship. At the time, I also collected the data for a paper on transport services, which we presented at the BIEE conference in 2003, and was the starting point for Chapter 6.

THE FINAL PHASE

Despite more encouragement, funding for the project seemed as elusive as ever. A small notice at the back of the *New Statesman* in November 2003 provided the boost of funds and encouragement needed to turn data into information and then a book. David and Elaine Potter, the former being the founder of PSION, the computer company, saw our graphs, realised they were trying to tell a story and encouraged me to do so. Their Charitable Foundation provided a sum to help a single researcher get started on a book. Without it, this book would probably never have gone beyond a set of graphs.

A modest contribution was also given to me by the Kuhbier Legal Consultancy in Brussels, an organisation that ceaselessly pushes for a level playing field and defends the opportunity for small technologies to compete in European energy markets. It was definitely phase three of the project.

As well as needing to understand the graphs, there were still many gaps in the data series. Most of the data collection, throughout the three phases, was undertaken in London as a member of the Imperial College Centre for Energy Policy & Technology (ICCEPT) and Environmental Policy and Management Group (EPMG). As a centre of academia, London provided two invaluable sources of information for this research – for the history of technology, the Science Museum Library based in Imperial College London, and for economic history, the Lionel Robbins Library at the London School of Economics.

By the summer of 2004, most of the data had been collected and it was time to take the laptop somewhere exotic to analyse it thoroughly and start writing. Jeremy Woods provided the connection with the University of the South Pacific in Fiji, and my office, complements of Mahendra Kumar and the Physics Department, was not far from the swimming pool. These two crucial months allowed me to formulate the ideas and float them by energy and economic analysts in developing country issues, such as Jan Cloin, Emily MacKenzie, Malcolm McKinley and Jonathan Frankel, and later Biman Chand Prasad and Mahendra Reddy.

On return, a central European contingent was receptive to the ideas. Arnulf Grübler, who had done so much research on the diffusion of energy technologies in the past, invited me to the Gordon Research Conference to present the latest results. This also led to an exciting exchange of ideas with Marina Kowolski-Fischer, Fridolin Krausmann and Heinz Schandl at the Institute of Social Ecology in Vienna.

The main ideas associated with long-run trends were starting to appear. Over the centuries, people had found more effective and, so, cheaper ways of providing services (heating, powering, travelling and illuminating) with their limited energetic resources. This meant that they could generate more services, but how much more would they consume? In many cases, the innovations transformed and radically increased consumption of these services – revolutions in energy services.

The old debate about 'limits to growth' was starting to raise its dismal, yet fascinating head. It also led to a couple more questions: if the growth makes us better off, why not? Well, the environment shows the scars of market failures received throughout the history of energy services. With this in mind, what should we do about it?

The data required a lot more management and the trends far more analysis. Historians, such as David Edgerton, John Langdon, Peter King, Jon Newman and Hans-Rolf Sieferle, have been consulted on specific events, and their clarifications have reminded me that any attempt to analyse the course of events in the history of energy services would only provide a weak and inadequate explanation. Also, four anonymous referees for the 2006 article in *The Energy Journal* and two for this book made many valuable remarks. Naturally, they (or any other person mentioned here) are in no way responsible for errors in this book.

And, this brings me to the issue of joint authorship with Peter Pearson. As the director of a thriving research group, duties have pulled him in all directions, much of them related to managing many other researchers. Since my move, in the Spring of 2005, to the University of the South Pacific, I have been refining the ideas for the book and preparing the chapters. Once drafts were prepared, they were sent to Peter for discussion. It was apparent, however, that his obligations were too demanding to embark on this phase of the project. His absence was sorely missed and the final product is a less-rounded piece.

At that point, it was necessary to take stock and assess whether this was the work of collaboration or of a single author. In addition to our joint work in Chapter 7, he provided me with useful comments for Chapters 3 and 4. Despite Peter's role in sowing many of the seeds bearing fruit in this book and our previous work together, for which I am deeply grateful, in writing the conclusion, it seemed clear that this book reflected personal research, ideas and views that make me solely responsible.

Finally, I would like to thank my extended family, Marc, Maggie and Raphie, Joan and Yvon, David, Dörte and Alexandre, for their curiosity in this project. And, a big shout goes out to Tanya O'Garra: for her drive, which has pushed me to write when it was tempting to lie in the hammock and just think about these issues; for her critical faculties, which have been a sounding-board for many of the ideas; and her patience, which has been necessary to deal with my ghostly

Preface

appearance after spending too many hours staring at data and graphs about the past.

Please consume the graphs in moderation.

Suva, Fiji
March 2008

PART ONE

INTRODUCTION

1. The Past, Present and Future of Energy Services

1. REVOLUTIONS IN ENERGY SERVICES

Hydrogen-fuelled vehicles, climate-controlled cities or interplanetary business trips are all ideas worthy of a Jules Vernes novel. Yet, over the next hundred years, these transformations, or others, might actually unfold and will seem obvious in retrospect.

Two hundred years ago, electricity, central-heating systems or intercontinental travel would have been seen as far-fetched to all but the most enlightened. Similarly, five hundred years ago, the steam engine, railway travel or gas lighting would have seemed like miracles. Nevertheless, over the last thousand years, humans have harnessed energy sources in ever-more dramatic ways, through the adoption of radically-innovative technologies.

However, improvements are not inevitable. Roman Britons lived in conditions far superior to those of inhabitants five hundred years later. In the early modern period, road and river travel deteriorated for over one hundred years before new institutions found solutions to the problems. Prior to the Industrial Revolution, the cost of heating, power and lighting also rose for generations.

2. THE UNBOUND PROMETHEUS

All life depends on energy for survival and growth. Humans are warm-blooded animals that need to maintain their body close to 37°C for survival. Relative to their weight and size, they have weak and short limbs, meaning that they can move little and slowly. For sensory information, they are also highly dependent on their vision. A human alone, unequipped, generates sparse heat, can power and travel little, and is at the mercy of the sun for all but the most basic functions. This human would, therefore, have been shivering, weak, geographically-constrained and half-blind. For most of their existence, this has been the begrudgingly-accepted experience of life for the majority of humans.

Transforming the human condition has depended on harnessing more energy, more efficiently. Humans have needed to eat food to warm their bodies and power their muscles. Sunshine supplied heat and light. The ability to reproduce fire from organic matter, such as wood, provided further warmth and light, a way to improve the nutritional value of food, and a method to transform materials. Better management of crops ensured more food to warm bodies and fuel muscles. The domestication of animals supplemented that diet and increased the human potential to generate stationary and mobile power. The discovery of fire, agriculture and animal-rearing and the diffusion of the ideas and skills led to major improvements in human survival and the expansion of human population (Cipolla 1962, Landes 1969, Smil 1994).

Through time, new means of harnessing energy were developed. In the last two thousand years, the introduction of watermills and windmills, the development of the steam engine, or the expansion of the electricity network and its applications are spectacular examples. The Industrial Revolution was, amongst other things, a shift from the organic energy system to a mineral one (Wrigley 1988). Especially since the Industrial Revolution, humans have found ways to enjoy lives that are comfortable, powerful and mobile, as well as independent of the sun's rhythms.

3. CHEAPER AND MORE ENERGY SERVICES

The importance of the energy system within the current economy and its impact on the environment has generated a keen interest in identifying future energy consumption trends and in formulating policies that pursue the objectives of sustainable development. As guides to the future and to policy-making, analysts have presented a series of scenarios, including road maps to decentralized power, low carbon or hydrogen economies (Flavin and Lenssen 1994, Rifkin 2002, Geller 2003, Vaitheeswaran 2005). Inevitably, the future energy system, especially if it will experience radical change, is highly uncertain and subject to many complex forces. Nevertheless, it is likely to be heavily influenced by the interactions within and surrounding the markets for energy. Thus, a fuller understanding of these markets will also be a valuable guide to the future and to effective policy-making.

Throughout history, the demand for energy has been driven by the needs and wants for heat, power, transport and light. To provide these services, it has been necessary to combine energy with the appropriate equipment, be it a hammer with muscular strength, a harness with horse power, sails with the wind, or a train with steam, diesel or electricity. New generations of energy technologies have tended to reduce the energy used per unit of service provided – more heat, power or light has been generated from one kWh of energy (Landes 1969, Smil 1994). Also, evidence suggests that individual energy prices have tended to fall and then stabilise in the long run (Krautkraemer 1998, Fouquet and Pearson 2003a). Both factors have effectively reduced the cost of producing an energy service. In many cases, cheaper energy services led to a rise in the consumption of these services, which in turn put upward pressure on energy used.

Despite the importance of energy service demand, it has hardly been analysed, due to the lack of data. Furthermore, until recently there was a lack of awareness of even the broadest trends in the long run cost of energy services. William Nordhaus (1997) painted the first brush stroke by factoring efficiency improvements from lighting technologies and fuels into the cost of lighting services in the USA over hundreds of years. He showed how focussing only on the trends in the price of lighting fuels ignored much of the welfare improvements related to technological innovation.

4. THE PURPOSE OF THE BOOK

To contribute to this new awareness and understanding, this book presents trends in the price and consumption of energy services in Britain over the last millennium, and investigates the influence of economic and technological developments on these trends. It seeks to understand: what drives the declining cost of energy services? What creates the rising consumption of energy services? What are the welfare implications of these trends?

Many lessons for current and future energy markets can be drawn from observing past experiences. Price shocks have been common throughout the history of energy, and are likely to occur in the future. The Oil Shocks of the 1970s were not apocalyptic, nor unique, but rather an important chapter in the history of energy. They should be compared with similar events to better understand the forces that lead to energy crises.

There are many parallels between past and present energy systems worth studying: the successful uptake or failure of a technology; associated problems of technological lock-ins and path dependency; the concerns and fears about the expansion of energy infrastructure; concerns about security of supply; the importance of market structure; the processes that enable markets to externalise the costs of energy service production; and the tendency for governments to influence markets. Furthermore, by observing and analysing the rapid uptake of technologies and energy sources for the provision of energy services, an understanding can emerge of when and why radical change in the energy system occurs.

As well as insights and understandings, building on Nordhaus' approach, this book offers a framework for understanding the long-run trends in energy consumption. Forecasters of climate change need to cast their eyes one to two hundred years into the future. Their models are based on energy consumption for similar lengths of time. An effective way of studying trends in energy use is by studying the relationships, first, between energy consumption, technologies and energy services, and second, between energy service consumption, economic growth and the cost of generating these energy services. Identifying trends in energy service prices and use can help forecasters better understand the drivers for energy consumption and, therefore, improve their scenarios of greenhouse gas emissions.

Finally, a broad perspective will be useful for considering resource abundance and scarcity. The 'limits to growth' debate can only be addressed from a very long run vantage point. Meadows (1992) and Ehrlich and Ehrlich (2004) were alarmed at the growing appetite of the global economy. Lebergott (1988), Simon (1996) and Lomborg (2001) have highlighted the apparent dramatic improvements in resource availability, environmental quality and standards of living, many resulting from technological developments. It is hoped that this book will add to the debate about: which wins out, in the long run, resource scarcity or technological progress?

5. WARNINGS

Data Limitations

Such a grand undertaking needs to be presented with humility and care. Data has been collected from many sources, often of dubious accuracy. The data has then been brought together to form time series despite the lack of consistency (of geographic boundaries or units of measurement) between data sources. While efforts have been made to select data from reliable sources and create consistency, this has been achieved only enough to present a single series. The discussion may appear to be providing accurate data, when the evidence is based, at times, on qualitative information or assumptions.

Some might question the virtue of producing estimates of costs and consumption patterns, when their reliability is questionable. Hatcher (1993 p.572) raises specific concerns about creating a single national price index for energy products in early periods. These concerns are well-accepted.

Indeed, the reader should not be fooled by estimates for individual years or believe the data is representative of all British consumers. They are, at best, approximations, especially before the nineteenth century. The presentation of supposedly accurate data is to paint a picture. It seeks to give the reader a feel for the cost of heating a home in the sixteenth century, of lifting a tonne of grain in the seventeenth century, of travelling to London in the eighteenth century or of illuminating a room in the nineteenth century, and to compare these with the equivalent costs at the end of the twentieth century. The reader should focus on trends rather than individual years. The importance is the changes in the orders of magnitude.

Scope of the Book

While this book will not, of course, do justice to the richness and complexity of the underlying behaviour and data, it tries to introduce readers to the dramatic changes and trends in the price of energy that the British economy experienced in its stages of development: from an agrarian, traditional economy, bounded by the productivity of a scarce resource – a fixed supply of land – whose flow of outputs had to supply all basic needs for food, clothing, housing and fuel (what Wrigley (1988) calls an "organic" economy), towards a new regime freed from these

Malthusian constraints. In this regime, the prospects for higher growth and living standards were transformed by the exploitation of a stock of mineral resources, coal, and by technological innovations, including the steam engine, that enabled the conversion of heat energy into mechanical energy and drove the mechanisation, urbanisation and industrialisation that led first to the Industrial Revolution, and later – via the discovery and exploitation of gas, petroleum and electricity – to the modern, 'post-industrial' economy.

This study will focus on how the price of energy and technological change influenced the ability to provide heat, power, transport and light and how this ability, coupled with demand-side elements, drove the consumption of energy services. It should be emphasised that the author does not argue that over such a long period, with its interplay of changing economic, technological, social, political and demographic forces and institutions, a single 'model' underlies developments in energy uses. He does propose, however, that throughout this period the influences of economic drivers of supply and demand (such as resource availability, technological change, trading opportunities, income and relative prices) and processes of market development and adjustment are discernible and significant.

Furthermore, the book does not attempt to analyse the influence of changing technology and energy use on economic growth and development. Many distinguished scholars have addressed the issue, and it lies beyond the scope of this book (for an excellent overview, see Stern and Cleveland 2004, as well as Cipolla 1962, Landes 1969 and Crafts 2004). It is hoped that the research will be of interest to them and contribute towards future explanations.

Author's Limitations

This book is the work of an energy economist drawing on the invaluable researches of economic historians. Inevitably, an energy economist's focus on the past will be quite different from the historian's view.

Also, an examination of such a rich and complex subject over a thousand years will omit many issues and factors and is constrained by the authors' capacities and knowledge. The economist is more likely to ignore important issues, fail to respect conventions and make crude generalisations. It is hoped that the readers will forgive the author his shortcomings and appreciate the gains are greater than the losses.

The author believes that in countries with long energy and environmental histories, it is worthwhile for economists to explore the behaviour of markets, prices and institutions over longer periods than has been the custom since the first Oil Shock of 1973–74. Such a study can help illuminate the past; it can aid understanding of how we got where we are today; and – at a time of unprecedented environmental challenges – it may help us map the pathways to different energy and environmental futures. Wrigley (1988 p.6) notes that: "We cannot choose but to be the inheritors of the industrial revolution; we can choose to know our inheritance better than we do". And Horrell (2003) argues that while we cannot prescribe from history, "it offers a storehouse of guidance, pointers as to what might be relevant considerations on conditioning and shaping outcomes. ... A lantern on the stern can help with navigation ahead".

6. DEFINITIONS

Energy Services

Before presenting an outline of the book, a few definitions may help explain the subsequent discussion on revolutions in energy services.

'Energy services' discussed throughout this book relate to services that traditionally required large amounts of energy for provision. Many services, from hairdressing to financial management, have required relatively small amounts of energy. To provide them, however, the availability and cost of energy has little impact upon the price of the service. For heat, power (stationary or mobile, that is, transport) and lighting, energy has been important in its provision and a major expense.

Goods and services in economics have most commonly been distinguished by the latter being immaterial. So, energy and energy-using equipment are non-durable and durable goods respectively and heating, power, transport and lighting are the immaterial services that drive demand.

Here, both firms and households produce energy services. Alfred Marshall suggested that "in one sense all industries provide services. Man cannot create material things" (quoted most recently in Jansson 2006 p.5). Workers generate heat and power to transform materials into new forms. Although certainly not part of the service industry, these workers' and their firms' services are of interest.

Similarly, Gary Becker (1976) saw households as producers of services. He was especially interested in how individual members of households allocate their time towards the production of 'basic commodities', 'characteristics' or services. Throughout history, members of households have spent more or less time combining energy and equipment to generate heat, power, transport or light. Households are both producers and consumers of the energy service.

Finally, energy services can be provided by a separate company for the consumption of a firm or a household. The most common example of this outside production of energy services historically was in the transport sector, where haulage companies, stagecoaches or railways sold carriage. More recently, energy service companies (ESCOs) manage the production of heat in buildings. Given their relative novelty, they hardly feature in this account of the last thousand years of energy services.

Revolutions and Trends

'Revolution' is a term frequently used by academics for dramatic intent. Large declines in the prices of important commodities need to be highlighted. They certainly do not mean they are revolutionary. More important than the price changes are their impacts. Here, they have been characterised as 'revolutions' when major transformations in the use of energy services occur. Thus, while they generally result from substantial drops in prices, revolutions in energy services can also ensue from changes in characteristics, such as ease of use or speed of travel, or institutional structures, including new legislation or social norms. Despite the ability to quantify price changes in energy services, qualitative transformations also feature in this analysis of revolutions in energy services.

The other term relating to long run energy services is (possibly) the opposite of revolution, 'trends'. Indeed, the study allows us to observe the long run path taken by price and consumption. A revolution suggests a break in the trend. Yet, here, presenting very long run economic behaviour enables us to consider the trends in revolutions and the trends including the revolutions. Thus, revolutions become recurring events – cycles of economic transformation.

7. OUTLINE

The book is in four parts, each with several chapters. Part One forms the basis for the study of the long-run trends in energy services. The second chapter briefly reviews the key ideas related to energy and technology at different stages of economic development, to resource availability in the long run, and to the demand for energy services.

The third chapter presents a brief summary of the approach used to analyse long run changes in price and consumption. It focuses more on the general sources, especially related to population, economic activity, general prices and energy, rather than energy services, because too much information early on gives the story away. A detailed discussion of data estimates would be presented later, either in the heart of the text or, where they detract from the flow, in the Data Appendix.

Part Two presents the revolutions in energy services. They can be seen as four case studies (Chapters 4–7), each addressing the forces influencing the price and consumption of individual energy services. Because they all deal with energy, there is some interdependence between the 'markets' for heating, power, transport and lighting. Yet, each service has important features and an evolution that distinguish it from the others.

Part Three analyses these trends in energy services. Chapter 8 examines why the price of energy services has a tendency to fall. It focuses on the two central factors producing the services, the energy and the knowledge embodied in human or physical capital. Chapter 9 investigates three related issues. First, there is a summary of long run consumer responses to changes in income and prices. Then, the chapter looks at the underlying demand for heat, power, transport and lighting. It considers whether the rising consumption for energy services is only driven by falling prices and rising income, or other factors. Finally, it questions how beneficial are these revolutions.

Chapter 10 presents estimates of the external costs of energy service consumption. It points to the potential improvements and damage from these revolutions. It also tries to identify the long run incentives externalising and internalising the costs of energy services.

Chapter 11 touches on the deeper forces of economic change, the institutions creating incentives and the organisations forming some of the rules of economic interaction and their reaction to others. They are fundamental to understanding the long run transformation of demand and supply for energy services. In particular, that chapter addresses the role and influence of government on the evolution of energy services.

Part Four draws together the revolutions and trends experienced in Part Two with the understanding developed in Part Three. Chapter 12 uses the ideas in the previous parts to discuss some future trends and revolutions in energy services. Chapter 13 discusses the implications of the understanding of Part Three and the trends proposed in the previous chapter for policy formulation. Concluding remarks are made in the final chapter.

2. Energy Demand, Technological Change and Economic Development

1. THE DEMAND FOR ENERGY

To repeat, this book tries to understand the impact of economic and technological development on the price and consumption of energy services. An interest in understanding the co-evolution in economic development and revolutions in energy services needs to consider our current knowledge of these relationships.

This chapter starts with a review of efforts to model energy demand through its key explanatory variables. The review leads to a discussion of the role played by appliances and technology, including the process of diffusion and lock-ins. It is followed by comments on the importance of efficiency improvements and of 'rebound effects', and on energy transitions. The chapter then summarises long run studies of the relationship between economic development and energy consumption, and of scarcity associated with energetic resources and environmental services.

Since the early 1970s, there have been a growing number of empirical studies of energy demand to estimate how consumers would react to changes in economic opportunities and constraints, especially GDP or income and energy prices (see, for instance, Berndt and Wood 1975, Griffin and Gregory 1976, Pindyck 1979, Beenstock and Willcocks 1981, Griffin 1993). The estimates gave support to theoretical suggestions that income elasticities are positive and own price elasticities are negative. It would be impossible to present a summary of all empirical work on energy demand (for the United Kingdom, see Barker 1995, Fouquet et al. 1997, Hunt et al. 2003).

For industrialised countries studied, income elasticities tended to be smaller than one. Using both OECD and non-OECD countries, Judson et al. (1999) provided valuable insights into the Engel curve (or income elasticity). In particular, for the whole economy, they concluded that income elasticities were lower at low levels of economic development, rising substantially at medium levels, and falling at higher levels.

Reviews of elasticities from numerous different studies do not, however, enable the observer to draw many conclusions about the nature of energy demand – especially since they observe different countries, different fuels and different sectors. Aggregate energy demand is the sum of the different fuels being consumed by many separate and heterogeneous activities. For modelling purposes, therefore, energy consumption must be split into separate sectors: residential, industrial, transport, commercial, agriculture, and so on. Such a split more accurately represents relatively homogeneous groups. Most groups, however, can be disaggregated further (Baker 1991). The transport sector, modelled as one entity, explains little unless one sub-sector, such as the road consumption, dominates. Industrial energy demand disaggregates in a similar fashion.

As GDP rises, income elasticities in the industrial sector grows towards one, then (at about £6 000) falls towards zero. Residential sector income elasticity appears to be constant at about 0.5, until it reaches about £6 000 (or $9 000) and then drops towards zero or even becomes negative. Income elasticity of energy demand in the transport sector does appear to fall at higher levels of economic development, but only slightly – from 0.75 to 0.50 (Judson et al. 1999).

Even within homogeneous groups the importance placed on each determinant varies substantially between different classes of consumer. The amount residential consumers demand energy depends on the specifics of many variables: income, socio-economic and demographic characteristics, physical structure of the house, price expectations and appliance ownership and purchase. The reaction to, say, a dramatic rise in electricity prices for a large, wealthy family living in its own gas centrally-heated home differs considerably from that of an unemployed person based in a rented flat with only an electric heater for warmth (Micklewright 1989). Similarly, the response of a peasant family in their medieval hall to a change in prices will be quite different from that of the millionaire in his modern penthouse apartment.

2. ENERGY-USING APPLIANCES

Central to the variation in consumer responsiveness to changes in constraints and opportunities is the role of appliances (Baker 1991). Whether a reader requiring light or a driver requiring transportation, consumers need to generate services with their appliances. The appliances, whether lamps using electricity or cars using petrol, provide the services by consuming energy. In other words, energy demand derives from a two-step procedure: demand for a service, which an appliance provides by using energy.

Energy consumption, therefore, depends on the services required and the rate at which they can be provided. The preference function is based on individual taste. The rate of provision, however, is based on appliances' efficiency and can sometimes be obtained (or at least proxied). For example, modellers cannot predict where a specific driver wants to travel to, but can predict the fuel used to get there, as it depends on the car's efficiency, which is a function of the distance it can travel (all other things being constant) on a litre of petrol. Thus, economists have started building models of energy demand, in part based on the rate of appliance efficiency.

So, derived demand now features prominently in discussions about energy modelling. Without using micro data, however, it is difficult to work directly with an appliance variable, since each machine uses energy at different rates depending on appliance depreciation, embodied technical progress and level of services required. The vintage capital approach tackles the problem by assuming there will be a continual replacement of appliance stock, which embodies state-of-the-art technical progress. Every firm – and, to a lesser extent, households – will, therefore, have some new, efficient appliance and some old, less efficient ones. The rate of energy-use is approximated from the expected age and efficiency of appliance stock.

Alternatively, modellers, such as Manning (1988), may avoid directly using appliance stock variables; instead, they use a variable which influences the cost function. Through time, the cost of providing a service becomes cheaper, since increasing the efficiency of an appliance equates to reducing the quantity of energy required. Modellers simply introduce a variable that reduces the cost of energy as efficiency grows.

But, how does efficiency change through time? In the past, modellers have included efficiency or technical progress as a time-trended deterministic variable. Its growth, or annual rate of cost reduction, is constant. Technical progress, however, depends on research and development (R&D). R&D is a function of investment, patent life, industrial structure and chance. Being highly volatile and unpredictable determinants, technical progress appears to be more appropriately modelled as a stochastic variable. Harvey and Marshall (1991) include such a stochastic variable, generated as a random walk with drift in their energy model. But, this assumes technical progress to be only neutral. That is, it affects all cost functions equally, though, in reality, it does not. Through time, technical progress favours certain fuels or appliances. Thus, as efficiency rises in certain appliances more rapidly than others the cost of running them declines faster as well. Like Harvey and Marshall's, certain recent models show that an efficiency variable should be included.

Including such a variable aids in the understanding of energy consumption. Its omission causes the price variable to be biased upwards, because an increase in appliance efficiency effectively reduces the cost of providing a service relative to its price (Manning 1988). Furthermore, fuel price and total expenditure fluctuations alter energy consumption indirectly, by affecting investment in appliance stock, as well as directly. The inclusion or exclusion of an appliance stock (or efficiency) variable, generally, determines whether price elasticities estimated are short or long run.

In the short run, when consuming energy-generated services, individuals depend on a fixed set of appliances. Because an appliance costs dearly to acquire, but considerably less to run, it often provides the required service for many years, even when alternative equipment could provide the service more efficiently or using a cheaper fuel. As Waverman (1992 p.7) comments, the services are provided by "long-lived durable equipment". As such equipment may not be replaced until it stops working, full adjustments to fuel price or total expenditure fluctuations occur only in the long run. Thus, 'sticky' (or slow adjusting) markets for energy-using appliances further characterise the demand for energy.

3. TECHNOLOGICAL DIFFUSION AND LOCK-INS

So, when trying to understand the evolution of energy use, it is valuable to examine any initial responses, rates of adjustment to the long run (i.e. the adoption of new technologies) and to test for possible long-term relationships between energy demand and its principal determinants. The diffusion process of a new technology (and the separate phases) can be represented through the dynamics of (pioneer and follower) demand and supply curves. After a period of R&D, which can last many years, a firm may innovate or invent a new technology. This supplier presents the new technology to the market. In absolute terms, the introduction of the technology will experience slow growth. The consumers of such products can be seen as consumer pioneers. Provided the demand grows satisfactorily, increasing returns to scale and declining costs can be achieved. This also leads to additional supply entering the market, driving down prices further. This pushes up the pioneer demand and leads to a large demand from followers (Geels 2005a).

The main incentive for a firm to provide new products to consumers is in order to differentiate its products from competitors and, therefore, increase its market power and profits. In this vein, the firm might invest in R&D activities. Resulting innovations with promise are, then, marketed through 'niche market' awareness-raising campaigns, such as advertisements and demonstrations. The campaigns will focus on identifying improvements in the quality or novelty of the new products' attributes – in comparison with previous and competing models, products or technologies (Bikhchandani et al. 1992).

In addition to general economies of scale, several factors will affect the willingness to supply the new product: costs of financing (depending on the estimated net present value of the project, availability of credit, interest rates, creditors' perception of the products' risk of failure and sensitivity to exogenous variables); costs of production (including the ability to mass produce products rather than on-site production, markets for materials used in the production process and market for relevant labour); costs of distribution (involving the supply infrastructure in place or required; the size of the product; the ease of stocking product); and the costs of awareness raising (Stoneman 2002).

As well as the costs, the expected revenue, market share and product differentiation are key to increasing supply. This would include whether the product can be marketed as a luxury good; if it can, a luxury good allows the supplier to increase the wedge between the supplier's cost and the retail price, thus increasing the potential for profits.

If sales in the niche market are considered satisfactory, after the initial sales period, the firm will continue to promote its product with the anticipation of further growth. This may attract interest from competitors to supply similar products. Factors such as the existence of patents, licensing legislation or other potential barriers to market entry will influence the degree of competition and the firms' ability to raise prices. This will naturally influence the rate of growth of consumption (Geels 2005b).

Joseph Schumpeter led the way in the economic analysis of technological change. He considered technological change as a process starting from invention to development to diffusion. In the 'invention' stage, new ideas were generated in the laboratory. Then, the applications were refined for customer use and then sold on the market for new goods. The diffusion stage involved the successful spread of the good or service through the economy. While the invention and development stages are crucial, economic analysis is more relevant to the diffusion stages where market forces of demand and supply play a greater role (Stoneman 2002).

Analysis of diffusion was refined with the introduction of epidemic models. The uptake of new goods or technologies in the past has been seen to follow an S-shaped curve. They represent the diffusion process as similar to the spread of infectious disease, where information about the new technology is like a 'disease', spreading from 'infected' individuals to 'uninfected' members of the population. The assumption is that, once they receive the information, potential customers will buy the new product. The rate of adoption follows the cascade effect of new information, at a rate that follows the 'logistic' S-shape curve. In other words, the standard diffusion is for the new technology to be adopted at first gradually and then with greater speed, until, beyond a threshold, the market is saturated. The plateau of the curve indicates the maximum potential for each technology, determined by the technical capabilities of the technology and the maximum size of the market (Stoneman 2002).

The stylised growth rates were supported by empirical research. They included studies on the diffusion of hybrid corn in the USA (Griliches 1957) on the diffusion of industrial innovations (Mansfield 1968) and on the diffusion of televisions throughout UK households (Bain 1964).

Many subsequently questioned the simplistic assumptions, the limited number of variables considered and the unrealistic treatment of information acquisition process (Stoneman 2002). New models incorporated a broader range of variables and decision-making processes of adopters. For instance, adopter characteristics influenced rate of adoption. More evolutionary models represented the diffusion process as endogenously driven and subject to bounded rationality (Sarkar 1998).

Numerous historians have explored the adoption of new technologies related to energy and considered the role technology played in driving economic development (Grübler 1998). These studies highlight the prominence of energy production, distribution and especially use in the history of major technological revolutions. Windmills and watermills were central to economic growth in the late Middle Ages (White 1941, Langdon 1991). Abraham Darby's invention, enabling iron smelters to use coke rather than charcoal, radically changed the economics and geography of iron-making (Hammersley 1973). The monumental steam engine, turning coal-generated heat into power, drove the Industrial

Revolution (von Tunzelmann 1978). Energy has provided many fascinating and valuable case studies to study technological change (Smil 1994).

Technological historians have used energy statistics to explore the factors that lead to innovation and to adoption, as well as the implications. They argue that much of the experiences of energy markets cannot be divorced from the technologies and appliances that convert the sources into services. And, implicit in the experiences are the continual attempts to improve the technologies and deliver better services (Rosenberg 1994). They also remind us that these improvements take place within an economic, political, social and cultural setting, and when economists try to make generalisations and extrapolate from past trends, they tend to ignore the settings (von Tunzelman 1978).

At the same time, technological historians have over the past twenty years been placing these improvements back within an economic context, showing that the agents responsible for the inventions and their diffusions are subject to incentives (Dosi et al. 1988). Numerous scientific and engineering developments led to major savings in the factors and, therefore, the costs of production. Particularly with process innovations, these have meant labour savings (Landes 1969), improvements in energy efficiency and shifts away from organic to mineral fuels (Wrigley 1988). The increased output and declining costs resulting from new technologies have, in turn, freed up resources for other pursuits. Thus, the economy has greatly benefited from both 'gap-filling' (or micro) inventions, which generate clearer productivity gains, and 'door-opening' breakthroughs (or macro inventions), which enable the economy to shift into new systems and avoid the diminishing returns associated with micro inventions (Mokyr 1990).

A rich array of energy technologies have been examined by Arnulf Grübler et al. (1999). As part of their generalisation about the up-take of new technologies, they identify two processes – diffusion and substitution. First, a technology can create a whole new market. Second, a technology can replace old ones in an existing market. Often, however, a technology can be involved in both. For instance, cars replaced trains as a vehicle for transport services, yet, they provided many new characteristics as well, redefining mobility.

Grübler et al. (1999) also point to the declining costs of technologies and the services they provide. At high costs, the technologies are appropriate only for niche markets and special demands. Then, as the costs fall, a pervasive diffusion takes place, in the case of successful technologies. Its pervasiveness leads to saturation, yet, in this stage, often costs can fall much further.

The trend in costs is often called the 'learning curve'. If sales in the niche market are sufficient, the unit costs of production are likely to fall. The 'progress ratio', which reflects the percentage decline in product price for every doubling in production, tends to be in the range of 70 percent and 90 percent (Dutton and Thomas 1984). For example, the model T Ford had a progress ratio of 86.6 percent, meaning that its price dropped by 13.4 percent for every doubling in output. The declining costs can also be the source of competition with incumbent technologies. This dynamic tension is often called the 'sailing ship effect', as the introduction of the steam ship was believed to have driven sailing ship companies to become more competitive, improving their efficiency and dropping prices (Grübler et al. 1999).

Grübler et al. (1999) propose three factors that are common features of successful technologies. First, a 'learning curve' implies that the costs decline. Second, the uptake model (that is, diffusion/substitution) represents the successful growth and dominance of the technology. Third, they also propose that 'technological clusters' are crucial to success, dominance and ultimately 'lock-ins' (that is, because of its pervasiveness, the technology and its cluster stifle new competition in that energy system or economy).

Technologies that form a cluster work together and support each other. The synergies across technologies imply positive externalities. An important type of technology that promotes technological clusters is infrastructure, which creates a network. The 'network effect' reduces the costs of technologies within the cluster, and increases the costs of incompatible ones. The growth of the railroads helped the expansion of the telegraph network. Increased use of telegraph services made it profitable to set up new railway tracks. Thus, compatible technologies co-evolve (Grübler et al. 1999).

Clusters imply that individual technologies developed in the same epoch as compatible technologies are likely to experience faster declines in their costs and to successful penetrate the intended market. An individual technology not forming part of a cluster will be less likely to successfully penetrate the market. It also means that they are likely to remain dominant longer, due to 'lock-ins', than if not part of a cluster.

This reminds us that no technology is destined to succeed, and circumstances can help it along its development path. Successful technologies depend on favourable complementary developments at different levels of the economic, technological and social systems (Geels 2002, 2005a).

The literature on the 'social shaping of technology' argues against technological determinism. It proposes that many paths can be taken and choices (conscious or not) made influence the path followed. Thus, society plays an important role in making choices that steer a technology's path (Williams and Edge 1996).

In particular, they propose that the development and the exact nature of technologies can be seen as a struggle between different organisations. Especially in the early stages of development, individual groups, such as marketing companies, given the role of awareness and information, can be crucial to the uptake of a particular technology. The final shape that a technology forms will, therefore, be moulded by different interest groups (Williams and Edge 1996).

4. ENERGY EFFICIENCY AND THE REBOUND EFFECT

Other features direct the evolution of technological development. The maximum potential diffusion for a technology (either to improve energy efficiency or to switch to a new source of energy) refers to estimates that are limited only by the technical capabilities of the technology and the maximum size of the market. Yet, many constraints stand in the way of reaching these maximum potentials.

The constraints will inevitably vary across sectors, companies and activities within companies. Generalising for so much heterogeneity can become difficult, although some attempts have been made (Reddy 1991). Much of the existing literature on constraints has looked at the 'efficiency gap', being the difference between the actual level of investment in energy efficiency and the level that would be most beneficial to the user. The gap is associated with two main factors, market failures and barriers (De Canio 1998, Brown 2001).

There are numerous situations where the market incentives fail to encourage improvements. Problems of 'principal-agent' theory, where the investor and the beneficiary of the savings are different, mean that the incentives to improve efficiency do not reflect the gains (Jaffe and Stavins 1994). Or, investors may be lacking the necessary information to make the ideal decision (Eyre 1997). Also, discount rates are often too high – discouraging activities that will take time to recuperate the investment (Hassett and Metcalf 1993). Another problem is the difficulty for low-income households and small firms to gain access to capital markets (Sutherland 1996). There may also be considerable uncertainty about key economic variables, such as future fuel prices, which are important for determining the savings made from an investment. Alternatively, there could be hidden costs. Finally, taxes and other regulation frequently distort incentives away from efficiency investments.

Market barriers do not focus on perverse economic incentives, but more on organisational or behavioural issues. Psychological barriers, limitations on people's ability to assess the benefits of investment, the form of the information on investments or the credibility of the informer can hinder decisions (Stern 1992). Another issue is that the rate of return expected for efficiency investments in companies appears to be consistently higher than for return on traditional capital investments (DeCanio 1993). Also, the social or cultural context within which decisions are made can positively or negatively influence households or managers in firms (Shove 1998). For example, this might relate to the structure of energy research and development (Lutzenhiser and Shove 1999) or to how previous experiences of related decisions will influence future ones.

In other words, numerous factors exist that limit the introduction of a technology, even when there is meant to be a direct financial gain, such as from lower expenditure on energy and, hence, a private benefit from these investments. These constraints can reduce the potential growth in the use of higher efficiency technology and, therefore, their market penetration.

Barriers can limit the total uptake of a new technology. They can slow its introduction. Despite potential barriers to the uptake of new technologies, when more energy-efficient appliances are bought, they reduce the amount of energy required per unit of service generated and effectively reduce the cost of producing energy services. It can be expected that they lead to reductions in energy consumption.

This expectation is tempered by the 'rebound effect', which was first observed by Stanley Jevons in relation to coal consumption in the 1860s – that is, an improvement in efficiency may lead to an increase in energy consumption (Khazzoom 1980, 1987, Brookes 1990, Grubb 1990, Saunders 1992, Herring 2000). It can be broken into at least three parts. First, in the direct effect, the efficiency improvement reduces the price of energy services and encourages a greater consumption of energy services. Overall, energy use would increase if the price elasticity of demand for services was greater than one – because then the increase in consumption of services and of energy would be larger than the decline in energy savings.

Second, in the indirect effect, the efficiency improvement reduces the price of energy services which enables consumers to spend more on other goods and services, which requires more energy to produce. Third, in economy-wide effect, cheaper energy services reduce the costs of producing many goods and services and, therefore, stimulate the economy, including energy-intensive industries. This boosts GDP and income levels, increasing the demand for energy services.

Much of the theoretical analysis of the 'rebound effect' has made two assumptions, limiting the nature and size of the feedback (Binswanger 2001). First, studies have often assumed that no substitutes exist for the service. Including substitutes for, say, car transport (such as riding a train) implies that proper consideration must be made for both the substitution and income effect. Strong substitutes imply that a large energy efficiency improvement in car use and the price of car transport will encourage a switch away from rail travel (implying an important substitution effect). The income effect depends on the proportion of the household's budget spent on the service and the tendency to spend a greater proportion of the budget on the service as income rises. Lovins (1988) argues that the income effect would be negative for car use, because it is an inferior leisure service. He suggested that energy efficiency improvements made people richer, encouraging them to pursue other, less energy-intensive activities and reducing the 'rebound effect'. While it may be empirically accurate, there is no reason to assume that all energy services are inferior services. Allowing substitution between services allows for a wider range of 'rebound effects' according to the size of the substitution effect and the sign and size of the income effect.

Second, studies often assume that energy is the only input in the production of the service. Yet, the service is provided through combining energy with equipment and, at times, a person's time. Newell et al. (1998) found that the nature of the technical change depended on energy prices. High prices tended to encourage energy efficiency improvements. Lower prices led to other technological change, especially related to time saving. Also, they find that these changes tend to require additional energy, implying a substitution towards a more energy-intensive production of the service. This substitution is compounded by the reduction in the price of the service and the 'rebound effect' related to time efficiency, which increases the consumption of energy further.

Greening et al. (2000) have brought together an extensive array of estimates of the rebound effect associated with energy efficiency improvements. They find that, while estimates vary greatly, the rebound effect is almost always less than the efficiency savings. So, an efficiency improvement tends to reduce energy consumption.

The studies brought together tend to focus on relatively recent cases of efficiency improvements. Mostly, these examples estimate the impact of 'micro' improvements. While modest changes tend to make up the majority of cases, radical (or 'macro') innovations are likely to exhibit different reactions from consumers, and deserve a separate analysis.

Ayres (2005) argues that more revolutionary changes in efficiency tend to feed through into larger energy consumption. He suggests that, whereas more mature industries tended to achieve energy savings, improvements early in an industry's development have generated large rebound effects.

5. ENERGY TRANSITIONS

In the context of energy, technological diffusion will either lead to efficiency improvements or switches between sources. While transitions exist between many different energy sources, the most dramatic and potentially destabilising for the economy has been the switch between traditional and commercial fuels.

In human history, two main energy systems have existed. The first can be called the organic energy system. For heat, it depended on biomass fuels, for power on muscle and then the force of wind and water, for transportation, again muscles, and for lighting, fats, either vegetable or animal. Because the energy resources were generated by mostly indirect solar radiation, in the form of the plants, animals and the hydrological circuit, flow of energy in any region was limited. This flow dictated the maximum energy supply. Given that land surface provided a source for capturing the sun, elements of the organic energy system were always in competition with one another – especially, agricultural and forest land (Pearson 1988, Leach 1992, Krausmann et al. 2003).

In periods of economic and population growth, the economy faced tensions between these two needs. These limits of flow and the tensions created strong limits to the potential growth of an economy. The only way to increase consumption of the service provided was by increasing the supply – capturing more sunlight, in its indirect forms – or by improving the efficiency of the energy technology, generating more energy services with the same flow of energy (Barnes and Floor 1996).

People's livelihoods have become strained by the lack of energy. Similarly, their health has been put at considerable risk. Also, inefficient equipment has increased the financial or time costs of energy use, implying a greater likelihood of lacking energy (Barnes and Floor 1996). Substantial rigidities and failures in organic energy markets mean that security of supply concerns have often been greater than in more commercial energy systems.

The second system can be described as the modern or mineral energy system. Instead of depending on the flow of energy from the sun, an economy can use stocks of fossil fuels, created from millions of years of decaying plants capturing indirect solar radiation. The main difference has been that this source was underground, rather than on the surface, thus considerably reducing the tension between fuel supply and agricultural production. Also, given the millions of years of accumulated fossils (or minerals), the stock of fuels was potentially very large. Finally, mineral supplies have tended to be associated with more developed markets.

While energy transitions tend to shift from traditional (that is, organic) to commercial (that is, mineral) markets, there is no rule about the process, nature or speed. For instance, some economies complete the transition in a couple of decades, as in the United States (Schurr and Netschert 1960), or a couple of centuries, as in Britain (Fouquet and Pearson 1998). Also, some parts of the energy system can remain heavily dependent on organic fuels, while other parts have long since switched to mineral fuels. It depends mostly, but not exclusively, on technological capabilities, economic incentives and institutional structures (Pearson 1988, Barnes and Floor 1996).

Another crucial factor has been economic well-being and development. Higher income levels have tended to be associated with more commercial fuels. Up to a point, agrarian economies have functioned relatively successfully within an organic system. The expansion of industrial sectors has required substantial amounts of energy that put strains on land-based resources. For example, Wrigley (1988) suggested that by 1800 to meet the British economy's energy demands with woodfuel, a forest the size of Britain would have been needed to be harvested each year.

6. ECONOMIC DEVELOPMENT AND ENERGY USE

Inevitably, energy consumption per capita and per unit of GDP changes at different stages of economic development. The evolution of energy use for a whole economy will depend on (and interact with) economic, social, demographic and technological activities and resource constraints. Long run adjustments to changes in output, income, prices, technology or climate can only be made gradually as new appliance stocks are accumulated and used.

Most studies seeking to understand energy use at new stages of economic development focus on cross-sectional analysis (Medlock and Soligo 2001). They suffer from inevitable limitations relating to differing economic and institutional structures. For instance, Judson et al. (1999) indicate that 96.5 percent of the variation in total apparent energy consumption was due to an individual country's characteristics. They find that, despite taking account of per-capita income, the USA's energy consumption is relatively high – and the reasons are that Americans drive great distances and own large, air-conditioned houses.

Long run studies of individual countries are especially valuable for a deeper understanding of the evolution of energy consumption at different stages of economic development. A few have provided evidence on the relationship between economic development and energy use (Schurr and Netschert 1960, Humphrey and Stanislaw 1979, Ray 1979, 1983, and Martin 1988).

Humphrey and Stanislaw (1979) and Martin (1988) examine energy intensity (that is, the energy use to GDP ratio) in the United Kingdom over the last two centuries, highlighting how, after a dramatic rise in the first half of the nineteenth century, the intensity fell. They attempt to stylise the changes in energy consumption associated with the transformation from an agrarian to an industrial to a service-based economy.

To describe the stylised relationship between energy use and the three different stages of economic development, it is worth commenting on the nature of their growth. Agrarian economies tend to grow slowly. When economic growth takes places it is often driven by increased productivity in the agricultural sector. These improvements can generate increased population, which in turn creates greater demand for agricultural products. This leads to a growth in the demand for energy. Nevertheless, the agricultural sector is not seen as energy-intensive, so economic growth in agrarian economy might be expect to lead to less than proportional increases in energy consumption.

Industrialisation involves the manufacture of products rather than the harvesting of crops. Manufacturing combines organic, mineral and man-made materials, often found in disparate locations. Acquiring organic materials would demand similar efforts to crop harvesting. Collecting mineral resources needs extraction – digging and hauling. Then, the disparately located materials need to be brought together. Once under one roof, the raw materials must be transformed into the desired product, such as metals, cement or glass. Large quantities of energy are required to extract, move and transform raw materials into a final product.

Other features that characterise an industrialising economy are a greater use of technology, rising personal wealth and disposable income, expanding and improving distribution and trade networks, rising and then stabilising population (declining mortality rates, then slowing fertility rates), migration from rural to urban areas and back to more rural areas (that is, there is an increased and then decreased density of population in certain areas). Many of the features tend to increase the demand for energy, either directly or indirectly. Therefore, during industrialisation, energy consumption tends to grow at a faster rate than the overall economy.

In the third phase of economic development, an economy's service sector is meant to expand. Most services depend to a great extent on human input, through the application of skills, rather than physical labour. It is, therefore, commonly accepted that post-industrial economies increase at a faster rate than their energy requirements.

To summarise, the relationship between economic development and energy consumption generally follows an S-shaped curve – first, income rises with limited response in energy consumption, then, with industrialisation, energy use increases faster, and finally, income rises with a little growth in energy requirements (Humphrey and Stanislaw 1979, Judson et al. 1999).

Rosenberg (1998) considers the role of electrification in reducing energy intensity. He argues that electricity offered characteristics that made other forms of energy imperfect substitutes. The pervasive diffusion of electricity-using technology helped increase the efficiency of the USA economy from the 1920s. In other words, this superior form of energy reduced energy intensity in maturing industrial economies.

Kander (2005) questions whether the anticipated reduction in energy intensity is due to a structural shift towards services. She reminds us of the risk of 'Baumol's disease', where the service sector only gives the appearance of growth. In the industrial sector, labour is replaced by machines, raising productivity and driving down the price of its products. In the service sector, human skills are required and a growing proportion of the work force shifts towards the service sector – thus, the service sector appears to be growing. Prices in the service sector rise relative to the declining price of industrial products, however. This leads to the conclusion that the industrial sector is likely to grow faster than the service sector, and service production is not growing relative to industrial activity. Her evidence from Sweden supports this view. Higher levels of economic development were associated with a shift towards lighter industrial activities. Thus, the majority of the improvements in energy intensity in this mature industrial economy can be attributed to lighter industrial activity and better resource productivity, in part due to the role of microelectronics, which corroborates Rosenberg's (1998) argument.

Few studies by energy economists have tried to draw this information together to build a picture of relationships between economic growth and development, resource constraints, energy use and environmental quality over the very long run. Fouquet and Pearson (1998) added the role of energy prices to the long run relationship between economic development and energy consumption. It supported the idea that the continuing structural shift in the economy, away from primary and secondary sectors and towards lighter industrial manufacturing and some tertiary sector activities, would increase the share of activities which tend to be relatively less heat- and power-intensive per unit value of output. In addition, there was an increase in technical efficiency of the appliance stock (including a growing reliance on electricity) and of electricity generation and supply.

7. RESOURCE SCARCITY AND ABUNDANCE

Fouquet and Pearson (1998) also indicated that energy consumption was bound by the tensions between the changing structure of economic activity and constraints on energetic resources. As an economy grows, it requires additional resources to support it. Where resources exist, the economy will expand. But, an economy can only expand to its resource limits. Then, signals of resource scarcity will occur – taking the form of economic, social or political pressures. The economy needs to find solutions to the problem of resource limits. The solutions can include creating or finding new resources, conquering new land to provide additional resources, increasing efficiency of resource yield, or altering the population's lifestyle.

Prices provide an economic indicator of a fuel's relative scarcity and value. As a reminder, Hotelling's principle, one of the foundations of modern resource price analysis, states that a non-renewable resource manager will have an incentive to extract resources as long as the rate of increase in future expected net prices (that is, price minus costs) is lower than the discount rate – the opportunity cost of not extracting and selling resources.

Expectations of relatively low future net prices will encourage additional extraction today and tend to put upward pressure on current production and supply. Rapid exploitation today will mean future fuel reserves will be lower, driving up expectations of future prices. If the expected annual rise in net prices becomes greater than the discount rate, managers will have an incentive to invest in fuel reserves by keeping them as stocks. With the stock limited, the expression for the equilibrium price path suggests that net real prices will be rising through time.

The basic model of resource extraction has been extended to incorporate numerous important variables: the existence of costs of exploration and extraction (the basic model assumes zero costs) and of a 'back-stop' technology (providing a more expensive yet inelastic fuel substitute); either increasing or decreasing marginal costs of extraction (because of greater difficulty in extracting the next unit and varying resource quality or due to technological improvements); changes in the discount rate; increases in reserves or in demand; market structure such as monopolies or cartels; and uncertainty about demand, reserves or institutions (Krautkraemer 1998).

All of these extensions alter the optimal rate of extraction. For example, a 'back-stop' technology provides the upper limit for the cheaper fuel's price; lower costs of extraction will lower the initial price, but raise the rate of growth in future prices; higher discount rates will have a similar effect; new discoveries will reduce the price range, as well as the rate; new demand will have the opposite effect; monopolies are likely to reduce the rate of extraction, creating a higher initial price with a lower eventual price. All these factors will have their role in determining the price path, which may be rising, downward-sloping or U-shaped (Fisher 1979).

Partly to test theoretical analysis and partly to provide a basis for forecasting, economists have examined long-run trends in energy prices and costs. A well-known study, *Scarcity and Growth*, by Barnett and Morse (1963) examined the real (inflation adjusted) average costs for a range of minerals, agriculture and renewable resources in the USA between 1870 and 1957. It found that prices had remained constant or fallen, except in forestry and for two out of thirteen minerals (lead and zinc).

Other studies by Smith (1978), Slade (1982) and Berck and Roberts (1996) examined non-renewable resource price trends, including oil, over periods of more than one hundred years. In some cases they fitted these data to quadratic (that is, U-shaped) trends; they found, however, that the coefficients of the quadratic trends tended to vary according to the samples. Pindyck (1999), analysing USA's oil, coal and natural gas prices over the 127 years in order to improve forecasting techniques, shows that, while a U-shaped regression may explain trends up to the 1980s, it dramatically overestimates prices in the 1990s. All conclude that the prices or the trends are stochastic, putting doubt on the certainty of rising long run price trends. Adelman (1996), considering consumer oil prices over eighty years and crude prices for more than one hundred and thirty years, found it difficult to reconcile the evidence with a theory that oil is a limited resource. Krautkraemer (1998) reviewed the literature and argued that the discoveries of new deposits, technological progress in exploration and in use, and the development of substitutes mean that the finiteness of resources does not directly influence the economic scarcity of the commodity.

It is possible, however, that around one hundred years is too short a time-span to reflect on the theoretical expectations. Despite the difficulties of creating them, and the compatibility of values within the series, a few researchers have presented longer price series. Hausman (1996) splices consumer and producer prices series to create a very long run series – from 1450 to 1988. He concludes that there is little evidence of rising fuel prices over 550 years, and that where particular fuel prices have risen, consumers have switched away from the dearer fuels.

Fouquet and Pearson (2003a) present an average 'energy' price. The overall 'energy' price series is particularly important in relation to concerns about energy scarcity and price; since for many purposes different fuels are substitutes, what matters in general is not so much the price of an individual fuel but the price of 'energy'. The price series assembled does not indicate the existence of a rising long run trend in the weighted average 'energy' price series over five centuries. Nevertheless, even the medium run can exhibit rising or falling trends that, with fluctuations, have lasted for well over a century.

The second half of the nineteenth century and the early years of the twentieth century were characterised by an increase in the real average 'energy' price. This coincided with a growing share of petroleum, gas and ultimately electricity in final user expenditure on energy over the period.

Underlying the substitution is the expectation of greater value (in the form of a higher level, quality or flexibility of energy services per unit of energy) by using petroleum products, gas and electricity and their associated production rather than from burning coal. Nineteenth and twentieth century experience, in particular, highlights the need for a better understanding of what has happened to the price of energy services over time.

While price reflects relative scarcity and value of energetic resources, the combustion of fuels has required the assimilation of the emissions. As the level of emissions grew, the capacity of the air and more recently the atmosphere to absorb this waste has come under strain, implying that the emissions imposed an external cost on society. This cost and tension indicates that the air and atmosphere's waste assimilation capacities has become increasingly scarce. David Pearce (2005) called the limits imposed on these public goods 'the new scarcity', in contrast to traditional resource problems.

The lack of markets for the environment implies that the scarcity has tended to be ignored by fuel users. Given this market failure, a role exists for government to create an institutional structure that will signal scarcity. Increasingly, governments are starting to require polluters to pay for their burden and to internalise the external costs imposed fuel users (Krautkraemer 2005, for instance).

The existence of an external cost implies that the social cost of energy consumption and service use is greater than the market price. It would be of value to identify the trends in the full social costs – in order to know whether the combined scarcities (that is, new and old) are rising or falling, and whether the economy is imposing an increasing burden on 'the new scarcities'.

8. INVESTIGATING ENERGY SERVICE DEMAND

The evolution of energy consumption depends on its changing relationships with technological innovation, with economic development and with resource scarcity. This chapter has sought to show that any interest in energy consumption needs to consider the relationship, first, between energy service consumption, economic growth and the cost of generating these energy services and, second, between energy services, technologies and energy consumption (Toman and Jamelkova 2003). Understanding energy services is especially important in the long run, as technological change radically changes consumption behaviour.

Yet, an investigation into energy services is appropriate in its own right. After all, services provided indicate more accurately the value generated from one tonne of coal or one kWh of electricity. Robert Ayres (2005) has regularly emphasised the importance of the difference between energy inputs and 'work' output. William Nordhaus' (1997) study of energy services showed the value of assessing trends in energy services. He identified how dramatically the price of lighting services has fallen, due to improvements in the efficiency of lighting technology, especially over the past century and a half. He also stressed the size of welfare gains resulting from the drop in the price of lighting.

In his analysis, he replaced energy consumption with energy service use as the source of utility (Nordhaus 1997). This implies that price and income elasticities of demand for services can be estimated in a similar manner to goods. However, little is known about the consumer responses to changes in prices and income. There is a need to begin studying the relationship between energy services and its key explanatory variables.

Standard economic theory considers marginal decisions, not dramatic changes in prices and income. The study of energy services is particularly valuable in the long run with the unfolding of major technological and economic transformations. They reflect dramatic changes in economic structure and revolutions in energy services. An analysis on this scale can be guided by marginal analysis, but, cannot be bound by its concepts.

Each market for energy services reflects the complex interactions of energy resources, technological development and institutions created to produce, trade and regulate energy. These interactions make up the system within which demand and supply meet, prices are set, and energy is produced and consumed. An understanding of this complex interaction and evolution will come from combining broad concepts of economic analysis with long run quantitative and qualitative information, a historical perspective and ideas from other social disciplines.

While few could do the subject justice, this book makes a crude attempt to investigate long-run trends in energy services. Using an extensive data collection, this book tries to identify very long-run trends in the price of energy services: do they reflect increasing scarcity or abundance to the consumer? What underlies these trends? To what extent do they reflect the full social costs of energy services? It also seeks to assess the response of energy service consumers to major reductions in energy service prices and to dramatic changes in economic activity and structure: what forces influence the responsiveness? Do these reductions and changes lead to improvements in well-being? And, finally, briefly, the book considers what role subsequent monarchies and governments have played in the trends in energy service prices, full social costs and consumption.

3.   Historical Data and Methods

1. A WEALTH OF INFORMATION

An exploration of trends in the evolution of the cost and use of energy services requires statistical information on prices and consumption of heating, power, transport and lighting fuels, on energy technologies and their efficiencies, and on variables that help to explain service consumption patterns, including – but going well beyond – population and income. Economists are increasingly exploring and refining the rich vein of information associated with the history of energy. Researchers have unearthed more data than might perhaps have been expected. Many in previous generations, including often meticulous local government and other responsible officials and employees, kept relatively good records of transactions relating to the purchase of heat, power, transport and light. In some ways, given the significance of energy to such a wide range of private and public activities, the recording of these data is not wholly surprising. The survival of a substantial volume of this information over the centuries is more so.

In the next section, the sources of our statistical data for general economic conditions related to the production and use of energy services are presented. There follows an outline of the sources for statistics on energy production, consumption and prices. The following section discusses how these energy data were combined with technological information on energy conversion and other efficiencies to estimate trends in energy services. The penultimate section highlights some of the complexities involved in trend estimation and discusses the need for caution when drawing inferences from data of variable quality and continuity.

2. GENERAL LONG RUN ECONOMIC STATISTICS

Long run economic analysis has benefited from the recent growth in the accessibility of historical time series, which may be partly in response to the rapid developments in the 1960s and 1970s in quantitative economic history and the growing application of econometrics and computers. In the last decade or so, it has benefited particularly from advances in information and communication technology.

GDP and Population

Officer (2007a) has brought together data from various sources to present data series for gross domestic product from the thirteenth to the twenty-first century. Snooks (1994) provides some additional detail on early GDP estimates. Snooks (1994) has also brought together data for population between the eleventh and the seventeenth centuries. Wrigley and Schofield (1981) gathered original data on population from 1541 to 1871. Mitchell (1988) provides the data afterwards. The data provides a rough guide to the trends in economic and demographic changes since 1086, when the Domesday Book produced the first census of population.

It is worth providing a brief review of these data series, since growth in economic activity and personal incomes, as well as population expansion and migration, exert significant influences on the demand and supply of energy services. The following discussion should be taken as a crude sketch and, for a more detailed explanation for long-run trends in population and economic activity, the reader should consult, for instance, Hatcher (1977), Wrigley and Schofield (1981) and Floud and McCloskey (2004).

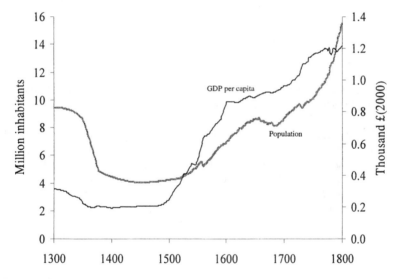

Source: Wrigley and Schofield (1981), Mitchell (1988) and Officer (2007a)

Figure 3.1 Population and Real Gross Domestic Product (GDP) per Capita in the United Kingdom (at year 2000 prices), 1300–1800

In the eleventh century, Britain was a relatively minor and subsistence economy on the edge of Europe, which was itself economically and politically less powerful than the Islamic or Chinese civilisations. Ideas and technical knowledge from distant lands were starting to be adopted in and benefit

European economies. Along with increased political stability, and a warmer climate, the medieval population and economy expanded.

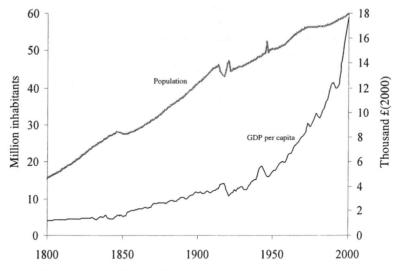

Source: Officer (2007a) and Mitchell (1988)

Figure 3.2 Population and Real Gross Domestic Product (GDP) per Capita in the United Kingdom (at year 2000 prices), 1800–2000

After centuries of invasion, the Norman conquest of England in 1066 created some political order. Improvements in agricultural productivity helped feed the growing population, and wool exports boosted the economy (see Figure 3.1). The 'Black Death', or the Bubonic Plague, struck in 1347–48 and approximately halved the population of Britain, tearing apart the feudal economy.

The fifteenth century was a period of demographic and economic expansion from a low base – taking two hundred years for per capita income and four hundred years for the population to reach its level at the height of the medieval boom in the early fourteenth century. Military campaigns, economic policies and the Reformation's switch to protestant religion under the Tudor monarchies helped direct growth throughout the sixteenth century.

The growing population led to a need for more agricultural products. Efforts to expand arable land or pastures and intensifying yield involved the adoption of new tools and products, the tendency to 'enclose' formerly common land (often for sheep) and the drainage of swamps. These activities particularly increased the production of wheat, minimising famines and exporting surpluses in years of good harvest, and tended to concentrate land ownership. The greater supply of food also enabled the population to expand rapidly in the eighteenth and nineteenth centuries (see Figures 3.1 and 3.2).

The British manufacturing sector was starting to develop, improving its productivity, and expanding. The emergence of an increasingly concentrated and mechanised industrial base – in the seventeenth and eighteenth centuries, in the form of cottage industries and, from the last few decades of the eighteenth century, as factories – transformed the British economy. The textile industry was the first beneficiary of mechanisation and the largest industrial activity, providing cloth for both domestic and foreign consumption. The coal mining and iron industry also grew, as it formed the fuel and the building blocks for the economy.

By the mid-nineteenth century, especially through its expanding colonial base, the British economy was the workshop and sweatshop for the world. The manufacturing sector produced and exported increasing quantities of goods. By the second half of the century, growth was leading to greater prosperity for the average population (see Figure 3.2). Expanding trade and communication networks were helping to import as well.

Economic activity and well-being continued to improve in the twentieth century, especially after the Second World War. The traditional heavy industries, such as coal, iron and steel, were in decline, often unable to compete with foreign counterparts. Other, lighter industries and the service sector grew providing the spectacular growth in GDP per capita.

Retail Price Indices

Since the earliest times, accounts of daily life in Britain frequently commented on the cost of living. One of the first British economic historians, Thorold Rogers, undertook a painstaking exercise over twenty years of trying to gather all the available evidence on the prices of agricultural products sold in markets around the country. His concerns were with the distribution of income and wealth and the objective in that study was to identify trends and changes in the cost of living over a series of several centuries. His work, presented in eight volumes (Rogers 1865–86), still offers, despite its limitations, a most accessible source of information on late medieval prices – from the eleventh to the sixteenth century.

In some large institutions, such as colleges, hospitals or government departments, it was custom to record all the expenditures. This might have been due to the need to be accountable to those paying the bills, be they wealthy parents or public authorities. The quantity and price paid per unit for foods, materials and fuels are, therefore, available, in some cases, for several hundred years from the sixteenth to the early nineteenth century. Despite the loss of many records due to fires, generally the result of the provision of some energy service, much information still remains. After eighteen years of interrupted research, and building on the foundation of Rogers' work, the then Sir William Beveridge (1894), collected and published in a single volume the data recorded by numerous institutions, mostly in southern and eastern England (see also Hamilton 1942). Like Rogers, his main driver was to analyse the trends and fluctuations in prices and wages.

Henry Phelps-Brown and Sheila Hopkins (1956) made interesting use of the data available in Rogers (1865–86) and Beveridge (1894). In this much-cited study, the authors created a set of time series that they combined to form a retail price index for England, dating back to the thirteenth century.

Since then, there have been efforts to incorporate a wider range of sources to reduce the bias in prices caused by the institution and region specific expenditures. Two interesting and recent very long run data sets are provided by Clark (2003) for agricultural prices and Officer (2007b) for retail price indices.

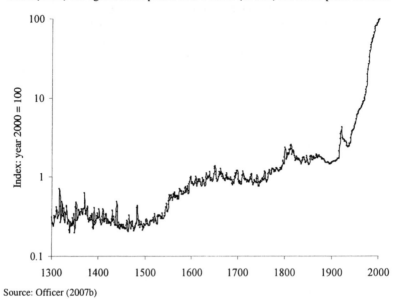

Source: Officer (2007b)

Figure 3.3 Retail Price Index (Year 2000=100) in the United Kingdom, 1300–2000

Figure 3.3 presents a retail price index series for 1300–2000, using Officer's (2007b) series. It shows a deflationary period after the Black Death until the beginning of the sixteenth century, fairly rapid growth in prices from about 1500 to the middle of the seventeenth century, then a century of slightly declining prices until about 1750. The second half of the eighteenth century was a period of rapid price increases. In comparison, the nineteenth century was more stable – up to 1850, prices mostly had a downward tendency, and then rose somewhat, falling downwards in the last quarter. The twentieth century experienced far more rapid price increases, as well as considerable volatility. This retail price index is needed, of course, to deflate any nominal, money-of-the-day price series into 'real' prices and is an important element in comparing the cost of lighting services over the last seven centuries.

3. STATISTICAL SOURCES ON ENERGY

This section introduces the data sources for energy prices and consumption, which underlies a great deal of the analysis. Much of this explanation is also available in Fouquet and Pearson (1998, 2003a). Chapters 4 to 7 use this data and convert them into trends in energy services, with additional data. Because an extensive discussion of these additional information sources would detract from the flow of the text, a full coverage of the data collection process has been placed at the back of the book (see the Data Appendix).

Energy Prices

Rogers' (1881–86) data included many types of wood for burning (e.g. bavins and faggots), as well as charcoal and coal. The volumes identified some extreme volatility in the price of woodfuels, the birth of the coal industry and the declining cost of that fuel through time, associated especially with the productivity improvements in shipping down the east coast towards London in the sixteenth and seventeenth century.

Fortunately, Beveridge (1894) also had substantial data on the price of different types of woodfuel, charcoal, coal and oils, as well as candles. The end of most series, in the first half of the nineteenth century, coincides with the initial switch to gas from coal ('town gas') in Britain for lighting; although there is apparently no evidence of the use of gas in the institutional records from which Beveridge drew the data for his series. Beveridge's data does witness the gradual substitution of woodfuels by coal for heating and cooking purposes.

The Phelps-Brown and Hopkins (1956) data included a cost of fuel and light series. It is made up from series for the price of woodfuels, coal, candles and oil for the early modern era, coal, kerosene and gas throughout the Industrial Revolution, and coal, petroleum, gas and electricity for the twentieth century.

The prices of charcoal and coal are based on weighted averages of the numerous price series available for parts of the period between 1400 and 1800 in the South of England. The weighting of various series tries to balance, as much as possible, the prices in Cambridge and London, two cities for which there is the most information, and the beginning of, ending of and gaps in the available series. For charcoal, the index reflects weighted averages of series presented in Rogers (1865–86) and Beveridge (1894).

Additional statistical information has become available in the 1980s and 1990s. For coal prices, the five volumes of the History of the British Coal Industry (see below) form the basis. The coal price series from 1440 to 1700 combines the series available in Beveridge (1894) and Hatcher (1993). For the eighteenth century, the series is based on the authoritative work by Flinn (1984 pp.303–4) and converts his series and previous ones into pence per tonne.

The price series that are presented are not national indices, at least until the nineteenth century; they are principally for the South-East of England. They cannot be considered definitive price series for these commodities in this region, either. They simply try to give the reader a broad comparison of the costs of buying a ton of charcoal and a ton of coal, taking account of general prices over the period. It also worth remembering that regional and national markets for fuels were a relatively recent development, predicated on the gradual spread of merchant shipping and of road, canal and railway networks, as Chapter 6 illustrates.

The price series for coal from the nineteenth century can be considered a relatively accurate national average. The series splices the Flinn (1984) index up to 1830 with a series in Church (1987) until 1883, followed by data presented in the Coal Statistical Tables (British Parliamentary Papers (BPP) 1902, 1926) up to 1913 and in the various editions of the Statistical Digests of the Ministry of Fuel and Power and of the *Digests of United Kingdom Energy Statistics* (known as DUKES) published annually by the Department of Trade and Industry (DTI)).

Petroleum prices are available from the 1860s when petroleum fuels were first imported. From data in a number of British Parliamentary Papers Statistical Abstracts, an estimate of the price of petroleum per tonne was generated by dividing the expenditure by the volume of imports. Until the end of the nineteenth century, the main petroleum product was kerosene (that is, paraffin in Britain), which was used for lighting. From 1903, the Statistical Abstracts (in the British Parliamentary Papers (BPP)) break down petroleum expenditure and volume into various constituent products – lamp oil or kerosene, motor spirit or gasoline, gas oil and fuel oil. Later, more products, including diesel and aviation fuel, were added.

Prices of town gas were available from 1823 for different companies, mostly in the South East of England, and were published in various British Parliamentary Papers. An average price series was created from these different companies for the period up to 1935. After this, the successive government ministries associated with energy provided United Kingdom gas price series.

The first British statistics on electricity prices date from 1898 and were prepared for the Administrative Council of London – and, therefore, reflect costs to Londoners rather than the whole of the United Kingdom. Following a gap of four years in the series, between 1919 and 1922, national electricity prices have been published from 1923 to date (in the annual DUKES and their precursor, the Ministry of Fuel and Power Statistical Digest).

This data collection has produced a number of long run energy price series. The charcoal price series runs between 1441 and 1830; that for coal, between 1441 and 2000; for petroleum, from 1860 to 2000; for town gas and (from 1969) natural gas, between 1820 and 2000; for electricity, from 1895 to 2000.

Fuel Production and Consumption

Just like most developing economies, information available about the production and consumption of traditional biomass-based fuels, like wood, charcoal and crop 'residues', such as straw or stalks, is very limited. Oliver Rackham (1980) has provided some evidence of how woods were used in Britain in earlier times. As a historian of ancient woodland, he provides evidence of deforestation in Britain, although the role of energy use, relative to the parts played by the spread of agricultural land and the use of wood for construction is unclear – a debate that has its modern counterpart in discussions about the occasionally exaggerated role of biomass energy in deforestation in developing countries.

Some estimates could be made based on evidence about the fuel's uses. For example, until the mid-eighteenth century, charcoal was a key input into iron smelting. Because there are relatively reliable data on iron production, it was possible to estimate the amount of charcoal used for iron smelting. An alternative approach was used to estimate domestic woodfuel use: a basic model of the relationship between income, prices and the consumption of wood for heating was built (see the Data Appendix for more detail).

Relatively early evidence of the production and consumption of commercially traded and priced fuels exists. The first official statistics on the coal industry began in 1854. To study the industry before this, economic historians have had painstakingly to search company and port authority records for estimates of production, exports and imports. John Nef made an impressive effort to pull together evidence on the industry and to chart the growth of the industry from its earliest times (Nef 1926).

The first port of call, however, was the five volumes of *The History of the British Coal Industry*, commissioned by the then state-owned British Coal. Fortunately they were completed before the company's demise after coal privatisation in 1994. They focus on the nature of mining activities, the industrial tensions and the market structure of the industry. They also, however, provide the most definitive attempts to estimate past coal industry statistics.

The first volume, by John Hatcher (1993), draws together a wide range of evidence on the birth and early development of the coal industry. Most of the data concern the cost and levels of production in specific mines, as well as imports into London and other receiving ports. Although the evidence is not at a national level, the data paint a picture of the expanding market for coal. Similarly, Michael Flinn (1984), covering the period between 1700 and 1830, provides a more complete picture of production and exports (and, thus, consumption) of coal in Britain. The other volumes of this history (particularly, Church 1987, Supple 1987 and Ashworth 1987) add to the series, although, from the nineteenth century to the present day, there are many publications that present similar data (see, for example, Mitchell 1984). Much of it stems from the government's annual statistical publications, initially the mineral statistics, then from the Ministry of Fuel and Power annual statistics, and (since the early 1970s) the *Digest of United Kingdom Energy Statistics*.

The other energy industries have generated statistics but, similarly, data for the early years are relatively unsatisfactory. The gas industry was not required to provide data until 1883. Until then, there is evidence of production levels in London from the early 1820s, which was thought to have produced and used around one third to one quarter of the gas in Britain. By the time national estimates are provided, the gas industry had been growing for about 70 years.

Consequently, much potential analysis of the industry must wait until researchers painstakingly collect company records and gather production estimates. From the 1890s, when production and consumption grew to new highs as the working classes adopted gas for lighting, a more satisfactory analysis is possible. Before the 1920s, the companies were meant to report to the Board of Trade, although this reporting did not always generate a complete picture. Afterwards, statistics for the gas industry (consumption, production and fuel inputs to production) are available from the Department of Trade and Industry (DTI 2001), and are highly reliable information. There are, however, limitations in our ability to analyse separately the purposes for which gas was used.

From the economist's perspective, petroleum was, until relatively recently, an imported commodity, which meant that greater care was taken to measure quantities, particularly for tax purposes. From virtually the first uses of petroleum products, as a lighting fuel, or later as a lubricant, a source of motive power or of heating services, there are estimates of supply in this country. And, while it is not always possible to apportion exactly imported petroleum to specific uses, a relatively detailed analysis of petroleum product consumption is possible.

By the time the electricity industry was developing, in the late nineteenth century, the collection of statistics was more common and systematic. Consequently, there has been a smaller lag between the industry's take-off and the availability of adequate information about production and consumption. As is the case in other industries, however, details about precise uses of electricity are not complete, and depend on infrequent surveys.

4. ESTIMATING THE PROVISION OF ENERGY SERVICES

While energy prices and consumption are of interest, the focus of this book is on investigating trends in energy service costs and use. William Nordhaus' (1997) analysis provides the basis for investigating trends. His analysis and other subsequent research into energy services are based on the consumer theory developed by Kelvin Lancaster (1971). Lancaster argued that individual goods are combinations of objectively measured characteristics (or attributes). So, for example, a fuel may be a combination of its energy content (e.g. joules per kilogram), purity, ease of transportation and environmental impact (e.g. carbon, sulphur, particulate, radioactive content). Consumer theory might more appropriately, but with increasing complexity, analyse the optimisation decision as a choice about how to maximise utility associated with buying goods to acquire the attributes and the services these attributes provide subject to the usual constraints.

The framework for investigating the demand for services also builds on Gary Becker's (1976) concept of the household production function. In his analysis, members of a household seek to combine their activities to maximise their well-being by producing services. The provision of services is subject to constraints imposed by income and time budgets and the costs of acquiring appliances and using energy, reflected through the pricing mechanism.

A simplified version of this analysis considers the situation where, in a specific context, each good (e.g. fuel) provides one service. In this case, when used for lighting in conjunction with an appliance, electricity provides one service, illumination. 'Lumen-hours' is an indicator of the amount of lighting in one square foot. The service consumption can be estimated through multiplying the energy consumption with the technical efficiency. If a household's consumption of lighting fuels is equivalent to 100 watts of electricity in one hour and the efficiency of an incandescent light bulb is 10 000 lumen-hours per kWh, then in this hour the household will generate 1 000 lumen-hours of lighting (see the data appendix for more detail on efficiency estimates).

This framework was presented for households. A similar approach can be considered for firms, who seek to maximise profits through their production of goods. To produce goods, they must initially produce 'input services', such as heat and power, from energy. Thus, firms also produce energy services by combining equipment and energy and, as the equipment's technology improves, it can reduce the cost of producing energy services and alter consumption accordingly.

These concepts provide the foundation for producing estimates of the long-run trends in heat, power, transport and lighting in the United Kingdom. The conversion of data on the cost and consumption of fuels into their equivalents in energy services required them to be combined with the energy efficiency of the equipment used for each service. Thus the estimates depend both on the energy data and on the technologies being employed to deliver the services.

Because of the varying nature of both the energy services and the data available, different approaches needed to be used for estimating the performance of different energy services. Service prices or consumption can, for example, be based on direct estimates of the service (that is, transport), or indirectly derived from the fuel consumed and the efficiency of technologies (that is, heating and lighting), or from the amount, size and use of the equipment generating the service, or a combination of the three approaches (that is, power).

'Useful heat', for instance, was estimated from fuel data and conversion efficiencies. Some estimates of the performance of various heating technologies were obtained. The efficiency of hearths, traditional fireplaces and more modern coal fireplaces, as well as gas and electric heaters, were then estimated through time. Then, it was necessary to make assumptions about the proportion of heating fuels being used by each technology. These assumptions were based on literature that revealed the prominence of particular technologies. With estimates of the efficiency of individual heating technologies and shares of the technology, it was possible to calculate the 'useful' heat generated from each technology. Using this approach, it proved possible to create long run series for the cost and consumption of 'useful' heating from the second half of the fifteenth century to the end of the twentieth century.

As a straightforward example, in the eighteenth century, a tonne of coal could be placed in a traditional fireplace and burnt, generating around 10 percent of a tonne of coal in terms of useful heat. With this information and the price of one tonne of coal (in 2000 money), estimated at £145, we can estimate the price of one tonne of coal equivalent of useful heat – about £1 450.

The amount of power provided was mostly estimated from the equipment used. For humans, animals, water- and windmills, and steam engines, evidence on the number of prime movers and their capacity was available. Assumptions were made about the frequency with which equipment was employed, based on literature suggesting rates of work, number of shifts per day or tendency to break down. For most of the twentieth century, there is direct evidence on the amount of power used by industry, although the share of electricity for power rather than other services needed to be estimated. The costs of power were estimated either directly (as wages in the case of human power or prices in the case of electricity) or from energy expenditure per unit of power (for animals and steam engines). It proved possible to construct series for the use of power, from the Domesday Book in 1086 to 2000, and for the costs from around 1300 (see, for instance, Langdon 1991, 2005).

For transport, more direct estimates were available. It is now common to publish information on the price and use in terms of tonne-kilometre or passenger-kilometre. Prices were presented from about 1300 and use of transport service from 1700.

Lighting costs and use can be calculated by combining the cost or use of a lighting fuel with its efficiency or the efficiency of the lighting technology. Estimates of the lumen-hours per 1 000 btu or British Thermal Units (and its equivalent in lumens per watt) for a particular generation of lighting technology were accessible. They were combined relatively easily to estimate costs of lighting between 1300 and 2000, and consumption between 1710 and 2000.

As mentioned above, a more detailed discussion of sources of information and estimates of energy service prices and consumption are included in the Data Appendix.

5. THE DATA

On Units of Measurement

Energy is a physical concept bringing together what once were considered separate phenomena, such as heat and power. Through time, different units have been used to measure energy. While under different physical conditions the conversion of those units varies, some standard conversion factors can be presented and will be adequate for the nature of this study. These will also be useful for the reader possibly more familiar with different units of energy from those employed in this book. More information can be found, for instance, in the *Digest of United Kingdom Energy Statistics* (DTI 2006).

1 kiloJoule (kJ)	= 0.9478 British Thermal Units (btu)
1 teraJoule (TJ)	= 9 478 therms

1 kilowatt-hour (kWh)	= 3 600 KJ
1 kWh	= 0.086 tonnes of oil equivalent (toe)
1 tonne of coal (toc)	= 0.588 tonnes of oil equivalent (toe)
1 tonne of oil equiv. (toe)	= 7.5 million barrels
	= 425 million therms
	= 12 700 GWh of electrical energy
	= 42 000 million cu ft natural gas
	= 1 200 million cu m natural gas

1 kW	= 1.134 horsepower (hp)
1 hp	= 550 lb lifted one foot in one second

1 megawatt (MW)	= 1 000 kW
1 gigawatt (GW)	= 1 000 MW
1 terawatt (TW)	= 1 000 GW
1 petawatt (PW)	= 1 000 TW

There has been an attempt to present consistent units of measurement to enable comparison across time. Following the *Digest of United Kingdom Energy Statistics*, the 'tonne of oil equivalent' will be the main unit of measurement of energy; in some cases, principally related to electricity, kWh may be used.

Similarly, units of length, weight and volume have varied greatly over the last thousand years and across trades, regions and countries. For much of the period of study, the imperial measurement system was used. Here, for the study to be of most relevance to the present day, the metric system is used. For instance,

1 kilometre (km)	= 1 000 metres (m)
	= 0.6203 miles
1 kilogramme (kg)	= 2.2046 pounds (lb)
1 tonne (t)	= 1 000 kg
	= 0.9842 (long) ton

Geographical Boundaries

One problem facing any study of long periods is the definition of geographical boundaries. As noted earlier, much of the data presented are for the South-East of England until the eighteenth century. Afterwards, more national data are available. For much of the statistics, the information relates to England until 1883, the United Kingdom including Ireland from 1883 to 1920, and the current United Kingdom (that is, England, Wales, Scotland and Northern Ireland) afterwards.

Population and the economy will differ considerably on these change-over dates. Thus, trends might appear to experience some discontinuities. These are inevitable parts of the make-up of historical change and analysis. The reader should be aware of such dates. Nevertheless, given the long-run trends being examined, most of these changes should have a limited impact on the trends and relationships.

Converting Data into Real Prices

Except where stated, all prices quoted throughout the paper are in real terms (that is, in £(2000) money). The retail price index (discussed earlier) is from Officer (2007b) shown in Figure 3.3. Thus, albeit with substantial reservations about whether price indexes have captured adequately the quality improvements that have flowed from technological change, the costs of using different energy sources and technologies are broadly comparable across time.

In personal correspondence, William Nordhaus has suggested using a wage deflator rather than a price deflator, especially over long periods. This is because, using a price deflator, if the good or service deflated has the same productivity increase as the average basket of goods and services, no productivity gain would be observed. The productivity gain should be seen if a wage deflator was used.

Another issue is that the retail price index may not take account of efficiency improvements in the technology of consumption for all goods included in 'the basket', as this study tries to do for energy and its services. Consequently, the retail price index may ignore substantial long run declines in the price of other services. This implies that using a retail price index probably overestimates the fall in the price of energy services.

Nevertheless, a price deflator was chosen to follow the convention of comparing the price (here, of individual energy services) with the average price for a basket of goods. Readers should be aware of these limitations on the accuracy of price estimates. Readers interested in converting to a wage deflator could convert the real prices (such as those presented in Tables A5 and A8) into nominal prices and then into wage deflated values (see Officer 2007b).

Quality of Data

Above, some of the historical information about energy use and prices was presented. The wealth of data is no longer quite so hidden in many different volumes across a series of obscure libraries. Instead, much of it is available in a relatively few volumes and some of it can now be accessed via the internet in a spreadsheet format. As in many areas of academic endeavour, improvements in information technology have reduced the cost of analysing information.

The quality of some of the available data is in question. Different variables are subject to different problems. For the price series, for example, there is a high degree of confidence that Westminster School or Kings' College paid the stated price for charcoal, coal or candles. There is uncertainty, however, about variations in the quality of the goods bought, a problem associated with any price series of several hundreds of years. In fact, we can expect more consistency in some of these data, than in many other recent series. Current price series are averaged across a far wider cross-section of observations, however. So, the historical data series available do suffer from being averaged across only a relatively small number of price quotations. Thus, fluctuations in data prices may be disproportionately subject to local variations (such as the College's regular supplier having staff shortages through a cholera epidemic) rather than more general issues. Nevertheless, the data series should provide a reasonable outline of long-run trends in fuel and light prices, provided not too much attention is paid to individual perturbations without further analysis and confirmation.

In a similar way, statistics on production and consumption become more reliable as we approach the twentieth century. The coal information after 1854 was official although incomplete. After 1870, it was intended to be the outcome of a thorough census and, therefore, quite reliable. Gas production and consumption data, however, only become satisfactory after 1882. Petroleum data, on the other hand, should be relatively accurate from its first days, the 1850s, because as indicated it was imported and, therefore, recorded by the more watchful eyes of the customs officers. Owing to its more recent introduction, electricity data can be seen as relatively reliable from its first major breakthrough.

The reliability of data on technical efficiency varies considerably. Over the centuries, many contemporary exercises have been performed to estimate the efficiency of particular pieces of equipment. These were often carried out by enthusiasts to emphasise and sell the virtues of their products, as well as by relatively disinterested scientists. Nevertheless, despite the risk of 'appraisal optimism', which persists to this day, the experimental approach indicates a relatively systematic form of measurement. The main limitation in the efficiency estimates we use relates in some cases or periods to uncertainties about the share of different technologies in use; these shares are used as weights in estimating the average technical efficiencies of a stock of energy using equipment.

The statistics that have been collected are from many diverse sources. Their accuracy is certainly in question. Despite changes and even fuzziness in geographical boundaries and variations and approximation in measurement units, efforts have been made to try to ensure broad consistency throughout the long run series produced. Although the data may be presented in a way that suggests they are accurate, the reader should consider them approximate. To repeat the discussion in Chapter 1, the reader is encouraged to focus on the broad trends and transitions and not on individual data points. The striking picture that appears in the following chapters is about how much and in what ways the costs, consumption and quality of energy services have evolved over the last thousand years.

PART TWO

THE PAST

4. Heating: Resources and the Environment, Abundance and Scarcity

1. THE NEED FOR HEATING

In the home, the demand for heating has been driven by the need to regulate body temperature and inner climate. Households have also required heating for processing and cooking food to be edible, more nutritious and tasty, and for preparing drinks. Recently, demand for warm water – to wash body, clothes and dishes – has also become more common.

Humans have sought to regulate their indoor climate. Their ability to keep warm depended on building shelters, as well as the use of other 'know-how', like wearing clothes or keeping active – or even getting more bodies in the room. They also combined equipment and fuel to provide heat. The amount of heating for cooking and washing a family required was affected by similar 'know-how', technologies and fuels.

If the price of heating fell because the fuel became cheaper and/or the equipment used less energy to produce useful heat, the family may have altered its inner climate, cooked more food or washed more. It might also have done so if the heater, cooker or washer required less time to prepare its use, was less effort to use, or was less smelly, noisy or ugly.

Until relatively recently in Britain, expenditures on core services like heating, cooking and washing formed a significant proportion of total expenditures for all but the most well-off families. Thus, any changes in the prices of heating or in wealth were likely to feed-through into a significant adjustment to a household's consumption of heating, cooking or washing.

Heating has also been central to many industrial and commercial activities. Like households, industries have needed heating to regulate temperature, serve food and drink or wash – or for different purposes, such as preparing and processing substances and materials, particularly minerals and chemicals. When workers' know-how, technology or fuels changed, industrial heating patterns tended to respond accordingly.

This chapter considers the evolution of the demand for heat in homes and industrial activities, as well as the consumption and cost of heating over the last seven hundred years. This evolution reflects, to a large extent, the dramatic economic, technological and social revolutions that interacted to provide the desired services and to stimulate their demand. Their enhanced availability and use in turn played an important role in promoting other economic, social and cultural changes. This chapter aims to explore this story.

The chapter begins in the medieval household and the basic biological need to regulate body temperature. This need creates a demand for cooking to improve its edibility and quality. The next section assesses the tensions between industrial expansion and resource scarcity, and the role of technological solutions. It also highlights the heavy burden industrial activities imposed on the environment and society. From the medieval economy to the Industrial Revolution, these tensions and burdens are examined in various industries, such as glass-making, and then in the production of iron.

Afterwards, the story returns to the household, which had benefited from the industrial expansion to improve temperature control, including insulation from clothing, climate control through shelters, and heating using fuels. Population growth and improvements in economic well-being generated rising demands for heating, causing additional strains on natural resources, as well as technological solutions. Finally, the chapter looks at the industrial demand for heating over the last two hundred years. It reflects on the dramatic transformations that have occurred, both in the need for heat and the way the heat was provided.

2. COOKING DEMAND BEFORE THE INDUSTRIAL REVOLUTION

Basics Needs

Lives in medieval[1] Britain were much harsher than they are today. The meeting of basic needs, such as food and shelter, could not be taken for granted. To consider the evolution of heat services, it is worth considering briefly the basic role heating provides in human survival.

Consumption of food, combined with oxygen, generates energy in the body. This metabolic activity produces heat to 37°C, which is central to a human's survival. Heat loss from a body (through radiation, convection and evaporation) is dependent on effort, but also air and radiant temperatures, air movement, humidity and clothing. So, for example, in cold conditions, the body starts to shiver to generate heat to maintain the desired temperature, whereas, in hot climates, it sweats to reduce excess heat. These extreme conditions put strain on the heart and, in cold conditions, lung, cardiovascular and respiratory problems are aggravated (Billington 1982 p.12).

A human's attempt to keep at the appropriate temperature depends, therefore, on successful management of three factors: food, clothing and climatic conditions. When one of these components changes or is lacking, the others will need to compensate, or health will be impaired. Given that food is also central to

---

1. Broadly described as from the eleventh to the fifteenth century, often linked to the periods from 1066 (crowning and death of King Harold II and arrival of William I, the Conqueror) to 1485 (death of Richard III at the battle of Bosworth Field).

providing the energy for muscular activity, the demand for food as a source of energy will be briefly discussed in Chapter 5.

The Demand for and Supply of Cooking

The majority of the poor and slightly wealthier craftsmen had few furnishings, principally for cooking, eating, seating, bedding and storage. Beyond food preparation and cooking, the wife's main domestic tasks, apart from child care, were floor sweeping, pot washing or scouring, and the heavy yet infrequent washing of sheets and linen. "At times of festival, humbler people could also 'exceed after their manner'. But most people, most of the time, lived on bread and oatcakes, pottage or porridge, 'white meats' (cheese, butter and eggs), bacon, and occasional poultry and butchers' meat, washed down with weak ale. Few kitchens had spits on which to roast meat. Most had pots and pans. Larger households baked their own bread and brewed their own ale. Most probably did not, carrying their prepared dough to a communal oven, as described above, or relying on bakers and alehouse keepers. All this took time; the fetching and carrying of water alone could take a good deal of time and energy" (Wrightson 2000 p.45).

Cooking and warming meals and especially floured grain, has been essential for improving digestibility, and, therefore, the ability to harness calorific and nutritional value from food. It improved the efficiency of food (or human fuel) consumption. The principal methods of cooking in Britain were boiling and baking. They remained the same for hundreds of years, only becoming increasingly sophisticated as the price of iron fell during the Industrial Revolution.

Pot boiling was the most common method, and relatively simple if a single 'dish' was to be cooked. It involved hanging a large pot from a wooden beam or later an iron rod above the fire. To control the heat, the pot was moved up or down onto hooks of different height. Water, grain or vegetables were placed in the pot, and left for long periods of time. The pot, however, created great heat, which made cooks 'hot and fretful', and could be ruined by spilling (Davidson 1986 p.46).

Baking was frequently done on a bakestone, where one big or several smaller stones were generally placed in the middle of the fire, absorbing the heat. Breads and cakes, as well as fishes and stews, were prepared on the stones. Later, as iron became more widespread, in wealthier homes, plates, girdles, or 'pots' (that is, boxes) could be placed above the fire. In other cases, earthenware ovens were placed above the heat (Davidson 1986 pp.49–50).

Often, though, baking took place on a larger scale. Communal and free-standing ovens, made of stone or brick, prepared a week's supply of bread for a small hamlet or village. To prepare such a large amount, an abundant supply of fuel needed to be collected. They also demanded considerable skill to operate. The process involved heating the fuel until it became red hot, removing it and cleaning the oven, then placing the dough in the oven and allowing the stones or bricks, which had stored the heat, to bake. Thus, the fuel needed to be prepared correctly, the fire managed, the heating process carefully timed, heat losses limited and loaves placed according to their size (Davidson 1986 pp.50–52).

Demand for Cooking Fuel in Medieval Times

The traditional fire was heated using biomass fuels – wood, charcoal, crop residue, peat or dung – in an open hearth. Before the thirteenth century, fuelwood and charcoal, the main fuels, were readily available, with their real prices remaining stable (Rackham 1980 p.167). Forests in the eleventh and twelfth centuries were still extensive and provided many of the resources required in a medieval household. In addition to its role in building shelter, wood was important for the manufacturing of furniture and tools. Forests were also the source of considerable food, both vegetable and animal. Naturally, they also supplied much of the fuel for cooking.

A village was often surrounded by fields, and then forests, creating roughly concentric circles around the dwellings. Consequently, it took time to reach the forest and access the resources it provided. Forest resources were not always common property, with freedom of access to those entitled to share such property, or open access resources, however. By the end of the thirteenth century, most forests still standing near urban centres were privately owned by nobility or royalty. Such woodland was, therefore, carefully reserved, and not available for general exploitation (Rackham 1980).

In times of population growth, such as in the thirteenth and early fourteenth centuries, forests were competing with other agricultural uses for peri-urban land exploitation. In such periods, agricultural land and produce were often seen as more valuable than forests and wood. Given the threat of serious food shortages if any year's harvest failed due, for example, to poor weather conditions, 'farmers' were likely to convert parcels of land, chopping down trees and digging up the roots to grow further crops.

As a result, wood was travelling greater distances before being used, adding to the cost. The cost of fuelwood faced by a region was dependent on the size of its forest, the users' ease of access to forests, the type of wood (e.g. firewood, underwood, faggots, charcoal) bought or collected and the demand for wood both as a fuel and for its non-energy purposes. At the peak of the economic cycle, between 1270 and 1320, concerns about fuel reserves grew, as demand appeared to be exceeding the maximum flow of fuel available from local forests, and supply was becoming less responsive to price changes. This led to modest and temporary real price rises (Rackham 1980 p.167).

Most medieval households were rural and, therefore, would have been most likely to collect their fuel themselves. The collection of wood was generally a time-consuming activity. Time spent gathering fuel was not available for other household chores. If it was the woman of the household, this might mean less time preparing food, cooking or cleaning. Further distances to acquire sufficient wood might mean reductions in calorie intake, nutritional value and hygiene, with major health effects. On the other hand, not having enough fuel to cook properly might reduce the nutritional value of a meal prepared, again with health effects. A careful balance needed to be kept to achieve the most desirable level of calorific and nutritional services – and not all were able to achieve it.

Galloway et al. (1996 p.456) estimated fuel consumption for baking in London in the late Middle Ages. Based on their per capita consumption figures, an estimate of English firewood consumption in 1300 and 1400 can be calculated. They suggested that in 1300 each person in London needed 280 kg of wood (equivalent to 75 kg of oil) per year for baking. This implied that baking in England required 2.68 million tonnes[2] of wood (equivalent to 800 000 tonnes of oil (toe)) in 1300. Due to the decline in population after the Black Death (mentioned in the previous chapter) and the associated fall in economic prosperity, per capita consumption fell to 200 kg of wood (58 kg of oil equivalent) per year, and baking consumption in England would have fallen back to 0.88 million tonnes (equivalent to 250 000 toe) in 1400.

3. MEDIEVAL AND EARLY MODERN INDUSTRIAL HEATING

Energy Scarcity in the Medieval Industrial Expansion

The main industrial activities in medieval Britain included the processing of food and drink, and cloth-making. Some other industrial activities, such as metal smelting, building and ship construction, required heat, although at that time their output and, thus, their inputs were on a relatively small scale (Galloway et al. 1996). On the whole, medieval Britain was principally an agriculture-based economy and less heat-intensive than future industrial economies, minimising the per capita demand for non-domestic heating fuels. The overall demand for heating tended to follow the growth in population and economic activity, while being subject to resource and technological limitations and development. The gradual rise in population and income throughout the late Middle Ages did drive up the demand for heating services (Hatcher 1993).

Using the same methods as for baking, which were based on the London per capita consumption in Galloway et al. (1996 p.456), it was possible to estimate industrial fuel consumption in England. In 1300, the brewing industry required around 3.58 million tonnes of wood (equivalent to one million tonnes of oil). Again, the fall in population associated with the Black Death reduced fuel consumption. By 1400, use in brewing had fallen to about 1.05 million tonnes (equivalent to 300 000 tonnes of oil). If fuels for baking and brewing accounted for one-half of non-ferrous industrial energy requirements in the late Middle Ages, other industries (that is, excluding baking, brewing and iron industries)

---

2. Many historical studies present weights in 'tons'. For consistency, throughout the book, the current unit of weight measurement, the 'tonne', will be used. One 'British long' ton is equal to 1.016 tonnes (see Chapter 3).

used over six million tonnes of woodfuel in 1300 and just under two million tonnes of woodfuel in 1400 (equivalent to 1.6 and 0.5 million tonnes of oil respectively).

In the twelfth and thirteenth centuries, the British economy was changed by what Carus-Wilson (1941) called the 'first Industrial Revolution'. Although industrial activity remained on a small scale in the twelfth century, it grew considerably, along with agricultural output (see the previous chapter). This led to a substantial rise in demand for farm produce and for basic industrial goods, such as textiles and tools, which in turn increased the derived demand for factor inputs into agriculture and industry, including energy services.

Population growth was responsible for much of the deforestation experienced in medieval times. Yet, increasing industrial activity was taking its toll on woodlands. Henry III (1216–72) observed the process of deforestation in his Kingdom. In 1232, he was told that a Westminster building project could not find the necessary timber in the forests of Windsor or Cornbury. Later, in 1252, he also discovered that in the Forest of Dean, the value of the wood that iron forges were consuming was greater than the value of the iron they were producing. He decreed that timber should not be used, because its value would triple or quadruple in a few years. Finally, in 1258, he ordered that sales of timber be halted, although it is not clear how successful the ban was (TeBrake 1975 p.350).

In 1290, and again in the early fourteenth century, Edward I imposed a ban on wood exports, indicating the authorities' desire to limit over-exploitation of forest resources and limiting their sales to the local economy. It was revoked in 1357, suggesting the end of any shortages linked, no doubt, to the huge decline in population and economic activity after the Black Death (Galloway et al. 1996 p.467).

For industrial activities and urban households, fuel would have been bought rather than gathered. The cost of carriage was often a large proportion of the fuel retail price. Transport costs fluctuated, due to factors ranging from weather conditions to wars; between 1330 and 1370, for example, the cost of transporting woodfuel overland to London doubled (Galloway et al. 1996 p.458). With poor quality roads, the most effective way of transporting fuel was by waterways. Where waterways were accessible, much greater fuel supplies became available. As a result of differences in these factors, conditions in fuel markets varied considerably between regions, as well as over time (see Chapter 6).

Transport costs also depended on the fuels carried. In particular, increasing amounts of charcoal, lighter than wood, were being prepared in forests before being transported to industrial and domestic users. While charcoal was of higher energy content than fuelwood, 30 MJ/kg and 20 MJ/kg, respectively (Simmons 1993), its low value in relation to its bulk and its tendency to disintegrate during journeys or under its own weight meant its range of distribution was only slightly greater than that of wood (Rosenberg 1998 p.18).

The Birth of Coal Use

Growing demands for traditional biomass heating fuels in the thirteenth century encouraged certain industries to start using coal. Most of the coal mines were in the North-East of England and in Scotland. This implied that in nearby regions or ones accessible by waterways, coal was available at competitive prices and was rapidly becoming the main fuel (Hatcher 1993 p.28). Even in the South-East of England, where the high travel costs meant coal was dear, consumers began to use coal (Hatcher 1993 p.22). Although sales at the time were relatively small, they developed a trade route that would become the key source of fuel to Southern England for nearly five hundred years.

Most industries used heat to transform raw materials. Before the sixteenth century, coal was considered inappropriate for many industrial activities because the fuel came into direct contact with the material being transformed; in the process it became contaminated by coal's by-products, especially at high temperatures. Coal was a potential alternative to woodfuels, however, for activities where there was no direct contact, if the raw materials were heated from below or if they were processed at low temperatures. In London, "coals in former times was onely used by smiths, and for burning of lime" (William Gray from 1642, quoted in Hatcher 1993 p.16).

The location of the fuel and the availability and nature of the material being processed and transformed were important influences on the location of industrial developments. In some cases, fuel and material were co-located. Limestone, often found by the sea, was prepared to make plaster for the construction industry. It required considerable heat and, given its proximity to coastal supplies of coal, those processing it had switched early on from biomass to coal. Salt made from sea-water and prepared on the coast also had easy access to coal supplies. Here, the importance of the demand for heating and the great difference in weight (and, therefore, transportability) between the material, sea-water, and the final product, salt, meant that the industry centred in the North-East of England, close to the most available fuel. Similarly, some industries, such as brickmakers and potters, began to locate near coal seams (Daunton 1995 p.209).

If the materials being prepared were evenly distributed around the country, and transportation was an issue, the choice of fuel depended on its local accessibility. This was the case for tallow, glue and soap makers, which located near the meat-markets to collect animal fats and bones, since theirs was not a raw material that could travel for any significant period untreated. The makers, therefore, would choose the fuel for processing according to availability; choices that reflected the local cost of heating.

In these cases, parts of the industry would have started using coal at the first signs of dearer wood or charcoal, while other firms would still have used woodfuels until well into the nineteenth century. In other cases, it was the consumer, along with the accessibility of fuel, which determined the choice of heating method. So, for bread baking, which required considerable heat, and brewing, which used less, fuel choice varied according the region. In other words, many factors determined a particular industry's transition from woodfuels to coal.

An Early Modern Energy Crisis?

After the recession following the Black Death (shown in Figure 3.1), the demand for heating fuels remained low for another century. Population remained small until the mid-fifteenth century (see Figure 3.1), and most industrial activities stayed on a relatively modest scale. Economic activity in the sixteenth century recovered dramatically, per capita GDP growing by about 1.5 percent per annum between 1490 and 1560. With similar technology and energy requirements per unit of output to two hundred years earlier, the demand for heating fuels also increased rapidly.

In the fifteenth and early sixteenth centuries, energy consumption was further encouraged by the relatively low real price of heating fuels (see Figure 4.1). While the average price of consumables in the South of England was creeping up from the beginning of the sixteenth century, nominal fuelwood and charcoal prices remained stable. Because population had remained relatively small, demands for agricultural land in the previous century had also been low; much of the peri-urban land had become wooded again (Witney 1990 p.39). With increasing population and income, the first pressures were put on agricultural resources, driving up prices. In real terms, fuelwood and charcoal prices were falling.

Some have argued that between the mid-sixteenth and mid-seventeenth centuries a national wood crisis occurred, which was one of the causes of the rapid expansion in coal production between 1550 and 1680 (Nef 1926). Hammersley (1973), Flinn (1978) and Allen (2004) questioned this conclusion, arguing that it was not so much a rise in the price of woodfuel as a decline in the price of coal that led to the expansion of the coal industry; their pint is corroborated by Figure 4.1.

The data does not support a woodfuel crisis from the mid-sixteenth century. Nevertheless, as Hatcher (1993 p.33) pointed out, throughout the sixteenth and seventeenth centuries, to meet growing demands for agricultural produce, many forests were being transformed into arable land. For instance, in the 1540s, nominal fuel prices rose dramatically, although average consumer prices soon caught up. Based on the data available, the real price of woodfuels was lower in the sixteenth than the fifteenth century.

Thomas (1986) argued, however, that, during the fifty years following Nef's period of crisis (in particular, from 1640), the British economy did suffer a severe scarcity of timber and fuel. The data shown in Figure 4.1 does indicate a rise in the price of fuels between the mid-seventeenth and mid-eighteenth centuries.

By the mid-seventeenth century, a growing demand for wood-based products, such as timber, may also have influenced fuel prices (Rackham 1980 p.166). Demand for timber grew considerably as a result of the expansion of the Royal

Navy, of other construction work[3] and of international trade. First, dramatic changes in defence policy during the Cromwellian Revolution, which promoted aggressive naval activity, led to major growth in ship production in the Royal Navy between 1640 and 1680. As well as the general increase in the use of wood products for this expansion, including the fuels needed to smelt iron, the Navy insisted on English oak for its ships (Thomas 1986 p.135). Second, the seventeenth century rise in international trade particularly for luxury goods imported from the Colonies and re-exported to Europe, promoted by a mercantilist Government, also increased the number of ships being built. In addition, rebuilding London after the Great Fire of 1666 also called upon substantial supplies of timber.

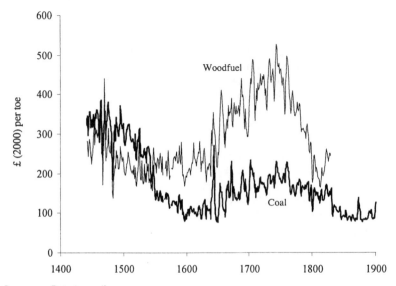

Source: see Data Appendix

Figure 4.1 Estimates of Charcoal and Coal Prices in the South-East of England, 1450–1900

Hammersley (1973) and Flinn (1978) cited the existence of examples of large wooded areas during that period as evidence of a lack of scarcity. The issues relate to the degree of deforestation and the distance of forests from centres of economic activity rather than to the complete extinction of forests. Indeed, transport was key to determining whether consumers faced abundance or scarcity.

Transport costs did play a crucial role in the price faced by the customer. Unfortunately, evidence (discussed in more detail in Chapter 6) does not help to

3. See also Machin (1977) for a critical discussion of pre-industrial house building activity, including Hoskins's thesis of a 'Great Rebuilding' in the period 1570–1640.

conclude. Cost of land carriage tended to rise between the mid-sixteenth and the early eighteenth centuries. This could have put upward pressure on the price of fuels at delivery. But, the timing does not match properly; the cost of carriage had been rising for one hundred years (from 1550) before it fed through into higher woodfuel prices (in the mid-1600s). If anything, it suggests that, despite higher transport costs, the price of woodfuel managed to stay constant, indicating that the production of woodfuel was in fact rising. And then, when land carriage costs start falling (around 1700), fuel prices continued to rise.

In any case, because of its bulk, all but the most modest woodfuel needs had to be supplied along rivers. Insufficient data on the cost of river carriage limits any comparison of trends. Yet, qualitative information on river transport proposes that the river network started to improve (albeit slowly) from the mid-seventeenth century. This would suggest that fuel scarcity was rising in the 1650s.

As Hatcher (1993 p.32) explained, because of its bulk, there was no national market for energy and each centre of consumption faced different constraints. It is, therefore, impossible to ascertain whether the whole economy experienced an energy crisis. The conclusion that can be drawn is that, to the consumers for which data on prices is available (mostly organisations in the South-East of England), individual fuel prices were considerably higher in the early 1700s than in the early 1600s. In other words, the increase in the demand for wood-based products and for agricultural land caused at least local wood shortages, which led to a rise in woodfuel prices between the mid-seventeenth and mid-eighteenth centuries.

In the early modern era, the urban market was comprised of homes and most industrial activities. The rural demand was for households and the iron industry, which was forced to locate in remote, highly-wooded areas to access sufficient fuel. The urban and rural markets did not encroach on one another. To consider the impact of the rising woodfuel prices, the three groups of consumers (the iron industry, other industries and households) need to be considered separately.

Estimates of (non-iron) industrial energy consumption for heating are presented in Figure 4.2. From 1550, an important price differential existed between woodfuel and coal (see Figure 4.1). Where substitution was possible many manufacturers started using coal, reducing their marginal costs of production. As Hatcher (1993 p.49) indicated, by the mid-seventeenth century, most industrial activities had made the switch to coal. By the time woodfuel prices started to rise, industry was hardly dependent on woodfuel. Thus, on the whole, general manufacturing in Britain did not face a woodfuel crisis in the seventeenth century. It was, however, subject to rising coal prices, which were due in large part to the growing demand for heating in households (discussed later).

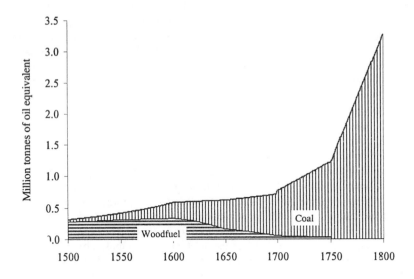

Source: see Data Appendix

Figure 4.2 Estimates of Non-Ferrous Industrial Woodfuel and Coal Consumption, 1500–1800

The Expanding Coal Market

As an illustration of the many industries that switched to coal, the glass industry provides an interesting example of the interplay of factors in creating opportunities and incentives for new technologies and fuels to be adopted. For centuries charcoal had been the only satisfactory source of heat for making glass and producing and preparing metals. In the middle of the sixteenth century, there appear to have been only two window glassmakers, based in the Weald[4] (Godfrey 1975 p.251). They used a great deal of wood in their processes. As well as the fuel, production required great skills in working the molten glass.

During Elizabeth I's reign (1558–1603), foreign glass-makers were welcomed into England in order to boost this infant industry. Production increased and with it the demand for heat and charcoal grew. In some places, between 1585 and 1615, the price of wood bought by glassmakers trebled. Because of the weak demand for window glass, producers were absorbing much of the increase in cost and facing declining profits. This problem was, to a considerable extent, caused by the industry's lack of mobility. Being fragile, glass could only be transported

---

4. The modern Weald is an area in southern England that lies between the chalk hills of the North Downs and South Downs, and across the counties of Kent, East Sussex, West Sussex and Surrey. In medieval times the extent of this wooded area was much wider than this.

short distances, and the industry needed to be close to the consumer. In such circumstances, wood supplies became quickly depleted (Godfrey 1975).

The technical problem facing the use of coal was that, if the glass was separated from the fuel to avoid contamination, insufficient heat was generated to melt the sand and alkali. The coal-using reverberatory furnace, patented in 1612, had a tall funnel shape to create a strong draught and a curved dome to send the heat back down onto the protected raw materials. Now, sufficient heat was created for the use of coal.

The introduction of this furnace into the window glass-making industry was not, however, solely due to fuel shortages. It stemmed from one firm's attempts to enter the monopolised (and highly lucrative) niche market of crystal glass. By developing this new process, they hoped it would be considered by government to be a separate industry, yet able to compete with the crystal monopolist. When this failed to convince government, the firm, Zouch, was forced to enter the less profitable, but larger, market for window glass (Godfrey 1975 p.252). Thus, the invention was not driven by a perceived need for a new fuel.

In fact, despite glass-makers' concerns about wood supply, the diffusion of the reverberatory furnace was initially tentative. The amount of coal required to create sufficient heat was so high that fuel costs were not lower than with charcoal. Over the following decades, as the process became more efficient, however, cost savings were made, the process became common and coal became the main source of heating for glass production. Output started to grow, and prices fell (Godfrey 1975 p.253). Crossley (1972 p.430) suggests that, "perhaps the most striking achievement of these glass-makers was their ability to sell, at steady or declining prices, a product of higher quality than traditional English glass. These points were interlinked: at the furnace, improvements in methods had the dual effect of keeping fuel costs to a minimum and of allowing higher standards of manufacture and, further, this qualitative improvement may well have had a part, along with price stability, in widening the market."

By 1640, the industry had grown to about 30 glasshouses, producing 9 000 cases of window glass (Godfrey 1975 p.251). The growth in the industry was principally due to the Elizabethan policy of welcoming foreign glass-makers to develop an infant industry in England. The invention was from outsiders trying to enter another market. But, the impact of this growth on forests without the switch to coal would have been important, and probably with serious incidental effects on other industries also using woodfuels. The new furnace also paved the way for other raw materials to be heated using coal.

The expansion of the coal industry started in the North-East of England. A catalyst for the expansion was the transfer of ownership from the Bishop of Durham to the merchants of Newcastle in the sixteenth century. Henry VIII's (1509–1547) Reformation meant that land owned by the Catholic Church was up for sale. While the Church was mining coal, the land and what lied beneath it was exploited more vigorously in commercial hands.

Coal output in the North-East of England, the main region of coal production, has been estimated at 45 000 tons (27 000 toe) at the end of the fourteenth century – 'a tiny amount' in comparison to production in the later Tudor and Stuart periods (1485–1714) (Hatcher 1993 p.29). Coal shipments from the North-East down the coast grew substantially throughout the sixteenth century. Considered an already important industry by 1500, the annual supply of coal from the Northumberland and Durham ports rose to 60 000 tonnes (36 000 toe) in 1560 (Hatcher 1993 p.45). By 1600, it was over 220 000 tonnes (130 000 toe); this averaged out at a growth rate of 4.5 percent per annum – far greater than the 2 percent annual growth rate in economic activity. Coal exports from the North-East of England rose to 500 000 tonnes (300 000 toe) by 1660 and temporarily peaked at 800 000 tonnes (480 000 toe) in the 1680s, a 60 per cent increase, falling slightly in 1700 (Hatcher 1993 p.45). By that same year, as a result of the growth of mining in other regions, especially Yorkshire, the west Midlands and Scotland, the estimated total consumption of coal for the United Kingdom was 2.6 million tonnes (1.5 million toe).

The major expansion of the industry was not the result of major innovations in method. Few barriers stood in the way of growth, and no major technical progress was called upon. If problems arose, such as when water flowed into the mines, they tended to be abandoned for other sites. Improvements in mining and distribution did occur, but most often in tiny ways. In the long run, the coal mining and supply industry was considerably more efficient in the seventeenth than the fifteenth century. Each man could produce more coal, but the main reason the industry expanded was simply because it used existing practices and multiplied the number of men and seams being exploited. The supply of coal was abundant, as was the men willing to work at the pit-face for a decent wage. They required little capital and, therefore, few funds for investment (Hatcher 1993 p.11).

Serious Concerns about Air Pollution

The medieval economy had started to use coal and the smoke emitted had been a local nuisance. A ban had been introduced on the use of coal in certain urban areas. The Black Death and the ensuing economic downturn reduced the pollution problem.

By the mid-seventeenth century, many major urban centres had switched to coal as their main source of heating – for example, John Gaunt asserted that, by 1665, "Sea-Coals ... are now universally used" in London (quoted in TeBrake 1975 p.338). By the seventeenth century, London was already famous for its smoke – compared with many cities on the continent (Brimblecombe 1987). The largest complaints were associated with industrial activities, such as brewers, lime-burners and soap-boilers, where coal use and smoke was concentrated. As domestic use grew it too became heavily implicated.

The smoke was seen as damaging to health – it was addressed in scientific debates at the Royal Society in the 1660s. John Evelyn highlighted the importance of air in the public's well-being, and that London's inherently good quality air was fouled by smoke from burning coal. He argued that the smoke entered the lungs and mixed with the blood, provoking catarrh and coughs (Jenner 1995 p.538). Meetings and masses were regularly disrupted with coughing and spitting. The seventeenth century economic statistician Gregory King had blamed smoke for the low fertility rate in London, while John Gaunt had commented that it was the source of high mortality rates (Jenner 1995 p.539-40). As Henry Oldenburg, the first secretary of the Royal Society, said, "ye corrosive Smoake of their SeaCoale, yt cuts off more than half their dayes" (quoted in Jenner 1995 p.547).

The smoke and its constituent pollutants had also been a burden for other reasons. It generally impaired visibility, corroded materials and affected plants and trees. It was seen to kill insects. The soot dirtied clothes, and ladies felt the need to clean their faces with crushed almonds (Jenner 1995 p.538).

Despite his interest in promoting woodland, Evelyn considered it unrealistic to seek a return to wood burning. Instead, he proposed moving all of London's polluting industrial activities downwind, beyond Greenwich; he also suggested this would create jobs for freighters carrying beer, plaster and soap into London (Jenner 1995 p.538). Here, as a precursor to later attempts at pollution control, the approach was to export and relocate the problem, rather than seek to address it at source.

It is important to appreciate, however, that some of the attempts to improve environmental quality were also driven by political interests. John Evelyn had returned to England from exile before the Restoration of the monarchy in 1660. He supported Charles II (1660–1685) and, in various pamphlets, argued that the King would cleanse the city both physically and politically (Jenner 1995 p.541). Swiftly after the Great Fire of London in 1666, John Evelyn had drawn up plans for a new London. In Charles II's speech about the rebuilding, he promised that "brewers, dyers, bakers and similar smoky trades ... would be banished from the Thamesside where a handsome vista would be erected in their stead" (quoted in Jenner 1995 p.550). Economic and legal reasons made this impossible, and consequently pollution continued unabated – though, at regular intervals, hotly debated.

Other cities were also suffering from the negative aspects of growing coal use. Estimates from the late fourteenth and from the seventeenth centuries indicate that parts of York were faced with growing and harmful levels of smoke and sulphur dioxide concentrations, and that the area of maximum concentration in the centre of the city was widening and shifting from the West to the South-East (Hipkins and Watts 1996). In addition to health complaints, the pollution was a regular concern for the preservation of the Minster, which has been in the centre of the city and, therefore, subject to high levels of damage over the last eight hundred years.

4. IRON IN AN INDUSTRIALISING ECONOMY

Charcoal Use in the Iron Industry

The iron industry, textile production and coal mining were the central pillars of industrialisation in Britain. The iron industry experienced two major transformations. The first took place in the Elizabethan period, while the second is the more famous expansion which coincided with the central period of the Industrial Revolution (King 2005).

Yet, until the second expansion, and a long time after other industrial processes switched use to coal and its main derivative, coke, the iron industry remained dependent on charcoal supplies for technological and then commercial reasons. This dependence forced the industry to migrate to increasingly-remote forests (Flinn 1978 p.142).

Strong and resistant, iron provided a key foundation and material upon which the rest of the economy was built and functioned. All sectors depended on iron. Innovations in agricultural technology and the rising demand for intermediate goods, such as axles, chains and bolts, and for consumption goods, such as cutlery, grates and firebacks, drove the growth in iron production (Thomas 1986).

In the early sixteenth century, the iron industry produced just over 1 000 tonnes of bar iron, virtually all of it in bloomeries,[5] located in the forests of the Weald, in Kent and Sussex. These installations undertook the whole production process, from smelting iron ore to producing cast iron to forging wrought iron (King 2005).

The smelting process involved combining iron ore with charcoal and limestone in a strong draught, often generated by water-driven bellows, to produce a great heat. The output, cast (or pig) iron, had a high (that is, 5 percent) carbon content, making it hard and brittle. It was only appropriate for certain uses, such as pots, stoves, firebacks, railings and cannons. Again using charcoal, the next phase of heating and hammering reduced the carbon content, converting the cast into wrought iron, which was more malleable. Wrought (or bar) iron was more suitable for other uses, including nails, locks and small arms. The next process was the manufacture of the iron into rods, through further heating, rolling and cutting in mills. These rods were then finally sold to ironmongers and smiths who shaped them into the desired object. This final process could use coal, given that the metal was not in direct contact with the fuel.

As these processes began to be performed in separate stages (in furnaces and forges) to improve the quality of iron, the bloomery lost its central role. In decline from the 1560s, it took another two hundred years for bloomeries to completely disappear. Nevertheless, by the end of the sixteenth century, they produced only a tiny fraction of the total bar iron production (King 2005).

---

5. A bloomery is a furnace in which iron ore is smelted and from which metallic iron is produced. Several chemical processes help to separate the iron from the other materials in the ore. The bloomery produced a porous mass of iron and slag known as a 'bloom'.

In 1600, furnaces smelted nearly 23 000 tonnes of pig iron and, refining it, forges produced more than 15 000 tonnes of bar iron annually. Thus, during what Joan Thirsk (1978a) described as the 'Age of Projects', between the middle and end of the sixteenth century, iron consumption per head of population doubled from 2kg to 4kg (King 2005 p.20).

Estimates of charcoal use per ton of pig and bar iron production are also available between the early sixteenth and late eighteenth centuries (Hammersley 1973). Combining iron production and fuel efficiency data makes it possible to estimate the level of charcoal consumption for the industry. On this basis, in the early sixteenth century, the (pig and bar) iron industry used just over 10 000 tonnes of charcoal (6 000 toe). As shown in Figure 4.3, consumption had grown nearly twelve-fold to 115 000 tonnes (70 000 toe) by 1600. Given the quantity of wood required, this would have involved the annual clearance or coppicing of 250 000 acres of land. To give a comparison, in 1700, around 10 percent of England's land was covered by trees and hedgerows and it amounted to 3 million acres (Hatcher 1993 p.55). In other words, around one-twelfth of the wooded land in the country was used to produce a relatively small amount of iron.

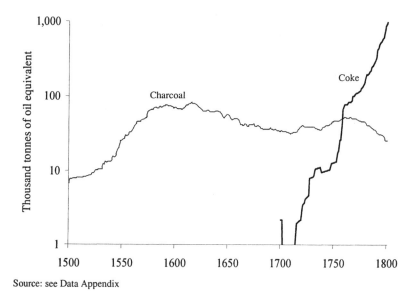

Source: see Data Appendix

Figure 4.3 Woodfuel and Coal Consumption in the Iron Industry, 1500–1800

Decline of the British Charcoal Iron Industry

After its spectacular growth in the sixteenth century, from the 1620s, the English iron industry started to stagnate and decline. The source of decline of the iron industry in Britain remains controversial. It coincided with a period of economic depression and the importing of Swedish iron (King 2005 p.20). Thomas (1986) argued that fuel scarcity was the main factor. He stated that, as the iron furnaces used greater quantities of wood, they were pushed to more remote areas. The price data presented in Figure 4.1 is not directly relevant to the specific 'rural' market of charcoal industry. In any case, each ironmaster faced different constraints.

The desire for cheaper fuel costs certainly existed. Whereas in the early 1500s it took more than ten tonnes of charcoal to produce one tonne of bar iron, by the mid-eighteenth century it took little more than three tonnes (Hammersley 1973). From the 1580s, ironmasters tried to smelt iron with coke (Flinn 1978 p.146).

Despite the dramatic rise in demand, the English charcoal iron industry never used more woodfuel than around 1620. That is, it only ever needed 250 000 acres of land (one-tenth of English wooded and hedgerow land) to produce its energy source. To a large extent, it failed to compete with the Swedish iron industry because charcoal was available in abundance in the Baltic and not Britain. It does appear that the case of the charcoal iron industry was one of facing resource constraints. Efforts were made to find solutions, yet no viable ones appeared until many decades later.

In 1700, pig iron production had fallen back to 18 000 tons and bar iron to 13 000. Charcoal use had fallen back to 55 000 tonnes in 1700, when much of the pig and bar iron used in Britain was imported. The forests of the Baltic were providing heat for the iron consumed in Britain. By 1700, half of the bar iron was of Swedish origin (King 2005 p.23). Charcoal iron production was labour-intensive; given the high wages in Britain, relative to foreign businesses, the domestic industry could hardly survive – and only did due to British import and Swedish export duties (Daunton 2002 p.212).

Over the next fifty years, the British iron industry suffered dramatic swings of fortune. In 1716, the government imposed an embargo on Swedish imports. It was introduced as a result of Swedish negotiations with the Catholics, and the British government feared it was to support the overthrowing of the protestant rulers – instead the Swedes were actually raising funds for their wars against the Russians. The loss of imports drove up iron prices, production of the existing industry and investment in new iron works. But, by the time many of the new works were productive, the embargo was lifted and the Swedes had returned, coupled with Russian imports. By 1735, British production fell back to its 1716 level of production, around 20 000 tonnes of pig iron (King 2005 p.8).

Iron demand increased in the 1740s, such that, by 1750, production had risen to 28 000 and 19 000 tons of pig and bar iron respectively. The industry consumed 77 000 tonnes of charcoal, of which two-fifths was for pig iron output. Consumption per head rose from 5kg in 1710 to more than 7kg in 1760, two-thirds of which were satisfied by imported fuels (King 2005 p.20).

The Switch to Coke

The revival of the British iron industry and the growth in demand for domestic fuels was initially gradual and then radical. Most agree that the use of coke for smelting iron spread slowly in the first half of the eighteenth century (Angerstein 2001 p.ix, King 2005). In 1709, Abraham Darby introduced a new method for smelting iron which used coke. He had been one of many, since 1580, that had brought out a patent to substitute away from woodfuels. In addition to the usual teething problems (Hyde 1973, Mott 1983), it seems, however, that his method was not more profitable than using charcoal for a long time. Based on Hyde's (1973) information, Figure 4.4 compares the variable costs of producing one tonne of pig iron using charcoal and coke.

Throughout the eighteenth century, to its demise, the production of pig iron from charcoal stayed relatively stable. The principle change in industry was the variable cost of producing iron using coke. In 1750, around 10 tonnes of coke were required to produce a single tonne of pig iron. By 1800, fuel requirements had fallen to around 4 tonnes of coke (Smil 1999 p.167). Inevitably, such efficiency improvements were reflected in substantially cheaper variable costs of production, increasing the incentive to build coke iron furnaces if needed.

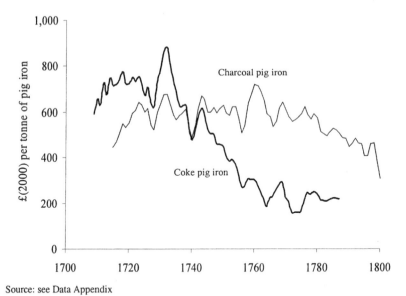

Source: see Data Appendix

Figure 4.4 Variable Cost of Charcoal and Coke Pig Iron Industries, 1700–1800

The new coking furnaces were relatively capital-intensive, requiring large investments. High interest rates made such risky investments difficult to fund. Another factor delaying uptake was that few had the technical expertise to oversee the installation of the coke smelting operations. The plant also required large supplies of fuel, far more than for an equivalent-sized charcoal plant. Thus, potentially large transport investments might be needed to provide the necessary coal (Hyde 1973 p.64).

Provided charcoal remained widely available, there was little incentive to build entirely new furnaces simply because coal was an abundant resource. Where deforestation made charcoal increasingly scarce, where labour costs made charcoal relatively expensive, and as the demand for iron products rose within Britain and with its trading partners, coal smelting became increasingly attractive.

The second half of the eighteenth century experienced dramatic growth – in 1800, pig iron production was 285 000 tonnes (see Figure 4.5) and bar iron output 70 000 tonnes. Consumption per head was close to 8kg (King 2005 p.25). It supports the traditional view that coal iron production began to dominate the industry in the second half of the eighteenth century.[6]

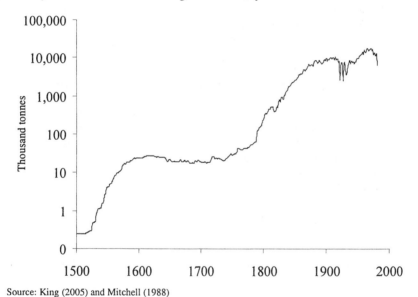

Source: King (2005) and Mitchell (1988)

Figure 4.5 Pig Iron Production, 1500–2000

Coal use in the iron industry began to grow first for pig iron production. It jumped nearly seven-fold from under 3 000 tonnes in 1750 to nearly 20 000 tonnes in fifteen years. Then, it kept on rising to 170 000 in 1800. By 1840, the coal-based pig iron industry's output was more than one million tonnes. This was

6. Growing concern in Sweden about the potential threat to their exports from the growth of iron smelted with coal in Britain inspired the Swedish Government and other bodies, like the Swedish Steel Producers' Association, to send travellers to Britain to engage in an early form of industrial espionage. Angerstein (2001) produced his remarkable diaries of his reconnaissance visits to industrial Britain, undertaken between 1773 and 1775.

one of the prime examples of the extraordinary production increases produced during the heyday of the Industrial Revolution.

This did not kill the charcoal iron industry for some time, however. The charcoal pig iron production had been in a decline since the 1750s, and by the 1780s it must have seemed that it was terminal, especially as its competing technology had been dominant since the 1760s. As demand grew and the variable costs of production fell (see Figure 4.4), it managed one last flurry. It was, however, its swan song.

Other parts of the charcoal iron industry followed. In the fining stage, the pig iron was heated to remove the carbon and converted to bar iron. Coal contained sulphur and would contaminate the iron, if in contact. To avoid damage, a method was devised in the 1780s that placed the iron in ceramic 'pots'. This 'potting' process grew in popularity, taking about 40 percent of the bar iron market. It never surpassed the charcoal industry though.

A more appropriate method was the 'puddling' process, which burnt the coal in a reverberatory furnace – that is, by reflecting the heat off the ceiling. But, Henry Cort's 'puddling' process was not an immediate success.[7] The process, in which 'plastic' iron was stirred and turned over in a reverberatory furnace, to expel the carbon and turn it into malleable iron, initially could not use 'grey' or high-silicon iron, which came from the production of pig iron using coke. So, the refiners had to go through a preliminary refining process.

In fact, the charcoal and coke pig iron had different properties, and the demand for these different types of iron reflected distinct requirements. The high-silicon content of coke pig iron added value and hence it was sold for higher prices, when used directly for cast iron products, such as stoves and firebacks. But, if it was used as an intermediary for bar iron, the high-silicon iron was of less value and sold for a lower price (King 2005 p.25).

The problems associated with the puddling process only lasted a few years, however. Once they were solved, the dominance of coal in the iron sector was complete. While charcoal iron production was about 15 000 tonnes in 1800, the puddling fineries grew from 10 000 tonnes in 1790 to 50 000 tonnes in 1800. Production doubled in three decades (with stagnation in the 1810s), reaching nearly 400 000 tonnes in 1840.

Energy Consumption of the Iron Industry

By 1800, the iron industry accounted for more than 10 percent of total British coal use, equivalent to one million tons of oil (see Figure 4.6). This growth continued unabated. By 1840, to smelt one million tons of pig iron and refine 400 000 tons of bar iron it needed nearly 9.6 million tons of coal (5.6 mtoe), converted into coke.

7. The story of Cort's processes for making wrought iron with coal, instead of charcoal, as the fuel and for rolling to bar iron, instead of finishing with relatively slow forge hammers, and of his struggle for recognition and reward, is told in Mott (1983).

In 1828, James Beaumont Neilson patented the hot blast technique, which transformed the iron industry once again. Until his ideas were understood, many ironmasters believed colder blasts improved the quality of their iron. They associated cold winter days with better output, and concluded that temperature must play a part. In fact, the crucial ingredient was dry air. For a given blast of air, the less humidity in the air, the more could be combusted (Hyde 1973 p.146).

The introduction of the dry 'hot blast' sharply reduced fuel costs. In five years, all Scottish ironmasters had adopted the technique. It changed them from a fringe supplier to the most competitive producers in Britain. Although slower to adopt the method in England and Wales, the hot blast accounted for 95 percent of output by 1860 (Hyde 1973 pp.149–5).

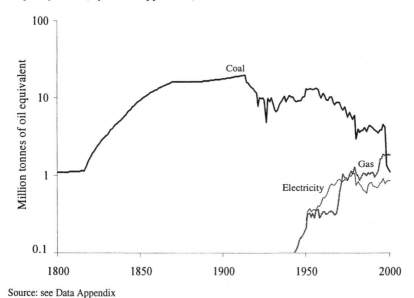

Source: see Data Appendix

Figure 4.6 Energy Consumption in the Iron and Steel Industry Industry,1800–2000

The fuel savings made from introducing the hot blast depended on the carbon content of the coal used. The high temperatures achieved with the hot blast meant that raw coal could be used instead of coke. Traditionally, the less carbon in the coal, the more coal was required to produce one tonne of coke. The new method avoided the coking stage, thus saving coal. In regions, such as Scotland, with low carbon content, great savings could be made. In South Wales, the coal had a high carbon content, and ironmasters benefited only a little from the hot blast. To a certain extent, the rate of adoption in different regions reflected the coal savings (Hyde 1973 p.157).

By the 1880s, one tonne of pig iron could be produced with about two tonnes of coal. These improvements were the result of technological development and industrial capacity. The greater the hearth, the more output a furnace could produce. These had increased from around 15 cubic metres in 1700, to 20 cubic metres in 1770 to nearly 100 in 1800. The size of hearths continued to expand, the largest reaching 250 cubic metres in 1850 and nearly 400 by the end of the nineteenth century (Smil 1999 pp.166–7).

As well as increasing the size and volume of hearths, ironmasters were raising the pressure in the furnaces and, so, the temperatures achieved. Just like the furnaces, the forges, set up to produce bar iron, also expanded – in number, size and output. The annual output of individual forges reached 50 000 tonnes of bar ion by the 1870s (Hyde 1973 p.176).

In 1870, the iron industry was producing six million tonnes of pig iron (Mitchell 1988 p.283). The whole industry consumed sixteen million tonnes of coal. The iron industry had become central to the economy, providing the building material for much of it, including the heating, power, transport and lighting equipment and infrastructure (see Chapters 5, 6 and 7). Thus, the ability to generate colossal amounts of concentrated heat at lower cost was embodied in the new equipment and infrastructure that was driving down the price of other energy services.

5. HEATING IN HOUSEHOLDS

Demand for Clothing

To complement food in helping to regulate body temperature (briefly mentioned earlier), efforts to reduce heat loss have been crucial to keeping the body warm. Across medieval Britain, "clothing provided the essential thermal protection from the elements … [A]ll wore shiftlike tunics of varying length over a shirt and hose. Cloaks provided further protection, especially if lined with fur" (Crowley 2004 p.7).

Traditionally, the average person wore much heavier clothing and was more active indoors than today. Heat was generated by being active. Fabrics kept bodies insulated. It has been proposed that that the average person before the twentieth century (and the advent of lighter clothing) lost less heat than today (Billington 1982 p.18).

The average person buying clothing in the medieval era had three textiles from which to chose. Worsteds were made of relatively light, coarse and 'dry' yarns. Woollens were woven from heavier and finer 'wet' yarns. Worsteds were cheaper than woollen garments. A third textile was made by combining the two.

Between the eleventh and the thirteenth centuries, the production of worsteds in England grew considerably (Munro 2006 p.3). As prices fell, more people were able to be clothed properly (that is, instead of wearing 'rags'), reducing heat loss. And, for all but the wealthiest, worsted garments sufficed, or were still the only choice.

Beyond the basic demands for protection from the cold, the provision of textile was for more subtle needs of comfort and conspicuous consumption. The quality of fabrics and their cleanliness were signs of wealth and status. Also, after the middle of the fourteenth century, gender distinctions were created, as men's tunics shortened (Crowley 2004 p.7). The ability to wear shorter tunics could well have been a fashion reflecting the ability to buy warmer fabrics and, therefore, wealth. Across medieval Europe, the English woollens were considered the finest and most expensive – especially those from the Welsh Marches, Herefordshire and Shropshire (Munro 2006 p.6-7).

In the tenth century, the introduction of mechanisation of the fulling process, needed for the woollens to make them more robust and heavier, reduced the costs of the garments by about 15 percent (Munro 2006 p.10). During the late fourteenth and early fifteenth centuries, most of the fulling in England was mechanised (see Chapter 5).

Woollens were still considerably more expensive, both because preparation processes were more extensive and the raw materials, such as the wool itself and dyes used, were more expensive. So, reducing the price of woollens may not have increased their consumption in poorer households. But, a decline in the price of woollens would shift some of the demand for clothing towards finer garments, reducing the demand for worsteds and, therefore, the price of the inferior garments. From the fourteenth century, the major improvements in the ability to provide better quality clothing and the cheapness of textiles enabled the British population to reduce heat loss.

Lighter clothing, and the ease of movement it provided, was desirable and, at times, a painful trade-off between warmth, comfort and fashion needed to be made. As lighter fabrics, such as linen and cotton, were supplied in Britain from the seventeenth century, they began to replace wool, but in colder weather or at cold times of day insulation was paramount. Inevitably, while the price was still high, the wearing of these fabrics was a sign of affluence. Then, as they became available at affordable prices in the eighteenth century, more people bought them. In *The Wealth of Nations*, published in 1776, Adam Smith explained that a "linen shirt, for example, is not strictly speaking necessary of life ... But, in the present times, through the greater part of Europe, a creditable day-labourer would be ashamed to appear in public without a linen shirt" (Smith 1776 Vol.2 B5 Ch.2).

Demand for Shelter

Another crucial way of ensuring body heat, especially in the British Isles, was to create adequate shelter. The Anglo-Saxon approach to shelter was to set wooden posts into the ground with planks covered in wattling, mud or turf. In medieval times, stone foundations replaced these lighter and more temporary structures (Crowley 2004 p.11).

It is interesting to consider the cost of remaining sheltered from the elements, as the quality of the home acts as a partial substitute for clothing and heating services. Clark (2002) produced several long time series for the nominal cost of renting constant-quality houses and an indicator of the average quality of housing. His nominal cost of renting series can be converted into a real price series by using the retail price index (Officer 2007b). The resulting real price series suggests that the real cost of housing in Britain, keeping quality constant, leapt up (by nearly 50 percent) in the 1670s. It then fell gradually until the end of the eighteenth century. In the first decades of the nineteenth century, it rose substantially (by more than 50 percent). Remaining constant for a few decades, the real cost of housing shot up again in the 1870s (increasing by about 50 percent). It only began to decline at the beginning of the twentieth century as more homes were built.

The quality of housing appears to have remained constant throughout the seventeenth century, and then improved considerably up to 1770 (30 percent, using Clark's (2002) index). The early Industrial Revolution was associated with a decline in housing quality, no doubt due to the rising cost of housing. After 1850, standards of housing began to improve again, such that by the end of the nineteenth century they had returned to the levels of quality appreciated by those living in the early eighteenth century – but now with many more living in urban areas.

The effects of the trends on heating can be mixed. On the whole, the level of protection and insulation from the elements will follow the overall quality of housing. For example, timber housing provided a shell to insulate the household from the cold and the humidity. Plastering improved the buildings resistance to the elements. Plaster was often made from limestone. Later, bricks were introduced to provide even greater protection from the outside world. Thus, better protection might have existed in the mid-eighteenth century and less in the mid-nineteenth century. On the other hand, the shift to urban areas and rising cost of renting reduced the average size of homes. Since dwelling sizes shrank, smaller spaces needed to be heated.

Gathering information about the quality of insulation through time is difficult. Ayres (2005) suggests that, in modern buildings, only 5 percent of the energy burnt converts into useful heat once the efficiency of the equipment and especially losses through walls and the roof have been taken into account. DTI (2003) presents trends in insulation between 1987 and 2001, which indicate that at the end of the twentieth century 10 percent of homes lacked any insulation and only about 15 percent had full insulation. Yet, it also suggests that the quality of the housing stock had improved greatly since the 1970s. Looking further back, homes were probably so poorly protected from the elements before the nineteenth century that the concept of heating was different – it was pointless to try to warm the ambient air, explaining why people kept warm through their proximity to a source (discussed below). Unfortunately, insufficient information exists to provide estimates of the evolution of insulation in Britain. The reader should be aware of this limitation when interpreting estimates of long-run trends in heating services.

Air Temperature

Another factor to consider is, of course, the outdoor temperature. Human existence revolved around the "basic dependence on nature and its rhythms which impose[d] fluctuations in life and labour, making the best of the season of fine weather and withdrawing when winter [came]" (Roche 2001 p.109).

From the seventeenth century, the Met Office (2006) provides records of average daily temperatures in England. In addition, evidence about average temperatures has been estimated back to the eleventh century. Although not as useful as variations below the average temperature (thus, highlighting extreme cold weather), this data provides indications of the need for shelter and heating over the long term

Air temperature during the twelfth and thirteenth centuries was exceptionally warm, averaging around 10°C around 1200 (Anderson 1981 p.2). This may have led to a lower demand for heavy clothing, shelter and fuel. Alternatively, it may have created an increase in people's expected ambient temperature for a number of generations.

During the second half of the fourteenth century, in addition to the devastation of the Black Death, populations had to get use to lower temperatures, as they fell back to the more normal historical average, around 9°C. Then, from the second half of the seventeenth century, people were faced with the hardship of the 'Little Ice Age'. The declining trend in temperatures – averaging a miserable 8°C at the end of the seventeenth century – undoubtedly led to a higher demand for heating (see Figure 4.7).

The trend was dramatically reversed rising to 10°C by the 1740s. From the 1750s on, for the next 130 years, the average temperature averaged 9°C, although with considerable fluctuation – some notable cold periods included 1782–85 and 1812–16 averaging around 8°C. After the late nineteenth century, temperatures in England were on an upward trend (or possibly a rise in the annual average to 9.5°C).

Also of relevance was humidity. Average annual rainfall is available from the mid-eighteenth century (Met Office 2006). Here, there were less clear trends. Most of the period of observation averaged around 900 mm of rain. It would seem that the 1780s and 1802–07 were fairly dry, often having less than 800mm per year; as were much of the 1850s, 1860s and 1890s. There were few clearly wet periods, apart from 1875 to 1883, when rainfall was around 1 000mm.

The evidence suggests that the need for shelter and heating was most pronounced in the second half of the seventeenth century, and perhaps the late 1870s (especially 1879, which experienced one of the coldest years, 7.4°C, and the wettest years, with 984mm of rain). It appears to have been of least need in the first half of the eighteenth century and twentieth century (1975–76 were warm, over 10°C on average, and dry, both less than 800mm of rain).[8]

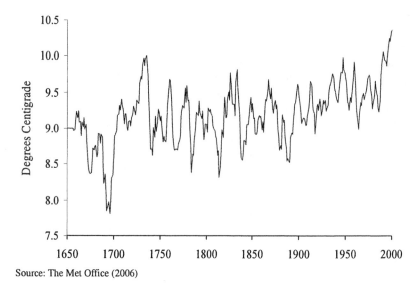

Source: The Met Office (2006)

Figure 4.7 Five-Year Average Air Temperature in Central England, 1650–2000

Demand for Heating

With considerable humidity and low outdoor temperatures, especially by twenty-first century standards, keeping the interior of a home warm was a necessary supplement to clothing and shelter. One commentator points out that "the demand for heat varies extremely in different individuals according to constitutional peculiarities, diet, clothing, and many other circumstances such as exercise, excitement and time of life" (quoted in Billington 1982 p.18).

Observations about preferences for indoor temperatures can show how demand for heat has changed. At the beginning of the nineteenth century, it was suggested that 15°C was an ideal temperature for dwellings. It was commonly believed that excessive temperatures indoors was unhealthy – although this may have been a form of cognitive dissonance to ensure that heating expenditure was kept down. "Sensitivity to cold and heat floats between the innate and the acquired: it is a profoundly cultural fact ... [and] a biological phenomenon" (Roche 2000 p.108)

In fact, until relatively recently, the concept of the demand for ambient heat appears to be inappropriate, especially in Britain. "Where heating was by means of braziers, fires and stoves, it was simple enough to approach the source of heat

8. Analysis searching for a possible negative (or positive) relationship between temperature and rainfall indicates that the correlation is non-existent.

if one was cold, or to move away if too warm...[thus,] temperature, in any modern sense, had no meaning..." (Billington 1982 p.17). It is suggested, therefore, that each person had some control over their own needs.

"The medieval hall and its open, chimneyless, hearth provide a baseline for studying ... the elementary comforts of warmth and illumination ... [Until] at least the sixteenth century, ... this single room provided the crucial space for domestic, social, productive and administrative purposes" (Crowley 2004 p.8). A distinct advantage of the open hearth was the economies of scale in fuel use it benefited from, which was important when entertaining and keeping warm large numbers of people, as was custom at the time.

In many instances, a household generated heat for cooking, which provided warmth – a positive secondary benefit. Often, additional heat was required; the fuel available dictated the amount of heat generated, but also the amount of clothing people wore, the level of their activity needed and the proximity they sat from one another and from animals. "[P]romiscuity and crowding served as all-purpose remedy for the cold" (Roche 2000 p.108).

Social interactions based around the need to keep warm, and the open fire, were very different to indoor dynamics experienced today. The general ambient temperature was of little interest to a person seeking warmth. An individuals' location relative to the heat source was central to keeping warm. There was an important hierarchy of placing by the fire – more respected members of the family and guests received the warmest seats. The lord of the house often sat back to the fire, in a large wooden chair, the heat permeating but not burning. 'Hearthmen' were those fortunate to be seated by the lord; some considered themselves happy to face a singeing fire. "Free bench" was a right given to widows, and referred to their privilege of being seated by the hearth (Crowley 2004 p.10). At the other end of the hall, the young were generally relegated to the edge of the halo of heat, probably wearing a lot of itchy and cumbersome worsted. Thus, a community's social structure and access to heat were intertwined.

As mentioned earlier, heating was first driven by cooking requirements. Probably the poor would make do with the heat generated from cooking, the food in their stomachs and the worsted on their backs. More wealthy homes would supplement that heat. Demand for further heat increased woodfuel consumption. Rising income also increased its consumption. Hatcher (1993 p. 31) proposes that population was the main driver for the rising demand for woodfuel in the sixteenth and early seventeenth centuries. Except for a valued guest, an additional person in the main hall was unlikely to increase the fuel consumption of the family. In the longer run, however, rising populations translated run into more households. Each home having a hearth, a fire was needed to be lit in it.

Smoke and the Demand for Ventilation

The fire had virtues. Yet, it is worth assessing the discomforts of early homes, partly to reflect on how far the average house has evolved. One Welsh thirteenth century traveller described the main hall he visited one night as having "a floor full of holes and uneven ... so exceedingly slippery with cow's urine and their dung" (quoted in Crowley 2004 p.4). He then explained how "a crone feeding a fire ... throw[s] a lapful of husks on to the fire, so that it was not easy for any man alive to endure that smoke entering his nostrils" (quoted in Crowley 2004 p.4).

Many homes did not have any provision for the escape of smoke. As the open hearth was the principal source of cooking and heating, the lack of a flue meant that smoke had a tendency to waft through the room before exiting through holes in the walls or ceiling. Breathing in wood smoke was of considerable harm to people's lungs. Life expectancy was greatly reduced by the burden it imposed.

Another problem was that fuel, such as wood or charcoal, consumed oxygen (2.5 kgs of oxygen for every kg of charcoal) and released carbon dioxide (3.5kgs), thus, the air frequently needed to be replaced both for the fuel to burn properly and for the inhabitants to breathe healthily (quoted in Fitchen 1981 p.498). Unfortunately, the warmer air was also most likely to escape out of holes provided for ventilation. Thus, there was often a trade-off between a warm room and a well-ventilated one.

The problems of smoke created some sophisticated solutions to improve ventilation and ensure fresh air (Fitchen 1981 p.500). One example was the louvre (from the French "l'ouvert": the 'open'). A tower-like structure, with a roof and openings on the sides, was placed in the middle of the ceiling and allowed the smoke to waft up from the hearth into the tower and out of these openings; its roof and position above the main ceiling minimised the wind and rain entering the hall, and introduced light. Even when the chimney grew in popularity, open hearths with louvres were being built for aristocratic and gentrified families, indicating that it was not an inferior technology (Crowley 2004 p.14).

Adoption of the Chimney

The Norman conquest of England in 1066 brought major transformations in architecture, including the chimney. The first chimneys were introduced into the keeps built by the conquerors in the twelfth century. These keeps were tall and thin to appear imposing and to tower over the common people. It was, therefore, not appropriate to build a wide hall with an open hearth. Instead rooms were stacked one on top of each other, making a chimney more appropriate for heating. Because a vertical chimney made the tower vulnerable, if attacked with missiles, they tended to be built rising obliquely through the keep. The consequence of this structure was that smoke could not travel vertically and the air differential was insufficient to create much of an upward draft.

The fireplace (with its chimney) was a poor supplier of heat. Even today's fireplaces tend to lose 86 percent of the heat through the chimney (Fitchen 1981 p.498). But the chimneys in the Norman keeps were inefficient providers of heat and poor extractors of smoke, due to their shape. In the thirteenth century, as the need to appear imposing subsided, such keeps reverted to open hearths, with chimneys in secondary rooms (Crowley 2004 pp.29–30).

The second generation of chimneys was associated with the decline of feudalism. By the fourteenth century, as knights with land increasingly paid their lords a fee to absolve them of military responsibility, lords hired other knights. As these additional warriors stayed for extended periods of time, they required accommodation. Chambers in multi-storey buildings were built to satisfy them. One of the features of these chambers was the chimneys, which were more appropriate than open hearths when small fires were needed. These hired men spent more time in their own chambers, as did the lord and his lady; all of them warmed by their private fires. Although the hall continued to be heated with an open hearth, it tended to be a less desirable place to be, certainly in terms of status (Crowley 2004 pp.32–6).

In the sixteenth century, architecture changed dramatically. The number of rooms in the average house increased, reflecting the separation of functions within the household, the desire for privacy and the emulation of noble houses. The 'axial' chimney provided the central structure of the building. It separated the parlour, which greeted guests at the front, from the hall, which was now smaller. Both tended to have fireplaces, ensuring more rooms could be heated. Furthermore, in wealthier homes, the kitchen was in another room at the back, thus reducing the need for heat in the hall. Finally, bedrooms were frequently above the hall and beside the chimney, benefiting from the warm air – though they sometimes had their own fireplace (Crowley 2004 pp.51–4).

Despite the increase in chimneys, many rooms were not heated. A study of houses in Norwich between 1580 and 1730 indicates that one-fifth of homes had three or fewer rooms, and the average number of fireplaces per house increased only from 1.1 to 1.3. Two-fifths of houses had between four and six rooms, and the average increased from 1.7 to 2 chimneys. Given that less than half the rooms were heated, it is not clear that the new house design led to better standards of comfort (Crowley 2004 p.56).

This problem may have been exacerbated by the introduction of the 'hearth' tax in 1662, which was meant to reflect wealth and certainly penalised the more modern architectural design, discouraging the installation of additional fireplaces. The tax (on fireplaces and hearths) increased the cost of heating homes by charging households two shillings (about £(2000)10) per fireplace. It was repealed in 1689 for its regressive nature for modest incomes (as the poor were exempt) and its intrusion on domestic spaces (Crowley 2004 pp.56–7).

The tax highlighted wealth distinctions and had its role in influencing technological choice. The poor only had one hearth. A further reason for the common household to have kept the open fire was the investment required for conversion. Few poor were likely to have new homes built, and, therefore, they kept the old design. But, this also implied the need to use wood in the fire, even when the cost of collecting or buying wood was expensive (in time or money).

By the end of seventeenth century, two-thirds to three-quarters of houses in England and Wales still only had one chimney. One-fifth had two chimneys. Less than one-fifth of the population had more than half of all the chimneys. Some homes had twenty chimneys (Crowley 2004 p.57).

To have an axial chimney was a sign of not being a poor labourer. "The central chimney symbolized control over the natural, human and economic processes that produced a respectable way of life" (Crowley 2004 p.70). Thus, many lower middle class families had their homes remodelled or rebuilt to reflect their status. But, as the expression goes, "it is easier to build two chimneys, than to maintain one" (quoted in Crowley 2004 p.58).

Fire was also important for health. In particular, common wisdom stressed their necessity to remove humidity from the house. The open hearth appears to have been superior for these purposes (Crowley 2004 p.57). Health perception, however, swung favour towards the chimney, in the eyes of the well-to-do. The chimney was far safer and produced less smoke and soot in the house. As filth was associated with poor hygiene and disease, methods that would minimise the level of soot were considered desirable, including the fireplace and chimney (Crowley 2004 p.72).

Chimneys came as a basic design of the building. When new houses were built, especially in the growing urban centres, they were designed with chimneys. This did make sense since, in most cities, coal had become the main fuel source by the seventeenth century.

The Switch to Coal

It seems that the evolution towards the (in some respects) inferior chimney design was driven by the need to assert status and the availability of fuel. Coal had been used for certain industrial activities for many centuries. It could not be burnt in an open fire. While fumes from wood fire were unpleasant, the noxious smoke most coals produced was hardly bearable indoors. Only once the chimney was introduced could smoke be removed from the house.

For a while, in England, woodfuel was burnt in the fireplace. The chimney, on its own, was not sufficient to enable households to use coal. A heap of coal lumped in a fireplace usually failed to burn. The dark fuel needed additional ventilation, using an iron grate. The coal could be placed in it, and air could rise from underneath, helping the coal to combust.

Coal consumption in urban areas grew substantially from the beginning of the sixteenth century. Based on evidence from the South of England, coal prices were falling substantially. Averaging about £300 per toe at the end of the fifteenth century, prices fell to about £250 by the early sixteenth century. Remaining constant for a few decades, they dropped to £150 per toe in 1550 (see Figure 4.1). Irrespective of its drawbacks, a commodity that halves its original price will generate important increases in consumption. By 1600, it had fallen to £100. For the next century, it fluctuated between £100 and £200, apart from during the civil war of the 1640s, when prices reached £270 per toe.

Converting fuel prices into effective heating, using the efficiency estimates for each technology, provides an indicator of the marginal cost advantages of using coal compared with woodfuel (see Figure 4.8). The open hearth was more efficient. But, as mentioned above, coal prices fell dramatically in the sixteenth century. This translates into a decline in the price of 'effective' heating from £3 500 per tonne of oil equivalent in 1500 to £1 000 in 1600. The open-hearth, using woodfuel prices for the South of England, remained oscillating around £1 500 for this period. Thus, in the South of England at least, coal became an attractive option, despite the poor quality of chimneys at drawing up the smoke.

As an illustration of the uptake of chimneys and coal use, a model of heating consumption was developed. Knowledge of coal consumption between 1500 and 1800 provided an anchor for estimating heating required. This produced an estimate for an average household in 1800. Variations in income, fuel prices and temperatures, as well as their associated elasticities, generated a 'back-cast' of heating consumption to 1500. The coal consumption was subtracted from this overall heating consumption estimate, and the residual was assumed to be woodfuel consumption.

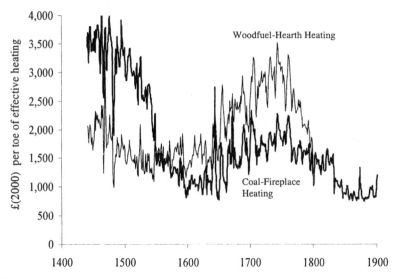

Source: see Data Appendix

Figure 4.8 Price of Domestic Heating using Woodfuel in an Open-Hearth and Coal in a Fireplace, 1450–1900

Again, the quantities presented in Figure 4.9 are purely indicative of trends. It has been suggested that in the mid-seventeenth century the two fuels shared equally the domestic market in England (Hatcher 1993 p.49). Times of hardship were experienced when supply networks were disrupted, as during the civil war coal ships had difficulty leaving or reaching ports. By the second half of the eighteenth century, domestic heating was predominantly dependent on coal.

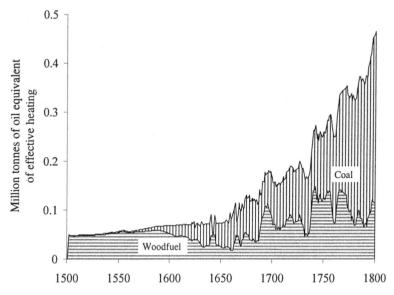

Source: see Data Appendix

Figure 4.9 Estimate of Domestic Effective Heating using Woodfuel and Coal, 1500–1800

As the market developed, the coal merchant had many varieties of coal on offer. Found in the North East, bituminous coal was the main supply for the East Coast, including London. When heated, bituminous coal tended to lump together. Lacking oxygen, it would stop burning, unless poked and separated. Thus, such fires needed constant attention.

Found in the Welsh mines, anthracite was far superior. Much cleaner, producing little smoke, it could burn all day with little attention. Its main disadvantage was lighting it. Often, other fuels needed to be used to start the fire. Also, there was far less of it. Thus, the higher value and lower supply drove up the price of the high quality coal (Davidson 1986 p.95).

So, apart from the wealthy, most households burnt coal that spread dirt and smoke, and required time-consuming chores of preparing, cleaning and tending to the fire. The average housewife needed to clean twice a day to stop the dirt spreading (Davidson 1986 p.95).

Despite their role in reducing indoor pollution, chimneys were far from being the perfect cure. Few masons understood the process of draughts in chimneys. This was compounded by poor craftsmanship. The upshot was that in many cases smoke 'backfired' and came into the house. Often, homes needed to hire the expertise of the over-demanded and expensive chimney doctors. In 1732, one chimney doctor charged two guineas (equivalent to about £220 in today's money) for curing one chimney (Cullingford 2000 p.37). Given that the average income was about £300 per year, this was only available to the wealthy. The alternative was simply putting up with poorly ventilated fires and smoke, with considerable long-term health implications. One book of advice from an elder man to his younger wife about man's needs suggests "a smoky chimney is in the top three things to irritate a man, along with a leaking roof and a scolding woman" (Crowley 2004 p.5).

An additional financial expense for chimneys more than one storey high was incurred by calling on the expert skills of the chimney sweep to remove trapped soot. This cost around 2 pence (equivalent to £2 in 2000 money) per chimney in 1589 (Cullingford 2000 p.7). Failing to call on his services would also lead to poor fires and much smoke, as well as the risk of the soot falling back down covering the room; even worse, excessive soot up a chimney could increase the risk of fires. A small house would need a visit every six to twelve months, producing two bushels of soot. A larger home tended to need four visits per year, producing a total of six bushels of soot (Davidson 1986 p.95).

Although some smoke wafted back into the room and plenty of soot got stuck in the chimney, most of it was deposited across the neighbourhood. The chimney was an example of an externalising technology. The fireplace with its chimney was an inferior source of heating. If woodfuels were burnt in a fireplace, the private cost of heating increased. But, of course, the chimney allowed coal to be burnt. Households very rarely used coal in an open hearth, because the full costs of burning coal – combining the price of coal, the heating efficiency and the smoke damage – were too great. But with a chimney, despite the reduction in efficiency, by about 1550, it became cheaper to use coal as a heating fuel and externalise the smoke costs.

The introduction of the chimney enabled a dramatic growth in the use of coal in urban households, with a substantial increase in air pollution. Although many of the complaints about pollution were focussed at the more obvious industrial activities, by 1700, more than half of the pollution was caused by the residential sector.

Resource Scarcity and Abundance

Between 1500 and 1700, the population doubled. The 1670s and 1690s were exceptionally cold (see Figure 4.7). The growing middle classes were appreciating a degree of comfort. The switch to coal in many households had alleviated some of the pressures on woodfuel resources. Yet, by 1700, fuel supplies, whether organic or mineral, had been stretched.

Just like in the organic energy system, the mineral energy system was subject to a rate of flow (that is, extraction and supply) of resources. Coal production had managed to increase since the fifteenth century, especially in the North-East, thanks to large reserves near the surface and close to the River Tyne. Its limits were being set by the depth at which water flooded mines and the distribution network.

As the easily accessible and extractable coal was used up, prices started to rise. As displayed in Figures 4.1 and 4.8, the price of fuels and heating more than doubled between 1640 and 1700. The rising price led to the search for solutions. In the case of coal, scarcity was only a readjustment, a call to increase the flow. The solutions do not always come quickly or smoothly, though.

From the early seventeenth century, wooden wagon-ways were developed to transport the coal across land. In many cases, they managed to reduce the cost of overland carriage. It was not, however, an ideal solution, as successful distribution depended on the appropriate terrain to deliver the wagons. Also, land owners, over which the coal travelled, charged high rents (Hatcher 1993).

Until the mid-nineteenth century and the development of railways, access to waterways continued to be essential to transporting such a bulky commodity. In certain areas, a canal could be built. These provided a vital link between certain centres of high production and others of high demand. Again, costs of carriage dropped.

This enabled new regions to become accessible. In the eighteenth century, other regions started to compete with the merchants of Newcastle. Pits opened up across the British Isles. In Scotland, Yorkshire, Lancashire, the West Midlands and South Wales, coal production soared between 1700 and 1830.

Another way to produce more coal was to remove the water flooding mines. An important technical development in the eighteenth century was the improved ability to pump water. Many deep veins remained untapped because they flooded, risking miners' lives. Manual labour or animals could pump, but only if the quantities of water filling the mines were relatively modest. Mines in the proximity of rivers could use waterwheels, increasing the volume of water extracted. The introduction of the steam engine, burning cheap coal, managed to pump far greater quantities of water. Improvements in power technology had a major impact on the production of coal. Similarly, the coal mining industry provided a boost to the demand for power (see Chapter 5) by investing in steam engines and enabling engine producers to achieve economies of scale. The mining industry also inadvertently (no doubt) created a huge demand for its own product.

The Need for Innovation

In addition to finding a greater supply, higher prices had stimulated efforts to reduce energy consumption for heating. Despite its central role in society, centuries passed with little effort to understand or improve the quality or efficiency of heating. The average person kept warm beside the fire, accepting its costs and its inadequacies. Indeed, "people lived in the civilisation of the open, free fire, with its habits, its repeated operations, its utensils, its need for constant maintenance in order to combat damp and cold, its ashes collected for use in major washing chores, for scouring pots and pans, and fertilising the kitchen-garden, its embers which had to be covered at night, its smoke which made one's eyes smart but protected hams, its pans hung from the pot-hanger and its pots entrusted to the fire-dogs" (Roche 2001 p.129).

In the eighteenth century, scientific endeavours finally sought to better understand the nature of domestic heating. Scientists, including Benjamin Franklin, wrestled with ways of reducing fuel consumption, of ventilating fires without creating cold drafts, of conserving heat lost up the chimney and of avoiding smoky chimneys. Between the end of the seventeenth century and the beginning of the nineteenth century, the efficiency of heating from fireplaces was estimated to have improved by 5 to 10 percent (Roche 2000 p.133).

As scientific understanding and engineering skills progressed, a range of heating technologies to replace the fireplace was on offer in the second half of the eighteenth century. Across Europe, major improvements had already been made in the development of the stove. A German proponent explained, "I like to warm myself beside my furnace (rather than before an open fireplace where one is often almost roasted in front while freezing behind) ... [with] a glowing and agreeable heat" (quoted in Roche 2000 p.128).

One promoter, John Durno, "developed his readers' technological literacy by comparing stove types: Gauger's (efficient but expensive), Desagulier's (ditto), Dutch and German stoves (efficient but made the room stifling), French ceramic stoves (ditto), and stoves used in shops and coffee houses (efficient but noxious from leaky stovepipes)" (Crowley 2004 p.184). This inventor and entrepreneur had refined Benjamin Franklin's Pennsylvania stove for use with coal for the British market. Its valued attributes were that fuel was consumed efficiently, cold air did not rush in the room to keep the fire alive, warm air was not lost straight up a chimney, heat was more evenly diffused across the whole room, smoke was removed and the fire could be appreciated through a sliding iron plate. And yet, the technology that became the standard of English domestic heating throughout the nineteenth century was Count Rumford's refinements on the common fireplace (Crowley 2004 pp.182–90).

In the 1790s and early 1800s, this anglophile American drew the British public's attention to the principles of effective heating. "The great fault of all the open fireplaces, or chimneys, ... is that they are too large; or rather, it is the throat of the chimney, or the lower part of the open canal, in the neighbourhood of the mantel and immediately over a fire, which is too large" (Rumford quoted in Davidson 1986 p.98). His role in improving British heating standards was crucial (Brown 1969).

Count Rumford, who had experienced the benefits of European and American heating technologies, knew that the British would not adopt the stove. It created "a confined atmosphere of suffocating air, loaded with perspiration of their own bodies, very injurious to the constitution" (quoted in Crowley 2004 p.188). "The English people thought that domestic space needed fresh air, lots of it, and preferably on the cold side" (Crowley 2004 p.188). Again, the concern for cleanliness and health appears to be an important influence on the preference of heating technology.

Another problem was the entertainment value. As a Frenchman at the time put it: "What a distance between a stove and a fireplace! The sight of a stove kills my imagination and makes me sad and melancholy. I prefer the sharpest cold to this tepid, dull, invisible heat. I like to see the fire, it stirs my imagination" (quoted in Roche 2000 p.128). It seems that the British needed to have their imagination stirred too.

Despite the fact that radiant heat provided one-third of the warmth that convective heat generated, the stove was considered inappropriate for British domestic life. Instead, Count Rumford explained the importance of radiant heat and adapted British fireplaces accordingly. He showed how more effective heating would be achieved by heating the back and sides of a shallow grate radiating the warmth off the back of the firewall. He also advised his public to build the fireplace with better radiating materials and colours; bright colours were more effective than dark, and stone or brick would give (rather than absorb) heat. Thus, to the British, his fireplace became a symbol of warmth and efficiency (Davidson 1986 p.98).

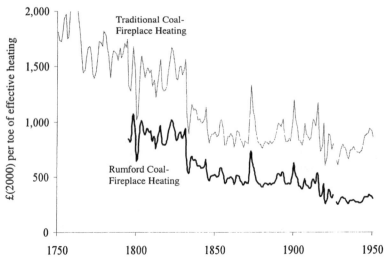

Source: see Data Appendix

Figure 4.10 Price of Heating using a Traditional Coal Fireplace and a Rumford Coal Fireplace, 1750–1950

The British fondness for fresh air and entertainment, for a fireplace rather than a stove, and the fuel efficiency losses entailed suggests that the fuel expenditure in Britain must have been low, relative to other household costs and relative to other countries in Europe or America. Given that coal in Britain was much cheaper than wood, this is probable. It also highlights that the heating experience combined many complex trade-offs, and, in some circumstances, the most fuel-efficient technology was not necessarily the most valued, and would not be adopted.

A few other technological developments also improved the ability to heat homes. Iron grates improved, providing better ventilation. For centuries, lighting a fire could be a tedious and even painful experience. Tinder and flint were scratched together to create a spark, which could take up to half an hour in humid and dark conditions. The introduction of friction matches in the 1820s saved households considerable time (Davidson 1986 p.96).

Converting fuel prices into useful heat underlines the major benefits of new fireplace designs (see Figure 4.10). The price of effective heating using a traditional chimney cost on average £1 300 per tonne of oil equivalent, whereas the new Rumford fireplace generated the same heat for £800 at the beginning of the nineteenth century.

Desired Warmth

As mentioned earlier, one observer at the beginning of the nineteenth century had suggested the ideal temperature was 15°C. By 1844, a commentator had proposed 18°C as appropriate (Billington 1982 p.18). Given the stagnation of income levels, the change in demand seems to be the result of declining costs of keeping warm. Another factor influencing the demand for heating was temperature, altering the difference between the desired warmth and the outdoors. Given the poor insulation in houses, low temperatures would seriously drive-up demand.

The consumption of coal by households in Britain had increased in waves. In 1700, a population of 8.6 million people needed 0.8 million tonnes of oil equivalent. With population rising, especially in urban areas, coal demand increased: domestic use was 1.3 mtoe in 1750 and 3.1 mtoe in 1800. Thus, per capita consumption rose from 0.09 toe in 1700 to 0.13 toe in 1750 to 0.2 toe per person in 1800. From the mid-eighteenth century to the second decade of the nineteenth century, income had hardly risen (see Figure 3.1). From the 1740s, temperatures fell, however, averaging around 9°C for the next 150 years (see Figure 4.7).

In the first couple of decades of the nineteenth century, average temperatures had dropped to about 8.5°C. Coal prices were averaging about £130 per tonne of oil equivalent, compared with about £170 per toe at the end of eighteenth century. Thus, inevitably, demand and consumption was relatively high then. In fact, despite rising income, consumption per person was lower in the 1830s and 1840s. It took until 1855, when income was 50 percent higher and coal prices on average 30 percent lower than in 1816, for domestic consumption per person to increase – to 0.32 toe. With a rising population in the nineteenth century and improvements in the heating technology, the amount of effective heating generated increased across the country (see Figure 4.11).

Coal prices had remained around £90 per toe for the most of the nineteenth century. Income was rising 20 percent higher in 1869 than in 1855, 25 percent higher again by 1887. Household consumption per capita continued to increase to 0.37 toe and 0.44 toe respectively. Despite rising income and relatively stable prices, per capita coal consumption had fallen in 1903 and only returned to its earlier level in 1913. The new century was a little warmer than the end of the nineteenth century.

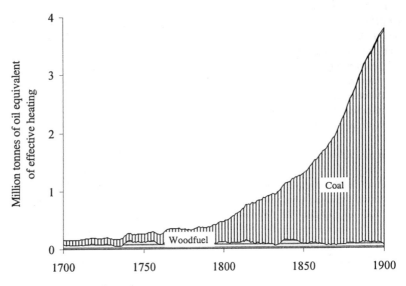

Source: see Data Appendix

Figure 4.11 Effective Heating from Woodfuel and Coal, 1700–1900

Cooking

An important transformation in the preparation of meals was the explosion in cast or wrought iron production during the second half of the eighteenth century. The 'open range' of ovens was an iron frame that could be adjusted over the fire. Often, boilers, for example, were added on the side. In 1830, one observer stated that it was "within the means of the poorest persons. To find a dwelling, however small, without an oven beside the fire, would be an exceedingly novel occurrence now-a-days" (quoted in Davidson 1986 p.60).

Increasingly, though for a long while only in wealthier homes, heating and cooking services were being separated. As the cost of iron fell further, more elaborate ovens were developed. At the end of the nineteenth century, the 'closed' range, or 'iron monster', offered an oven that sealed the fire inside, with a hot plate on top. The most popular tended to be the 'combination' range, which had sliding doors to close off or expose the fire – something close to British folks' hearts. Its advantages over the open range were significant though. Several dishes could be cooked at the same time. The process was also less hot and sweaty (Davidson 1986 p.62).

From a fuel cost perspective, though, the closed range had problems. Iron was not the ideal material for cooking. It absorbed far too much heat, giving it off slowly, and warming-up the room rather than the food. As Count Rumford had suggested, stone or brick ovens were more desirable. The marketers often used his name to sell their products despite the fact that they tended to ignore many of his recommendations, because it was cheaper to use iron (Davidson 1986 p.63).

Also, the maintenance of such cookers was time-consuming. It involved regular removal of oven parts, raking of ashes, cleaning of flues, stripping off the grease and polishing. The success of the cooker was due, in large part, to effective marketing to wealthier families that had servants. And in the north of England, well into the twentieth century, most families still used the open range ovens (Davidson 1986 p.63).

Competition from Gas Cookers

The growing use of coal, as well as raising fears about fuel availability, was intensifying the smoke problem. In a sense, the solutions proposed for pollution paved the way to improvements in resource availability, although, at first, it accentuated the problem by increasing the demand for coal-based fuels.

The rising problem of air pollution (discussed in more detail in Chapter 10) began to offer a few solutions in the second half of the nineteenth century. Gas had been developed as a cooking and heating source as well as a means of lighting. Various reasons kept early demand for these services low, however. The first was that the flow of heat was poorly understood, hindering the efficiency of the cookers and heaters. Also, early gas heaters lacked flues and the purity of the gas sold was not always of high standard. Finally, the gas industry had focussed on the lighting market (Billington 1982 p.172).

So, up to the 1870s, gas from the coking process had been used almost exclusively for lighting purposes. In fact, until then, customers saw gas cooking and heating as "expensive, ineffective and possibly dangerous" (Thorsheim 2002 p.399), and only a few enthusiasts tried to dispel this belief (Davidson 1986 p.66). When electricity began to threaten the lighting market, the gas companies began to promote its products' virtues to reduce the pollution from coal used for cooking and heating (Thorsheim 2002 p.395).

The relationship between gas companies and smoke-abatement societies flourished. The companies made important financial contributions towards promoting the importance of reducing pollution. And, gas and coke were suddenly "the radical cure of that great bugbear of ... winter existence, a smoky atmosphere" (Preece quoted in Thorsheim 2002 p.393).

Strong marketing was needed, however, to convince people of its virtues. In one example, a wife, delighted by her time-saving gas cooker, needed to place the food by the open fire just before her husband returned from work every day, because he thought the gas was poisonous; she continued the masquerade until the day he died (Davidson 1986 p.67).

When, gas cooking took off in the 1890s, it offered many advantages (Clendinning 2004). No longer was there a need to lug coal around, to tend the fire or to perform the daily maintenance chores. One cook claimed that "those who adopt gas in the kitchen will find themselves freed from all that trouble, dirt and uncertainty in working which attend a coal kitchener" (Sugg quoted in Davidson 1986 p.63). They also reduced the 'unpleasant experience' of dealing with undesirables involved in the coal trade (Thorsheim 2002 p.393).

In the 1890s, the gas companies had introduced 'penny-in-the-slot' meters, which was ideal for poorer consumers that would not be able to invest in the gas supply equipment. Another effective service was the rental of cookers, attractive to those again reluctant or unable to buy outright. An example of the growth was in Newcastle-upon-Tyne where rentals increased from 95 in 1884 to 1 035 by 1890, to 3 297 in 1910, and on to 16 110 in 1920 (Davidson 1986 p.67). So, when gas companies started marketing the concept, it was not as a high luxury service for a while, reaping profits, until the costs of manufacturing fell sufficiently to sell to customers with lower means of payment. Instead, gas cooking very quickly became a mass market service (Clendinng 2004).

This was reflected in the uptake of the technology. In 1898, one household in four had a gas cooker. Then, the total number of gas cookers doubled in three years; so, in 1901, there was one gas cooker in every three homes. By 1939, there were up to nine million gas cookers, meaning that three-quarters of households had one. The main limitation to saturating the market was the supply of gas. During the Second World War, in London, 81 percent of the homes were using gas for meals. In rural Gloucestershire, only 3 percent were (Davidson 1986 p.68).

Electric cookers were introduced swiftly after gas cookers became popular but, because of unreliable electricity and cookers, as well as high prices and the fact that the rings were slow to heat-up, they did not take off immediately. The fall in electricity prices in the late 1920s and the halving of the cost of cookers in the ten years leading to 1935 boosted sales. In 1936, only 6 percent of families used electricity for cooking. By 1948, 19 percent did. Then, it rose to 30 percent in 1961 and 46 percent by 1980 (Davidson 1986 p.71).

Gas Heaters

By the twentieth century, apart from in a few poorer quarters or rural areas, ovens had fully divorced the cooking from the heating services. Given the concern about pollution, marketers also tried to convince the British public to use gas for heating. Considerable effort went into creating visible flames and radiant heat, clearly important features for the British market. By the early 1900s, efficiencies of 30 percent were achieved for the radiant heat, plus 25 percent from warmer air. In comparison, today's gas heaters achieve 50 percent through radiance, and 10 to 15 percent through convection (Billington 1982 p.172). Nevertheless, as shown in Figure 4.12, estimates indicate that in the early 1920s gas heating was considerably more expensive than a traditional coal fire.

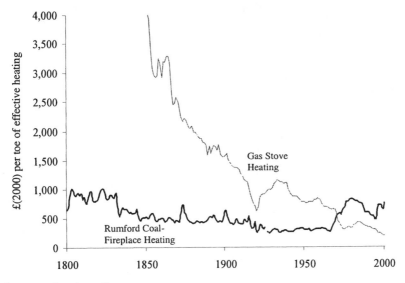

Source: see Data Appendix

Figure 4.12 Price of Heating using Coal in a Rumford Fireplace and Gas Stoves, 1800–2000

Inevitably, the uptake of gas heating was slow. In 1939, gas provided only 18 percent of the demand for heat. Electricity provided a modest 2 percent. Coal and coke provided virtually all the rest of the demand for heat (Davidson 1986 p.100).

The growth in the demand for gas in the first quarter of the twentieth century created a surplus of coke. And yet, the use of coke in homes had not been properly developed until the 1920s. Adjustments needed to be made: widening the space between the grate's bars to increase the air flow and help the removal of ash; deepening the 'fuel bed' to allow more coke to be burnt, as coke needed higher temperatures than coal to combust properly; additional refractory material to increase the burning temperature and protect the fireback. At the time, coke was 20 percent cheaper than coal; once households had time to make the modifications, demand grew. In the 1930s, the new domestic coke fires were being installed at a rate of 100 000 per year (Billington 1982 p.88).

The introduction of the Clean Air Act in 1956, following the deadly Big Smog four years earlier, enforced the need for smokeless fuels. This finally excluded the use of raw bituminous coal in homes, after about five hundred years. Anthracite coal, semi-carbonised briquettes, or coke could be used instead (Billington 1982 p.88).

Production of Coke and its Pollution

The fuel substitution that occurred to reduce pollution was not a complete solution. The coking process was a highly polluting activity, as it carbonised the coal, removing the impurities which were released as toxic gases and as tar. Due to the fumes, compared with the average labourer, coking and gas workers were thirty times more likely to suffer lung cancer (Thorsheim 2002). Heat exhaustion, skin conditions (resulting from contact with tar) and accidents were also common ailments amongst these workers.

It was said that fumes from the coking process "harmed plants and trees, sullied clothing, tarnished brass and copper, discoloured paint, and impaired human health" (Thorsheim 2002 p.386). A high cost was placed on living near a gas works, driving away all that could afford to move, creating "neighbourhoods of squalor, poverty and disease" (Thorsheim 2002 p.386).

The manufacture of coke and gas also generated considerable solid waste that either was poured in rivers (despite being banned from 1847) or left to contaminate the ground, leaving a long-term legacy; for instance, sixty years after ceasing activities, 6 000 gallons of coal tar were removed from a former site of the Gas Light and Coke Company in Westminster – it then became the site for Department of the Environment offices in Marsham Street (Thorsheim 2002 p.387).

Frequently, the companies faced threats of legal action. In one case in 1847 the company paid £500 to a brewery complaining that its well water was unfit for use (Thorsheim 2002 p.388). Where compensation was paid for the damage, a form of internalisation of the external costs was taking place. In most cases, however, victims could not threaten these companies, and the environmental costs remained externalised. Indeed, coking and gas companies tended to build installations in areas where land was cheap and residents had little influence (Thorsheim 2002 p.389).

Gas had been a solution to a major urban environmental problem. But, it resolved the problem by externalising the costs. By externalising the costs, it altered the costs faced by the consumer and society. This increased the consumption of the product, enabling producers to achieve economies of scale. Driving the costs even lower meant further consumption, which imposed a greater burden on society.

Twentieth Century Domestic Heating

At the beginning of the twentieth century, coal still strongly dominated the heating market in Britain. Fireplace technology continued to progress, and coal heating was between 15 to 20 percent efficient in the 1930s. After the Second World War, most households still used coke or coal as their main source of cooking and heating. By then, efficiencies of up to 30 percent were reached with better control of the combustion process and reduced unwanted air leakages (Billington 1982 p.87).

At the end of the nineteenth century, Siemens had confidently stated that it was "not far distant when gaseous fuel will almost entirely take the place of solid fuel for heating, for obtaining motive power and for the domestic grate" (Billington 1982 p.172). This forecast was a little optimistic about the timing.

The development of pressure boilers and central heating systems for homes led to the first major switch of heating fuel in three hundred years. Central heating systems could run on all fuels, but gas was most effective. In the 1970s, the discovery of natural gas in the North Sea provided the boost needed. The price of effective heating using gas central heating became cheaper than using coal (see Figure 4.13).

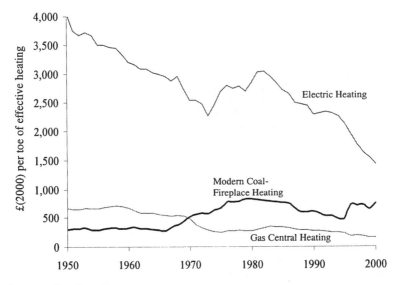

Source: see Data Appendix

Figure 4.13 Price of Heating using Coal in a Modern Fireplace, Electric Units and Gas Central Heating Boilers, 1950–2000

The proportion of homes with central heating systems rose from one-third in 1970 to one-half in 1976. The uptake continued, reaching 80 percent in 1990 (Miller 1993a p.47). In the twenty years leading up to 1980, households made the transition from coal to natural gas (see Figure 4.14). At the end of the twentieth century, natural gas provided around three-quarters of the fuel for heating homes and, because of the efficiency of its system, almost all of the effective heating.

The ability to keep a home warm has also depended on the characteristics and quality of the building. For instance, flats tend to have lower heat losses, as they were less open to the elements. The growth of semi-detached houses in suburban areas has tended to increase heat loss. On the other hand, new buildings have had to comply with regulations, including those related to insulation. Insulation, especially in lofts and wall cavities, and improved glazing has radically reduced heat loss. Forty percent of the housing stock in Great Britain was built before 1945 and only 14 percent was erected after 1984. Overall, heat loss in the average building has declined substantially since 1970 (DTI 2003 p.29).

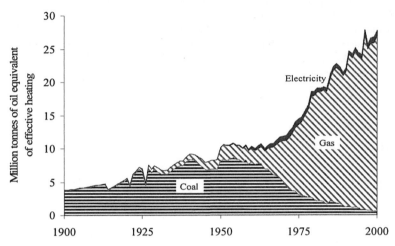

Source: see Data Appendix

Figure 4.14 Effective Heating from Coal, Gas and Electricity, 1900–2000

The introduction of central heating, along with better insulation, has transformed comfort levels in the United Kingdom. As early as the beginning of the twentieth century, some Americans, where central heating was already being introduced, had higher standards of comfort – expecting 21°C as a desirable temperature in homes and other buildings (Billington 1982 p.19). Higher summer temperatures may also have made American comfort levels higher than British standards. USA building engineers began to introduce guidelines on comfort levels. It appears that cultural influences both from the lay-person and the engineer were important for influencing British standards – "the changes begin first in hotels, and progress downwards though public buildings, offices to schools and homes" (Billington 1982 p.19). The rise in ambient temperatures was associated with the desire to wear lighter clothing, which coincided with the introduction of man-made fibres (Billington 1982 p.20). At the end of the twentieth century, British buildings tended to be heated to 23°C. This trend was partly reflected in the amount of effective heating over the twentieth century, which approximately trebled in the first half and then trebled again in the second half.

6. INDUSTRIAL HEATING IN THE TWENTIETH CENTURY

The Decline of the Iron and Steel Industry

Throughout the nineteenth century, Britain led the world in industrial production, supplying iron sheets, plates, bars, rails and wires. In 1870, it produced six million tonnes of pig iron – half of the world's pig iron and steel[9] (Musson 1979 p.174). As the demand for industrial products and, therefore, production grew, the need to apply heat to materials and substances increased. Metal manufacturing had been the most heat-intensive industry. Coal consumption for the iron industry in 1870 was over 16 million tonnes oil equivalent. This was about 45 percent of all non-domestic heating consumption, one-third of all heating consumption and one-quarter of Britain's final user energy requirements.

The heating and fuel requirements of the iron industry were astonishing. While some regions started to stagnate as their iron ore reserves depleted, others, such as Cleveland, started expanding massively. Many manufacturers incorporated the major innovations introduced in the mid-nineteenth century, such as hot blasts strengthened by steam engines pumping air and using waste gases. They increased the throughput of air, size, pressure and heat produced (Musson 1979 p.172).

Since completing the switch to coal, it had suffered few major problems about resource availability. In the late nineteenth century, because of the growing demands for coal to provide energy services, resource availability concerns were being raised – but they were certainly not of the severity that the industry experienced in the seventeenth century. The industry continued to introduce improvements in fuel efficiency. The desire to cut costs had been the driver for many inventions, as fuel was still a large proportion of the total costs. Increasingly intense competition, especially from abroad, was driving the need to reduce costs.

Metallurgic chemists were searching for new, more efficient ways of producing iron and particularly steel. In the 1850s, Henry Bessemer proposed a method of extracting the carbon from pig iron by blasting air directly into the molten metal as it came out of the furnace. In the 1860s, William Siemens introduced the open-hearth method also for producing steel. The Siemens method involved placing the pig iron in an open bath and using a gas furnace to remove carbon (Musson 1979 p.172).

Both techniques had their advantages. Britain tended to adopt the open-hearth process, which could be economical at smaller scale. It was a slower, more controlled process than the Bessemer technique, enabling the forger to determine the quality of the output more accurately. This was more appropriate to the demands for steel associated with the shipbuilding, engineering and other

---

9. Wrought iron became increasingly produced as 'steel'. In earlier times, pig iron was generally refined into bar iron but, as the output of refined or de-carbonated pig iron took on many different forms, more 'steel' was produced.

industries. It also took advantage of cheap skilled labour of which there was plenty in Britain at the time (Musson 1979 p.175).

Production of pig iron rose from six to ten million tonnes between 1870 and 1913; at the same time, steel soared from 0.22 million to nearly eight million tonnes (Musson 1979 pp.174–5). Despite the major increase in production over that period, coal consumption only rose by one-quarter, reflecting efficiency improvements that were being made in the industry (see Figure 4.6).

By the end of the nineteenth century, however, other countries had caught up with Britain, in terms of output and technology, and the industry was starting to import innovations from abroad. By 1913, Britain had lost its world share, producing 14 percent of the pig iron and 10 percent of the steel (Musson 1979 pp.174–5). Fuel savings could not stop the declining demand for British iron and steel. Some have argued that there were managerial failures. Mostly, the declining share reflected circumstances: Germany and the United States had more resources and a larger and growing demand with an industry protected by their government. Britain had a relatively modest iron ore base with a small internal market. The internal demand for iron and steel was not growing as it did in the nineteenth century. Many of the needs appeared to have been met – people had ovens, pans or kettles; there were wires, pins and needles aplenty; bridges, railways and ships were ubiquitous. Decline (or at least, stagnation) seemed inevitable.

Heating in General Manufacturing

Despite iron and steel's prominence in history books, other industries consumed nearly half of the coal supplied in the United Kingdom up to the nineteenth century, and about one-third afterwards. General manufacturing, and especially non-ferrous metals, was a major consumer of energy and crucially dependent on heating for its processes. Copper production grew from about 500 tonnes in 1700 to 12 000 tonnes in 1850. The industry found it was cheaper to transport the ore from Cornwall, Devon and Anglesey to the coal fields of South Wales and the West Midlands, where the copper ore was smelted (Musson 1979 p.104). During the same period, tin output quadrupled to 6 000 tonnes. Meanwhile, lead production more than doubled, reaching 65 000 tonnes (Musson 1979 pp.103–4).

Much of the metal produced in Great Britain was for the export market. It was valued at £240 million[10] in 1850. For example, the tin-plate industry rose nearly ten-fold from 1800 to 1850 and about 60 percent of it was sold abroad. The iron and steel industry exported another £600 million. Following the 1843 abolishment of the ban on exports of mechanical engineering output to protect British knowledge, £95 million worth of machinery was sold abroad (Musson 1979 p.120). The cheap mineral resources provided the low-priced materials and heat that made Great Britain the metal producer for much of the world's economy in the mid-nineteenth century.

---

10. As a reminder, unless specified, all price values in the book have been converted to the year 2000.

Another large user of heat for its transformative processes was the chemical industry. The chemical industry provided major inputs for textiles, which was by far Great Britain's largest export industry – more than £4.3 billion in 1850 (when the economy's GDP was around £40 billion). The inputs had benefited from major innovations, such as vitril 'sours', synthetic sodas and chlorine bleach. The industry also provided major components for the soap, glass, pottery and paper industries. Chemicals were used by the metal, tanning and brewing industries, as well as in the production of gunpowder, oils and paints (Musson 1979 pp.120–21).

In 1800, coal consumption for non-ferrous industries was little more than three million tonnes of oil equivalent. By 1870, although not as meteoric a rise as the iron industry, it increased to nineteen million. This was 40 percent of all of Britain's heating fuel needed and 30 percent of all of its final user energy required. The growth in fuel consumption continued to thirty million in 1913. This represented 44 percent of heating fuel and 24 percent of energy in the United Kingdom.

Resource Scarcity and Abundance

Clearly, in the nineteenth century, coal fuelled the economy. From 1800 to 1900, coal consumption for heating outside the domestic sector had grown from four million to fifty million tonnes of oil equivalent (see Figure 4.15). It was, of course, the source of warmth in homes. And, by the end of nineteenth century, coal was required for far more than just heating. It was the basis for power and transport in Britain. Coal was also exported in increasing quantities. Between 1800 and 1900, production of coal had increased from 8 million to 130 million tonnes of oil equivalent.

Could the coal industry continue to meet an apparently ever-expanding demand? Stanley Jevons was interested in 'The Coal Question?' He noticed that the demand for coal had increased dramatically over the last several centuries. Supply had, on the whole, kept up with demand and, at times, even led to abundance. He was aware of the likelihood of the declining output per unit of effort as more remote seams were exploited. He also understood that prices created incentives for solutions. Indeed, technological progress could provide both a solution to increasing the supply of resources in mining and to declining consumption of resources per unit of service. But, he also appreciated that an industry that found ways to supply more and consumers that required less would create downward pressure on the price, encouraging further consumption. He stated in relation to the manufacturing sector that "[i]t is wholly a confusion of ideas to suppose that the economical use of fuel is equivalent to a diminished consumption. The very contrary is true" (Jevons 1865 Ch.VII p.III). He, therefore, wondered how and when would the growth in coal consumption slow.

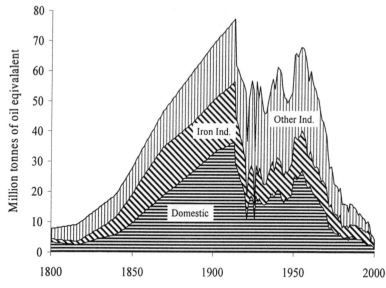

Source: see Data Appendix

Figure 4.15 Estimates of Coal Consumption in Different Sectors, 1800–2000

Decline of Heat-Intensive Industries

Three economic transformations provided the answers to Jevons' question. First, resource and material efficiency progressed. As has been the case throughout much of industrial history, the heating service provided by energy has become more efficient over the years. Similarly, less iron and chemicals are required for the same purpose today than during the Industrial Revolution. Engineers understand better the strengths and limits of materials – when Isambard Kingdom IBrunel built his great bridges, he wanted to be sure they would not collapse, so he built them strong. Today, Ave Orup, or the many other structural engineers, needs less steel and other materials for a similar bridge.

Second, there was a shift away from coal – as was seen by the growth of gas heating in households. This started out as a way of converting the coal into a gas to isolate the pollution. Eventually, though, natural gas replaced town gas and genuinely reduced the use of coal. In a similar way, industrial activities also transferred their use of coal for heating from a direct to an indirect source, through the medium of town gas and electricity; then, coal stopped being used even in an indirect way (see Figure 4.16).

The other transformation was the decline of heat-intensive industries in the United Kingdom mentioned above. The iron and steel industry had experienced dramatic fluctuations in the interwar period. Heat demand and energy consumption followed these fluctuations. The First World War and its immediate aftermath had generated much demand. But, this had led to overcapacity in the early 1920s, which gradually got used up; then the Great Depression threw the industry into decline again. The Second World War was another period of high demand.

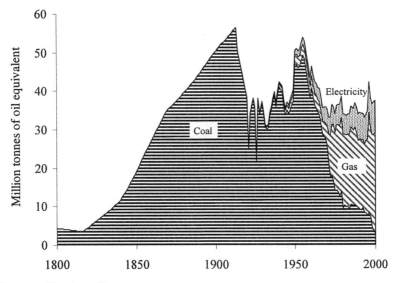

Source: see Data Appendix

Figure 4.16 Estimates of Heating Fuel Consumption in Non-Domestic Sectors, 1800–2000

Since the 1600s, metal manufacturing, especially iron and steel, had been a major user of energy for heating. The relative decline of manufacturing after the Second World War has led to a reduction in the demand for fuels, particularly coal and coke. Total industrial consumption of energy in 1960 was equivalent to 90 million tons of coal (53 mtoe) and peaked at over 110 million tonnes (65 mtoe) in 1973; since then, it has fallen virtually ever year, and now stands below 60 million tons (35 mtoe). After 1913, coal and coke in the industrial sector declined and were eventually replaced by petroleum, which tripled between 1960 and 1973 to nearly 50 million tons of coal equivalent (29 million tons of oil). In the early 1970s, natural gas began to penetrate; and gas and electricity increased, while overall energy consumption was falling. Although today, with a wide range of energy sources, industrial activity is still an important user of energy, its energy consumption is unlikely to revert to the upward trend of the previous four hundred years.

Improvements in Environmental Quality

The polluting properties of coal made it unattractive for homes and many industrial activities. The chimney enabled the pollution to be removed from the home and, thus, coal could be used for cooking and heating. The burden of coal smoke pumped out of chimneys became an environmental problem that had few solutions until the incentives for companies were appropriate. Coking and gas companies found ways to encourage the use of 'cleaner' gas.

While gas had some favourable characteristics, the cost differential was too great for most activities to abandon coal combustion (see Chapter 10). The London fogs were notorious, and city dwellers preferred to move out of town and commute to have some respite. This spread of cities, in large part due to the introduction of suburban railways (see Chapter 6), helped reduce the concentration of air pollution resulting from households.

Most efforts to reduce pollution from industrial activities in the nineteenth century had failed due to public authority's priority to economic development. The Big Smog of 1956 catalysed the public willpower to force stricter regulation on both households and industrial polluters. They coincided with the major switch away from coal towards natural gas for heating, shown in Figure 4.16.

Traditional air pollution problems have been on a steady decline since the 1950s. This has substantially reduced acid rain and carbon dioxide emissions. Whereas once, heating was the cause of much of the environmental pollution caused in Britain, its social burden has been declining, due to the fortuitous discovery and exploitation of natural gas reserves in the North Sea.

7. LONG-RUN TRENDS IN HEATING

Looking at the average price of fuels used for heating over the last five hundred years, no very long run trend appears (see Figure 4.17). It fell between the mid-fifteenth century and the end of the sixteenth century. Reflecting rising woodfuel and coal prices, the average price started to increase until the second half of the eighteenth century. By then, the shift to coal was near complete and the average price fell.

From the mid-nineteenth century, average prices started rising, associated first with a rising coal price and, at the turn of the century, a rising share of the more expensive, yet cleaner gas. In the 1960s, the price of heating fuels was higher than most peaks in the fifteenth and the eighteenth centuries. Since the 1980s, the price of natural gas has fallen. The fluctuations in the average price of heating fuels do signal periods of scarcity and abundance. They also obscure the story by conflating resource availability and shifts to more valuable fuels.

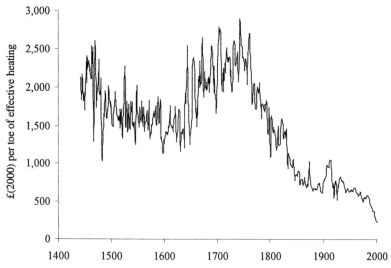

Source: see Data Appendix

Figure 4.17 The Price of Heating Fuels (£(2000) per tonne of oil equivalent), 1450–2000

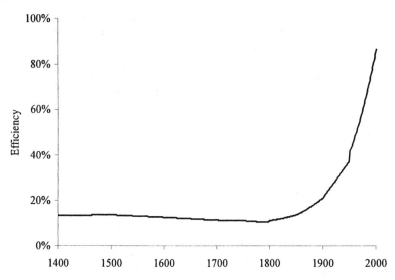

Source: see Data Appendix

Figure 4.18 The Efficiency of Domestic Heating Technologies, 1400–2000

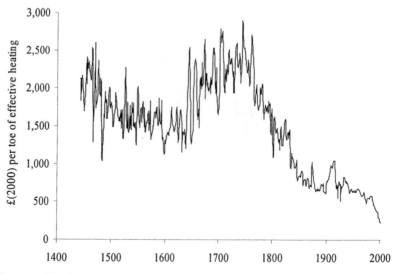

Source: see Data Appendix

Figure 4.19 The Price of Heating (£(2000) per tonne of oil equivalent of effective heating), 1450–2000

For industrial activities, it is difficult to present long-run trends in efficiencies of technologies because of the variety of different activities. Certain activities, such as the iron industry, exhibited considerable improvements in efficiency. In households, an estimate of long run efficiency was produced and presented in Figure 4.18. It indicates clear trends in the conversion of fuel to heating. After the modest decline associated with the shift from the hearth to the early chimney, major improvements were made in the use of coal in fireplaces during the nineteenth and twentieth centuries. The introduction of gas heaters also improved efficiency, culminating in the central heating boilers used today.

For the domestic sector, it was possible to create an estimate of the price of producing 'effective' heat, combining the fuel costs and the efficiency of conversion – see Figure 4.19. While it fails to include quality of thermal insulation in the building stock, it indicates the marginal costs of keeping a house warm over time. A clear rise in heating prices in the seventeenth and eighteenth century is discernable, resulting from the higher energy prices and accentuated by less efficient chimneys. From the late eighteenth century for one century, the price of heating fell dramatically as both fuel costs and efficiency favoured the consumer. Another dramatic reduction occurred at the end of the twentieth century with the introduction of natural gas central heating.

Heating use reacted to the price of the service, as well as changing demands due to rising income and characteristics related to the equipment and fuel. As for the price, heating provided and consumed[11] was estimated by combining the fuel consumed and the efficiency of conversion. In Figure 4.20, three phases can be discerned in the rate of growth of heating consumption. Up to 1650, consumption increased gradually. Between the late seventeenth century and the last decades of the eighteenth century, it accelerated, despite the higher price of heating. Then, for the next two hundred years, heating use climbed at a constant rate.

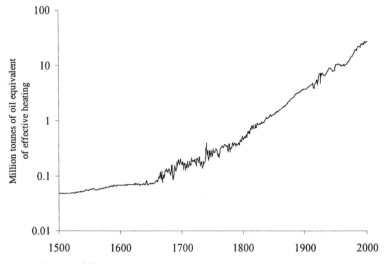

Source: see Data Appendix

Figure 4.20 The Consumption of Heating (million tonnes of oil equivalent of effective heating), 1500–2000

It should be remembered that woodfuel consumption was modelled on economic activity for industrial heating and on income for households, as well as the price of woodfuel for both. Coal estimates are from other researchers' assumptions about the share of total consumption.

In 2001, heating was still central to many productive activities. Two-thirds of energy used in industry was for heating purposes. Of the 29.5 mtoe used, one-third was consumed for high temperature heating, especially in the iron and steel, non-ferrous metals, chemical and cement industries. Food and drink, as well as plastics, chemicals and mechanical engineering, use considerable energy for low temperature processes – this purpose was responsible for one-quarter of industry energy requirements. Space heating used about 10 percent of energy consumed in the industrial sector (DTI 2002).

Looking at the service sectors, heating was nearly always the main driver for energy use. In retail, hotel and catering, and warehouses, heating used half of the

---

11. Thermal insulation might be incorporated to capture the difference between production and consumption of heating.

all energy consumed. Two-thirds of all the energy in health, education and government was consumed for warming buildings (DTI 2002).

Table 4.1 Non-Transport Energy Consumption by Energy Service (mtoe), 2001

	Residential	Services	Industry	Total
Space Heating	26.3	11.6	3.1	41.0
Water Heating	11.5	2.0	-	13.5
Cooking/Catering	2.4	1.9	-	4.3
Lighting and Appliances	5.9	3.3	0.3	9.5
High/Low Temp. Process Use	-	-	17.2	17.2
Motors & Drivers	-	-	2.4	2.4
Drying/Separation	-	-	2.1	2.1
Other	-	1.9	4.3	6.2
TOTAL	46.1	20.7	29.5	96.3
Heating % of TOTAL	87.2%	74.9%	68.8%	78.9%

Source: DTI (2002)

Table 4.1 shows that proportion of energy used for heating in the United Kingdom in 2001 – the residential sector, 87 percent; the services sector, 75 percent; and industry, 69 percent. The residential sector accounted for over half of the 76 mtoe used for heating in the United Kingdom; industry required one-quarter and service sector one-fifth.

8. CONCLUDING REMARKS

Every society requires heating services, both for industrial and domestic purposes. In the home, heating supplied for cooking also met some of the needs for personal warmth. As income grew and cheaper fuels became available, heating began to be used to improve comfort levels in the home. The shift from the open hearth to the chimney was not a heating efficiency improvement. It did, however, create an opportunity to use coal, since it reduced – and also effectively 'externalized' – the smoke pollution, which was too great to bear indoors without a chimney. By about 1550, the price of heating using coal in a fireplace with a chimney fell below the price of heating from woodfuels burned in an open hearth. The chimney was also an important symbol of status; the open hearth was used by commoners. Thus, declining prices, externalized pollution, as well as growing economic opportunities for social mobility, boosted the demand for the new technology and the substitute fuel, coal.

Other technologies were very slow to enter the British market. Count Rumford's late-eighteenth century design improvements to the coal fireplace were the most radical home heating change between the seventeenth and the twentieth centuries. Eventually, in the early twentieth century town gas entered the heating market, mainly in reaction to the threat of electricity entering the lighting market.

With the exploitation of large fields of natural gas in the North Sea in the 1970s, the demand for central heating truly took off, providing substantial declines in the price of heating. The real price of producing heat in households fell thirty-five-fold over the last six hundred years. The price of energetic resources declined. Efficiency of conversion increased seven-fold. This means that the real price of heating fuels in 2000 was about half of their price in the early fifteenth century – in tonnes of oil equivalent, woodfuel was then £300 per tonne, while in 2000 natural gas was about £120 per tonne.

The shift to coal use in industry was also a gradual process reflecting the different requirements and characteristics of every activity. Each industry made the transition once the appropriate technology became available and the commercial incentives made using the technology worthwhile – in the case of the iron industry, the delay between innovation and sufficient incentives was more than fifty years. In some industries, like the lime-makers, the fuel did not come in contact with the material being transformed, and coal could be quickly introduced.

For others, ingenious devices, such as reverberatory furnaces, were developed, first, in the glass-making industry, then for non-ferrous metals and, finally, at the end of the eighteenth century, the iron industry began to use coal, in the form of coke. This boosted British iron production, which became one of the pillars of the Industrial Revolution. Industrial production and coal use continued to grow through the nineteenth and into the twentieth century.

At various times over the last three hundred years, concerns about availability of resources have been raised. In the long run, the coal industry managed to meet the growing demands. Relatively cheap and stable coal prices were the cause of other concerns as the environmental burden grew. The generations living in urban Britain in the nineteenth century suffered greatly from ever more heating and its outputs.

After the Second World War, heat-intensive industries began to decline and, therefore, so did the demand for industrial heat. Throughout the twentieth century, industrial heat demand has also shifted away from coal towards gas. These structural transformations reduced the resource and environmental pressures that this industrializing economy imposed.

The shift from wood-based fuels to coal enabled the price of heating in both industry and households to fall substantially. In turn, this may have contributed significantly to the United Kingdom's economic advantage over other countries, enabling it to industrialize before any other nation. It did, however, impose a heavy burden upon its society, largely for environmental reasons but also in terms of effects on communities that grew heavily dependent on coal mining and that suffered as the industry declined during the second half of the twentieth century.

5. Stationary Power: Technology, Economies of Scale and Novel Attributes

1. THE NEED FOR POWER

Humans, before the development of the steam engine, did not live in an absence of power to move and modify nature. Crops were sown and reaped, and fabrics were turned into clothing. More dramatically, bridges and cathedrals were examples of pre-Industrial Revolution feats of engineering that depended upon the ability to harness vast amounts of energy to move nature.

Power has been central to the production of goods and to driving the economy. In an agrarian economy, most of the power provided was likely to be destined for the agricultural sector. During phases of proto-industrialisation and the Industrial Revolution much of growth in power use was in the manufacturing sectors. In this chapter, agricultural and industrial power needs are the focus.[12]

The story begins with the major transformations in the provision of power to agricultural production in the medieval economy. It focuses on the evolution of power provision – from human and animal power to the harnessing of water and wind, from the steam engine to the power station. It examines the changing availability of resources used as energy to provide power, and considers the efficiency with which prime-movers generated power. Together, the cost of energetic resources and efficiency indicate the price of producing power. The long-run trends in the price and provision of power are identified.

2. ANIMAL AND HUMAN POWER

Animal Technology and Power

The collapsing walls of the subsistence feudal system across Europe created greater incentives to produce beyond the needs of the manor and trade excess

---

12. The major omission in this chapter is the transformation of domestic life and work through the use of appliances. See, for instance, Cowan (1983), Davidson (1986), Mokyr (2000) on the impact of technologies and knowledge on domestic labour. Another missing story is the evolution of military power and the ability to harness energy explosively (see MacNeil 1982, Landers 2003).

supplies for a profit. In medieval Britain, the growing population needed to be fed, creating an increasing demand for bread, the main food source. This demand required ploughing of fields, reaping of crops and crushing of grain. On the edge of a blossoming European trade network, the quality of British wool was to be England's source of wealth. Both crushing grain and fulling wool required high levels of power (Langdon 1986, 2003, 2005).

A major catalyst for the upheaval of the economy at the end of the first millennium was the major transformation of agriculture. It began in the early Middle Ages and took many centuries to spread across Europe and Britain. Technologies for agriculture were highly dependent on the location and its characteristics. Crops, soil, inclination of the land and rainfall affected the exact tool to be used for the task. This meant that modifications, refinements and improvements, as well as their diffusion, were very gradual (Mokyr 1990 p.32).

One of the crucial introductions in the early Middle Ages, which became widespread by the tenth century in Britain, was the use of the heavy plough. The ancient plough, brought to Britain by the Romans, was inappropriate for the clay soils of Northern Europe, leaving many lands uncultivated or using slash-and-burn techniques. The heavy plough that cut and furrowed in certain British fields during the tenth and eleventh centuries was placed behind wheels and oxen (Mokyr 1990 p.32).

Prior to the Norman invasion, the ox was the main source of power. In the fields, they provided decent, steady work rates, and their role in providing power increased considerably. An estimate for England at the end of the eleventh century suggests that oxen provided 70 percent of the animal power capacity (Langdon 1986 p.19). In the Domesday Book, there were 81 184 plough-teams identified. Given that each team was comprised of eight animals, there would have been 649 472 oxen or horses – nearly one animal for every two people.

From Langdon (2006), each ox was assumed to provide more than 380 watts. Smil (1994) indicates that a weak horse could provide around 500 watts of power. Horses represented 22 percent of the ploughing animals on the farm in 1086 (Langdon 1986 p.255). Combining the percentage of oxen and horses with the strength of each animal, and multiplying by the total number of animals, produces an estimate of the potential capacity of 270 MW. Based on an assumption that each animal worked 300 days per year for six hours per day, oxen and horses could generate 385 GWh of power every year at the end of the eleventh century.

The Horse Revolution

Various technological improvements in horse management during the Middle Ages allowed "substantial, even massive, introduction of the horse to general draught work" (Langdon 1986 p.19). The first of those innovations was the horseshoe. Humid soils wore out horses' hooves, causing splinters. The nailed horseshoe protected hooves, and became common around the ninth century. The other crucial improvement was the harness. Until its introduction, a metal bar was placed across the horse's chest and windpipe, strangulating it, and reducing its efficiency by about 80 percent (Mokyr 1990 p.36).

In the twelfth century and thirteenth century, the number of horses used began to increase. As mentioned before, in 1086, only 22 percent of the draught stock used was work-horses. A peasantry, seeking to meet the demands of the faster-paced twelfth century economy, began to use mixed teams of oxen and horses. By 1300, horses made up 40 percent of the animal power-base (Langdon 1986 p.255).

Gradually, specialisation took place according to the conditions. The two animals were suited to different soils, and regional diversity reflected this: in the midlands, heavy clay fields were hard for horses; the stony chalk grounds of the Chilterns or Yorkshire were slippery for oxen; on drier and lighter soil or inclined terrain, horses were preferred. But, physical factors were not the only determinant. Horses were generally more expensive to buy and to look after. They were, however, more versatile. Also, the market for horses by the late Middle Ages was well developed, and the price range for horses varied greatly. So, despite generally higher prices for horses, even poor peasants could afford a low quality horse (Langdon 1986 p.272).

Little evidence remains of animal numbers in the medieval and early modern era. A basic model estimates the role of animal power (see the Data Appendix). Given the success of using horses for power in the late medieval period, animal capacity would certainly have increased. On the other hand, since there was evidence of land scarcity at the time and the more powerful horse replaced some oxen, it is assumed that the animal population rose by only one-third. This was equivalent to 370 MW of capacity, generating 530 GWh of power.

Human Effort

In the medieval economy, oxen and horses added greatly to the existing work done by humans (Campbell 2003). Since the principal activity in the pre-industrial economy was the sowing and reaping of crops in the fields, most of the active population would have been involved in agricultural production. The active population in the seventeenth century – and probably before then – has been estimated at around three-quarters of the total number of people (Petersen 1995 p.246). Thus, estimates of the effort provided can be estimated as an indicator of power provision.

The population at the time of the Domesday Book was around 1.5 million (Snooks 1994). Although effort varies with the type of work, on average a human generates around 50 watts of power at work (Smil 1994). Given that about three-quarters of the population would have been working manually, the potential power was equivalent to almost 70 MW. Given the relatively large number of festivals and holy days, and seasonal variation in agricultural activities, they probably worked intensively about 1 500 hours per year – five hours per day for 300 days (Voth 1998 p.39). At this rate, they would have generated 50 GWh of power (see Figure 5.1).

By 1300, the population had quadrupled to six million, offering a possible 270 MW of capacity, generating 200 GWh of power. Thus, human and animal power could have generated around 730 GWh of power at the end of the eleventh century – 11 percent of the total economy's power provision coming from human muscles and 80 percent originating from animal hooves. In other words, the introduction of oxen to assist human limbs in the Middle Ages dramatically increased the economy's ability to generate power.

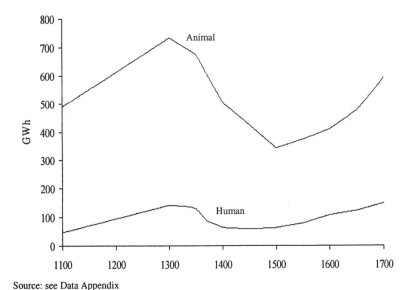

Source: see Data Appendix

Figure 5.1 The Provision of Human and Animal Power, 1100–1700

Food Demand and Supply

As mentioned in the previous chapter, food has provided the basic source of energy for human survival. A basic minimum of energy intake of food was about 2 000 dietary (that is, kilo) calories, equivalent to 0.2 kg of oil, per day (Smil 1994). Food also acted as the source of energy for muscular activity. Different conditions altered the metabolic rate. A human at rest generated and used up considerably less than a person involved in light work, or someone busy with heavy toil (Billington 1982 p.11). To generate more power required more food to be consumed.

Clearly, even when performing muscular exertion, a considerable amount of the energy was required for basic biological functions. To be accurate, therefore, any estimate of the energy required to drive muscular power should subtract this base level of energy consumption (Campbell 2003). Nevertheless, to provide any muscular activity, a person needed to consume enough energy to meet both basic biological and physical labour requirements. Here, it will be assumed that, if humans (and animals) were providing power, the energy required was equivalent to their daily calorific intake (that is, both biological and labour needs).

Despite its fundamental role in providing fuel for the human and animal power, this is not the place for a formal discussion of the evolution of agriculture since medieval times.[13] Here, only a few general points will be made about the changes in the ability to produce agricultural products, which may also provide insight into the relationship between technological development and growing consumption.

Until the nineteenth century and arguably the twentieth century, the ability to generate and consume sufficient calories in Britain has been a central economic and social issue. In the fields of medieval England, the energy produced per worker was rarely far greater than the amount needed to feed each person. Thus, it was very much a subsistence economic system (Woolgar et al. 2006).

In periods of growing population, such as between the twelfth and the mid-fourteenth centuries, food demand inevitably rose. There were two methods of generating more food. First, the yield per acre could be increased by planting better seeds, growing more calorific foods, spreading fertiliser on fields, or improving the organisation of fallow and cultivation. In particular, efforts would have been made to grow crops that provided the highest yields of calories relative to the surface area. In the Middle Ages, grains, such as wheat, barley, oats and rye, were the main food source. The high calorific density of grains made them an efficient source of food-energy, especially where land was limited and yields poor.

Major technological developments took place in the twelfth and thirteenth centuries, such as the shift from the hook plough to the wheeled plough pulled by animals, mentioned above. It improved weed control and increased labour productivity in the fields. Similarly, the shift from two- to three-field rotation also increased yield, distributed labour needs more evenly around the year and improved the nutrient balance of the soil. Without these technological and managerial innovations, agricultural output would not have managed to meet the demands of a growing population (Langdon 1986). In turn, such developments most probably spurred further growth in population.

The second option was to increase the size of the land under cultivation – by reclaiming forests (see the previous Chapter), fens or other waste land. In medieval times, expansion – increasing the available land – was the common option. The growth in population well into the fourteenth century drove a major process of land reclamation (TeBrake 1975 p.347).

At the same time, pressure and incentives to grow crops led to the conversion of unproductive lands. Evidence suggests that crop yields per acre fell between 1230 and 1350, as increasingly marginal and infertile lands were being used. This was exacerbated by the conversion of pasture lands to grow crops, reducing the livestock per acre and the relative amount of fertiliser available. An estimate suggested that around three acres of land was needed to nourish one person. As

---

13. See, for instance, Allen (1994), Overton (1996).

population grew, some communities could not ensure this rate; and given the declining yields, much of the population was struggling to intake enough calories. The unusually wet spring and summer of 1315 ruined many harvests. With insufficient reserves, and unsatisfactory yields over the next couple of years, many starved. Afterwards, food shortages were common. Malnutrition started to slow the medieval population rise (TeBrake 1975 p.353).

Fourteenth century Europe and Britain appears to have reached a high level of over-population relative to the agricultural production. Despite the technological improvements, production was insufficient to meet the growing demands. Declining yields, due to the pressures on agriculture, made matters worse. By the early fourteenth century, extreme climatic conditions reduced harvests, creating a dearth of grain and famine, raising mortality rates (Chavas and Bromley 2005).

The Economy after the Black Death

In 1348–49, a Great Plague spread across Europe, reducing the European, as well as British, population by around one-half. A plague on such a scale inevitably destroyed most enterprises. Well-established trade networks lost much of their markets. The need for so much power to produce bread and wool disappeared. In fact, the low populations coupled with the relatively abundant land meant that after the 1370s, the price of grain fell too (Clark 2003).

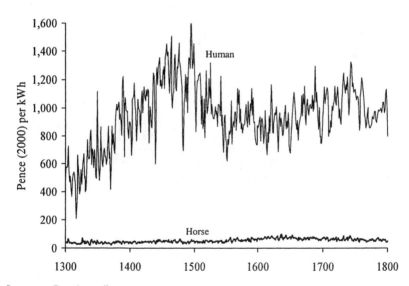

Source: see Data Appendix

Figure 5.2 The Price of Human and Horse Power, 1300–1800

Another important implication of the decline in population was that labour force was in short supply. Wages and earnings rose substantially in the fourteenth and fifteenth centuries (see Figure 5.2). For activities in which the two were substitutes, it was usually cheaper to use an animal for power than a human, further discouraging the use of human power and encouraging a greater use of animals.

Despite the shift towards animals, with smaller population and economy, far less power was required. Given the decline in the demand for power, attempts were made to find markets for horses. The growing city of London had a large demand for meat, and the excess supply of horses seems to have met part of it (Langdon 1986 p.262). Another use of cheap horses was for military ambitions. Henry VII (1485–1509) brought a revival of military and economic ambitions in the final quarter of the fifteenth century. This created a great demand for horses, especially since many got killed in battle. Given the poor quality of the horse-stock in England at the time, many horses were imported (Edwards 1983).

Inevitably, the new uses for horses had transformed a situation of overabundance into one of scarcity. While horses were in large supply in the fourteenth century, an excess demand existed in the fifteenth, sixteenth and seventeenth centuries. While the great variety of horses makes comparison difficult, evidence shows that the excess demand fed through into prices. A horse bought in 1350 would cost £(2000)500 per kW of capacity. By 1650, the price of horses had risen to £(2000)800 per kW (see Figure 5.3).

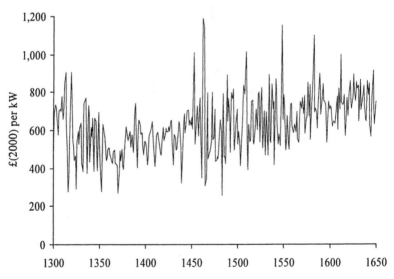

Source: see Data Appendix

Figure 5.3 The Price of a Horse (per kW), 1300–1650

The Black Death slowed the introduction of horses on farms. The percentage of horses used for draught purposes remained at 40 percent throughout the fourteenth century. By the end of the sixteenth century, however, two-thirds of animals working on the farm were horses (Langdon 1986 p.255).

Over the two hundred years after the Black Death, the growing use of animals in general brought additional nitrogen to the land. This, in turn, increased the value of producing protein-rich foods, such as beans and peas, rather than corn as fodder (Allen 2004 p.17). Between 1300 and 1800, wheat productivity increased by two-thirds – from 12 to 20 bushels of wheat per acre (Allen 2004 p.2). Much of this improvement in the efficiency of agricultural production was associated with the increased use of nitrogen. The main sources of the nitrogen were, therefore, from legumes (e.g. beans, peas, clover and turnips) fixing or capturing loose nitrogen in the soil and from manure.

The shift away from the production of fodder drove up the cost of using animals, however. Fodder was the principle expenditure to maintaining a horse. Hay or grass was central to a horse's diet. Yet, the low calorific content of hay increased the amount of time a horse needed to eat to meet its daily requirements, reducing work-time. Often, a grain, generally oats, and a legume, such as peas and beans, supplemented the hay, speeding up the 'refuelling' process (Turvey 2005 p.50).

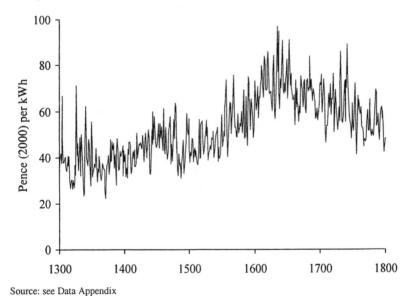

Source: see Data Appendix

Figure 5.4 The Price of Horse Power, 1300–1800

An estimate of the fodder mix of hay, oats and peas from the fourteenth century was used to estimate the cost of 'provender' for a horse between 1300 and 1650 (see Figure 5.4). In 1300, one kWh of power produced by a horse cost around 40 pence. The cost of feeding (and maintaining) a horse increased by about 30 percent during the first half of the fifteenth century. After falling again, from 1550 to 1650, the cost of horse power nearly doubled.

The price of horses and the cost of maintaining one had increased substantially between the fifteenth and seventeenth centuries. Yet, with the growth in commerce in this time came a renewed demand for power. From the second half of the seventeenth century, the expansion of horse-trading fairs across the country helped meet this growing demand. Better horse-breeding created a rich variety of horses to meet all needs. In particular, breeders managed to double the power of the strongest horses. By the beginning of the eighteenth century, an estimated half of one million horses lived in England and Wales; a large proportion of which were used for ploughing the land (Edwards 1983). This new stock of horses would have created a capacity of 390 MW, generating 600 GWh of power.

The Industrious Revolution

The rising cost of using horses and the declining cost of hiring labourers after the fifteenth century meant that a proportion of the growth in the demand for power was met by human power, and new ways of harnessing it.

The population grew gradually after the Black Death and pay for a labourer was 'good'. At its peak, in the second half of the fifteenth century, human power could cost 1 400 pence per kWh generated (see Figure 5.2). Between 1450 and 1650, the population had doubled, increasing the labour supply. Consequently, the cost of hiring humans for power had fallen to around 800 pence in the first half of the seventeenth century.

Most of the population, outside the urban centres, was involved in agricultural production or related crafts. In 1520, around 15 percent of rural households were undertaking manufacturing activities (Wrightson 2000 p.41). The proportion of the rural population still involved in mainly agricultural activities fell from 70 percent in 1600 to 60.5 percent in 1670 (Wrigley 1985, Wrightson 2000 p.172), and is thought to have fallen to 55 percent in 1700 and 46 percent in 1750 (Wrightson 2000 p.235).

In 1520, of the 2.4 million inhabitants in Britain only 5.5 percent of the population lived in urban areas with populations of more than 5 000 people; this share rose from 8 percent in 1600 to 13.5 percent in 1670. Urban population rose to 17 percent in 1700 and 21 percent by 1750 (Wrigley 1985, Wrightson 2000 p.172). The urban populations were far more likely to be involved in non-agricultural occupations. These occupations reflected the goods and services of growing importance at the time: manufacture of textiles, clothing, leather, wood and metal; production and retailing of processed food and drink; the building trade, including carpenters, masons and plumbers; entrepreneurial and distributive roles, such as merchants, grocers and clothiers; and finally the professionals – the lawyers, clergy, physicians and apothecaries.

It appears that the amount of time spent working in the agricultural sector remained relatively constant between the fourteenth and the nineteenth centuries at about 300 days per year (Voth 1998 p.39). The major changes in time expenditure were in the manufacturing sector. In addition to an employer's threats of redundancy, the appearance of new commodities, such as tobacco and sugar, in the seventeenth century created an increase in the labourer's desire for such products. This growing desire led to a rise in the willingness to supply labour for income generation. It led to a growth in the amount of hours worked by the head of the household and an increased use of women and children for productive activities (De Vries 1993).

In the industrial sector, before mechanisation, work-time and effort varied significantly during the week. Saint-Monday (the tendency of taking-off Monday to recover from the weekend) was followed by a sluggish mid-week, and led to frenetic end of week, generally finishing on Saturday, to meet production targets. The Industrial Revolution transformed irregular work patterns into rigid time structures (Thompson 1967).

The reduction in abstention from working on Mondays and of the fall in the number of holy days in the eighteenth century increased working hours for men from under 3 000 hours per year in 1750 to over 3 500 by 1800. Some have also associated this change with additional food consumption and energy, thus, allowing for more active hours (Freudenberger and Cummins 1976). Thus, throughout the eighteenth century, men worked more regularly and harder, and more women and children were employed directly in the production of goods (De Vries 2006 p.50).

The increased productive activity occurred initially within the home. While many households remained outside the market, a growing number became specialised in a particular activity. This 'putting-out' system enabled households to produce a particular good or component of a good (De Vries 2006 p.48). Adam Smith (1776), in his discussion of sources of economic growth, focussed on how manufactures broke down the production process into a series of many little tasks. The division of labour enabled each worker to be extremely skilled at a particular part of the production process – be it for making nails, cloth or pans. This greater skill reduced the effort required, enabling faster production. In the 'proto-industrial' period, the focus was on producing more in the same time, rather than the same amount in less time, and driving down the costs of production.

Better skilled labour also played its part in increasing the output relative to the effort put in. Apprenticeship was central to the training of children and young men. Without a binding contract guaranteeing some return on the investment, few tradesmen would have been willing to share their skills with young men who were likely to leave once the training was complete and work for higher pay. Passed down from the craft guilds of the Middle Ages, a national system of technical training was introduced in the second half of the sixteenth century. This system provided a legal contract between apprentice and master. It played a major role in promoting the development and spread of skills across Britain, and its success grew over the centuries (Humphries 2006 p.75).

Power-Saving Devices

The separation of tasks brought improvements in production. Further major reductions in the costs of production were the result of power-saving devices. Most activities still depended on manual work using tools and devices to assist in the task. Most often, wool was hand-combed and yarn was spun on a wheel with a foot peddle. Weaving used hand looms, and dyeing and shearing was also based on manual processes (Musson 1979 p.45). A key development for the textile industry was the introduction of the flywheel in the late Middle Ages. The wheel tripled the rate at which yarn could be spun, compared with the classical hand-held distaff-and-spindle (Mokyr 1990 p.51). Similarly, the horizontal frame loom considerably improved the process of preparing woollen garments (Musson 1979 p.47).

Various devices introduced for their efficiency were faced with hostility. The gig-mill, which was often water-powered, was banned by Parliament in 1552 and by royal proclamation in 1633. Introduced to England in the seventeenth century, the engine-loom, which could weave dozens of braids at the same time and could use hands, feet or water for power, received strong opposition (Mokyr 1990).

The reduction in labour per unit of output created considerable fears about unemployment. Such concerns could often be short-sighted, however, since reduction in costs could lead to greater demand, thus employing potentially more workers. Naturally, in the short run, a conservative approach guaranteed a status quo in the level of employment (at least, temporarily), while the new device depended on fickleness of the market forces (and few were likely to understand how they worked). In the long run, the cautious approach would probably imply that the business was eventually no longer able to compete with those that had adopted the new techniques, leading to declining demand and employment. The only way a company could fail to adopt without experiencing a decline was by providing a higher value product resulting from its production process. This depended on the existence or the creation of a demand for the higher value product. Thus, if it was adopted and improved production, a new technology created change – how exactly changes occurred depended on the producers' and consumers' choices. Despite the potential long-term benefits associated with any device, workers faced with a new invention understood it had the potential to replace human power.

In the medieval and early modern era, guilds played an important role in protecting the interest of their members. They have frequently disrupted the uptake of power-saving devices. In other cases, they did help to promote technological development, through their role in training craftsmen, disseminating knowledge and protecting the inventors. In particular, after the late Middle Ages, they tended to be more promoters than a hindrance to change (Epstein 1998 p.694).

3. THE WATER AND WIND POWER REVOLUTION

Water Power

The water mill had been in Britain at least since Roman times. Its principal role had been to crush grain. During the seventh to the tenth centuries, ideas about how to improve the harnessing of water power spread across Europe. The main improvements included better overshot wheels to catch the water, and gearings for horizontal and vertical waterwheels, which enabled greater use on fast- and on slow-flowing rivers (Mokyr 1990 p.34).

The strength of water for providing power was impressive. A hard-working human might generate around one hundred watts of power, and cattle no more than four hundred watts. The traditional waterwheel that would have been used in late medieval and early modern times could produce two thousand watts. From this power, around 100 kg of grain could be crushed in one hour; a donkey might crush about 10 kg, and a human only 3 kg (Smil 1999).

Growing populations created rising demands for power, which made it worthwhile to use these improved methods of harnessing nature's strengths and, therefore, to make the large investments. The expansion of the watermill in Europe created an opportunity to generate far more power than had been previously possible. Some have called it a "medieval power revolution" (Holt 1988 p.147), with major implications for the economy – described as the "industrial revolution of thirteenth century" (Carus-Wilson 1941).

Agrarian and Industrial Markets for Power

The mills, driven by the strength of rivers, were, in medieval times, used for only a few repetitive activities, particularly crushing grain to make bread and malt for ale. In fact, the first census of the British economy in the Domesday Book provided evidence of the number of mills in England. In 1086, it was estimated that 6 082 mills were in use, all driven by water. Most of these mills were used for grinding grain to feed the population.

Given that for the majority of the population, efforts or income went towards ensuring sufficient food, demand for bread was relatively stable. This made the mechanisation of grain-grinding a potentially profitable investment. As population grew during the eleventh and twelfth centuries, the number of mills to feed the population increased.

The introduction of the windmill created a new boost to investment in power services. Combining the concept of the waterwheel with a sail was recorded first in 1185 (Mokyr 1990 p.45). Attracted by the expectation of major profits from cheap power, many lords swiftly invested in the new technology. By 1300, at least 2 000 windmills had been installed in England (Langdon 2005 p.35).

In addition to grain crushing, fulling began to use water power increasingly in Britain. Clothing, and wool in particular, was the only other product with a large enough demand in medieval times to warrant investing in mills – except in special circumstances and only where water power was plentiful.

Combing, spinning and weaving were the three principal steps to preparing textiles. To avoid damage and entanglement in these processes, however, oils had to be applied to woollen textiles. This additional stage involved placing the woollen textiles in a tub of water and pounding them, aided by heat and pressure. As well as removing the oil, fulling compressed the garment, making it more robust and heavier (Munro 2006 p.8).

Fulling new wool required heavy scouring and pounding to remove dirt and oils, and to force the fibres together. Hands and clubs have been used since ancient times, while most of the fulling was done by walkers in great tubs. Human power was central to cloth making (Holt 1988 p.152).

This manual process added around 20 percent of the cost of the original textile. A mechanised fulling process was developed in the tenth century in Florence. It enabled the fulling costs to fall by three-quarters. This mechanisation spread across Europe and, in the late fourteenth century, most of the fulling in England was mechanised (Munro 2006 p.10).

Heavy manual and foot pounding to clean wool began to be replaced by the repetitive power of the watermill from the second half of the twelfth century (Holt 1988 p.153). Although there were hardly any at the end of the eleventh century, by the end of the twelfth century there were more than 500 fulling mills across England (Langdon 2005 p.35).

If we take a look at the overall power production and use in medieval times, a clear picture emerges. The twelfth and thirteenth centuries experienced considerable economic growth. By 1300, there were an estimated 10 000 mills in operation, one-fifth of which were powered by wind (Langdon 2005 pp.13–19). Given that the new mills were probably larger than earlier ones, the supply of power more than doubled.

Since there were around 100 mills used for non-fulling industrial activities, total industrial mills at the end of the fourteenth century was about 6 percent of the total number of mills in operation in England. So, while wool production was significantly affected by the growth of mills in the late medieval period, claims of an 'industrial revolution' seem an exaggeration, particularly in comparison with the far greater demand for power for agricultural needs.

The Economic Structure of Mills

Mills were major investments in the Middle Ages. Building the waterwheel and the house and preparing the millstones were large undertakings. At the beginning of the fourteenth century, the average watermill would cost about £(2000)2 800 per kW of capacity (Langdon 2005 p.179). Windmills tended to cost half. At the time, the cost of a horse (or an ox) was around £(2000)700 per kW.

The total investment in milling capital was around £(2000)112 million in 1300 (Langdon 2005 p.179). Many lords and other entrepreneurs were willing to invest such vast sums of money because of the large perceived returns. Once built, the mill owner incurred low variable costs. Animals required daily fodder and care, as well as labourers to direct them. A mill could run for years with only minor repairs and with relatively few paid hands to manage it. In 1300, at its medieval peak, between 15 000 and 25 000 people worked in the milling industry (Langdon 2005 p.237). This suggests that only one to three people were required to run each mill, each with a capacity varying from 2 to 10 kW.

Mills could operate as part of various economic entities. Mills were often part of a 'demesne'. At first, the mill provided power services for the lord's farm. It then was made available for all households living in the manor. In fact, they were usually obliged to use the lord's mill, which could work as a monopoly, creating profits for the lord and tensions between classes (Langdon 2005 p.17).

During the eleventh and twelfth centuries, demesnes, as economic systems, fell into decline. Increasingly, lords would lease out the mill to a family who would manage it as an independent economic entity for extended periods or often as hereditary tenure. These tenants would, therefore, provide power services in return for a payment (in-kind, such as grain, or in money).

Throughout the thirteenth century, when clear profits were being made by the tenant millers, lords would frequently try to repossess the mills. It would seem, however, that they did not always succeed, and over the next couple of centuries, tenant mills grew.

In addition to the mills set up on manors, certain boroughs built mills. They were usually very large by the standards, providing power services for local residents. They often exercised their monopoly rights very strongly, again creating tensions between owners and residents. Finally, smaller household mills existed. Driven by hand or horse, they were set up to crush grain. They often operated illegally, and lords or the borough owner sought to confiscate them (Langdon 2005 p.18).

Decline in Mill Activity

The first half of the fourteenth century was a period of considerable uncertainty for the milling industry. Economic stagnation made a number of the mills commercially non-viable. Many mills went into disrepair, often – especially between 1315 and 1317 – the result of severe flooding. With dwindling profits and relatively large costs to fix any mill wear and tear, many mills fell into disrepair and abandon. After a while, a second-hand market in spare parts, stripped from the abandoned mills, kept the profitable ones turning (Holt 1988 p.161).

In addition to the many grain-crushing mills, some were set up for fulling wool. In the fourteenth century, the centres of cloth production shifted away from the eastern lowlands to the western hills, where the costs of generating power were much lower, and from towns to rural areas, reflecting the growth in cloth export rather than for local consumption (Carus-Wilson 1941 p.45). By 1330, there were more than 200 recorded fulling mills (Holt 1988 p.154), with an equivalent of 400 kW of power capacity.

By the mid-century, the number of mills in use fell by about 5 percent in ten years. After the Black Death, they dropped a further 5 percent. Corn-mills were most sensitive to the decline in population, as their demand depended on mouths to feed. Some corn-mills were converted to fulling stations. The number of fulling mills grew by about 50 percent between 1350 and 1390 (Langdon 2005 p.35).

In 1390, a new period of economic depression, associated with the 'great bullion famine', drove down the number of mills further. Windmill owners seem to have suffered greatly; the number of windmills fell by about 30 percent. In many areas, windmills complemented watermills in the crushing of grain, and they were first to be abandoned. In the Eastern regions, where windmills were the only large source of power, little decline was experienced. By 1450, windmills (in all of England) provided only 12 percent of the total power, compared with 21 percent in 1300 (Langdon 2005 p.35).

In 1450, grain crushing mills, powered by either water or wind, had stabilised at 75 percent of the level in 1300. Given that population had halved, this was potentially more flour for each person. The major attraction of the mill was that it was labour-saving. In a time of labour shortages, a high value was placed on using the mill rather than any human or animal activity for power (Langdon 2005 p.301).

Non-fulling industrial demand for power had been on a gradual decline since the early fourteenth century and, between 1390 and 1450, all industrial mills had also fallen slightly, due mainly to a strong contraction in non-fulling mills after 1410. Still, industrial mills had doubled their share of demand for power from 1300 (6 percent) to 1450 (12 percent). By the mid-fifteenth century, the total number of mills had fallen by about 20 percent relative to the early fourteenth century – to around 7 500 mills (Langdon 2005 pp.35–41).

This was the lowest point in milling activity for nearly three hundred years. Afterwards, the number of grain mills remained constant, at least for the next hundred years. On the other hand, from the mid-fifteenth century, fulling mills began to grow a little, then stagnated for another forty years. From the 1490s, fulling demand for power increased substantially – by 50 percent to 1540. Since the early fourteenth century it had more than doubled and, by the mid-sixteenth century, was the source of nearly one-fifth of the total demand for water and wind power in Britain (Langdon 2005 pp.35–42).

Non-fulling industrial milling grew sharply from 1460 to 1500 and 1515 to 1530, increasing eight-fold in that time. A growing source of water power use was in Cornwall where it was used for crushing, cleansing or bellowing tin ore. A few were also being used for bellowing fires to smelt iron. Demand for non-fulling industrial power was still only one-twentieth of the total share by 1540 (Langdon 2005 pp.41–2).

Grain demand had fallen from 94 percent to 77 percent of the total demand for grain between 1300 and 1540. So, nearly one-quarter of the milling power was for industrial activities. The total demand for power was around 12 percent lower. But, since population was still 45 percent smaller than in 1300, each person had more food and clothing, and there was plenty to export (Langdon 2005 pp.28–35).

Water Power in the Early Modern Period

The role of the grain mill in the economy had already been well-established by the fourteenth century, and was further consolidated over the next two hundred years. The demand for power to grind grain continued, but income and price elasticities for bread were low. So, demand grew gradually with the rising population. This demand or its supply did not, however, change greatly over the following centuries. Power provided for grain-crushing appears to have about doubled between 1540 and 1760.

During the Early Modern era, there were few major changes in the market for power, even in the industrial sector. The beginning of the sixteenth century saw a modest growth in the demand for water-powered fulling. European demand provided a huge impetus for textile industrial activity and by the end of the fifteenth century, 90 percent of all English exports were for wool products; and, by the end of the seventeenth century, half of all wool production was exported, and a quarter of all manufactured goods (Musson 1981 p.26). And yet, in 1760, more than two hundred years later, there were an estimated 1 800 textile mills – barely 10 percent more. The major difference though was their size – each mill had a capacity of around 11 MW, generating about 40 GWh (Kanefsky 1979a p.338).

Other industrial activities certainly grew more. The number of non-fulling mills increased from around 400 in 1540 to 1 300 in 1760. By then, 430 mills were used for bellowing metal works (discussed in the previous chapter); 300 were drawing water from mines and crushing the ore; 370 were crushing pulp into paper (Kanefsky 1979a p.338).

The Role of Water Power before the Industrial Revolution

Water, and to a lesser extent wind, provided an important amount of power before the Industrial Revolution. A broader picture shows, however, that they were far from being the main source of power. At the end of the eleventh century, humans provided about one-tenth and animals eight-tenths of the power (see Figure 5.5 and Table 5.1). During the 'power revolution' of the late medieval period, it would seem that the share of water power hardly changed. If there was a 'power revolution', it was driven by animals.

After the Black Death, human muscles were in short supply. Other sources of power were in excess capacity. Water- and windmills increased their share. The proportion of animal power seems to have stabilised after the Black Death at about two-thirds of the economy's power supply. Improvements in tools, the division of labour and longer hours worked led to an early 'Industrious Revolution', as the role of human effort increased its share of total power provided during the sixteenth and seventeenth centuries.

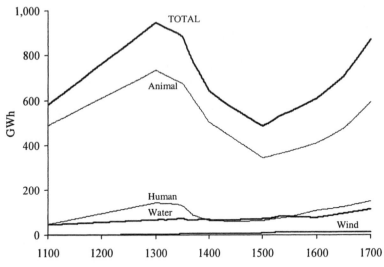

Source: see Data Appendix

Figure 5.5 The Provision of Power, 1100–1700

Total power provision rose from just above 500 GWh in 1100 to 800 GWh in 1300. Power provision slumped back, after the Black Death, to about 500 GWh in 1500. The expansion of the economy in the fifteenth and sixteenth centuries was paralleled by the growth in power provision – by 1700, 900 GWh of power was generated.

Table 5.1 Estimates of the Share of Power Provided by Different Sources in Late Medieval and Early Modern England, 1100–1700

	1100	1300	1500	1700
Human power	11%	25%	18%	22%
Animal power	80%	66%	67%	64%
Watermill power	9%	8%	14%	12%
Windmill power	0%	1%	1%	2%

Source: see Data Appendix

A final consideration is the total amount of power per person. Significant changes in power provision for each inhabitant would be an indicator of a 'power revolution'. Based on the figures presented, in 1100, each person benefited from the provision of more than 300 kWh of power per year. By 1300, it had fallen to

130 kWh. Clearly, as the population quadrupled but alternative power sources to supplement human limbs did not increase as much, there was a decline in supply.

In 1500, as population was lower than two hundred years before, power provision returned to about 230 kWh per person per year. As population grew, even with the economy expanding with the development of the proto-industrialisation, it would seem that the per capita provision of power in 1700 had fallen again to around 160 kWh per year.

The estimates of power provision shown in Figure 5.5 indicate that water and wind power were not the dominant sources of power in Britain. As stated, though, they played an important role in a few key sectors. This implied that, in those sectors, power costs and, therefore, prices of commodities were considerably lower than if mills had not been introduced. They also freed human and animal power to be employed in other sectors. This was nearly 100 GWh of power and more than 10 percent of the total power provided in the English economy at the end of the seventeenth century.

In 1700, the economy had nearly the same population as in 1300, around six million inhabitants. Animals, which provided the main source of power, were twice as expensive to buy and to maintain as in 1300. The population had slightly more power in 1700 – about 20 percent. In the eighteenth century, the economy was at the dawn of a far greater expansion in population, however. If a new 'power crisis' was to be avoided, new ways of 'fuelling' the demand would need to be found.

4. POWERING THE INDUSTRIAL REVOLUTION

The Waterwheel

Throughout the medieval and early modern period, waterwheels had changed little. They were small and simple, made of wood, catching water at the bottom of the wheel (that is, undershot) and had few gears for transmitting power. Since the late Middle Ages, some creativity had been directed towards finding new uses for wheels – increasingly being applied to fulling cloth, pumping water, crushing mineral ores and materials, sawing wood and operating machines. During the seventeenth century, the more efficient, overshot wheels, which caught the water in buckets at the top of the wheel, were becoming popular. In the eighteenth century, the thriving technological and economic spirit led to major innovations and investment in the harnessing of water power (Buchanan 1994 p.46).

During the second half of the eighteenth and the nineteenth centuries, water- and windmills underwent dramatic improvements in their ability to harness energy (Reynolds 1983). Water power also benefited from developments in metal construction and an understanding of water flow and regulation. Windmills improved "with its easily controlled patent spring sails and its self-regulating fantail mechanism and centrifugal governor" (Buchanan 1994 p.47).

A little information exists about the costs of water power during the Industrial Revolution. The wheel was often the largest expense. In the eighteenth century, from a broad range, the average price for a wheel was £(2000)3 800 per kW (Kanefsky 1979a p.164).

The price of a wheel did not seem to have benefited greatly from economies of scale. In fact, some evidence suggests that the unit price of a wheel could increase with power. In one example in mid-Wales, the price per kW of a 35 kW wheel was double the price of 6 kW wheel – the total cost of the first wheel was twelve times the latter (Kanefsky 1979a p.164). Price did vary according to the materials used. For instance, basic wooden wheels were quite cheap. Composite and iron wheels were pricier.

The waterwheel was not the only expense, however. In some instances, more expensive power resulted from other factors being dear. In one detailed example in 1884, a 180 kW wheel cost just under £(2000)1 550 per kW. The 'water privileges and land' were nearly the same. Another major expense was the cost of the weir and a tunnel to direct the water, and a building to house the wheel. The total cost was equivalent to £(2000)1.1 million – thus, £(2000)6 400 per kW.

In addition to the cost of the buying and installing a wheel, there were interest and depreciation expenses to consider. While they differed greatly, nominal annual interest of borrowing funds for watermills was generally around 5 to 10 percent, and the rate of depreciation was about 5 percent (Kanefsky 1979a p.167).

Finally, there were the costs of running a mill. They included charges for the use of water, the hiring of relatively unskilled labour to maintain and operate the mill, and lubrication and general upkeep. These costs were modest – no more than £(2000)670 per kW (Kanefsky 1979a p.172). It would seem that the cost of generating power from water was very approximate. The main reason was that it varied greatly according to the conditions – especially the wheel and the location.

Incorporating all the costs discussed above, a rough estimate of the cost of water power in the mid-eighteenth century was 160 pence per kWh (Kanefsky 1979a p.164). This estimate includes both capital and operational expenditure, making a comparison with human and animal power cost difficult and potentially misleading. As a reminder, in the middle of the eighteenth century, the running costs of human power were around 1 000 pence (2000 money) per kWh (see Figure 5.2) and of horse power were 60 pence per kWh (see Figure 5.4). For a comparison, a crude indicator of the running costs of water power (based on the labour and maintenance expenditure mentioned above, working 300 days per year for 10 hours per day, which is probably a minimum for an industrial activity) was 20 pence per kWh. In other words, a waterwheel, once installed, generated very cheap power.

Technological innovation appears to have driven down the price. Dramatic improvements in wheel efficiency were the brainchild of Joseph Smeaton's better designs and his use of iron rather than wood wheels. These improvements, along with cheaper iron and lower maintenance costs, drove down the cost of power. It has been suggested that a best-practice wheel in the 1780s allowed the cost per unit of power to fall to one-third of its cost in 1750 (Freeman and Louç   a 2001 p.162).

Capital and Running Costs of Steam

Around the turn of the eighteenth century, a series of experiments on the power of steam led to one of the most dramatic transformations in economic history. In 1698, Thomas Savery used steam to create a vacuum that then worked a pump. A few years later, Thomas Newcomen developed the first steam engine with piston. His machine heated up a cylinder which created a change in atmospheric pressure, pushing the piston. Because the cylinder was cooled and reheated for every pump of the piston, the atmospheric engine was extremely energy inefficient. Nevertheless, the engine worked and was, therefore, of interest in locations where fuel was virtually free. Coal mines, which needed to pump out water, were the first demand for the steam engines (von Tunzelman 1978 p.187).

In 1768, James Watt patented a steam engine with a separate condenser. This avoided the problem of reheating the cylinder with each stroke. Therefore, the Watt's non-atmospheric engine reduced the amount of heat and fuel required to produce a given amount of power. This greater fuel efficiency enabled his engine to be in demand beyond the coal mines (von Tunzelman 1978 p.187).

In the 1780s, two machines were developed that further improved the potential use of heat-generated power. The first machine applied the pumping mechanism to a rotary motion, which could turn wheels. The second machine drove two pistons – a first piston was pumped in a high-pressure cylinder and, on the release of the steam, it pushed a second lower-pressure cylinder (Mokyr 1990 p.85).

Just like water power, the costs of power provision depended on the fixed or capital costs, annual expenses and running costs. The fixed costs naturally involved the price of materials, the boiler and other machinery. They also included the efforts of installing and housing the engine. Often the latter could double the fixed costs. For the average Newcomen engine, though, the metal parts were around 60 percent of these costs; the boiler about 15 percent; and the buildings another 35 percent (Kanefsky 1979a pp.150–51).

In the mid-eighteenth century, for a small engine, with a 30-inch cylinder, capable of 6 to 8 kW, the fixed costs were around £(2000)80 000 – or about £(2000)10 500 per kW. The larger engines, 70-inch cylinders, generating 35 kW, cost around £(2000)4 000 per kW (Kanefsky 1979a p.151).

At the end of the eighteenth century, a small Boulton & Watt engine of around 4 horsepower, including the building, cost around £(2000)9 300 per kW. A larger one, able to generate 35 kW, cost about £(2000)5 300 per kW (Kanefsky 1979a p.156). Crucially, customers paid a substantial premium for the Boulton & Watt patent – around one-third of the price of the engine (Kanefsky 1979a p.155). Once the patent expired in 1800, the cost of machinery and power fell substantially (Kanefsky 1979a p.156).

Taking the average engine used in the cotton textile industry, the long run
trend in capital costs of steam engines shows a strong decline (see Figure 5.6). In
1760, the cost of capital was above £(2000)5 000 per kW. By 1800, the capital
costs had dropped to one-third – to around £(2000)1 500 per kW. Costs stagnated
in the first half of the nineteenth; only in the 1850s and 1860s did they start
falling again and, in 1870, the costs were around below £(2000)600 per kW.
Again, costs stayed static – they only fell at the very end of the nineteenth
century. By the beginning of the twentieth century, it cost under £(2000)400 to
generate one kW – a twelve-fold decline in one hundred and fifty years (Crafts
2004).

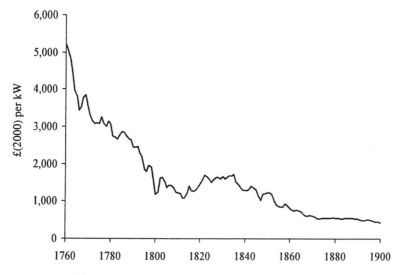

Source: Crafts (2004), see Data Appendix

Figure 5.6 The Price of a Steam-Engine (per kW), 1760–1900

Newcomen's steam engine patented in 1718 had a thermal efficiency of only
0.5 percent. Although by 1792 Watt had increased the thermal efficiency ten-
fold, diffusion of steam-power remained limited to activities where coal was
cheap and easily available in large quantities. Developments, such as the high-
pressure stationary engines, improved the efficiency to 17 percent by the 1830s.
These improvements encouraged technological diffusion to many new activities
and rapid growth in the demand for heating fuels (Anderson 1993).

Evidence on running costs highlights the dramatic improvements in energy
efficiency. In 1760, an estimate of the labour and fuel costs of generating one
kWh of power was around 450 pence (see Figure 5.7). The costs fell to about 100
pence by 1800. After some volatility, in the first half of the nineteenth century,

the costs dropped to around 30 pence by 1870. In 1910, the costs had halved again to around 15 pence per kWh.

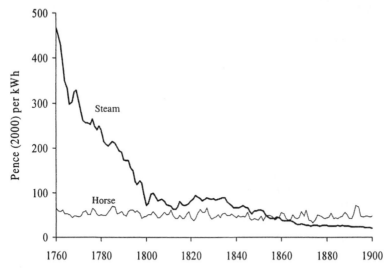

Source: see Data Appendix

Figure 5.7 The Running Costs of Steam and Horse Power, 1760–1900

Characteristics of Competing Technologies

The costs of power equipment ranged widely according to the scale, location, designs, materials and businesses involved. Nevertheless, around the turn of the nineteenth century, the capital costs of power from water and steam were broadly similar (Kanefsky 1979a p.170). It is clear, however, that the running costs of a waterwheel were much cheaper (Kanefsky 1979a p.171). The crude estimate above suggests that it was around 20 pence per kWh in the 1750s, and it no doubt dropped in subsequent decades.

By the mid-eighteenth century, numerous technologies were able to produce power and they competed amongst themselves for demand. In most cases, however, the nature of the demand for power dictated the type of technology to be used. For small needs, of less than 3 kW, or skilled tasks, human effort tended to be employed. If the chore was done repetitively, it was probably more appropriate to use horses, donkeys or oxen. When more than four to six animals were needed, problems of coordination and of directing the power arose, constraining the scale of the activity (Kanefsky 1979a p.138).

For larger tasks, water or wind had generally been the only option. Windmills could provide power for needs of up to 6 kW. Wind was intermittent and, therefore, was only appropriate for users that could adjust their activities to the fickleness of the wind. Grain-crushing was relatively flexible. Wind power also meant that power users did not need to be by a water source, expanding the distribution of power.

On the other hand, for activities that used water in the process, such as fulling and paper pulping, water sources were needed and they were more likely to combine this need with its power source. For demands that required regular power, such as mines, where intermittent power would have left spaces filled with water and potentially drowned miners, the reliability of the power source was essential. Also, mines often sought large quantities of power. Thus, waterwheels, generating up to 30 kW, did the work.

During summer months, when water flows could slacken considerably, mines would fill with water, leaving potentially rich veins untapped. By the 1710s, the existence of a reliable source of power enabled miners to go deeper, and ultimately transformed many other activities. Despite the relatively limited applicability of the Newcomen engine, around 75 machines had been installed by 1730 (Kanefsky 1979a p.139).

The steam engine had been a valuable tool for pumping water. In the 1740s, this task helped iron and brass works address the problem of their bellows spluttering during the summer months. Steam engines could pump water over the waterwheels, providing power. By the 1760s, these recirculating engines had become common in metal works and were spreading to the textile industry (Kanefsky 1979a p.140).

Many were reluctant to use steam directly. The nature of the motion was paramount to providing good quality work, and they believed that nothing compared to the smooth running of a waterwheel. This belief was held in a number of industries. Furthermore, the waterwheel was a far simpler technology than the engine, reducing the likelihood of breakdowns (Kanefsky 1979a p.141).

Steam engines did, however, provide two attributes that made it of great value to a number of power users – flexibility and reliability. Power was no longer limited to being by a source of running water. Also, the steam engine was less constrained by the size of the wheel, enabling greater power to be generated, once the technology evolved to larger scales. The other key characteristic of the steam engine was that it was less susceptible to unexpected stoppages. Thus, in many cases, steam was used as the back-stop technology, either directly or to turn the waterwheel.

Large-scale power provision was no longer dependent on geography and season. It could spread across the whole country and be used all year. Throughout the eighteenth century and first half of the nineteenth century, the economy was divided according to the different power sources and their demands. Much of the textile industry stuck to the water-powered regions. The mining and the metal works, which could not move towards the water, brought the power sources to them.

The Demand for Power

In the early days, the main users of steam power were in the coal mining industry where coal was a virtually free resource. The collieries' demand for power was so large and the lack of water power so great that, by 1760, much of it was met by steam power (Kanefsky 1979a p.148). Around 300 water mills pumped mines, virtually all of them helping to extract coal, with a joint capacity of about 4 MW. So, not including the large role played by humans and animals, water and steam power each provided about half of the power. This would have been equivalent to about 20 GWh at a time when 7 million tonnes (4 mtoe) was being raised (Flinn 1984 p.252).

The dramatic expansion of the coal mining industry required vast quantities of pumping, as it sought deeper mines. In 1870, it was producing 120 million tonnes of coal (70 mtoe) (Church 1987 p.25). By then, the coal mining industry had installed 224 MW of power, providing about 460 GWh.

In other mines, the demand for power was smaller and the cost of coal greater. The installed capacity in non-coal mines was only 45 MW. Most metal mines still depended on water wheels. Cornish mines, however, needed larger amounts of power, and adopted steam relatively early (Kanefsky 1979a p.148).

Iron smelting also required large quantities of power for bellowing its furnaces (see the previous chapter). Because of the large demands, the industry quickly adopted steam engines – by 1800, most of the industry used steam rather than water power. In 1870, in its blast and puddling furnaces, the iron industry used nearly 245 MW.

In the textile industry, the size of the mills and the demand for power grew considerably between 1760 and 1870. In the mid-eighteenth century, only fulling used water power. It generally required about 6 kW. Other activities, such as spinning and weaving, were done by hand or foot. In the 1760s, flax was starting to be stretched and linen finished on larger scales (Kanefsky 1979a p.145).

By the 1770s, cotton spinning was being mechanised (for wool, it did not occur until the 1820s). Each of the individual tasks required little power, but could be multiplied many times to meet the needs of the producer. By the nineteenth century, the average cotton factory was around 200 kW (Kanefsky 1979a p.146).

The cotton industry was an early exception to the conservatism of many entrepreneurs. The industry had grown rapidly in the latter stages of the eighteenth century, through the innovations in spinning and weaving techniques, which drove down textile prices (Wrigley 1962). This stimulated considerable new demand. And in the early nineteenth century, the steam engine began to replace water power in order to drive larger numbers of spinning and weaving machines ever faster.

The whole textile industry also started using steam in the first half of the nineteenth century. It had been requiring relatively large amounts of power already. By 1838, when detailed statistics became available, three-quarters of textile mills activity was driven by steam. While the woollen industry still had nearly half of its activities powered by water, the cotton and worsted mills were four-fifths steam-powered.

In other industries, the demand for power varied according to the processes. The paper industry had been a large user of power for hundreds of years. Into the nineteenth century, it still stamped the paper with waterwheels. In the 1820s, a new machine, calling on greater power, was introduced and diffused. By 1870, the average mill was over 75 kW and the industry used around 25 MW of capacity, three-quarters from steam (Kanefsky 1979a p.149).

Another example of a large user of power was the gunpowder industry. Although it was the source of the first use of explosive power, it remained a large user of water late in the nineteenth century. Gunpowder had tended to be made in rural areas, near sources of water – for power and safety. Placing a steam engine in a gunpowder factory was considered dangerous (Kanefsky 1979a p.149).

Initially, the traditional main user of power, grain milling, did not feel the need to adopt the new technology. This reluctance was a combination of economic factors, since coal was not necessarily available abundantly near agricultural locations, and of conservative behaviour on the part of millers. By nineteenth century standards, corn and grain mills tended to be rather small-scale activities. In villages across the country, small mills of around 15 kW would grind grain from local farmers to local customers, minimising the need for transport. In cities, mills tended to be larger, averaging more than 30 kW. It was only after the 1870s and the large imports of American and Russian grain that concentrating flour milling, and using steam, became a major advantage (Kanefsky 1979a pp.143–4).

The Expansion of Power

For most of the first Industrial Revolution, broadly between 1760 and 1830, the largest provider of direct power was still animal muscles. Human labour was second. The physically active population was around three-quarters in the seventeenth century, and had fallen to one-half by the middle of the nineteenth century (Crafts 1994 p.46). In the first half of the eighteenth century, human power provided around 340 GWh (0.34 TWh) of power (see Figure 5.8). Despite the decline in the active population, a quickly rising and increasingly 'industrious' population nearly doubled the power provided – to more than 600 GWh by 1800. It increased further, peaking in the 1840s at around 1 300 GWh (or 1.3 TWh), stabilising up to the turn of the century, and declining thereafter. By 1850, time spent working appears to have fallen to about 3 200, dropping to 2 700 hours in 1900 and around 1 500 hours by the end of the twentieth century (Voth 1998 p.40).

A considerable volume of increased inputs came in the form of animal power. In fact, it could be argued that the Industrial Revolution was powered not so much by steam, water or even humans, but by horses. Animal population and power supply increased continuously throughout the eighteenth and nineteenth centuries. In 1700, approximately 400 000 horses (Edwards 1983) provided 600

GWh. By 1811, when reliable data was available, around one million horses (Thompson 1976 p.80) generated about 1 500 GWh (or 1.5 TWh). Horse power continued to grow, generating more than 4 000 GWh of power in 1900.

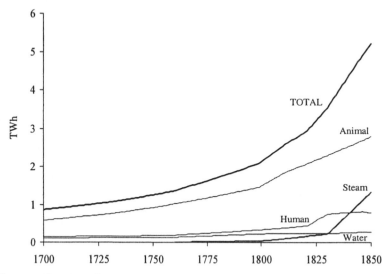

Source: see Data Appendix

Figure 5.8 The Provision of Power, 1700–1850

Table 5.2 Estimates of the Share of Power Provided by Different Sources, 1700–1900

	1700	1750	1800	1850	1900
Human power	22%	19%	17%	14%	4%
Animal power	64%	70%	70%	51%	23%
Watermill power	12%	10%	11%	5%	1%
Windmill power	2%	1%	0.5%	0%	0%
Steam power	0%	0%	1.5%	30%	71%

Source: see Data Appendix

In 1750, humans and animals provided nearly nine-tenths of the power provided in the British economy (see Table 5.2). By 1850, their share had fallen to two-thirds. Yet, the major transformation was in the second half of the nineteenth century. The process of industrialisation, which had begun with human and animal toil, and also depended on the strength of water, created demand for ever-more power. "Three criteria came to be regarded as essential in any source of power developed to meet these novel demands. First, it had to be available in volume, so small-scale or marginal energy-converters were not encouraged at this stage. Second, it had to be reliable, as the drainage of mines and the smooth running of factories came to depend utterly upon it. And thirdly, the power source had to be reasonably accessible, both physically and intellectually; it needed to be easily obtainable, and capable of being moved, reassembled and maintained without insuperable difficulties" (Buchanan 1994 p.46).

The introduction of the steam engine would eventually convert the coal mining industry from an important supplier of energy into the heartbeat of an entire economy and era. And, despite this apparent growth, and its potential benefits, its uptake was in fact slow. After all, the first steam engines were used in the first decade of the eighteenth century. In 1760, barely 4 MW of capacity was installed, not even providing 1 percent of the total installed power in Britain. At the turn of the century, steam only powered 3 percent of Britain's total. It took until 1830 for steam engine capacity to have caught up with water power, both with around 125 MW. Most industries were conservative in their strategies (Berg 1994) and savings in power costs from using steam-powered engines were achieved in steps as new generations of engines improved energy efficiency (von Tunzelmann 1978).

So, the major growth in steam power took place one hundred and thirty years after its introduction. By 1850, steam power (with over 800 MW of capacity) finally dwarfed water power (164 MW), and had overtaken human and animal power as the largest source. Steam provided 41 percent of the total power.

Yet, almost half of all steam power at that point was in the mining and cotton textile industries. Only in last quarter of the nineteenth century did steam power spread in a large scale to most industries. In areas with plentiful water, such as Yorkshire and the West Country, water turbines continued to provide a significant amount of energy. Steam power was also replacing large amounts of human and animal power. By 1900, human and animal power provided only one-quarter of the total. Steam dominated, generating more than 70 percent of Britain's power needs.

Total Power in Britain

Between 1760 and 1830, that is, the first Industrial Revolution, total power provision increased from about 850 GWh to nearly 2 400 GWh – almost tripling at an annual rate of 1.5 percent. Population had more than tripled. At the beginning of this revolution, every year, 12 kWh were generated per person. At the end, there were 10 kWh provided. Thus, the first Industrial Revolution can be seen as a period when the average person had less power to meet his or her needs.

The period of major growth in power provision was the second half of the nineteenth century (see Figure 5.9). The most impressive phase was between 1870 and 1900, when total power provided nearly tripled, at an annual rate of 3.5

percent. Population only increased 30 percent. By 1900, nearly 40 kWh per person were generated – four times more than in 1830.

The major transition in energy use between the eighteenth and the nineteenth centuries was in the use of heating fuels (rather than agricultural products) to generate power services, after the introduction of the steam engine. Nevertheless, human effort in general, animal power in agriculture, and water in the industrial sector continued to provide substantial amounts of energy until the end of the nineteenth century.

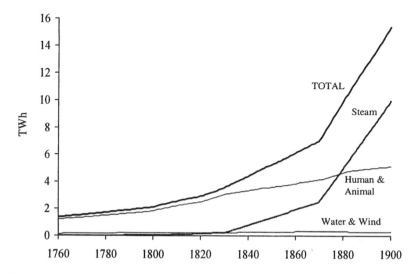

Source: see Data Appendix

Figure 5.9 The Provision of Power, 1760–1900

5. INTO THE TWENTIETH CENTURY

Steam Power Expands

Steam continued to power the British economy well into the twentieth century. Further technological improvements improved the efficiency of the steam engine. For instance, the pumping of a piston was wasteful of energy, because of the inertia associated with constantly changing the piston's direction. The introduction of steam turbines allowed for a less wasteful rotary motion (Kanefsky 1979a p.188). By 1907, the new steam turbines already provided around 400 MW of power (Musson 1979 p.168).

In 1870, the majority of power capacity was destined for three sectors, the textile, metal and coal mining industries. The textile industry had around one-third of the total installed capacity, and the metal and coal mining industry almost one-fifth each (Kanefsky 1979b p.373). By 1907, the main user of power was the metal industries with 30 percent, the textile industry had fallen to one quarter, and the mining industry was still one-fifth.

The growth in steam power capacity was dramatic. In 1870, about 1.5 GW was installed; by 1907, there were nearly 7.2 GW of steam power capacity installed. After 1870, other traditional sources of power for stationary activities had started to decline as steam started to dominate the market. Water power had fallen from around 170 MW in 1870 to about 130 MW in 1907. Wind capacity had halved in the period, down to under 4 MW. In fact, the newly developed internal combustion engine provided more than water and wind put together. Although it failed to develop into an important source of stationary power, in 1907, gas and petroleum products could be used with 500 MW of engines (Kanefsky 1979a).

In 1870, steam provided 62 percent of final user stationary power; by 1900, it drove 85 percent. Total primary power reached the 20 TWh level; final user power was over 15 TWh. The use of steam power grew between 1870 and 1900 by an annual rate of growth of 4.5 percent.

The Flexibility and Mobility of Electricity

As steam power became truly dominant, a new source was starting to threaten its position. Although electricity's primary source of power was also heating fuels and steam, the customer saw a completely different energy source, thanks to a series of revolutionary innovations (Musson 1976).

Michael Faraday's discovery of electromagnetic induction in 1831 paved the way for the invention of the dynamo. The dynamo was central to the generation of electricity both in motors and in power stations. By the 1880s, they were providing electricity on a commercial scale, and would soon revolutionise the use of power. The growth of a market for electricity began properly in the 1890s with the development of coal-fired steam generators, and benefiting from the introduction of steam turbines, which were well-suited for electricity generation (Musson 1979 p.194).

As electrification of industry increased, it led to major changes in the production process itself. For instance, traditionally, a factory was designed around a single power source. A large waterwheel or a steam engine provided the power down a long line of machines. Initially, the electric motors that replaced steam engines followed this design. However, large energy savings could be achieved if a series of motors each powered only a few machines. It became appropriate to fit each machine with its own motor. This shift reduced the amount of energy required for the power generated and allowed greater flexibility in the production process (Devine 1983).

Yet, arguably the most important characteristic of electricity was its mobility. To use steam power, an engine was needed nearby. Instead, electricity could be produced in one location, fed along a wire, and used in another, with only minor losses of power. While larger companies produced their own electricity, many smaller ones quickly depended on a central supplier.

The Growth of Power Stations and Supply Networks

Initially, technological complications made the central supply of electricity difficult and the uncertainty of commercial viability implied that electricity generation was a risky business. Yet, by the late 1880s, more than 80 companies or local authorities provided electricity from a central power station. Ten years later, most towns in Britain had at least one power station (Byatt 1979 p.25).

Limited to small areas on the network, power stations supplied varying standards of electricity, which was subject to frequent interruptions. In London alone, there were at least fifty generators, using twenty-four different voltages and ten frequencies. And, the increase in the scale of individual power stations was impressive – for instance, the City of London Company increased the size of its station from 1.5 MW in 1896 to 23 MW in 1907 (Jones 1989 p.89). The expansion of the industry enabled the price of electricity to drop considerably at the end of the nineteenth century. It fell from about 200 pence per kWh in 1883 to 115 pence in 1900 (see Figure 5.10).

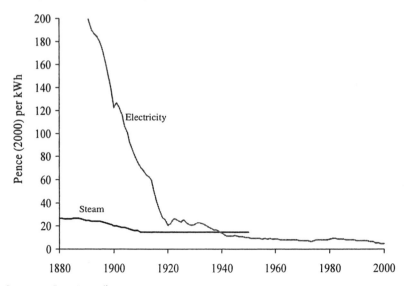

Source: see Data Appendix

Figure 5.10 The Running Costs of Steam Power and Price of Electric Power, 1880–2000

For customers, flexibility and mobility made electricity valuable. For the producer, the inability to store electricity drove up the costs. Large reserve capacity was needed to deal with demand peaks. The introduction of off-peak pricing in 1900 helped shift some of the demand away from peak periods. Power stations still needed to keep large levels of extra generation to avoid black-outs – in 1920, the load factor (that is, the ratio of capacity used to the total available) was 30 percent (MoFP 1951 p.110).

Technological developments led to the generation of a more homogeneous, reliable and time-saving energy source. Electricity prices fell further – down to 70 pence per kWh in 1910 and to 20 pence by 1920.

The Electric Growth of Power

The main demand for electricity at the beginning of the twentieth century was for transport and lighting. The use of electrical power had made only modest in-roads in the market for industrial power. Slow progress in industrial electrical power was not surprising given the large investment in steam power. The total electricity generating capacity was about 1.75 GW (that is, 1 750 MW) – of which 58 percent was in power stations, 35 percent were in industrial firms, and the rest were for railways and tramways (Musson 1979 p.170).

The introduction of electricity for power did provide a major boost to certain industrial activities. Many of the older industries were showing signs of stagnation. Agricultural and woollen mills had been in decline for a while. The textile industries in general, mining sector and metal manufacturing began to falter, particularly after the First World War, as world trade and exports weakened. The spread of electric power in industry occurred during the interwar period. Steam for direct power finally lost its dominance – 60 percent of industrial power was electrical by 1930. There was, however, a striking difference between industries. The old textile industry still used direct steam for more than 60 percent of its power. The degree of electrification in the engineering, shipbuilding and vehicles was 95 percent (Musson 1979 p.353).

The dramatic uptake of electrification of the economy coincided with the beginning of the twentieth century. In 1900, less than 1 percent of the power came from electricity. Before the First World War, it was just under 10 percent. By 1930, just under 40 percent of industrial power was from electricity. By the 1960s, most of the United Kingdom's industry was driven by electrical power.

Since electrical power replaced steam (rather than acting as a complement), the total consumption of power increased less dramatically. Total industrial power rose from about 8.5 TWh in 1900 to nearly 14 TWh in 1930 – an increase of 64 percent or a modest annual growth rate of 1.6 percent (see Figure 5.11). In the 1930s, in the face of the Great Depression, electricity consumption doubled. It was the ideal time to scrap steam engines and replace them with more flexible electrical power.

By 1950, total power consumption was around 23 TWh. The post Second World War boom created an impressive increase in the demand for industrial power, nearly tripling to 1970 – rising at annual growth rate of 5 percent. In the last thirty years of the twentieth century, consumption tripled again to more than 140 TWh.

By 2000, the demand for power was very different from the beginning of the century. The iron and steel industries consumed 6 TWh of electricity. The once powerful textile industry required about 3.5 TWh. Mechanical and electrical engineering were still major users of power, needing 16 TWh. The largest single industrial user of electricity was the chemical industry – with 23 TWh. The food and drink, and the paper and pulp industries both consumed 11 TWh (DTI 2003), although electricity has been used for heating and lighting as well as powering devices.

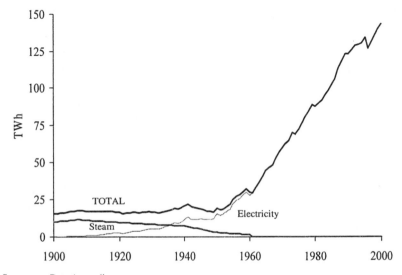

Source: see Data Appendix

Figure 5.11 The Use of Stationary Power in the Industrial Sectors, 1900–2000

Much of the increase in power consumption was in the commercial sector, which consumed in 2000, nearly 70 TWh. This was a fifteen-fold increase on 1950 – equal to an annual growth rate of 5.6 percent. Of course, just like in the industrial sector, it would be hard to separate-out the electricity consumption of power for office machinery and computing, as well as heating and lighting.

Fuel for Electricity Generation

The impressive rise of electrification shadowed the decline of the steam engine. Yet, the role of steam power was not lost. It stood behind the scenes rather than in front. Electricity was a form of energy with a high degree of added value. Flexibility and mobility were highly desirable attributes for energy. To create such a valuable 'good', several stages of transformation were necessary before the energy was provided to the customer – coal was mined, then steam was created in the power station, and the electricity fed down a wire.

For a long time, electricity extended the importance of coal. In 1945, it provided more than 95 percent of the energy for electricity (see Table 5.3). But by 1960, the share was just above 80 percent, with most of the rest being provided by oil. It fell down to 70 percent in 1970 with oil and nuclear power providing the rest.

More recently, a greater shift away from coal was observed – from 75 percent of the total inputs in 1981 to 65 percent of the total in 1991 to 28 percent of the total in 2000. Between 1981 and 1991, nuclear power rose from 15 percent to 23 percent of the total and, between 1991 and 2000, natural gas increased from less than 1 percent of the total to 38 percent (DTI 2001). This shift has been mainly due to successive United Kingdom government's support for nuclear power until the mid 1990s and to the privatisation and liberalisation of the electricity supply industry which encouraged generators to use CCGT (Combined Cycle Gas Turbine) plants, because of lower costs of installation and because of the incumbent's desire to create over-capacity discouraging market entry (Newbery 1996).

Table 5.3 United Kingdom Fuel Input for Electricity Generation (as a percentage of total), 1895–2000

	1895	1905	1914	1929	1939	1945	1960*	1973*	2000*
Coal	100	100	100	99.7	95.9	96.9	81.7	62.6	31.0
Oil	-	-	-	0.3	0.1	0.1	15.5	25.4	1.5
Natural gas	-	-	-	-	-	-	-	0.9	39.0
Hydro	-	-	-	1.0	4.0	3.0	0.7	0.5	1.0
Nuclear	-	-	-	-	-	-	1.7	10.5	21.0

Note

* The percentages may not add up to 100 percent because of small proportions of other fuels and imports being used.

Source: Mitchell (1988 pp.263–64) and DTI (2001)

The twentieth century was characterised by a near-complete dependence on heating to generate power. On the whole, economic activity expanded rapidly throughout the century and demand for power followed. Expansion was delayed by the First World War and the great depression and, consequently, power-related coal consumption started to decline, not returning to its 1913 level until the early 1950s. By then, cheaper prices for alternative energy sources and the diffusion of technological innovations, especially refinements of electricity generators and other electrical devices, were important stimuli for the increased diversity of energy sources, the long-term rise in overall energy use and the decline in coal use.

6. LONG-RUN TRENDS IN STATIONARY POWER

At the beginning of the story, at the time of the Domesday Book, power provision was about 500 GWh. Eighty percent came from animal power, mostly oxen, the rest evenly shared between humans and water mills. Evidence available in the Domesday Book suggests that each person benefited from the provision of more than 300 kWh of power per year.

A rising population enabled more power to be produced. But, the growing labour force needed to be fed, and was in competition with animals for the principal source of energy, the land and its food. The animal population could not grow as much as humans, such that, by 1300, two-thirds of the power was from animals, and two-fifths of that from horses; one-quarter was provided from humans and one-tenth from water- and windmills. The average person only had 130 kWh of power per year and the whole economy generated around 800 GWh of power. To generate the total power, 1.7 mtoe – more than 20 000 GWh – of energy in the form of food and fodder was required; that is, almost 0.18 toe per person – or 2 MWh.

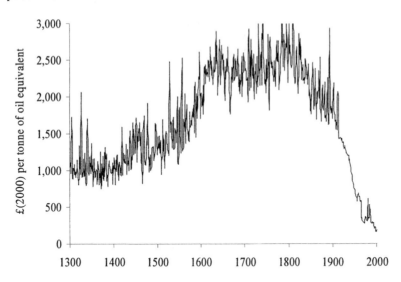

Source: see Data Appendix

Figure 5.12 The Price of Stationary Power, 1300–2000

Increasing pressures on land limited the supply and drove up the prices of agricultural products, leading to malnutrition and death. Following the Black Death (see Chapter 3), the population approximately halved, increasing the cost of human power. This improved labourers' standard of living and encouraged the use of animals. Yet, there was still excess capacity. New markets for animals, in transport, war and meat, were developing, using-up the surplus power. Total power provision fell to about 500 GWh in 1500.

The expansion of the economy in the fifteenth and sixteenth centuries created new demands for power. The rising population also needed to be fed, driving up the cost of maintaining animals. This fed through into a rising cost of generating power (see Figure 5.12). Yet, better horse-breeding created more powerful animals, providing much of the growth in power. The supply of power from water- and windmills grew as well. Mills found demands for power beyond the traditional grain-crushing, first, for fulling wool, then for bellowing metal-workers' fires and miners' water pumps. By 1700, 900 GWh of power were generated.

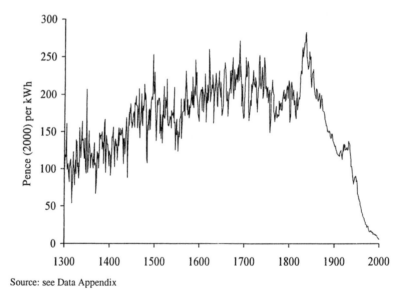

Source: see Data Appendix

Figure 5.13 The Fuel Costs associated with Stationary Power, 1300–2000

At the beginning of the eighteenth century, the population was similar to in 1300, around six million inhabitants. Despite improvements in strength, horses (per unit of power) were twice as expensive to buy and to maintain as in 1300. The population in 1700 had about 20 percent more power available. It consumed a similar amount of energy to generate this power per person. But, in the first half of the eighteenth century, the British economy was about to experience a much greater expansion in population and, to avoid the likely 'power crisis', new ways of 'fuelling' the demand needed to be found.

The price of power fuels had been rising since the sixteenth century (see Figure 5.13). The main fuels for power were food and fodder. Given the growth in both human and animal populations, the prices of agricultural products were rising. This was especially a concern for businesses seeking to use animal power, since the fuel costs had to be covered by the owner. Just like for heating, organic energy sources for power were very expensive in the seventeenth and early eighteenth centuries.

The logistics of controlling horses limited the maximum power that could be harnessed by animals in one location. So, horses provided a lot of power in a decentralised manner. A key development, therefore, was the improvements in the design of waterwheels. New designs enabled much greater power to be harnessed in a particular location. The ability to concentrate vast amounts of power in one space enabled power to be centralised, transforming the nature of economic production.

And, even more crucially, the introduction of steam engines, first, for pumping water out of coal mines, where the fuel was virtually free, enabled economies of scale and technological improvements to be achieved. Until the mid-nineteenth century, though, they were far less efficient than horses at converting energy into power (see Figure 5.14).

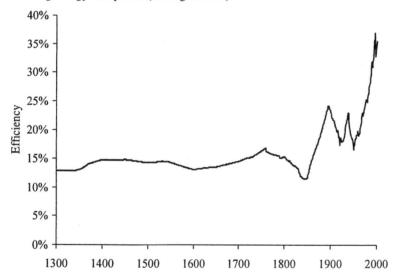

Source: see Data Appendix

Figure 5.14 The Efficiency of Stationary Power Provision, 1300–2000

In 1800, the steam engine provided a modest 2 percent of the total power. Animals, mostly horses, provided 70 percent. Humans and watermills generated the rest. All together, these bodies and machines created around 2.1 TWh of power (see Figure 5.15).

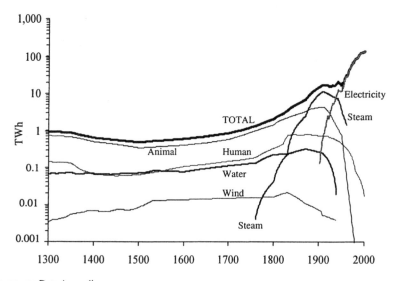

Source: see Data Appendix

Figure 5.15 The Provision of Stationary Power, 1300–2000

The next hundred years experienced the transformation of power provision and of the whole economy, thanks to the steam engine. Despite its inefficiencies, coal was (about twenty times) cheaper per unit of energy than food and, by the second decade of nineteenth century, was starting to compete with the running costs of horse power. In the second half of the nineteenth century, major improvements in efficiency enabled steam power to become cheaper and much of the economy centralised its production around the steam engine.

By 1900, more than 70 percent of power was generated by the steam engine. The horse provided a little under one-quarter. Nearly 19 TWh were produced in total, allowing 450 kWh per person. The total energy used (food, fodder and mostly coal) was equivalent to 10 mtoe or 0.24 toe per person – little more than in 1300.

The introduction of electricity provided even greater increases in power provision and equally important transformations of the production. Increasingly efficient central power stations and integrated networks of supply led to economies of scale and declining costs of power. By 2000, power provided had risen to more than 140 TWh, about 2 300 kWh per person. Generation of this amount of power used 36 mtoe of energy, principally from coal, natural gas and uranium. For each person in 2000, 0.6 toe of energy were used for power.

In 1300, the price of power was around 150 pence per kWh. In 1700, before the Industrial Revolution, it had risen to 250 pence per kWh. Major improvements in the efficiency of power technologies and the availability of cheaper sources of energy, by switching from food to fossil fuels, drove down the cost to 160 pence per kWh by 1900. Then, the power revolution heralded by electrification pushed the cost below 20 pence per kWh. The cost of power fell twelve-fold from the beginning of the Industrial Revolution. Lower prices created greater consumption. Power provision rose 120 times since 1700 (See Figure 5.15). Per capita, income increased twenty-fold (in some part due to the steam engine (Crafts 2004) and electrification (Rosenberg 1998)).

7. CONCLUDING REMARKS

This chapter explored the evolution of power provision in Britain. The first episode in the long story in power provision touched on the medieval era. Technological developments, especially the increased use of animal power, improved agricultural productivity. This led initially to food surplus, but eventually to a growing demand due to a rising population. Resource pressures generated further advances in technology and field management. Eventually, population rose further and, faced with extreme climatic conditions and with disease, population fell and remained low for an extended period.

Very basically, Malthus proposed that rising population and demand would outstrip supply, leading to famine, and then a decline in population and demand. Crudely, Boserup argued that rising population and demand would create pressures on supply, which would lead to technological solutions, and higher supplies. Both Malthusian and Boserupian scenarios appear to have occurred during the late Middle Ages (Boserup 1965, Chavas and Bromley 2005).

Although arguably less pivotal than animals in the agrarian economy, watermills introduced from the eleventh century played an important role in the power revolutions in Medieval and, especially, industrialising Britain. In the late Middle Ages, they reduced the cost of producing grain, the basic staple for the population. After the Black Death, many mills were no longer needed for grain crushing, and shifted to the fulling of wool, lowering its cost and boosting exports. This power surplus helped boost the economy, increasing demand for manufactured goods, and related energy services.

This development included the demand for iron which, although very heat-intensive, depended on power for stoking the fires and shaping products (see Chapter 4). Water mills provided much of the power. Also, they were pivotal in pumping water out of coal mines, increasing accessibility to deep coal reserves, and weaving textiles. Technological improvements of water wheels were crucial to providing cheap power at the on set of the Industrial Revolution.

Yet, central to the story was the potential power that was unleashed by the introduction of the steam engine. Its first niche was the pumping of water out of coal mines, where the engines' inefficiency was of little concern. This phase allowed the technology to be refined, and be adopted by the textile industry, where huge amounts of power were required. The introduction of coal combustion for power services reduced the pressures on harnessing energy from limited land and water.

With further refinements and economies of scale, around one hundred and twenty years after its first use in industry, the steam engine started to become a general purpose technology, both for stationary power and transport. The growth of the coal industry enabled fuel costs to stay low and, even, fall substantially with subsequent generations of steam engines. The declining cost of power transformed the manufacturing sector.

Electricity was even more radical. For several decades, the price of power was not cheaper with electricity. Production was more flexible, however. Steam engines provided power from a central source with each worker or power use linked by a series of belts. Electricity was more simply passed down wires, allowing, for instance, each worker to have personal control of the power used, rather than working at a centrally-directed rate determined by the machine. Work in a factory was also much safer, as 'wired power' avoided the accidents caused by highly-strung belts snapping. Although difficult to show (in graphs of long-run trends), production was more efficient and the working conditions were greatly improved.

6. Transport: Infrastructure, Technology and Novel Attributes

1. THE DEMAND FOR MOBILITY AND CARRIAGE

Travel has brought people to new locations – to work, to talk, to see. In the past, when travel was costly, people had workstyles and lifestyles that minimised the need for transport. Work was in or near the home. People socialised with family and neighbours. Sedentary work and lives did not create much need for travel.

Cheaper travel created an opportunity for workstyles and lifestyles to change. As they changed, they required greater levels of mobility, generating demands for more transport services.

Similarly, if distant goods were costly to carry or ship, local alternatives were found – to eat, to work with, to entertain. As distant goods became cheaper, partly because of the declining cost of transport services, people could consume from a wider range of sources. The demand for transport services associated with freight was probably less dependent on workstyle or lifestyle, because moving goods imposed fewer constraints on people's behaviour and time. Consequently, freight transport use could increase without people switching to new workstyles or lifestyles; however, switches were likely to lead to changes in haulage services.

Transport has been provided by the directed use of power. The direction of power and of travel was dependent on the infrastructure set up – be it a road, a rail or a river. Thus, the history of transport was determined by the infrastructure built and networks formed.

It was also affected by the co-evolution of vehicles and vessels to carry people and goods. Their ability to carry and to travel along the network was vital at reducing the cost of travel, and altering the characteristics of the experience – including the speed of delivery and the protection of passengers and goods.

Another key feature of the vehicle or vessel was its ability to convert the energy used into a source of power for transport. Engineers capable of improving the design of vehicles, including their engines, played a central role in driving down the cost of transport.

A source of energy powered the journey. For much of history, energy sources providing stationary power and transport were similar and often interchangeable. Yet, with the increased sophistication of infrastructure, technologies and markets, stationary and mobile power evolved separately. Their experiences and lessons to be drawn have been very different.

This chapter examines how the transformation and expansion of infrastructures, mode of transports and energy sources have provided transport services over the last seven centuries. The radical transformations and expansion have created cheaper transport services and the opportunity for dramatically different ways of working and living, and much greater mobility. These have been central to many of the economic, social and cultural revolutions over the last thousand years.

The chapter begins with the early forms of freight and passenger road transport services. It then looks at river and canal networks. This is followed by a discussion on the evolution in the technology, institutions and costs of sea-freight. This completes the sections covering traditional forms of energy.

Afterwards, the chapter examines the introduction of fossil fuels to the provision of transport services. This was heralded by the growth of the railway network. In the wake of this expansion, other modes of transport are considered, including horses, canal barges and steam-ships. A discussion follows about the transformations in the twentieth century with the advent of the internal combustion engine and air travel.

2. EARLY TRANSPORT SERVICES

Basic Transport

The ability to move people and goods has been central to many economic activities. Legs provided the original technology for transportation. An average human could walk about four kilometres in one hour on a path (Leunig 2006 p.645). On muddy paths or hilly terrain, the going was much slower. For faster travel, running has been an option, but not over long distances.

A person could carry goods, but, over longer distances, the load was rarely more than 20 kg (Smil 1994). Through time, man has found methods of enduring the loads – such as the pharmacological powers of certain plants. Nevertheless, carriers quickly appreciated that domesticated animals were far better suited for carrying and pulling loads.

A packhorse could carry one-eighth of one tonne. Far more efficient, however, was to pull a load placed on wheels. If roads were in good condition, a wheeled carriage could pull over one tonne. In specific locations, such as mines, an iron rail was placed on the ground to reduce friction, and a horse could pull up to eight tonnes (Crompton 2005 p.3). Thus, a horses' potential, when friction was reduced, was spectacular – up to 800 times more than a man carrying a pack.

Obstacles to Travel

Most roads created a lot of friction, however. The rain on earthen roads, especially in winter, made the wheels stick in the mud, reducing loads and speed. Getting bogged down on muddy roads delayed convoys further. During winter months, roads could become unusable. Thus, trade routes were all but closed down during these periods.

The quality of paths and roads in early Britain were crucial to the cost of carriage and, ultimately, the growth of transport. Responsibility for the maintenance and improvements of roads in the medieval economy fell on local parishes. They generally financed their projects through local property taxes and conscripting residents for up to six days of free labour per year (Bogart 2005a p.441).

In pre-industrial Britain, the cost of carriage depended on the quality of roads and the available technology, as well as the burden of predation – that is, the loss of goods or money by force. The cost of losing goods or having to pay to not lose them was the greatest source of uncertainty associated with transportation. The violent capture of goods was exercised by both brigands and noblemen. It was legal (and even considered a respectable activity) if the local ruler consented (Kohn 2001 p.4).

The costs of predation were the immediate loss of goods, and potential injury. In an attempt to reduce the risk of being a victim and the ensuing costs, travellers protected themselves by hiring additional men and weapons. Protection costs also included the time wasted finding alternative routes. One major indirect cost was associated with the economic burden of convoys. They imposed delays from organising a convoy and travelling at the speed of the slowest vehicle. It also led to market instabilities as products arrived in large quantities of abundance and then periods of scarcity, while waiting for the next convoy.

Government officials were frequently involved in the practice of seizing items of value, or in payment for exemption. In England, this was the most common form of predation. The monarchies had imposed their rule on the roads and waterways of the land, and travel was relatively safe from brigands compared with Europe. Thus, a price was paid for safe travel – 'the royal prises' (Kohn 2001 p.5).

According to contemporaries, tolls were "everywhere for everything" (Leighton in Kohn 2001 p.10). Their success in making travellers pay depended on the ability to create effective barriers to passage. On roads, they were placed at fords, bridges, mountain passes or any location creating a bottleneck. Bulk goods tended to be targets for tolls because they were less able to avoid tolls – they, therefore, paid a relatively large toll burden. To minimise the tendency to bypass the toll, authorities often introduced laws about what routes travellers could take.

Yet, when comparing the burden of brigands and tolls, both are methods of capturing value from the consumer and are, therefore, ways of redistributing wealth. But, they have different effects. Violence causes considerably greater damage than tolls. It leads to arms races, which is a burden to both brigands and travellers. It also causes great uncertainty – to both parties.

Tolls redistribute the wealth, but at lower cost. Thus, policing land and waters, reducing the number of brigands, and creating tolls to capture benefits were an improvement. It captured value in a less damaging manner, converting "uncertain losses into inevitable expenses" (Kohn 2001 p.17). Compared to continent travellers, England benefited from safer roads and more certainty about the cost of travel.

Transport Costs

In the short run, changes in the cost of tolls or predation tended to dominate the variance in transport expenses. For instance, in times of unrest, these costs could be substantial. Yet, long-run trends in transport services depended on the decline in the cost of carriage as infrastructure, organisation and technology improved (Kohn 2001 p.2). When no losses were incurred, about three-quarters of the cost of carriage by packhorse was associated with provender – mostly fodder, such as hay, grass and straw, but also bedding and general care (Gerhold 1993 p.16).

Rough estimates of the cost of transporting heavy goods in the late medieval period can be presented. In current terms (that is, 2000 prices), hiring a team to carry bulky goods along a road to a nearby market or manor in the early fourteenth century cost about 150 pence per tonne-kilometre travelled (see Figure 6.1).

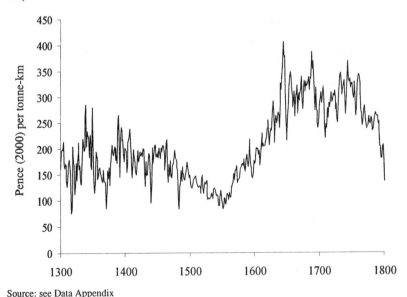

Source: see Data Appendix

Figure 6.1 The Price of Road Freight Transport Services, 1300–1800

This cost would have incorporated a series of technological improvements in horse management during the Middle Ages that enabled "the substantial, even massive, introduction of the horse to general draught work" (Langdon 1986 p.19) including transport services. As mentioned in Chapter 5, the horseshoe and the harness radically improved the animal's performance, reducing the cost of carriage.

Demand for Transport Services

The reduced cost and increased ability to carry goods and travel thanks to the revolution in horse management was certainly a boost to the medieval economy and created a desire for mobility. In medieval times, wealthy families appear to have been relatively mobile. One example was the choice of furniture amongst bourgeois and noble families, which gave priority to its portability – as the Latin and French for furniture, meubles (that is, movables), indicates. The other main passengers travelling in pre-industrial Britain were soldiers, administrators (including tax collectors) and pilgrims. No doubt, the crusades, which created a vast demand for transport were enabled by better methods of travel. Their demand for transport may also explain the State and the Church's role in infrastructure investment, such as roads and bridges (Kohn 2001 p.3).

Yet, until the nineteenth century, most of the population travelled little, rarely seeing neighbouring villages, let alone market towns. Transportation services were mostly to move goods. The major changes in transport services that occurred before the expansion of railways did not affect the mobility of the majority of the population, as they provided carriage for the wealthy and improved trade networks around Britain, as well as Europe and the world (Masschaele 1993).

The market for goods haulage could be split in two – according to the bulk of the commodities and the urgency of delivery. The costs of delivering heavy goods, such as fuel and raw materials, were high compared to the costs of production. Finding the cheapest mode of transport was essential for heavy good carriers.

Consumers have not always been after the lowest cost, though. For some, a trade-off existed between the costs and other attributes. For instance, people transporting perishables and high value goods, such as expensive fabrics, spices and mail, were concerned about speed of delivery – either because they were concerned about rotten produce or the risk of predation. The price per kilometre travelled reflected technological improvements from the perspective of the costs of supplying the service. Yet, to the consumer, the same service provided, at the same price, but in less time, was seen as a superior service (other attributes being equal).

An attempt was made to quantify the gains in transport services from improving the speed of technologies. Although more sophisticated methods have sought to estimate the social savings and consumer surplus associated with innovations in transport services (Leunig 2006), here, a crude indicator incorporating cost and speed was estimated. To take account of long run changes in infrastructure and modes of transport, separate indices of road quality and technological improvements were created, and then used to determine travel speed, based on anchors, from estimates of the speed of travel in the early fourteenth century and in the seventeenth century (Masschaele 1993). Both anchors indicate that the average speed of travel was about two kilometres per hour. Combining this information with the price of transport services, an estimate of carriage per kilometre-hour is presented (see Figure 6.2).

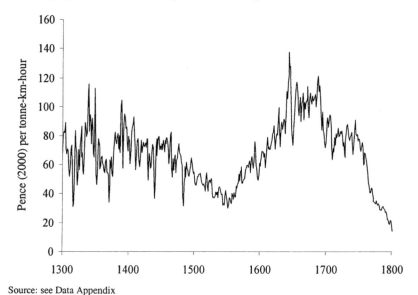

Source: see Data Appendix

Figure 6.2 The Price of Road Freight Transport Services Including Speed, 1300–1800

The Declining Quality of Infrastructure

Price appears to have fluctuated considerably around the time of the Black Death (that is, in the mid-fourteenth century), when nearly half the population died. The cost of carriage fluctuated between 70 pence and 280 pence per tonne-kilometre. Incorporating speed accentuates the cheapness of travel in parts of the early fourteenth century – with prices below 60 pence per tonne-kilometre-hour. In the fifteenth century, starting from a high level, the trend in prices was downwards, falling to below 40 pence per tonne-kilometre-hour (or about 100 pence per tonne-kilometre) at the time of the religious reformation introduced by King Henry VIII (1509–1547).

Certain technological improvements would have accelerated the pace of transport. The introduction of axles to control steering and brakes encouraged the use of carts instead of packhorses. Later, in 1618, the ban on the use of four-wheeled wagons was lifted. It was introduced to reduce damage to roads (Gerhold 1993).

Yet, the speed of travel declined a little and the cost of carriage rose considerably from the second half of the sixteenth century. Since the fifteenth century, the economy was expanding and road use was increasing. No doubt, the heavier loads, initially caused by the use of carts and later by four-wheeled wagons, were causing more damage. There was also evidence that the quality of rivers for transport was declining, creating a shift towards roads and increasing the burden on roads.

At the same time, the main institution responsible for transport infrastructure was losing power. It has been argued that selling-off church lands meant that many of the roads, once maintained by the clergy, went into disrepair for nearly two hundred years (Masschaele 1993). Local parishes were constrained in their ability to finance road maintenance. Charging residents in money and time created tensions within the community, discouraging all but the most necessary repairs. Another problem was the difficulty of coordinating between parishes, which tended to leave bordering areas uncared for. Thus, rising demand for and declining supply of road maintenance could only lead to worsening roads, slower travel and greater costs of carriage (Bogart 2005a p.442).

By the mid-seventeenth century, price of carriage increased to more than 300 pence per tonne-kilometre – triple its value one hundred years earlier (see Figure 6.1). It actually peaked in the 1640s, during the Civil War, when carriage cost more than 400 pence. Incorporating speed of travel, the price of transport increased from as low as 30 pence per tonne-kilometre-hour in the 1550s to more than 130 in the 1650s (see Figure 6.2).

3. TURNPIKES AND STAGECOACHES

The Creation of Turnpikes

The dramatic decline in the quality of roads and rising cost of transport services was signalling that the small public institutions responsible for maintaining roads, the parishes, were not able to keep up with the growth in traffic. New institutions needed to be developed to provide adequate infrastructure (Gerhold 1996).

Turnpike trusts were private enterprises set up to improve the quality of roads by using hired workers and by charging travellers for use. Given the right by Acts of Parliament to charge users, trusts managed to borrow money on the basis of future tolls, creating an innovative way of generating funds to take-on major infrastructure projects (Albert 1972).

Those that paid for the construction and the protection of the road had some way of covering building costs. Once built, however, tolls tended to be used as a source of revenue rather than a method of only covering costs and financing basic maintenance (Kohn 2001 pp.11–12). As the cost of travel fell, demand for travel grew, and, with a greater consumer surplus, incentives for institutions to capture the benefits increased. The natural monopoly created by transport networks led itself particularly to capture.

Like many innovations, turnpikes were a potential threat to some. As Pawson (1984 p.63) put it, placing a "toll on the highway altered the common right of free passage". Some parliamentarians opposed their introduction. Riots against gates being placed on roads broke-out (Albert 1979).

Yet, most of the time, the rates charged reflected ability to pay. Tolls discriminated against the wealthy with wheeled carts, waggons travelling to markets and outsiders. Packhorses carrying coal or cloth on their back were often offered concessionary rates; they benefited less from turnpike improvements than wheeled vehicles. Local residents were usually not charged, especially if on foot. On the whole, residents also benefited from the creation of turnpikes. They no longer had to pay in money and time for the wear-and-tear of roads caused, to a large extent, by outsiders (Pawson 1984 p.62-3).

An Expanding Network

During the second half of the seventeenth century and the eighteenth century, many turnpikes were created, roads were improved and tolls were placed. Before 1750, the focus was on the busiest roads, such as those leading into London. By then, around 5 000 kilometres of roads had been 'turnpiked' (see Table 6.1). The next twenty years were a frenzy of road improvements, forming a network of around 20 000 kilometres. The main addition was the dense web in the West Midlands and the North – the new industrial heartland. Considerable expansion continued until the beginning of the nineteenth century. By 1800, there were nearly 30 000 kilometres of private roads.

Table 6.1 Length of Turnpike Roads, 1720–1770

Year	Length (km)	Year	Length (km)
1720	800	1750	5 400
1730	3 100	1760	14 700
1740	3 700	1770	21 400

Source: Pawson (1977 p.154)

Although local parishes still played a small role, much of the technical improvements in roads during the eighteenth century were the result of turnpikes. Better road surfaces, such as those introduced by McAdam, enabled heavy traffic loads to be sustained, and reduced the friction between wheels and road. Turnpikes also invested in better drainage systems, protecting the roads and increasing their lifespan. On a tar-macadamed road, a horse could pull a waggon with two tonnes, which was probably double what it achieved on the poorer quality roads. Thus, they dramatically improved transport services, especially for wheeled vehicles, enabling horses to carry greater loads, faster (Crompton 2005 p.3).

Since the overall costs of using and maintaining horses, especially provender expenses, accounted for four-fifths of the costs of operating long-distance waggons, firmer roads and easier gradients were two key factors that reduced the number of horses required per load and the price of transport. Refinements in horse-breeding in the second half of the eighteenth century improved the efficiency with which provender was converted into power. Finally, as companies grew in size, they were able to achieve economies of scale in the provision of carriage services (Gerhold 1996 pp.499–504).

The Price of Transport

Turnpikes appear to have been responsible for about half of the reduction in carriage costs, which fell around 40 percent in that period, and passenger travel times, which fell 60 percent (Bogart 2005a p.443). Yet, the cost of carriage stabilised, rather than fell, at a high price (around 300 pence per tonne-km) between the mid-seventeenth and mid-eighteenth centuries (see Figure 6.1). The decline in costs coincided with the major expansion of the network in from 1750.

For passengers, prices (per kilometre) changed little in the seventeenth and eighteenth centuries. The first regular stagecoach journeys (from London to Chester in 1657) provided evidence of the cost of people travelling. Clearly, considerable variation in prices existed according to the number of passengers in the stagecoach, its comfort and whether the passenger was by the window or stuck in the middle. For around two hundred years, average prices and speeds can be estimated, based on more than a dozen regular services between London and provincial towns, as well as between the burgeoning industrial towns of the midlands and Lancashire (Hart 1960). Up to 1800, the cost of travelling by stagecoach ranged from 50 to 60 pence per kilometre (see Figure 6.3). As competition for services grew, especially at the end of the eighteenth and the beginning of the nineteenth centurcies, prices fell to 40 pence. But, over the next twenty years, prices doubled (to be discussed later).

Modest improvements in travel speeds were achieved in the first century of stagecoaches and turnpikes, especially on routes near London (Bogart 2005b p.496). By 1750, stagecoaches were averaging speeds of 5 kilometres per hour. Crucial was that, as 'cruising' speeds increased, fewer nights were spent in inns along the way (increasing average speeds, and reducing the overall cost of travel). For example, the London to Chester route, 290 kilometres long, took six days in 1657; in 1704, it took four days. By 1837, passengers could expect to reach Chester in 22 hours. A journey from London to Oxford took 36 hours at the end of the seventeenth century; it took only six hours in the first half of the nineteenth century (Hart 1960). The second half of the eighteenth century and early nineteenth century were times of major road and technological improvements. By 1830, average speeds were around 15 kilometres per hour.

These developments had major implications for the cost of travelling a kilometre-hour (see Figure 6.3). The price peaked at over 20 pence per kilometre-hour in the 1690s. But faster times led to important reductions – down to 13 pence in 1750 and to 4 pence by 1800.

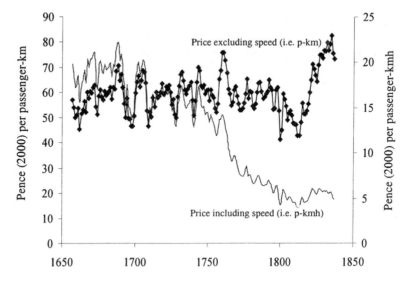

Source: see Data Appendix

Figure 6.3 The Price of Road Passenger Transport Services Excluding and Including Speed, 1660–1830

Greater Mobility and Trade

Until the seventeenth century, passenger transport, apart from the few wealthy, was limited to military, fiscal and spiritual purposes. As the middle class grew, a wider demand for mobility developed, creating a need for a more regular form of transport services (Hart 1960).

Stagecoach use reflected the dramatic growth in use of transport services and in personal mobility from the seventeenth century (see Figure 6.4). In 1715, around seven million passenger-kilometres were travelled on stagecoaches. By 1775, stagecoach services were providing over fifty million passenger-kilometres (Chartres and Turnbull 1983). Over the next fifty years, personal mobility had been revolutionised, with 1.6 billion passenger-kilometres using stagecoaches, and nearly the same again through private sources of travel. So, by 1815, horse-drawn travel generated more than three billion passenger kilometres every year. Interestingly, for the next twenty years afterwards, travel use stagnated, at a time of considerable economic growth and growing prosperity, but rising prices of transport services (see Figure 6.3).

The growth in freight use was similar during the eighteenth century. Ignoring speed, since most of the goods carried were non-perishables, like coal, wool or iron, the price of land freight fell from more than 300 pence in the 1760s to under 150 pence per kilometre by 1800 (see Figure 6.1). For bulk goods, where travel cost was an important component of the total cost, the price of many goods fell in Britain during the second half of the eighteenth century.

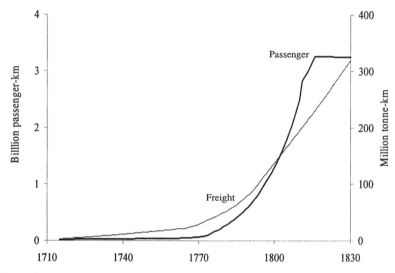

Source: Chartres and Turnbull (1983), see Data Appendix

Figure 6.4 The Use of Land Passenger and Freight Transport Services, 1715–1830

More goods were available and cheaper. The number of retail outlets increased dramatically from the late eighteenth century (McKendrick et al. 1982). Advertising promoted all sorts of new products, convincing people to buy (Walsh 2000). The desire to consume spurred the Industrious Revolution (DeVries 1993). Households entered the labour market, received a regular income and were able to buy goods. A key force in the process of industrialisation at the end of the eighteenth century was the transport revolution.

As for passengers, freight transport activities soared. In 1715, freight service provided about three million tonne-km. Services increased to forty million, sixty years later, and on to 225 million by 1815. This growth continued – by 1830, horses were providing nearly 320 million tonne-km worth of carriage (Chartres and Turnbull 1983).

Whether for goods or passengers, the equipment needed to meet this growing transport service were the horse and a vehicle. The horse population exploded. In 1811, the first year for which estimates were formally made, nearly half of one million horses were used for pulling stagecoaches, riding and carrying goods (Thompson 1976 p.80). A broad estimate of energy consumption for 1811 was that road passenger transport used around 130 000 toe and land freight around 90 000 in the form of fodder. It might be expected that, at the time, freight services were more demanded by the economy and demanding to the energy system than passenger transport, especially since the role of roads in transport history has been given its due importance (Pawson 1977, Freeman 1980). Nevertheless, it is commonly accepted that, before the introduction of railways, most of the goods for British consumption were carried along rivers, canals, coasts and across seas (Dyos and Aldcroft 1969 p.81, Bagwell 1974 p.60, Crompton 2005).

4. THE RIVER AND CANAL NETWORK

The Great British Waterway

While roads provided an important means of travelling or moving goods across the country, waterways also served this purpose, often with far less effort required, although more slowly. As mentioned before, the transport system was, to a large extent, separated in two. For more precious commodities, sometimes perishable, possibly at risk of theft, speed of delivery was valued. Passengers also preferred to reach their destination quickly. In these cases, the improving road system with its 'swift' coaches was the appropriate mode of transport. For heavy or bulky goods, where the transport costs were a large proportion of the final price, cheap methods of distribution were vital. Here, the waterways were more appropriate (Barker 1989 p.87).

Historically, coasts and banks of rivers have been a frequent location for settlements, as they benefited from relatively easy access. Britain, and especially England, was also endowed with many naturally navigable rivers. Being a narrow island, much of the country was on the coast or an estuary. For instance, London, despite being more than 60 kilometres from the coast, was at the beginning of the wide Thames estuary. This position enabled seagoing vessels to navigate as far up the river as London Bridge (Barker 1989 p.87). For centuries, the coast and river networks supplied many of the goods that were not locally produced.

Despite the relative ease of distribution, navigating along the rivers required skill to deal with the changing flows. The shape of valleys and twisting meanders meant that rivers rarely followed straight lines. Consequently, river transport was slow, especially when going against the current, and trade limited to areas near the waterways.

Source of Power

The simplest source of power to drive a boat along a river was a rower. Of course, in one direction, the current might pull the boat downstream, thus, gravity and water flow provided the power. This was a free source of energy. Yet, up the river, a man needed to row, and the stronger the current down, the harder was the rower's task up-river. This meant that, on faster currents, trade happened mostly in one direction – downstream towns benefiting from cheaper goods. On more modest flowing rivers, where trade went both ways, the rower's muscle pushed the load.

On some rivers, towpaths that could accommodate horses existed. On a tarred road, a horse could pull a waggon with two tonnes. On an iron rail, it could drag eight tonnes. Along a river, a single horse could move twenty tonnes (Crompton 2005 p.3). In other words, river carriage could be up to ten times more efficient for heavy loads.

Another advantage of river transport was that it could deal with growing trade. On a road, greater loads put additional pressure on the surface, reducing its quality. The load in a boat could be increased without damaging the infrastructure (Crompton 2005 p.3).

Cost of Carriage

Because it was far less effort to row or pull a heavy load down and even up a river than along a road, carrying goods on waterways was generally cheaper than over land. Some suggest water transport was, at times, ten times cheaper (Jones 2000). Far less evidence on the cost of water carriage exists, however. Looking at the data from Rogers (1865–86), it would seem that road and river costs (of carrying one tonne of goods for one kilometre) were in the same order of magnitude. The few data points that have been found indicate that the cost of water carriage (for heavy goods) was, nevertheless, cheaper than land transport in most periods. In the mid-fourteenth century, river carriage was around one-quarter of the price, averaging 40 pence per tonne-km compared with about 150 pence on land.

Thanks to the low cost of river transport, far more goods, especially heavy ones, such as fuel and materials, were traded around England. These vital transport networks enabled cities to be supplied in food and fuel from much greater distances and allow these urban centres to expand far more than if limited by land transport (Galloway et al. 1996).

The price differential between land and river travel varied considerably though. In the mid-sixteenth century, road transport was cheap (by its own standards), falling to 100 pence. It seems that river costs had also dropped, to about 30 pence. Undoubtedly, a fine boost to the Tudor economy.

But, before this, Britain went through a phase of expensive transport. Based on the little evidence available, the cost of carrying goods down the river had reached 120 pence per tonne-km, when road transport was around 200 pence.

More Declines in the Quality of Infrastructure

At the end of the medieval period, obstructions to rivers became a major concern to traders. Often the problem was that mills were installed to capture the water's power (see Chapter 5), blocking the passage of vessels. Clearly, there was a conflict between those that harnessed the river as a source of power and those that used it as infrastructure for travelling. Other obstacles included the growing number of fish-traps set up. Crown commissions were created to address obstructions. Despite, at times, radical action (such as allowing the destruction of mills and fish-traps), it appears that the Crown was unable or unwilling to deal with many obstructions (Jones 2000 pp.69-71).

The evidence indicates that, between the late thirteenth and the fifteenth centuries, river navigation in England became less frequent. This was the result of the growing number of obstructions and the declining population after the Black Death. In some cases, the obstructed rivers did not become navigable again until the eighteenth century (Jones 2000 p.72).

In addition to the physical obstacles faced, tolls often existed on rivers. While they were higher on the Thames, in the sixteenth century, Gloucester charged boats travelling along the Severn – it charged 270 pence per tonne for every ship with timber, 200 pence for firewood vessels, and 200 pence on other goods (Willan 1937 p.69). In this case, the revenue was used to maintain local quays and bridges.

The general evidence, thus, supports the view that waterways deteriorated during the second half of the fourteenth century and the fifteenth century. The cost of river transport rose in the early fifteenth century – between 40 pence and 110 pence. Furthermore, in this period, it was cheaper to use roads than to rivers. Thus, it appears that the cost of carriage (of heavy goods) favoured waterways up to the mid-fourteenth century and from the beginning of the sixteenth century, and in between that period, roads were cheaper. This no doubt led to a reduction in the amount of waterways travel and increase in land carriage during the fifteenth century. This might also have worsened the quality of roads between the second half of the sixteenth century until the introduction of turnpikes.

River Improvements

From the beginning of the seventeenth century, efforts were being made to address the problem of river navigation. For instance, barges could only travel up the Thames as far as Henley until the mid-sixteenth century. By the seventeenth century, towns beyond this point received considerable business by barge – suggesting that either river improvements were eventually made or barges evolved to be able to complete the journey (Rogers 1886 p.758). Between 1660 and 1750, forty rivers were improved, creating a network of about 2 200 kilometres of waterways (Crompton 2005 p.2). Despite a lack of data, it seems that between the sixteenth and early nineteenth centuries, the price of river carriage varied between 20 and 50 pence per tonne-km; considerably lower than the 120 pence which faced customers in the mid-fifteenth century.

Gradients posed a major barrier to ensuring waterways were navigable. Slopes made currents too strong for waterways to be used in both directions. Locks, introduced in the seventeenth century, provided a solution. Yet, early locks were slow, substantially increasing travel times.

Also, awkward meanders were cut-through, shortening travel time along rivers. Thus, the river improvements enabled more rivers to be travelled, further up stream and with larger boats. Throughout the seventeenth century, the number of towns within 20 kilometres of England's river network increased dramatically. Without the expanding river system, cities, such as London which increased from 40 000 to 600 000 during the sixteenth and seventeenth centuries, would have suffered severe limits on the supply and far higher prices of food, fuels and materials (Willan 1964).

Canal Investment

Canals were only created when or where river improvements were not possible. Yet, once the potential benefits of building water access were appreciated, the Canal Age began. The explosion of investment in canals indicated the pent-up demand for water transport that existed in the mid-eighteenth century.

The first canal was built to enable Liverpool to have direct (that is, water) access to coal. The city was a major centre for salt production. Without a river coming from the nearest coal mines, the heat-intensive industry was dependent on fuel transported at high cost by land. Other local industries also suffered from high fuel costs. In 1755, the merchants of Liverpool managed to convince Westminster of the need to build a waterway linking the city to the coalfields. In late 1757, the Sankey canal started moving goods into the city. Compared to the colliery price, the cost of coal carried overland often tripled the price paid by the customer. Once the canal opened, households in Liverpool were able to buy coal at only an 80 percent mark-up (Barker 1989 p.89).

The network of canals expanded greatly throughout the eighteenth century. Its expansion has been associated with the distribution of goods with low value relative to their volume – such as coal and iron (Wrigley 1994). Many canal owners were also land owners likely to benefit from the cheap distribution of the coal in their mines (Hawke and Higgins 1981). One such example was the Duke of Bridgewater's canal from a coal face in Worsley to Manchester – reducing the price of coal by 50 percent. Thus, industrialisation of Britain benefited from the expanding network of canals, which distributed bulky goods the breadth of the country.

After the more well-known Duke of Bridgewater canal was completed (in part) in 1761, a series of joint-stock companies were set up to build canals over the next twenty years. After a brief lull, the 1790s was a period of intense canal building. In 1830, when most of the canal building had been completed, the waterway network had reached around 6 500 kilometres (Crompton 2005 p.2).

Cost of Carriage along Canals

While the lack of data was also a limitation to examining the impact of canals, it appears that the price of carriage fell substantially around the turn of the nineteenth century. In 1781, on the Birmingham canal, the cost carrying one tonne of non-perishable goods for one kilometre was 50 pence. By about 1810, heavy freight on the London-Reading canal was charged 23 pence per tonne-kilometre. The same goods on the same route appear to have cost 31 pence in 1828 and 37 pence in 1852. The principal reason for the rising price of canal transport was the fixing of prices by railway companies to match the cost of using trains for carriage – this will be discussed later (Barker 1989 p.89).

Canals played an important role in the supply of heavy goods, especially for certain strategic economic centres. This was especially true for coal – as the Duke of Bridgewater put it, every canal "must have coals at the heel of it" (quoted in Crompton 2005 p.4). Many of the most successful canals did carry the coal from the pits to centres of demand for heating and later power. By the end of the eighteenth century, Liverpool was the third largest city in England due to its iron, copper, pottery, glass and salt manufacturing, and fuelled by the Lancashire coalfields. The canals kept the price of coal and, therefore, of heating low in many regions of Britain, especially south Lancashire, West Midlands and South Wales, where coastal and natural waterways were not adequate.

To some, the canal was an extension of the existing waterway network – albeit an important extension, tripling the size of the transport infrastructure (Barker 1989 p.90). To others, it was a major improvement in the potential of water transport. Canals were designed for carriage – straight with good towpaths and no obstacles, they could be travelled equally well in both directions. Along well-maintained towpaths, a horse could pull up to thirty tonnes – 50 percent more than along a river, and 500 percent more than on a tarred road. They also linked together important distribution routes, minimising the fickleness of natural water currents (Crompton 2005 p.3).

Limitations of Canal Services

Yet, canals could only avoid hills and mountains by going around them, or gradually following their course, extending their length and cost of construction considerably. Another problem was that, in the summer, droughts limited water supply to a point where the canal was not usable (Freeman 1980 p.26).

Similarly, canals were more subject to freezing than flowing rivers. For instance, in Lancashire between 1771 and 1831, in half of those years the canals were frozen and, thus, not navigable at least twenty days in a year. On average, half of the days in December, these canals were closed. In some unusually cold years, canals were closed for up to three months. The 'Little Ice Age' reduced the reliability of delivery by canal (Freeman 1980 p.25). Thus, the canal, although a major improvement in transport services, still relied on horses for power, water as its medium of transport and weather conditions to ensure delivery.

5. THE GROWTH OF SHIPPING

The Costs of Carriage at Sea

The expansion of the road and river networks was preceded by a greater development on the seas. Shipping provided a boost to the economy by exporting textiles and importing goods available cheaper abroad. As the population of the British Isles grew, resources, such as land, were in greater supply abroad. Shipping enabled the use of timber and iron from Sweden, for instance, without impinging on domestic soil.

To provide transport services, the same three factors of production were needed – infrastructure, equipment and a source of power. The sea provided the basic 'infrastructure'; only along the coast could this infrastructure be improved. The vessel carried the goods and people through the water and harnessed the power to move the ship. For centuries, most seafaring vessels depended on wind for power – free to use but unreliable. Technological improvements in the ability to move ships, to carry goods and people, and to harness wind reduced the costs of transport.

Given the low expenditure on energy and the relatively simple vessels used in early days, the main cost of sailing ships was labour. Examples of shipping expenditures show that hiring and feeding a crew for a single voyage could be equal to the price of the ship – and given that the investment in a ship could be spread over many voyages, the main cost of carriage was indeed the men and their skills (Kohn 2001 p.18).

These expenditures included the running of the ship, which varied with the length of the voyage. The costs of loading and unloading the goods were fixed and, therefore, reduced the price per tonne-kilometre for longer voyages. It was important to ensure that labour was used efficiently, and as little time as wasted as possible.

The duration of the voyage was naturally a key determinant of the cost. The duration was extremely variable, determined by the winds. Technology limited the speed with which ships could harness favourable or work against contrary winds. Medieval vessels were poor at sailing into the wind. Technology was also crucial to its ability to weather storms. Early modern ships could only do a little more in the face of a squall than their predecessors, and often needed to find refuge. So, the unreliability of the energy source imposed high risks on shipping companies (Kohn 2001 p.22).

Timing and organisation were, therefore, central to the cost of shipping. Ships needed to be as full as possible, in order to spread the cost of hiring the crew. Yet, filling the ship was difficult, especially as it had to be done in both directions. This could mean waiting in harbour for freight, or moving from port to port in its search. To ensure the appropriate buoyancy, it was also necessary to mix the cargo – a balance of cheaper, heavy goods with expensive, lighter products. Efforts to coordinate the supply of shipping services with needs for carriage was crucial to minimising costs, and a source of great wealth, if done successfully (Kohn 2001 p.19).

In addition to minimising inefficient capacity utilisation, another risk was the potential loss of the cargo or even the ship. Poor design, bad craftsmanship and deteriorating conditions led many ships to sink or run aground. This problem was compounded by unable, drunken, disorderly or uncooperative crews.

One potential alternative to the sailing ship, and its unreliable energy source, was the galley. Crews rowing, combined with more modest sails when winds were favourable, allowed for a more reliable, flexible and manoeuvrable vessel. It tended to be smaller and, because of the larger crews and their rations, unable to carry much freight. In the eleventh century, the average galley carried only one-eighth of one tonne per man. The space problem was compounded by the higher labour costs. On the other hand, large crews, as well as manoeuvrability, ensured that it was less easily caught and more protected (Kohn 2001 p.23).

By the fifteenth century, some galleys could carry up to 300 tonnes, or 1.5 tonnes per man. Even the modest sailing ships of the thirteenth century could reach ratios of between 5 and 8 tonnes per man. By the fifteenth century, the larger sailing ships had increased their 10 tonnes per man and up to 13 tonnes per man in the sixteenth century (Kohn 2001 p.24).

Thus, for a while, choice of energy source depended on the type of goods ferried. Luxury goods, such as silks, spices and bullion, called for human power, ensuring fast, dexterous and secure vessels. Heavier and bulky goods were only commercially viable with the slower, less reliable sailing ships. Given that more primary commodities made up the majority of trade, most of the vessels were sailing ships.

Size was another investment decision. Larger ships were more efficient and safe. Yet, most of the ships in England were small. This reflected that for short distances, smaller vessels were more practical. Many harbours could not accommodate larger ships implying that, even for long haul trips, vessels remained small. This factor was also relevant for the crucial issue of capacity utilisation. While some sailing ships freighted more than 200 tonnes in the sixteenth century, the average ship sailing between, for instance, Bordeaux and English ports, was about 20 tonnes. So, although larger ships were technologically feasible, they proved in many cases unprofitable (Kohn 2001 p.26).

Piracy and Privateering

The source of power and the means of harnessing it were vital to the costs of carriage. Like on land, without a safe infrastructure, transport was expensive. To compensate for poor infrastructure, additional equipment and power needed to be used. Unlike on land, however, little could be done about the sea itself to make it a better infrastructure for travel. Yet, ships could be made sturdier, seas could be charted, sextants could be studied and lighthouses could be built all to act as guides across dangerous seas. Thus, a central feature of managing to reduce the cost of sea transport was reducing the risk of losing goods.

One of the greatest threats at sea in the early days was the risk of predation. On the high seas, it was harder to guard against illegal capture of goods. Nevertheless, as the size of the navy increased and technology improved in the sixteenth century, piracy declined. On the other hand, privateering, or capture with royal consent, grew. Royal consent was given for several reasons. First, if a citizen had been victim of piracy (or of unpaid debts) from another nation, this person could be given consent to repossess goods carried by a citizen of that country. Second, in times of famine, countrymen were encouraged to acquire food and goods by any means possible. Finally, the most common source of privateering was while the country was at war. Enemies were a target for attacks and looting. Merchants, faced with disruptions due to war, could turn their attentions to capture rather than trade. This was a highly profitable, legal business. Inevitably, the cost of transport during wars was extremely expensive (Kohn 2001 p.6).

Protection was provided by the crew. Thus, bigger ships – in addition to being harder to board – carried larger crews, insuring greater protection. Despite the lack of manoeuvrability of sailing ships, they sometimes travelled in convoys to ensure economies of scale in protection through mutual assistance in case of attack. By the sixteenth century, guns and cannons became sufficiently accurate and reliable to be used on the seas, therefore improving ship protection. They did, however, increase the might of pirates (Kohn 2001 p.8).

For certain problems, protection could be guaranteed for a fee. For instance, ships carrying wine from France, Portugal and Spain (upon which much of our early transport data was based) were at risk of running aground in Brittany. Goods lost aground there were captured by local officials or militia. The Duke of Brittany opened an office in Bordeaux to enable ship owners to pay for a letter insuring safety from capture in case their goods ran ashore (Kohn 2001 p.9).

In general, though, tolls at sea were harder to impose. They tended to be paid in the harbour – encouraging smaller, more valuable goods to be smuggled through undetected or on nearby beaches. Tolls also led to indirect costs. Substantial efforts, such as lobbying, threats and wars, were put into freeing travellers, companies, or countries from the burden of tolls. Naturally, if successful, these costs avoided paying the toll.

Sharing the Risk

Many of the ships were initially small, and owned by the mariners, who moved from port to port searching cargoes. As the ships grew in size, the value of the cargoes increased disproportionately. The ships, such as those in the modest wine trade, carried goods whose value was many times the price of the vessel itself. This implied that great risk was being carried by the ship owners. Yet, it was their merchant customers who owned the cargo and, therefore, also faced large risks.

Methods of reducing risk needed to be developed. The first method, developed in the late Middle Ages, was part-ownership, whereby several merchants joined their money to build a large ship. Later, it became popular to introduce shares, so that investors – frequently unrelated to the trade – put money forward to invest. The attraction of the investment was that it could often be paid back in a single voyage, thus, the promised returns were very large. This method enabled smaller investors to join in, who could buy and sell shares quickly. Ultimately, an even broader spread of risk was achieved through the introduction of marine insurance, which divorced the risk of failure of the business from the loss of cargo and ship. Nevertheless, marine insurance was slow to catch on in Britain (and Northern Europe). This has been attributed to the importance of lower value and lower profit Northern trade, making insurance too expensive. It could also be related to the nature of losses in the North – lower risk of piracy and higher risk of shipwrecks (Kohn 2001 p.32).

All this spreading of risk meant that certain inefficient decisions to deal with the risk, including breaking-up the cargo into several smaller boats, could be avoided. Thus, these practices encouraged the use of larger, more efficient vessels, which drove down the cost of transport services.

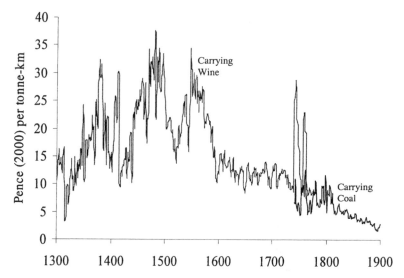

Source: based on Menard (1991) and Harley (1988), see Data Appendix

Figure 6.5 The Price of Sea Transport Services, 1300–1900

The Cost of War and Piracy

The burden of war and piracy can be gathered from the trends in the transport costs, based on data from the wine trade (Menard 1991). Conflicts between the

French, English and Flemish at the beginning of the fourteenth century were reflected in relatively high costs – around 15 pence per tonne per kilometre carried (see Figure 6.5). The price fell – to 5 pence – during a brief period of peace between 1315 and 1330.

The Hundred Years' War drove up the price again, reaching 30 pence in the 1380s. Falling back with the return of peace, it moved to around an average 15 pence for the first half of the fifteenth century. Weakened English and French governments meant they could do little to prevent piracy and their burden. Price steadily rose throughout the century, reaching over 30 pence at the end of the fifteenth century.

It only began to decline with better policing of the seas in the sixteenth century. Even then, the prices were still high – around 20 pence. Again, prices soared with new wars with Spain. It finally dropped in the 1590s, after defeating the Spanish Armada. Throughout the seventeenth and eighteenth centuries, prices fell gradually below the 10 pence mark.

Technological Development

In a business where the consequence of an inappropriate innovation was loss of the ship, caution was inevitable. As a consequence, smaller boats were transformed more readily and were more specialised. Larger ships tended to follow standard lines, to avoid the risk of being inappropriate for certain trades, commodities or journeys, or of being lost against some rocks.

Technological improvements were driven by economic forces. For example, the decline in timber supply in Britain encouraged the adoption of 'skeleton' ships rather than shells, which had existed for a long time in the Mediterranean. Demand was particularly important to the technological changes. Bulk goods, which dominated the market in and around Britain, had small profit margins. The 'cog', a round ship, was developed in the thirteenth century most probably for the ease of loading and storing wine. After refinements and diffusion, it became a standard design for centuries. Finding methods to carry more goods and reduce labour costs were key to success, and technology helped (Walton 1987 p.127).

The full-rigged ship started out in the business of carrying bulk goods. It eventually became invaluable in the trans-oceanic voyages. In fact, the combination of safer seas and technological advances were responsible for a dramatic decline in freight charges (at least in the wine trade (Menard 1991)) during the second half of the sixteenth century. From a peak in the late 1540s of 34 pence per tonne-kilometre, the price fell to an average below 15 pence in 1600 (see Figure 6.5).

The diffusion in technology benefited from the nature of the business. Ship builders were often also the carpenters on board. As they travelled, and came into foreign ports, they learnt the techniques adopted abroad. These could then be adapted for domestic needs and diffused. Before the fifteenth century, the Mediterranean and the North were two separate trading areas, with their own technologies. Once trade routes interconnected, major technological advances occurred, as each region incorporated the others' ideas. By 1500, all variations in designs reflected local demands rather differences in knowledge (Kohn 2001 pp. 39–40).

Shipping in the Seventeenth and Eighteenth Centuries

The introduction of the Dutch flyboat in the late sixteenth century had a major impact on the shipping trade. The flyboat had a flat bottom, was long relative to its width and was light, because it had done away with the construction and equipment required for protection. These features made it ideal for the carriage of bulk commodities.

In waters that were properly policed, such as coastal Britain, which was safe from piracy since the beginning of the sixteenth century, the flyboat could carry far more goods than its predecessors. Before being adopted in Britain, the English needed 30 men to crew their 200 tonne ships, while the Dutch only needed a dozen men, because of the reduced need for protection and the easier sails used. Goods could be delivered by flyboat for often a third to half of the cost of other ships (Walton 1987 p.127).

Using the wine trade as an indicator of declines in transport charges in protected waters, there is evidence of a gradual decline (Menard 1991). At the beginning of the seventeenth century, freight charges averaged just below 15 pence per tonne-kilometre. By the mid-eighteenth century, the average had dropped to below 10 pence (see Figure 6.5).

In less protected waters, piracy and privateering were rife. For instance, most of the ships in the North American Colonies and especially in the Caribbean were heavily protected with guns and men. The flyboat there was very slow to be adopted, and only once better law enforcement insured safety (Walton 1970 p.127).

Other technical improvements helped reduce the cost of freight. Wind was a free resource and efforts were made to find more effective ways of capturing the winds. The introduction of the jib and headsails, as well as the helm wheel, enabled ships to sail more easily into the west-prevailing winds. These innovations enabled mariners to alter their routes and save considerable time on each journey. Costs fell in many transatlantic businesses during the seventeenth and early eighteenth centuries, such as the tobacco trade. Such improvements provided the boost for the growing number of journeys, distances travelled and goods carried (Menard 1991 p.261). This was reflected in the increased carrying capacity of registered ships in Britain since the mid-sixteenth century, shown in Figure 6.6.

Based on the registered tonnage, a bold attempt has been made to estimate water freight services (see the Data Appendix). Although this was a very crude estimate of goods lifted, it does help to identify the scale of water-based transport services (see Figure 6.7). For instance, it suggests that in 1760, at the beginning of the Industrial Revolution, the estimate of river, canal, coastwise and sea trade amounted to 4 billion tonne-km (btk).

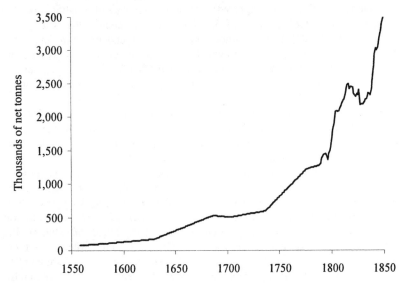

Source: collected from Davis (1962), Mitchell (1988) and Hope (1990)

Figure 6.6 The Net Tonnage of Registered Ships, 1558–1850

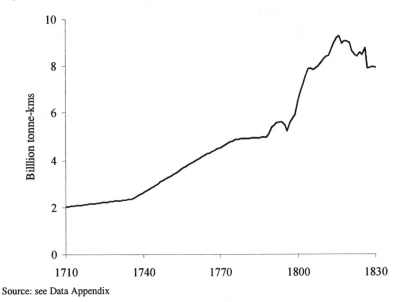

Source: see Data Appendix

Figure 6.7 Estimate of the Use of Water Freight Transport Services, 1710–1830

At the time, the carrying capacity of registered ships in Britain was just under 1 million tonnes, lifting (an estimated) 12.5 million tonnes and freighting them an average (extrapolated) distance of 350 kms. As a reference, the British coal production in 1760 was 6.3 million tonnes, and around one-third of it was shipped along the East Coast of England – the distance between Newcastle and London was about 500 kilometres. An estimate of 4 btk for 1760 seems plausible, certainly the correct order of magnitude. In 1830, it was estimated that 8 btk of goods were freighted.

The estimate of road freight was 20 and 320 million tonne-km in 1760 and 1830, respectively. According to the estimates presented, therefore, during the Industrial Revolution, around twenty times more goods were freighted along and across water than over land.

Up until the early nineteenth century, transport services – both on land and in the sea – were bound by relatively limited and unreliable sources of power. The wind pushed seafaring ships, and animals pulled barges and waggons. There were, however, substantial efforts to improve services. They focussed little on altering the source of power though. Instead, they relied on altering the technologies that harnessed the power and modifying the infrastructure to direct the power. Organisational and institutional transformations were paramount to the improvements that took place in the Early Modern era. To truly revolutionise transport services, however, new sources of power were needed.

6. THE RAILWAY MANIA

Expansion of the Railway

The harnessing of power from heating fuels to create steam was the break-through needed to revolutionise transport services. Since the eighteenth century, a steam engine had been used as a stationary source of power in a growing number of activities (see Chapter 5). Directing its power along an iron rail was an effective way of harnessing the steam generated by coal for transport purposes and of minimising the friction associated with land transport. The steam-driven railway paved the way for a new era in transport services.

When Richard Trevithick placed the steam engine on rails in 1804, it ignited the interest of engineers to find the solution to a series of problems relating to engines, wheels and rails. The Stephensons' Rocket became the locomotive to drive the spectacular growth in railways between 1825 and 1850 (Mokyr 1990 p.128).

The railways enabled passengers and goods to be pulled along with far less friction than wheels on roads. Yet, in the early 1820s, when the first railed route, the Stockton & Darlington Railway, was being planned, it would have still made commercial sense to have horses pull the load along a road. By the end of the decade, many entrepreneurs had been convinced that the railroads were a source of great profit.

Railway companies were generally a group of private individuals anticipating profits from reducing the cost of freighting goods and from selling seats to passengers. They were willing to take on the early costs of surveying and buying land upon which to build the tracks. They were, however, reluctant to be faced with complete liability for their businesses, and Parliament was ultimately responsible. This position would have been the opportunity for Government to influence the expansion of railways, including the promotion of compatibility in the construction of lines. It failed to do so. The railroad manias in the 1830s and 1840s that followed created a patchwork of different tracks and gauges, delaying the linking up of the regional routes. Slowly, integration took place. While most companies set out with the intention of building a particular line, by the mid-century, they were merging with expectations of economies of scale (Hawke and Higgins 1981 p.256).

Investment in railway capital – including the land, tracks and the rolling stock – was impressive. For instance, the length of the network expanded from 40 kilometres in 1825 to more than 150 kilometres in 1830, increasing sixteen-fold in the 1830s, and then another four times in the 1840s, to nearly 10 000 kilometres (see Table 6.2).

This vast rail network being developed was already greater than the canals and about one-quarter of the size of turnpiked road system by 1850. Most of the main lines had been built. An important feature of the service to customers was the integration of the network through the organisation of a Railway Clearing House from 1842, enabling a passenger or item to be paid for the entirety of the journey, rather than having to pay a multitude of tickets from each company (Hawke and Higgins 1981 p.236).

Table 6.2 Expansion of the Railway Network in kilometres, 1825–1900

Year	Length (km)	Year	Length (km)
1825	40	1850	9 700
1830	150	1860	14 500
1835	540	1870	21 700
1840	2 400	1880	24 900
1845	3 900	1890	26 700
-	-	1900	29 900

Source: Mitchell (1988) p.541

The Cost of Railway Transport

The cost of using trains in the very early days of railways was expensive, greater per kilometre than using stagecoaches (Schivelbusch 1988). Naturally, in the early period, customers were paying for large capital expenses, hence the high prices. At the same time, the costs between the two modes of transportation had to be comparable for sufficient number of customers to be willing to shift

towards railways, companies to cover their investment and out-compete the
incumbent technology.

By the time annual data on railway prices was available, in 1843, the cost of
travelling one kilometre was 34 pence (see Figure 6.8). The price per kilometre
for stagecoaches never dropped below 40 pence and, in the 1830s, the price was
around 75 pence.

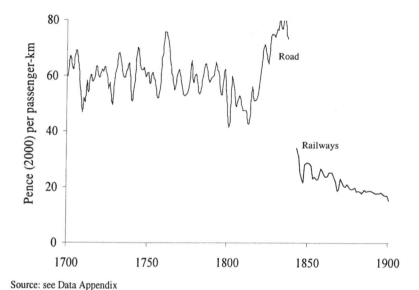

Source: see Data Appendix

Figure 6.8 The Price of Land Passenger Transport Services, 1700–1900

It appears that coach companies quickly realised they could not compete with
the railways. Having invested in equipment and horses that would soon be of
little value, they drove up the price to make as much money in as little time. The
effect was naturally to encourage a swifter shift towards railways than if coach
companies had sought to compete creatively (Hart 1960).

With declining costs and increasing speeds, by the 1840s, railways were
providing a superior service to the wealthy and middle classes. Indeed, "the
greater speed of railways than of coaches made travel a commodity available to
people who would not otherwise have considered it as a possible item for
expenditure..." (Hawke 1970 p.191).

Evidence on travel times helps incorporate speed into the transport price
(Leunig 2006 p.646). The price (factoring-in speed) falls considerably – from 1.4
pence per kilometre-hour in the early 1840s to 1 penny by 1850. In the last years
of data for stagecoaches, in the 1830s, the price was around 5 pence. For first-
class travellers, railways also offered greater comfort and more frequent travel
(Leunig 2006 p.638).

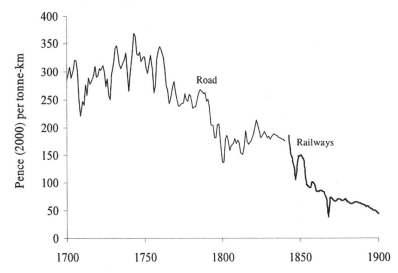

Source: see Data Appendix

Figure 6.9 The Price of Land Freight Transport Services, 1700–1900

For the carriage of goods, the railway also seems to have been an improvement over the road. In the 1830s, the cost of horse-pulled goods travelling one kilometre was around 200 pence (see Figure 6.9). The cost by rail fell sharply from 185 pence in 1843 to 94 pence in 1855. On a price-basis alone, railways were certainly competitive with horses by the 1840s. Indeed, the long distance horse-haulage practically disappeared swiftly, yet shorter distance still survived well into the twentieth century.

The price of traffic in ships along the coast was certainly cheaper than the railways – Figure 6.5 indicates the price of carrying coal by sea was around 5 pence per tonne-km in 1850. Canals also seem to have been cheaper than railways for the carriage of goods during the nineteenth century. Around 1810, heavy goods cost 23 pence per tonne-km along waterways. The charges increased in 1828 to 31 and 37 pence by 1852 (Jackman 1960 pp.728–737). They, nevertheless, show that canals could compete with railways, at least when speed of delivery was not important.

Fuel expenditure for early locomotives was relatively high. In 1840, around 0.3 million tonnes of coal were used on the railways. At the time, they provided about 0.33 billion passenger-km and 0.16 billion tonne-km – or 1 100 passenger-km and about 500 tonne-km per tonne of oil (based on Church 1987 p.19).

To provide a simple comparison with the other costs of rail transport and with other transport services, it was assumed that the share of railway company receipts for passenger and freight services was similar to the energy consumption between the two services. This indicated that around two-thirds of the fuel would have been used for passenger travel, in which case 0.33 billion passenger-kilometres consumed 200 000 tonnes of coal and 0.16 billion tonne-kilometres required 100 000 tonnes. Thus, one tonne of coal could move around 1 700 passenger-kilometres, or 1 500 tonne-kilometres. Given that coal prices were about £(2000)62 per tonne at the time, this would mean that the fuel cost of one passenger-kilometre (and for one tonne-kilometre) was about 4 pence – a small fraction of the price of transport services in 1840.

Despite considerable benefits from introducing railways, many groups resisted the expansion. For example, canal owners and carriers realised they were in competition with the freight transport services offered by trains, and voiced their concerns. Similarly, turnpike owners and financiers petitioned against the expansion of railways. Coaching companies appear to have fought less strongly for the defence of their industry – although lobbying would have been a costly strategy especially given their expectations about their ability to compete with railways and the future of their industry (Hart 1960).

Many farmers near large centres of population also feared the loss of their monopoly in the supply of markets, as produce could be brought from greater distances. Land owners felt that they would suffer from the expansion of rail transport, "disfiguring the landscape, destroying the privacy and seclusion of their estates, and causing a great decrease in the value of their land" (Jackman 1960 p.497) and demanded compensation for their troubles. Some towns, such as Northampton, Maidstone, Windsor and Eton, objected to the railways. In Oxford, dons felt that access to London, and its loose morals, would corrupt the minds of young students. They were banned from travelling on trains for many years and the station placed at considerable distance from the town (Jackman 1960).

Consolidation

Nevertheless, the railway expanded. By 1900, the length of network had tripled in fifty years. It reached over 32 000 kilometres at the beginning of the First World War (see Table 6.2).

Fuel efficiency improved, particularly in the 1850s and 1860s. By 1870, one tonne of coal could move 3 000 passenger-kilometres or 3 700 tonne-kilometres – with the same assumptions as above. This increased more modestly to nearly 3 400 passenger-kilometres or almost 4 500 tonne-kilometres in 1900. Thus, the fuel expenditure per kilometre had dropped from between 3 and 4 pence in 1850 to 1.3 and 1.6 pence in 1870. It fluctuated between 1 and 2 pence per kilometre afterwards, depending on the price of coal.

Railway prices continued to fall. In 1850, a passenger would pay 29 pence per kilometre. One tonne of freight cost just under 150 pence per kilometre. By 1870, prices had fallen 20 percent for passenger travel and 50 percent for freight. In 1900, they fell another 34 percent (to 15 pence) and 38 percent (to 44 pence) respectively.

In the latter part of the century, an important change in railways' role was when the owners began to appreciate, under threat from Government, that third-class customers were a large potential market. Walking (or riding on a slow waggon) was the only alternative for most poor. Improving the quality of the service to and encouraging the use of railways for poorer members of the population saved them time and opened up many opportunities. These time-savings (rather than the direct cost reductions of travelling) were the greatest contribution to social well-being (Leunig 2006 p.651). Thus, the railways started out as an improvement on the stagecoach for the wealthy. They ended up providing a new service to the masses, transforming the nature of mobility and even society.

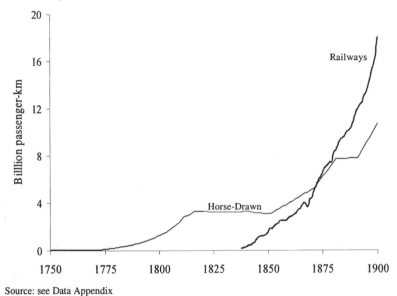

Source: see Data Appendix

Figure 6.10 The Use of Land Passenger Transport Services, 1750–1900

Factoring in the speed of travel, the fall in prices was even greater. From 1.3 pence per kilometre-hour and 7 pence per tonne-kilometre-hour in the early 1840s to 1 penny and 5 pence by 1850, to below 0.35 pence and just above 1 penny in 1900. Thus, taking account of the time saved, passengers could travel for 40 times and 10 times more cheaply than two hundred and one hundred years before. Freight was 70 times cheaper than two hundred years earlier, and 12 times less than one hundred years before.

Inevitably, the use of transport services exploded. In 1850, there were already one billion passenger-km and one billion tonne-km (see Figure 6.10 and 6.11). Railway freight was larger than horse-drawn carriage had ever been. It rose to just under 30 billion tonne-km in 1900. Passenger-km also increased to 18 billion.

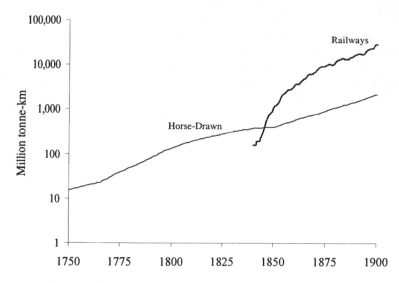

Source: see Data Appendix

Figure 6.11 The Use of Land Freight Transport Services, 1750–1900

Between the mid-eighteenth and mid-nineteenth century, Britain went from an economy with modest transport services providing local needs to a network of roads, rails and canals ensuring fluid distribution across most of the country. And, in the second half of the nineteenth century, railways created a rapid, integrated network that converted a patchwork of regions into a single economy (Crompton 2005 p.5). The consequence was an increased mobility of people and goods.

7. OTHER FORMS OF TRANSPORT IN THE NINETEENTH CENTURY

The Return of the Horse

Although the steam engines had replaced horses as the prime mover, the latter provided an important role in the nineteenth century economy. To a great extent, the railways and horses were complements rather substitutes. The railways had created a huge growth in the movement of goods and people, often large distances. Those goods and people needed to get to the railway stations. Thus, demand for horses to provide transport services grew, becoming more specialised on shorter journeys.

Horses were capital investments that – combined with fodder, harnesses and a cart – could transport people and goods. Like other equipment, the investment depreciated in value and had a limited lifespan – averaging between five to eight years after acquisition, which happened, generally, at the age of five (Turvey 2005 p.41). Their mobility enabled a thriving second-hand market to develop. But, each horse had special characteristics: their ability to work varied – sometimes they were ill, some were temperamental or lazy; also, irrespective of their workload, they required feeding and care on a daily basis (Turvey 2005 p.38).

In the 1890s, the supply of omnibus horses from America grew. The decline in the cost of freighting across the Atlantic and the decline in the demand for such horses in American cities, because of the major expansion of the electric streetcar, enabled prices to fall. This led to a rapid growth in the horse-drawn street car in Britain (Turvey 2005 p.56). This was a great example of how one economy 'benefited' by acquiring cheap technology from another economy, because the latter had invested in new, 'superior' technology. However, the low cost locked the first economy into the old and 'inferior' technology, while the latter economy profited from having found a healthy market for its old technology and modernised its technology.

It should be noted that, at the beginning of the twentieth century, although horse-power was responsible for less than one-tenth of freight transport, it still provided more than one-third of all passenger journeys, through horse-drawn buses, trams, hackney carriages (that is, taxis) and private carriages, as well as horseback riding (see Figure 6.10).

The Bicycle

In the early nineteenth century, mechanical developments had created a simple way of harnessing the power of human muscles, increasing the speed of travel and distances that could be achieved. The introduction of the bicycle chain meant the enormous front wheel was no longer necessary to harness muscle power, making travel far safer. Safety was also enhanced by the use of brakes. The increased number of roads being covered with tarmac and the introduction of the pneumatic tyre improved cycling conditions considerably. Thus, for small distances, the bicycle was a cheap and effective mode of transport. By the 1870s, the bicycle was the main source of transport for a large proportion of the population.

Waterways

The canal still suffered from problems associated with weather conditions and difficult terrain. Yet, the efficiency with which a power moves a weight was still greater on waterways than on a rail. Barges were cheaper and faster to depreciate than railway waggons. Canals were considerably cheaper to maintain than railways. Thus, wherever canals had the opportunity to exploit these inherent advantages, they managed to provide carriage of heavy goods at lower cost (Bagwell 1974 p.157).

The growing success of railway companies in the mid-nineteenth century enabled them to acquire many canals. In 1846 alone, they managed to control 1 200 kilometres of waterway or around 20 percent of the whole network. By 1865, over 30 percent of canals were in railway hands. Early fears of the monopoly powers of the railways led to the creation of the Canal Carriers Act in 1845 which only allowed existing canal companies to acquire or lease waterways. By then, however, many of the railway companies had acquired canals and had changed their names to reflect their business on the waterways. They were, therefore, able to invest in more canals and did so. Only in 1873 were mergers forbidden, except with Parliament's consent (Bagwell 1974 p.158).

Apart from a few exceptions, there was no separation of tasks between modes, despite the advantages of rail for passengers and canals for heavy goods. The outcome was a period of intense competition between railways and canals for both markets. This generally led to the absorption or leasing of the canal by the railway (Bagwell 1974 p.160). In many cases, the takeover was the result of canal owners panicking and believing their business was doomed, offering the waterway at very attractive prices – this was especially the case during the Railway Mania (Bagwell 1974 p.163).

Often, the railway owned part, but not all, of important routes. When deciding whether to carry goods partly along tracks and partly through water or entirely by rail, they naturally chose the latter. The result was a lack of interest in the care of canals owned by railways. Repairs or ice breakage on these canals were slow (Bagwell 1974 p.161).

More aggressively, to shift demand to trains, railway companies also drove up the price of tonnage on their section of the canal. One salient example was the joint acquisition of the Rochdale canal by a series of railway companies in order to place prohibitive prices on this form of transport. In another example, on the 230 kilometre Birmingham canal, the 10 km stretch owned by the London and North Western Railway cost one-third of the price of travelling the whole distance (Bagwell 1974 p.162).

During the second half of the nineteenth century, the role of waterways in transport services declined significantly. This was in large part an inevitable consequence of the growth of railways. The extent of the decline was also the result of poor canal management and government policy, and the aggressive strategies of the railway companies. In 1845, the tonnage carried by canals and railways was roughly the same (Bagwell 1974 p.157). Assuming similar distances for canal and train journeys (although canal journeys were probably a little shorter), around 0.2 billion tonne-kilometres were achieved on waterways. By 1898, canal freight was close to the horse-drawn haulage and one-fifteenth of the carriage provided by the railways – around 1.6 billion tonne-kilometres.

Canal carriage increased modestly into the twentieth century, and started to decline substantially after the First World War (Bagwell 1974 p.157).

Shipping Technology in the Nineteenth Century

Despite the growth of roads, railways and canals, shipping services dominated the supply of goods throughout, into and out of Britain. Based on goods lifted, broad estimates of international trade and coastwise carriage were possible from the mid-nineteenth century to the present day. For instance, international trade and coastwise commerce was about 5.6 btk and 6.1 btk in 1850, at a time when most of the freight was powered by the wind (see Data Appendix).

Steam engines had been used on land since the early nineteenth century. Similar attempts to use steam on the water were equally successful. By the 1850s, steamships had proven their technical capabilities for long distance journeys, such as across the Atlantic. Their speed and, thus, timing of arrival were reliable. Building such a ship was extremely expensive, however. In some cases, steamships cost 50 percent more than the equivalent sailing vessel (Dyos and Aldcroft 1969 p.239).

Even if the building costs were not a problem, the engines, boilers and fuel storage used up most of the ships' carrying capacity. The engine could take up to half of the total space in the vessel. The first steamships were also extremely fuel inefficient. The first Cunard steamship used 650 tonnes of coal, having a total weight-lifting capacity of 880 tonnes. On long journeys, especially to the Far East, few coaling stations existed, limiting the routes these ships could follow (Dyos and Aldcroft 1969 p.240).

Why would anyone invest in such an inefficient ship? Perhaps the builders of steamships hid or were overoptimistic about the ship's fuel requirements. More crucial, though, was that such a ship did increase the reliability of travel, given that wind was so intermittent. To ensure accurate timing, particularly for perishable goods, for passengers and for communication, people were willing to pay high prices.

For instance, Cunard benefited from favourable mail contracts with the British Admiralty. This strongly subsidised the shipping technology. It has been argued that without these subsidies, Cunard would not have succeeded as a company. Furthermore, given its ultimately powerful position in the shipping business, it drove out potentially more innovative companies, and held back technological improvements (Dyos and Aldcroft 1969 p.239).

Reductions in the cost of construction and operation were key to its success. In particular, ways of increasing the vessel's carrying capacity needed to be found. Iron ships weighed a quarter less than an equal sized wooden one. Iron's strength allowed for larger ships to be built (Dyos and Aldcroft 1969 p.240).

Yet, the use of iron in ships was adopted slowly. Iron tended to corrode quickly, reducing the ship's lifespan. Also, shipyards were used to building wooden ships; the skills and techniques necessary to build iron hulls had to be developed. In the mid-1860s, wooden sailing ships still provided virtually all the bulk goods, which made up the majority of demand for transport services.

Soon, though, the iron ship proved its worth. The Great Eastern, completed in 1857 by Isambard Kingdom Brunel, was a commercial failure and an engineering success, because it created a model of how large iron vessels could be built. Gradually, too, engine power and efficiency increased. Boiler pressures quadrupled in the thirty years leading up to the early 1870s, reducing the coal consumption by half. This was crucial given that fuel was responsible for up to 50 percent of the total cost of a voyage (Dyos and Aldcroft 1969 p.241).

The opening of the Suez Canal in 1869 marked the beginning of steamship dominance. Contrary to the difficulties of stocking coal along the long coasts of Africa, the Suez was ideal for refuelling along the way. In 1870, the total tonnage of steamships being built was greater than that for sailing ships. By the end of the 1870s, steamships monopolised the market for high class freight, passengers and mail. And, by 1883, there were more steam vessels than sailing ships in Britain (Dyos and Aldcroft 1969 p.241).

The Sailing Ship Effect

It has been argued that the threat from steamships from the 1840s created incentives for sailing ships to innovate. Compared with thirty years before, the sailing ship of the 1870s was faster and could carry twice as many goods with half the number of men. The low unit cost of bulk goods made sailing ships commercially viable. As the market for grain and coal expanded dramatically during the second half of the nineteenth century, wind power held on to an important share of the transport market (Dyos and Aldcroft 1969 p.241).

New technological developments put an end to the survival of the sailing ship, however. The new 'triple expansion' engines developed in the 1880s eventually reduced coal consumption by half compared to the high pressure boilers, and ten-fold relative to the early engines (Dyos and Aldcroft 1969 p.241). Coal consumption per unit of power had fallen from 1 kg per Indicated Horse Power (IHP) in 1871 to 0.7 kg in 1885. By 1913, this had fallen 0.56 kg per IHP. Along with the faster speeds these engines generated, and the increased availability of cheap steel, steamships now provided a low cost transport service (Mohammed and Williamson 2004 p.197). Figure 6.12 reflects the initial increase in sailing ships despite the introduction of competition. Given that stagecoaches were such poor competition for steam power on land, the longevity of the sailing ship was a testament to the value of having free wind power, even if it was unreliable.

Other advances in metallurgical, chemical and engineering sciences were also vital for improvements associated with the declining costs of iron and of steel ship construction and with the better performing engines. For instance, the introduction of steel in the late 1880s eventually reduced the weight of the hull by 15 percent and increased the cargo capacity, thus improving fuel efficiency further. Growing ship size meant that these efficiencies were consumed by a growing volume of trade (Mohammed and Williamson 2004 p.197).

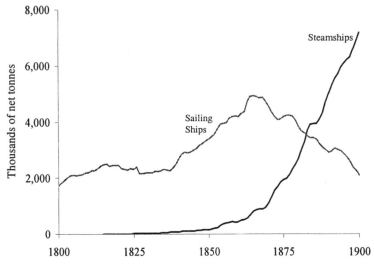

Source: Mitchell (1988)

Figure 6.12 The Net Tonnage of Registered Ships, 1800–1900

Thus, steamships' early success was in finding a niche, luxury market, in which customers were willing to pay high prices for a particular attribute, principally timing. This early revenue supported the business, and enabled sufficient economies of scale and technological developments to be achieved. In turn, the steamship was able to gradually increase its competitiveness relative to the sailing ship.

These competitive forces had favourable effects for the cost of travel. The price of sea carriage at the beginning of the nineteenth century was between 5 and 10 pence per tonne-kilometre. By the end of the century, it was between 1.5 and 2 pence (see Figure 6.13). Inevitably, sea travel increased dramatically during the century.

With a declining price and an expanding economy, carriage along and across waterways continued to grow in the nineteenth and twentieth centuries. Displayed in Figure 6.14, goods lifted rose from 14 btk in 1850 to 70 btk in 1900. As a comparison, the amount of railway freight went from 1 btk to 30 btk in those same fifty years.

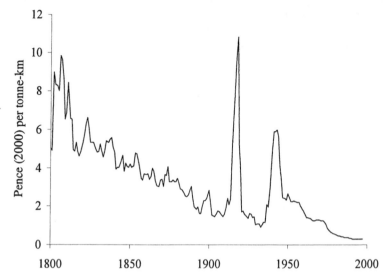

Source: based on Harley (1988) and Mohammed and Williamson, see Data Appendix

Figure 6.13 The Price of Sea Transport Services, 1800–2000

Source: see Data Appendix

Figure 6.14 Estimate of the Use of Water Freight Transport Services, 1850–2000

Apart from during the major wars, the trend was still very much upwards, driven by a process of expanding international trade networks and globalisation. By 2000, more than 300 btk of goods were lifted. Until the last decade, no real substitute to sea freight existed in the United Kingdom. The introduction of the channel tunnel enabled the railways to compete with ships for the distribution of international trade, although the growth of this substitute has been limited by the size of the tunnel.

8. PERSONALISED TRANSPORT

The Birth of Car Demand

Back on land, improvements in road surfacing and lightweight steam engines in the nineteenth century had led to the introduction of steam-driven road vehicles. A few even provided services between major cities, travelling at around 25 kmh and carrying more than a dozen passengers. Powerful lobbies, including many landowners, who had invested in railways were able to introduce legislation against motorised road transport. Some of the legislation required vehicles to travel at no more than 5 kmh and to be preceded by a man walking and waving a red flag. These tricks managed to stifle the advance of road technology for over half a century (Bagwell 1974).

The introduction of the internal combustion engine in the last decade of the 1800s created a new opportunity for road transport to grow and compete with railways. Before the First World War, except in a few cities where buses were introduced, the main demand for motor transport was for 'pleasure driving' (Bagwell 1974 p.221). The car manufacturer was selling to wealthy motorists to speed around the countryside.

The number of private motor cars in Britain grew spectacularly. In the first year for which data exists, 1904, there were 8 000 cars. By 1910, 53 000 had been sold – a six-fold increase in six years. By 1914, 132 000 cars were on the roads – a sixteen-fold rise in ten years (Mitchell 1988 p.557).

The demand for fuel to drive cars was also impressive. In 1910, 0.21 million tonnes of motor spirit were used. By 1914, consumption had risen to 0.45 million tonnes. It should be noted that in those four years, there was 2.5 times more cars but only 2.16 times more motor spirit used. So, fuel consumption fell from 4 000 litres to 3,430 litres, hinting at possible early efficiencies or changes in driver behaviour (King 1952 p.551).

The roads, developed for horse and carts, were inappropriate for cars. Early tourist driving through the countryside caused large amounts of noise and generated large amounts of dust. Lord Montagu of Beaulieu believed that the dust was "the cause of nine-tenths of the unpopularity of motor cars" (quoted in Bagwell 1974 p.217). The value of property on popular routes, such as the London to Portsmouth road, fell by up to one-third in the 1910s (Bagwell 1974 p.217).

Another problem associated with the motor car was the class tensions it created. Lord Asquith suggested that "the manifestation of wealth in the form of ostentatious expenditure on motor cars was one of the reasons for the current industrial unrest" (Bagwell 1974 p.217). One example of these tensions was played-out between local policemen and wealthy motorists. Most cars could travel much more than the twenty miles per hour (32 kmh) speed limit introduced in 1903, and motorists enjoyed taking advantage of their technological powers. The police, mostly of working class backgrounds, took considerable pleasure in waiting for speeding rich to impose a substantial fine. The Automobile Association (AA) was set up to hire 'scouts' to warn members of speed-traps. The waving of flags as a warning was deemed an obstruction of police activities. Instead, scouts saluted passing members, unless the police were waiting; the motorist then pulled over and the scout could warn the motorist in more subtle ways. Motorists managed to win another battle in the class struggle when, in 1930, speed limits were abolished, except in residential areas (Bagwell 1974 p.219).

Yet, before that, in 1909, Lloyd George introduced a petrol tax of 3 old-pence per gallon (£(2000)0.13 per litre) and an annual vehicle licence according to the size of the engine. The revenue helped support a Road Fund. In its early years, the Road Board, which used the revenue, chose to reduce the mud and dust by improving the surface of existing roads. More than £(2000)125 million was spent on the problem in the four years before 1914 – or £(2000)30 million each year for the 100 000 motor cars on the roads. Thus, although this investment benefited motorists, their money (£300 per car) also helped minimise some of the main external costs they imposed on society at the time.

Fuel Costs

The costs of actually driving a car were more concealed but depended to a large extent on the price of petrol and the efficiency of the vehicle. Presented in Figure 6.15, petrol (that is, 4-star) prices were around 60 pence (2000) per litre in 1910. They peaked in 1917 at over 125 pence per litre, as a result of supply disruptions associated with the war. Part of the rising cost was due to the taxation introduced in 1909, and then doubled (in nominal terms) in 1915; the duty was then removed in 1921. By 1923, the price had fallen to 60 pence and, for three decades, fluctuated around this value, despite duties being re-introduced (BPP 1915, 1926).

Fuel-related travel costs followed these patterns. In 1910, a driver spent around 25 pence to travel one kilometre (see Figure 6.16). With the soaring wartime fuel prices led to a cost of over 80 pence. By the mid-twenties, and until after the Second World War, the cost settled at about 10 pence per kilometre. In fact, the cost had dropped to the point where it was competing with train journeys, which were around 7 pence per kilometre.

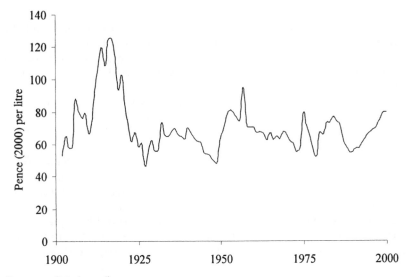

Source: see Data Appendix

Figure 6.15 The Price of Motor Spirit, 1905–2000

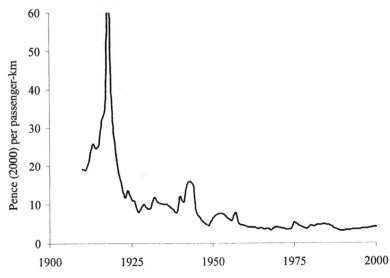

Source: see Data Appendix

Figure 6.16 The Fuel Costs of Car Transport, 1910–2000

Expansion of Car Demand

In 1924, there were just under half of one million cars on the road. In 1938, nearly two million cars sped around Britain (see Table 6.3). In that period, motor spirit consumption increased from 1.6 to 4.4 million tonnes. Each car consumed only 2 300 litres per year, a 50 percent decline on use in 1924 (BPP 1926, King 1952).

These significant improvements were likely to have been the result of the vehicle licence. From 1909, cars with around 30 horsepower (22 kW) were charged four times as much as cars with less than seven horsepower (5 kW). From the 1920s until the Second World War, the licence was changed and motorists paid one old pound Sterling per horsepower (around £(2000)470 per kW). The taxation system (inadvertently) encouraged the manufacture of moderately-powered cars. These vehicles consumed less fuel and were especially popular when the price of petrol was high and the economy was sluggish, as in the 1930s. The under-10 horsepower (7.5 kW) cars increased their share of the total market from one-quarter in 1927 to over 60 percent in 1938. A large factor in this change was the growth of middle class car owners (Bagwell 1974 pp.215–9).

Table 6.3 Number of Road Vehicles, 1905–2000

Year	Millions	Year	Millions	Year	Millions
1905	0.016	1930	1.05	1970	9.9
1910	0.053	1940	1.42	1980	14.6
1920	0.187	1950	1.97	1990	19.7
-	-	1960	4.90	2000	23.2

Source: Mitchell (1988)

Public Transport

The introduction of the internal combustion engine was much slower for commercial vehicles. In 1913, only one-third of the motor vehicles produced in Britain were for commercial purposes and these were mostly buses and taxis (Bagwell 1974 p.222).

In many of the larger cities, well-developed tramways limited the need for motor buses. In addition, the narrow streets of many urban centres meant that motorists could not take advantage of the vehicles' superior speeds. Some of the first adopters of the motor bus were in more rural areas where train connections tended to be very slow. In fact, before the First World War, the largest investors in buses were the rail companies. Buses enabled better connections between rail lines. Often, this enabled companies to assess the viability of building a new line. In other cases, it helped deal with peak demands for transport or specialised needs, such as during summer holidays (Bagwell 1974 p.224).

In other words, compared with the railways, the motor vehicle provided an additional attribute, flexibility. Plans could be adjusted to deal with changing circumstances. The introduction of the motor bus created a swifter, more flexible transport network.

Fuel and Rubber

Demand for the delivery vehicles was slow, however. For smaller businesses in the early days, it was unclear in what technology to invest. Steam, petrol or electric powered vehicles all competed in the market for hauling goods. Each manufacturer sold its van's virtues, and hid its flaws. It was common to see motor cars sitting on the side of the road, the victim of unreliable mechanical parts or poor driving, and of a lack of engineers able to fix them. For a while, each technology grew, trying to break out of its niche applications. In 1918, Harrods' delivery services depended on 80 electric vehicles – they were cheaper to run and maintain than motor vans. As late as 1919, some steam buses were still carrying passengers through the streets of London (Bagwell 1974 p.222).

Another factor that delayed the adoption of motor vehicles was the major cost of tyres. In 1906, a London bus's expenditure on four solid rubber tyres was 4 old-pence per mile (70 pence (2000) per kilometre). More long-lasting pneumatic tyres were only introduced by Dunlop in 1916. With economies of scale in the production of rubber tyres, the cost had fallen in 1932 to 0.10 old-pence per mile (1 penny (2000) per kilometre). The rubber costs had fallen seventy-fold in twenty-six years (Bagwell 1974 p.222).

The hidden costs of rubber were also enormous, however. Some of the most brutal colonial regimes were driven by the lucre earned from rubber production. For instance, one estimate placed the death toll from the harsh regime in the Belgian Congo, much of it driven by the exploitation of rubber plantations, at ten million (Hochschild 1998 p.233).

The development of the car provides an interesting example of the early externalities caused by new technologies and, in some cases, the possible solutions that can be created. The freedom to drive cars reaching impressive speeds was inevitably going to cause considerable external effects. As mentioned before, the dust caused by cars was a source of great annoyance. Noise and smell also made shopkeepers dislike the motor van – "it barked like a dog, and stank like a cat" (quoted in Bagwell 1974 p.222). Another major problem with cars was the speed at which they travelled and the accidents that resulted.

The Dominance of the Roads

In the 1950s, the price ((2000) per litre) of motor spirit leapt up to over 80 pence, peaking at 94 pence in 1957 as a result of tensions in the Suez Canal, before falling gradually until late 1973. In 1975, it reached 80 pence, dropping and rising to 75 pence in 1985, and then falling after disputes over OPEC production quotas.

Improvements in fuel efficiency and then declining fuel prices had driven down the fuel costs of travelling by car to 5 pence per kilometre in 1950. Around the same time, the cost had fallen below the price of taking the train. Since then, the price of travelling by car had declined gradually as a result of improvements in fuel efficiencies. By 1965, it was below 3 pence per kilometre. The total costs of motoring dropped below 20 pence after the Second World War, and to just over 10 pence by 1965. This was still more expensive than taking the train – although, naturally they had other benefits, such as flexibility and privacy, which were hard to measure.

Fuel costs and, therefore, total costs of motoring rose a little higher in periods of high oil prices – yet, these were negligible variations in historical terms. High oil prices have led to a demand for improved fuel efficiency of vehicles. This has come in the form of more efficient motors, and smaller and lighter vehicles, lowering the marginal costs of transport (IEA 2004).

Similar to the early years of motoring, fuel costs at the end of the twentieth century seem to have been about one-quarter of the total motoring expenditure (see Table 6.4). Private motoring has entailed other costs, such as repairs, insurance and road tax. In 1998, they amounted to one-third of the total annual costs (ONS 2002a). Despite the dramatic decline in fuel costs, they still accounted for one-fifth. Expenditure on the car and spare parts was just under one-half of annual expenditure in 1998. So, at the end of the twentieth century, capital expenditure was the major component of the total annual costs of private motoring.

Table 6.4 Shares of Motoring Costs for Average Households, 1971–1998

	1971	1981	1991	1995	1998
Motoring costs - Motor vehicles & spares	48.2%	42.6%	38.6%	40.7%	45.0%
Motoring costs - Petrol & engine oil	27.9%	29.1%	26.8%	23.7%	21.5%
Motoring costs – Repairs & insurance	14.5%	17.1%	15.1%	16.9%	15.3%
Motoring costs – Vehicle tax	5.1%	5.1%	5.4%	5.2%	5.2%
Motoring costs – Other	4.3%	7.4%	14.2%	13.4%	13.0%

Source: based on data from ONS (2002a)

A calculation of the annualised costs, assuming a lifespan of the car of eight years, suggests that fuel costs accounted for one-quarter of the costs of motoring at the beginning of the twentieth century. The average price of a car in 1910 was about £(2000)25 000, falling to just over £(2000)10 000 by the early 1930s (Foreman-Peck 1981 pp.264–5), and has dropped only modestly since. When prices of cars fell in the 1930s, fuel costs became a significantly larger share of the total annualised cost of private transport until they started to fall in the 1990s as efficiency improvements and fuel prices dropped.

Finally, in 1987, after the fall in oil prices and rising train fares, car travel was momentarily cheaper than using the railways. Since then, they have been roughly the same, although in the late 1990s, average car prices appear to have risen. When oil prices were lower, as they were during the 1990s, this created a demand for larger vehicles and more accessories, such air conditioning and convertibles; these drove up car prices and then fuel cost of the vehicle.

The Grand Shift Back to Roads

Road transportation was the main source of transportation for people (see Figure 6.17). At the end of the twentieth century, around 600 billion passenger-kilometres were in cars; 50 billion were from public road transportation (that is, buses and coaches). The total amount of transport service was around 720 billion passenger-kilometres. Personal travel had increased more than 350 times in the last two hundred years and 35 times in the last one hundred years.

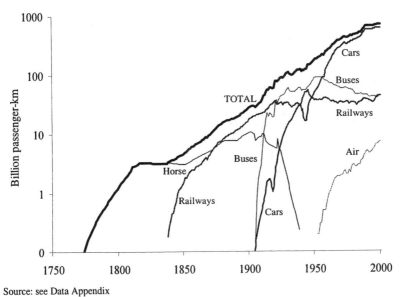

Source: see Data Appendix

Figure 6.17 The Use of Land Passenger Transport Services, 1770–2000

Underlying the more modest declines in goods-haulage from trains was the massive substitution of total transport services back to roads, as well as the use of waterways (including coastal services) and pipelines. Roads ensured 120 million tonne-kilometres of carriage; waterways 60 and pipelines ten billion. That is, in 2000, companies provided 250 billion tonne-kilometres of goods transport service. Excluding the huge role played historically by water, freight transport was one thousand times greater than two hundred years ago, and twelve times greater than one hundred years ago.

Trains and Ships

Throughout the twentieth century, apart from in the thirties when they rose, railway prices per kilometre remained relatively constant and average speeds rose. Prices per passenger kilometre-hour fell nearly three-fold from around 0.35 pence in 1900 to about 0.16 pence in 1950, and have fallen a little since then, currently at 0.1 pence. After the impressive fall in the nineteenth century, freight prices were the same in 1900 as in 1950, at 1 penny per kilometre-hour. Since 1950, however, they dropped five-fold, down to 0.2 pence per tonne kilometre-hour by the end of the century.

Despite these dramatic declines in these transport services, railway passenger-kilometres have only doubled, to 38 billion, since 1900 (see Figure 6.17). Another ten billion passenger-kilometres were provided by urban underground services. Freight tonne-kilometres increased from 30 in 1900 to 36 billion in 1950, and halved by 2000.

The dominance of British ship-making continued until the First World War, when the shipyards kept producing steam vessels, while foreign dockyards gambled with diesel (combustion) engines. It has been argued that many in the British shipping industry had formed close ties with the coal industry and were, therefore, suspicious of and reluctant to adopt diesel engines. Diesel quickly proved its superiority during the First World War, but by then many competitors had leap-frogged the British industry (Mohammed and Williamson 2004 p.199). Once again the risks and hazards of war drove-up the price of sea carriage. There was a five-fold increase in prices during the First World War, and a tripling by the end of the Second World War. Afterwards, freight transport services along the sea and especially across seas continued to grow. It rose from around 80 btk in 1950 to almost 325 btk in 2000 (ONS 2002b), considerably more than all other forms of transport together.

9. FAST, LONG-DISTANCE TRAVEL

Having seen the dramatic progress made in moving people and goods across land and sea, technological developments in the twentieth century have enabled air travel. Although flights in air balloons were achieved as early as 1783, when the Mongolfier brothers rose into the sky, the Wright brothers' invention in 1903 paved the way for large-scale air travel. Once again, developments following the mass investment during the First World War created a boost in transport technology.

Some believed in the market for regular flights. But, although technically capable, the commercial viability of these lines was poor, before the Second

World War. At the time, planes were unreliable and expensive, and were hardly faster than the trains unless crossing water or travelling more than 300 kilometres. They competed with new, faster trains and the cheap coach routes. Providing no cargo services and generating few mail contracts, there was nothing to cross-subsidise passenger transport. Load factors were generally far less than 50 percent (Pope 1989 p.113). In the early days of the airlines, the government had a preference for leaving carriers in private hands, which tended to go bankrupt.

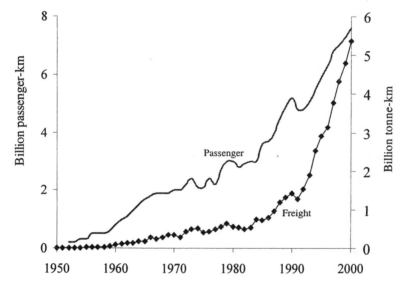

Source: Great Britain Transport Statistics (DoT 2002)

Figure 6.18 The Use of Air Passenger and Freight Transport Services, 1950–2000

Of the little government money supporting the airlines, most of it went into international flights, which were seen as more prestigious and strategically important. After the Second World War, the market for long-distance travel began to develop. The introduction of the jet engine enabled faster, larger capacity and more comfortable planes provided a better quality of service and declining prices. Rising income, more annual vacations and tour operators selling the virtues of exotic destinations created a mass demand for leisure travel (Pope 1989 p.114).

Air travel grew impressively in the second half of the twentieth century. In 1952, airplanes were responsible for 0.2 billion passenger kilometres – this was equivalent to only one-tenth of 1 percent of the total travel associated with British transport. In 1960, the amount of air travel had quadrupled. By 1980, three billion passenger kilometres were being flown – another near quadrupling in twenty years (see Figure 6.18). In 2000, there were 7.6 billion passenger kilometres. There was thirty-eight times more air travelling than in the early 1950s. It still only accounted for about 1 percent of the total market for British passenger transport (DoT 2002).

Despite the growth in passenger behaviour, the rise in air cargo was more spectacular. It had increased thirty-eight fold between 1950 and 1990. It nearly doubled again in the 1990s – having increased seventy-five times in fifty years. Air cargo also provides 1 percent of the total freight service in Great Britain (DoT 2002).

In line with travel, fuel consumption rose considerably after the Second World War. In 1950, less than 0.5 million tonnes of fuel was used for air travel – in 1952, around 200 passenger-kilometres could be travelled with one tonne of fuel. Fuel consumption reached two million in 1960, just over five million in 1980 and nearly twelve million in 2000 – a twenty-four fold increase in fifty years (DTI 1997, 2001). With one tonne of fuel, more than 600 passenger-kilometres can be travelled.

10. LONG-RUN TRENDS IN TRANSPORT

The growing use of horses, with better harnesses to avoid suffocating them and horseshoes to strengthen their hooves, reduced the cost of transport and increased the speed and probably provision of carriage in the thirteenth and fourteenth centuries (see Figure 6.19). Adoption of wheeled vehicles to pull goods and people, rather than packhorses which carried them, improved the efficiency of transport services, especially on decent roads.

By the sixteenth century, the demise of the Catholic Church after Reformation and the inability of local parishes to keep up with the growing pressures put on roads by carriers, led to a major decline in the quality of roads, leading to more expensive and slower transport. The formation of turnpikes to improve roads and charge travellers transformed the transport network. Around the same time, major river improvements were being undertaken to address demands for cheap goods carriage. From the seventeenth century on, major infrastructure projects created a much sturdier road, river and then canal network. The cost of carriage and speed of delivery improved substantially, leading to a growth in the number of travellers and goods pulled (see Figures 6.17 and 6.20).

On the high seas, the gradual reduction in the number of wars and in piracy (illegal or government sanctioned) reduced the number of men and guns required on board. To minimise risks, major improvements in the organisation of shipping enabled ships to carry more goods and people. Finally, and in large part resulting from these reductions in risks, the adoption of new vessels and masts, to capture the power of the wind, drove down the cost of and increased the level of long-distance transport (see Figures 6.19 and 6.20).

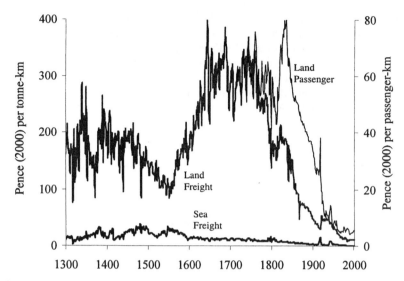

Source: see Data Appendix

Figure 6.19 The Price of Land Freight and Passenger Transport Services, 1300–2000

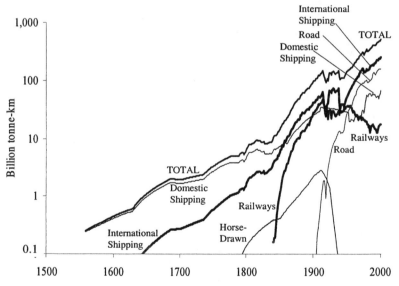

Source: see Data Appendix

Figure 6.20 The Use of Land and Sea Freight Transport Services, 1550–2000

The introduction of steam engines to rail and sea transport in the first half of the nineteenth century meant that coal rather horses and wind could power the next revolution. In Britain, coal was cheap. And, entrepreneurs were plenty to build railways that would eventually form a vast network and to invest in ships to bring home many exotic goods (see Figure 6.20 and 6.21). Costs fell and speed of delivery increased. Released from the limitations of horse population and wind speeds, far greater quantities of energy and power could be used for transport services (see Figure 6.22).

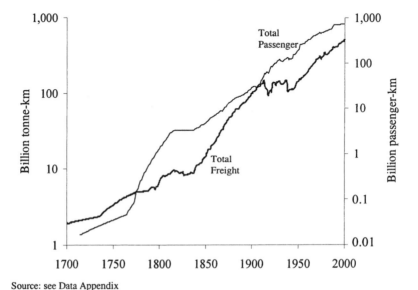

Source: see Data Appendix

Figure 6.21 The Use of Land, Sea and Air Freight and Passenger Transport Services, 1700–2000

The next revolution was the diffusion of the internal combustion engine. It was first the toy of the rich. After the First World War, however, demand from middle classes grew. Similarly, buses began to replace horses on shorter journeys and trains on medium distances. The flexibility the internal combustion engine offered was the main driver for a new demand. By the end of the twentieth century, the low marginal cost of the car travel had created a consumption of travel unimaginable even one hundred and certainly two hundred years ago.

Finally, the airplane also revolutionised transport in the twentieth century, providing much faster delivery for long distances. Again, this form of travel grew out of the demand for luxury and exotic destinations. Demand for air travel is still predominantly for leisure purposes, but prices have fallen to a level where long-distance tourism is available to most of the population. Consumption has grown considerably in the last twenty to thirty years, and is likely to continue further.

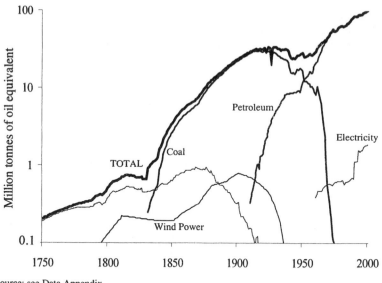

Source: see Data Appendix

Figure 6.22 Energy Use for All Transport Services, 1750–2000

11. CONCLUDING REMARKS

This chapter sought to present the cost and use of an energy service, transport, over the very long run. Fundamental were the investments in infrastructure, the adoptions of new transport technologies and the markets for energy sources. The shift from horses to railways to cars and sails to steamships to diesel engines dramatically transformed the nature, cost and use of transport services and, with them, the whole economy and society.

Creating a solid, reliable and effective infrastructure has been fundamental to driving down the cost of transport services. Historically, the investment on transport infrastructure has been important. Yet, there has been considerable fluctuation over time. While there was little evidence on the size of investments, it is clear that during the first half of the sixteenth century insufficient road maintenance was provided. Small, public institutions, the parishes, were expected to provide the public good, but were failing in their duty. The consequence was a declining quality of roads and a rise in the cost of moving people and goods.

It highlighted the inability of the existing institutions to provide all road infrastructures. This created a new set of institutions, turnpikes, which were private companies providing semi-public goods. They also could charge customers for the privilege of using the infrastructure, thus, they could build and maintain roads with new methods of financing.

By the mid-eighteenth century, the amount of investment on transport infrastructure was around £100 million (in 2000 prices), most of which was spent on parish roads. By 1800, the expenditure (in real terms) was only slightly higher, but now almost the same was spent on turnpikes and canals as on parish roads. By 1850, investment on these three types of infrastructure was almost double (Hawke and Higgins 1981 p.229). Furthermore, in 1850, expenditure on railways was triple that on other transport infrastructure. As an example of the scale of railway investment, in both 1846 and 1847, more than £2 billion was spent.

In addition to the financial investment, considerable energy mostly in the form of heating of iron was used to create the infrastructure. Thus, when considering the energy consumed on transport services, a large amount of energy has been embedded in the infrastructure.

The control of a strategic part of infrastructure created considerable economic power. Once they had built their route, the owners of turnpiked roads, canals or railroads generally faced little competition. Where they did, as the railway companies with stagecoaches or canals, they quickly were able to out-compete the incumbent. The control of a route enabled them to increase the price of using the particular route.

Consequently, the natural monopoly created by transport networks led itself particularly to capture of consumer surplus. Thus, the growth in transport services led to an increase in institutions specialised in capturing the benefits – from brigands, pirates to government tolls, from private turnpikes to railroad barons. Ultimately, all this capturing behaviour meant less benefit to the consumer and, in part, society – either due to a smaller consumer surplus, which benefited the 'prey' (but probably increased income and social inequality), or from lower levels of transportation (and in the case of freight, lower consumption), which was a loss to society.

In addition to the infrastructure, vehicles and vessels were fundamental to improving the services available. They provided the link between the infrastructure and the source of energy, as well as being the carrier. The cost of a vehicle had generally been a significant investment for a company and certainly a household. A horse and cart were many years of salary for the average family. Today, a car is a fraction of an average family's yearly salary. Consequently, there has been a major change in the number of people owning vehicles and, therefore, able to travel independently.

Yet, vehicle investments have been and still are large purchases. Once investment in a technology has been made, this mode of transport will probably be used for its lifespan. The bigger the investment and longer the lifespan, the greater was the tendency towards conservative decisions. And, the conservative customer was likely to follow the crowd. If a number of individuals bought a particular vehicle, it provided a signal to other potential customers about its value, thus raising its demand further. A successful stagecoach, car or airplane would breed more sales and increasing the likelihood of dominance as the main source of transport for a particular service.

The availability of cheap incumbent technology (or sources of energy) could lead to further lock-ins to old technologies. The rebirth of the demand for horses in the 1890s was a classic example of how one economy 'benefited' by acquiring cheap technology from another economy, because the latter had invested in new, 'superior' technology. However, the low cost locked Britain into the old and 'inferior' technology, while the USA's economy profited from having found a healthy market for its old technology and modernised its own technology.

Energy provided the power that moved the vehicle along the road or rail and the vessel along the water. For much of this story of transport services, the horse (on land) was the main source of mobile power. Undoubtedly, considerable sophistication in horse-breeding and selection of horses for appropriate tasks by the nineteenth century made it difficult to use a cheaper, more efficient source of power.

Yet, ultimately, the generation of heat for power became the choice for transport since the mid-nineteenth century. The use of fossil fuels, their declining price and increased efficiency, has enabled the cost of transport to fall dramatically and travel to grow to levels unimaginable even during the Industrial Revolution.

The appropriate combination of infrastructure, mode of transport and energy were required to provide transport services. Combinations have varied considerably through time. The most basic paths and rivers required a great deal of energy to move a load or a person. The development of better, turnpiked roads or canals enabled the horse pulling the load to double its efficiency. Safer seas allowed for new ship designs that could carry far greater loads. Thus, there was considerable substitution between factors of production of transport services.

In most cases, the very long run trend has been towards improving the infrastructure and the design of vehicles and vessels, and reducing the energy component per unit of transport service. One explanation is that energy expenditure was the main factor determining marginal cost. Each additional kilometre travelled costs directly, in terms of the expenditure on energy. On the other hand, the infrastructure and vehicle created fixed costs of transport. As the total number of kilometres travelled increased, these fixed costs per kilometre travel fell, enabling the transport system and users to invest in better infrastructure and vehicles. Thus, the incentive within the transport system was to drive down the energy input by improving infrastructure and vehicles and reduce the fixed costs by increasing the amount of transport. Thus, there was a drive towards always travelling cheaper and more.

The increased demand for passenger transport has resulted from the growing number of people and places wanted to visit. At a local level, expanding urban (and suburban) centres, commuting to work, and large and distant sources of produce have made people need to travel more on a daily basis. The amount of time spent travelling remained relatively unchanged since the beginning of urbanisation – the willingness to spend time travelling a constant.

At an international level, growing populations, opening-up of markets and borders, emigration of family and friends, expansion of companies, better means of communication and powerful mediums for selling the virtues of tourism and travel were some of the reasons for the growing demand. At the same time, the capacity for travel was expanding and the cost of travel was declining.

Where there was a new, cheaper transport technology, opportunities for cheaper travel emerged. Companies invested in the prospect of growing consumption. But, they also needed to advertise their goods and services, be they car manufacturers or airline companies. Demand for transport needed to grow to meet the supply.

Travel was inherently connected with ways of working and living. Experiences outside these ways were not of great interest and, therefore, rarely in people's imagination or wants. So, before transport technologies were introduced, there was generally not an important potential demand for these technologies.

In some cases, a potential demand for transport might have existed. The birth of canals providing cheap coal to cities that were not linked to mines by waterways is an example of demand for transport. This demand existed because these cities were aware that some regions benefited from waterway (that is, river) access and, therefore, the entrepreneurs of Liverpool and Manchester imagined the potential gains if they too were connected.

In most cases, however, demand for cheap travel was lacking. It is questionable whether the burgeoning middle classes in the seventeenth century anxiously awaited the arrival of regular passenger transport services on turnpiked roads. Instead, entrepreneurs probably took a gamble when setting up the London-Chester service. Once stagecoaches were introduced for certain routes, and the middle classes became aware of the benefits of meeting a potential client or visiting a 'distant' relative, demand grew. Thus, the take-off of this new technology – or others, such as the railway or the car – started with a very low, niche demand, and the entrepreneurs providing new services needed to create more demand – through driving people's imagination and wants and ensuring prices were low enough for the service to be part of their workstyle or lifestyle. Once this demand had been created and people had used the services sufficiently, people expected these services as part of their workstyle and lifestyle.

Transport was a service that moved people and goods around. The reason for travelling was to be in a new location – to work, to talk, to see. When transport costs were high, substitutes would be found for these objectives. Less flexible labour meant lower skilled workers were acceptable. When seeing someone in person was costly, more modest forms of communication were acceptable. Similarly, if distant goods were expensive to haul or ship, local alternatives were found – to eat, to work with, to entertain. Conversely, each time transport services were revolutionised, becoming cheaper and faster, life and work was transformed.

7. Lighting: Competing Technologies and New Energy Sources[14]

1. THE SEARCH FOR BETTER LIGHT

Over the last three centuries, industrialised societies have been freed from dependence on sun and moonlight for illumination: technological innovation, mass production of lighting appliances, expansion of energy infrastructures and networks, falling costs of fuels, rising incomes and social and cultural change have revolutionised our desire and ability to illuminate. Substantial economic welfare, resource and environmental consequences have flowed from these changes in lighting services.

The chapter starts by considering the process of illumination using candles. It then touches on the changes in price and use of candlelight resulting from technological developments and taxation during the eighteenth century. In the streets particularly, oil lamps tended to be used before the nineteenth century. Policies related to the expansion of street lighting are covered first, then the major role of gas in this process. This is followed by the development and growth of electricity for lighting. Finally, the trends in lighting prices and use over seven centuries are reviewed.

2. CANDLELIGHT BEFORE THE EIGHTEENTH CENTURY

Throughout history, light has been valued in households, in workshops, as well as in commercial and ecclesiastical buildings, in streets and along the coasts. Before the sixteenth century, lighting methods and costs are thought to have been broadly similar for indoor and outdoor technologies, except for the need to cover outdoor lights from wind and rain (O'Dea 1958). Apart from the central light generated by the fireplace for cooking and heating (see Chapter 4), up to the nineteenth century (Meadows 2001) candles provided the main source of artificial lighting in Britain.[15]

---

14. This chapter is a revised version of the paper co-authored with Peter Pearson and published as 'Seven centuries of energy services: the price and use of light in the United Kingdom (1300–2000)' *The Energy Journal* 27(1) 139-77. It was chosen for the *Campbell Watkins Award for Best Paper* in the journal in 2006.
15. Although in warmer climates oil lamps were preferred because candles tended to melt, in Britain

Most candles were made from tallow, or animal fat, which was relatively smoky and smelly compared with, say, the finer beeswax, which was too scarce and costly for all but the rich and the church. The relatively poor quality of tallow as a light source was illustrated in Robinson Crusoe (Defoe 1719, ch.5): "I was at a great loss for candles; as soon as ever it was dark, which was generally by seven o'clock, I was obliged to go to bed ... The only remedy I had was, that when I had killed a goat, I saved the tallow, and with a little dish of clay, which I baked in the sun, to which I added a wick of some oakum, I made me a lamp; and this gave me light, though not a clear steady light like a candle."

Many of the rural poor made their own form of candles, known as rushlight (Eveleigh 2003). They collected rushes (or pine splints where marshes and reeds were not accessible) and spent evenings stripping the reeds (except for a small strip to support the pithy centre) and dipping them in tallow, which was often gathered as a by-product from cooking meat. A home-made rushlight avoided the expense of purchasing tallow candles, as the (urban) poor tended to do, which led to possibly misplaced criticism from Gilbert White, who averred that the latter were "always the worst economists" (O'Dea 1958 p.42). A 50-60cm rushlight would burn with a clear light for between 45 minutes and an hour and, unlike tallow candles, did not need to be trimmed every quarter of an hour (Meadows 2001, Woodcock 2002). For every pound of rush, six pounds of animal fat was used; 1½ pounds of rushlight would last a family one year (O'Dea 1958, drawing on Gilbert White[16]).

Assuming that in 1300 a family would have generated light from a small wood fire (say, of 1 kg with an energy density of 12 MJ per kg), producing around 8 lumen-hours per day (Nordhaus 1997) and might have used the equivalent of 1½ pounds of tallow candles per year, generating around 150 lumen-hours per year, that is, about 0.4 lumen-hours per day, for a total of 8.4 lumen hours per day. In other words, this crude estimate suggests that, at the beginning of the fourteenth century, including light from wood fires, a household would have consumed around 3 000 lumen-hours[17] of artificial light per year.

In towns, in particular, wax and the cheaper tallow candles were also commercially produced and sold in the fourteenth century. Royal consent was granted for these activities in the second half of the fifteenth century (O'Dea 1958 p.38).[18]

---

this was rarely a problem – especially during the colder period between the fifteenth and nineteenth centuries (Anderson 1981).

16. This comes from Gilbert White's remarkable 1775 description of rushlight making, printed in 1789 in his Natural History of Selborne. His comment possibly ignores the costs that poor (urban) dwellers faced, in money and time, of obtaining rushes and tallow and preparing the rushlight. Eveleigh (2003 p.6) quotes William Cobbett's view that poor labourers often had little meat and hence surplus fat with which to make rushlights.

17. A lumen-hour is a measure of illumination. As a reference, one million lumen-hours is equivalent to a one hundred watt incandescent bulb burning for one hundred hours.

18. The craft guilds of tallow and wax chandlers enforced trade regulations and sought to advance their members' interests. Monier-Williams (1973) dates the first articles of the Tallow Chandlers of London back to 1300. He also describes periods of price and export control of tallow by the City of London, during the fourteenth to the sixteenth centuries.

From the fourteenth to the sixteenth centuries, there seems to have been a general decline in lighting price from tallow candles, which was likely to have stimulated consumption. Over that period, the cost of lighting approximately halved – from around £20 000 to £10 000 per million lumen-hours (see Figure 7.1).

Candle efficiency is thought to have improved at a modest rate (Bowers 1998), which for this analysis is assumed to be 0.1 percent per year – or about a 10 percent improvement every century. Tallow candles would have generated with an efficiency of about 15 lumen-hours per kWh at the beginning of the fourteenth century, and about 25 lumen-hours per kWh by the end of the eighteenth century (Nordhaus 1997).

The cost of lighting also depended on the cost of the main fuel source, tallow. Despite much regional variation, tallow candles fell over that five hundred year period from around 70 to 20 pence per kWh – probably associated with a decline in the cost of livestock (Thirsk 1978b). Candlelight seems to have been at its cheapest for several centuries between the 1530s and the 1560s (at the end of King Henry VIII's reign (1509–47) and the beginning of Queen Elizabeth I's reign (1558–1603)), averaging around £10 000 per million lumen-hours.

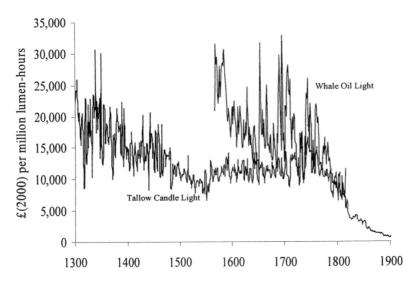

Source: see Data Appendix

Figure 7.1 Price of Lighting from Tallow Candles and Whale Oil (£(2000) per million lumen-hours), 1300–1900

This is likely to have encouraged rising levels of per capita consumption of artificial lighting. With a soaring GDP (see Figure 3.1), it was probably a time of growth in production and of great improvements in lighting standards. After the

1560s and up to the end of the seventeenth century, the cost of candle lighting stayed relatively constant, at about £12 000 per million lumen-hours. With rising population (from about five to about nine million people) and per capita real GDP (from about £600 to £850), the total use of lighting was likely to have risen further.

3. CANDLELIGHT IN THE EIGHTEENTH CENTURY

A Petition

From the Manufacturers of Candles, Tapers, Lanterns, Sicks, Street Lamps, Snuffers, and Extinguishers, and from Producers of Tallow, Oil, Resin, Alcohol, and Generally of Everything Connected with Lighting.

To the Honourable Members of the Chamber of Deputies.

Gentlemen:

You are on the right track. You reject abstract theories and little regard for abundance and low prices. You concern yourselves mainly with the fate of the producer. You wish to free him from foreign competition, that is, to reserve the domestic market for domestic industry.

We are suffering from the ruinous competition of a rival who apparently works under conditions so far superior to our own for the production of light that he is flooding the domestic market with it at an incredibly low price; for the moment he appears, our sales cease, all the consumers turn to him, and a branch of French industry whose ramifications are innumerable is all at once reduced to complete stagnation. This rival, which is none other than the sun, is waging war on us so mercilessly we suspect he is being stirred up against us by perfidious Albion (excellent diplomacy nowadays!), particularly because he has for that haughty island a respect that he does not show for us. [A reference to Britain's reputation as a foggy island].

We ask you to be so good as to pass a law requiring the closing of all windows, dormers, skylights, inside and outside shutters, curtains, casements, bull's-eyes, deadlights, and blinds —— in short, all openings, holes, chinks, and fissures through which the light of the sun is wont to enter houses, to the detriment of the fair industries with which, we are proud to say, we have endowed the country, a country that cannot, without betraying ingratitude, abandon us today to so unequal a combat.

Bastiat (1845 I.7.1)

Taxing Light

Frederic Bastiat's (1845) petition was directed towards the protection of industries in France. French candle-makers were not as fortunate as their British colleagues. As well as being subject to a great deal of fog (see Chapters 4 and 10), at least in towns and cities, in 1696 prosperous lovers of natural light faced the introduction of the Window Tax.

At the time, residents paid a tax of two shillings, four if they had between ten and twenty windows and eight if they had more than twenty windows in their house. In (2000) money, two shillings was equivalent to £8 for a house with less than ten windows, when the average annual income was nearly one thousand pounds – thus, about 1 percent of income. It was revised downwards in 1747, by which time smaller houses were exempt. It was intended to reflect the wealth of the inhabitants, as proxied by the number of windows in the house. Inevitably, it "operat[ed] as a tax on light, and a cause of deformity in buildings" (Mill 1909 p.3.27), but was retained until well into the nineteenth century. For most, though, windows remained a luxury until the end of the eighteenth century, creating a need for artificial light in the daytime (Woodcock 2002 p.4).

Moreover, at the beginning of the eighteenth century, in Queen Anne's reign (1702–14), a tax on candles (and other articles of general consumption) was proposed to help fund the war of Spanish Succession. Shortly after, some retailers raised candle prices by an amount equal to the proposed tax (suggesting a fairly price inelastic demand).

In 1709, the tax was actually imposed and the cost of lighting rose (Dowell 1965 p.307). A duty of 4 pence per pound was placed on wax candles and one-half of an old-penny on tallow candles, equivalent to a tax of about £1 000 for a million lumen-hours, or a 10 percent increase. This fed through into the (ten-year) average real price, which rose by nearly 50 percent between 1700 and the mid-1740s (see Figure 3.3).

The tax was followed by fairly heavy regulation – although households were allowed to make their own rushlights, as long as they were "not for sale, of small size, and only dipped once in or once drawn through grease..." (Dowell 1965 p.308). This change in relative prices may account for their apparent resurgence in poorer households during the eighteenth century (Woodcock 2002 p.4).

The tax was criticised by commentators, including Adam Smith (1776), on grounds of its regressive nature, its effect on the price of labour, its tendency to encourage fraudulent production of candles at the expense of honest chandlers, and the cost of regulation. The duty on candles was not fully repealed until 1830 (Dowell 1965 p.310).

Conveniently, the tax collection data provided a first indicator of national candlelight consumption (Mitchell 1988 p.398): in 1711, around 30 million pounds of tallow candles generated some 17 billion[19] lumen-hours (see Figure 7.2). Up to 1750, overall candlelight consumption appears to have changed little, however. There must have been considerable upward pressure on demand from a

---

19. Billion is 10^9 or one thousand million.

more than 20 percent rise in per capita income over that period. Nevertheless, since population rose by around 10 percent to 10 million, per capita lighting consumption seems likely to have fallen. With the window and candle taxes increasing the cost of natural and artificial light, the first half of the eighteenth century might be seen as another kind of 'dark age'.

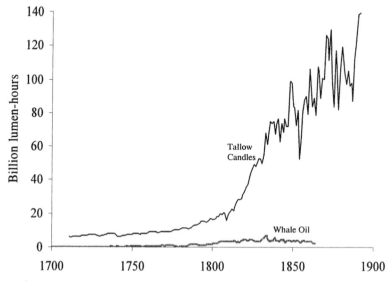

Source: see Data Appendix

Figure 7.2 Consumption of Lighting from Tallow Candles and Whale Oil (billion lumen-hours), 1711–1900

Developments in Candle Technology

It has been suggested that there was no improvement in the quality of lighting during the period of the candle tax, and considerable developments in technology once it was repealed in 1830 (Dowell 1960 p.310). It might be expected, however, that tax-induced price increases would create incentives to improve the efficiency of lighting provision.

Evidence suggests that the quality of candles did improve dramatically between the end of the eighteenth century and the mid-nineteenth century. Moulding processes and plaited wicks were developed and refined, which reduced the cost and improved the efficiency of candlelight provision (O'Dea 1958 p.54, Eveleigh 2003 p.19). These improvements meant that tallow candles in the 1830s could produce light with an efficiency of 75 lumen-hours per kWh compared with the 25 lumen-hours at the end of eighteenth century (Nordhaus 1997 p.36).

Across Europe, where similar taxes had been imposed, efforts were made to better understand the burning properties of fats. By 1840, the firm of Price's Candles were able to build on the French chemist Chevreuil's research on fatty acids, carried out in the 1820s in collaboration with Gay Lussac (Eveleigh 2003), to refine tallow and vegetable oils to produce a harder, pure white fat known as stearine; it made candles that burnt brightly with little smoke or smell (Newman 2003 p.12).

As a result of these technological improvements, the real price of candlelight fell from around £15 000 in 1760 to below £4 000 in the 1820s. Lighting use probably doubled to 15 billion lumen-hours in the second half of the eighteenth century (see Figure 7.2). With population rising by 50 percent between 1750 and 1800, this would represent a substantial increase in per capita consumption. By 1820, over 60 million pounds (or 27 000 tonnes) of tallow candles produced about 35 billion lumen-hours. Candles continued to be a main source of lighting up to the mid-nineteenth century and afterwards were valued as complements to other lighting methods.

4. OIL LAMPS BEFORE THE NINETEENTH CENTURY

Regulation on Street Lighting

The oil lamp was another important source of lighting services. Vegetable oils, principally colza oil from rapeseed, cabbage, kale and the root of the swede in Britain, were said to "burn exceedingly well" in lamps (Nash in BPP 1816 p.177). "Colza lamps provided the great link between the primitive form of teapot- and saucer-shaped lamps and the highly efficient paraffin lamps of the mid nineteenth century. They represented the application of mechanical ingenuity to the provision of better domestic lighting, for the oil lamp as an efficient means of lighting really dates from the end of the eighteenth century" (Meadows 2001 p.7). However, colza oil was at times of limited availability for lighting, because its main use was for cleaning good quality wool and consumption depended on the larger market for textiles (see Chapters 4 and 5). It was used mostly indoors because it tended to congeal in cold weather (Mellish in BPP 1816 p.189).

The most basic lighting oil was fish oil, particularly cheap in coastal areas. When the candle tax was introduced, households were only allowed to use oil lamps if they were fuelled by 'fish' oil. The smell and bad quality of illumination meant it was a poor-person's fuel, however.

Whale oil represented an improvement on fish oil – and since whales were thought to be fish, the candle tax regulation did not prohibit its use (Jackson 1976 p.20). Oil from the right whale was a common source of lighting from the sixteenth century.

From the eighteenth century until the early nineteenth century, oil from sperm whales was the product of choice for lamps, because of its better quality illumination, although it never provided more than half of the lighting associated with whales. Sperm oil was used almost exclusively for illumination. In addition to the oil, spermaceti wax, found in this whale's brain cavity, was made into candles that gave light that was better than that from traditional tallow candles – and equivalent to but less costly than that from beeswax candles.

As with candles, demand for all forms of lighting had been rising since the fourteenth century. Greater household wealth demanded better ways of keeping active after sunset (Jackson 1976 p.56). Mechanisation and growth of the textile industry created a need for lighting to extend factory working hours. And urbanisation, as many left the countryside, called for improvements in street lighting, mainly to enhance public safety.

The illumination of town and city streets, and other public space, became an important driver for technological and institutional change. In the first decades of the fifteenth century, town lighting regulations began to be introduced, requiring certain citizens, such as innkeepers, to place a 'lanthorn' in front of their doors. This probably also reflected a decline in the cost of lighting in the early 1400s, which would have made such regulations less onerous than before.

In 1599, in what Monier-Williams (1973 p. 87) calls "a landmark in the history of street lighting", an Act of Common Council required every householder in the City of London, "from the first day of October until the first day of March to cause a good and substantial lanthorn and a candle ... to be hanged without their doors ... every night when the moon shall be dark." Over the decade, many towns and cities introduced regulation requiring all (non-poor) citizens on main roads to provide light in front of their buildings (Falkus 1976 p.252, Monier-Williams 1973 p.79). This remained the main basis for regulating street lighting until the end of the seventeenth century. As the rate of urbanisation increased (for example, London's population had grown two and a half times during the seventeenth century), lighting became increasingly seen as one of the basic amenities that local authorities should be responsible for providing.

Table 7.1 Street Lighting in London, 1599–1809

	Pre 1599	1599– 1662	1662– 1694	1694– 1736	By 1736	By 1750	By 1809
Hours per year	189	303	351	750	4 000	4 000	4 000
Lamps				1 000	4 800	15 000	35 000

Source: Falkus (1976 p.261)

Throughout the seventeenth century there was a shift towards oil lamps for street lighting, especially after major reductions in the cost of whale oil throughout the century and efficiency improvements in the 1680s. Despite great volatility, the price of whale oil lighting fell from more than £25 000 per million lumen-hours in the sixteenth century to between £10 000 and £15 000 in the mid-eighteenth century (see Figure 7.1).

Many of the larger, higher quality oil lamps for street lighting were too expensive for private supply, and contractors began to take responsibility for supplying lighting services in London. Fierce competition existed between lighting entrepreneurs (Monier-Williams 1973). Their initial success in improving street lighting led to many towns around the country following London's example. By the early eighteenth century, most towns had companies responsible for supplying streetlight (Falkus 1976 p.257).

In the first few decades of the eighteenth century, to cover the expenses and fund extra lighting, towns across Britain started raising lighting rates more systematically. By 1736, parts of London had lighting 365 days a year. Despite attempts by the Company of Tallow Chandlers, particularly in the 1680s and 1690s, to prevent competition from new lamps, such as the lamp with a convex (bulls eye) lens patented in 1684 (Monier-Williams 1973), lighting companies invested in many new lamps (see Table 7.1). In the second half of the eighteenth century, most important towns adopted Improvement Commissions responsible for a standard supply of public amenities. Street lighting improved substantially in this period, although the level of illumination was poor compared with later periods (Falkus 1976).

Protection of the British Whale Oil Industry

Given the growing importance of street lighting, efforts were made to develop a national industry that could ensure a secure supply of fuel. As early as 1673, a protectionist British government imposed a nine pound per ton tax on Dutch imported whale oil, when the price per ton was about twenty-one pounds (£2 100 in year 2000 money, and equivalent to £16 000 per million lumen-hours).

Shortly afterwards, an infant British Colonial (mainly North American) whaling industry flourished, supplying most of the British demand for whale oil. By the 1720s this industry's heavy whaling activity drove the price down to seven pounds per ton (Jackson 1976 p.51). However, this soon led to a shortage of coastal whale stocks and higher prices, creating a demand for larger whalers seeking stocks further afield.

In 1732, the government introduced a key incentive for the whaling industry, a bounty of 30 shillings per ton of the vessel's weight for every voyage of an appropriately qualified ship – evidence of the growing dependence on oil imports and concern about supply shortages. In 1749 the bounty was raised to 40 shillings (£200 per tonne in (2000) money). The payments were lowered after 1790 and abolished in 1824 (Barrow 2001).

In the 1750s hostilities between the British and the French over North American territories interrupted the supply routes to English ports, creating further opportunities for a British whaling industry. But, when Franco-British hostilities ended in 1763, the Colonists again became for a few years the main whale oil suppliers. The War of American Independence (1775–83) came at a price to the whalers, now paying a heavy import duty on what had become foreign rather than colonial products. John Adams, the future second president of the United States, lobbied the British Government: "... you prefer darkness, consequent robberies, burglaries and murders in your streets, to the receiving, as a remittance, our spermaceti oil" (Jackson 1976 p.70). The lights did not go out completely, however, since many of the main whaling families moved to England.

Yet, consumption patterns were closely influenced by the political interruptions and influences, and by industrial developments. In 1750, around 370 million lumen-hours were generated from about 3 000 tonnes of sperm and other whale oil; and while other whale oil made up nine-tenths of this total, sperm oil was about twice as effective in providing illumination. By 1774, the oils (30 percent from sperm oil) generated nearly three times as much, just over one billion lumen-hours. In 1781, lighting from sperm and other whale oils fell back to less than 300 million lumen-hours, perhaps leaving the streets in some darkness, as John Adams had predicted. Once hostilities ceased though, sperm and other whale oil imports resurged, with light output reaching more than 1.8 billion lumen-hours by the late 1780s.

The growth in lighting was the result of increased supplies of oil at declining prices and major efficiency gains in energy conversion. Improvements in oil lamp technology from the 1770s included Leger's 1783 invention in Paris of the flat-wick lamp, the Swiss chemist Argand's 1780–84 invention of the Argand lamp, with its round tubular wick with a hollow centre, giving a double air supply from inside and outside, a chimney placed over the flame for better aeration and a mechanism for raising and lowering the wick, and then the 'bird-fountain' feed, which ensured that there was always the same level of oil in the reservoir, providing a better supply to the wick (O'Dea 1958 p.40, Meadows 2001).

These improvements doubled and, eventually with refinements, tripled the efficiency of oil lamps. As a result, the price of lighting from lamps fell substantially over that period, from about £15 000 per million lumen-hours in 1750 to around £5 000 by 1820. After a sluggish end of the eighteenth century, with consumption at about 1.7 billion lumen-hours, the trend in consumption reverted upwards, rising to about 3.4 billion lumen-hours in 1805 and 4.7 billion lumen-hours by 1820 – around 8 percent of overall lighting. By then candles provided less than 60 percent of lighting. Thus, already, about one-third of lighting was provided by a new source of energy, gas.

5. LIGHT IN THE GAS ERA (1820-1920)

The Expansion of the Gas Network

In 1800, an average family generated just under 50 000 lumen-hours of light per year, although most of this would still be a valued by-product of cooking and heating, rather than an energy service sought directly. This estimate was founded on the assumptions: (a) in 1800 domestic consumption of coal was about 5.6 million tonnes and the population was about 16 million (or roughly 4 million households) – hence the average family might have used 1.4 tonnes of coal per year (with an energy density double that of wood and the same lumen-hours per watt) and, therefore, generated about 45 000 lumen-hours per year (or 120 lumen-hours per night) from coal fires (see Chapter 4); and (b) an estimated national consumption of artificial light of around 20 billion lumen-hours from other sources, of which half (following the domestic sector's share of total coal consumption at the time) was consumed by the domestic sector, then each household might have generated 2 500 lumen-hours. Adding these together, an average household would have generated around 47 500 lumen-hours of light.

Up to the latter part of the eighteenth century, the active production of artificial light was based on relatively primitive fuels and technologies, mainly tallow candles and fairly basic oil lamps. These technologies required frequent manual re-stocking and were awkward. Oil lamps smoked in draughts, were difficult to supply with the correct rate of fuel, and would smell bad when cheaper oils were used (Bowers 1998). Candles required frequent wick trimming to avoid smoking and guttering, which tended to generate sparks.

The threat of fires and economic loss was constant. For instance, The Great Fire of London in 1666, which was meant to have been caused by a lantern knocked-over, led to an enormous amount of damage. The economic cost was estimated at over £900 million in 2000 currency. 13 200 homes were lost – equivalent to £350 million in lost rent. Public buildings were destroyed, many goods were moved, and many goods were destroyed or looted – each of which was estimated at around £180 million. The number of human (and animal) lives lost is unknown (Tinniswood 2003). In time, factories developed safety regulations, took out insurance policies and frequently kept their own fire engines (Falkus 1982 p.220).

Increasing demand for higher-quality lighting, as well as dissatisfaction with existing technologies, had generated a large body of research into developing better illumination (Falkus 1967). From the 1770s, the Royal Society handed out many prizes and awards for lighting improvements. Similarly, the number of lighting patents rose dramatically, 14 in the 1790s and 29 the next decade (Falkus 1982 p.218).

And, when the by-products of the coking process were used for lighting, the Times claimed that "there is nothing so important to the British Realm, since that of Navigation, ...[as] the grand discovery of the Gas Lights" (quoted in Falkus 1982 p.226). William Murdoch lit the Soho works of Boulton and Watt with gas in 1803, with a light equivalent of 2 500 tallow candles, at relative costs said to be about £600 per year for gas and £2 200-3 000 for candles (Gledhill 1999 p.6).

In 1812, Frederick Winsor's Gas Light and Coke Company received the first charter to supply parts of London and, after eighteen months of errors in equipment investment and design, the market for gas lighting grew quickly as prices fell. In 1820, gas lighting cost around £3 000 per million lumen-hours. By 1840, it had fallen to £1 300 and then, by 1850, to about £500 per million lumen-hours (see Figure 7.3).

The dramatic price decline was to generate the first of three phases in the demand. Gas lighting rose ten-fold – from around 25 billion lumen-hours in 1820 to 250 billion in 1850 (see Figure 7.4). The growing wealth and associated desire for comfort, the accelerating industrialisation and the increased urbanisation of Britain were factors driving the demand. Initial demand was for public street lighting, commercial establishments (especially shops), and some wealthy households. By the 1840s, middle class families were starting to use gas in their homes (Williams 1981).

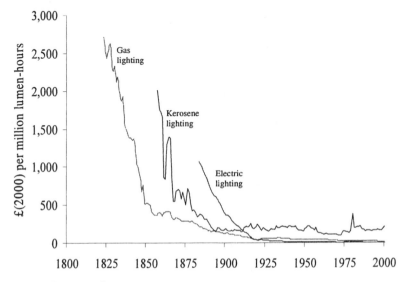

Source: see Data Appendix

Figure 7.3 Price of Lighting from Gas, Kerosene and Electricity (£(2000) per million lumen-hours), 1820–2000

In the mid-nineteenth century, the demand for all forms of lighting was growing. Candles and oil lamps continued to be the main source of illumination for many, particularly poorer households, as they could not afford the infrastructure costs required for gas use. The dramatic improvements in tallow candles, generating about 75 lumen-hours per kWh, meant that candlelight had become much cheaper – with costs nearly halving between 1800 and 1830 to £4 000 per lumen-hour (see Figure 7.1).

Price's Candle Company, established in 1830, grew rapidly, particularly after its new 'composite' candles, made from a mixture of refined tallow (stearine) and coconut oil, and enhanced by plaited wicks, were widely used to celebrate the eve of Queen Victoria's wedding to Prince Albert in 1840 (Eveleigh 2003, Newman 2003). Throughout most of the second half of the nineteenth century, candlelight cost less than £1 500 per million lumen-hours.

Despite the competition, candlelight consumption increased from 20 billion lumen-hours in 1800 to 75 billion lumen-hours in 1830 and, at times in the second half of the nineteenth century, it rose to nearly 100 billion lumen-hours (see Figure 7.4). While it had lost much of its share of the market to gas (77 percent) by 1850, it still provided more than one-fifth of the lighting in the United Kingdom.

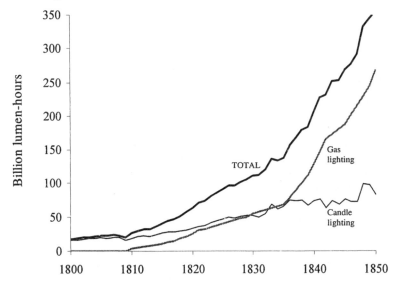

Source: see Data Appendix

Figure 7.4 Consumption of Lighting from Gas and Tallow Candles (Billion lumen-hours), 1800–1850

The Birth of the Oil Industry

Reichenbach and Christison had both discovered paraffin (that is, kerosene) and its properties in 1830. A Scot, James Young, then devised a process for extracting oil from "cannel coal" (now thought to be oil shale): filing his patent in 1850, he used the word "cracking" to describe the splitting of the oil into its component substances, one of which was kerosene (Meadows 2001 p. 10).

In the nineteenth century, the main petroleum product for the consumer was kerosene for lighting. Given the high substitutability between candles and different oils for lighting, because the capital costs were so low, consumers were highly sensitive to price variability. With a rising average income level in the second half of the nineteenth century, the demand for kerosene was potentially very high. The key problems for the petroleum industry and the consumer were the price volatility and the varying quality, which could have explosive consequences. Thus, kerosene demand grew slowly at first (Yergin 1991).

The discovery of oil in Burma in 1854 and Drake's Well in Pennsylvania in 1859 heralded a new phase in the history of energy. It started modestly, however, in the market for lighting, mostly for poorer households unable to afford the costs of installing gas. The growth of the petroleum industry from the 1860s signalled the abundant availability of a lighting fuel that required little equipment and infrastructure (Yergin 1991 p. 22).

Throughout the 1870s and 1880s numerous oil fields were discovered, in Texas and in Russia, increasing supply and putting downward pressure on prices. The evolution of petroleum industry was exemplified by one of its founding fathers. In the 1860s, John D. Rockfeller, who owned an oil refinery firm, observed the damaging effects of price volatility and poor kerosene quality on both the producer and the consumer. As other refineries went bankrupt, he would buy-up the available capital at low costs. Rapidly, he owned a large proportion of the refinery business in the Midwest of the United States. With a control over much of the supply of kerosene, he reduced output and raised prices, earning substantial profits and offering the consumer some price stability (Yergin 1991).

Another of Rockfeller's strategies was to enter the market for kerosene distribution directly to the consumer. His refineries would supply his distribution outlets at a lower price than to his rivals' shops. His shops, therefore, faced lower marginal costs than his rivals. To reduce the consumers' uncertainty about the products being bought, Rockfeller guaranteed an oil of a fixed quality – a 'standard' oil. His product, which was sold in its famous blue tin can, was rapidly being differentiated from other kerosene. The demand for his product grew substantially in the 1880s and 1890s. A differentiated product enabled him to raise prices a little further and earn more profits. These lower average costs for its refineries, lower marginal costs for his shops and a differentiated, quality product for the consumer meant that Rockfeller could watch his competitors either become part of the Standard Oil Company or fall out of the market. He had created a natural monopoly through his control of the inputs of production (Yergin 1991).

In the 1860s, the price of lighting oil lamps using kerosene was more than £1 500 per million lumen-hours (see Figure 7.3). Eighty patents a year relating to oil lamps were applied for between 1859 and 1870 (Meadows 2001 p.12). From the 1870s, kerosene, which was cleaner and cheaper than colza oil, became the main fuel for lamps; "by 1846 colza oil was only a third of the cost of sperm oil and the latter became obsolete" (Meadows 2001 p.18).

The rapid expansion of the petroleum industry described above drove down prices. By 1870, £500 worth of kerosene would generate one million lumen-hours, while by 1900 the cost had fallen to around £200. Consumption responded accordingly. In 1870, kerosene lamps, with a lighting efficiency of about 159 lumen-hours per kWh, generated about 3.3 billion lumen-hours. The following decade saw a six-fold increase to nearly 20 billion lumen-hours. It tripled throughout the 1880s and then more than doubled in the 1890s, as it reached over 1.5 trillion[20] lumen hours in 1900 (see Figure 7.5).

---

20. Trillion is 10^{12} or one million million

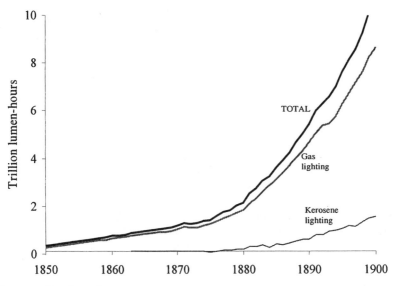

Source: see Data Appendix

Figure 7.5 Consumption of Lighting from Gas and Kerosene (trillion lumen-hours), 1850–1900

Refinements in Gas-Lighting Technology

Despite the threat of kerosene's growth, capturing 14 percent of the lighting market in 1900, the gas-lighting industry was to show its resilience, taking an 81 percent share in 1900. After 1850, gas prices were initially stable with even a slight increase in the mid-1860s. Then lighting costs began to fall again – to about £270 per million lumen-hours by 1880, £170 by 1890 and just over £125 by 1900 (see Figure 7.3).

While the price of gas as a fuel changed little through the second half of the century, gas lighting efficiency tripled after the introduction of the incandescent mantle (Nordhaus 1997). This was invented in the 1880s by Carl Auer von Welsbach, using chemical substances (eventually thorium and cerium oxides) to create a mantle that would fit around the flame from Bunsen's aerated gas burner. Gledhill (1999 p. 14) suggests that it was the appearance of electric light in the 1870s that offered the incentive to improve gas light through enhanced incandescence.[21] He remarks on the rapid uptake of incandescent burners in Britain: the numbers sold grew from 20 000 in 1893, to 105 000 in 1894 and then tripled to 300 000 in 1895.

---

21. This is effectively a suggestion of a 'sailing-ship' effect (where an incumbent technology, threatened by a new technology, improves dramatically (see Chapter 6, Geels (2002) and Schivelbush (1988)).

Gaslight consumption grew dramatically in the second half of the nineteenth century. Because demand was mostly non-industrial, it was less vulnerable to fluctuations induced by business cycles. In every decade of the second half of the nineteenth century, growth always averaged more than 60 percent. In the 1850s, consumption grew by 140 percent and, in the 1880s, by 156 percent. In 1850, an estimated 267 billion lumen-hours of light were produced. By 1900, it had increased to 8.65 trillion lumen-hours, a 32-fold rise at an average annual growth rate of over 12 percent from 1850 (see Figure 7.5).

Once again, declining cost was central to the major switch towards gas but was not the only factor. By the turn of the century, working class living standards had improved substantially, and with them demands for better quality lighting. Also, the introduction of the 'coin in the slot' meter attracted many new customers, as they did not have to pay for the installation costs (which the gas companies covered in return for higher prices). First used in London in 1893, by 1914 two-thirds of customers used it. In that time, the London Gas Company's customers quadrupled from fewer than 300 000 to over 1 280 000, representing most of London's households (Matthews 1986).

6. THE EXPANSION OF ELECTRIC LIGHTING

Technological Competition

The dominance of gas in the lighting market at the turn of the century was already under threat from the next technological revolution. Electricity had shown promise since the eighteenth century, and Humphrey Davy demonstrated the electric arc at the Royal Institution in London in 1810 (Bright 1949 p.22).

However, lighting applications only began to be commercialised in the mid-nineteenth century. Arc lighting was used increasingly from the late 1860s for illuminating large areas, like markets, stations, stadiums and lighthouses (Bright 1949 p.29). For example, Crompton imported Gramme generators and arc lights from Paris, developed improved arc lamps and in 1879 illuminated the Henley Regatta and the grounds of Alexandra Palace with them (Bowers 1969 p.20). Arc lighting had large economies of scale but was impractical for indoor lighting, especially in dwellings.

Much innovative effort went into "subdividing the electric light" (Bright 1949 p.34, 58) in a way that enabled individual control of the lights, a task that many eminent electrical engineers thought impossible (Byatt 1979 p.15). In the late 1870s, Swan, in the United Kingdom, and Edison, in the USA, led the field of inventors working on incandescent lamps. They succeeded in patenting the incandescent light bulb.

With subsequent developments in generation and transmission, it enabled electricity to brighten up shops, offices and homes (O'Dea 1958). Crompton and Swan joined forces in 1880, to make lamps, lamp fittings and generators, and in

1882 made the first major installation of incandescent lighting in England, at the Law Courts in London (Bowers 1969 p.22, Byatt 1979 p.16).

In spite of early difficulties with public supply (Hannah 1979 p.6), by 1888, more than 80 private companies and local authorities were supplying electricity; and by the mid-1890s most towns had an electricity supplier. By the end of 1903, only two towns of more than 100 000 people lacked a supply, although even as late as 1910, only a small proportion of houses were lit by electricity (Byatt 1979 p.25).

Electricity prices fell from around £2 per kWh in 1883 to just over £1.15 by 1900. Lack of storage capabilities, however, forced companies to keep a reserve capacity for unexpected surges in demand and to limit the frequency of 'black-outs'. So, despite the introduction of off-peak pricing in 1900, the need for reserve capacity kept upward pressure on the price of electricity. Nevertheless, prices continued to fall to £0.70 per kWh in 1910 and £0.20 per kWh in 1920.

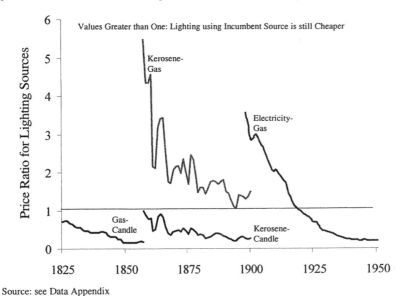

Source: see Data Appendix

Figure 7.6 Price Ratio of Lighting from Competing Energy Sources, 1825–1950

Meanwhile, the efficiency of electric lamps was improving. In 1879, the carbon filament lamp generated less than 2 000 lumen-hours per kWh. By 1897, efficiency had more than tripled to 7 000 lumen-hours per kWh, with the introduction of the osmium filament lamp, and over 10 000 lumen-hours per kWh when gas-filled tungsten lamps were invented in 1913 (O'Dea 1958).

Declining energy prices and rising technical efficiency led to a dramatic fall in the costs of electric lighting services. Starting in the mid-1880s, from over £1 000 per million lumen-hours, which was four times more expensive than gaslight, the cost of electric lighting dropped to about £360 by 1900 (see Figure 7.3). The decline continued down to £180 in 1910 and below £35 by 1920 – less than one-twentieth of what it had been thirty years before. By then, in cost terms, after nearly four decades incandescent electric lighting had finally caught up with gas lighting, as Figure 7.6 shows.

And electric lighting companies had been chasing a moving target. At the beginning of the twentieth century, the gas lighting industry had also achieved major improvements: refinements associated with the gas mantle meant that, compared with lamps from the 1880s, by 1920 three times as much light could be generated from the same amount of gas, and until then gas managed to out-compete electricity. The cost of gas lighting had fallen from £125 per million lumen-hours in 1900 to £35 in 1920 (see Figure 7.7). Gas lighting consumption peaked at over 20 trillion lumen-hours in 1920 (see Figure 7.8).

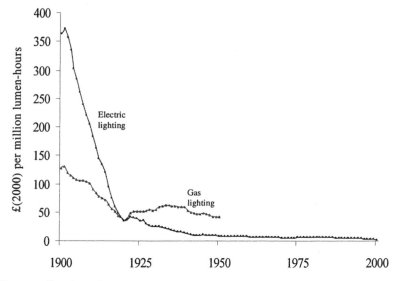

Source: see Data Appendix

Figure 7.7 Price of Lighting from Gas and Electricity (£(2000) per million lumen-hours), 1900–2000

Initially, the demand for electric lighting was in streets and other outdoor locations. In 1895, consumption was about 45 billion lumen hours, which was less illumination than was generated from candles. Consumption increased more than five-fold in five years, seven-fold in the first decade of the twentieth century, and then just over three-fold in the second decade, to 6 trillion lumen-hours by 1920 (see Figure 7.8). This was nearly a third of the consumption of lighting from gas. And, yet, by as late as 1919, only around 6 percent of households were wired to an electricity supplier (Jones 1989 p.89).

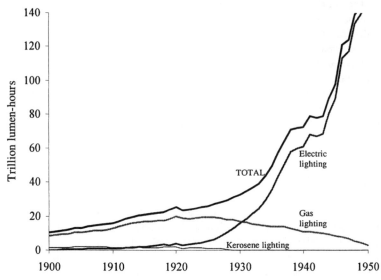

Source: see Data Appendix

Figure 7.8 Consumption of Lighting from Gas and Electricity (trillion lumen-hours), 1900–1950

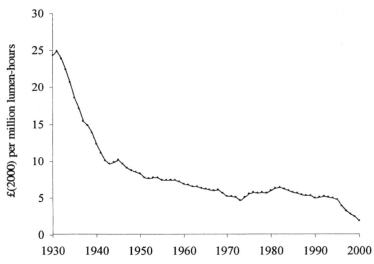

Source: see Data Appendix

Figure 7.9 Price of Lighting from Electricity (£(2000) per million lumen-hours), 1930–2000

The industry was severely affected by a lack of coordination, with many companies using different voltages and frequencies. Better coordination would enable companies to link up their distribution networks, minimising the extra reserve capacity required – since the likelihood that all areas connected suffer unexpected surges in demand at the same time fell as the number of connected areas increased. In 1933, the National Grid was completed, saving electricity suppliers substantial capital, fuel and running costs. These savings led to another drop in prices (see Figure 7.9). Falling prices from 1933 to 1942, coupled with the mass production of electrical appliances, increased the demand for electricity. By 1938, two-thirds of United Kingdom houses had electricity supply, consuming nearly 100 trillion lumen-hours.

Post-War Expansion

Low electricity prices, coal shortages and cold weather after the Second World War helped electricity consumption to rise to three times higher in 1948 than it had been in 1938. The government was catalysed into nationalising electricity production and supply (see Chapter 5). In April 1948, the 200 companies and 369 local authority undertakings, along with the Central Electricity Board and almost 300 power stations, were transferred to the new British Electricity Authority (Hannah 1982 p. 7).

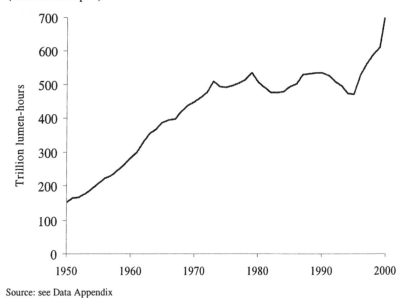

Source: see Data Appendix

Figure 7.10 Consumption of Lighting from Electricity (trillion lumen-hours), 1950–2000

The period up to the first oil shock of 1973–74 saw declining costs of electric lighting. With minimal improvements in incandescent light bulb efficiency (now around 12 000 lumen-hours per kWh) but increased commercial and industrial use of fluorescent tubes, there were major increases in the consumption of light – from 200 trillion lumen-hours in 1945 to 1 000 trillion in 1973 (see Figure 7.10).

From 1973 to 1995, there was no increase in consumption – and only a little cyclical fluctuation. Then, since the advent of compact fluorescent lights (CFL), which in the early 1990s produced 62 000 lumen-hours per kWh, and the decline in electricity prices that gradually fed through from the liberalisation and re-regulation of the electricity supply industry in 1990, the amount of light provided started rising once again. By the late 1990s it was estimated that the average household in the United Kingdom used 720 kWh on lighting – over 10 million lumen-hours – per year (Palmer and Boardman 1998).

8. LONG-RUN TRENDS IN LIGHTING

Figures 7.11 and 7.12 show a relatively modest decline in price of lighting fuels (in pence (2000) per kWh) and proportionately smaller increase in efficiency of lighting appliances (in lumen-hours per kWh) between the sixteenth and the eighteenth centuries. The price of lighting fuels (associated with the shifts from tallow candles to oil, gas and then electricity) fell considerably in the second half of the nineteenth century, and then rose (from the use of high-value electricity, which also had a high initial price) and fell in the twentieth century.

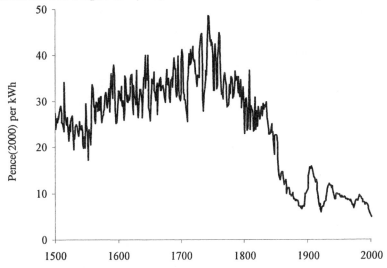

Source: see Data Appendix

Figure 7.11 Average Price of Lighting Fuels (pence (2000) per kWh), 1500–2000

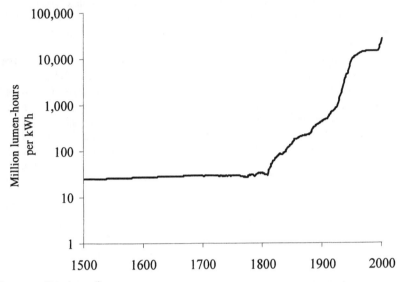

Source: see Data Appendix

Figure 7.12 Average Lighting Efficiency (million lumen-hours per kWh), 1500–2000

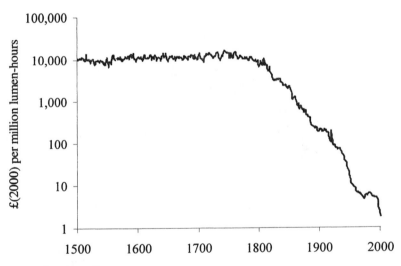

Source: see Data Appendix

Figure 7.13 Average Price of Lighting (£(2000) per million lumen-hours), 1500–2000

There are, however, dramatic improvements in efficiency in the nineteenth century (fourteen-fold) and the twentieth century (nearly seventy-fold), indicating the major role played by technological and institutional innovation, especially over the first fifty years of the twentieth century. The shift to electricity at the beginning of the twentieth century supports the argument that while the average price of energy can rise, the consumer can still benefit, as long as improvements in energy conversion continue to reduce the price and/or enhance the quality of energy services.

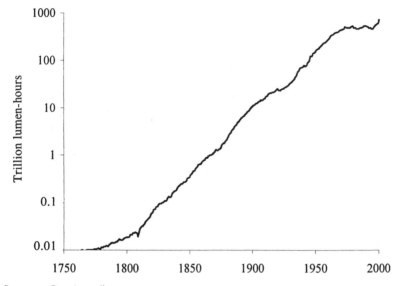

Source: see Data Appendix

Figure 7.14 Consumption of Lighting (trillion lumen-hours), 1750–2000

Combined together, the fuel price and the efficiency series provide an indicator of the price of lighting services (in £(2000) per million lumen-hours). As Figure 7.13 indicates, by 1800, lighting (costing about £6 600 per million lumen-hours) cost one-sixth of what it had in 1300. But by 1900 it cost one twenty-fifth of what it had cost in 1800 – and by 2000 the cost of lighting in the United Kingdom was £1.7 per million lumen-hours – one one-hundred and sixtieth of what it had been in 1900.

As show in Figure 7.14, the consumption of lighting grew rapidly throughout the nineteenth century, hardly surprising given the significant decline in both fuel prices and rise in efficiency of lighting. The price of lighting continued to fall in the twentieth century, mostly due to the decline in electricity prices, and consumption followed, although at a slightly slower rate than during the previous century. Lighting prices stabilised in the 1970s, and so did consumption. Consumption was revitalised by the introduction of CFL in the 1990s.

9. CONCLUDING REMARKS

The history of artificial lighting in the United Kingdom illustrates the kinds of dramatic and often surprising improvements that can be achieved in energy services – and that are likely to continue to flow from ongoing and future developments in lighting and associated technologies. As Grübler et al. (1999) have shown, explorations of historical patterns are central to anticipating developments in future energy systems and their environmental impact. This study of artificial lighting corroborates their conclusions: (i) accumulated experience and learning of technologies creates reductions in cost and improvements in performance; (ii) there are regular patterns of technological competition; and (iii) synergies lead clusters of technologies and infrastructures to co-evolve. The evolution of lighting markets certainly saw both the rapid emergence of new technologies (benefiting from accumulated experience in niche markets and synergies with other technologies) and the dominance – and sometimes lock-in – of incumbent technologies for long periods.

One lesson, as we have suggested, is that using past trends to anticipate future developments is risky: it might be appropriate, if we are in a period of technological and infrastructure lock-ins, or misguided, if new technologies, fuels and synergies are being or are likely to be discovered. The evolution of markets for lighting services seems to have experienced a number of 'punctuated equilibria' (Gould 2002). Rather than a continually and gradually changing system, periods of stability were disrupted by dramatic transformations, resulting from major innovations in energy and/or technology markets and their associated institutions.

Indeed, it can be suggested that we have seen four distinct revolutions in lighting services. The first occurred in the second half of the eighteenth century. Between 1750 and 1800, the price of lighting halved, as the cost of candles and oil fell and the lighting technologies improved. These changes resulted from a combination of changing supply-side factors, such as production technologies and methods, and rising demand, due to rising income and other influences, in the context of expanding markets. Lighting consumption (mostly from tallow candles, as well as whale and vegetable oil) rose six-fold in this period.

The second revolution (between about 1810 and 1850), associated with the introduction of gas lighting, left the price of lighting eight times lower. Consumption rose twelve-fold. By the mid-nineteenth century, gas made from the coking of coal produced three-quarters of United Kingdom lighting. The third revolution (from 1860 to 1900) resulted from the second wave of gas and the expansion of kerosene markets. The cost of lighting fell six-fold. These developments were of considerable benefit to the middle and lower classes, respectively, and represent a kind of 'democratisation' of access to relatively affordable artificial lighting. Consumption increased twelve-fold. By the end of the nineteenth century, gas provided around four-fifths (82 percent) and kerosene one-sixth (15 percent) of lighting services in the United Kingdom. The fourth revolution (from about 1920 to 1950) saw the large-scale introduction of electricity. Prices fell twenty-fold, and consumption rose ten-fold. At the beginning of this phase, gas provided 80 percent of the lighting in the United Kingdom but, by the end, electricity generated 99 percent.

Table 7.3 shows the changes in the lighting sources over time, as well as their efficiencies. It indicates how energy sources that were virtually not in use, then became the dominant source in less than fifty years. Thus, energy technologies and systems that seemed eternal, to those living at the time, could be replaced in a few decades. One might wonder about the next revolution in lighting services. While compact fluorescent lighting (CFL) is in the process of reducing the costs of illumination again, another revolution will come. And, when it comes, possibly from solid state lighting technologies, such as Light Emitting Diodes (LED), Organic Light Emitting Diodes (OLED) and other developments, we can expect dramatic declines in the price of lighting services (US Department of Energy 2003, *The Economist* 2002). Based on past evidence, new technologies and falling prices provide an opportunity for dramatically increased current uses of lighting, for finding creative new uses, for redefining the lighting experience (and standards), and for becoming increasingly wasteful. We can expect similar although not identical revolutions in other energy services.

Table 7.2 Percentage Share (Sh) and Average Efficiency (Eff)* of Lighting in the United Kingdom, by Sources**, 1700–2000

	Candles		Whale Oil		Gas		Kerosene		Electricity	
	Sh	Eff	Sh	Eff	Sh	Eff	Sh	Eff	Sh	Eff
1700	99%	28	1%	20						
1750	95%	29	5%	21						
1800	90%	37	10%	56		68				
1850	21%	76	1%	76	78%	186		112		
1900	1%	80			82%	497	15%	246	2%	1 310
1950					1%	887			99%	11 660
2000									100%	25 000

Notes

* Efficiency is presented in lumen-hours per kWh.

** These estimates ignore the proportion provided by fish and vegetable oil, and from indirect sources, such as cooking and heating fires.

Source: see Data Appendix

In homes and businesses before the nineteenth century, people lived and worked to the rhythms of the sun and moon. Cheaper lighting – and greater wealth – were opportunities to 'lengthen the day' both in the factory and in the kitchen (Bowers 1998). Improvements in access to and in the affordability and quality of lighting transformed the economy and society – longer and safer working hours, new tools for marketing, better conditions for learning, and safer streets. They may have also changed the way we think about and sense the world – less dependent on the sun and moon, less afraid of the dark and distancing ourselves from the communal fire, less tactile and more visual (Verdon 2002). Today, most homes, businesses and streets in the United Kingdom seem lit sufficiently for most requirements. People are no longer in awe of our ability to create light. So, when prices fall and incomes rise further, consumption will grow, but probably not with the dynamism that illuminated the industrial revolution.

The demand for lighting evolved as income rose, innovation proceeded, lighting service prices fell and attributes associated with the fuels and technologies changed and were refined. While hard to estimate, especially in the early periods, given the patchiness of the data, the long run evolution of demand for lighting has also been influenced by non-price variables (Wilms and Mills 1995). The development of markets for candles and oil enabled many families to reduce their time spent preparing rushlights, freeing them for other activities. The introduction of gas was of major benefit to lighting large areas, including factories, as the heat generated by sufficient candles to provide illumination was frequently unbearable (Bowers 1998). Similarly, candles and oil lamps were the source of many fires, mostly avoided with gas lighting. The introduction of electricity provided other valuable attributes. Large-scale gas lighting, for example in theatres, created heat and depleted oxygen. Simply flicking a switch to turn on the electric lamps made lighting up a room much easier. It also reduced the amount of preparation, maintenance and cleaning required, as well as the smell of burning tallow candles, animal or vegetable oil or gas (O'Dea 1958). Thus, the growth in the demand for new or enhanced attributes has always been important for the successful introduction or failure of a new lighting technology. The measures of the cost of lighting services in this chapter do not themselves take proper account of the effects of technical change on the full range of attributes that affect the quality of lighting services.

Through technological, market and other institutional and public policy developments, the ability to live and work in a well-illuminated environment has radically transformed the economy and society of industrialised countries. The economic and technological history of light in the United Kingdom shows how a focus on energy service provision – rather than just energy markets – reveals the remarkable declines in costs and increases in consumption that have been achieved, especially since the nineteenth century. Today, one lumen-hour costs almost one twenty-thousandth of what it cost seven centuries ago, and almost one three-thousandth of what it cost in 1800. The average British family uses 200 times more light per year (that is, around 6 million lumen hours), while the United Kingdom economy consumes around twenty-five thousand times more light than it did in 1800.

PART THREE

ANALYSIS

8.   Producing Cheaper Services: Energy and Knowledge

1. THE PRODUCTION AND SUPPLY OF ENERGY

Heating, power, transport and light all experienced dramatic transformations in the process and costs of production. They were the result of changes in the energy, equipment (or physical capital, including the technology and, in some instances, the infrastructure) and skills (or human capital) used. This chapter draws together the experiences from the four different services and investigates the forces underlying the production of energy services. First, the features that have characterised energy markets over the last seven hundred years are identified. Then, the chapter assesses the evolution of knowledge production and its importance in the provision of energy services.

Energy, the Product

One important feature is that the nature of the energy used and the process of preparation to generate services has evolved greatly over the last thousand years. For instance, organic fuels were often collected from nearby thickets or forests by the members of the household or a local cutter. Wood might be chopped into pieces for better management of the fire. It might also be dried to improve combustion. They received little transformation before use.

Over time, the raw product was increasingly modified. Additional preparations could considerably improve the quality of the fire and even the final product. For industrial processes, such as iron smelting, wood was first placed on a low heat to remove the impurities, producing charcoal. As a result of the need for this process, a small, yet significant charcoal-making industry developed around the edge of forests. Although denser than wood (in terms of energetic content), charcoal was fragile and could only travel short distances before decomposing. This constrained industries dependent on charcoal to locating near the energy source. The depletion of wood stocks also required the industries to move to find new fuel locations.

The growth of coal mining enabled a relatively untransformed fuel to be used in basic heating purposes. For industries such as iron smelting, once coal could be used, it needed to be purified into coke. Coal and coke were able to travel greater distances than wood and charcoal, respectively, altering the relationship between the fuel supplier and consumer. The growing mobility of energy led to the development of major mining and coking industries that were tied in to the expanding trade networks.

Initially, food (whether for humans or animals) was the 'fuel' for generating power. The preparation of food evolved considerably – from raw ingredients to cooked meals. Wind and water flow were additional sources of power. Then, the growth of the steam engine enabled coal to generate heat and power. Each source of energy altered the constraints and costs the consumers faced in the production of power. Until the twentieth century, transport used the same sources and was bound in similar ways.

Sunlight was the key source for lighting, imposing life's rhythm. Man was able to 'lengthen the day' with animal fats and vegetable oils. They required a little more preparation than heating fuels. Then, mineral-based fuels began to be used. Gas, as a by-product of the coking process, began to be fed through pipes and burnt. Then, kerosene was lit in poorer homes. Kerosene was also a manufactured fuel, through the refining of crude petroleum.

Then, the era of electricity generation began. The production of electricity depended on coal first, on refined petroleum fuels, on natural gas, on uranium, or on flows of energy, such as water or wind. The process of distribution of electricity required considerable transformations (into smaller voltage) before the customers could use this source of heat, power and light.

Energy carriers have been adapted to the changing technologies and markets, as well as to the ease of distribution and of use. They have become increasingly value-added for the consumer. That is, the raw energy source has undergone increasingly sophisticated transformations and refinements to improve the provision of the final service. They have also shifted away from organic sources to mineral fuels, easing the pressure on land availability and competition with living space, and separating agricultural production from energy provision.

The Availability and Production of Coal

Arguably the most important issue related to energy resources is their availability and the ability to exploit them. Scarce energy translated into higher fuel prices and, all other things being equal, of the related service. Abundant resources often implied cheap energy and services.

Traditional energy resources depended on the land available for fuel production. Given the static nature of land, provided limits were not reached, the flow of energy into the village (or economy) tended to be relatively constant. There were methods to increase the flow of energy by using new land (taken from nature or from other communities). In general, though, fuels for heating and food for power essentially competed for land. The rising population, the expanding economy and the associated growth in the demand for heat, power and transportation during the sixteenth to the eighteenth centuries put increasing pressures on the availability of land for food and fuel.

The introduction of mineral fuels reduced the burden imposed by a constrained land on a growing population. Yet, in the same way that the production of biomass energy provided a flow of resources, the extraction of mineral resources created a flow. The stock of reserves was converted into a flow, through the carriage of coal vans and later trains full of coal, tankers freighting oil or pipelines supplying natural gas. That is, extraction rates and supply infrastructure determined the flow of energy.

In medieval times, many of the coal seams lay over Church land, with limited exploitation of the resources. Reformation enabled the crown to take ownership of those lands and sell them to entrepreneurs. The coal industry began to open these mines and expand to meet the growing demands for heating.

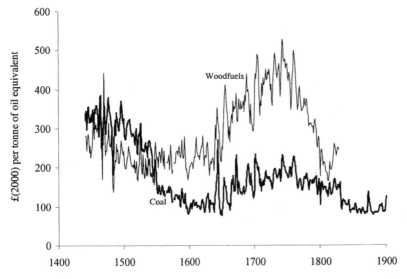

Source: see Data Appendix

Figure 8.1 The Price of Coal and Woodfuels (£(2000) per toe), 1440–1900

From the fifteenth century to the end of the seventeenth century, the coal mining industry expanded from a niche business to one of the major generators of wealth in the North-East of England. As demand grew in the seventeenth century, however, coal supply was inadequate and prices started to rise. This created incentives to exploit new knowledge. A series of innovations transformed the coal industry into one of the pillars of the British economy. First, the development of pumps to remove water from mines enabled much greater depths to be achieved. This was accomplished most successfully with the use of the steam engine in the eighteenth century. Second, Britain discovered that its vast energy reserves were not limited to the North-East. A number of regions started to compete with the Newcastle trade. The coal industry transformed itself from a localised business to one of the leading sectors of the economy. Third, transport routes were dramatically improved. The improvements to rivers and building of canals enabled industrial regions to reduce the cost of heating services. Also, along the coast economies of scale were achieved by increasing the size of ships carrying the goods (Hatcher 2003).

Despite only small technical improvements in production methods, large and accessible reserves, a diversity of types and qualities of coal, a big labour force to draw from and improving means of transportation, enabled coal supply to expand in line with the growing demand (Church 1987). This ensured that real prices remained relatively stable throughout much of the nineteenth century (see Figure 8.1). As the century wore on, however, a continually growing price-inelastic (domestic and international) demand for coal coupled with antiquated extraction techniques, more powerful trade unions and attempts towards collusive behaviour amongst large suppliers put upward pressure on prices (Church 1987). The growing demand for coal in the nineteenth century created concerns about the scarcity of coal (see, for example, Jevons 1865 for a response to these concerns) and the possibility of upward pressure on prices. One of the problems associated with the production and supply of energy resources is that they often require long term investments. For the coal industry, there was, at times, a delay between the signal of scarcity and the change in flow of resources resulting from higher investment in extraction, from hiring more miners and finding new seams. Consequently, by the 1870s, the average coal price in the United Kingdom exhibited increased volatility.

There was, however, no clear trend in prices. At the end of the nineteenth century, the British coal industry still benefited from vast accessible reserves. At the pit face, the principal method of extraction was the miner's pick and shovel. Efforts to mechanise coal extraction were slow, and the British coal industry failed to use more efficient mechanical techniques; as late as the 1930s, when other coal mining countries such as Germany and Belgium were fully mechanised, less than 40 percent of United Kingdom coal was cut with mechanised cutting equipment and conveyor systems (Jones 1989). Instead, its expansion was the result of a large unskilled labour force willing to work long periods underground. In 1830, there were around 100 000 miners, by 1870, nearly 400 000 and, by 1913, over one million (Church 1989 p.12). These characteristics enabled the industry to expand supply to meet demand without raising prices.

Coal production peaked in 1913, and began its decline. The First World War encouraged foreign consumers of British coal to look for other suppliers. From the end of the nineteenth century to 1940, real coal prices kept rising, driving up the price of heat and power. And, between 1950 and 1973, coal prices were rising relative to petroleum products, encouraging consumers, where possible, to use liquid fossil fuels (see Figure 8.2). Much of this rising price was not really a result of rising scarcity, but due to the market power of the British coal mining industry until the 1990s and its privatisation (Ashworth 1987, Robinson 1991).

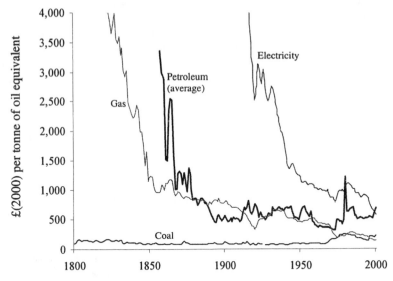

Figure 8.2 The Price of Energy Sources (£(2000) per toe), 1800–2000

The Availability of Petroleum Resources

The evolution of petroleum products, availability and market structure followed a different path. In particular, the location of accessible resources when first used on a large scale implied that petroleum needed to be imported into Britain. Thus, many of the factors influencing the production of energy services related to petroleum occurred beyond the British Isles.

The first oil fields to be exploited on a large scale were in Pennsylvania, in the North East of the United States, in the 1860s. Just after the American civil war, large numbers of migrant workers searched for jobs. Coupled with growing immigration in nearby New York, there was a large and cheap labour supply available for the exploitation of petroleum. With low wage rates, the early petroleum industry had a large and disposable labour force, and little equipment. This meant that the fixed costs of petroleum extraction were low and, therefore, many companies could quickly seek to exploit new discoveries (Yergin 1991).

After a discovery, oil supply would rapidly rise, driving down prices (see Figure 8.2). Intense drilling activity reduced the pressure in an oil field and, consequently, the total potential output of a field. Rapidly a field would dry up and prices would shoot up. As well as a failure to exploit all the available resources, this market structure would create considerable price volatility, substantial bankruptcy and unemployment problems. In a period of pro-competition ideology, the USA government did not see a role in minimising production losses, price volatility or social problems (Yergin 1991).

The pressure on prices after the diffusion of the internal combustion engine had started to be alleviated by Amoco's invention in 1913 of a new method of 'cracking' petroleum, enabling more of the crude to be turned into gasoline. So, short-run inelasticity of supply had driven up prices, but in the long run supply met demand.

Also, gradually, more oil fields were discovered in the USA, in the Soviet Union, in Romania, in South America, in Asia and in the Middle East which meant that despite an impressive growth in demand, prices managed to fall gradually from the 1930s to the 1960s. As discoveries were being made in increasingly isolated regions of the world and at greater depths, capital costs increased. This meant that production costs were increasingly at the initial stages of production. Thus, there were declining long run average costs and increasing returns to scale. Only a few companies could profitably operate in the oil production market.

Another cycle observed is that there have been periods of energy scarcity and of abundance. In periods of scarcity, prices rose, increasing the incentive to supply more resources. Producers were encouraged to find more resources. Thus, their objective was to increase the flow of resources. Periods of energy scarcity also could lead markets to develop more efficient technology and offer substitute fuels.

Times of abundance have generated incentives to create demand, use more resources, but not necessarily become less efficient. Markets tended to find ways to use more resources. Low prices encouraged consumers to increase heat or the power intensity of industrial activities and heating of households and buildings. Energy producers sought to increase demand and sell their resources. In other words, scarcity and abundance have promoted greater energy production.

Ownership of Oil Reserves

Throughout the twentieth century, the United Kingdom, along with many other countries, was becoming increasingly dependent on oil imports for strategic aspects of their economy. Any shortages could have major cost implications for economic activity. During the Second World War, both Germany and Japan, which did not have access to any important oil fields, created military strategies that were guided by their needs to acquire of petroleum supplies. Germany set out to control the oil fields of Romania, and later those of Baku; Japan was after those in Java and Sumatra. Both countries invested large resources in the development of synthetic fuels – trying to reduce their dependence on petroleum products. Neither controlling inputs nor creating substitutes were fully achieved, and have been seen as major factors in the outcome of the war (Yergin 1991).

An important feature of the evolution of world oil markets was the changing ownership of extraction rights and the power of the supplier to dictate prices. In the early days, especially outside the USA, at least, part-owned British companies like Royal Dutch/Shell, the Anglo-Persian (later called BP) and the Turkish Petroleum Company sought extraction rights from the ruler of the countries with potential oil fields, such as Sumatra, Java, Saudi Arabia, Persia, Iraq, Bahrain, Venezuela and Mexico. For a small fee or percentage of the sale price of oil, these companies could, once oil was found, exploit the country's mineral resources (Yergin 1991).

In 1938, after a change of government, Mexico decided to take over the rights to all mineral resources, which were being exploited mainly by Royal Dutch/Shell. This created a precedent for other new governments around the world to nationalise crude oil production or request at least larger shares of the profits. In 1943, Venezuela made a part ownership deal; Saudi Arabia did the same in 1950 with a company jointly owned by Exxon, Mobil and Texaco. The next year, Iranian oil fields were nationalised completely. In 1960, the Organisation of Petroleum Exporting Countries (OPEC) was formed. This gave a potentially unified voice to about 40 percent of world production. By 1970, OPEC countries produced more than half, and a far greater proportion of exports (Yergin 1991).

Supply had continued to grow and prices continued to fall; by 1970, prices in real terms were almost one-third of the level in 1920. Not only had gasoline demand grown, but fuel oils were starting to replace coal in the heating of homes and electricity generation – economies were becoming very dependent on oil supplies.

Some countries were beginning to appreciate the danger of oil shortages, which were appearing. The nationalisation of Iranian fields in 1951, the Suez Crisis in 1956 and the Six Day War in 1967 had all been signals of potential crises. The latter experience showed that interruptions of oil supplies could occur, as Saudi Arabia, Kuwait, Iraq, Libya and Algeria banned shipments to the USA, United Kingdom and Germany because of their involvement with Israel. Arab production was down 60 percent. Further more aggressive nationalisations in Iraq (1968) and in Lybia (1969) also highlighted the tension between exporting countries and petroleum refinery and distribution companies. In the 1950s and 1960s, because supply was substantially in excess of demand, any interruptions were temporary and had little impact on prices (Yergin 1991).

Many countries were seeking ways to reduce their dependence on imported oil. The first temporary measure against shortages was to stockpile oil, although this policy was not truly effective until the early 1980s. Far more promising for the United Kingdom were the geological surveys which indicated that below the North Sea large supplies of fossil fuels could be exploited. The United Kingdom, along with Norway, started discovering oil in 1969, which provided some relief from foreign supply shortages. The extraction costs of North Sea oil were still far higher than the Middle East oil, and would only be economically viable at higher prices.

Other means of reducing oil dependence were also followed. As well as many other countries, the United Kingdom was looking for natural gas as a heating substitute. It also started developing a nuclear power programme, hoping to generate electricity from uranium.

Nevertheless, by 1973, all industrialised countries were increasingly dependent on foreign and especially OPEC oil. In all sectors, the price of oil relative to fuel efficient technology favoured an inefficient use of oil. Expanding demand associated partially with rising disposable income led to an oil consumption increasing from under 10 million barrels per day in 1950 to 20 million in 1960 to over 50 million in 1973. The world market was changed in the early 1970s by the USA becoming a net importer of oil, when it had previously been the largest exporter. Either current demand growth rates or the excess supply had to come to an end. Prices were starting to signal the need for rationing – they were starting to rise from the beginning of the 1970s. They rose from $1.80 per barrel in 1970 to $2.18 in 1971 to $2.90 in mid-1973 (Yergin 1991).

Saudi Arabia, rather than the USA, had become the country that would increase production to meet unexpected increases in demand. This powerful position would soon be used for economic and political objectives. Individual OPEC countries, seeing that distribution companies were earning substantial profits, demanded a greater percentage of the revenue from petroleum sales to customers. The oil distributors realised that to avoid losing complete control, they needed to join forces and act as a monopsony. So, the Front Uni tried to bargain with OPEC as a whole, rather than have to deal with some of the more difficult countries, like Libya and Venezuela, on an individual basis (Yergin 1991).

At the beginning of October 1973, OPEC ministers met the oil companies in Vienna to discuss OPEC's share of sales. Negotiations collapsed. On October 16, ministers decided how much of the oil price would go to the producers – $5.11 per barrel. At the same time, Egypt and Syria attacked Israel starting the fourth Arab-Israeli War. Saudi Arabia and a few other OPEC countries decided to impose a complete embargo on the USA and the Netherlands, until their policies in the Middle East became more pro-Arab. In other European countries and Japan, lighter embargoes were imposed according to their policies in the Middle East. Production in the OPEC countries was set to fall by 5 percent per month (Yergin 1991).

While OPEC countries had tried embargoes in the past, they had failed because of the excess supply. With a lack of alternative sources of supply on the world market in late 1973, such an embargo was likely to be more successful. Furthermore, because of the short-run inelastic demand, common production quotas would drive up the price proportionally higher than the decline in consumption; producers' revenue would rise. Prices increased to $5.12 in October and to $11.65 in December. Earnings from OPEC exports rose from $23 billion in 1972 to $140 billion in 1977 (Yergin 1991).

OPEC ministers voted to end the complete embargoes in March 1974, after pressure from the Egyptian leader, Anwar Sadat, who believed the embargoes to be potentially damaging to Arab interests in the long run. Post-embargo, OPEC realised it now had the power to influence the course of world oil markets; Saudi Arabia and Iran produced half of OPEC's oil exports and the key players. The

Shah of Iran wanted to drive up prices to earn more revenue. Sheik Yamani, the Saudi Arabian oil minister, preferred price stability, which would be achieved by increasing production when other nations tried to drive up prices. In 1975, prices were $11.46 and, at the end of 1977, $12.10. As the Shah realised increasing prices were not the answer to his country's problems, he too sought price stability. OPEC, with some dissenters, followed (Yergin 1991).

In December 1978, after disgust over the Shah's treatment of their religious leader, Ayatollah Komeini, the workers on the Iranian oil fields went on strike – exports stopped until the middle of 1979. Exports from other countries rose to meet this fall in supply, but world production in January 1979 was still 2 million barrels per day short of the level at the end of November (Yergin 1991).

This led to a period of panic. OPEC countries no longer could stabilise prices as each of its members tried to raise its prices to make more revenue. Industrialised nations, with their growth in demand having returned after the initial shock of 1973, tried to stockpile as well as trying to meet their normal consumption. Prices of petroleum products had risen 60 percent in a few months. Despite attempts by Saudi Arabia to create stability through OPEC meetings, the price of crude oil was $32 per barrel in June 1980 (Yergin 1991).

In September, Iraq declared war on Iran. Both countries' production virtually stopped – 15 percent of total OPEC output. Prices rose, but less dramatically than in 1979, mainly because industrialised countries were now in a recession and countries used their stockpiles to moderate the missing supply. Another OPEC meeting was concluded with further price rises – to $36 (Yergin 1991).

October 1981 was the last month for a long time in which prices rose, however. The 1970s had turned potential oil fields into economically viable supplies. Major new fields in Alaska, Mexico and the North Sea were to add an extra 7 million barrels per day to the world supply by the early 1980s. Being outside OPEC, the owners of these fields would enter the market at lower prices. The power of OPEC was waning. Many countries had developed conservation programmes; the price ratio between energy and efficient technology had shifted, favouring efficiency. Heating demand increasingly used gas. Nuclear power was becoming another way of generating electricity (Yergin 1991).

OPEC introduced new quotas, but accepted the need to reduce prices. By the mid 1980s, the effectiveness of their quotas, though, was declining. There were too many competitors and substitutes. Saudi Arabia had played the stabilising producer, like Standard Oil had, but at a considerable expense. It decided to retake its lost market share. In December 1985, the price fell to below $10.

The Oil Shocks of the 1970s act as a reminder of a potential close relationship between market structure and the availability of resources. Energy production and supply industries are some of the most powerful sectors in the economy. Several of the energy companies are amongst the top ten most valuable on the planet. Such economic (and even political) power has the potential to influence medium- and even long-run trends in energy markets.

Industrial Concentration

Although there has been some evolution in the nature of the fuels supplied, energy producers sell relatively simple and homogeneous commodities. The lack of innovation potential in the product means that driving down costs and improving image are the main objectives. Driving down prices involves achieving economies of scale, through discovering large new energy resources and selling increasing quantities, and producing with more efficient processes.

A feature of the modern energy system has been the tendency for economies of scale to create a monopoly supplier, or at least only a few suppliers. The introduction of new energy sources can create competition, but it appears that eventually the drive is for the concentration of production and supply. Fewer companies can compete in an expanding and now globalising market.

The production and supply of energy has become more capital intensive. Numerous factors are likely to have influenced the trend. This is in part due to the nature of energy reserves. As David Ricardo argued about resource exploitation, the lowest-hanging fruit were picked first. More distant resources were sought afterwards; in the case of energy reserves, they tended to be deeper too. Energy production required more capital to exploit the resources – whether setting up bellows to pump in air or steam engines to suck out water in coal mines, oil derricks or North Sea oil platforms.

Capital intensification has been partly due to the increasing dependence on technology in the provision of power, for which energy production and supply was dependent. In addition, the rising cost of labour has encouraged managers to substitute workers for machines where possible. Also, as easier reserves have been exploited, more distant and less accessible resources were used. Whether the deserts of Arabia, the depths of the North Sea, the arctic wastes of Siberia or Alaska, these tended to be less hospitable locations for humans. This raised wages further. Machines could do more of the work. Another probable reason was a managerial preference. Mining has certainly experienced its share of industrial tensions. Thus, there may well have been a preference for machines that do not complain.

High infrastructure costs associated with the development of integrated production and managerial techniques, advertising strategies and supply networks have also led to increasing returns to scale. All of these have tended to create a 'downward sloping long run average cost curve' – as a firm increased production, its unit costs continue to fall. Thus, if one firm produced more petroleum than others, its cost of producing each barrel would be lower than its competitors. With lower unit costs, it could sell at a price at which its competitors made a loss, and they would eventually go out of business, creating a natural monopoly.

Back in the nineteenth century, Standard Oil controlled most of the production and supply of kerosene and other petroleum products in the USA. This market power and its potential abuse led to considerable jealousy from other entrepreneurs and concern from the public and politicians. Increasing pressure to intervene and develop anti-Trust legislation eventually led in 1911 to a Supreme Court ruling forcing Standard Oil to break up into separate competitive firms. The largest part became Standard Oil of New Jersey, and known as Exxon (Esso in Europe); Standard Oil New York was known as Mobil; Standard Oil of Indiana, Amoco; Standard Oil of California, Chevron. By then, other companies, most notably Shell in the United Kingdom and Royal Dutch in the Netherlands (the two soon merged), had made discoveries in other parts of the world and had been weakening Standard Oil's monopolistic control of resources and revenue. Interestingly, in recent years, we have seen a large merging of many oil companies (BP with Amoco, Exxon with Mobil), which reflects the tendency towards declining long run average cost curves and natural monopolies (Yergin 1991).

The intensification of capital in the production and supply of energy can slow responses to changes in demand. Larger firms are likely to be slower to adjust to market fluctuations, increasing the lag between price fluctuations and producer responses. Market rigidities reduce the speed of adjustments to changes in demand. Rising demand create increased prices, which only slowly lead to investments in additional energy. Thus, energy markets will tend to experience longer periods of high prices and low prices as markets become increasingly rigid.

A consequence of large suppliers has been a concentrated degree of economic power. The consumer faced with strong suppliers has had little choice but to accept higher prices than would have existed in a competitive market. This has created a role for government to regulate energy suppliers. For domestic energy firms (such as a gas or an electricity company), they have had their powers limited by a stronger State. In the case of huge multinational corporations (like the oil companies), this can be harder – given the power they yield, large energy companies can even often influence government policy. As wealth is captured by large energy suppliers, and away from the public, such economic power is unlikely to maximise net social benefits.

Competition and Amalgamation in the Electricity Supply Industry

One of the consequences of high capital investment for energy distribution has been the technological lock-ins this has created. A large infrastructure made it hard for the electricity industry to replace the gas network. Since its inception in the nineteenth century, the electricity industry has experienced considerable changes in structure and ownership. Initially, each user generated its own electricity. Due to the great economies of scale, the power station increasingly replaced the self-generating consumer. Given the importance of creating a distribution network, natural monopolies tended to occur in the supply of electricity from a central source. Private companies and local authorities were both venturing into the production and provision of electricity.

By the 1920s, the great benefits from linking the nation into a single, homogeneous network were becoming apparent. High demands in one region could be compensated for by lower consumption in another. The attempt to create a national grid highlighted the need to coordinate electricity production and distribution at a national scale.

After the Second World War, the call to bring numerous industries into public hands led to the amalgamation of electricity generation and supply into the Central Electricity Generating Board (CEGB) along with its regional distributors. Thus, electricity was formally a public monopoly.

This experience continued until the privatisation and the liberalisation of the industry. The process that began in 1989 was protracted, in large part due to the complications of separating the nuclear power industry and turning it into a commercially-attractive business (Surrey 1996).

An important feature of the transformation of the electricity industry was creating competition. The strategic incentives upon liberalisation led to the 'dash-for-gas', which pushed the fuel mix away from coal, the dominant source for over a century. Combined-cycle gas turbines (CCGT) were the cheapest way of generating gas and could be installed quickly. Once the European Commission had removed its moratorium on using natural gas for electricity generation, the two privatised incumbent electricity companies, formed out of the sale of CEGB, sought to create over-capacity in the industry, which was best done through installing CCGT. The independent power producers sought to enter the market, which could also be done by building natural gas power stations (Newbery 1996).

The supply industry entered a phase of competition. Electricity prices fell. Quality of service may have improved. The competitive drive was over-shadowed by the liberalisation occurring at the wider European level. As Europe slowly worked its way towards a single market for electricity, the large players have appeared to dominate, and slowly stifle competition.

From a longer-term perspective, in a number of energy industries, there have been cycles of increased competition and concentration. These cycles have often been related to government intervention in altering the market structure, seeking to reduce the economic power of these industries.

Long-run Trends in the Price of Energy

Prices are presumed to reflect a fuel's relative scarcity and value. The nature of individual commodities, the availability of resources and the suppliers' market power are factors that have influenced the trends in prices. Considerable debate has surrounded long-term trends in non-renewable resource and energy prices energy prices, which might be expected to become scarcer as the stock is used up. The evidence is inconclusive, yet there has been little sign of growing scarcity in the long run (Krautkraemer 1998, Fouquet and Pearson 2003a).

A prominent feature of the trends in energy prices was the dramatic declines in prices in the early expansion phase of the associated industries, such as the coal, gas, petroleum and electricity. Figure 8.1 shows the declining price of coal in the sixteenth century, and Figure 8.2 identifies, from 1820 to 1850, this effect for gas, in the second half of the nineteenth century, for kerosene (the main petroleum product used at the time) and, in the first half of the twentieth century, a similar drop in electricity prices. This decline has been associated with economies of scale in production and supply.

A second phase tended to be associated with more gradually declining prices. Coal prices stabilised in the seventeenth century and again in the nineteenth century. Gas prices did so from the 1850s, oil prices from 1900 and electricity from 1950. The second phase has been a period of industrial consolidation, where fewer economies of scale could be achieved.

In the third phase, resources might begin to hit limits of availability (designed by the production capacity) and prices stabilise and may start to rise (slightly). At this point, if the industry shows resilience, producers may find additional resources, and prices fall again, as the coal industry did in the eighteenth century and the oil industry in the 1920s and the 1980s. Consumers might substitute away from these fuels. In the case of woodfuels, from the seventeenth century, coal from the nineteenth century, and petroleum from the end of the twentieth century, there were signs of upturns but little evidence of systematic rises in prices.

A fourth phase could be included as an extreme case where physical resource limits are being reached. This would occur if insufficient resources were found to meet demand and no alternative sources existed at a comparable price. The big debate amongst historians can be characterised as whether the substitution from woodfuels to coal happened in 'phase four' (as Nef (1926) argued) or phase three (Flinn 1984). It seems clear that given the existence of coal as a cheap alternative to woodfuel (at least, in many sectors), the transition took place not as an energy crisis, but as a gradual process.

Table 8.1 The Price of Energy Sources (£(2000) per toe), 1300–2000

	1300	1500	1700	1750	1800	1850	1900	1950	2000
Heating Fuels[a]		235	245	267	119	106	167	280	158
Power Fuels[b]	940	1 215	2 450	2 505	2 635	1 815	1 790	700	185
Transport Fuels[c]	675	840	2 400	2 720	2 280	1 525	1 350	583	795
Lighting Fuels[a]	4 640	3 180	4 550	5 010	3 025	2 625	1 570	1 170	532

Notes

a – £(2000) per tonne of oil equivalent (for households).

b – £(2000) per tonne of oil equivalent; energy cost of wind and water assumed to be zero.

c – £(2000) per tonne of oil equivalent (in passenger travel).

Source: see Chapters 4-7 and Data Appendix

Another important observation was the absence of a clear rising trend in the weighted average 'energy' price series for individual services over five centuries.

However, there have been extended periods of rising average prices. From the end of the sixteenth century, the price of average fuels for the four energy services appears to have risen. The rise was accentuated in Figure 8.3, compared with previous attempts to observe this trend (Krautkraemer 1998, Fouquet and Pearson 2003a) by the inclusion of several organic fuels (including basic food and fodder) rather than simply woodfuels. The trends reflected a tension between rising population and economic development into heat-, power- and transport-intensive activities, on the one hand, and the finite availability of land.

Breaking down the average energy price into the average price of energy sources by individual energy services helps understand the trends (see Table 8.1 and Figure 8.3 – Figure 8.5 provides more detail). For heating, a solution was being offered in the form of mineral fuels. Until the nineteenth century, they were not an option for power, transport and lighting. The use of power was able to expand through harnessing the force of water. At sea, the wind did the work.

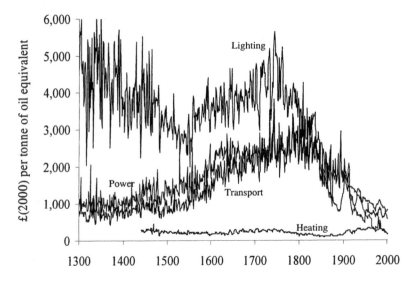

Source: see Chapters 4-7 and Data Appendix

Figure 8.3 The Price of Energy Sources by Energy Service (£(2000) per toe), 1300–2000

So, non-organic energy sources were available. It seems, though, that limits were technological and logistical. In some cases, such as the iron industry, coal could not be used. In others, large supplies of water power were not in desirable locations, and transport costs did not warrant shifting production to remote areas – in the case of the textile industry, the savings sufficiently important and the demand large enough to justify remote production.

Even agriculture experienced major transformation, associated with enclosures and technological development, which helped reduce the pressure, initially (Allen 1994). It appears that, by the second half of the seventeenth century, the average price of power and transport, both still highly dependent on agricultural products for energy, started to stabilise. Thus, by the mid-eighteenth century, the tensions between economic growth and resource scarcity were not so strong.

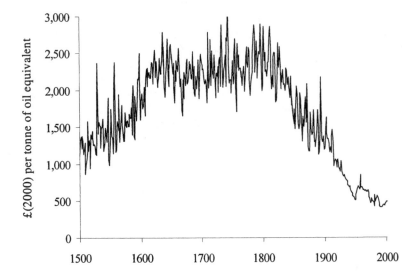

Source: see Chapters 4-7 and Data Appendix

Figure 8.4 The Average Price of Energy (£(2000) per toe), including Agricultural Products, 1500–2000

But, demand for new goods was increasing at the time of the Industrial (or Industrious) Revolution and, without the non-organic fuels and their technologies, growth would have created tensions. So, the Industrial Revolution was facilitated and possibly allowed by the adoption of technological solutions, including the switch to coke in the iron industry.

Shown in Figure 8.4, the average 'energy' price, including agricultural products, did present a striking shape. It rose up until the end of the seventeenth century, as resource scarcity associated with land increased. The improvements in agricultural productivity for power and transport provision and the shift to coal in heating stabilised the 'average' price. The use of coal with the introduction of steam engines for power and transport, as well as gas for lighting, drove down prices. The shift to other fossil fuels and access to greater supplies of resources have kept pushing the price downwards throughout the nineteenth and twentieth centuries.

Some might question the appropriateness of including agricultural prices in the 'average' price of energy. Food and fodder provided the 'fuel' for human and animal power. Table 5.2 suggests that human and animal power provided more than 80 percent of the power for the British economy into the nineteenth century. To ignore this dependence, as well as their fuels, is to heavily bias any estimates of 'average' energy prices.

The third issue that appeared from looking at the long-run trends in the average 'energy' price in Fouquet and Pearson (2003a) was a major increase in the second half of the nineteenth century and the early years of the twentieth century. Figure 8.4 shows that, once agricultural products are included as fuels for power and transport, this effect disappears.

Yet, this point should not be ignored. For the two services not dependent on food or fodder, a rise in the average price of heating energy sources from the mid-nineteenth century occurred due to the introduction of gas and electricity (see Figure 8.5 – note the different scales). Energy for lighting also experienced a peak, which reflected the introduction of electricity.

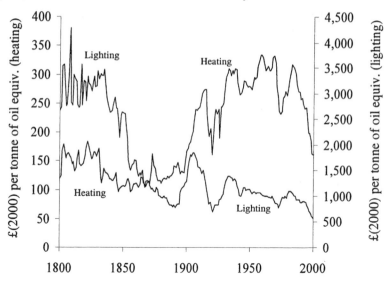

Source: see Chapters 4-7 and Data Appendix

Figure 8.5 The Price of Heating and Lighting Fuels (£(2000) per toe), 1800–2000

At the end of the nineteenth and early twentieth century, energy systems were dramatically altered by large-scale substitution towards more expensive but higher 'quality' fuels. It was reflected in the growing share of gas and ultimately electricity in final user expenditure on energy over the period. So, a possible explanation for the appearance of a rising 'average' energy price at the end of the nineteenth century in Figure 8.5 and in Fouquet and Pearson (2003a), rather than being associated with rising scarcity, was the growing value consumers placed on the energy being consumed. This implies that studying energy price as an indicator of scarcity can be misleading, because of the rising value of a tonne of energy. This supports Nordhaus (1997), who argued that using energy prices (rather than service prices) ignores the impact of technological development.

Some points can also be made about the trends in energy prices for individual services, which can be discerned in Figure 8.3. The price of heating fuels in households actually fell during the fifteenth to the mid-seventeenth centuries, due to the increasing share of cheaper coal. Prices then leapt, staying high until the mid-eighteenth century. Despite the shift towards coal, the rising price of woodfuels appears to have imposed a rising average price – coal prices were relatively constant (in real terms) for those centuries. By the beginning of the nineteenth century, virtually all households had shifted towards coal. Then, from the end of the nineteenth century, the more valuable and expensive commodities entered the market for heating. First, gas was used in heating, then eventually electricity, to be dominated today by gas in central heating systems.

The fuels for power and transport were quite similar until the twentieth century. Humans and mostly animals provided power until the steam engine arrived. Consequently, fodder (e.g. oats, maize and hay) and food reflected the price of fuelling power into the twentieth century. For stationary sources, wind and water also generated considerable power – here, the price of these energy sources is assumed to be zero. Then, coal began to provide the heat that powered the steam. Per unit of energy, coal was far cheaper than horse fodder or food for humans – around one-tenth of the cost. The rising average price of power and transport into the nineteenth century was represented by the continuous growth in the price of food and fodder into the nineteenth century, as well as the increased price of coal between 1600 and 1750. Until the end of the nineteenth century, the price of power was dominated by these expensive fuels to drive humans and animals. The expenditure on food and fodder for power are comparable (over £(2000)5 billion each per year in the second half of the nineteenth century) and dwarf expenditure on coal for steam engines and for electricity generation. At the end of the twentieth century, more expensive and effective natural gas began to be used, alongside coal, driving up the average price of power fuels. Yet, these pressures had minimal effect compared with the decline in the use of animals and humans, which enabled the cost of fuels for electricity generation to influence the average series.

For transport, similarly, horse fodder dominated the average price series. The growing use of coal in trains from the mid-nineteenth century pulled down the average price. Nevertheless, even by 1900, more money was spent on horse fodder than on coal in the transport sector. Then, the share of the petroleum products for buses and cars grew, replacing horse fodder and coal, and by the 1930s, fuel costs had fallen dramatically. Petroleum fuels naturally dominated the market for transport and, therefore, reflected a middle ground between expensive horse fodder and cheap coal.

Before the nineteenth century, most illumination resulted from fires and tallow candles from animal fat. It fluctuated through the centuries, rising somewhat in the mid-nineteenth century. Animal fat (per unit of energy) was an expensive source of illumination. A hundred years later, gas was used widely and kerosene (or paraffin) was starting to light poorer homes. Although expensive in their first years of use, these new fuels soon became cheaper than fat. In the same way, the introduction of electricity drove up the average price of lighting fuels, because it was initially very expensive but fell fast. By the end of the twentieth century, electricity had taken-over the whole market for lighting sources and its price had fallen considerably.[22]

To summarise, while trends in fuel prices were hidden behind considerable volatility, three issues stand out. First, with the introduction of a new fuel, its price tended to fall, then stabilise (see Figures 8.1 and 8.2). At that point, the threat of shortages either led to more supply, efficiency improvements or substitution to other fuels.

Second, the average 'energy' price, including agricultural products, reflects the relationship between economic activity and resource availability (see Figure 8.4). The growing tensions associated with land use did create a problem for generating power and transport, and to a lesser extent heating and lighting. In the eighteenth century, institutional and technological solutions were found, which appeared to keep a balance between energetic resources and demand. In the nineteenth century, further technological solutions alleviated the tensions, and enabled the average price of energy to fall.

Third, for energy services, especially heating and, to a lesser extent, lighting, power and transport, there was an upward trend in average energy prices during the second half of the nineteenth century and much of the twentieth century (see Figure 8.5). This reflected the shift to energy sources that were more expensive per unit of energy, but that were used in combination with technologies that managed to produce significantly more services per unit of energy.

While energy has become cheaper in the very long run, the markets fluctuated between periods of energy scarcity and of abundance. In periods of scarcity, prices rise, increasing the incentive to supply more resources. Producers were encouraged to find more resources. Thus, their objective was to increase the flow of resources. Periods of energy scarcity also led markets to develop more efficient technology and offer substitute fuels.

Times of abundance have generated incentives to create demand, use more resources, but not necessarily become less efficient. Markets find ways to use more resources. Low prices encourage consumers to increase heat or power intensity of industrial activities and heating of households and buildings. Energy

---

22. In estimating the price of the fuels for different services, there might seem to be an inconsistency. For power, coal (and then natural gas) was considered the fuel for generating electricity; whereas, for lighting, electricity is the energy source in the twentieth century. However, power is used for lighting, just like heating is used for power. Thus, coal is the fuel for power, and electricity the fuel for lighting.

producers sought to increase demand and sell their resources. In other words, scarcity and abundance promote increasing energy production.

Yet, on the whole, energy prices have been declining with structural shifts reflecting greater value. Where prices exist, the market system worked to minimise scarcity and increase abundance. There have been rigidities in the system, reflecting the increasingly capital intensive industries, and causing price hikes. Nevertheless, energy has become less scarce.

Efforts have been made to provide more value added energy. Producers have increasingly tended to refine the raw energy material, improving the quality of the service. The shift to electricity has epitomised this trend, providing a highly flexible source for services. Thus, considerable knowledge is embodied in the final energy consumers receive today.

2. KNOWLEDGE FOR ENERGY SERVICES

Basic Knowledge

Technological and institutional innovations that led to better ways of producing energy services reflect improvements in knowledge (Chen 1994, Fri 2003). Before investigating the evolution of knowledge in providing energy services, first, it is worth defining knowledge.

A clear difference exists between knowledge and information. Knowledge can be described as the accumulation and classification of information (von Tunzelmann 1995 p.5). Here, what is of interest is the knowledge that enabled the production of energy services, heat, power, transport and light. For instance, it includes an understanding, scientific or intuitive, that a fire needs oxygen to burn. It also involves converting that understanding into a practical technique for oxygenating the fire. To ensure a healthy flame, people or boilers have needed to find an appropriate way to ventilate the fuel. Poor ventilation or too much wind would have killed the fire. Similarly, useful power has been generated through the combination of effort and knowledge. Effort can be considered the brute or raw power. Knowledge has been necessary to direct the effort. For instance, if a carpenter tried to drive a nail into the wall without direction, the powerful swing of his hammer would leave the nail sticking out of the wall – and him with a sore thumb.

Knowledge comes in various forms – as skills associated with human capital or technology in physical capital. If a miller was standing at a distance from a sack of grain, he would have needed a lot of effort to lift it. If he moved closer and in front of the sack, bended his knees well, far less effort would have been required. The use of a little bit of common sense reduced the miller's work considerably. Alternatively, the miller could have tied the sack to a rope passing it through a pulley above, reducing his effort. 'Human capital' describes know-how and skills accumulated for the process of producing the services. The accumulation of information for the creation of knowledge benefits from economies of scale: the more you know, the faster you can assimilate new information and learn.

Knowledge can also be embodied in physical capital. A tool or machine contained the ideas at a particular moment in time. New generations of technologies included additional sets of information and instructions, reflecting the development of scientists', engineers' or designers' knowledge (Stevens 1996).

The information encoded in technology was generally hardware – fixed and inflexible, implying that to incorporate new knowledge, old equipment needed to be scrapped and new technology acquired. Human capital was certainly more flexible. New information could be incorporated within human capital through experience, training or education. The embodiment of knowledge was, therefore, important for the accumulation of new ideas and the nature and evolution of energy service production (Chen 1994, Fri 2003).

The provision of energy services in the household depended greatly on the family members' skills. Sowing and reaping crops, building a healthy fire and preparing cooked meals were essential skills. Such skills were generally passed on down the generations, from father to son and mother to daughter. It was a know-how that was learnt young and carried throughout life.

While to current generations the skills needed may not appear very great, they were not trivial and were crucial to the household's well-being. Without well-honed skills, the quality and quantity of food and heat prepared were low. Poor domestic skills led to bad health, reducing the potential to produce food or earn a living and imposing a greater burden on the household. Survival was dependent on producing the most food from the land, the most heat from the fuel and the most nutrition from the food.

Innovation and progress in domestic skills tended to be very slow. The passing-on of domestic skills was an oral tradition. The parents' cognitive abilities limited the stock of knowledge supplied. The potential for skill development was also bound by the children's learning capabilities and their dexterity.

Furthermore, knowledge formed part of the family's tradition, creating the rules about how 'things are to be done' – for survival. Tradition built on the past often had a tendency of being wary of novelty. Only the most open of minds could have incorporated new ideas into a traditional system and felt confident enough to develop such skills within a strongly traditional community. Thus, traditional domestic skills, including those related to producing energy services, tended to progress very slowly.

The Guilds

The ability to produce energy services was as important for manufacturing activities. Although commonly accused of creating barriers to competition and promoting rent-seeking behaviour, the principal role of craft guilds was to train and develop skills in particular trades.[23] They enabled families to increase the efficiency of skilled labour in their domestic workshop (Epstein 1998 p.687).

Workshops needed skilled labour to make products of consistent quality and increase output. The artisans would frequently pay their apprentices below the going rate to recuperate the investment costs of the training, which encouraged apprentices to move to other employers. This fear, in turn, reduced masters' incentives to fully train their apprentices. Most guilds sought to limit the poaching of trained apprentices amongst workshops, protect the apprentices from excessive abuse and, therefore, promote proper training (Epstein 1998 pp.691–2). Thus, guilds were systems for ensuring the production of knowledge in the form of human capital.

Passed down from the craft guilds of the Middle Ages, a national system of technical training was introduced in the second half of the sixteenth century. This system provided a legal contract between apprentice and master, ensuring the stability of the relationship (Humphries 2006 p.75).

It played a major role in promoting the development and spread of skills across Britain, and its success grew over the centuries. Crafts provided an information pool and network for a particular supply of skills across regions. In the seventeenth century, about two-thirds of the English male labour force had been trained in the apprenticeship system in one of the major cities (Rappaport 1989 p.77). While networks were limited and far from efficient, the distribution of information helped signal changes in the demand for the skills and, therefore, provide a supply, if necessary (Epstein 1998 p.694). Searchers wandered the country assessing practices and demands. Journeymen, either as part of a guild or as independents, travelled the country to provide their skills. Thus, the guilds provided a means of distributing knowledge (in the form of human capital) across the country.

The distribution network could and would also have applied to new techniques and technologies. Guilds have frequently been associated with stifling innovation. They did both: they opposed certain technologies, and were responsible for the invention and diffusion of others. Evidence also suggests that, in the face of growing competition and expanding markets, the guilds' barrier to technological innovation declined after the later Middle Ages (Epstein 1998 p.694). Furthermore, craft guilds did "increase the supply of technology in three ways: by establishing a favourable environment for technical change; by promoting technical specialization through training and technical recombination through artisan mobility; and by providing inventors with monopoly rents" (Epstein 1998 p.701). Thus, the two opposing forces of a monopolistic support system for invention and of the demand for ever-wider competitive markets in skilled labour provided a healthy source of technological innovation and diffusion (Epstein 1998 p.704).

---

23. Guilds were rarely involved in price-fixing activities, because (it would seem) the costs of enforcing the prices were too high (Epstein 1998 p.688).

Lack of information makes it difficult to present a clear case that guilds were responsible for the dissemination and even progress of knowledge on the production of energy services. Undoubtedly, though, apprentices did learn valuable skills about how to use fire and power for their crafts. In fact, "the success of coal-using processes was largely governed by the skills possessed by the key workers involved" (Harris 1976 p.19). It would seem that Britain's long tradition of industrial apprenticeship was vital to the evaluation, modification and employment of coal fuels for heat and power.

Given their reputation for slowing the introduction of new technologies, guilds were probably a powerful force in encouraging knowledge to be embodied in human rather than physical capital. However, ultimately, the crafts that had been learnt helped men on the shop-floor alter the tools and machines. Thus, many of the skills and understanding of processes associated with energy services developed by the craft guilds were central to the development of new technologies for heating and power (Harris 1976 p.19).

Science and Invention

Creating and developing useful new technology has generally been a lengthy and expensive activity. Research and development often required high fixed costs: a lot of money was spent to hire scientists and engineers, to develop new technologies, but it was not always certain what would be the outcome – thus, developers faced considerable risk.

In addition, earning benefits from a new idea have always been difficult in an unregulated context. A new tool or machine could be bought (at the market price) to use the novel idea. The ability to replicate a good idea was often easy, and did not require paying the inventor a large sum to show how the idea worked. In an unregulated market, an inventor could rarely cover the costs of investment required to research and develop a new idea for a practical purpose.

As was discussed with regards to the investment of human capital, an unregulated market for knowledge production discouraged the development of new ideas. Monarchies were convinced of the benefit of protecting the inventors' investment. While the origins of the patenting system are obscure, the first known patent in England was granted in 1449 to a Flemish-born glazier for his method of making stained-glass windows at Eton College (UK Intellectual Property Office 2006).

From the 1560s, the Tudors granted monopolies on manufactures and trades, as well as inventions. After a flurry of protectionism and its abuses, James I introduced the Statute of Monopolies in 1624. It outlawed all monopolies, except "for the term of 14 years or under hereafter to be made of the sole working or making of any manner of new manufactures within this Realm to the true and first inventor" (UK Intellectual Property Office 2006).

Thereafter, patents developed as part of the legal system, argued by lawyers and attributed by judges for clearly outlined new inventions. As a result, the patent on Arkwright's spinning machine in 1785 was voided because it was invented ten years earlier. In 1796, James Watt's extensive litigation to defend his patent on the steam engine established that improvements on existing technologies were sufficient grounds for a permit (UK Intellectual Property Office 2006). Another major development was the dramatic streamlining and reduction in the cost of the patent application in 1852.

This institution was set up to encourage the development of new ideas and, despite its flaws, was successful in increasing the production of knowledge (Epstein 2004). In the seventeenth century, on average, three were granted per year. There was an important growth in the number of patents granted during the eighteenth century. Between 1720 and 1760, the authorities allowed around eight per year. In the 1760s, the average increased to twenty per year. The production of knowledge grew – an average 30 in the 1770s, 50 in the 1780s and 65 in the 1790s (see Figure 8.6).

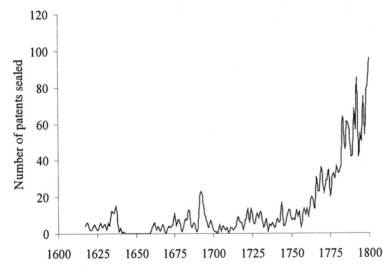

Source: MacLeod (1986)

Figure 8.6 The Number of Patents Granted, 1616–1800

Knowledge created to reduce the costs of producing energy services increased too. Inventors requesting patents had to explain the nature of their invention. Some indicated their inventions would directly save labour or fuel or increase power. Table 8.2 presents evidence on the number of patents given for improving energy service provision before and during the Industrial Revolution. Knowledge embodied in physical capital for energy service production rose substantially during the second half of the eighteenth century – nearly doubling in the 1760s and increasing by about half every subsequent decade.

Information is also available about what the new knowledge embodied in physical capital replaced. 'Labour saving' devices can be considered either a substitution in the source of energy, from muscular power to another source of power (such as water or steam), or a substitution in the source of knowledge, from human capital to technology embedded in the physical capital. In the former case, knowledge was still required to enable the substitution in the source of power. However, since human power was the least efficient source of power (even less efficient than the early steam engines), 'physical' knowledge was reducing the amount of energy required and was, therefore, a substitute for energy. In the latter case, 'physical' knowledge was clearly replacing human skills and know-how. These two cases were the reason for about one-third of grants leading to cheaper energy services in the first-half of the eighteenth century and, more generally, around 5 percent of total grants attributed.

Table 8.2 Percentage and Number of Patents Granted Reducing Costs of Energy Services, 1660–1800

	Labour Saving	Fuel Saving	% of Total Patents for Cheaper Energy Service	No. of Patents for Cheaper Energy Service	% of Total Patents for Improved Production	Total no. of Patents
1660–1719	4.1%	11.2%	15.3%	52	12.4%	339
1720–1729	10.4%	32.8%	43.3%	29	34.3%	67
1730–1739	7.4%	16.7%	24.1%	13	20.4%	54
1740–1749	4.6%	10.3%	14.9%	13	18.4%	87
1750–1759	5.6%	10.3%	15.9%	17	18.7%	107
1760–1769	5.5%	6.7%	12.2%	31	13.4%	254
1770–1779	8.8%	5.4%	14.1%	50	11.9%	354
1780–1789	6.2%	8.1%	14.3%	85	14.1%	594
1790–1799	11.8%	10.2%	22.0%	168	15.2%	762

Source: adapted from MacLeod (1986 p.100)

'Fuel saving' technology acted unambiguously as a substitute for energy. In the 1720s, one-third of all inventions were introduced to reduce fuel used.

Generally, in the first half of the eighteenth century, these fuel savings represented about two-thirds of the new knowledge to reduce the cost of energy service provision and 10 percent of all patents. In the second-half of the century, the relative share of fuel-saving inventions appears to have fallen. Yet, in absolute terms, though, they increased seven-fold between the 1750s and the 1790s, from 11 to 78 patents.

Cheaper energy services were highly desirable. Similar efforts were being directed towards inventions that more indirectly reduced the total cost of energy services. If the production process was improved ('increase output', 'reliability of equipment' or 'regularity of product'), this would have reduced indirectly the expenditure on energy services, because less heat or power would be needed to produce a good. More reliable processes decreased the amount of heat or power required to manufacture a good. Increased output generally benefited from economies of scale. In such cases, knowledge reduced the energy services required to produce one good. A reduction in the unit cost of a good will lead to an increased production, putting upward pressure on the demand for energy services – the degree of pressure depending on the share of total expenditure dedicated to energy service production and the price elasticity of demand for the good.

The need to reduce the cost of energy services at the beginning of the eighteenth century was alarming. Vital was the attempt to replace energy with knowledge embodied in the equipment. The price of woodfuel and of coal doubled between 1600 and 1750. This fed through into a substantially higher cost of heating. The cost of keeping a horse had doubled from the sixteenth to the beginning of the eighteenth century. Even the price of hiring labourers rose a little in the seventeenth century. Thus, the average cost of stationary power had risen greatly. Similarly, the cost of transport and of lighting had risen in the seventeenth century too. It is probable that many of the inventions were reflecting an accumulation of concerns about ways to reduce the cost of energy services, including fuel savings and switching towards physical capital.

The ability to create new knowledge was dependent on the conditions at the time. In particular, the cost of acquiring and spreading knowledge was declining in the eighteenth century. By the 1750s, most engineers and entrepreneurs shared similar technical vocabulary. This reduced the cost of converting knowledge into technology, and in marketing the technology (Mokyr 2004 p.39). Similarly, technological knowledge became increasingly subject to property rights, through better enforced patents and industrial secrecy, creating greater benefits from developing new ideas and technologies (Mokyr 2004 p.37). Other incentives also existed; prizes and awards from various organisations, such as the Royal Society, provided a source of funding and of raising awareness (Mokyr 2004 p.44). Finally, the growing industrialisation created a clear avenue to convert ideas into technologies and marketed commodities.

At the same time, the demand for knowledge grew. More information about scientific and technological ideas was being disseminated. The improved printing press reduced the cost of raising awareness. New institutions were formed that were promoting the advancement of science and involved in specialised journals, public demonstrations and networking (Mokyr 2004 p.45). They also encouraged private manufacturers to advertise their technologies. Thus, new communication systems provided more information and, in turn, created a demand for more knowledge.

Technological development that took place before the mid-eighteenth century was built on a narrow scientific foundation. That is, many of the technologies were developed through experimentation rather than theoretical underpinning. "When no one knows why things work, potential inventors do not know what will not work and waste valuable resources in fruitless search of things that cannot be made ... The range of experimentation possibilities that needs to be searched over is far larger if the searcher knows nothing about the natural principles at work ... But the gradual and slow widening of the epistemic [or scientific] bases of the techniques that emerged in the last third of eighteenth century saved the process an early death by exhaustion" (Mokyr 2004 p.32). In other words, earlier inventions and developments led to improvements but rarely fostered further improvements; whereas later inventions led to virtuous circles of scientific and technological development. This is an argument to explain why many new energy service technologies were developed over the last two hundred years.

The Cost and Diffusion of New Technologies

This trend does not, however, explain why the devices were adopted, and at a faster rate. More inventions do not directly mean more knowledge was used to produce energy services. In some instances, diffusion of new ideas took place many years after the invention (such as Darby's coke iron-smelting process). It is worth re-examining the factors that drove the diffusion of new technologies – the supply of and demand for energy service equipment.

Producers of energy-using equipment followed similar objectives to most firms – they sought to maximise profits, most effectively in the long run, by gaining market share. Driving down production costs was one approach. Differentiating their equipment from how consumers perceived other firms' products was another powerful tool in achieving these objectives. This was done through a combination of methods, including image creation (e.g. advertising and public relations) and adjusting the product design (modifying existing features of the existing equipment and adding new attributes). Product differentiation enabled companies to create a growing demand for their products – driving up their market share, allowing them to increase price above their competitors' prices, price discriminating amongst consumers by offering a range of equipment with subtly different attributes, all in the name of profits (Agrawal and Gort 2001).

Market conditions dictated the company's adjustments to product design. For example, if the price of energy and, therefore, of the main service was rising, it had an incentive to incorporate more energy-efficient technology, driving down the price of energy services. When the price of energy services was falling, either because of declining energy prices or of the recent adoption of technical efficiency equipment, then consumers were more likely to be interested in new attributes, often requiring more energy. Thus, the market reacted to the price of energy services with suppliers of energy technology providing a central feedback loop in the market adjustments in the face of resource scarcity or abundance. They drove down the price of energy services if resources start to become scarce, and drove up the demand for energy service if resources start to become abundant.

This proposition depends on the power of markets to react to these incentives. Medieval markets were rigid at times, less capable of responding to the signals. The early modern economy was more capable of converting the signals into the appropriate reaction – more efficient technologies when prices are high and a broader range of attributes when prices are low. Thus, the development of markets created a mechanism for adjusting to resource scarcities and the appetite to consume ever larger amounts of resources.

Mokyr's (2004 p.37) concept of 'Industrial Enlightenment' involved engineers and entrepreneurs adopting a scientific method, scientific mentality and scientific culture to their activities. For the entrepreneurs, this included a keener eye on market developments, thanks to the improving communication systems. Also, a stronger drive for profits may have led to a greater responsiveness to opportunities.

There was also a growing demand for new technologies. Households and firms had been constrained in their ability to produce energy services. The doubling of fuels between 1600 and 1750 meant expensive heating. Horse and human power were also dear. Similarly, the cost of transport and of lighting had increased throughout the seventeenth century. In a general sense, the growing incorporation of knowledge in equipment was a way to consume cheaper energy services and, ultimately, allow many households and firms to use far greater amounts of heat, power, transport and light.

Households and firms required energy services. The cost of new energy service equipment was high, especially for households. For instance, a fireplace was an important portion of the cost of a whole house. Many poorer households burnt fuel in hearths, sometimes with painful consequences, when using coal. A horse in the early modern era was the equivalent of around one year's salary for the average worker. Until the mid-nineteenth century, most households continued to produce energy services in a similar fashion to their ancestors.

At the time, the demand for new energy technologies was greatest in the industrial sectors. They required large quantities of heat and power for their iron and their textiles. New technologies, such as the reverberatory furnaces, waterwheels and steam engines, could generate large quantities of heat and power.

Naturally, they required large capital investments. In 1760, one kW of power (which was a little more than the average horse's strength) from a steam engine was more than five times the average person's annual salary. Thus, to generate large quantities of power (and heat, as well), and reap the potential benefits, required huge sums of money upfront, or a trusting lender.

Central to the introduction and uptake of new technologies was the potential for economies of scale in the production of energy service equipment. As production increased, the unit cost of production tended to fall. Figure 8.7 shows the decline in the cost of steam engines per kW of power provided. In the first few decades, dramatic declines in costs were achieved. During the first third of the nineteenth century, costs stabilised. Then, a further decrease was achieved with a new generation of steam engines. This was combined with a major push in the demand for steam engines, which enabled economies of scale, driving down the cost of diffusing knowledge.

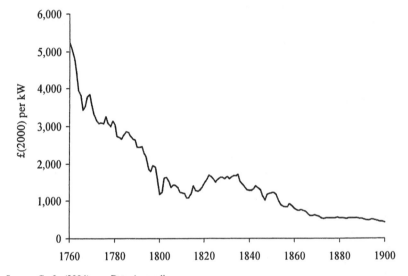

Source: Crafts (2004), see Data Appendix

Figure 8.7 The Price of Energy Equipment: The Steam Engine (per kW), 1760–1900

This was a crucial difference between knowledge in human capital and in physical capital; the former could benefit from economies of scale in its production. Cheaper machines meant that the cost of acquiring knowledge embodied was falling. As the market for equipment developed, with the expansion of markets and manufacturers, the cost of knowledge fell.

Especially from the eighteenth century, there was also a major growth in the demand for information. This was associated with rising population, production and trade. For the merchant, information was money, in the form of better accounts and understanding of trade patterns, and reduced risk. For the authorities, information was power and control, through a great awareness of revenue income and expenses, and ways of minimising social unrest and improving public health. The military and other professions, including farmers, craftsman, lawyers or health services, valued improvements in the supply of information (Headrick 2000 p.9).

The communication systems that were being developed in the eighteenth century helped raise potential users' awareness of new technologies. The factors that led to more science were the drivers of technological diffusion. In other words, the declining costs of searching for (and the rising supply of) information on technological improvements increased the ability to acquire new energy-using equipment and reduced the risks involved.

Another factor was that technology enabled knowledge to be acquired without the owner or user of the equipment being aware of the nature of the knowledge. The cotton mill worker could use steam-powered fulling equipment without any knowledge of heat exchange and the scientific fundamentals that would be needed to understand it. "The practical fruits of the insights of this knowledge to technology may still be available just as if everyone has been taught advanced physics" (Mokyr 2004 p.7). The transition of knowledge in a 'black box' avoided human beings having to undertake large investments in human capital to use each piece of technical knowledge. Thus, technological diffusion reduced the cost of knowledge diffusion and saved vast amounts of effort.

The Skilful Revolution

The growth in population from the fifteenth century and the improvements in agricultural production pushed people to search for work in towns. The cost of hiring humans for power had fallen to around 800 pence per kWh in the first half of the seventeenth century. Because there was a greater supply of workers and their demand for goods and income had increased, throughout the eighteenth century, men worked more regularly and harder, and more women and children laboured increasingly for the production of goods (De Vries 2006 p.50).

Yet, in the face of large competition (from other labourers), one strategy for workers was differentiation. Improving skills enabled workers to be more valuable to their potential employers. Similarly, as the technology developed and production processes became more sophisticated, it was essential for employers to have workers that could use the machines effectively. The introduction of new technologies and use of new fuels transformed the provision of heat and power. These altered the demand for skills in the production of energy services and industrial activity in general. For instance, working a fire and iron took great skills. An ironmaster from the eighteenth century described the art: "A Furnace is a fickle mistress and must be humoured and her favours not to be depended upon. I have known her (to) produce 12 tons per week, and sometimes but 9 tons, nay, sometimes but 8, the excellency of a Founder is to humour her dispositions, but never to force her inclinations" (Fuller quoted in Hyde 1973 p.9).

Shipbuilding had been an important traditional craft, requiring fine carpentry skills. While the industry had spread across the country, downstream of London Bridge on the Thames had long been one of the most successful bases for traditional shipbuilding in Britain. The craftsmen, once rewarded for their ability to shape wood, were no longer in great demand. The availability of large quantities of wrought iron, which was rolled into plates that could be riveted together, transformed shipbuilding and its location in the middle of the nineteenth century. New skills were needed. Similarly, poorer access to coal and iron had meant that, despite its prominence in the development of machine tools, London lost its role as a centre for shipbuilding (Buchanan 2003).

Similarly, the steam engine killed the demand for certain skills and created new ones. In the shipping industry, maritime engineers were especially sought-after. And, unskilled engine-room workers replaced able-bodied seamen, whose skills were in the manipulation of sails. Instead, those skilled sailors that worked on steamships earned substantially more than their sailing ship counterparts (Chin et al. 2004).

The increased investment in technology during the Industrial Revolution created a demand for workers with considerable skills for the provision of energy services. Entrepreneurs needed men that knew how to keep a fire burning, and paid handsomely for the skills. Thus, many men learned the trade and were rewarded.

It would be hard to estimate whether the level of human capital per unit of energy service actually increased. It may not have, given the rapid rise in energy services provided. Nevertheless, in the early days of industrialisation, there was some complementarity between human and physical capital.

As industrialisation and technologies progressed, the ability to stoke a fire and similar energy services were incorporated in the machine. Physical capital became a substitute for human capital. Expertise shifted to areas where machines could not replace humans. One such area was the creation of physical capital. Another expertise was in the maintenance and repair of technology.

Opposition to New Technologies

Despite the demand for new skills, there had been a decline in the need for human capital associated with energy service provision since the Industrial Revolution. The cost of disseminating knowledge in physical capital fell compared to the equivalent cost passed through human capital. So, some skilled workers lost their job in the face of competition from a machine. These workers may have discovered that the skills they had spent many years developing were obsolete. In other cases, less-skilled labourers were replaced by a few skilled workers and their machines.

Various devices introduced for their efficiency were received with hostility. The gig-mill, which was often water-powered, was banned by Parliament in 1552 and by royal proclamation in 1633. Introduced to England in the seventeenth century, the engine-loom, which could weave dozens of braids at the same time and could use hands, feet or water for power, received strong opposition.

The reduction in labour per unit of output created considerable fears about unemployment. Such concerns could often be short-sighted, however, since reduction in costs could lead to greater demand, thus employing potentially more workers. Naturally, in the short run, a conservative approach guaranteed a status quo in the level of employment (at least, temporarily); while the new device depended on the fickleness of the market forces (and few were likely to understand how they worked). In the long run, the conservative approach would probably reduce a company's competitiveness – compared with firms that had adopted new techniques – leading to declining demand and employment. The only way a company could fail to adopt and not decline was by providing a higher value product resulting from its production process. This depended on the existence or the creation of a demand for the higher value product. Thus, if it was adopted and proved to improve production, a new technology created change – how exactly changes occurred depended on the producers' and consumers' choices.

The decline in human capital meant that individuals had less of an understanding of the way of providing the service. This could increase the vulnerability of individuals when circumstances changed, such as price increases or shortages. Knowledge diffusion in a 'black box' could also lead to the alienation of the individual from the technology, as it carried knowledge that its owner was not privy to.

Another fear associated with new technologies was that traditional knowledge would be lost. Skills about ways of keeping warm, lighting and burning fires, cooking food and washing clothes disappeared. Much of this human capital that ensured efficient use of energy with little technology was lost, when the service became so cheap with machines.

New technologies have altered the boundaries of possibilities. They have enabled consumers to produce more services with the same amount of energy. They have transformed the type of workers that were needed to produce goods. They have led to opposition because the technologies reduced the number of workers needed, impinged on lifestyles or caused environmental damage. Innovations have also altered the incentives facing producers of existing equipment, and have created competition between technologies.

The Growth of Science: on the Shoulders of Giants

As the sophistication of technologies increased, high levels of expertise were required to produce advances in knowledge. To improve on existing techniques, observation alone was rarely sufficient. A theoretical underpinning of the knowledge was required to create improvements or radical changes. So, while in the eighteenth century, technical knowledge led to scientific understanding, by the second half of the twentieth century, science drove technology (Mokyr 2004).

Late in the nineteenth century, science became institutionalised. Universities stored the current state of scientific knowledge. They pushed forwards the boundaries of science, which improved technology. They also passed on the scientific and technical knowledge required to use increasingly sophisticated equipment.

Similarly, advances in technology were institutionalised. Universities, firms and governments began to set up research laboratories for the pursuit of knowledge. Each of them competed and, at times, cooperated in research, development and demonstration. The amounts of physical and human resources invested have been spectacular. The potential benefits from patented technological improvements were vast, both financially and in terms of the influence over the market.

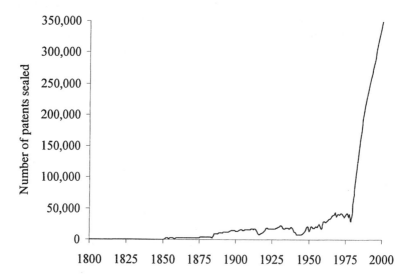

Source: UK Intellectual Property Office (2006)

Figure 8.8 The Number of Patents Granted, 1800–2000

Knowledge production has also become an international process. Organisations from different countries have been sharing ideas and competing for prizes and global markets. Knowledge production has increased dramatically as a result of the international spillover of ideas. This globalisation of science is reflected in Figure 8.8, which shows the explosion in the production of knowledge in Britain since the nineteenth century.

Improvements in Energy Technologies

Table 8.3 presents the trends in energy technologies. As might be expected, through time, equipment uses the energy more efficiently. From the beginning of the nineteenth century on, the average efficiency for a particular service always improved.

Heating became less efficient through the increased use of the chimney which replaced the open hearth. The switch, and consequent reduction in efficiency, enabled coal to be burnt, reducing the economy's need for products that directly converted solar radiation into products. Then, the improvements in the efficiency of heating in the last two hundred years have been substantial – from 11 percent to more than 85 percent, when the economy moved from the simple coal-burning fireplace to the gas central-heating system. Knowledge about directing heat and minimising loss in the conversion of fuel into heat was central to achieving these greater efficiencies. Thus, compared with buildings two hundred years back, households can expect dramatically greater heat per tonne of energy input (see Figure 8.9).

Table 8.3 Long-run trends in the Energy Technologies, 1300–2000

	1300	1500	1700	1750	1800	1850	1900	1950	2000
Heating[a]	13	13.5	11.2	11	11	13.5	21	41	86
Power[b]	11	15	15.5	17	17.5	15.5	28	23	32
Transport[c]			13	16	21	8	8	22	25
Lighting[d]	19	22	27	29	36	190	500	11 600	25 000

Notes

a – % of energy converted into heat.

b – % of power generated per unit of energy used.

c – passenger-kilometre per tonne of oil equivalent; transport only includes transport on land.

d – lumen-hours per kilowatt-hour.

Source: see Chapters 4-7, and Data Appendix

For much of the last thousand years, power and transport was generated by converting agricultural products, which captured solar radiation. Around one-tenth of the food or fodder was converted into power. This conversion rate was similar to the one provided by heating methods in the early modern era. It changed only gradually with the increased use of horses that were bred for specific purposes. The early steam engines were quite inefficient, reducing the average efficiency of power and transport conversion in the nineteenth century. Just like chimneys, steam engines allowed the use of fossil fuels, which reduced pressures on land per unit of service. Through time, their efficiency improved forty-fold in two hundred years after the beginning of the Industrial Revolution. Then, the introduction of electricity transformed the provision of stationary power, allowing a system reliant on a central source of supply, achieving major economies of scale, coupled with distributed points of use. At first, centrally-supplying power stations were less efficient than contemporary steam engines, thus, they reduced average efficiency once again. Through time, electricity generators have improved their conversion of fuel into power.

For non-stationary power, technological developments associated with railways and on roads, such as the internal combustion engine, led to substantial efficiency improvements for land-based transport in the twentieth century (see Table 8.3). For goods carriage, seafaring has provided most of the transport services in Britain. Thus, the introduction of steam and using it to replace sailing ships that harnessed the wind's power implied a drastic decline in the efficiency of transport services in the nineteenth century (see Figure 8.9).

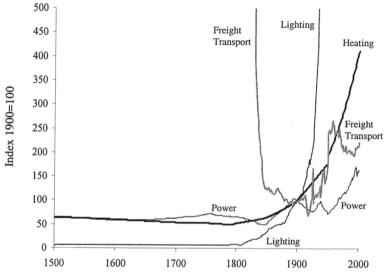

Note

* freight transport includes sailing ships.

Source: see Chapters 4-7, and Data Appendix

Figure 8.9 The Efficiency of Energy Technologies*, 1500–2000

Similarly, lighting was initially provided by animals – from cattle, sheep or whale fat. This fat was the share of energy remaining in the animal's body after consuming plants that did not get converted into heat, power or other basic biological functions. Of course, fat was an indirect way of providing heat, by making the animal more efficient at keeping or insulating the warmth it produced. This fat provided tallow or oils. Some oils also came directly from plants, such as the rape seed. During the nineteenth and twentieth centuries, the shift from tallow to gas to electricity (especially with today's compact fluorescent lighting) has enabled humanity to generate nearly one thousand times more light per unit of energy.

In most cases, the cost of energy was a major part of the overall expenditure on the service and, consequently, encouraged efforts to reduce the cost of the service. Yet, developments have directed changes in technologies towards a less efficient use of energy. Possibly the most interesting case is when efficiency worsened. In the case of heating, this was due to the shift from the open hearth to the fireplace. This appeared to be a retrograde move, as the chimney, especially in its early years, was quite inefficient. It required more fuel to generate the same amount of heat. Yet, there were several clear reasons for the shift in technology. A crucial reason was that the chimney enabled the smoke associated with fuel combustion to leave the room or hall – burning wood in an open hearth created a smoky room, with considerable health effects. This was undesirable. Using coal in an open hearth would have been a deeply unpleasant experience. Thus, when the chimney began to be adopted on a large scale in Britain from the sixteenth century, it was the only way to burn coal, which was a far cheaper fuel than wood (even considering the modest loss in efficiency for producing heat, discussed in the chapter on heat). The chimney also reflected a certain status in society and became fashionable then – it distinguished the middle classes from the labourers (Crowley 2004). Thus, the fireplace, though less efficient, provided additional attributes of value to the user: social status and externalising the costs of smoke.

The conversion of energy was probably worsened when steam power (for stationary or moving purposes) replaced water power (for stationary power) and wind (for transportation). Reliability of service provision was improved – water and wind power were intermittent, whereas steam could be created whenever a stoker had coal. There were, therefore, important characteristics of the technology that made it desirable. So, in a few examples, therefore, the market has followed a less efficient path. But, it generally improved the broader quality of service provided.

The twentieth century has witnessed some quite important improvements in the efficiency of energy technologies. In heating, refinements in coal and gas heaters during the first half of the twentieth century drove up the efficiency considerably. Then, in the last quarter, the introduction of the central-heating gas boiler converted enabled very high conversion of energy into heat. Similarly, steam engines were reaching more than 20 percent efficiency in the early twentieth century. The introduction of central generators and the distribution of power in the form of electricity improved the conversion rate. While coal power stations had improved considerably, the use of combined-cycle gas turbines improved efficiency substantially.

Physical laws do limit scientific progress – for instance, improvements in heating cannot rise too far; vehicles cannot travel faster than the speed of light. When or if the limits will be reached, perhaps scarcity of knowledge production in that field will be experienced. Once these physical limits have been encountered, the economy is likely to face severe constraints on growth, making resources scarce.

3. LONG-RUN TRENDS IN PRODUCING ENERGY SERVICES

The Price of Energy Services

Looking at the trends in the average cost of energy and the average efficiency of energy technologies suggests that the former consistently declines or the latter always rises. To consider them separately ignores the underlying drivers for demand, the provision of cheaper services.

Before the Industrial Revolution, there were striking fluctuations in the prices of energy services. For instance, one can discern a rise in the price of services leading up to the Industrial Revolution. The average price of power increased during the seventeenth century and first half of the eighteenth century, reflecting the changing cost of generating power from humans and horses (see Figure 8.10).

In the case of heating, the price did rise before the full switch to coal and the diffusion of the more efficient Rumford fireplace (see Figure 8.7). Families still using woodfuels experienced substantial increases in costs; some of them were burning the wood in highly inefficient old chimneys.

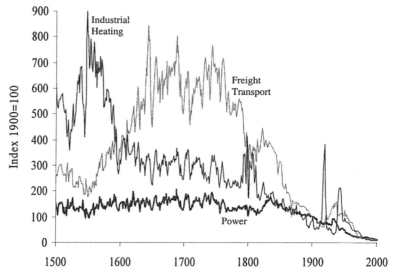

Source: see Chapter 4-7 and Data Appendix

Figure 8.10 The Price of Industrial Energy Services (Index 1900=100), 1500–2000

An interesting example was the rise in the price of freight transport services during the seventeenth century. The evidence is based on the series for freight transport, which stretches back to the thirteenth century, rather than passenger transport presented in Table 8.4, which only goes back to the mid-seventeenth century. The explanation for the dramatic price rise appears to be associated with the growing use of roads of worsening quality. These transport services have been dependent on a network of roads. The church was responsible for looking after the roads, before its dissolution under King Henry VIII. For a long period, no clear body was responsible for maintaining roads, and they were left to local communities. It appears that they failed to provide an adequate service. The introduction of turnpikes in the seventeenth century was a reflection of the desperate need for institutions to provide these public goods – in this case, in private hands. Once turnpikes became widespread in the eighteenth century, the price of transport services fell substantially (Jackman 1960).

Table 8.4 The Price of Energy Services (Index 1900=100), 1300–2000*

	1300	1500	1700	1750	1800	1850	1900	1950	2000
Heat		225	275	300	140	110	100	80	28
Power	85	155	160	165	105	150	100	50	12
Transport[a]	390	360	690	790	330	260	100	75	20
Lighting		950	1 115	1 170	570	300	100	6	1

Notes

* – values are rounded up or down for easier interpretation of changes.

a – land transport price.

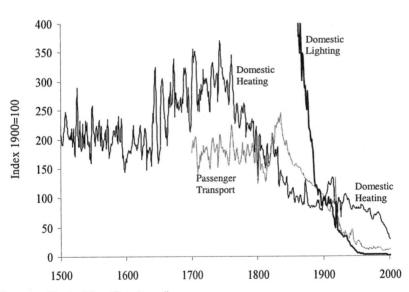

Source: see Chapter 4-7 and Data Appendix

Figure 8.11 The Price of Consumer Energy Services (Index 1900=100), 1500–2000

Sea freight transport also exhibited periods of high prices (in Figure 8.10). These were mostly associated with wars and privateering. The high risks of loss of ship and cargo drove up the costs of shipping. In times of peace, the price fell back to its base level. Yet, seafaring experienced the earliest declining prices of all energy services. A first feature of the freighting on the seas was its dependence on a free resource in large supply, the wind. Expansion of freighting services did not lead to increased constraints on the availability of resources. Prices could remain relatively stable, despite expansion, and then started to fall – before other energy services. One reason was that carpenters who worked on boats often travelled with the crew. They were able to visit foreign countries and observe knowledge used around Europe. Thus, by the sixteenth century, new shipping techniques were being adopted to improve carriage, speed and navigation. Prices were also falling because of the methods of reducing risk. The knowledge learnt in the seafaring trades was a precursor to the major changes that would occur in other activities and energy services.

The development and meeting of scientific, engineering and marketing skills at the time of the Industrial Revolution fed through into declining prices of energy services. In those last two hundred and fifty years, the cost of generating useful heat has fallen more than 10-fold. To generate a unit of power costs 50 time less. To travel one kilometre is 150 times cheaper. To produce the same quantity of light, it costs us 8 000 times less.

Despite the existence of considerable volatility in the original data series, the evidence presented in Table 8.1 shows that energy prices for heating and lighting fuels tended to drop before the sixteenth century, rise until the mid-eighteenth century, and fall with the beginning of the Industrial Revolution. For most of the services, despite the large-scale substitution towards more expensive but higher 'quality' fuels, there was a downward trend in average energy prices during the second half of the nineteenth century and much of the twentieth century. From the beginning of the nineteenth century on, the average efficiency for energy services always improved. This means that, since 1750, apart from a brief period of stagnation in the first half of the nineteenth century for power and transport, Britain experienced consistently declining prices of energy services.

4. CONCLUSION

The Growing Dominance of Knowledge and Technology

A series of revolutions transformed the way energy services have been provided over the last thousand years. Both energy and knowledge have played their part in determining the paths of energy services. Energy markets over the centuries have been characterised by a series of major trends and recurring issues. The trends have included, on the one hand, the shift to less expensive fuels, such as fossil fuels and, on the other, the supply of increasingly value-added energy products, epitomised by the popularity of electricity. Another trend was the increased capitalisation of energy industries, enabling economies of scale and engendering technological lock-ins.

Energy markets have also been subject to cycles. First, cycles of increased competition and concentration have altered the relationship between consumer and supplier. Second, the economy has experienced periods of energy abundance and scarcity, with altering impact on human welfare and economic activity.

Despite an overall tendency towards declining individual energy prices, periods of scarcity have created incentives to develop knowledge about how to find more resources, distribute them more swiftly and use them more effectively to provide energy services. In particular, considerable knowledge has been involved in the improving energy-using equipment. Technology embodied the knowledge that created better ways to heat, power, transport and light. As knowledge became easier to reproduce, it increasingly replaced energy in the production of energy services.

Although it is hard to present figures for the 'cost of knowledge' – here, 'knowledge' refers to techniques to improve the efficiency of energy use – it can be argued that the costs of reproducing information have fallen over the centuries, and particularly since the Industrial Revolution. Two modes of carrying knowledge relating to the generation of the production of energy services – human and physical capital – competed.

There has been a shift from human capital to physical capital, from skills about how to stoke a fire, drill a hole, drive a vehicle or light a room to a machine that can do it for the consumer. Knowledge was expensive to pass on when carried in people's heads. Traditionally, considerable skill was required to improve the quality or level of energy service, as well as the physical equipment. Human capital, and the labour, in time spent, made energy services costly. To employers, human capital had a further cost – the skilled energy service provider had additional bargaining power because of his knowledge.

Knowledge 'in a box' has become relatively cheap to reproduce, thanks to the Scientific and Industrial Revolution, and subsequent developments in engineering. The spread of books and literacy helped both modes, but the cost of investing human capital still experienced high marginal costs – teaching an additional person new skills was costly. On the other hand, the marginal costs of producing an additional machine carrying the knowledge about improving the provision of heat, power, transport or light were very low, especially as economies of scale occurred. The expansion of markets, resulting from wealthier consumers and bigger integration, has led to a larger demand for technology which made it worthwhile to pursue research and development in order to improve equipment.

Also, the cost of producing 'energy-efficient' knowledge fell relative to the price of energy. Energy prices have fluctuated over the last seven hundred years. While there have been more periods of decline than of increase in energy prices, the costs of knowledge production most probably fell relative to energy prices. As a result, there was a tendency to substitute knowledge for energy in the production of a unit of heat, power, transport or light.

This implies that the provision of each unit of energy service has become increasingly capital-intensive. Consumers faced higher fixed costs relative to marginal costs. As the size of firms and wealth of households increased, they were able to invest in larger equipment to generate energy services. This was aided by the increased credit availability and declining discount rates (partly due to lower interest rates, greater information dissemination about equipment, and general risk).

With the increased acquisition of equipment, the consumers of services became the producers. These producers were more in control of the cost structure they faced. In particular, at times, when the energy prices rose, so did the marginal cost of the service. During extended periods of high prices, consumers sought to reduce their energy dependence, through efficiency and conservation.

When prices fell, investing in less efficient technology meant increasing the amount of energy required, thus increasing the marginal costs of energy service production. Thus, even in periods of energy abundance and low energy prices, individuals tended not to invest in purely less efficient technology. When they did, it was as a result of investing in technologies that provided the services with additional attributes (to be discussed in the next chapter). In other words, when services were self-produced, consumers were unlikely to be willing to increase their marginal costs of production, at least not without compensation in the form of additional attributes. Thus, the increasing role of knowledge tended to keep the price of energy services low, increasing the consumption of energy services.

Is there a problem with generating our energy services with too much knowledge? The economy is knowledge-dependent. This knowledge is embodied in the technology. Thus, the consumer (and producer) of the energy service does not understand or control the necessary knowledge. Consumers are certainly alienated from the means of producing their services. Although a potentially undesirable situation, humans would not be capable of carrying all the knowledge necessary to produce energy services generated today. Vulnerability is just one of the prices for cheap heat, power, transport and light.

The economy produces more knowledge than is used. Today, many car companies are investing in developing the car of the future. Many possible futures exist – one car type will come to dominate. Knowledge production experiences increasing returns to scale, and leads to path dependencies. The economy follows only one path and it is impossible to know which will become the path followed or the car developed into 'the winner'. Thus, our economic system needs to produce too much knowledge, much of it abandoned. Yet, this inefficient process may be expected to achieve some economic development and progress.

On the other hand, all possible paths have the potential to create valuable ideas. Knowledge that has been used for the technological path chosen, such as the internal combustion engine in the early twentieth century, is well understood by a large body of engineers. Excluding cataclysmic events, this knowledge will remain in the economy's collective memory. The knowledge associated with technological paths not followed may tend to be forgotten – for instance, some of the information about harnessing wind in a sail or cars running on electricity has been lost. Avenues not followed by the present energy system may be valuable in the future. There is undoubtedly an option value related to retaining this knowledge, though probably no private incentive to do so.

A further consideration is the path followed. Knowledge can lead to many different paths associated with the use of energy services. Certainly not all possible paths of knowledge and technology development will be socially desirable. The market is likely to fail to ensure that the socially desirable path will be chosen (discussed in Chapter 10).

Cheaper Services

At this point, it is worth drawing a few conclusions from this chapter. The first conclusion is that focussing exclusively on energy prices (as economists have tended to do, due to a lack of data) risks ignoring part of the story. For instance, deducing that rising energy prices have been the result of increased scarcity might be correct, as in the case of some woodfuel in the eighteenth century, but it might also be misleading. At the end of the nineteenth and in the early twentieth century, higher prices reflected more valuable energy sources, using more efficient technologies, generating far greater energy services.

Similarly, the second conclusion is that considering only the trends in efficiency of technologies (as engineers and historians of technology might do, again due to a lack of evidence) might ignore the nature of the fuels being used, their prices and the systems within which they operate. The rare declines in efficiency, as in the switch to the fireplace or the steam engine, reflect characteristics of the technology and fuels they use.

Looking at the services that consumers seek to produce tells a different story. As Nordhaus (1997) highlighted, the fall in the price of services has been far greater than that indicated by the price of the fuel. The welfare improvements will have been far greater than expected. People have been able to heat their homes, push and pull objects, move people and goods, and light their homes far more cheaply. This has radically altered people's lives.

Two factors can make that happen. Each technological wave enables these people to provide these services increasingly cheaply. And, major transformations and economies of scale achieved in energy markets can lead to lower service prices. The following chapter will investigate the forces driving the increasing use of technology and consumption of energy services.

9.   Consuming More Services: Growth, Saturation and Novel Attributes

1. CONSUMPTION OF ENERGY SERVICES

Income and Economic Development

From the eleventh century to the mid-fourteenth century, both population and economic activity appear to have been rising relatively rapidly. Then in 1348 the 'Black Death' (bubonic plague) killed more than half the population and cut population and economic activity back to the levels of two centuries earlier. Figure 9.1 presents estimates of population and real gross domestic product (GDP) per capita (at year 2000 prices) for the period 1300 to 2000.

At least three features of the chart require comment. First, population took nearly four centuries, and per capita real income almost two centuries, to recover to their pre-1348 levels. Second, per capita income increased relatively rapidly in the sixteenth century and at a slower rate in the century after. And third, population increased relatively rapidly from the second half of the eighteenth century, partly in response to the rises in living standards associated with the Industrial Revolution. The most dramatic growth in economic activity and income levels was from the mid-nineteenth century and especially since the Second World War.

GDP in the United Kingdom has risen dramatically over the last five hundred years. In 1500, GDP per capita was at a level of around £250 per capita, lower than the poorest countries in the world today. By 1700, it had grown to around £1 000 per person per year. In 1870, it had reached around £2 500. Before the Second World War, it was just under £5 000 per person per year. By 2000, per capita income had reached £18 000 per person, nearly 70 times higher than five hundred years before and had increased 18-fold in three hundred years.

While the causes of economic development are hotly debated, key to the growth were the increased productivity in the agricultural sector, dramatic expansion of the industrial sector (especially, the textile and the iron and steel industries) and considerable growth in the service sectors. These factors in the growth of the British economy have been reflected in the changing structure of economic activity. Other features that characterise the development of an agrarian to an industrial to a service economy were the greater use of technology, rising personal wealth and disposable income, expanding and improving distribution and trade networks, rising and then stabilising population (declining mortality rates, then slowing fertility rates), migration from rural to urban areas and back to more rural areas (with major changes in population density in certain areas), and a growing demand for services and, thus, resources.

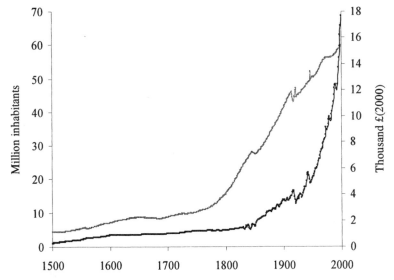

Source: Snooks (1994), Wrigley and Schofield (1981), Mitchell (1988) and Officer (2007a)

Figure 9.1 Population and Real Gross Domestic Product (GDP) per Capita in the United Kingdom (at year 2000 prices), 1500–2000

Consumption of Energy Services

In addition to a growing economy with higher income levels creating a rising demand for heat, power, transport and lighting, the declining price of energy services will have led to an increased consumption of services. The increase in consumption will have occurred because (as discussed in Chapter 8) it became cheaper to use heat to produce goods and keep a house warm, for instance, so firms and households would have tended to use more heat (and less of their substitutes). It will also have occurred because cheaper services made consumers relatively wealthier, thus, increasing consumption of most goods and services.

Over the last five hundred years, consumption of energy services has risen dramatically (see Table 9.1 and Figure 9.2). Power provision for 'industrial' purposes increased more than 200-fold since 1500 and 120-fold since 1700. Carriage of goods (on land and on the sea) has increased nearly 250 times in three hundred years.

Table 9.1 The Consumption of Energy Services (Index 1900 =100), 1300–2000

	1300	1500	1700	1750	1800	1850	1900	1950	2000
Heating[a]		1.3	4.1	5.9	12.2	34	100	266	726
Power[b]	6.7	4.3	7.7	11	17.7	39	100	194	944
Passenger[c]			0.06	0.1	4.5	16	100	683	2 565
Freight[c]			2	3.3	6.7	15	100	148	524
Lighting			0.06	0.1	0.2	3	100	2 362	11 910

Notes

a: domestic heating; b: power for all non-domestic sectors; c: land transport.

Household consumption of effective heating has increased 500-fold in five hundred years and 175-fold in three hundred years. Ignoring the role played by the ships, passenger travel increased more than 40 000-fold since 1700. In that time, lighting consumption rose 200 000 times.

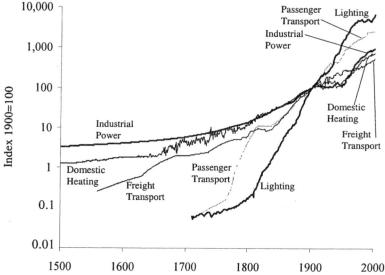

Note

'Industrial Power' includes all sectors except for the domestic sector.

Source: see Chapters 4-7 and Data Appendix

Figure 9.2 Consumption of Energy Services (Index 1900=100), 1500–2000

Service Consumption per Capita

One impression that Figure 9.2 creates is of permanently increasing consumption of energy services. The only exceptions were to transport during the Napoleonic

Wars, heating, power and freight transport at the beginning of the twentieth century, and lighting after the Oil Shocks. Each service has had its moment of stagnation, but they have been rare.

Consumption could have been driven by a growing population, a rising income level, a declining price of services (due either to declining energy prices or efficiency improvements) or changing tastes. In many cases, it would have been a combination of all factors. Complex inter-relationships between factors may also exist. For instance, the 'rebound effect' identifies an energy efficiency improvement that generates a general rise in economic activity and GDP, which feeds through as an increase in service consumption, thus, putting upward pressure on energy consumption. Alternatively, major technological developments are likely to alter people's awareness, attitudes and tastes, which could create a demand for specific services. Finally, rising income levels may stimulate changes in the price of energy leading to the development of new technologies, or changes in consumers' tastes.

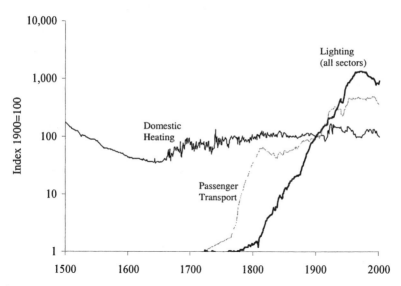

Source: see Chapters 4-7 and Data Appendix

Figure 9.3 Consumer Service Use per Capita (Index 1900=100), 1500–2000

Although the data can be considered a satisfactory reflection of long-run trends, annual changes in variables are not to be trusted. Because of the unreliability of the data presented, econometric exercises for identifying the influence of individual factors are impossible. Thus, a crude decomposition has been used to identify the possible influence of factors. To be specific, consumption of services will be stripped of the effects of population, then GDP and finally prices.

Population has quadrupled, from roughly 15 to 60 million people over the last two hundred years. Calculating the consumption of services per capita provides an almost identical pattern to overall consumption, suggesting that population was not a major driver for variations in consumption. Observing the trends in services of domestic heating, passenger transport and lighting helps understand the changes people experienced over the centuries, so it is worthwhile examining consumer per capita service use per capita (in Figure 9.3).

For consumers, the rate of growth of per capita use of domestic heating appears to have been relatively constant from the mid-seventeenth century. Despite a rising price of woodfuel and a declining average efficiency due to the gradual shift to chimneys, away from hearths, comfort levels increased in the mid-seventeenth century. The price of household heating settled from the 1680s and fell after the mid-eighteenth century. The price then fell considerably until the mid-nineteenth century, and intensity rose ten-fold. After a modest decline, prices declined rapidly at the end of the twentieth century, due to the introduction of central heating. Interestingly, heating per capita grew greatly. Thus, each person in 2000 benefits from around 200 times more effective heat in their household than in 1700.

Passenger transport exploded between the 1750s and 1800, due to the development of stagecoaches. With declining prices, it also increased, in bursts of 30 years, in the mid-nineteenth century and then at the turn of the century, as a result of railroads. Passenger transport expanded again between 1945 and the 1960s due to the growth of cars. A person at the end of the twentieth century travelled around 3 000 times more than the average person at the beginning of the eighteenth century.

Lighting prices fell steeply from the 1830s. This created a dramatic increase in lighting per capita. With limited improvements in lighting technology during the twentieth century (until the last decade), lighting per capita stabilised in the second half of the century. From the 1830s to the 1930s, homes, streets and towns in the Britain were lit up. Between 1700 and 2000, each person in the United Kingdom consumed 200 000 more lighting.

Consumer Responses to Income and Prices

Each consumer clearly benefited from a great deal more heat, transport and lighting over the last five hundred years. What factors were consumers responding to and by how much? As mentioned above, given the quality of the data, econometric analysis was not attempted on the data. Nevertheless, comparing changes in price and income with per capita consumption provide some valuable information, focussing on changes in orders of magnitude rather than marginal changes in behaviour.

A comparison will be made of the actual changes in consumption with a 'counter factual' consumption level if demand had both a price and income elasticity equal to one. This exercise will be executed for the eighteenth, nineteenth and twentieth centuries and the second half of the twentieth century, as represented in Table 9.2.

Table 9.2 Actual and Counter Factual (C.F.) Increase in Energy Service Consumption per Capita to Income and Price Changes, 1700–2000

	1700-1800		1800-1900		1900-2000		1950-2000	
	Actual	C.F	Actual	C.F.	Actual	C.F.	Actual	C.F.
Heating	3.0*	2.5	8.2**	4.0	7.3	18	2.7	10
Power	2.3*	1.9	5.6**	3.1	9.4	42	4.9	14
Passenger	75***	1.8	22***	3.5	26	44	3.8	7
Freight	3.4*	2.7	15**	8.2	5.2	38	3.5	32
Lighting	2.8*	2.5	595***	2.9	120	646	5.0	25

Notes

* joint (that is, income and price) elasticity greater than one.

** joint (that is, income and price) elasticity around two.

*** joint (that is, income and price) elasticity very large.

Source: see Chapters 4-7 and Data Appendix

This comparison will help identify during which periods consumers were highly responsive to changes in income and prices. The most striking observation is that consumption was elastic in the eighteenth century, very elastic in the nineteenth century and not elastic in the twentieth century, possibly becoming even less elastic since the middle of the twentieth century.

In the eighteenth century, household[24] heating consumption per capita tripled. If the demand for heating had had an income- and price-elasticity of one, then consumption would have risen 2.5-fold in that period. Heat consumption was slightly more responsive during the eighteenth century. The average consumer in the nineteenth century was far more responsive to price and income changes. On the other hand, despite a considerable increase in heating consumption in the twentieth century, the consumer was relatively unresponsive to the large rise in income and fall in heating prices. Similar patterns of consumer responses occur for each of the services. Energy service users in the nineteenth century responded strongly to changes in budgets and price changes.

Again, we can say little about price and income elasticity individually, but it would seem that there were differences between services. Industrial users, mainly power and freighting, were less responsive to changes. Consumers of heating, transport and lighting were a little more sensitive. The most responsive was passenger transport. It is not clear to what extent the lack of data on water transport for passengers overstates the increase in consumption. It is probable, however, that, whereas freighting services used water carriage a great deal,

---

24. The large number of different industrial activities using heating meant that no single indicator for industrial heating could be created.

passengers increased their mobility dramatically with the introduction of stagecoaches and of railways.

Service Intensity

It may seem frustrating to know that the nineteenth century was a period of extreme responsiveness to changes in price and income, yet not know whether it was due to the economic growth and wealth or due to prices. Although discerning accurately elasticities will be impossible, a little more analysis is possible. By observing consumption relative to GDP, we can gather an impression of the role of GDP and, consequently, the role of prices or tastes.

Power intensity (shown in Figure 9.4) fell dramatically from the sixteenth to the mid-seventeenth centuries. This indicates that the rise in economic activity was important for the increase in power consumption from the sixteenth to the twentieth centuries, represented in Figure 9.2. Yet, relative to other services, this growth rate before the nineteenth century was quite weak. In fact, Figure 9.4 suggests that, over these five hundred years, power's role weakened in the sixteenth century, perhaps as industrialisation required other services.

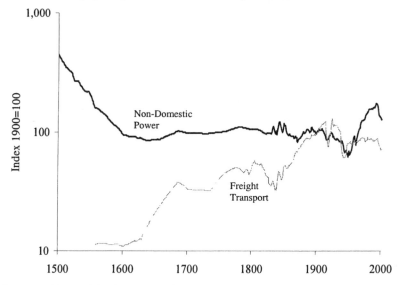

Source: see Chapters 4-7 and Data Appendix

Figure 9.4 Industrial Energy Service Intensity (Index 1900=100), 1500–2000

Also, the price of power increased between 1500 and 1700. Then, during the eighteenth century, the price of power fell, yet power intensity hardly changed. Apart from a peak in the early 1800s, the price of power continued to fall with the switch from food and fodder to coal as the main fuel. Yet, as a proportion of

GDP, power stayed relatively constant, declining slightly in the second half of the nineteenth century. Power intensity increased with a decline in the price of power, the electrification of the economy and the expansion of service industries in the first half of the twentieth century.

In the early seventeenth century there was a major increase in freight intensity, due to the growth of shipping (see Figure 9.4). From the mid-eighteenth century, freight intensity increased again. At the same time, the price of transport fell rapidly with the development of turnpikes and expansion of sea merchants. Then, freight intensity halted briefly at the beginning of the nineteenth century indicating that, during this period, the growth in freight use shown in Figure 9.2 was due to rises in income. From the mid-nineteenth century until the turn of the century, freight intensity exploded (see Figure 9.4). Thanks to the introduction of railways, freight prices collapsed.

This evidence suggests that economic activity was not the dominant influence in the growth of freight services, at least until the twentieth century. By 1900, much of the dramatic changes had taken place. Prices continued to fall in the twentieth century, yet, freight intensity changed little. In other words, the growth in freight service use in the twentieth century was due to growing economic activity.

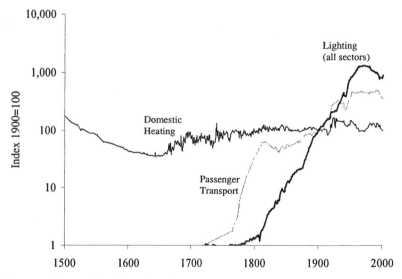

Source: see Chapters 4-7 and Data Appendix

Figure 9.5 Consumer Energy Service Intensity (Index 1900=100), 1500–2000

Overall, the carriage of goods was radically transformed in two phases. Industrialisation involved a dramatic increase in the amount of raw materials and manufactured goods that were moved around the economy. This process was completed at the end of the nineteenth century, and further expansion of the economy no longer required moving proportionally greater amounts of raw materials and manufactured goods.

The heating intensity of households fell substantially during the sixteenth and the first-half of the seventeenth centuries, as shown in Figure 9.5. Prices were relatively stable in the 1500s and even declining in the first half of the 1600s. In Figure 9.3, per capita heating increased, however. Thus, rising wealth drove up demand for heating then. Intensity increased considerably at the end of the seventeenth century, increasing gradually in the eighteenth century and stabilising in the nineteenth century. Between 1650 and 1800, domestic heating consumption increased due to income, as well as from changes in prices and tastes.

Interestingly, though, price of heating increased between 1650 and 1700, then decreased after 1750. In the second half of the seventeenth century, heating intensity rose despite a rise in prices and, in the nineteenth century, with declining prices, heating intensity did not change. Thus, it would seem that, ignoring the influence of income, there was a growing desire for heating in the seventeenth century and a declining desire in the nineteenth century.

Passenger transport intensity rose dramatically in the eighteenth century. The price of passenger transport changed little during the eighteenth century, suggesting there was a growing desire for mobility, exclusive of income changes. Prices then rose up to the 1830s, which led to a decline in travel. With the introduction and expansion of railways, prices fell yet intensity grew only gradually.

The first half of the twentieth experienced a leap in passenger transport intensity. Prices fell considerably, suggesting much of the rise in passenger transport was due to price or preference changes. From 1955, passenger intensity remained constant. Travel per capita (in Figure 9.3) rose consistently during this period, suggesting much of the growth was due to rising disposable income. For most of that period, prices were stable, except during the oil shocks. It suggests that, between 1973 and 1986, consumers were willing (or had no choice but) to pay extra to keep their mobility.

Lighting intensity grew between the end of the eighteenth century and the 1970s. During this extended period, the price of lighting fell almost constantly, thus, it was a major driver of consumption. From the 1970s, intensity fell, despite only a slight and temporary increase in prices. It would appear that consumers learnt to want less light, or conserve more.

Expenditure on Services

Previous sections provide impressions of the trends in consumption, per capita consumption and intensity. Building on these impressions, the patterns in service expenditure relative to GDP will help separate the influence of responses to price changes from consumer willingness to pay for service. It may also help identify interesting features of the economy and the role of energy services.

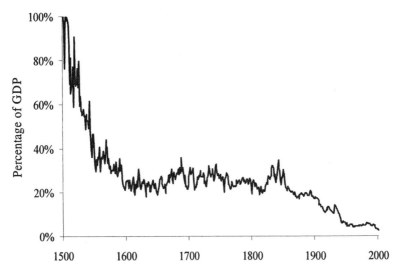

Source: see Chapters 4-7 and Data Appendix

Figure 9.6 Non-Domestic Power Expenditure relative to Total GDP, Percentage, 1500–2000

Figure 9.6 suggests that an economy which spent most of its income on power, principally humans and animals to mostly work in the fields, and pay for the food and fodder to keep them, was a subsistence economy. It just managed to breakeven. In some years, more was spent on power than was produced. Although this could be due to data limitations, it highlights the possibility that, at times, the economy was not subsistent.

The major decline in expenditure on power as a share of GDP, due to lower wages and cheaper agricultural products, observed in the sixteenth century, freed-up funds for other purposes, presumably shelter, textiles and manufactured goods – and military ambitions. The next decline in power expenditure was from the mid-nineteenth century, enabling another large share of expenditure to be spent on other activities and products. Thus, according to this evidence the major changes in power in Britain occurred in the sixteenth century, enabling a shift out of agriculture, and from the 1830s to the 1920s, which completed the process of mass production.

Expenditure on freight transport grew rapidly from the eighteenth century (see Figure 9.7). Despite falling prices, expenditure rose, showing a growing desire for freight services or the benefits of trade. It increased substantially in the nineteenth century, with the introduction of railways. Again, prices were falling. The movement of goods, often heavy raw materials and manufactured goods, became a major function of the economy. A further peak was observed in the early twentieth century, associated with the shift to expensive petroleum in goods vehicles. The importance of freight services has declined considerably from the 1950s, however.

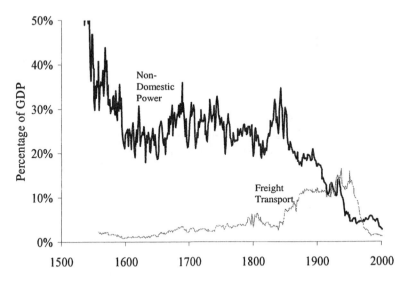

Source: see Chapters 4-7 and Data Appendix

Figure 9.7 Industrial Energy Service Expenditure Relative to Total GDP, Percentage, 1500–2000

Domestic heating benefited from the shift to cheaper coal from the sixteenth century, and there was a major decline in expenditure on household heating relative to GDP (see Figure 9.8). Then, the major increase in the seventeenth and eighteenth centuries was, in part, due to a modest increase in the average fuel heating prices and consumer insensitivity to these prices. Yet, the increase probably also reflected a consumer desire for the appearance of greater comfort (Cowley 2004). The burgeoning middles classes were seeking to emulate wealthier citizens and distinguish themselves from the commoner. A greater standard of domestic comfort – including the building of a chimney and the use of coal – was an important way of stating social mobility in early modern era.

From the mid-eighteenth century, household expenditure on heating fell. In the 1930s and the 1980s, there were peaks in heating expenditure relative to GDP, which seem to reflect rises in fuel prices. Nevertheless, during the twentieth century, average heating prices were cheaper than in the nineteenth century, yet expenditure relative to GDP was higher. This indicates that the twentieth century was a second wave of willingness to pay for warmth and comfort.

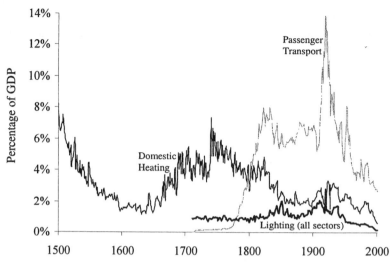

Source: see Chapters 4-7 and Data Appendix

Figure 9.8 Consumer Expenditure Relative to Total GDP, Percentage, 1500–2000

After the first wave of comfort came an increased expenditure on energy for mobility in the latter part of the eighteenth century. Travel prices were stable, removing their influence. From the 1770s, people wanted to travel more. In the nineteenth century, expenditure stabilised. Prices rose before the railways, and fell afterwards. Intensity dropped a little before and rose a little afterwards. Thus, surprisingly, the railways did not intensify people's desire for mobility.

2. THE ROLE OF ENERGY

Energy Consumption

For much of the last five hundred years, energy consumption has been on an upward trend, driven by economic and population growth. It may have increased due to declining energy service prices, due to cheaper fuels or from the 'rebound effect', associated with, first, a 'greater than one' price elasticity of demand for energy services, second, an increase in the production of other goods requiring more energy, and third, a boost to the economy increasing the demand for energy services and the related energy (see Chapter 2). It will also have resulted from shifts in demand due to changing preferences, which could coincide with new technological improvements combining greater energy efficiency and desirable attributes.

Figure 9.9 represents the trends in industrial power, heating and freight transport. In 1500, the amount of energy used for industrial heating and power was already substantial, much of it part of an organic energy system. Estimates have included, as best as possible, organic energy sources. As a result, the growth rate during the Industrial Revolution was not as spectacular as has often been suggested, because of the substitution of mineral for organic fuels.

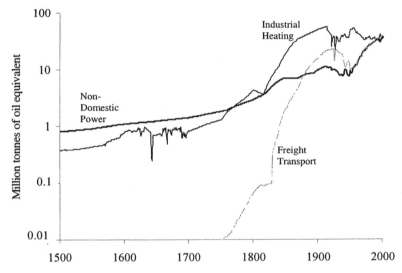

Source: see Chapters 4-7 and Data Appendix

Figure 9.9 Industrial Energy Use (million tonnes of oil equivalent (mtoe)), 1500–2000

The rate of growth of energy for power did accelerate during the Industrial Revolution, yet only modestly. Man and animal required substantial amounts of energy, in the form of food and fodder. The steam engine consumed more coal. Yet, as its uptake accelerated, its efficiency increased, implying that between 1800 and 1900 the consumption of power increased twice as fast as the energy use for power. The use of electricity for industry from the Second World War led to an acceleration in the amount of coal used for power. After the Oil Shocks, energy consumption on industrial power slowed dramatically.

Energy consumption for industrial heating grew very slowly up to 1700. It then increased substantially up to 1800, requiring more energy than power. Heating fuel use grew rapidly between 1820 and 1870. From the First World War, fuel used for industrial heating stayed relatively constant (with a small peak reflecting the rebuilding of the United Kingdom after the Second World War).

Energy use for freight increased rapidly, with the exception of the Napoleonic Wars, until the First World War. This growth was amplified by the switch from sailing ships with low energy inputs from harnessing the wind (here, not estimated) to steam and its heavy consumption of coal. By then, the energy used to move goods around the country was approaching the amount of fuel used for power. Freight fuel use stabilised, until the mid-1980s, when it started growing again.

Up to the twentieth century, passenger transport energy consumption grew in a similar way: rapidly (see Figure 9.10). The difference was that fuel used for passengers continued to grow at a fast rate. After the Second World War, passenger fuel consumption surpassed freight use, and was three times as large in 2000, overtaking domestic heating consumption.

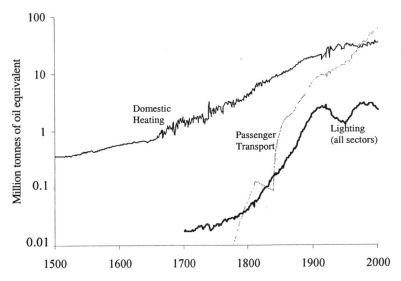

Source: see Chapters 4-7 and Data Appendix

Figure 9.10 Consumer Energy Use (million tonnes of oil equivalent (mtoe)), 1500–2000

Fuels used for heating in households and firms were similar in 1500. After some fluctuations, especially associated with the 1640s Civil War, domestic use grew at a relatively steady rate from the second half of the seventeenth century until the Second World War. The shift to natural gas and later central heating systems appears to have increased the provision of warmth with no additional fuel.

Fuel consumption for lighting grew steadily in the eighteenth and rapidly in the nineteenth centuries. It dropped between the two World Wars, rising again from the 1950s peaking in 1978, and starting to fall in the 1990s.

Energy Intensity

Energy intensity is a frequently used indicator for observing the role of energy in the economy. Yet, the fluctuations in energy intensity are poorly understood. Much of the discussion in this book highlights the importance of services in driving energy behaviour. In particular, although tempting to ignore the break-down for lack of data, energy intensity can be seen as a function of service intensity and of the service to energy ratio.

The amount of energy required for power per pound of GDP declined almost continuously since the sixteenth century (see Figure 9.11). The only exceptions were slight increases in the second half of the seventeenth century, between 1760 and 1780, between 1820 and 1850, and, more significantly, between 1945 and 1973 – periods of critical importance in Britain's economic history. They were also the only periods of increased power intensity in the last five hundred years (see Figure 9.3). Between 1820 and 1850, the average energy efficiency of power services declined, with the diffusion of highly inefficient steam engines.

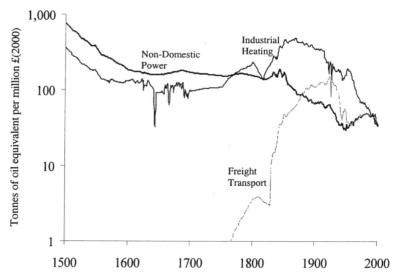

Source: see Chapters 4-7 and Data Appendix

Figure 9.11 Industrial Energy Intensity (tonnes of oil equivalent (toe) per £(2000)million), 1500–2000

Industrial heating fuel use intensity also fell during the sixteenth and seventeenth centuries. As industrial heating generated many different outputs, there is no single indicator of heating consumption to understand the source of the decline. From the mid-eighteenth century, however, energy intensity for heating increased considerably. The iron and other metal industries were certainly major sources of economic value during the Industrial Revolution. Yet, after 1870, the role of energy for heating in the economy declined.

Energy used for freight services increased rapidly into the 1800s and again from the 1840s with the introduction of railways and steamships, which replaced sailing ships. This energy intensity fell throughout the twentieth century – freight service intensity did too.

At home, during the sixteenth century, energy used relative to income declined (see Figure 9.12). It gradually increased from the end of the seventeenth centuries, until the 1820s. Energy used for heating fell relative to income – this was reflected in a stable trend in service intensity (see Figure 9.5) and an improving energy efficiency of heating.

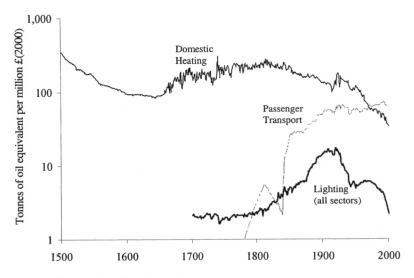

Source: see Chapters 4-7 and Data Appendix

Figure 9.12 Consumer Energy Intensity (tonnes of oil equivalent (toe) per £(2000)million), 1500–2000

Energy for passenger transport increased with income rapidly up to the 1850s. The growth was associated with increased fodder for a huge horse population and, at the end of this phase, inefficient steam trains. After a brief break, energy use compared with income increased from 1870 to 1930 – more fodder, more coal, and then petrol. Fuel intensity grew again from the 1970s, dipping in the late 1990s. The oil shocks appear to have had little impact on the consumption of transport services or its fuel.

Fuel for lighting relative to income grew rapidly from the 1800s until 1913. It then fell in the 1920s, increasing again from 1945 and then stabilising in 1973. In other words, for most of the twentieth century, despite declining service prices, energy consumption for lighting has been falling relative to income.

The 'Rebound Effect'

Given the interest in the 'rebound effect' (see Chapter 2), it is worth analysing these trends. Without econometric analysis (and reliable data to base it on), it would be impossible to properly infer the importance of the 'rebound effect' in history. A starting point for a crude analysis is a study of energy intensity trends.

A main reason for energy consumption to have risen through time is economic and population growth. Energy intensity estimates remove these influences. Thus, any additional increases would have been due to falling energy service prices or (non-growth related) shifts in demand.

In a few periods in history, sectoral energy consumption increased faster than economic and population growth: industrial heating (1700s to 1850s), industrial power (1920s and 1930s), freight transport (1710s to 1810s and 1840s to 1930s), passenger transport (1710s to 1810s and 1840s to 1920s, 1950s to 2000), domestic heating (1670s to 1920s), lighting (1810s to 1910s). While this approach may not capture all cases of 'rebound effects', it helps to identify a number of possible ones.

But, before moving forward, it is obvious to ask whether they were phases of energy efficiency improvements. While some industrial activities may have been getting more efficient in the eighteenth century, the iron industry was becoming less efficient, as it starting using coke. Between the 1810s and 1850s, however, by which time most iron furnaces and forges were dependent on coke, substantial efficiency improvements were achieved (see Chapter 4). In the early 1900s, industrial power saw substantial reductions in efficiency, with the introduction of power stations, followed by improvements (see Chapter 5). Both freight and passenger transport experienced improvements in the efficiency of horse carriage with the development of turnpikes, then a worsening with the introduction of railways, followed by further improvements as steam power was refined; modest efficiency improvements in vehicles were achieved in the second half of the twentieth century, especially after the Oil Shocks (see Chapter 5). Average domestic heating efficiency worsened in the seventeenth and eighteenth century as more people shifted to fireplaces and their wasteful chimneys (see Chapter 4). Lighting experienced transitions to new energy sources and greater efficiency (see Chapter 7). So, in many cases where the energy intensity increased, there was an energy transition leading to a reduction in energy efficiency and then an important improvement (Table 8.3 and Figure 8.9).

To consider whether a 'rebound effect' occurred, it is first necessary to compare the trend in energy prices (see Table 8.1 and Figure 8.3) with the one for energy intensity. The only cases selected in which the rising trend in energy intensity was similar to or weaker than the trend in energy prices were associated with the diffusion of electricity in industry (despite being a strong candidate for the 'rebound effect'), the desire for greater comfort in the eighteenth century and the expansion of car use at the end of the twentieth century (see Table 9.3). But, examining energy intensity implies that any economic growth leads to a proportionate rise in the service and energy consumption. If energy and service responsiveness to economic output and income grew at a slower rate, then the rise in energy consumption would have large relative to the fall in energy prices, suggesting the possibility of an increase in energy use attributable to a 'rebound effect'. These cases remain uncertain.

The following cases experienced a greater rise in energy intensity than the fall in energy price: industrial heating (1810s to 1850s), freight transport (1710s to 1810s and 1840s to 1930s), passenger transport (1710s to 1810s and 1840s to 1920s, 1950s to 2000), and lighting (1810s to 1910s). A greater rise in energy intensity than the fall in energy prices would suggest a 'rebound effect' and/or a shift in demand; the shift in demand may be the result of valued attributes related to the introduction of the new technology associated with the 'rebound effect' or driven by external factors, such as separate economic, social or cultural developments.

Table 9.3 Evidence of the 'Rebound Effect'

Sector	Period	Growth in Energy Intensity	Fall in Energy Prices	Rebound Effect (RE) or Other Factor
Industrial Heating	1700s-1850s	Medium	Small	Economic Development
Industrial Power	1920s-1930s	Small	Medium	Possibly RE
Freight Transport	1710s-1810s	Extreme	Rise in Prices	Economy-Wide Effect (RE)
Freight Transport	1840s-1930s	High	Small	Economy-Wide Effect (RE)
Passenger Transport	1710s-1810s	Extreme	Rise in Prices	Direct Effect (RE)
Passenger Transport	1840s-1920s	High	Small	Direct Effect (RE) and Time Saving Effect
Passenger Transport	1950-2000	Small	Small	Possibly RE and Demand Shift
Domestic Heating	1670s-1800s	Small	Small/Medium	Demand Shift
Lighting	1810s-1910s	High	Medium	Direct Effect (RE) and Demand Shift

Source: see Figures 9.11, 9.12, 8.3, 8.9

As mentioned above, the 'rebound effect' can be the result of a direct effect (that is, a 'greater than one' price elasticity of demand for energy services), an indirect effect (that is, an increase in the production of other goods requiring more energy) or an economy-wide effect (that is, a boost to the economy increasing the demand for energy services and the related energy). Given some understanding of the cases (see Chapters 4 to 7), it might be possible to explore further the nature of the effect. Ironically, the limitations of this analysis can also give clues to the nature of the impact of technological change.

Just as the responsiveness of energy demand to economic growth could have been less than one (possibly at the time of electrification, rising comfort and expansion of the car), it could have been greater than one as a result of structural shifts in the economy. Industrial heating (1700s to 1850s) was probably not a case of the 'rebound effect'; instead the economy shifted to more energy-intensive industries, such as iron production.

Economy-wide effects are associated with higher GDP levels, which affect energy intensity. So, focussing on intensity hides the scale of any economy-wide effect. Despite the problem of analysis, freight transport intensity increased greatly. Freight transport (1710s to 1810s and 1840s to 1930s) was probably associated with substantial economy-wide effects, as the declining prices of the service stimulated trade, commerce and the whole economy and, thus, the demand for freight services.

Often, technological innovations may achieve time-savings, instead of or as well as energy efficiency improvements. Passenger transport (1710s to 1810s and 1840s to 1920s) did experience radically greater desire for mobility, especially from the time savings it generated – particularly for poorer people at the end of the nineteenth century (Leunig 2006). This was probably a classic case of time-saving technological change encouraging the production of a service (mobility) in a more energy-intensive way (that is, using coal steam engines) and creating dramatic increases in the demand for the service, partly due to the 'rebound effect' of time-efficiency (Binswanger 2001).

In some cases, the income effect of the demand for a service can be large enough to influence the 'rebound effect'. Lighting (1810s to 1910s) was associated with a desire to 'lengthen the day' (Bowers 1998). The dramatic reductions in the price of the service achieved positive and important income effects. Consumers were also swayed by a rising demand for lighting and the social and cultural opportunities it offered (Schivelbusch 1988).

In the cases discussed, many forces were at work simultaneously influencing energy consumption. The population and economy was growing. The price of energy may have been falling. Technological progress may have been leading to improvements in energy efficiency or to savings in time. To disentangle all these influences properly, econometric analysis would be necessary. Given the nature of the data, this was not possible. Instead, some very crude methods were used to identify the existence and types of 'rebound effects', as well as other factors, such as structural shifts in the economy or cultural transformations driving demand.

In many cases throughout history, energy efficiency improvements may not have led to 'rebound effects'. There were 'border-line' cases, such as the electrification of industry, the shift to greater comfort and the expansion of private vehicle use, which should be considered in more detail. In other cases, especially associated with transportation and lighting, the 'rebound effect' was probably large and greater than the energy savings.

The Energy Intensity of the Economy

Looking at the overall energy intensity of the economy, the pattern has been distinct, and can be stylised. The agrarian economy was heavily energy-intensive. The organic proto-industrial phase was not. The industrial economy was energy-intensive. The post-industrial economy has been far less energy-intensive.

A striking feature, shown in Figure 9.13, was the dramatically large amounts of energy used to produce one pound (Sterling) of GDP in the sixteenth century. The data is, once again, a possible culprit. Yet, the data does have some basis in numbers quoted from the time. As long as the estimates do not overestimate the actual levels by three-fold, the early sixteenth century economy was very energy-intensive.

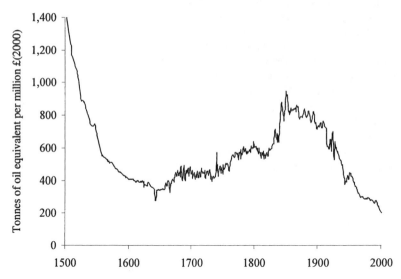

Source: see Chapters 4-7 and Data Appendix

Figure 9.13 Energy Intensity (tonnes of oil equivalent (toe) per £(2000)million), 1500–2000

One explanation is that following the Black Death, the population was under five million and the economy had collapsed. Resources were available. Both industrial power and heating intensity fell. Food and fodder was relatively cheap in 1500. Population and the economy grew a great deal throughout the sixteenth century. The price of food and fodder increased considerably by 1600, and the price of power rose too. In particular, the number of horses became more productive.

Basic activities of agricultural production, cooking and brewing required considerable amounts of energy. They were essential for survival, yet generated only a small GDP. The growth in GDP in the sixteenth century was associated with other activities, such as textile. Textile required a little extra power, and boosted the value of the economy steadily.

Having considered the shift from the agrarian to the proto-industrial era, the Industrial Revolution needed great quantities of energy, aided by the gradual shift towards fossil fuels. The dominant trend in the price of heating, power, transport and lighting was downwards during the twentieth century. Yet, energy intensity has fallen consistently since the 1860s.

Looking at productive activities, energy intensity for power declined consistently, while energy intensity for industrial heating and freighting increase during first and second phases of industrialisation (from about 1760 to 1870). During the third phase (1870–1913), fuel intensity for heating declined and for freighting continued to grow. The shift towards the 'post-industrial' economy tended to imply a decline in energy intensity for production.

For direct consumption, energy intensity associated with domestic heating, passenger transport and lighting all increased with a growing standard of living up to the 1870s. Requirements for mobility were most abrupt. Then, from 1870, heating consumption relative to income started to decline, and growth for transport slowed, while the 'democratisation' of lighting increased fuel consumption. After 1913, consumption relative to income tended to fall for all services.

The ability to produce heating, power, transport and lighting has become increasingly dependent on knowledge. The economy also is becoming more dependent on knowledge to produce goods and services.

Energy Consumption of the Economy

Having noticed the improving energy intensity of the economy since 1870, it is important to point out, however, that energy consumption has been rising (see Figure 9.14). In the nineteenth century, energy consumption increased eight-fold, particularly due to the fuel requirements for manufacturing. Final user energy consumption doubled during the twentieth century. Energy use for all services increased, especially for transport services.

Knowledge has enabled the economy to produce heating, power, transport and lighting more cheaply and with less energy. Yet, the economy has been growing so fast, especially in the second half of the twentieth century, that the overall effect has been to consume ever more energy.

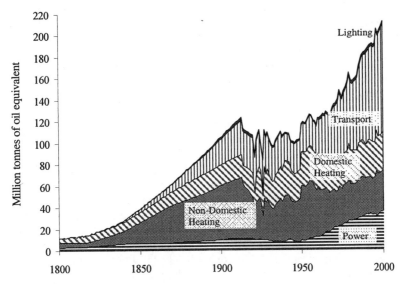

Source: see Chapters 4-7 and Data Appendix

Figure 9.14 Final User Energy Consumption (million tonnes of oil equivalent), 1800–2000

3. DEMAND FOR ENERGY SERVICES

In many studies of major transformations, the role of the consumer is given little emphasis. Changes are seen as coming from the supply side, and the demand tends to follow. While this is often the case, it relegates demand to being passive. Demand evolves, and this evolution has major implications for these transformations.

Demand is of great importance, influencing incentives for new supply-side developments. Ultimately, the reason for being interested in these major transformations is the welfare improvements bestowed on the population. It is, therefore, worth considering the value of the revolutions in energy services.

The Basic Needs

Man, a warm-blooded animal, with weak and short limbs and highly dependent on its vision, has been requiring energy services for certain basic 'needs'. Heating has been an important service in the household. A key driver of the demand for heat has been the need and desire to regulate body temperature and inner climate. While there were basic biological requirements, the demand for heating has shown itself to be surprisingly subjective. It has varied greatly with age, health, personal experiences and habits. Before the mid-nineteenth century, 15°C appeared to be a desirable temperature in a house – any warmer would be harmful to one's health. This ideal temperature has risen with the falling cost of heating and habits have followed.

Naturally, outdoor temperatures and humidity have had a major impact on the demand for heating to the desired temperature. Given that the desired and outdoor temperatures have varied considerably over the centuries, demands have greatly varied.

Throughout history, when heating was not easily possible, people have used other ways of staying warm than simply fuel and associated equipment. Shelter, furnishings and clothing helped reduce the demand for heating, by improving the efficiency of the heat. People have also stayed warm by keeping active, huddled or inebriated. Thus, there have been substitutes for 'fuel' heating.

Another central demand for heating in the household was for cooking food, to be edible, more nutritious and tastier, and preparing drinks too. Gradually, warm water was also used to wash body, clothes and dishes. Heating was also central to many productive activities. Either it was needed in the same way – to regulate temperature, serve food and drink or wash – or for different purposes, such as preparing substances and materials, particularly metals and chemicals. When workers' skills, technology or fuels changed, their heating patterns varied.

Power was also vital to producing goods. In the agriculture sector, power was needed for ploughing fields, reaping crops and crushing grain. It was also needed for crushing grains. Mining also required power to work through the earth and lift minerals and ores to the surface. In manufacturing, textile preparation and making required large amounts of power. In addition, many industrial activities needed to move and shape materials.

Mobility of people and resources has been vital to the emergence of an economic system. The market depends on moving goods to meet the consumer. The consumer has also sought to travel, for economic activities and leisure.

Humans have a relatively well developed sense of vision. This has been of great benefit in performing tasks during daylight hours. But, humans are diurnal, and have been quite inept at night. When artificial light was not available, activities that required seeing were hard to complete and encouraged the pursuit of tasks manageable in the dark. Some activities could then be done in the daytime rather than at night, or were less frequently practiced. Artificial illumination has been crucial to improving mankind's ability to achieve objectives at night.

The Relationship between Economic Development and Energy Services

Having examined the trends in energy service and energy use, it is possible to draw some broad conclusions about the relationship between economic development and the demand for energy services, at least for the United Kingdom.

First, the interaction between variables will be analysed. Econometric analysis would be necessary to identify the direction of causation associated with economic development, energy service prices and energy service demand. Unfortunately, this data does not seem robust enough for the task.

Most probably, each variable influenced the other two. Economic development increased the demand for energy services; it also helped produce knowledge and achieve economies of scale which drove down the price of energy services. Prices clearly increased the quantity demanded, and probably boosted economic development. Similarly, consuming more energy services could have driven economic development, and could also have achieved economies of scale pushing down prices.

Yet, if a chain of causality had to be imposed, it may be that (a) economic development increased the demand for energy services, which led to (b) economies of scale in production of technologies and pressure on resources, encouraging the development of knowledge to improve energy efficiency, that drove down the prices of energy services, which (c) reduced the cost of producing goods and service in the economy, driving up the use of energy services and boosting economic development.

If this is a plausible – and perhaps the most powerful – chain of causality, then to understand the evolving demand for energy services and energy, it is useful to focus on stages of economic development and their influence on demand. This is especially relevant for energy services used for productive activities. The following discussion focuses on them, while the subsequent sections analyses (principally, but not exclusively) the evolution of demand for energy services associated with immediate consumption.

So, second, it might be valuable to consider how the demand for individual services changed at different stages of economic development. The evidence provides a useful guide for stylising the relationship between economic transformations and individual energy services.

It would appear that power was the predominant energy service at early stages of economic development. The agricultural economy depended on working and moving the land, and crushing grains.

Mining and industrial activities also required large amounts of power. However, the thermal transformations needed for metals and other goods called upon growing demands for heating. Proportionally, industrialisation was associated with a decline in power demand and a rise in heating demand. Similarly, an agrarian economy functioned at a relatively local level, using nearby produce. The industrialising economy was dependent on expanding networks of trade and commerce, which required increasing amounts of goods carriage. Demand for freight transport increased.

As the industrial economy matured, the need for power and heating declined. This was reflected in the data and in wider economic transformations that occurred after the First and Second World Wars. The economy also experienced a growth in the import of goods, many of which required considerable heat and especially power. A driver for the imports was the cheaper cost of power, in the form of labour in poorer countries.

The post-industrial economy (described broadly as the period after the Second World War) saw a continued relative decline in the demand for industrial power, heating and freight transport. It is important to keep in mind, though, that, in most phases of economic development and for most energy services, consumption of services and energy grew.

Saturation

Economic growth and development gradually fed through into rising income, which allowed mankind to afford a little more of those necessities. As income rose further, a person's ability to consume greater amounts of goods and services increased. Thus, households heated more, travelled more and lit more.

Yet, Engel's Law proposes that, as income rose, the demand for basic needs tended to fall, as they were fulfilled. A greater share of a person's budget could be spent on wants not previously afforded. This can be explained by the declining marginal utility of a particular good – consuming increasing amounts of a good brought decreasing rewards for each unit of the good consumed. When the benefit gained from consuming a further unit of the good fell below its price, a 'saturation' level had been reached and the consumer was unlikely to consume more of the good, even as income rose.

At the market level, consumers for non-durable goods, such as energy, might be expected to experience saturation, meaning that, at a certain level of income, demand began to stabilise or even fall. Similarly, the demand for durable goods, such as a cooker or a cart, followed a similar pattern as most of the population had acquired the good. At that point, demand should have stabilised, supply only meeting replacements as the durable goods break down.

A similar saturation effect would have followed after the price of a particular good fell dramatically. Because of the resulting improving income and tendency to substitute towards the good, its consumption increased considerably. As more of the needs associated with the good were met, such as increased heating from using more energy, demand for the good became satiated.

So, it can be expected that, after a major rise in income, improvements in an energy technology or declines in the price of energy, consumption of the energy services would increase until demand eventually became saturated. At the point of saturation, consumption would stabilise.

Given this tendency, at the end of the twentieth century, the consumption of industrial products per person might have been expected to stabilise. Indeed, the amount of money spent on manufactured goods has fallen in the second half of the twentieth century. This was not due to a decline in consumption, however. In fact, consumption has 'mushroomed'. Rowthorn and Coutts (2004 p.767) show that "what it reflects is a rapid fall in the relative price of manufactures. Rising imports from low-wage countries, together with rising productivity at home, mean that manufactured goods in the advanced economies are now so cheap that consumers can buy a lot more of these goods while spending a smaller fraction of their income on them."

Similarly, the evidence in Figure 9.2 shows that consumption of energy services has continued to grow. Incomes have risen greatly and prices of heating, power, transport and lighting have fallen dramatically over the last five hundred years, and yet per capita consumption of these services does not appear to be satiated. To better understand the trends, it is worth exploring what has driven the demand for energy services.

Basic Needs and Lifestyles

The basic needs of food and shelter have driven simple demands for heat and power. Self-sufficiency meant that these requirements were traditionally supplied from local surroundings, limiting the need for transport services. Similarly, artificial lighting, if considered necessary, was provided by local resources, either from the fire in the hearth or from reeds collected and prepared. Such demands for heat and power, as well as transport and light, increased with population, and were inelastic to changes in income and prices, where they existed.

Most demands for energy services revolved around ways of living and working (Schipper and Meyers 1992). Life in an agrarian community, for instance, required certain, although modest, amounts of heat, power, transport and, to a lesser extent, light. 'Lifestyles' and 'workstyles' determine how people behaved. They, and the communities formed around lifestyles, also provide information about people's values and their needs, forming their tastes and preferences. Thus, these habits drove demands for goods and services, including the amounts of heat, power, transport and light (Schipper and Meyers 1992).

Nevertheless, lifestyles and workstyles created limits to the goods and services required. An agrarian lifestyle and workstyle demanded far less of any energy service than, say, the 'jet-setting executive'. In fact, it would be near impossible for a person in an agrarian community to consume the amounts of energy services required by the air-conditioned, globe-trotting executive. Much of the saturation in demand associated with rising income reflected the limits imposed by lifestyles and workstyles.

To increase consumption dramatically, mostly because a new attribute became available in the consumption or production technology, lifestyle or workstyle had to change. Over the last seven hundred years, the United Kingdom has experienced a vast rise in the use of heat, power, transport and light. The growth in energy service consumption has driven and been driven by changes in lifestyle and ways of working.

Humans have always been animals of habit. They adapt to their budget and surroundings, and seek to improve their well-being within the context. Changing the way people live and work required considerable effort to adapt. Change involved risk and imposed substantial uncertainty, as well as physical and mental stress. Thus, many humans have been prone to certainty and security over change and uncertainty.

Humans are also social animals. Ways of living and working – the type of house and work, the structure of the household and workforce, the means of producing services for the house and the work – form some of the strongest social bonds. To change lifestyles was to break the social rules. To break the rules was to risk being cast out of the familiar social structure.

Breaking the rules of a social setting often came at a high price. Yet, some people rejected habit or sought new experiences. Others may have wanted to move to a perceived higher social status. New experiences or social mobility must have been important drivers for changing lifestyles and workstyles, some of which required a far greater consumption of services.

Consuming Beyond Basic Needs

A first wave of demand beyond basic needs in medieval England was for fabrics. The growth in population had lowered wage rates and the introduction of mills had supplemented human and animal power. Some of the mills, rather than crushing corn, were used for fulling wool, and their owners needed sufficient demand for it to be profitable. Lower costs of power were enabling the economy to produce textiles, in addition to grain-crushing. Cheaper textiles allowed more people to have several garments. The existence of a surplus of fabrics, beyond the most basic needs, created a desire to improve one's appearance, and domestic comfort. Threat from the potential mobility of lower classes meant that the upper classes had to distinguish themselves. Finer fabrics and their cleanliness were signs of wealth and status (Crowley 2004 p.7).

The growth in textiles for clothing and bedding created an increased demand for power – for their production. It also increased the demand for transport. In the case of more expensive textiles, it involved shipping goods from the continent, especially Holland, where the finer fabrics were made. The economic revival in the sixteenth century started with similar demands. Clothing provided the most public source of distinction. Furnishings also enabled peers to admire and appreciate a host's success.

As the disposable income of the middle classes rose, other goods were brought into the house, which had a more practical nature. Initially the influence appears to have been that the desire for goods drove the rise in income. Before the advent of the growth in the production of goods, households had had little reason to need money. The growing desire for the acquisition of commodities led to a need for money, and the 'Industrious Revolution' (De Vries 2006 p.63).

A clear relationship has existed between rising income, the production of goods and the consumption of energy services. The introduction of new heating methods associated with the reverberatory furnace had a major impact on the availability and cost of products in the sixteenth century. The pans, pots and kettles, as well as the cooking stove itself, called on a greater production of copper, brass and iron. Demand for metals was also growing for agricultural and industrial tools. The increase in iron production was dramatic. In 1500, 1.7kg of iron was consumed per person in England. By 1600, 4.2 kg per person were consumed (King 2005). At the time, this was a healthy growth – 1 percent per year for a whole century. Inevitably, the demand for heating (from charcoal) grew substantially.

From the mid-seventeenth century, households have been willing to spend more on heating fuels, as a proportion of total GDP (see Figure 9.11). This was at a time when the price of heating was rising (see Figure 9.1). It also reflected a shift towards the use of chimneys, which was described as a sign of social distinction (Cowley 2004). A growing middle class with greater wealth was emulating the upper class and distinguishing itself from the poor, who stayed warm by a hearth.

Social status has been one of the most important drivers of novel consumer behaviour. The desire to be respected, through the appearance of social importance, could well explain much of the growth in the demand for energy services (and other goods and services) above the rise in population.

New textiles from India arriving in the 1690s created a striking example of the desire for distinction and its impact on shifting demand. For most of the seventeenth century, commentators argued that the wealth of the nation was best served by ensuring that exports were stronger than imports. Demand was considered inelastic and grew in line with population growth. It was only in the last decade of the seventeenth century, as manufacturing output grew and their products were bought, that some wondered about the wealth-generating nature of increasing demand. "When the maverick spirit of fashion revealed itself in the craze over calicoes the potential market power of previously unfelt wants came clearly into view. Here was a revolutionary force. Under the sway of new consuming tastes, people had spent more, and in spending more the elasticity of demand had become apparent. In this elasticity, the defenders of domestic spending discovered the propulsive power (and the economic advantages to the nation) of envy, emulation, love of luxury, vanity and vaulting ambition" (Appleby 1976 p.505).

Although gaining weight, for much of the eighteenth century the growing middle classes, traders and businessmen gaining wealth chose to refrain from ostentatious behaviour, perhaps reflecting their strong protestant values (Mason 1981 p.86). For the landed gentry, the belief in the wealth-generating power of the consumers through emulation was morally and politically threatening. To accept this belief was also to support the idea that people could achieve social mobility through spending. It implied that social classes were determined by spending patterns. And, a "democratization of consumption" (Appleby 1976 p.515) was to undermine the British system of social control. When Mandeville's *Fable of the Bees* published in the 1720s hinted that the whole British population was addicted to luxury, it received violent attack from many parties.

It was only in the 1770s that this idea gained intellectual support, most famously from Adam Smith's pen. "The pursuit of luxury could now be seen as socially desirable, for as growth of new wants stimulated increased effort and output, improved consumption by all ranks of society would further stimulate economic progress" (McKendrick et al. 1982 p.19). A growing middle class in

Britain was also providing a conduit for social mobility and has been associated with changes in demand.

The Creation of Markets

Economic change has often been attributed to supply-side transformations. Lower costs of production were partly because of cheaper heating, power, transport and even lighting and, therefore, manufacturers benefited from the technological innovations and the decline in the price of energy sources. With some capital to invest in knowledge, combining skills and equipment, manufactures could be set up. During the proto-industrial period, households could specialize in the manufacture or refinement of some minor goods, such as pins, nails or buttons. With the growing demand experienced in the eighteenth century, most households entering such business ventures were likely to earn profits, which could in turn provide them with many of those desired goods or with an education for their children.

Alternatively, the money could be invested back into the business. As the economy grew, larger sums of money were being earned and an entrepreneur could invest in equipment providing greater quantities of heating or power. Metal-works or textile factories with the latest equipment could produce output at a much lower unit cost. And, as the industrialization expanded, the cost of acquiring such equipment fell, allowing more to invest and earn large profits (see Figure 8.7).

As a result, towns and regions flourished on the back of the greater investment and the demand for new products. "Birmingham's prosperity was built on the manufacture of buttons and buckles and candlesticks, or that Sheffield grew on the profits of cutlery, or that Staffordshire owed its prosperity to crockery, or that Manchester mushroomed on the cotton that provided the mass market for fashionable prodigality at the end of the eighteenth century" (McKendrick et al. 1982 p.31).

The expansion during the eighteenth century enabled far more goods to be consumed. Iron consumption per person doubled in the eighteenth century (King 2005). Again, the demand for heating and its fuels soared, increasingly using coke.

More exotic products were being consumed in vast quantities. In the last fifteen years of the eighteenth century, tea consumption per person grew by more than 70 percent and purchase of printed fabrics more than doubled (McKendrick et al. 1982 p.29). Much of this benefited from and increased the demand for cheaper sea transport, as goods were shipped around the world.

The growth of the manufacturing sector and the specialization of regions to particular types of products created a huge growth in the demand for freighting services. Between 1715 and 1775, it grew at a staggering rate of 4.5 percent per year, rising from 3 million to 40 million tonne-kilometres. It continued at the same rate up to 1815, moving 225 million tonne-kilometres. Up to 1840, the rate was a healthy 2.5 percent per annum and, by then, horses moved 400 million tonne-kilometres of goods every year.

Commercialization was assisted by the dramatic falls in the price of freight transport services associated with the introduction of railways. The rise in the amount of goods distributed around Britain in the nineteenth century was spectacular – from 1840 to 1850, total freight rose from 400 million to 1.5 billion tonne-kilometres, a rate of 14 percent per annum. By 1900, freight had expanded to over 30 billion, or a rate of 6 percent per year.

Much of the decline in production costs resulted from economies of scale. Investing in large energy-using equipment was only profitable when many units were sold. Increasing production in line with the growth in consumption attributed to the price elasticity of demand for goods would hardly have generated the economies of scale that ensued.

Demand had to be created. Consumers needed to be informed about goods available, their attributes, their prices and their distributors. They also needed to be told about how their lives would be improved by these goods – greater comfort, longer leisure-time or higher social standing. Consumers' imagination needed to be led to new worlds of possibility.

The growth of advertising played a vital role in directing preferences. Advertising was, however, quite different in the eighteenth century from the approach used in the nineteenth and especially the twentieth century. The power of influence occurred in the shop than through the media.

In the eighteenth century, few products were marketed by the manufacturers. Goods bought in markets and increasingly in shops were non-standardized and of varying qualities. Consumers entered a shop uncertain of the product that would be bought and selected according to availability. They learnt to assess quality on sight, rather than be dependent on brand loyalty (Walsh 2000 p.80).

While many shops appeared uninviting with goods hidden on shelves, the shopkeeper's role was to present goods from behind the counter, provide information about the different products and be open to bargaining. This was the opportunity to promote new products to customers. The art of persuasion was vital to sales figures. Even if customers chose not to buy immediately, attention to the customer would often bring loyalty to a particular shop, generating future sales (Walsh 2000 pp.88–91).

To attract customers in the first place, shops became more extravagant. Interiors followed the latest fashions. Fronts and window displays were enticing. In grim and dark times, the most effective tool was lighting. From the brightest candles to the gas lighting and then to electricity and even neon, shops seeking to entice customers and marketing in general were willing to pay for the latest advances in lighting technology.

Once in the shop, the presentation of goods was also a source of information on customers' preferences, which could be used for restocking and for relaying modifications to the manufacturers. With close attention to the customers, they were in a position to influence products. Such methods were high-cost ways of disseminating information, however. The costs involved considerable investment in human capital, the shopkeeper. It also limited the spread of advertising to actual customers. The growth of newspaper publications offered the means to reduce the costs of information supply and increase the potential demand.

While newspaper advertising started in the mid-seventeenth century, it only became the main source of advertising in the nineteenth century. Before then, most of the consumer goods advertised in newspapers were books and patented medicines, which were distributed nationally (Walsh 2000 pp.83–7).

As the size of individual manufactures expanded dramatically in the late eighteenth and nineteenth centuries, their products had a chance to be sold in a number of different retail outlets. This was the opportunity for producers to advertise, creating loyalty to a product rather than a shop.

One of the implications of larger-scale advertising was that information flowed only in one direction, from manufacturer to customer. The growth in the unit size of manufactures, partly due to the high fixed costs of producing heating and especially power, provided cheaper products, yet reduced the influence of customers on manufacturers. On the other hand, it could be argued that it was only wealthy individuals that had access to shops in the eighteenth century and influence on product design. Less affluent customers never had influence over attributes; at least, as the costs of production fell, they could start to afford goods and services.

Reductions in the costs of producing industrial heating and power during the eighteenth and nineteenth centuries enabled a dramatic growth in the production of consumer goods. They also benefited from economies of scale of production. Among other things, this created the capitalist class, who with wealth behind them could acquire equipment to produce dramatically cheaper energy services than had been previously possible. Complementing producers, suppliers, with a little money placed in the media, could advertise products creating a demand for their goods.

Conspicuous Consumption through Energy Services

Energy service revolutions have been associated with the uptake of new technologies by a segment of the population – the haves; in the meantime, there were many that were still using the old technology – the have-nots. In the first instances of private ownership of a new technology, only a few could afford the equipment. Then, as economies of scale were achieved, a few more could purchase it. This meant that substantial differences in the ability to generate energy services at the domestic level existed. Thus, the revolutions created inequality – well-being in the haves and dissatisfaction in the have-nots.

In turn, some might argue that the laggards were less driven by technological advancement and material wellbeing than the leaders, thus they suffered less from not 'having'. For some, this was certainly true; for others they may have been limited financially or, possibly swayed by advertising or the desire for conspicuous consumption, they tied themselves into jobs or credit schemes that were ultimately not in their long-term best interest.

Given that mobility involved travelling around and, therefore, being seen, transport was also to be a source of conspicuous consumption. Means of personal carriage had for hundreds of years been a signal of social position. Before the twentieth century, few households owned a method of personal transport. More recently, individuals have been able to afford certain equipment. Ownership of technology has remained a sign of wealth and, therefore, of success.

Lighting captured people's imagination and attention. The first markets for most new lighting technologies were in very public locations. In the early nineteenth century, gas-lighting was the pride of the towns and the dignitaries that had made it possible to illuminate their streets. Later, it was essential to have their city glowing with electricity. Today, the big cities at night are peppered with bright colours, reflecting their magnificence.

Similarly, for punters, it was 'a must' to be seen in the new theatre with new gas-lighting. And, of course, electricity was next. Today, lighting is central to the successful design of a theatre or restaurant in London, or around the country.

Conspicuous consumption played a vital role in the introduction of technologies. Luxury items could be produced in limited editions at high prices, earning substantial profits for the entrepreneurs. Thus, the existence of a niche market with high profit (per item) allowed companies to sell the equipment and achieve economies of scale. If people did not seek to enhance their status by the acquisition of new technologies, it would have been difficult to find a segment of the market that was willing to pay to achieve the economies of scale. It was the rich and socially mobile, and the advertising companies (and the large corporations paying the publicity), that enabled new technologies to spread.

The Creation of New Characteristics

The desire for social status did drive the demand for some early consumers of new technologies and, therefore, potentially radical changes in energy service use, lifestyles and workstyles. Others that led or followed were attracted by new characteristics the new technologies offered. These new characteristics, in turn, could lead to major economic or social transformations.

Some new technologies radically altered the methods of production. The introduction of coke-smelting in the iron industry transformed the production process from "a simple shed containing a 'finery' fire, one or two 'chafery' fires, and single water-powered hammer ... [to] two or three small 'refining furnaces', as many as a dozen puddling furnaces, and several large shingling and stamping hammers driven by a steam engine ... The forge had clearly become a more mechanized and generally more complex operation than its eighteenth century predecessor" (Hyde 1973 p.121).

Embodying knowledge in the equipment rather than in the mind of the worker had major implications for the methods of production. Three production systems worked throughout the pre-industrial period: the urban craft guilds, the rural 'putting-out' system known as proto-industry and the factory system. Each produced in parallel for around five hundred years. The factory system existed, but was a small source of production until the nineteenth century. The proto-industry involved widely distributed production units with poorly skilled labour. As a result, they were not well-suited for accommodating new techniques and technologies. Innovation tended to lead to structural changes. "Because major technical change caused either labor skilling or capital intensification, proto-industry displayed a tendency to move either 'back' to craft production, 'forwards' into factory industrialism, or 'sideways' into sweatshops" (Epstein 1998 p.706).

The steam engine worked best on a large scale. Production was structured around many shafts providing the power from a central system. The great explosion in the use of power in the twentieth century was due to the new opportunities electricity offered. The flexibility of electricity enabled individual units of production to work more independently. This connection to electrical wires altered factory production.

Another radical social transformation resulting from the adoption of new energy-using equipment was the adoption of the chimney. Access to heating around the hearth reflected social status – the lord or elder would sit close, but not too close, to the fire, with subordinates nearby. The introduction of chimneys enabled smaller, more private sources of heat. The chimney-fire was, until the increased availability and decline in the price of coal in the sixteenth century, a more expensive source of heating.

Similarly, most households could not afford a horse and carriage. People walked, if they needed to go anywhere. By the seventeenth century, the concept of businesses taking people places developed, enabling upper and middle classes to travel. Before the introduction of the stagecoach, only soldiers, tax administrators and pilgrims saw the world. The railway increased the ability to travel further. Lower costs later in the nineteenth century meant that virtually everybody could afford a trip, at least once.

Travel, however, was on other people's terms – the stagecoach or the railway dictated the route. The introduction of the bicycle gave the average person his or her first feeling of freedom of mobility. It was for short distances, generally on roads not designed for the poor suspension the bike provided. The popularity of the car in the 1930s was spectacular. Its main attraction was the freedom of travel.

The flip-side of privacy and freedom has been a schism within the community. Many of the forces that kept social structures together were the lack of ownership over energy technologies, requiring communities to share equipment, responsibilities and cooperate. The decline in the cost of equipment meant that private ownership was possible and cooperation (related to certain technologies) was no longer necessary. The decline in cooperation, compromise and shared experiences weakened the bonds of communication, trust and of social capital.

Other bonds have formed in their place. Distant relatives and friends have become more accessible. Regional and national bonds have been strengthened by the expansion of transport and communication networks. Across Britain, people's way of dressing and speaking became more standardised after the introduction of cars (Bagwell 1974 p.232). This has helped create a broader social and cultural identity – people were no longer from a little village yonder, but from Yorkshire, and then later, England, and after, Britain. Thus, although controversial, mobility may have ultimately led to a decline in general xenophobia, and a greater trust for outsiders.

New characteristics of energy technologies and services have been both a driver for new lifestyles and workstyles, and an effect of greater consumption. These characteristics have played a vital role in the transformation of the economy and society, and should be expected to continue to stimulate future revolutions.

4. WELFARE EFFECTS OF GREATER CONSUMPTION

Improvements in Welfare

In the debate about long-run trends in well-being, two extreme camps oppose each other. The first camp has presented examples of a world that has become increasingly spoilt and lives impoverished (Ehrlich and Ehrlich 2004). The other, often including many economists, has argued that people today live in a world of progress, and associated higher levels of well-being (Lebergott 1988, Simon 1996, Lomborg 2001).

The starting point for investigating the decline in the price of energy services was that traditional indicators of retail price indices failed to highlight the welfare gains associated with technological progress and underestimated the declines in the cost of living and, therefore, improvements in the standards of living (Nordhaus 1997). People today do live in an economy that provides far cheaper heating, power, transport and light than one, two or five hundred years ago. This also reduced the costs of other goods and services. So, individuals have been living in greater comfort with wider possibilities and more experiences. On this count, as Nordhaus (1997) argues, the improvements in material and physical wellbeing are underestimated – strengthening the belief in progress.

Unbound Prometheus

An assumption of economic analysis is that more consumption leads to greater well-being. Yet, despite an increase in energy service consumption over the last 300 years, a question mark remains about whether this has fed through to a genuine improvement in well-being over the last three hundred years.

For a time, technological improvements must have had substantial effects on the human condition. Technical progress was initially associated with rises in population, rather than improvements in standards of living (Mokyr 1990 p.288). Then, as population growth rates slowed, the technical progress translated into rising individual material well-being. Jordan (1993) indicates that the quality of life improved during the nineteenth century. These improvements were basic standards of hygiene, levels of education, but also ability to alleviate the harshness of existence. Veenhoven (1995), building on Maslow's hierarchy of needs, argues that "money enhances happiness when it can add to the satisfaction of basic needs for food, shelter and clothing".

Most probably, life today is better than it was in 1700. Yet, once basic biological needs for food, shelter, clothing and health care are met, and a standard of living providing some leisure and recreational time exists, evidence suggests that further consumption does not provide increased satisfaction (Diener and Diener 1998). Levels of well-being at the beginning of the twenty-first century are not necessarily higher than in the 1950s (Oswald 1997). It is worth commenting on the factors that might have improved well-being, and to what extent energy services played a role in raising it.

Indicators of 'happiness' provide some evidence on overall well-being. In the United Kingdom, the proportion of individuals claiming to be 'very happy' appears to have risen from the late 1940s, after the Second World War, until the late 1950s. Then, throughout the 1980s and 1990s, the proportion began to fall slightly (Layard 2004 p.249). They are hardly accurate indicators of general well-being. Furthermore, they only represent 'happiness' for a 'brief' period. They provide, however, our only indicator of long-run trends in general well-being, no matter how crude they are, and during a period of dramatic growth in energy service consumption.

Similarly, it would be facile to suggest that the level of energy service consumption would be central to general well-being. Yet, comfort and mobility could be considered important objectives in the pursuit of material wealth. The consumption of energy services can also act as a proxy for broader material wealth and the services it provides. The paradox is that, in the last fifty years, material wealth has been rising yet subjective well-being has hardly been affected by it. And, the paradox is even more acute if we take account of the dramatic improvements in services resulting from technological improvements. For the brief period for which evidence exists, a striking conclusion is not how much standards have improved, but how little technological improvements and material wealth affect general well-being.

Welfare Improvements Beyond Basic Needs

It is worth considering reasons why cheaper and more energy services are pursued, and what are the implications. Technological improvements and cheaper services have had some effect on well-being. However, the relationship between energy service consumption (or general goods and service consumption) and happiness (and, no doubt, general well-being) does not seem linear.

Another basic assumption in economic analysis is the tendency towards declining marginal utility of consumption. The marginal utility of energy services has, no doubt, been declining and this should have been expected. Each additional unit of energy service generated less utility or happiness. Individuals were receiving less and less satisfaction from producing more heat, more power and more light.

Each subsequent revolution in energy services led to less welfare gains. Given the dramatic increases in consumption and declining marginal utility, by the end of the twentieth century greater consumption cannot be expected to greatly improve people's lives.

At what point in the economic development of the United Kingdom were basic or absolute needs fulfilled: the completion of the Enclosures Act, which increased agricultural yields, the end of the First Industrial Revolution, or the introduction of the Welfare State? Beyond this point, perhaps around the mid-twentieth century, long run 'happiness' levels were not directly affected by technological improvements and the additional services these provided.

Relative Wealth

Recent surveys indicate that 'happiness' is affected by a series of factors – financial situation, family relationships, work, community and friends, health, personal freedom and personal values (Layard 2004 p.64). Financial situation is, therefore, important. And, cheaper energy services, for instance, lower the cost of living, which should improve individuals' financial situation.

How individuals form beliefs about their financial situations is important for understanding the impact of cheaper and more services on well-being. While absolute wealth may be important, especially at very low levels of income, relative wealth appears to be a far greater determinant of 'financial situation' (Layard 2004 p.42).

Individuals compare their wealth with their past wealth and other people's wealth. They use these reference points to form expectations about the current situation. Achieving these expectations provides a level of happiness, and failure to achieve them creates disappointment (Frank 2001).

New experiences create future expectations. The following experience reflects the rising expectations of energy services associated with technological improvements: "I grew up without central heating. It was fine. Sometimes I had to huddle over the fire or put my feet in a bowl of hot water, but my mood was good. When I was forty, I got central heating. Now, I would feel really miserable if I had to fight the cold as I once did. In fact I have become addicted to central heating" (Layard 2004 p.48).

When a new technology is acquired, the level of energy services produced provides temporary happiness. Once the individual has adapted to the new level of services, it forms the basis for expectations of future consumption and experiences. Provided the person consumes the new level of consumption, then the individual's happiness returns to a prior level of happiness – determined by other factors, mentioned above (Kasser 2002).

People that lived in the thirteenth or eighteenth centuries formed their expectations of service consumption, in part, on their own technological and material surroundings. Thus, the impact of these surroundings on their level of 'happiness' may well have been similar to individuals in the twentieth century who experienced far richer surroundings.

Individuals also form their expectations on the basis of other people's wealth and consumption. Keynes (1931 p.365) proposed that needs "fall into two classes – those needs which are absolute in the sense that we feel them whatever the situation of our fellow human beings may be, and those which are relative only in that their satisfaction lifts us above, makes us feel superior to, our fellows." A new technology is acquired and higher levels of services are produced. Others observe and seek to emulate, forming their own expectations. In this case, attempts to increase wellbeing through consumption are based on outdoing or keeping up with the Joneses and are fuelled by low levels of self-consumption and dissatisfaction (Offer 2006).

Conspicuous consumption provides a powerful method for raising people's awareness about how others appear to be living and consuming. Onlookers will tend to create new expectations about how they themselves should consume. Naturally, advertising provides a role in raising awareness and expectations.

Expectations of Growth

To a certain extent, the increase in consumption following each technological revolution was asssisted by entrepreneurs seeing abundant resources and seeking opportunities to create markets. Using advertisements, they highlighted inequalities in consumption and raised people's expectations. New expectations drove the demand for services when before the willingness to pay was very low.

In turn, new technological revolutions are fuelling the economic system. "In multiplying the power of production, men and women also multiplied their desires" (Nye 1998 p.68). A climate of change creates expectations of technological improvement. This implies that without improvements people will be disappointed, lowering levels of happiness (Offer 2006).

Abundance, created by more resources or efficient technology, enables individuals to achieve or go beyond their expectations. Such situations create happiness. Once they have adapted to the higher level of consumption, expectations are revisited and new standards need to be achieved. On the other hand, periods of scarcity lead to under-achievement and unhappiness. People might reduce expectations. With lower expectations, 'tightening the belt' would no longer be disappointing. Yet, generally, individuals find it harder to lower expectations than to raise them. If expectations rise more easily than they fall, phases of scarcity and abundance will tend to create lower welfare than stability, where expectations remain constant.

Volatile energy markets create situations of scarcity and abundance, and phases of disappointment and unhappiness. Similarly, technological revolutions create periods of inequality. Some, who have acquired the latest technology, consume large quantities of energy services. Others observe and raise expectations. While waiting, they feel frustrated and unhappy. For many, given that happiness is associated with relative wealth, those with large levels of consumption are happy with this inequality. Those consuming less probably raise their expectations more easily than those consuming more would lower theirs. If so, those consuming less suffer more from the inequality than those consuming more benefit. Thus, the cycles of inequality brought on by energy service revolution generate phases of unhappiness.

Welfare Impact of Creating New Wants

Major reductions in the price of energy services can lead to excess supply and create a need for new ways of using energy services. If the price fall is small or gradual, the increase in service can be used for traditional purposes. For instance, the economy has uses that were marginally uneconomic at a slightly higher price, but now become worthwhile. If the price fall is larger or faster, all the demands for traditional purposes are willing to be met, leaving an excess supply of service at a particular price. This can either drive the price down further or encourage entrepreneurs to find new ways of using the service. For example, lighting has met demands for visibility, and is creating demands for aesthetic lighting.

A consequence is that the faster the fall in price, the less probable the new uses will be applied to socially valuable objectives. Why? Various arguments could be put forward. First, with considerable slack in the system (that is, higher supply than demand), any uses for the services that exist will be taken advantage of – many of these may not be very valuable uses, but simply they are 'in the right place, at the right time'.

Second, entrepreneurs, in the pursuit of profit, and aware that low prices mean new opportunities for large consumption and revenue, will be searching for new ways of using the services. Entrepreneurs' creations will be driven by expectations of customers' potential demands, but this process is fairly random – if new uses are found, whether of great value or not, they will be marketed as valuable. And, marketing can create a demand. Here, 'excess is the mother of invention'.

Third, when prices fall quickly, society has less time to shape the technology. The market shapes the technology. Entrepreneurs will be in a hurry to get their new uses of a service out on the market. The greater the potential profit, the more pressure entrepreneurs will put on legislators to allow the new uses to be adopted. Thus, the speed of the price fall reduces society's role and increases the market's role in shaping the technology.

With time, new valuable uses may be found. Because of technological, institutional, behavioural and cognitive lock-ins, however, the socially undesirable uses will not necessarily become obsolete with time, but will in fact remain part of the uses.

Galbraith (1970 p.153) provides a summary of the ambiguity of welfare improvements associated with greater consumption. "As a society becomes increasingly affluent, wants are increasingly created by the process by which they are satisfied. This may operate passively. Increases in consumption, the counterpart of increases in production, act by suggestion or emulation to create wants. Or producers may proceed actively to create wants through advertising and salesmanship. Wants thus come to depend on output. In technical terms it can no longer be assumed that welfare is greater at an all-round higher level of production than at a lower one. It may be the same. The higher level of production has, merely, a higher level of want creation necessitating a higher level of want satisfaction."

5. CONCLUSION

Why Not Consume More?

Throughout history, humans have been seeking ways to meet basic needs. The processes surrounding the Industrial Revolution transformed humans' ability to achieve those needs. By the second half of the twentieth century, nearly all individuals in the United Kingdom had the means and the ability to meet their basic needs associated with heating, power, transport and artificial lighting. For instance, people starving or freezing to death has become very rare. For most in the United Kingdom, the end of the twentieth century was a time of consuming well beyond the basic needs.

Having also considered the influence of cheaper energy services on welfare, William Nordhaus' thesis of improvements in well-being from the declining price of energy services is true. Yet, it is not the whole story.

When disposable income rises, people are willing to buy more of the necessities and start to acquire luxuries and novelties. Certain energy-using equipment, which was once too expensive, becomes affordable. People have become able to own most energy service equipment, rather than be dependent on, say, public transport. Yet, few own airplanes. Few can afford to own one. As income grows and prices fall, consumers will ask 'why not?'.

Furthermore, the price of energy services has fluctuated greatly over the last five hundred years. The fluctuations have been in large part due to the dynamics of demand for services and supply of energy. When heating becomes cheaper, people consume more. If lower prices last a while, say, a couple of years for the average consumer, then longer-term decisions are made on the basis. Perhaps fuel efficiency is less of a priority, and the number of additional features becomes important.

Yet, "sensitivity to cold and heat floats between the innate and the acquired: it is a profoundly cultural fact ... [and] a biological phenomenon" (Roche 2001 p.108). Past behaviour forms the expectations of future behaviour. Greater consumption creates 'need inflation'. Expectations create routine and habits. People's routines, time structures and lifestyles are based around these levels of services. Habits form about the current levels of heating, of mobility and of lighting. When prices of services start to rise, the consumer is faced with tensions. Sacrifices need to be made. There are expectations about the consumption of goods and services. They ensure a type of lifestyle. A particular lifestyle acts as an indicator of well-being and social status. Reduction would be both a physical and symbolic drawback. In turn, the pressure to make sacrifices calls for another solution – find a way to keep the same lifestyle. This desire to keep the same lifestyle creates demands to improve the efficiency. Thus, incentives will exist to develop and commoditise knowledge to ensure lifestyles remain unharmed.

The New Economy

Despite the decline in price and income elasticities in the twentieth century noticed in Table 9.2, the economy is consuming ever more energy services and more energy (as shown in Figure 9.14). Engel's Law proposes that individuals should be consuming relatively less of these relatively basic needs compared with their income, and Figure 9.5 confirms it. Yet, to repeat, individual consumption has not stopped and probably will not stop.

There have been forces at work since before the Industrial Revolution that encourage continual consumption of services and energy. These forces appear to have become stronger, however, which means that despite a tendency towards saturation, consumption continues to grow. What are these forces?

First, individuals are making more decisions about the acquisition of durable goods. The expansion of the economy, in terms of the number of consumers and how much they consume, has enabled the producers of equipment to achieve economies of scale more quickly. There are more cheap durable goods. Also, disposable income has risen rapidly in the last fifty years, and consumers have been able to acquire far more goods, partly out of desire for the service, partly out of the status it portrays and even partly out of the need to find something to do with that money.

Second, as disposable income has grown, so have the opportunities to part with that income. The retail and marketing revolution was borne out of the desires to capture upper and then middle class income. In the last fifty years, disposable income has increased dramatically in the last fifty years. The economy has been developed in a manner to promote the acquisition of durable goods and consumption of ephemeral goods and services. The entrepreneurs and marketing departments are at work convincing people of the improved lifestyles and well-being from greater acquisition and consumption.

Third, in turn, beliefs and expectation have formed that technological solutions can avoid lifestyle sacrifices. This may have resulted from the advances in science and technology. It may have also been a marketing ploy in itself. It may perhaps have been that people's attitudes have changed.

When resources become scarce, knowledge will be directed towards finding ways to use them more efficiently. When resources become abundant, creativity will be directed towards finding ways to use them. In an economy geared towards selling more goods to consumers with rising income, the likely trend will be towards greater consumption. As Alfred Marshall said (1949 p.186), "The whole history of man shows that his wants expand with the growth of his wealth and knowledge."

In the last fifty years, in particular, the economy has been geared towards the alleviation of sacrifices and the pursuit of happiness, through greater consumption. The evidence, once again, confirms that it has been successful in consuming more. It also appears that it has helped temporarily alleviate sacrifices. It is questionable, however, whether, in the last half-century, technological progress and dramatically cheaper energy services have achieved happiness.

10. External Costs of Cheaper and More Energy Services

1. THE EXTERNALISATION PROCESS

Large supplies of energy resources and knowledge about how to generate energy services have led to dramatic reductions in costs of providing heat, power, transport and lighting, and have enabled major increases in the consumption of these services. Yet, some of the costs were passed on to society at large in the form of environmental pollution.

This chapter investigates how much of the full social costs were externalised, and the impact externalising costs had on the rate of adoption of new technologies. It also considers the forces at work to internalise the costs.

The Transition to Coal

Woodfuel fires, especially in hearths, created large amounts of smoke, which often remained trapped in poorly ventilated rooms. These fires led to many acute and chronic respiratory conditions, reducing the health of already malnourished populations suffering from other ailments.

In principle, a smoky room was not a 'negative externality', since the victim was also the polluter. In this sense, the polluter took account of the victim's health damage. In an attempt to generate heat, he was aware that he would have to endure unpleasant smoke. It was just a cost of generating warmth.

High discount rates, due to poverty, lack of information about the long-term health damage and poor markets for alternative fuels forced households to pollute themselves. Market failures did exist, however, and they probably limited a household's ability to make fully informed and satisfactory choices.

The problem of smoke from the hearth led to solutions to improve ventilation and ensure fresh air (Fitchen 1981 p.500). Many different louvre designs were placed in wealthier ceilings. The poor simply placed holes in the wall, which led either to too little smoke leaving the room or too much cold entering it (Crowley 2004 p.14).

The other solution to ventilation was the chimney. A chimney with a good draught would remove most of the smoke without properly entering the room. Coal's smoke was far too toxic to be left to slowly exit a room. The smoke needed to be extracted, and the chimney offered the way out. It also implied that households could burn coal instead of woodfuels.

One of the key attractions of the chimney was its ability to drive the pollution outdoors, to externalise the costs of coal smoke. Despite the fireplace with its chimney being an inferior source of heating, it enabled coal to be burnt. A household that used coal in an open hearth would face the full costs of burning coal – that is, combining the price of coal, the heating efficiency and the smoke damage. This would be a cheap, yet painful price to pay for a warm house. As the costs of coal smoke were generally passed on to the urban environment, the private cost of using coal was considerably lower than woodfuel by the mid-sixteenth century.

The introduction of the chimney enabled a dramatic growth in the use of coal in urban households, with a substantial increase in air pollution. Although many of the complaints about pollution are focussed at the more obvious industrial activities, by 1700, more than half of the pollution was caused by the residential sector.

Estimating the External Costs of Coal

As pollution concentration worsened, both from household and industrial pollution, the health effects were intensified. The number of deaths associated with respiratory diseases increased. Although smoke was not the only cause of respiratory mortality and morbidity, it was undoubtedly an important factor. The annual rate of deaths from bronchitis nearly tripled in the second half of the nineteenth century, rising to nearly 3 deaths per 1 000 people (see Figure 10.1). As a comparison, the crude (that is, all causes) mortality rate for India in the 1980s was 10 deaths per 1 000 people (Maddison and Gaarder 2002 p.17). In 1891, more than 15 000 people died from bronchitis in London alone (see Registrar General 1992).

To provide a long run perspective on the external costs of energy services, the health effects of air pollution were estimated. Data was available on the concentration of pollutants related to coal burning emissions. This was not the case for other fuels and their emissions. For other energy sources, recent economic costs of pollution were used.

One tonne of coal burnt in one location would have had a different impact on the environment and human health than others. Concentrations of toxins in the air would have determined the link between emissions and their effect. So, in urban areas, additional pollution would have created a higher level of concentration.

The approach used here was to measure the marginal external cost of using an additional tonne of coal. Maddison and Gaarder (2002 p.9) suggested that 55 percent of total suspended particulate (TSP) concentration was smoke. Thus, the estimates of smoke concentration presented in Brimblecombe (1987) were divided by 55 percent to calculate the total suspended particulate in London between 1700 and the present. At its peak, in the late 1800s, it was more than 600µg/m^3 (micro-grammes per cubic metre). As an indicator, current emissions in Delhi, one of the most polluted cities in the world, is around $370\mu g/m^3$ in the 1990s. For all of the nineteenth century, London pollution was higher than Delhi's current emissions. In the 1990s, the London average concentration of PM_{10} was only $27\mu g/m^3$ (Maddison and Gaarder 2002 p.10).

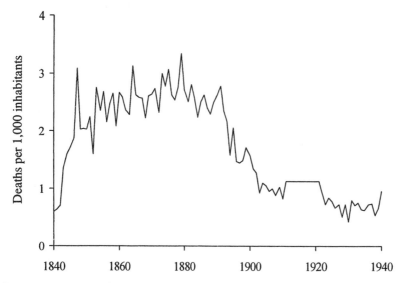

Source: Case and Harley (1958), Registrar General (1992, and each year between 1840 and 1910)

Figure 10.1 The Rate of Respiratory Diseases in London, 1840–1940

The number of deaths caused by the high concentration of pollutants can be estimated. Analyses of dose-response functions vary according to factors, such as the proportion of vulnerable members of the population (e.g. infants and old people). There is also uncertainty about the linearity of the relationship between concentration and effect. Here, it is assumed that it increased with concentration. For example, the coefficient is higher for Delhi than Bombay, reflecting its greater concentration. The demographics for Indian cities today (with a high proportion of young and few old) are likely to be closer to London in the nineteenth century than most industrialised countries today. Thus, in the eighteenth century, the lower coefficient (similar to Bombay) was used; in the early part of the nineteenth century, the middle coefficient (similar to Delhi) was selected. For the extreme values in the 1880s and 1890s, a higher pollution coefficient was assumed. For the second half of the twentieth century, a lower value like one in a transition economy was chosen (similar to Krakow in Poland).

Having taken a dose-response coefficient series, the number of premature deaths was estimated. At its peak, in 1890, the model suggested that around 40 000 people were dying from smoke pollution each year in the United Kingdom. To compare this with actual deaths, at the time, more than 100 000 people died annually from (acute and chronic) bronchitis, in a population of about 40 million (Registrar General 1992). This suggested that either the 'highest coefficient' was too low or around 40 percent of bronchitis deaths were due to air pollution. Infections, poor diets and smoking were also major contributing factors and it would be inevitably difficult to extract the impact of each factor. Since the modelled values are based on coefficient estimates from epidemiological studies, they provided a broad and acceptable indicator of the impact of pollution from coal combustion.

A benefit transfer was performed going back in time for the United Kingdom. Pearce and Cowards (1995) used a figure of £2.25 million as the value of a statistical life in the United Kingdom for 1993. Since per capita income was lower in, say, 1920 than in 2000, a smaller budget was available to individuals for reducing the risks of dying. This decline in budget was reflected in the lower value of a statistical life in earlier years. Assuming a constant income elasticity of the demand for avoiding mortality risks, this value was reduced by the lower income per capita before 1993. Thus, a series for the value of a statistical life was estimated back to the seventeenth century. For instance, the value of statistical life was calculated to be £170 000 in 1700,[25] and £630 000 in 1900.

Combining the value of a statistical life with the number of deaths provided an estimate of the economic cost of air pollution. For instance, in 1700, the health loss was around £100 million. As population and deaths rose, it increased to £750 million by 1800. Dramatic concentrations experienced in 1900 produced an economic cost of nearly £25 billion – at a time when the economy (that is, GDP) was valued at £140 billion. In 2000, the economic loss was around £4 billion, due mainly to the rising value of a statistical life.

Trends in the External Costs of Coal

The final step was to convert this economic loss into an external cost per tonne of coal consumed. The price of coal halved between 1750 and 1850. The external cost of coal consumption remained relatively constant during the eighteenth century, at around £50 per tonne. It then increased to almost £200 by 1850s, and falling back to £150 by 1900. It was around £70 in 2000 (see Figures 8.1 and 8.2).

Pollutant concentration was important for determining the external cost. The decrease in the price of coal raised the consumption of coal and, therefore, increased the concentration of pollutants and the external cost of coal. To coal consumers, air was effectively a free resource to be polluted – despite the fog outside their windows, no market signals indicated that it was failing to assimilate the smoke and becoming scarce, no pricing mechanism was creating incentives to ration consumption.

The opposite effect would occur when the price increased for sufficiently long a period. Thus, one might expect the full social cost to be more stable in the

---

25. As a reminder, all values are in £(2000).

long run than the prices. When the energetic resource became expensive and consumption and emissions lower, the assimilative capacities were less in demand.

The coal price reflected scarcity associated with the use of energetic resources. The full social cost incorporated the scarcity of other resources, such as the air's capacity to assimilate smoke (see Figure 10.2). For instance, when the scarcity of coal fell, it increased the scarcity of clean air. The full social cost of consuming coal remained relatively stable throughout the eighteenth century (around £(2000)1 5000 per effective tonne of coal equivalent – see Chapter 4 for a discussion on the units). It then soared in the nineteenth century, reflecting the far greater health cost of burning coal.

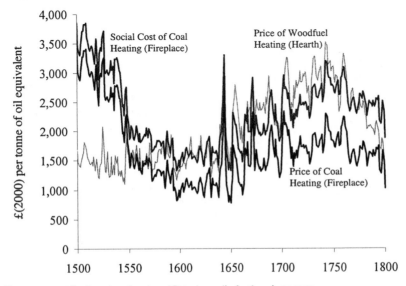

Source: see text for the external costs and Data Appendix for the private costs

Figure 10.2 The Social Costs of Woodfuel and Coal Heating, 1500–1800

While the full social cost of heating increased somewhat over the centuries, an even more dramatic change occurred in relation to who carried the burden of the cost. At the beginning of the eighteenth century, most of the cost was borne by the consumer. By the mid-nineteenth century, society paid the majority of the cost.

When resources appear to be free, there will be a tendency for them to be over-used. Technologies that help use free or cheap resources will be valued. Thus, there is a tendency towards externalising the cost of energy or energy services. Consumers do not, in general, seek to pass costs on to society. In fact, when the demand for coal began to grow in the sixteenth and seventeenth centuries, the external cost of coal were probably relatively small – and certainly less than one-third of the social cost. The lack of signals reflecting the scarcity of waste assimilation did allow consumption to grow despite a rising cost, however.

Shifting the burden away from resources from land and towards resources devoted to waste assimilation meant that the social costs of heating from coal fires were cheaper than from wood. This enabled the subsidisation of the economies of scale and learning-by-doing in the development of coal-using technologies. Given the importance of reducing costs at early phases of technological development to create a market and achieve economies of scale, technologies that can externalise the costs increase their likelihood of being adopted.

Life in the Big Smoke

Life started to be influenced by the rhythm of smoke plumes. Pollution varied according to the time of day, of the week and of the year. Smoke coincided with domestic and industrial peaks of fuel consumption. As fires were rekindled around 6am, emissions began. Factories' boilers started an hour later. The thickest smog occurred around 11am when boilers and lunch preparations were in full flow. In the afternoon, the fumes improved, until 5pm, when dinner was prepared. As fires were put out, the night was relatively free of smoke (Mosley 2001 p.50).

Weekly rhythm also followed household and industrial activities. Measurement of pollution intensity in Manchester between September 1914 and May 1915 shows the weekly pattern. A clear Sunday, with an index of 170 is followed by a bleak Monday (indicating an index over 200). Tuesday and Wednesday were the darkest (with indices around 250). This coincided with post-weekend laundry chores and industrial activity. Factories slowed down as the weekend approached, due to stoppages and short-time workers, who did their hours early on in the week. By Friday and Saturday, the pollution index was below 200 (Mosley 2001 p.52).

The smoke pattern also followed the seasons. Summer was the clearest period, as homes did not require coal for space heating. The increased sunshine also helped burn holes in the clouds. Yet, even then, the smoke often hid inhabitants from sunshine. Spring and autumn fires were needed, and the problem worsened. But, in wintertime, smoke was an ever-present mass, varying in thickness according to the time of day and of the week. At that time of year, in the industrial centres of Britain, the sun never shined through (Mosley 2001 p.52).

The soot deposited in the house required constant cleaning – using up much of the household's time. While many housewives abandoned any attempt at cleanliness, some took on the battle. "There were housewives who finally lost real interest in anything save dirt removing ... Two of these compulsives left us for the 'lunatic asylum', one of them ... still washing her hands like a poor lady Macbeth" (quoted in Mosley 2001 p.56).

Outdoors, the soot blackened the walls of buildings and covered vegetation. Fashions followed. Victorian ladies tended to wear grey simply because colourful clothes would become layered with soot (Brimblecombe 1987).

As ever, the market did find a way to make a profit out of the problem. Chimney sweeping became a booming industry. Soot was also a valuable commodity. It was used as a fertiliser, as a dye and in soap. In the eighteenth century, 500 000 bushels (which was around 10 000 tonnes) were traded in London every year (Cullingford 2000 p.25).

Coking and the Externalisation of Costs

Just like households, industrial energy users experienced a similar route to the transition to coal. For some industries, the fuel was not mixed with the material to be heated and transformed. In such cases, the transition to coal from woodfuels was relatively straightforward. When the price of coal per unit of heat was lower than the equivalent price of woodfuels, coal could be used. After all, the cost of smoke from either source could be easily externalised and pumped into the neighbouring air.

The manufacturing of certain goods, such as food and drink preparation, were affected by the coal smoke. It altered the quality of the product. For these industries, they needed to wait for the introduction of chimneys to minimise its effect. They also needed to force an evolution in the taste of consumers. In time, as more manufacturers used coal for heating, customers learnt to accept the taste of coal smoke in their stew and beer.

For a third set of industries, the fuel was directly mixed with the material being transformed. To use coal, the impurities needed to be removed. The coking process extracted them, leaving a relatively pure carbon fuel. In addition to the coke, the industry produced large quantities of by-products. A market was eventually found for the methane produced, first, for lighting and then for heating. Coke and town gas became popular as cleaner, 'smoke-free' alternatives to burning coal for heating. Thus, the coking industry found a way to reduce the pollution generated by the final consumer.

The coke and gas industry were responsible for some of the greatest levels of pollution, however. Large quantities of toxic gases and tar were released into the neighbourhood, either in the air or in rivers. Thus, the coking process removed the pollution from the final consumer and transferred it to the producer, creating areas of highly concentrated pollution, sacrificed for the benefit of generating heat and light (Thorsheim 2002 p.386).

When considering the external costs associated with town gas, the same method used for the estimates related to burning coal was followed. It was assumed that town gas was produced in urban areas, thus, the pollution was concentrated – rather than emissions for the combustion of coal which occurred across the country and, therefore, were partly dispersed in rural areas.

The estimate of the total external cost of town gas in 1850 was £250 million and increased to £1.5 billion in 1900 – one-twentieth of the damage caused by heating. Much of those costs were for the provision of lighting. In 1830, when gas lighting had completed a first phase of expansion amongst the wealthier streets and homes of Britain, its price (per million lumen hours[26]) was nearly £2 300. To provide the same amount of light using candles was £4 000. At the time, to produce enough gas to generate one million lumen-hours would have led to about £2 200 of damage. Including the external costs of gas production nearly doubles the full social cost of lighting to £4 500. In other words, accepting that candles have minimal external costs, gas lighting in 1830 was not cheaper to society than using candles.

By 1850, the external costs were responsible for two-thirds of the social cost of gas lighting. By then, the private marginal costs had fallen to £500. The social costs of gas lighting were less than half the cost of lighting with candles. It still meant, however, that for every million lumen hours burnt by a lord or wealthy businessman, it caused £1 000 of damage in the poorer neighbourhoods of the city, where the gas was produced. For every 30 million lumen-hours, another poor person died of a respiratory disease.

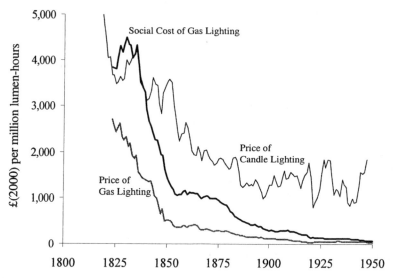

Source: see text for the external costs and Data Appendix for the private costs

Figure 10.3 The Private and Social Cost of Gas and Candle Lighting, 1800–1950

To some extent, the costs of air pollution were factored into decisions. The property and rents in neighbourhoods around the gas works were cheaper than in

---

26. It should be remembered that one million lumen-hours is the equivalent of a one hundred watt incandescent lightbulb lit for one hundred hours.

many other parts of a town. Poorer people could benefit from cheaper rent there. Thus, there was a trade-off between cheaper housing and poorer health.

One set of victims would have been the owners of property when the gas works were installed. They would have found the value of their property falling due to the air pollution and the declining demand to live in the neighbourhood. The owners would have to lower the rents. In many neighbourhoods, the 'type' of people living there influenced the value of property, and the value would have declined further as poor families moved in.

Although tenants could benefit and owners lose out from the introduction of a major industrial site, such as a gas works, two related factors limited the outcome. First, market failures existed in housing. In housing markets with rising populations, as was the case in the cities in Britain during the nineteenth century, the landlords tended to have more power over rents than the tenants. Also, the poor had less information about the health impact of air pollution – possibly having an inappropriately low perceived cost associated with air pollution. The lack of information limited their ability to make a beneficial trade-off between cheap housing and bad air.

Second, there was a dynamic nature to the pollution. Given the housing market rigidities, further pollution was likely to be imposed on the poorer population. The trade-off made (between housing and the environment) was at a particular time. But, the town gas companies continued to increase production and cause more damage. For certain segments of the population, with little option to find new accommodation and little market power, they were unlikely to be compensated for worsening air quality with declining rent.

So, the pollution from gas works imposed a burden on the initial owners of property who saw the value of their assets decline, as well as a transaction cost to tenants that chose to move to a cleaner neighbourhood. A subsequent burden was imposed whenever the gas works drove up production, resulting from an increase in the demand for lighting. This raised the level of damage, reducing the value of property to the owners and the health of residents. Who lost out most depended on the market for housing – given the unfavourable conditions for the poor in the nineteenth century, the poorer tenants were likely to experience a worsening trade-off between rent and pollution.[27]

The Steam Engine and Pollution

The steam engine revolutionised the provision of stationary power and transport in the nineteenth century. Yet, for the first hundred years of steam engines, coal consumption for power purposes was relatively modest, despite their inefficiencies. In 1800, steam engines consumed 750 000 tonnes of coal. One-third of that fuel was in the coal mining industry. Given that mining was often away from urban centres, the pollution was less harmful.

---

27. Though tallow may not always have been the choice for the wealthy, it provides an interesting comparison.

The estimates of the external cost of stationary steam engines were based on the same approach and assumptions as for gas works – the same proportion of coal used in populated areas: 40 percent in 1800 and 70 percent by 1900. For railway steam engines, it was estimated that one-third of railway activity was in metropolitan areas. For ships, it was assumed that the smoke dispersed at sea, causing no damage – despite the reality that great ships idling in port might have contributed to pollution in certain towns and cities. The proportion of emissions in urban areas was then multiplied by the amount of coal used for each service.

In 1760, stationary steam engines were estimated to be responsible for £3 million of damage. Converting these estimates into marginal external costs, until the 1820s, they added an extra 100 pence per kwh on the social cost of power. In 1760, this amounted to 20 percent of that social cost. But, by 1800, the price of stationary power had fallen to below 100 pence for one kwh. The external cost accounted for half of the social cost. As the price fell, consumption of power increased and more of the burden of steam engines was carried by society.

The rising efficiency of steam engines put downward pressure on both the price and the external cost. The growing urban population raised the health effects of one tonne of smoke. Throughout the nineteenth century, despite the growing urban population, the improvements in steam engine efficiency managed to keep the ratio of private to external costs about equal.

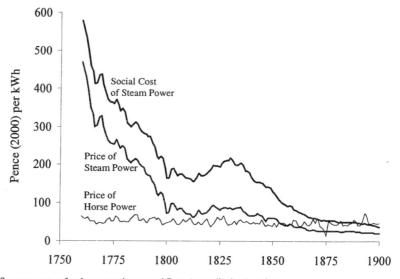

Source: see text for the external costs and Data Appendix for the private costs

Figure 10.4 The Private and Social Cost of Horse and Steam Power, 1750–1900

The social cost of stationary power fell from more than 500 pence per kwh in 1760 to less than 200 pence in 1800. It was around 130 pence in 1850 and down to 40 pence in 1900. The declining price had driven up the consumption of power, imposing ever greater burden on society. The total external cost of stationary power was £30 million in 1800. This increased to £600 million by 1850 and £1.2 billion in 1900 – one-twentieth of the damage resulting from heating (but still nearly 1 percent of the economy's value).

The Internal Combustion Engine

The development of the internal combustion engine transformed transport services. To some extent, it took some transport users away from the railways, removing some of the pollution caused by coal steam and, more recently, diesel and electric engines. Nevertheless, the internal combustion engine, driven mostly from petroleum products, has generated a new set of pollutants and toxins, leading to new diseases.

Particulate matter (PM), traditionally called 'black smoke', is still seen today as a major health problem. It is linked to bronchitis and other respiratory problems, leading to restricted activity, hospitalisation and many deaths. Particulate matter is graded according to its size. Measurement of PM_{10} indicates the concentration of particulate matter less than 10 micrograms; as scientific instrument becomes more sophisticated, observers are able to measure smaller sizes of particulate matter, such $PM_{2.5}$ and $PM_{0.5}$. The size of the matter is important as smaller PMs can travel deeper into a human's lungs, thus irritating highly sensitive parts of the body, increasing the likelihood of damage. As well as coal, the combustion of petroleum products has been responsible for particulate matter emissions. A growing proportion has been escaping from road vehicles. The introduction of the catalytic converter has helped reduce the problem, substantially reducing particulate matter.

Other more modern pollutants – lead, carbon monoxide and volatile organic compounds – were linked to the use of petroleum products especially in road transport and resulting emissions have risen over the last one hundred years. Perhaps the most harmful substance was lead. It has been associated with damage to brain development in children. The switch from leaded to unleaded petrol in cars has led to a 70 percent fall in lead emissions between 1985 and 1990 and the fall continues. Also, in the last five years of the century, carbon mononxide and volatile organic compound (VOCs) emissions fell around 20 percent because of the use of catalytic convertors and a shift to diesel engines.

The direct effects of nitrogen oxides are more ambiguous. They may be related to breathing problems but studies are inconclusive. NOx emissions are mainly linked to the creation of acid rain and ozone. These emissions have been rising up to about 1990 when the introduction of catalytic convertors on cars, as well as the use of efficient CCGT plants for electricity generation, have reduced emissions. In 1995, road transport was responsible for 46 percent of all NOx emissions and electricity generators for 22 percent.

Volatile organic compounds (VOCs) such as butane, benzene and ethanol, are most renowned for their role in the photochemical production of ozone. A wide range of economic processes emit VOCs, many of which are not related to energy services, such as the production of solvents. Nevertheless, road transport has been responsible for 30 percent of all VOC emissions. VOC emissions peaked in 1990 and declined slightly due to catalytic convertors.

Ozone results from the interaction of NOx with VOCs, with sunlight as a catalyst, and forms just above the earth in the troposphere – as opposed to the ozone in the stratosphere. Road vehicles have been the main source of both NOx and VOCs and, thus, because of the importance of sunlight, most of the problem of ozone in the United Kingdom has been in the South East. The main damage from ozone is damage to crops and lung diseases (including lung cancer), which have been associated with long exposures to high levels. Levels of tropospheric ozone have been increasing especially over the last 10-20 years but may now be stabilising as a result of slightly declining NOx and VOC emissions.

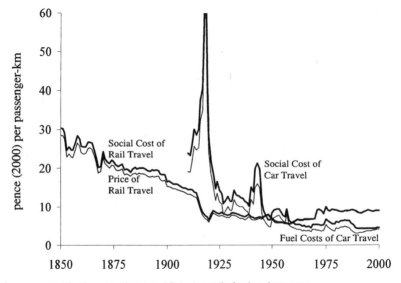

Source: see text for the external costs and Data Appendix for the private costs

Figure 10.5 The Private and Social Cost of Railway and Car Passenger Transport, 1850–2000

For petroleum products, Johansson et al. (1996 p.76) presented estimates of the marginal external costs of traditional (that is, leaded) motor spirit, unleaded petrol and diesel. The values available were for the early 1990s. Since most of the damage was associated with health effects, and especially premature deaths, the economic cost in each year needed to be calculated. A benefit transfer (back in time) was performed on the values presented in Johansson et al. (1996 p.76) taking account of the lower value of a statistical life (as was done for emissions from coal combustion).

Compared to the price of transport services, external costs have been small (see Figure 10.5). Until the 1920s, for both rail and car travel, the external cost tended to be around 5 percent. Since the 1950s, however, as the fuel costs of car travel have declined, the share of external costs has increased to around one-quarter.

These unit costs were multiplied by the amount of leaded and unleaded petrol used to quantify, for example, the total external cost of car use – £1 billion in 1950, nearly £10 billion in 1988 and down to £2 billion. This dramatic decline is principally due to the dominance of unleaded petrol in the 1990s, which has been one-fifth of the marginal external cost of leaded fuel.

Impressive was the cost associated with diesel vehicles, which produce high levels of particulate matter. In 1950, they were responsible for £400 million of damage; this increased to £20 billion in 2000. All petroleum products consumed in the transport sector caused an estimated cost of £2 billion in 1950 and £33 billion in 2000, which became the largest source of health damage (by value).

Electricity Generation

Electricity revolutionised the provision of power and lighting. The main source of energy to generate electricity was coal until the end of the twentieth century. The level of sulphur dioxide (SO_2) concentrations (as well as emissions) tended to follow the trend in smoke emissions as the sulphur content in coal is far greater than in other fossil fuels. Emissions, therefore, fell from the late 1960s. Nitrogen oxide emissions, considered more harmful to health than smoke or SO_2, result from the burning of all fossil fuels and, therefore, have probably been rising continuously since the switch from biomass to fossil fuels hundreds of years ago. In recent years, much of the recent growth in emissions is associated with electricity generation, and road transport has caused most of the emissions. Greater efficiency from combined cycle gas turbines (CCGT) and low NOx burners in electricity generators and catalytic converters installed on cars have started to reduced emissions and concentrations.

Just like town gas, consumers of electricity were free from pollution. Emissions concentrated near the power stations. The method for estimating the external costs of electricity were similar to those of town gas. Since coal was the main source of energy to generate electricity, external costs were estimated based on emissions associated with coal pollution. Until the 1950s, coal was responsible for at least 95 percent of the energy generating electricity. Before the 1990s, and the growth of natural gas, it provided the majority of the energy. Thus, until 1995, the external costs can be considered relatively reliable, and over-estimated somewhat afterwards.

The price of power from electricity in 1900 was 120 pence per kWh. The external costs resulting coal emissions were 200 pence per kWh (see Figure 10.6). In comparison, the external cost of power provided by a steam engine was 20 pence per kWh. The social cost of using power from electricity was eight times greater than from direct steam engines. This disparity reflected the technical and market inefficiencies in the provision of power from electricity by burning coal then.

The external costs of electricity fell four-fold, and the price of electricity fell six-fold in twenty years. The social cost of electricity was 50 pence per kWh. By 1950, market and technical efficiencies helped drive the social cost down around 15 pence per kwh – 60 percent of it due to production costs.

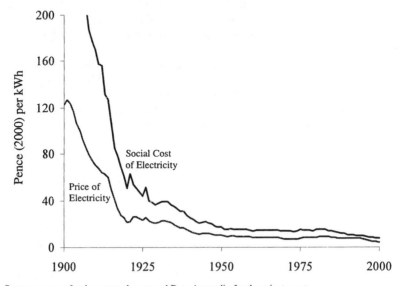

Source: see text for the external costs and Data Appendix for the private costs

Figure 10.6 The Price and Social Cost of Electricity, 1900–2000

Based on the coal air pollution emissions, electricity generation was estimated to be responsible for £300 million of external costs in 1900 at its beginning and £1.5 billion in 1950. It reached more than £5 billion in the 1970s before improving its efficiency and using cleaner fuels – in 2000, it generated £2.7 billion in external costs.

These estimates of external costs exclude the burden imposed by the several other types of energy-related environmental pollution, including acid rain and greenhouse gases, both of which follow to a large extent the trend in air pollution. In terms of impact, there is a difference between the local concentration of the pollutant and regional or national level of emissions. While for direct air pollution concentration is crucial to health effects, the level of emissions is important for acid deposition.

Acid rain occurs when SO_2 or NOx enter rain droplets and transform into acids. Acid deposition can also occur when SO_2 and NOx are moved by winds without being linked to rain and transform into acid upon deposition. Crucial, therefore, to determining areas affected by acid rain are the location of SO_2 and

NOx emissions and wind patterns. In Britain, winds tend to come up from the South-West driving acid rain north. This leads to acid deposition in the Highlands and Scandinavia where the vegetation and animals are more sensitive to changes in the acidity of the soil and water, thus, causing more damage. The main damage from acid rain is increased acidity in lakes and forests, killing certain plants and animals, and corrosion of buildings. Acid deposition does appear to have been declining over the last twenty years mainly because of the falling levels of SO_2. This is mainly due to the reduction associated with electricity generation.

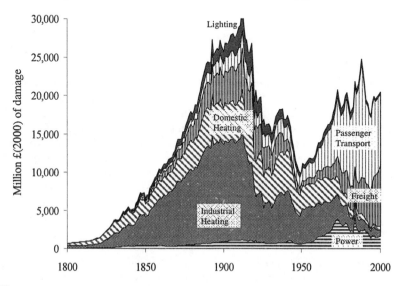

Note

'Industrial heating' includes all sectors except the domestic sector.

Source: see text for the external costs and Data Appendix for energy consumption estimates

Figure 10.7 The External Cost (of Air Pollution) from Energy Services, 1800–2000

Trends in External Costs from Energy Services

The estimates have shown that the energy services have been responsible for a large amount of air pollution with severe consequences for the public's health. Although not formally discussed, perhaps the single largest source of damage was industrial heating, and the iron and steel sector in particular. Around 1900, industrial heating was estimated to be responsible for nearly £15 billion of damage (see Figure 10.7). After the First World War, the consumption of coke for iron and steel halved, with huge benefits to society – increasingly, these metals have been imported, thus exporting the damage.

Around the same time, transport services, mostly due to freight of goods, caused up to £7 billion in damage. The impact of goods carriage declined somewhat in the middle of the twentieth century. It has started to increase again reaching nearly £8 billion in 2000. In turn, passenger transport has become the main source of damage. It reached nearly £15 billion in the 1980s. The introduction of lead and catalytic converters has substantially improved the damage – estimated at £10 billion in 2000. As a whole, air pollution damage caused by energy services was responsible for around £20 billion at the end of the twentieth century.

Greenhouse Gases and Climate Change

Greenhouse gases include carbon dioxide (CO_2), methane and nitrous oxide. The former is in far greater a quantity than the other two and is the main cause of concern for atmospheric pollution. Carbon dioxide has been emitted as a result of the combustion of all fossil fuels. Since the transition to coal in the sixteenth century, carbon dioxide emissions have been rising in Britain. Lighter fuels (e.g. natural gas) emit considerably less carbon dioxide per unit of energy. This has led to a slower growth in emissions in the twentieth century (see Figure 10.8), and even a decline from the 1980s. This decline was at a more moderate rate than the drop in air pollution in the twentieth century. Also, it is unclear whether this is a permanent downturn or a temporary downward shift, as was seen after 1913. One reason to believe the fall in carbon dioxide was temporary is the growth in energy use in the transport sector which shows little sign of slowing (see Figure 9.14).

Greenhouse gas emissions have added to the stock of gases in the atmosphere. Rising concentrations are expected to lead to changes in the climate. The effects of a changing climate are large and diverse and consequently there will be some areas that benefit but many will incur large costs (Tol 2002). Based on current projections of economic activity and fuel use, studies have estimated the costs associated with a doubling in CO_2 concentrations leading to a 2.5°C rise in global average temperature. The IPCC has valued (on an economy similar to today's) the costs of such a rise to be an annual reduction of 1 percent to 1.5 percent of national GNP for developed countries and of 2 percent to 9 percent for developing economies. This adds up to an annual reduction of 1.5 percent to 2 percent gross world product (GWP). In general, income and economic development mostly increase the causes and reduce the impact of climate change. These estimates try to incorporate market and non-market costs, as well as the costs of adaptation. Naturally, these estimates vary according to the changes and vulnerability of the region.

Measuring the long run trend in the costs of pollution related to climate change is complex. It is unclear what would be the impact of one tonne of carbon dioxide emissions. It would be even more complex to estimate the evolution of this cost.

The costs of air pollution were related to the relationship between the demand for waste assimilation, or the level of smoke emissions, and nature's ability to absorb the pollution. And, this changed dramatically between 1750 and 1850, tripling in value.

Is it possible that pollution related to climate change is on the verge of a similar growth in the costs? As emissions grow dramatically (at a global level), the impact grows rapidly. Climate change modellers propose that the impact will be large. If we are on the threshold, in a similar place to air pollution in Britain in, say, 1800, will economic costs soar?

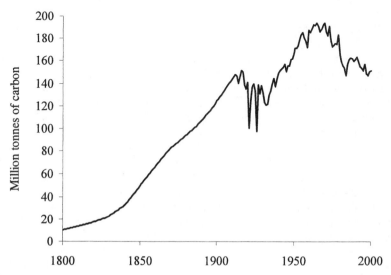

Source: Pearson and Fouquet (2003)

Figure 10.8 United Kingdom Carbon Dioxide Emissions (million tonnes of carbon (mtc)), 1800–2000

Externalising the Costs of Nuclear Power

Finally, it is worth making a brief comment about an alternative to fossil fuel power stations, as a possible solution to greenhouse gases. The introduction of nuclear power in the 1950s was advertised as a way to provide cheap, reliable electricity.

At the time, the environmental benefits were not a major factor in driving the policy towards the use of uranium as a fuel for generating electricity. During the second half of the twentieth century, the share of electricity generated from nuclear power stations grew.

For most of that period, the nuclear power industry has been in public hands. It was able to develop through the support of government, and ultimately the taxpayer and society. Large amounts of public funding went into the research and development of nuclear power. Large funds went into the building of installations. More funds collected from electricity customers (for the Non-Fossil Fuel Obligation) have been set aside as liabilities for the treatment of waste and decommissioning of power stations. The actual costs of treatment and decommissioning are unknown, and will be incurred for hundreds of years into the future. Given the opaqueness of government support for nuclear power and the uncertainty of future liabilities, it was impossible to quantify the trends in private cost of producing electricity from nuclear power. Nevertheless, the final bill, per kwh, for nuclear power is likely to be far greater than for other sources of energy (Mackerron 1996).

For other sources of energy, the external costs could be estimated relatively easily. The estimates are certainly not accurate, but they provide the correct order of magnitude. For nuclear power, the social costs are deeply unknown. The damage done from radioactivity leaks has been hard for epidemiologists to quantify and even harder for economists to monetise. Similarly, the risks of further leaks, major accidents or nuclear proliferation create a level of dread in the public that has been estimated as high compared with other industrial hazards, yet is difficult to monetise. In other words, the past, current and future external costs cannot be measured to a correct order of magnitude.

The inability to identify the damage and even provide a 'ball-park' figure for the external costs creates an opportunity to externalise the costs. Historically, the coal industry, the coke-and-gas industry or the petroleum have all benefited from the inability to identify and quantify damage to minimise concern and detract opposition. In some cases, the external costs were very high; in others, not. Their economic and political influence enabled them to pass on the costs to society. The nuclear industry stands in a similar position. Whether the full social benefits outweigh the full social costs is unknown, but their incentives to externalise as much of the costs as possible are certain.

The Incentive to Externalise Costs

There is an incentive for individuals and, especially, companies to pass on their costs to others, if they can get away with it. They will seek and welcome new processes and technologies that allow them to substitute external costs for internal costs.

Once the opportunity exists to externalise costs, a power struggle ensues between the 'polluter' trying to pass on the costs and the 'victim'. The victim is hoping to detect the external costs, attempting to halt the imposition of these costs and, at the very least, demanding compensation for the costs. Compensation means that the 'victim' has partially or wholly passed the costs back to the source, thus, they have been re-internalised. The success of the victim will depend on the science, the legal system and his/her economic and political power.

If the 'polluter' manages to pass on the costs, the victim is burdened by these extra costs. For example, a company builds a new factory with emissions that the local residents have to put up with. Gradually, the pollution is factored into the system: maybe the value of the house falls because it is in a polluted area. Naturally, this is an additional burden imposed on the victim. But, future transactions will have taken account of the external costs imposed on the system. So, if a person buys the house, it will be bought more cheaply than if those negative attributes did not exist. In other words, the house buyer made his/her decision with full knowledge of the pollution. In many cases though, the initial victim is not aware of the external cost (e.g. non-visual pollutants).

Information is crucial for enabling potential victims to avoid the burden of external costs. Science might help in discovering new external costs that were previously imposed. Companies will have an advantage in developing technologies where the degree of information about the potential external costs is extremely low. An example of this might be nuclear power in the 1950s or GMOs today. It increases the chances of being able to pass on the costs to others in the power struggle. Given these incentives, it is likely that the economy will move towards new, low information technologies because they increase the probability of being passed on to others and, therefore, of being adopted.

2. ECONOMIC DEVELOPMENT AND EXTERNAL COSTS

In a number of cases, environmental damage has been found to increase in early stages of economic development, eventually reaching a peak and then falling continuously; thus following an inverse-U relationship, the Environmental Kuznets Curve (EKC). The trend in air pollution will be compared with population and economic activity (Grossman and Krueger 1995, Panayotou 1997).

Air pollution damage associated with energy services cost about £(2000)20 billion at the end of the twentieth century. Relative to the overall population, it was not as high as during the dramatic increase experienced at the end of the nineteenth century (see Figure 10.9). The reduction in coal use, especially related to industry, drove down the average damage per person.

Yet, the rise in pollution damage per person from 1950 does hint at a more complex story. Environmental pollution appeared, caused major damage, eventually was addressed, and disappeared to a large extent. The problem seems to be solved. New concerns appear in their wake, however. The reduction in air pollution from coal use was associated with the decline in steam-driven railways. They were replaced by the internal combustion engine and petroleum fumes. These, in turn, have increased dramatically. So, environmental problems at different levels of economic development can be seen as a series of EKCs, one falling, the next one peaking, and the subsequent one rising.

Looking at the evolution of the economy, though, per unit of economic output or income, this is relatively low compared with the end of the nineteenth century (see Figure 10.10). This estimate suggests that, at the time, the environmental

damage of air pollution was equivalent to one-fifth of Britain's GDP. The social
burden of economic development was huge.

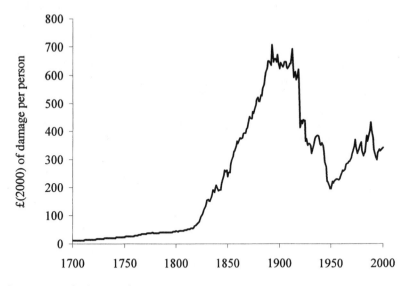

Source: see text for the external costs

*Figure 10.9 The External Cost (of Air Pollution) from Energy Services per
Capita, 1700–2000*

Empirical analysis and the discussion of trends in environmental pollution
above suggest that there exists an inverse-U relationship between economic
development and environmental quality. Air pollution rose and then fell. Acid
rain probably peaked in the mid-nineteenth century, before falling. It is a little
early to know whether greenhouse gases will follow a similar course.

There have been several possible explanations offered for the relationship.
First, economic development has been associated with a shift from agriculture to
heavy and then light industry, and to commerce and services. Each of these
sectors has different pollution intensities and is associated with different types of
pollution, but, generally, heavy industry imposes the greatest weight on the
environment. Second, for certain activities, such as those associated with energy
use, there was a shift towards higher quality products (e.g. from biomass to fossil
fuels to electricity). And, in some case, higher quality products may also,
coincidentally, have a lower impact on the environment – as has been the case for
energy.

Third, as income rises, households have more time and money to be
concerned about the environment – there is a 'positive' income elasticity for the
environment. Fourth, as income rises, households may have become more
concerned and interested in the environment – perhaps there was a 'greater than

one' income elasticity for the environment. While the former explanation seems obvious, the latter might be seen as politically incorrect to say that 'poorer people care less for the environment'. Fifth, and possibly helping to justify that last statement, communities with higher incomes have tended to have a greater awareness, information, education and knowledge of environmental pollution, risks and hazards.

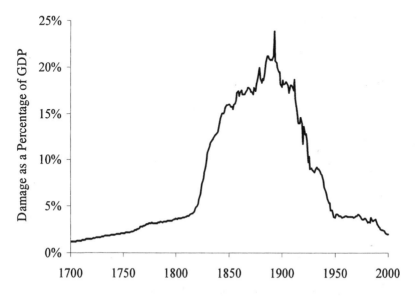

Source: see text for the external costs and Data Appendix for energy consumption estimates

Figure 10.10 The External Cost (of Air Pollution) from Energy Services as a Percentage of GDP, 1700–2000

Sixth, wealthy economies have exported polluting industries to poorer countries. Seventh, as more 'cleaner' technology has been produced and used, the costs fall. This has meant that as the economy has developed it will benefit from economies of scale in the production of 'clean' technologies. Eighth, more open and democratic political systems have been more willing to reflect the concerns and sufferings of the public. And, finally, there may be a greater capacity for politicians and authorities to reduce distortions and internalise externalities via regulation.

The history of the United Kingdom suggests, however, that it probably followed a relatively polluting path towards economic development: at an early stage of economic development, it became a major polluter; the turning point related to air pollution occurred around the 1920s, probably at a high level of economic development. This polluting path may be because of the large reserves of coal and possibly the relatively cheap energy services in the United Kingdom;

or because, as the first industrialised nation, Britain was locked-in to unclean and inefficient energy technologies; or due to the British lack of concern for certain environmental problems.

3. INTERNALISATION PROCESS

Early Air Pollution Abatement Efforts

Some of the explanations suggest that it may be useful to explore the existence of a shadow market for environmental quality. The inverse-U path could be seen in part as the result (and the many factors as determinants) of dynamic processes underlying the demand for and supply of environmental quality (Pearson 1994, McConnell 1997, Neha and Plassmann 2004). Having examined the supply of environmental quality above, here, it is proposed that a demand for reductions in environmental damage have existed for hundreds of years, that the demand has changed through time, and that it has played a role (if indirect) in determining the level of external costs imposed on society.

As early 1285, a Royal Commission found that it was indeed the switch from woodfuel to coal that was responsible for the increase in air pollution attributed to lime burners. Although an agreement ten years later established that smiths were not to work at night, it failed to abate the growth of air pollution in the Middle Ages. By 1307, Edward I banned the use of coal in lime kilns, for its "intolerable smell ... to the annoyance of the magnates, citizens and others ... and to the injury of their bodily health" (quoted in TeBrake 1975 p.340).

Indeed, London was already famous for its smoke, compared with many cities on the continent (Brimblecombe 1987). The largest complaints were the result of industrial activities, such as brewers, lime-burners and soap-boilers, where coal use and smoke was concentrated.

The smoke was seen as damaging to health – it was addressed in scientific debates at the Royal Society in the 1660s. John Evelyn highlighted the importance of air breathed in determining well-being, and that London's inherently good quality air was fouled by smoke from burning coal. He argued that the smoke entered the lungs and mixed with the blood, provoking catarrh and coughs (Jenner 1995 p.538). Meetings and masses were regularly disrupted with coughing and spitting. Although suspect, Gregory King had blamed smoke for the low fertility rate in London. More probable, John Gaunt had commented that it was the source of high mortality rates (Jenner 1995 pp.539–40). As Henry Oldenburg said, "ye corrosive Smoake of their SeaCoale, yt cuts off more than half their dayes" (quoted in Jenner 1995 p.547).

The smoke had also been a burden for other reasons. It generally impaired visibility and corroded materials. It was seen to kill insects. The soot dirtied clothes, and the ladies needed to clean their faces with crushed almonds (Jenner 1995 p.538).

Despite his interest in promoting woodland, Evelyn considered it unrealistic to seek a return to wood burning. Instead, he proposed moving all polluting industrial activities downwind, beyond Greenwich; also suggesting this would create jobs for freighters carrying beer, plaster and soap into London (Jenner 1995 p.538). Here, the approach was to export the problem, rather than seek to reduce it.

Others proposed the use of coke. Just like charcoal, burning coal over a low and gradual heat would carbonise the fuel, removing impurities and fumes from the point of use (Brimblecombe 1987 pp.30–31 and Jenner 1995 p.548).

It is important to see, however, that attempts to improve environmental quality were driven by political interests. John Evelyn had returned to England from exile at the time of the Restoration of the monarchy. He supported Charles II and, in various pamphlets, argued that the King would cleanse the city both physically and politically (Jenner 1995 p.541). Thus, ulterior motives drove much of the attempts to reduce environmental pollution.

Swiftly after the Great Fire in 1666, John Evelyn had drawn up plans for a new London. In Charles II's speech about the rebuilding, he promised that "brewers, dyers, bakers and similar smoky trades ... would be banished from the Thamesside where a handsome vista would be erected in their stead" (quoted in Jenner 1995 p.550). Economic and legal reasons made this impossible, and inevitably pollution continued unabated – though, at regular intervals, debated.

Other cities were also suffering from the negative aspects of growing coal use. Estimates from the late fourteenth and seventeenth centuries indicate that parts of York were faced with harmful smoke and sulphur dioxide concentrations, and that the area of maximum concentration in the centre of the city was widening and shifting from the West to South-East of the city (Hipkins and Watts 1996). In addition to the health complaints, the pollution was a regular concern for the preservation of the Minster, which has been in the centre and, therefore, subject to high levels of damage over the last eight hundred years. Swansea, home of much of the early British copper industry in the late sixteenth century and the early eighteenth century was affected by levels of air pollution (Newell 1997).

The Battle to Reduce Pollution in the Nineteenth Century

The Alkali Act of 1863 created the foundation for much of Britain's air pollution legislation in the twentieth century. It was also an example of the relationship between the demand for legislation and the difficulty of reducing pollution (Dingle 1982).

Because of the concentrated nature of the pollutants, including "a fuming, poisonous ... solution of hydrogen chloride" (Wohl 1983 p.225), the alkali industry was one of the first to be faced with stringent legislation. The Alkali industry in St Helens expanded sharply in the 1820s. The gentry lived downwind from the industrial centre. Deeply concerned about the rental and capital value of their properties, they were able to put pressure on government to investigate and tackle the problem. Lord Derby chaired the investigation and R. Angus Smith, the leading environmental scientist of the Victorian era, headed the commission inspection, specifying the industry standards to be met and fines for failure.

Smith's advice to manufacturers on newly developed methods for minimising waste helped reduce the level of pollution. The offensive by-product could be converted into chlorine, making a new product and, therefore, pollution unprofitable. The new legislation and inspectorate, therefore, managed to reduce the problem. As the industry continued to grow, however, even firms complying with legislation were causing harm. In addition, some of the original pollution problems were not included in the legislation and, therefore, were leading to great damage. In addition, some of the efforts to reduce gas emissions simply led to liquid wastes, turning nearby steams sulphuric. The problem declined at the end of the nineteenth century, not through legislation, as the industry contracted (Hassan 1997 p.10).

A more broad air pollution problem was associated with coal combustion (Clapp 1994). Urban centres were expanding at a dramatic rate during the nineteenth century. Industrial activity and population required power and heating and were generating increasing amounts of air pollution. Controlling air pollution associated with coal burning depended on passing a series of difficult hurdles – from scientific understanding to technical solutions to legislation and enforcement (Bowler and Brimblecombe 2000).

First, it was necessary to convince authorities of the benefits of pollution abatement. Benefits depended on identifying a relationship between pollutant and disease. In the nineteenth century, two competing models of disease formation existed. Leibig's model proposed that decay was the source of infections. Its policy implications complemented the 'miasma' theory, which advocated purity and flushing away dirt. Pasteur's model argued that infectious diseases resulted from specific microbes. While by the 1880s, the latter theory had the support of considerable empirical evidence, many in the mid-nineteenth century believed in the former theory. Thus, numerous experiments and observations related to the understanding of air pollution were guided by their theoretical beliefs, potentially delaying a formal understanding of the impact of air pollution on health.

Second, techniques need to be introduced to measure the level of pollution, preferably identifying toxins of direct relevance to the theory and scientific understanding. Measurement instruments started to be developed in the mid-nineteenth century. These were crude tools that captured suspended particulates on a fine tissue, and not other potentially more harmful substances. Another problem that has always plagued pollution control is the inability to identify culprits. Nevertheless, from the 1840s, scientists could begin to observe levels of air pollution concentration, enabling attempts to correlate doses and responses, and the establishment of pollution targets.

Abatement Technology

The next hurdle was the introduction of solutions to pollution problems. This was the cost-side of abating pollution. Solutions appeared gradually. "By the 1840s, it was possible to design furnaces that consumed a great proportion of their own smoke" (Hassan 1997 p.5). A few devices were tried early on and found to be unreliable and expensive to set up and use. These unfavourable experiences gave business a justification for its long term reluctance to seek solutions (Mosley 2001 p.144).

Observers argued that the principal source of smoke was feeding too much coal into the boiler. Some activities, such iron smelting, required periods of intense heat and, therefore, inevitably generated large amounts of smoke. For most activities, though, the consistent supply of fuel into the boiler was key to regular steam, smooth power and little smoke. Thus, promoters of smoke abatement tried to explain that reducing pollution would actually save industrialists money.

Failure to achieve these objectives was, in large part, down to the stoker. While the practice required skill, "this backbreaking task was as poorly paid as ever in the late nineteenth century, and still involved exposure to intense heat, undoubtedly contributing to the sluggish pace of smoke abatement" (Mosley 2001 p.154). Stokers were classed as unskilled workers, and they performed their tasks accordingly. In fact, they were often paid a commission by coal merchants according to the amount of fuel used.

Abatement societies encouraged the use of mechanical stokers, organising exhibitions and competitions for the most fuel-efficient machine and publishing information on the cost-saving potential. Yet, when mechanical stokers were introduced in factories, those placing coal in the devices were accused (by smoke abatement enthusiasts) of overloading the machines (Mosley 2001 pp.147–54). Another problem was that, although the machines performed well initially, they soon broke down, given that they were exposed to such extreme temperatures.

After the weak response of industry to mechanical feeders, enthusiasts tried to educate stokers about the value of good fuelling techniques. They tried to create certificates for stokers and encourage higher salaries. This too received indifference from employees, who argued there was no demand (Mosley 2001 p.155). They clearly remained unconvinced that raising the level of human capital and paying higher wages would reduce their fuel costs. The growth of trade unions in the late nineteenth century made industrialists wary of creating another skilled profession.

Legislation to Reduce Air Pollution

The development and diffusion of smoke-abating techniques and equipment could have provided a voluntary method towards smoke abatement. As this approach failed, new skills and technologies might make industrialists fight less hard for the status quo. So, the next hurdle to reduce pollution was the introduction of legislation, setting standards and penalising offenders.

Inevitably, industrialists created great opposition to the introduction of legislation, especially if it required changes in their activities. Supported by these captains of industry, John Bright, a well-known Manchester MP in the mid-nineteenth century, was proud of his skills and success-rate at defeating national bills to control manufacturing pollution (Hassan 1997 p.9).

Government considered that pollution was a local problem, best addressed by the appropriate authorities. This meant that the struggle to argue the case for legislation had to be done by a multitude of minor abatement associations across the country.

Throughout the nineteenth century, a series of different organisation put pressure on local authorities. The Smoke Abatement Associations became increasingly popular at the end of the nineteenth century. Mostly in vain, they sought to find ways to convince government of the magnitude of the problem.

The most basic legislation to deal with the problem was banning a particular industry or process – hardly a solution, but a way of reducing pollution in a particular area. This was the most common method of addressing pollution until the nineteenth century.

Yet, the economic imperative meant that it was hard to deny firms the right to produce. In fact, a common approach to the pollution problem in the nineteenth century was containment. It ensured that middle-class suburbs and countryside were unharmed by industry's expansion. Rather than banning activities, they were tolerated where they already existed. This meant that polluting industries concentrated in particular areas. They were generally working-class areas.

Another approach was to fine industries that failed to make efforts to reduce their smoke. For instance, the Police Act introduced in Manchester fined thirteen cotton mills in 1845 £2 each (Mosley 2001 p.144). There was a concern that imposing heavy fines would harm industry, reducing employment and competitiveness (both at a local and national level), rather than promote the demand for solutions to the problem. Needless to say, such 'powerful' incentives failed to alter the behaviour of industry and it continued to pollute where it could.

The Big Spread and the Big Smog

A growing problem, however, was the domestic fire. Increasingly dense populations were, on cold days, producing higher concentrations of smoke, even on Sundays and during strikes.

Smoke was driving wealthier populations out of the city. A member of a Manchester smoke abatement society noted that the "pollution of the atmosphere had done much to lessen the pleasure of residence in the city, and had thus driven away to Cheshire and other places, men of position, education and wealth" (quoted in Hassan 1997 p.21). The introduction of railways from the suburbs into the city centres had enabled residents to seek refuge far from the smoke, sewers and crime. The migration of homes had reduced the density of population, spreading the pollution.

Expanding transport systems was allowing cities to sprawl. Yet, while the transport infrastructure could accommodate more people, the environment may have been less capable of assimilation. More households required more heating and power.

In special cases, dramatic concentration levels were recorded. The worst recorded case of the famous 'pea soup' fog occurred in early December 1952, a period of particularly cold and unfavourable meteorological conditions. Smoke remained trapped throughout London and 4 000 additional deaths were reported in the city over a couple of days.

This event was, however, one of the last examples of high smoke concentrations. The 1960s were the start of a period of reduction in the smoke emissions, partly due to a ban on the use of coal for domestic fires in urban areas. Despite examples such as in 1952, it is generally believed that smoke concentrations started to decline around the turn of the century.

This century's decline in concentrations was mainly, first, the result of a migration of homes towards the suburbs (and, thus, a decline in the density of population in cities), which helped reduce concentration; and, second, a decline in many heavy (and energy-intensive) industries (as shown in Figure 10.7). There was also an attempt to shift industrial activities out of the cities and an increased efficiency of industrial boilers. More recently, there has been considerable benefit from the continued shift away from coal, especially associated with the use of nuclear power and then natural gas for electricity generation, and the use of petroleum for transportation.

Policies related to air pollution during the second half of the twentieth century were based initially on the creation of a legislative framework which set a constitutional right to air quality standards. A Clean Air Act was introduced in 1956 as a reaction to the big smog of 1952 which killed so many people. This was followed by numerous amendments leading to and amalgamated into the current Environment Act of 1995 (Ashby and Anderson 1981, Williams 2004).

In the 1980s, much of the pressure to set target reductions in emissions came from other countries. This included the Scandinavians (who were concerned about British acid rain harming their lakes and forests) and the West Germans (who had introduced Flue Gas Desulphurisation units on their coal-burning power stations to reduce emissions, raising the price of generating electricity and, thus, reducing the competitiveness of their products). This international pressure led to the creation of an international convention. The Convention on Long Range Transboundary Air Pollution (LRTAP) was proposed in Geneva in 1979; the United Kingdom signed in 1982. This set an international framework for agreeing to reduction protocols. In 1985, the first protocol proposed was to reduce sulphur dioxide by 30 percent of the 1980 level by 1993. The British government did not sign. Within the European Community, pressure was mounting for the British to accept targets. After many rounds of negotiation to introduce the Large Combustion Plant Directive, in 1988, the United Kingdom agreed to reduce its electricity generation and large industrial SO_2 emissions by 20 percent of the 1980 level by 1993, by 40 percent of the 1980 level by 1998 and by 60 percent of the 1980 level by 2003. This change of stance by the British coincided with plans to privatise the electricity supply industry, thus, the costs of reducing emissions would not be incurred by the public sector. Ironically, the ability to achieve these emission targets was in part the result of privatisation which encouraged the dash for gas. It was also the result of an increasing share of nuclear power and a decline in heavy (and polluting) industrial activities (Williams 2004).

International pressure also led to targets being set for NOx emissions. The second LRTAP Protocol signed in Sofia in 1988 agreed to stabilise 1994 emissions at 1987 level. The EC Large Combustion Plant Directive also agreed to reduce NOx emissions by 15 percent of the 1980 level by 1993, by 30 percent of the 1980 level by 1998 and by 45 percent of the 1980 level by 2003. Although it is unclear whether the UK will make these targets, the introduction of catalytic converters and CCGT power stations will help towards these targets. In terms of policies to achieve environmental targets, the former was an example of a command and control policy which did improve air quality (although at an unknown cost) and the latter an example of how unrelated market forces can lead to a relatively cost-effective emission reduction (Williams 2004).

The Road to Kyoto

At the end of the twentieth century, greenhouse gases emissions became a greater concern than air pollution or acid rain. The economic consequences of climate change are considerable and diverse. Climate change is likely to have an impact on agriculture and forestry, aquatic and coastal ecosystems, mountains, human infrastructure, energy service demand and human health (Tol 2002). A changing climate and environment is also likely to creating tensions and disputes associated with resource availability, increasing the chance of international conflicts.

Despite the difficulty of quantifying the damage associated with climate change, many policy-makers accept the need for greenhouse gas abatement. Because the atmosphere is a globally free-access resource, significant abatement will only be achieved by the commitment of many countries to reducing their emissions. This has been one of the stumbling blocks towards major abatement targets. Many of those policy-makers believe that without multilateral reductions, abatement will have little effect.

At the Earth Summit in Rio in 1992, politicians met and signed the Climate Change Convention. It states that governments have a responsibility for a sustainable management of the atmosphere, and introduced a framework for agreeing national reductions on greenhouse gas emissions. Its aim is to stabilise greenhouse gases concentrations in the atmosphere at a level that will prevent dangerous anthropogenic interference with the climate. In an attempt to start to agree on how to stabilise concentrations, a proposal was made to stabilise CO_2

emissions at the 1990 level by 2000. While many signed this proposal, it was a non-binding agreement and few achieved this target.

National leaders then met for the third Conference of the Parties (COP) to the Climate Change Convention in Kyoto in December 1997. This attempted to agree to legally binding targets, dealing with a basket of greenhouse gases rather than just CO_2, for targets up to 2012 that might be more ambitious than previous targets. The protocol set legally binding targets for OECD countries to reduce their collective basket of greenhouse gases. Some of the key targets are, for the EU, to reduce emissions by 8 percent below 1990 levels; for the USA, a 7 percent reduction below the 1990 levels (although the USA has decided to not sign the protocol); for Russia, a stabilisation at the 1990 level. For the protocol to become a reality, it needed the signing of sufficient countries to ensure that they represent 55 percent of total emissions associated with the protocol. In 2005, sufficient countries signed, making the Kyoto protocol legally binding. Thus, a token and modest effort to try to abate climate change had begun; it is probable, however, that, like in the past, major costs will not be imposed on polluters, and only reductions that can be achieved at minor additional costs will be incurred.

The Demand for Environmental Quality

The evidence above identifies the existence of a demand to remove the more damaging effects of energy services. Yet, because of the lack of sufficient signals and especially incentives to allocate and ration resources, the economy has tended to supply an insufficient level of environmental quality. The price of energy services facing producers has encouraged them to produce a greater level of energy services than the socially optimal level.

The inability to directly signal preferences to the supply-side has led to a demand for environmental legislation, which can in turn influence supply. The combination of legislation and the threat of enforcement have, at times, created incentives for polluters to internalise some of the costs, and improved the supply of environmental quality towards a more socially desirable level – where the demand and supply meet.

The supply of environmental legislation can be considered the outcome of the interaction of the demand (from the public and various pressure groups) for and the supply (by policy-makers and politicians) of environmental legislation (Keohane et al. 1998). The British Government has tended to develop energy-environmental policies that influenced three key markets. First, the traditional approach – often linked to the concept of Best Available Technology Not Exceeding Excessive Cost (BATNEEC) used in the United Kingdom during parts of the twentieth century – tried to specify the type of technology energy users could use. More generally, the regulators could change the constraints in the market for energy technology by creating incentives to use certain pieces of more efficient equipment (either in terms of energy or environment) or by encouraging manufacturers to supply equipment of a certain standard.

Second, policy could affect the market for energy. These effects could either focus on the energy producers, which leads directly to higher supplies of environmental quality (such as in relation to radioactive waste) or influence the producer (as in standards on electricity generators that feed through to the use), or directly influence the consumers (such as environmental taxation).

More recently, a third market, for environmental pollution permits, has been considered open to influence. It could be argued that the lack of any regulation on pollution was the most common 'policy' throughout the history of British environmental policy. It was a choice to allow the supply of pollution permits to adjust (in a perfectly elastic way) to the demands to pollute and ensure that the price of each permit was effectively equal to zero – thus, not harming economic development, at the expense of people's health. More recently, government has realised it can impose a fixed supply curve, setting the level of pollution.

This conceptual framework could, therefore, be argued that the level of environmental quality and cost of achieving it reflected the indirect interactions of the demand for and the supply of environmental quality. It would be valuable to consider how demand and supply will change and how they will interact in the future. For example, rising standards of living or greater awareness of physical damage associated with certain pollutants are likely to raise the public's willingness to pay for environmental quality. This could impose pressures on policy-makers to introduce legislation to raise environmental standards. Higher environmental standards are likely to lead to higher costs of either prevention or remediation. Changes in pressure groups, in the media's approach to the public's concerns or in the reflection of public preferences through political processes are likely to alter legislation related to the environment. Such changes are likely to increase the incentives for energy service users to internalise some of the external costs and supply a higher level of environmental quality, thus increasing the total costs of abatement (that is, environmental liabilities). Alternatively, policy-makers are moving towards more market-based instruments to achieve environmental standards. These instruments can achieve similar standards as traditional 'command-and-control' measures, but at lower costs to polluters. This movement may put downward pressure on external costs.

4. CONCLUSION

Major economic and social transformations have resulted from the availability of energy resources and the development of new technologies. Yet, while the energy efficiency of technologies has improved, it had limited environmental benefit during the Industrial Revolution. In the nineteenth century, the reductions in energy service prices led to vast increases in consumption, which were far greater than the environmental gains of efficiency.

Markets have an incentive to externalise the costs of energy service production. Technologies and fuels that manage to externalise the costs are more likely to be adopted. The costs have been passed on to society in general, although often on to the politically weaker or poorer segments of the population.

Can it be seen as the price to pay for cheaper heating, power, transport and light? Society carries some of the cost for private producers and consumers. A problem is that the costs of externalisation are not distributed evenly. The least economically and politically powerful groups carry the greatest burden. Another problem is that the benefits of cheap consumption are not spread equally either. Powerful firms producing energy and technology are able to capture high profits by externalising the costs. Their sales and profits would be far lower if the full costs were paid by consumers.

Markets have failed to respond adequately to the public's demand to reduce these costs. One of government's roles has been to reduce the costs of pollution associated with energy and energy service production. Despite this intent, the political influence of industry and the priorities of government have made intervention slow and limited. More recently, government has agreed to make polluters internalise the external costs, although again action has been modest.

Ultimately, the market has been mostly ambivalent to the damage caused by energy services, once they were externalised. Despite this, there has been an evolution towards a declining impact of energy services. Historically, the technology was more capable of using a solid fuel, than a liquid, and certainly not a gas. It has been mainly good fortune that has driven consumption from coal to petroleum to natural gas, from the polluting to the cleaner fuel.

Nevertheless, the market was not completely ignorant of the value that consumers placed on smokeless fuel. Once a certain level of disposable income had been reached, consumers and society were willing to pay for cleaner fuels. A cleaner fuel as a substitute for a more polluting one can be sold with added-value. It has become a new market in itself. Thus, the declining environmental impact of energy services does appear to reflect the priorities of the public, first for development then a cleaner environment.

Indeed, social pressures to reduce external costs today and the existence of technologies to exploit cleaner fuels mean that a return to use of coal would be politically unacceptable, without a method of removing the carbon from the fuel. It may become more politically acceptable if the availability of cleaner fuels declines and their price rises. Nevertheless, history has shown that markets have consistently, if sometimes slowly, found new supplies or new solutions to the resource availability problem, if not to the environmental problem.

11. Policies Influencing the Trends in Energy Services

1. THE EVOLVING ROLE OF GOVERNMENT

Although the evolution of the provision and consumption of energy services has been driven by the decisions of millions of individuals, certain organisations have had the power to influence market forces and sway the trends. The previous chapter reflected how the externalisation of costs of energy service production could encourage the uptake of particular technologies and fuels, such as coal, coke, gas, petroleum or uranium. Through these externalising technologies, the interests of organisations, such as those of fuel producers, were met. The well-being of energy service consumers was also met. This came at a cost to society, however.

This chapter reviews the extent to which market forces were enhanced or hampered by government, in a manner that altered the long-run trends in energy service prices and consumption. Given the importance of energy services in driving the economy, there has been considerable debate about the role of government in managing the production, supply and even consumption of energy. If past governments were successful in influencing long-run trends in energy services, this analysis might provide some evidence on the process of achieving revolutions in energy services – whether to radically increase the availability of energy services, to move towards a low carbon economy or to pursue a path of sustainable development.

A history of British energy policies is beyond the scope of this chapter. Instead, this chapter selects important trends related to government intervention, providing evidence of the influence of policies for long-run trends in energy service price and consumption. They will help to draw conclusion about the evolving role of government and its ability to initiate revolutions in energy services.

Priorities at Different Stages of Economic Development

The organisation of centralised decision-making has been both imposed on and sought by the public. Whether a monarchy or government, the source of decision-making has had roles expected of it by the people. Yet, like all organisations, government action works to secure, maintain and re-enforce its own objectives.

In the case of the monarchy or government, the main objective has been political power. In some cases, this objective was best served by improving society's well-being, but it has not always been the case.

At different stages of economic development, government priorities and influence on behaviour have changed. Government initially played basic roles, such as defence, law and order, and justice. It also sought to manage the economy. This included the protection of its population against famine and the promotion of economic activity – especially of exports, as a source of foreign revenue (Coleman and John 1976).

In early stages of economic development, the monarchy or government was a relatively weak organisation. Its objectives and scope of influence were limited. As the economy developed, new demands were made of government, and it also took on more roles. Its expanding role required greater funds (Jupp 2006).

Government's promotion of economic growth and development has helped to protect its position. At times, this coincided with encouraging cheaper provision and greater consumption of energy services. For instance, ensuring homes and industries had heat, power, transport and lighting was important for the economy. Although many other concerns and priorities fought for their attention, governments that appreciated the role of energy services were more likely to be successful at protecting the economy and, thus, their position than others.

2. MARKET PROTECTION

Monopolies and Technological Policy

In the mid-sixteenth century, English concerns about the cost and vulnerability associated with importing foreign products, as well as a growing inactive poor population, led to a policy of promoting national industries. The issue of imports was particularly alarming for the expanding military campaigns, which were imposing huge burdens on the government debt. In the 1549 *The Discourse of the Commonwealth of the Realm of England*, it was noted that the cost of iron, oils (principally for cleaning cloths, but also lighting) and certain agricultural products had risen by a third in the previous seven years (Thirsk 1978a p.30).

For these key products, and many others, the government, first of King Henry VIII (1509–47) and then following monarchs, appreciated the importance of welcoming foreign craftsmen to set up their trade in England, of introducing and diffusing the skills required to produce their goods and services, and of protecting a burgeoning national industry. Such positive policy could certainly bear fruit. For example, in 1544, Henry VIII invited foreign gun-founders and gunsmiths to the Sussex region, where iron ore and charcoal were relatively abundant – at the time, there were three furnaces established in the region; by 1548, more than fifty furnaces were active in the region (Thrisk 1978a p.27). This helped to reduce the cost of using certain key products, limit the risk of supply shortages either for economic or political reasons, and in hiring the unemployed which could otherwise cause social unrest.

Another lesson learnt from continental economic policy was the value of not only welcoming experts, but of giving them special status. The first patent of monopoly was introduced in 1552 for glass making. The invention of window glazing was the result of competitors trying to enter the more lucrative crystal market. The development of the industry was principally due to the Elizabethan policy of welcoming foreign glass-makers. These favourable incentives enabled Britain to switch to coal in the production of glass and eventually other goods (see Chapter 4). Without the incentives, many industries would have been stuck with production processes dependent on biomass fuels.

In the early days of the patent scheme, it appears to have worked relatively well. The foreign artisan was encouraged to introduce his technologies and practice his skills with a degree of monopolistic power, often paying the government for the privilege and, thus, helping to reduce the government's debts. At times of high demand, these monopolists would hire many labourers to assist in the work, who would then be in a position to use their learnt skills to set up their own trade. Due to the lack of resources of the foreign artisans to guard the secrets and protect their rights, the scheme promoting the introduction of new techniques and technologies also allowed for their diffusion (Thirsk 1978a p.59).

By the 1580s, however, the scheme was becoming less successful and facing considerable criticism. Many wealthy and influential entrepreneurs received patents, and had far more ability and power to enforce their rights, sending agents around the country to gather information and threaten adopters of the new technology. This process was also promoted by the practice of giving creditors of the realm monopolies as a form of debt repayment. Thus, political pressure, especially in 1597, 1601 and 1621, was put on the government to change the laws. In 1601, Queen Elizabeth I (1558–1603) admitted that many of her patents "had not proved beneficial to her subjects as she had intended, but had injured many of the poorer sort of her people" and declared many of those void (Thirsk 1978a p.98).

After James I (1603–25) chose to continue the practice of patents of monopoly to increase government revenue, further opposition developed. In 1624, a bill against monopolies was passed (after an initial failure), which limited grants to genuine inventors and then only for fourteen years. This certainly improved the development of new industries and technologies, although it did not stop the existence of corporations (of trades).

The Patent System

The patent system was transformed in the seventeenth century from a method for providing market protection for 'special' producers to a way for technological developers to appropriate some of the benefits of their ideas. Producers of knowledge had a better chance of earning a return from the developments.

Many of the important innovators in energy services, such as Boulton and Watt, have sought and received a temporary monopoly in the supply of knowledge, and its associated technology. Indeed, during the eighteenth century, patents (in general and related to energy services) were granted at a rate that greatly outstripped economic growth (see Chapter 8).

This improved the system for encouraging the dissemination of knowledge in the form of physical capital and radically reduced the cost of energy services. The ability to reproduce knowledge by placing it in physical capital transformed the ability to produce energy services. Knowledge could be commodified, bought and acquired in an instant. Traditional knowledge about the provision of efficient energy services depended on teaching and learning.

While innovation does not lead necessary to diffusion, it opens the door for the possibility of technological revolutions. Given the huge importance of knowledge in the provision of energy services, the creation and refinement of the patent system can be considered one of the most important influences government had in promoting revolutions in energy services.

3. SECURITY OF SUPPLY

Early Policies related to Supplies

The regular and secure provision of agricultural products as 'fuel' for humans and animals has been a crucial part of most governments' policies in lesser developed economies. It would be impossible to cover this effort, but it is worth remembering that it could be part of the production of power, in particular.

Yet, as discussed in Chapter 4, the expansion of arable lands to meet the needs of a growing population placed pressures on land, which created concerns about wood supplies for heating. The British government was beginning its policies to intervene in the supply of energy associated with heating. In the medieval and early modern era, this focussed not so much on supplying fuel, as on banning the destruction of forests. Given the weak role of central government at the time, they tended to be localised bans and to be ignored.

In the seventeenth and eighteenth centuries, the British government continued its efforts to minimise imports and increase its national industries. With the rising demand for street lighting, one such example was the attempts to maintain a British whaling industry (see Chapter 7). This episode shows the British government has had a strong aversion to importing energy sources – either because of the balance of trade or the vulnerability to foreign supplies.

It is also unclear whether this concern was exacerbated by the fact that the main consumer of whale oil was local authorities for street lighting. Had consumption been paid outside of the public purse, perhaps government would have been less concerned about ensuring domestic suppliers. The lack of instances when the British economy depended on foreign energy imports limits our ability to conclude.

Britain has had the good fortune of having large deposits of energy under its soil. So, once the economy completed the transition to fossil fuels, the pressures on land, sea and organic fuels declined. Thus, in only a few instances, did the United Kingdom have to suffer the discomforts of importing energy.

British-Owned Petroleum

During the nineteenth century, the British government had already shown interest in the growing imports of petroleum-based products, predominantly for lighting purposes. British companies, such as Shell and Burmah Oil, were already involved in the business. As petroleum-based products started to be used for transport services at the beginning of the twentieth century, the government cast an even keener eye. As the Royal Navy started using oil for its battleships, it began to lend a hand too (Yergin 1991 p.159).

In his bid to ensure government's protection of the Anglo-Persian Company in 1913, Winston Churchill stated that "if we cannot get oil, we cannot get corn, we cannot get cotton and we cannot get a thousand and one commodities necessary for the preservation of the economic energies of Great Britain" (quoted in Yergin 1991 p.160). He added that the Admiralty should become "owners or, at any rate, the controllers at the source". The British government invested the equivalent of about £120 million in the company (Yergin 1991 p.161).

Continuing to be majority shareholder in the company that became British Petroleum (BP), the government continued to control a large share of the production of oil destined for the United Kingdom market. In the early 1970s, its involvement in oil markets intensified when a series of oil discoveries were made under the North Sea. In order to control supply and to benefit from the potential profits, it formed a new company, the British National Oil Corporation (BNOC), which reserved the right to buy 51 percent of the oil produced in the British North Sea (Yergin 1991 p.670).

Following the Oil Shocks of the 1973, the British government was able to influence world oil prices through its ability to supply such a large amount of oil. While oil prices were high, this was an attractive position to be in. As oil prices started to fall in the mid-1980s, it was no longer in its interest to buy oil at a high price and sell it for less. Margaret Thatcher abolished the company in 1985 (Yergin 1991 p.746). From 1979, her government had also been selling its shares in BP. So, in the 1980s, the British government radically reduced its involvement in the economy's supply of oil. Despite a greater sense of control over energy security at some crucial periods of the twentieth century, it is doubtful whether the long run outcome for the consumer would have been very different if policies related to oil supplies had been less involved.

Nuclear Power

After the Second World War, many forces came together to create a desire to produce electricity from atomic energy. A belief (or a promise) in the low cost of nuclear power, growing concerns about oil imports, political pressures to use nuclear fission for civilian purposes and generate a secure supply of weapon-grade plutonium all played their part in formulating electricity generation policy.

The investment in research and development to generate nuclear power technology could only be funded by a very large organisation, such as government. Government's expenditure is not known, but must have been very large (Cowan 1990). In addition to the public funding to develop the knowledge and technologies to compete with conventional power stations, funds were (and still are) required for processing waste and fuel, and the decommissioning of power plants.

Before parts of the electricity supply industry were privatised, the CEGB, as a monopoly, could set prices to cover costs associated with the different methods of power generation. From 1990, to subsidise waste and decommissioning activities, the government introduced the Non-Fossil Fuel Obligation (NFFO) which involved a levy of 12 percent to all electricity customers, and helped fund renewable sources of power. While the actual economics of nuclear power has been opaque, due to a lack of information on costs, nuclear power has tended to be more expensive than coal and certainly natural gas power (Mackerron 1996 p.249).

Because the very large development costs were covered mostly by the taxpayer, rather than the power consumer, the costs of power provision in the United Kingdom only rose slightly due to the use of nuclear power. Undoubtedly, though, the government's involvement was crucial for the existence of a nuclear industry in the United Kingdom and for its role in the generation of electricity. Also, at the end of the twentieth century, the resulting fuel mix, which included around 20 percent nuclear power, probably led to lower emissions of air pollution and carbon dioxide than if the government had not developed a support for the nuclear industry.

4. REGULATING MARKET STRUCTURE

A less drastic form of concern about security of supply has been the management of market structure. A concentrated supply of energy sources, as has often been the case, leads to positions of power. The first consequence of concentration is economic power, often exercised by raising prices of energy and stifling competition. The second consequence is political, often resulting from the financial might of the large energy supplier, and its generation of economic wealth and employment, frequently in regions highly dependent on these activities, such as mining. This power can, at times, stand in the way of energy consumers' and government's objectives.

Until the twentieth century, government had little influence over the market for power, outside of its protection of patents, which were important for the likes of Joseph Smeaton and James Watt. The lack of coordination in the distribution of electricity had created a need for government direction. With different companies using various voltages and frequencies, and a patchwork grid across the country, the government was instrumental in linking up the separate distribution networks. This helped reduce the extra reserve capacity required and, thus, lower capital, fuel and running costs. In other words, power distinctly benefited from a coordinated effort through public hands.

A socialist attitude towards industry swept through Britain after the Second World War. The main energy suppliers were to be consolidated into publicly-owned monopolies. British Coal was experiencing a declining demand due to a downturn in heavy industrial activities. The company was facing competition from foreign producers and other fuels for generating power. It was also observing the growing willingness of government to reduce air pollution. It was responsible for a huge number of mines and men, which were gradually to be closed and laid-off respectively. The more gradually it could be done, the less political tension these regionalised unemployment crises would create.

British Coal did have a preferential demand coming from the Central Electricity Generating Board (CEGB). The newly amalgamated electricity production and supply industry in the 1940s used mostly coal in its power stations. The CEGB was in a very different position, having to find ways to meet the demand, and expand capacity. Its objective was to provide electricity and minimise black-outs, and was not under deep pressures of efficiency and price reduction (Surrey 1996).

In the 1980s, the mood had changed, and the British government felt that "the business of government was not the government of business" (Lawson quoted in Newbery 1996). It was time to privatise these monoliths. The lack of drive to become efficient had kept the prices of energy sources in the United Kingdom high. This may well have had an impact on the competitiveness of British industries abroad.

Privatisation and then liberalisation of coal, gas and electricity markets led to increased competition and declining energy prices. The integration of European energy supply industries into a single European market will certainly reduce the potential for the British government to influence energy markets.

5. PROVISION AND TAXATION OF PUBLIC SERVICES

Transport Infrastructure

A central role of the public authorities has been the provision of public goods and services, especially in the provision of transport infrastructure. One of the first services government provided was to police roads and waterways. The British government's success in reducing the level of brigandage and piracy dramatically reduced the risk and, therefore, the cost of carriage and travel. Security came at a price, however, as tolls sprang-up 'everywhere' and government needed to fund its public service.

Both brigands and tolls are methods of capturing wealth from the consumer, yet, with very different effects. For instance, the violence associated with brigands led to loss of limbs and lives, to the need for expensive protection and to a great deal of uncertainty and stress. Tolls caused no physical damage or need for protection, and more certainty about expense. Tolls enabled government to capture wealth, which is destined to be redirected for future 'public services'. Thus, government's role in policing land and waters, reducing the number of brigands, and creating tolls to capture benefits did lead to a long run reduction in the risk and cost of carriage and travel.

While transport networks were relatively safe in Britain, they were not always in good condition. As discussed in the transport chapter, local parishes were responsible for maintaining and improving roads. Reformation stripped the Church of its land, creating a vacuum in the provision of these services. The growth of transport in the early modern era became too great for local authorities responsible for the task. Especially for roads linking towns, privately-owned turnpikes provided the solution. Thus, the lack of public involvement in transport infrastructure led to a rise in the cost of transport.

It is inappropriate to consider that this incident was a case of government having an influence over long-run trends. Instead, it was a case of market failure to provide transport infrastructure, creating a role for government intervention. The lack of intervention eventually led to private organisations seeing opportunities for profit through the provision of transport infrastructure and charging users for its use.

From the second half of the seventeenth century, local authorities were responsible for considerable improvements to waterways. Many towns became far closer to the river network, able to supply goods to major towns and cities, especially London. These improvements substantially reduced the cost of carriage in the seventeenth and eighteenth centuries.

Yet, their improvements were ultimately limited by the size of the authority and the resources they could collect. Like turnpike trusts before them, private organisations were able to gather sufficient financial capital to expand and improve Britain's waterway network. They tended to focus on economically strategic links, connecting for instance energy reserves to centres of industrial activity.

Transport infrastructures in Britain continued to be privately developed throughout the nineteenth century. Railway lines tended to be installed by the companies running services, also creating local private monopolies. It was only with the introduction of roads associated with the combustion engines that government took a more direct role in providing the infrastructure. This increased involvement reflects the larger size of government in the twentieth century, and its greater ability to invest in major developments.

Public Lighting

Another energy service where the local authority's role varied through time was for lighting (see Chapter 7). Naturally, indoor lighting was sought and provided by the individual managing the building. Outdoors, responsibility was more ambiguous.

In the fifteenth century, regulations were being introduced about public spaces. Certain citizens, such as innkeepers, were required to light the area outside their main door. Although modest private contributions to a public service had appeal, in practice, the quality of service provision varied dramatically. As towns and cities grew, the need for a more organised approach to public lighting needed to develop. Urbanisation also implied that the authorities were growing in size, collecting more revenue and, therefore, able to invest in larger projects. By the beginning of eighteenth century, local authorities were increasingly supplying light or hiring private companies on their behalf.

Capturing Wealth through Energy Services

As was mentioned above, local authorities and the government had services to provide and needed revenue to fund them. Thus, one of government's key activities throughout time has been developing the most effective ways of capturing a share of the public's wealth.

The size of government has been a crucial determinant of the share it captured. The larger the government, the more revenue it has needed to fund its activities. Also, the larger the government, the more developed and sophisticated it has been at capturing wealth.

During the fifteenth and sixteenth centuries, the British monarchy was involved in a series of wars that needed funding. Although various methods were employed, the provision of monopolistic privileges was an effective way of capturing wealth, especially from the richer members of society. This system was abused to the point of being detrimental to the economy, and was abolished, except in cases of knowledge creation requiring a patent. In other words, government's search for methods to raise revenue was often at the detriment of cheaper energy services.

Later, in the middle of the seventeenth century, greater public expenditure required further revenue. The Hearth Tax was developed as an additional way to capture wealth. It acted as an income tax, as richer citizens were likely to have installed more hearths in their house than poorer people. Naturally, it discouraged the building of hearths and chimneys, thus, forcing many homes to be colder than would otherwise have been the case.

In a similar vein, and for new military activities, the government sought to collect funds by charging people according to the number of windows they owned. The Window Tax lasted for more than 130 years, and severely curtailed the access to natural sunlight. It was as if the British government had acquiesced to Frederic Bastiat's (satirical) petition on behalf of the chandlers, who complained against foreign and unfavourable competition, from the sun. Inevitably, citizens suffered from a lower amount of lighting than if a standard income tax had been introduced. They were also victims of the Candle Tax, which made matters worse.

6. SOCIAL AND ENVIRONMENTAL PROTECTION

Imposing Safety Standards

One of the greatest social costs associated with energy services has been the health costs and lives lost from coal mining. The billions of tonnes of coal consumed over the last five hundred years required millions of miners. Of those, most suffered health-related damage, and thousands died in mining accidents.

The growth in the coal industry came at a price to mining regions, in terms of lost lives. Throughout the nineteenth century, there were increasing pressures for government to demand basic standards of safety in mines.

Some mine owners might have argued that, in a competitive market, suppliers of labour select the level of risk and wage compensation that suited them. In this argument, those that worked far underground in unstable mines were willing to take greater risks for larger returns. Labourers could select their tasks and jobs according to a series of characteristics, including the level of risk. Coal miners, facing greater risks, would be paid more than the coal owner's butler. Safety legislation would stop risk-taking miners from earning higher wages. This argument ignored the market structure of the coal-mining industry. Often a coal mine was the main employer in a town. It was the main demand for labour, and could dictate the working conditions.

It would be interesting to note whether mines that were the dominant employers in a town forced their workers to take greater risks and compensated them less. In other words, these mines were able to reduce their costs of coal mining by keeping lax safety standards. They were, therefore, able to pass on some of the costs of mining to their employees in the form of greater health problems, injuries and lives lost. The process of externalisation of cost of energy services, which was discussed in relation to environmental problems, could be applied to wider social issues.

Whether due to a 'failure of the market to allocate workers to their optimal wage for the level of risk faced' or the alarming social cost or the existence of relatively straightforward and low-cost solutions, the government began to introduce legislation to protect miners' lives in the nineteenth century. Although they did not avoid all deaths, the series of legislations imposed on the industry did work towards reducing the social cost of energy services. From an examination of the British Parliamentary Papers, it appears that efforts to minimise lives lost in mining accidents was by far the single most important issue the British government sought to address in relation to energy industries during the nineteenth century.

While these policies had important bearings on the well-being of workers, they did not radically alter trends in energy service prices or consumption. They may have raised the share of the social costs of producing coal that was covered privately (that is, by the management) and passed on partly to consumers rather than by a part of a society (that is, the workers). It is unlikely that the higher costs to meet safety standards fed through into a significantly different mix of fuels to meet energy services – the additional costs were not sufficient that they reduced consumption in the short term or were responsible for the shift away from coal in the long term.

Environmental Standards

As was discussed in Chapter 10, the costs of consuming energy services were also passed onto society. In a similar way, especially in the nineteenth century, the public was concerned about air pollution. Yet, efforts to reduce environmental damage were less successful and far more gradual than for safety in the production of coal.

What can justify the more rapid 'internalisation of costs' related to safety than for the environment? The most obvious factor was the different costs of the solutions. Safety could be achieved relatively cheaply. Solutions proposed to reduce pollution tended to lead to important increases in the costs of energy services.

Another factor was the priority associated with the concerns. Both related to health damage and lives lost. The difference was in the ability to prove the cause of morbidity and mortality. A miner buried under thousands of tonnes of coal was unquestionably due to an accident in a pit. The coroner assessing the cause of death of a street vendor that keeled over from coughing was unlikely to claim that the death was due to inhaling coal smoke. Proof of the cause of damage or death has been a powerful tool in avoiding legislation. All industries – whether related to coal use, petroleum refineries, nuclear power or electricity distribution – have used science (and the lack of proof) to protect themselves from unfavourable legislation.

Similarly, politicians have conveniently chosen to use the same science in the way it suits them best. It required little courage for politicians to introduce legislation that imposed minor costs on an industry and substantially improved the life expectancy of a large number of workers. A far more difficult decision was faced by politicians that were asked to improve life expectancy through reduced air pollution at the expense of the economy. These politicians needed to balance the costs and benefits (to society or to themselves) of such legislation. Proposals made that imposed genuine costs have consistently been quashed. The policies introduced to date have imposed little additional cost on the economy. In other words, policies related to energy services have consistently prioritised economic rather than social or environmental objectives.

7. CONCLUSION

The Objectives of Government in relation to Energy Services

Many different facets of the markets related to energy services could be candidates for government intervention. It is possible to split the objectives of policies related to energy services into three categories: those external to the energy system, those internal to the energy system and those related to sustainable development.

First, the British rulers had a basic role of protection – physical and then economic. At times, it could help achieve these objectives by meddling in markets related to energy services. It sought to develop policies that touched on energy issues although their objectives were external to the energy system. The energy market was important and could generate large revenue for the government. Taxation of energy use was an effective way to improve the government's budget, even if it distorted the energy market. Also, given the size of imports and exports of energy around the world, attempts to balance the trade deficit may have involved dealing with energy markets. Similarly, given their importance, altering energy markets could improve the country's competitiveness relative to trade partners. Finally, altering the markets could be politically attractive and generate popularity amongst the electorate – at least, once it was important.

Through time, especially in the twentieth century, the importance of energy services became an objective in its own right. The main objectives of this category of policies was keeping prices low for the consumer, ensuring the quality of supply provided was adequate and reliable, containing the power of the large suppliers, and protecting the development of any infant energy industries that might be valuable in the long run.

Finally, alongside policies internal to the energy system, the British government has been forced to address the social and environmental effects of energy services. This category of policies could be seen as related to 'sustainable development'. They have been concerned with the better long run management of resources related to energy, taking account of the social and environmental issues generally ignored by markets. This has included dealing with sections of the population (often the poor and the elderly) and regions that lack adequate energy supplies and consumption, which would have reduced their well-being and their development. This also involved addressing problems about the damage caused during the extraction of minerals (such as river pollution caused by the mining industry) and the distribution of fuels (such as oil spillages), and of air pollution, acid rain and climate change (discussed in Chapter 10).

Influence on Trends

Over the last five hundred years, the energy system has evolved dramatically towards providing cheaper and consuming more energy services. The path followed has been driven by the market – its producers, suppliers and consumers. It has been constrained by the energy resources accessible and the infrastructure set up. It has been directed by new knowledge from the creativity of scientists and entrepreneurs. It has also been swayed by the hand of the large organisations and the State.

The early influence of the British government on trends in energy services was extremely inconsistent. There was little attempt to promote cheaper energy services. They sought other objectives, such as military security and economic development, and the markets related to energy services were simply a way to achieve them. Policies were introduced and repealed with relatively little awareness of their consequences. Higher priorities often led to policies disruptive for energy service markets.

It is difficult to assess the actual impact of policies on trends. Counterfactuals would need to be developed for each policy. And, the long-run impacts are clearly ambiguous. For instance, taxation of heating or lighting technologies and fuels certainly raised the price of these services, discouraging consumption for extended periods. They may have encouraged efforts to innovate and the adoption of new technologies. Those disruptions no doubt altered the course of trends in energy services – yet, probably only modestly.

In other cases, such as the policing of roads or the inability to maintain them, the costs of carriage and travel were dramatically changed. New technologies and organisations were formed around these changes. The impact on long-run trends was significant, severely altering the history of transport services.

Even more recently, as government sought to address the specifics of energy service markets, it was not necessarily consistent. In general, government decisions and policies appear to have been reactive to demands by contemporary influential individuals or organisations. The nature of democracy implies that governments and ideologies replace each other relatively quickly. The post-Second World War experience in the United Kingdom shows how drastically the incentives and State involvement can change in less than fifty years.

Looking at the medium run, policies can hinder or enable the adoption of a particular technology. Specific technologies and fuels can be sensitive to economic, political or even cultural conditions prevailing at the time of development. From the beginning of human existence, there have always been ways of heating, creating power, transporting and lighting. Generally, for a new technology or fuel to be introduced, an incumbent one had to be replaced. This required the achievement of important economies of scale. They, in turn, created lock-ins, making it harder for the next generation of technologies and fuels to replace it. Thus, the economy was clearly directed down a specific path. Increasingly, only a large player, either a multinational corporation or government, has sufficient access to funds to achieve the economies of scale necessary to compete or even replace an existing incumbent. The example of nuclear power shows both the extent and the limits of State involvement in trends.

A longer-run perspective does allow us to question the lasting influence of policy. The evidence suggests that there has been a near irresistible force pushing towards cheaper and more energy services. A government would find halting this force a promethean task. Government can do little against the general trend in services.

Nevertheless, policies can change the specific path taken. They can influence the technologies and fuels selected. They can determine who will benefit from cheaper and more energy services. In particular, they can determine the proportion of the costs that will be covered by producers, consumers and the burden placed on society at large.

PART FOUR

THE FUTURE

12. Future Trends in Energy Services: Continuity and Change

1. CONTINUITY

Evolution and Revolution

This chapter considers future trends in energy services, based in part on the analysis of past experiences. Naturally, it does not try to gaze into the crystal ball and claim to know what will happen. Instead, it only tries to show how the ideas developed in this book could be used to anticipate future trends.

The path an economy follows will be directed by the momentum of the past and of the changes people of the future will create. Wrigley (1988) described the processes surrounding the Industrial Revolution as the result of "continuity, change and chance". This encapsulates the forces that will be at work forming the future.

The unfolding of past events and of those associated with future energy services could be characterised as following a series of 'punctuated equilibria' (Gould 2002). Extended periods of continuity will probably be disrupted by major transformations. The 'punctuations' are the revolutions. Yet, even these radical disruptions are likely to lead to a rigid system and entrenched behaviour. For contemplating the future, it is appropriate to focus first on the current momentum of the incumbent energy system.

Projections of Energy Services

It has been seen that energy consumption in this modern energy system tends to grow, following the rate at which population and economic activity expands, which drive the demand for energy services. This relationship has been tempered somewhat by variations in the prices of energy services – higher prices naturally mean lower consumption. Thus, the central issue is to anticipate the rate of growth of the economy and population, and the change in the real price of energy services, then feed this information into identifying trends in the use of heat, power, transport and light, and in energy consumption.

If the present system for providing energy services remained unchanged, it would be a relatively straightforward exercise to predict long-run trends. Without technological development, energy service prices would fluctuate with fuel prices. These would be determined by resource availability, costs of production and distribution, market structure and the demand for energy services, which drives fuel use. Modest energy efficiency improvements could also be considered part of the existing system, and put downward pressure on energy service prices, but these are relatively gradual and predictable improvements and can be incorporated in projections – see, for instance, Fouquet et al. (1997) for a summary of this process for energy demand forecasting.

Assuming a constant population (in year 2000), and the same declines in prices, rates of growth in economic activity and elasticities as in the 1950–2000 period, forecasts of energy services and energy can be computed. Annual growth of GDP per capita would be 2.5 percent and the annual fall in service prices would vary between 1.5 percent for passenger travel and 4.5 percent for freight transport. Energy efficiency changes varied from a modest decrease for passenger transport to an annual improvement of 1.8 percent for lighting. The joint (that is, income and price) elasticities would be based on the actual estimates presented in Table 9.2.

Table 12.1 Service and Energy Consumption Forecasts up to 2050 (assuming the same rates as in 1950–2000 period)

	Joint Elasticity	Annual Rise in Price	Total Rise in Service Use	Annual Rise in Efficiency	Total Rise in Energy Use
Heating	0.27	2.2%	270%	1.5%	130%
Power	0.35	2.9%	490%	0.9%	300%
Passenger	0.53	1.5%	380%	-0.2%	410%
Freight	0.11	4.6%	350%	-0.2%	390%
Lighting	0.19	4.1%	500%	1.8%	200%

Source: see text and Chapter 9

The assumptions and the results are presented in Table 12.1. They indicate service and energy consumption up to 2050, assuming the same changes as between 1950 and 2000. Inevitably, under these assumptions, the consumption for all services increases considerably. The final column shows energy use consumption. The resource requirements and environmental effects using the current fuel mix would be quite serious. Within the current energy system, this implies dramatic increases in total energy requirements and in carbon dioxide emissions.

Naturally, this series of estimates is neither reflecting the current system nor necessarily the revolutionary changes that might occur. In particular, prices fell more dramatically for certain services and economic activity grew more between 1950 and 2000 than might be anticipated up to 2050. Efficiency improvements, especially those that occurred in heating and lighting, may not be experienced again.

Reaching Mineral Limits

Energy resources and supply will also be important in directing the current trends. However, the on-going debate about whether the global economy is likely to 'run out' of fossil fuels does not seem to be constructive, as opposing camps refuse to consider each others' points (Arnott 2002, Ahlbrandt 2003). As most economists argue, a genuine exhaustion of fossil fuels would be unlikely. First, even if oil and natural gas reserves currently appear limited, coal reserves are enormous, and are likely to remain untapped. The debate needs to focus on the lighter fossil fuels and their long run future. Second, the extraction costs of oil reserves vary greatly, and many reserves are not commercially viable at present. If global reserves available at current prices start to dwindle, oil or natural gas prices will rise, more costly reserves will be extracted and then stabilise once sufficient additional reserves are extracted.

When the economy was dependent on organic energy sources, the price of energy services did rise for an extended period. Heating, power and transport services did rise before the adoption of coal in many industries and households for heating and eventually for power and transport. The higher service prices led to a substitution to alternative energy sources where possible. Aspects of the economy, including the British iron industry, suffered from the lack of technological substitutes and solutions had to be found, by importing iron from Sweden and by eventually developing and adopting new technology.

These experiences might be relevant for the present and the future. As more expensive reserves are extracted, higher prices will encourage producers to find more oil and natural gas reserves, as well as alternative energy sources and technologies, and discourage some consumption (despite low price elasticities of demand for oil and natural gas-reliant services) and promote substitution to alternative energy sources. Prices may have to rise as a gradual shift to alternative sources is made. Sectors where solutions cannot be found will probably suffer most, intensifying the search for innovation. If the lighter fossil fuel reserves do start lacking, the market is likely to provide solutions, but the transition may be painful for some sectors.

The availability of energy resources has played a crucial role in influencing past trends, outside of phases of major technological transformations. They have also been central in facilitating service revolutions, especially with the shift from organic to fossil fuels.

Given this discussion, it is worth briefly considering future international energy reserves and supply. The amount of energy reserves required will depend on the demand for heating, power, transport, lighting and other energy services. Heating in the United Kingdom currently depends mostly on natural gas. Power is driven by a mix of sources: coal, natural gas and nuclear. These fuels also drive the electricity for services such as lighting and powering appliances, including computers. Transport services are dependent on petroleum products.

Within this context, the discussion in this book has focussed on the United Kingdom's demands. Despite its remarkable reserve of resources, foreign energy has played an important role for centuries. The country was dependent on the supply of Swedish wood for iron imports, of Burmese or Persian petroleum for lighting and transport and of colonial labour for all sorts of primary products. Some of these were not factored into the country's energy balance, although arguably should have been.

Today, the market for energy does not function on a national scale, but on an international and even global scale. While the British economy has been predominantly self-sufficient throughout its history, it might not continue to be. Coal reserves are plentiful. Petroleum and natural gas supplies are seen to be smaller, especially at the current rate of consumption – although assumptions that contemporary rates of consumption will continue in the long run have often been mistaken.

Indeed, coal reserves did not run out, despite fears that they would in the nineteenth century. Global oil stocks continue to expand in line with consumption, offering thirty years of proven reserves. To predict absolute energy scarcity is misguided (Rogner 1997). To believe that because supply has mostly out-stripped demand in the past, it will continue, might be seen as complacent. Yet, the technology involved in exploring and extracting reserves improved dramatically in the last one hundred years. A small fraction of the Earth's crust has been explored for fossil fuels. While it may be considered technologically unfeasible and ecologically undesirable to hunt all the ocean floors, strong incentives will exist for oil and natural gas companies and countries to ensure that regular supplies will continue in the current energy system.

Infrastructure

Five hundred years ago, the British economy used mostly woodfuel for its supply of heating. The flow of energy depended on the stock of wood and its rate of growth. The flow also varied with the number of boats or carts able to carry the wood. If consumption outstripped growth, as it did in iron-smelting regions, prices would rise, at least locally. Yet, except in times of war or harsh winters, the flow would usually continue.

The flow of energy resources to meet service demands depends on the infrastructure installed. Currently, it includes the tankers, pipelines and cables. As the global economy grows, requiring more services, it also needs more energy. The flow of energy supplied varies with the size of the infrastructure and its ability to expand.

As in other periods of history, the economy is currently locked-in to an energy supply system. Infrastructure was expensive to install and will be to replace. The greater the economies of scale achieved from the infrastructure then the harder it will be to substitute it. The current supply infrastructure, especially for natural gas and electricity, which involves a physical network, can be considered to contain a strong momentum. That is, it has an ability to maintain its fundamental role in the economy even if the prices of natural gas and electricity rise. Yet, evidence from the energy industry shows that large infrastructure investments can be installed to replace an incumbent technology, if profit and the potential for expanding market share are expected.

Market Structure

An interesting issue is the importance of market structure in long-run trends. Like the availability of resources and the infrastructure, the market structure influences prices during the status quo, when no competitive threat exists to the existing technologies.

Given the tendency towards economies of scale in the production and supply of energy, market concentration is likely. Although an oligopolistic situation has often been the outcome in unregulated energy supply industries, like the current global oil market or the European electricity market, concentration can result in a monopoly supplier.

Yet, market structure itself should not be expected to be a major determinant of long-run trends in prices. Since the expansion of energy supply industries several hundred years ago, the market structure varied between extremes of competition and monopolies. The price offered by an unregulated monopoly is bound by the cheapest potential supplier. If the monopolist's price exceeds the next cheapest (potential) supplier, the beginnings of competition will probably ensue. Thus, unregulated the price stays within a boundary. If regulation does exist, the difference in price of energy services between competition and monopoly will be even smaller. Empirically, the variation in the prices of energy services over a period of fifty or one hundred years has been dominated by the influence of knowledge production and greater supply of fuels. The market structure has played little role in the long-run trends.

The existence of powerful monopolies can, however, influence technologies adopted. It can support research and development into specific technologies, and enable economies of scale to be achieved. The decline of the coal and nuclear power stations showed that, in the long run, however, if the monopoly is not sanctioned by the State, commercially non-viable technologies are likely to engender competition from companies using cheaper technologies. Similarly, monopolies can stifle the adoption of new technologies. So, although market structure may have a short-run bearing on consumer satisfaction and a longer-term influence on technological development, its importance in identifying current trajectories is secondary.

The Consumer

There has been evidence that as an economy develops its needs for particular energy services changes. For instance, an agrarian economy is relatively power intensive. This does not mean it consumes a lot of power, but relative to GDP it does tend to. An economy in the process of industrialising needs large quantities of heating to produce the metal that forms the infrastructure of the economy. The

United Kingdom also reduced its need for heat and power by importing many goods.

As the economy moves towards a post-industrial economy, it is less clear to what extent the economy will depend on energy service consumption. Some might argue that eventually consumers will stop wanting more heating, more power, more transport and more lighting. Certain of the wealthiest consumers provide an indicator of future consumption of services. They consume far greater amounts of heating, power, mobility and lighting than the average person. It suggests that the saturation effect is not overwhelming. It might work at a marginal level – that is, the assumption of declining marginal utility – but not at the wider scale when an individual completes a shift in lifestyle.

It would appear that the ability to consume greater quantities of services still acts as a signal of social status. These wealthy consumers also provide the role models for others to emulate. Greater consumption will be a driver for many people's efforts to become wealthier. Thus, as the average consumer becomes wealthier, he or she will seek to consume ever greater amounts of services as an act of emulation and, ultimately, as the objective of his or her desires.

Expectations and drivers of wealth imply that technological developments, including energy efficiency improvements, will feed through into greater service consumption. And, no doubt, a combination of cheaper services, greater income and changing lifestyles will create greater consumption of energy and other environmental resources.

Welfare

Given this tendency towards greater consumption of services, it is worth considering whether these will feed through into greater well-being. The discussion in Chapter 9 proposes that, at the current levels of per capita consumption enjoyed in the United Kingdom, the basic physical 'needs' of heating, power, transport and light have been addressed.

Beyond these basic needs, well-being is derived, in part, by a person's expectations about consumption. These expectations are formed by a person's beliefs about the appropriate level of consumption. While other factors will influence expectations, an important determinant will be other people's consumption. Thus, as wealthier people are seen to consume more services, a 'poorer' individual's expectations of what they themselves should consume tends to rise. Inevitably to meet those expectations, consumption needs to rise.

Before expectations were raised, a lower consumption achieved an initial level of well-being. Once the expectations were raised, satisfaction dropped. Satisfaction returned to its initial level upon increasing consumption to the new expected level. Well-being has been kept on a constant compared with original expectations. This means that the well-being generated from services, per unit of service consumed, falls – a form of 'expectations inflation' which reduces the value of services.

So who benefits? The companies that manage to sell more service-providing equipment and energy receive more revenue. If their financial share of the economy rises, the shareholders of these companies will be relatively wealthier enabling them to consume more goods and services compared with other people.

2. FUTURE REVOLUTIONS IN THE UNITED KINGDOM

Inevitable Change

The current momentum will direct the provision and consumption of energy services on a path that is similar to the present one, only people will consume more services and energy. Evidence from the past provides one certainty, however: change. The existing energy system will eventually be transformed by a series of technological, marketing and institutional revolutions.

Organisations, institutions and technologies appear to be locked in to an existing system. Considerable imagination is necessary to conceive of a different system.

Historically, one factor that caused change in the economy was the physical world. The physical world has always been in a state of flux. And, the economy depended on natural resources. A number of resources, such as agricultural and forestry products, grew according to temperature, solar radiation and humidity, which are never constant. One of the foundations of an economy was in continual flux. Nevertheless, it has tended to vary around an average supply of products, reducing the likelihood of unexpected fluctuations. Also, developments in agricultural and forestry techniques have helped control and minimise the variation. Finally, the importance of these renewable resources within the economy has been declining and the economy has developed through its use of mineral resources, industrial production and service provision. Thus, through technological and institutional development, the economy has become less subject to fluctuations caused by the physical world.

Flux also exists in the human world. Organisations have an interest in creating change, allowing individuals to alter their social status. Smaller organisations can grow, increasing their revenue and power, capturing a greater proportion of the economy's wealth. As long as individuals strive for advancement, either in absolute or relative terms, we can expect economic change.

Another source of change is beliefs and knowledge. The imagination of scientists and engineers, and of entrepreneurs indicate that new technologies will be developed and new arguments for using them will be presented. Organisations can find and develop new ways of completing tasks, either through new technological, managerial or institutional change.

The development of new knowledge will be central to change, breaking-up existing structures and leading to revolutions in energy services. The price of energy services will fall, and our consumption of energy services will rise. More slowly perhaps, yet probably equally inevitably, energy consumption will increase.

If – or, given past experiences, when – new technologies replace parts of the current energy system, it is unlikely to be an immediate overhaul. A new technology, infrastructure or energy source starts modestly. It offers special attributes or characteristics to the user which justifies the higher prices that he or she is willing to pay. They may also be willing to accept certain limitations – such as less accessible refuelling networks.

An example of niche markets is the large number of technological innovations introduced for military purposes, where strategic concerns justify spectacular budgets. The modest growth created by the niche market may lead to economies of scale being achieved, to interconnections between technologies, infrastructures, fuels and the wider economic and social system, and to a raising of awareness about its special or novel characteristics, reliability and other features. In a few cases, niche innovations find developments for broader (e.g. civilian) use.

For them to develop, further economies of scale, interconnections and awareness need to be achieved. If this stage proceeds successfully, the new technology becomes a contender for replacing the existing technology. Competition between technologies (and the organisations that represent them) can be fierce, reflected in the 'sailing ship' effect. Out-competing the incumbent technology will be necessary for a replacement.

Whether this leads to an overhaul of the whole system or only a part depends on the role this new technology plays, whether it can be accommodated within the incumbent system or not. Its likelihood of success probably increases the more easily it fits within the existing system. Consequently, major overhauls of the whole system are uncommon.

The Future of Energy Services

When conceiving of the future, two views tend to be taken. Some believe that we have reached a point at which little will change in the future. These people cannot imagine transformation or change. This perspective suffers from a lack of imagination. History shows that the only thing we can be certain of is change.

The second category of people will tend to imagine specific, dramatic transformations, often associated with considerable optimism or pessimism. Probably the reality lies in between continuity and change, between optimism and pessimism. Here, we can only outline some possible avenues of change in energy services (see, for instance, Flavin and Lenssen 1994, Rifkin 2002, Geller 2003, Vaitheeswaran 2005, for studies of possible future energy systems).

For heating, major transformations are possible. Humans have an ideal body temperature, which might suggest limitations on the growth in demand. Yet, the provision of heat has evolved from generating heat at a 'point-source' to warming a space. This change can be extended. Instead of warming homes, whole urban centres could be climate controlled. Across the world, from

Montreal to Hong Kong, there is increasing evidence of this behaviour. As the price of heating falls, our ambitions to warm our surroundings will expand.

Similarly, on warmer days in the United Kingdom over the last decade, the demand for cooling has been growing spectacularly. Huge efforts have been put into cooling in the past. In the nineteenth century, ice was broken-off icebergs in the Arctic and shipped around the world to cool gin and tonics and their consumers in Colonial India. More often, less energy-intensive methods were used, like staying near water or using shade. As cooling and refrigerating technology improves, and the price falls, simpler methods will be abandoned and energy-intensive techniques increasingly adopted. The trend towards influencing the temperature of larger areas and more cooling is likely to increase the demand for climate-control services and energy use greatly.

Power services have radically changed over the last two hundred years, from horses and rivers to steam engines and on to electricity. One direction for change is likely to be in the modes of generating electricity. The central generation of power might be seen as a limitation for certain consumers. Individual households may seek to generate their own electricity. This might be combined with the heating system. Combined heat and power (CHP) has certainly advantages over existing methods of provision these services, although it has not yet swayed many consumers. As capital costs decline, uptake could grow.

Similarly, net-metering is creating incentives to transform the process of electricity generation. Being able to sell excess electricity onto the grid could decentralise power production. The grid would become more a receiver and redistributor of excess electricity than a basic supplier of electricity.

These incentives are also likely to help the growth of small-scale renewable electricity generation. Their growing popularity, especially encouraged by favourable policies, could achieve significant economies of scale. For instance, if costs fall sufficiently, legislation might force them to be introduced in many new buildings.

Despite its popularity, electricity does still have limitations. One valuable source of future knowledge development would be improving the storage and carriage of power. Electricity was seen as a way of improving the flexibility of factory production, compared with the steam engine. The fuel cell is but one example of the possible methods in which power could become more flexible.

More transportable power sources will be of importance for transforming vehicles. Electric vehicles with better performing batteries could transform the service, especially if additional attributes make them superior to existing combustion engines. Consumers may be willing to pay for more reliable and cleaner vehicles that can be connected to the grid. Electric vehicles could be a future step. This would create a dramatic increase in the demand for electricity and, thus, power, which in itself would revolutionise the provision of power (Romm 2006).

Given the vast evolution in travel in the last five hundred years and especially in the last one hundred years, perhaps more than any other service, transport will experience radical transformations. Some talk about cars on rails, improving the efficiency and safety of motorway travel.

Another possible change is associated with air travel. Most air travel is owned by companies. A growing number of people own their private jet. Along with the yacht and the football team, this is indeed a sign of wealth and success. Many aspire to this status, and, in time, they could reach it. Thus, we can expect far more private air transport, perhaps for even relatively small distances. Naturally, this will dramatically increase fuel consumption per passenger-kilometre travelled.

On the other end of the scale, airplanes that can carry nearly one thousand passengers from London to Sydney without refuelling are being tested. This is likely to reduce the cost and time to travel long-haul, increasing the overall passenger-kilometres. And, although the Concorde failed to create a long-haul commuting elite, airplane commuting is likely to become more common.

Space tourism has become a reality. When Charles Darwin travelled to the Galapagos, the cost of the journey was similar in real terms to what the first space tourist paid. Cruises to exotic locations are frequent. Companies are now inviting passengers to sign up. Prices for travelling into space are likely to fall considerably (McKee 2005).

Some are claiming land rights for the moon or planets. The USA government has indicated that 'space is the next frontier' and it intends to defend its rights in space. Colonisation is likely to happen. Biologists are considering the process of developing and protecting life on the moon and planets. Entrepreneurs are assessing the value of resources there. Once inter-planetary travel starts to grow even a little, economies of scale will be achieved, cost will fall, technologies will improve, and consumption will increase further.

The nineteenth century observed a dramatic increase in the carriage of goods. In the twentieth century, passenger transport grew spectacularly. It is probable that the twenty-first century will see vast increases in the 'transport of information'. Networks have been set up to accommodate an increase in traffic, but as the costs of computing and communication fall, the demands on these infrastructures will grow.

Internet hotels, buildings set up to house computers, require large amounts of energy. In addition to the power they consume, the smooth functioning of these computers depends on fans and other cooling devices. As these sites multiply, so will their demand for energy.

The mid-twentieth century saw the consumption of light grow only modestly. Demand appeared to be saturated. During the last decade of the twentieth century, the introduction of compact fluorescent lighting (CFL) enabled prices to fall and consumption to grow. This has stimulated the market, enabling additional attributes and refinements in the quality of the service to be offered to customers. In particular, we are already observing how lighting is 'not just lighting'. For instance, lamps are sold for special markets. The 'Seasonally Affected Disease' (SAD) sufferers are recommended lamps providing a more complete spectrum of light, which replicate better natural sunlight.

In terms of the energy used, major transformations may also be afoot. For agricultural products, customers are increasingly demanding and willing to pay more for special characteristics. Consumers have moved beyond the need for simple calorific content, and desire more 'value-added' foods, with subtle tastes and health-enhancing properties, as well as being organically grown.

Is this a potential development for energy products? Consumers may increasingly demand 'superior' quality and varying characteristics associated with their energy products. The market for 'green' electricity reflects the existence of a willingness to pay for these 'healthier' (and possible ethical) niche products.

3. FUTURE ENERGY SERVICES IN DEVELOPING ECONOMIES

Given that the case studies investigated the United Kingdom from an agrarian to a 'post-industrial' economy, the analysis provides potential insights for developing economies. For instance, it was found that power was the predominant energy service at early stages of economic development. Mining and industrial activities also required considerable power. Yet, relatively, industrialisation was associated with a rise in heating demand. Also, the industrialising economy was dependent on expanding networks of trade and commerce, which required increasing the demand for freight transport. It is important to keep in mind, however, that despite shifts in the importance of particular energy services, the tendency was for the consumption of all energy services and energy to grow.[28]

The Process of Industrialisation

One of the key drivers for the demand for heating has been associated with the transformation of materials. During the nineteenth century and early twentieth century, the main demand for heating and energy in Britain was for industrial and especially metal production. Metal manufacturing required large amounts of heating to reach temperatures capable of transforming the materials.

Much of the metal was used to create an infrastructure upon which the economy could produce other goods. The infrastructure consisted mostly of iron and steel – in buildings, including factories and warehouses, in railways and in pipes. So, one of the first stages of industrialisation was built on this metal infrastructure, and it required a huge energy investment.

Today, China and India, and many more countries, are in a process of industrialising. An important part of that development process involves the

---

28. It should be stressed that the following discussion does not question the virtue of developing economy expansion and does not recommend any particular path; it only tries to build on the analysis to offer some impressions of the trends ahead in these countries.

production of metal. While an industrial economy in the twenty-first century is not as dependent on iron, steel, or other metals for its infrastructure, these countries will inevitably be needing metals on a scale that will dwarf the demands in nineteenth-century Europe and America. That metal will require impressive amounts of heating. The principal sources of heating are still fossil fuels. Thus, industrialisation experienced in developing economies at the beginning of the twenty-first century will consume large amounts of fossils fuels.

Catching the Power Wave

Once the infrastructure has been set up, (stationary and non-stationary) power can play its role in moving materials, products and people around it. The characteristics of electricity, such as its flexibility, make it an increasingly attractive source for non-stationary power. Thus, the provision of power and electricity generation is likely to continue soaring too. For instance, in just one year, in 2005, China installed the equivalent of the United Kingdom's total generating capacity.

For power, a wider selection of energy sources is available than for heating. The timing of energy constraints can have even longer-run implications than in the market for heating. That is, at a time when major power station installation decisions are being made, gas supplies are becoming increasingly constrained, particularly in Asia. These possibly short-run constraints will encourage the building of more coal power stations than if gas prices were lower. Thus, given that installed capacity locks the economy into a fuel mix for power generation, short-run constraints will have medium-run (that is, twenty to thirty year) implications for the environment.

Yet, the power revolution that will unfold in developing countries offers an opportunity for large investment in new and renewable technologies. Excluding hydropower, costs of renewable technologies in the first decade of the twenty-first century are greater than for fossil fuel generation. This implies that developing economies are unlikely to invest greatly in renewable technology. However, the beginning of the twenty-first century is likely to be a time when huge investment is being made. Once these countries have installed capacity, opportunities on such a scale will no longer exist.

If there were investment in renewable technology on a level to meet a significant share of these expanding economies' power generation, there would certainly be constraints on materials, facilities and expertise, causing delays and higher costs. It would, however, generate huge investment in these technologies, enabling economies of scale that may begin to rival fossil fuel power generation. This would lower the price of renewable power increasing the overall global investment in renewable technologies.

It is important to consider the effect a rising demand for renewable energy will have on fossil fuel prices, encouraging greater consumption of coal, oil and gas. In fact, if power demand is price elastic, as it might well have been in Britain during the nineteenth century (see Chapter 9), then renewable technologies could increase the consumption of fossil fuels.

Provided power demand is not highly price elastic, there will be significant positive externalities from major investment in renewable technologies. These will lower the demand for fossil fuel. This may have considerable geo-political benefits. It will also reduce emissions by both the developing countries and by all other countries, once economies of scale have been achieved.

So, the mass-scale adoption of renewable technologies in developing economies is likely to create large long run global benefits. Unassisted, developing economies are unlikely to adopt cleaner technologies, however. The costs of adoption are focussed on the developing economies, while the benefits are spread widely across the globe. A clear market failure exists in the adoption of renewable technology.

The benefits of addressing this market failure are time-specific, because of the window of opportunity. Developing countries are in a process of electrification. Decisions are made in the short run that will have major long run implications. A global political process, associated with the Post-Kyoto Protocol negotiations, could be developed that would create the incentives for the large-scale investment in low-carbon technologies in economies in the process of rapidly expanding their power sector. It could either extend the concept of the Clean Development Mechanism (CDM) or involve the direct support (for the positive externalities) from already industrialised countries.

A Transport Revolution

Similarly, as a developing economy's production grows, demand for freighting will soar. Whether by road or rail, much of this is dependent on oil. The supply of goods will come initially from within a country's own borders, keeping the demand for freight transport relatively low. But, as the economy develops and income levels rise, an increasing amount of the demand will be for imported goods, which require more energy services and fuel.

Also, consumers want freedom and mobility. Rising income levels are feeding through into a transport revolution in developing countries. Most importantly, acquiring a car is a symbol of social status. There is clear evidence of the growth in the demand for cars in China. This will feed though into an expanding network of roads, of passenger-kilometres travelled and of energy consumed. Tourism, especially to distant destinations, is another important signal of success. Thus, there is likely to be a huge increase in global air travel.

The environmental implications of the growing use of cars and air travel in developing economies are important. At a local level, air pollution is likely to have a severe impact on public health. At a global level, the additional carbon dioxide emitted from the developing economy transport revolution will put pressure on any attempts to stabilise global emissions and concentrations.

Yet, here, again, the huge expanding market of developing economies is an opportunity to achieve economies of scale in the production of energy technologies. New technologies using low-carbon fuels, for instance, could be promoted. But, because of the current costs and availability of these technologies, and the lack of present political involvement on this topic in developing economies, most probably, the benefits will be reaped by the manufacturers of the incumbent technology, the internal combustion engine, which will only make competition from alternative technologies and energy sources harder.

Spreading the Light

The average non-electricity-using household consumes a tiny share of the amount consumed by those supplied with electricity (Mills 2002). One-third of the global population still uses non-electrical energy sources to generate light – in large part, with kerosene lamps rather than compact fluorescent lamps, which are vastly more efficient. Households around the world are estimated to consume $48 billion worth of kerosene. This represents 20 percent of the global lighting expenditure (estimated at $230 billion), but only 0.2 percent of the lighting consumed (Mills 2002). Clearly, access to modern lighting services is a key issue in many of the poorest parts of the developing world.

Rising income in developing economies and declining costs of lighting services through electrification can be expected to lead to dramatic increases in lighting consumption. Considerable economic and social benefits can be reaped from raising the level of illumination in these countries.

4. REVOLUTION OF THE ECONOMIC SYSTEM

The economies of the future will be transformed by a whole series of changes in energy and energy services. The actual direction taken, the infrastructure, technological and institutional lock-ins that will actually occur will depend on market forces and the influence of organisations and institutions. It will be the outcome of the continuity of the current energy system and the change created by new knowledge, organisations and institutions, and chance. It is anyone's guess what will actually happen.

Even though the discussion above has been about revolutions, it assumed that the households and firms in the United Kingdom function within the current basic economic structures of 'late-twentieth century Western capitalism'. These do create powerful incentives for change – for new technologies to be developed, for entrepreneurs to promote them and for consumers to use them.

The late twentieth century in many Western economies offered a picture of stability and growth. To a certain extent, we have a tendency to forget the transitory and fragile nature of the world we live in. The spectre of catastrophic destruction – either through 'mutually-assured destruction' (MAD), global terrorism or severe climate change – has created another image, where basic technologies, economic organisations and institutions could be radically different or even temporarily absent.

Perhaps, the Western economic civilisation will collapse in eighty or two hundred years. It is possible that our great-grandchildren will live at a time equivalent to the Dark Ages following the fall of the Roman Empire. The Dark Ages suffered from the loss of considerable technical and institutional knowledge, and lives were harsher, with a lesser ability to provide heat, power, transport and light (and many other goods and services). Maybe, institutions will be formed that will discourage and even stifle creativity.

Yet, an even broader perspective than the one presented in this book, that is, say, over the last ten thousand years, shows that the drive towards economic trade and the development of technologies, organisations and institutions are fundamental to human evolution (Sahlins 1972, Barbier 2005). In other words, despite the risk of global wars or cataclysmic environmental conditions, humans will have a tendency to adapt to their new surroundings and use their knowledge to achieve the service they want. In times, they will seek cheaper ways to provide services. The available resources and institutional structures they inhabit will determine their drive to seek cheaper ways and their success.

13. Policy Discussion Related to Long-Run Energy Services

1. GOVERNMENT'S OBJECTIVES AND ROLES

This chapter outlines some of the issues that the book raises in relation to the formulation of long run policies. This chapter cannot provide an in-depth guide to formulating such policies, however. Instead, the focus is on questioning some of the pre-conceived views about policies, which may help in the debate towards policies addressing 'sustainable development'.

One of government's key (presumed) responsibilities has been to enable the population to achieve the highest level of well-being in the long run. In particular, it has sought to ensure the well-being of its people, not necessarily only consumers of energy services. This difference implies that it should promote behaviour that can produce, distribute and use energy and the related services in ways that will not be compromised in the long term, or that are 'sustainable'.

As mentioned in Chapter 11, the government faces a constantly evolving series of demands and sources of influence. It needs to appreciate that issues that are of burning importance in one year may become irrelevant a decade later, only to be topical after several decades. It also needs to understand how different players' influence changes at different phases of economic waves. If it becomes excessively bogged-down in the short run, it will fail to see the wider picture.

Each revolution is a shake-up. New organisations are vying for affluence and influence. The sources of power change, and government needs to anticipate what issues are important and which players are influential, and alter the rules and incentives. Similarly, if it seeks to stimulate revolutionary changes it must create the correct incentives understanding the long term issues it faces. Ultimately, while it needs to address certain short-run issues, the government must learn to stand above them to address long-term policies.

2. CHEAPER AND MORE ENERGY SERVICES

Addressing 'Traditional' Energy Policies

Each technological revolution has created and will create a new period of abundance, a new phase of wealth. The benefits are often reaped over decades.

The voting population does not live in the long run, however. Their problems and concerns are day-to-day issues of wanting declining prices and improved service quality. For instance, regulation will still be necessary to avoid the abuses of the tendency towards market concentration and power. In the short run, higher prices, due to supplier power, will lead to consumer dissatisfaction. After all, regret theory reminds us that losses are more painful than gains (Kahnemann 1999). So, policy needs to ensure that the consumer is not becoming worse-off.

So, government will still need to address short- and medium-run energy policies. This will involve protecting infant industries, where genuine positive externalities exist. It will seek policies to encourage a balanced fuel mix that increases the security of supply. It will continue to encourage market liberalisation and address issues associated with market concentration.

The government cannot ignore the short run. Yet, short-run policies need to be developed in a flexible way that enables it to alter or even repeal them as the economic context changes. Nationalisation may have been an appropriate policy in the 1940s, yet the benefits of industry consolidation were less obvious, thirty years later. Similarly, government seeks to promote the positive forces of competitive markets without generating the dark sides. Competition in electricity supply industries has led to cases of dishonest and fraudulent behaviour. Also, because of the nature of declining long run average costs in energy supply industries, competition can lead to natural monopolies. Thus, although a government may want to believe in the immortality of its policies, it needs to appreciate that their value depreciates.

The Longer-Run Perspective

In a sense, governments' responsibilities towards energy services are likely to get harder. It needs to meet all the 'traditional' policies, in a flexible way, and place them within a longer-run perspective. They need to ensure that short-term policies do not clash with longer-term objectives.

On the other hand, some short-term sacrifice may be needed for long-term gains. At times, simply because of market fluctuations, consumers will face higher prices than they are used to, and will complain. Two features are inevitable. First, energy markets tend to be quite rigid, because of the lags between reactions to incentives and the completion of associated investment projects. This rigidity tends to lead to volatility. Higher prices are inevitable.

Second, consumers tend to adapt their consumption of energy services to the prevailing prices. Their expectations will be based on this consumption. When prices rise, consumption falls (either of energy services or other goods or services sacrificed instead), then expectations fail to be met. Consumers are unhappy, and complain.

So, no matter how low prices fall, consumers will accommodate to the lower prices, and be disappointed when prices do rise. In a democratic system, the politician will need to be seen to react to a 'crisis'. Despite the pressure to react, the markets are likely to provide the best reaction in the long run, except in specific cases.

If a government genuinely seeks to avoid price hikes, it should know that they will occur. Then, the best approach is to pre-empt. If positive externalities exist from smoothing out the peaks and the troughs, because market failures associated with rigidities and discount rates, then government can seek solutions, such as creating incentives for stock-piling. It can also involve allowing consumers to be more resilient to price rises.

Energy efficiency may be desirable in the short run because it will temporarily reduce energy consumption. Energy efficiency improvements may not reduce energy consumption in the long run, due to the rebound effects. First, they reduce the price of energy services, thus encouraging consumption of more services and, thus, energy. Cheaper ways of producing energy services also provides a boost to general economic activity, which feeds back into a greater demand for energy services. Finally, if due, say, to saturation of the specific service, energy consumption does not increase, then this implies excess supply of energy and prices will tend to fall, encouraging an increase in the consumption of other energy services. Thus, governments seeking to reduce fuel dependency or emissions should be aware that programmes promoting energy efficiency improvements are only likely to have short- to medium-run effects.

Often though, in the interest of long run objectives, governments try to select the technology of the future. Because the introduction and development of new technologies occurs in a series of phases, each with very different determinants of success, it is difficult for a government to 'pick winners'. Early phases of development can be supported by government and even, to a certain extent, controlled. Later phases depend on the market adopting the technology.

Drastic measures, such as the creation of artificial demand by requiring the use of the technology, can be introduced. It may be a desirable policy to achieve an objective of transforming the energy system. However, this will place a burden on the economy, if the ensuing costs of use and the price of services rise. Thus, government-induced technological innovations often involve economic sacrifices.

Its best bet is to encourage all 'doors' to be opened and see which door is chosen. Yet, there is a fear that that the market will choose the wrong door. Once 'through the door', technological 'lock-ins' are formed, moulding the energy system for the next twenty to fifty years.

Lock-ins have had a 'bad press' since the concept was popularised (Arthur 1989). They do, however, reflect the fact that a particular set of companies, infrastructures, technologies and energy sources have create synergies that have reduced the costs of providing energy services (Geels 2005b). They offer major benefits; in addition to the lower costs, they provide stability and low risks to energy service consumers.

The government should appreciate that markets move from system to system, a revolution followed by a period of consolidation, transformed again by the next revolution. Market forces will push us on to the next system, and beyond. The best that government can seek to achieve is to direct these forces in the long term interest of the public, avoiding being swayed by powerful and self-interested pressure groups.

3. POLICIES TOWARDS 'SUSTAINABLE' ENERGY SERVICES

Shifting to a Sustainable Path

Historically, the role of government in energy service markets has been negligible until the twentieth century. Intervention from the mid-century was a radical change from previous lack of commitment. Although the British government has sought a more hands-off approach at the end of the twentieth century, it is increasingly involved in creating a picture of the future energy system. In historical context, this ambition is bold, if not unprecedented.

A longer-run perspective will help to address issues that the markets tend not to take into account, because of market failures and high discount rates. A longer perspective will enable government to understand and take account of the momentum of waves of technological diffusion and economic cycles. It might highlight the importance of timing in policy-making.

It is generally uncommon for governments to develop programmes that have very long run benefits. The nuclear power stations were built with the intention of producing electricity in ten to fifteen years. Certain government's space programmes work on scales of over twenty years. Cases of working towards long run and inter-generational policies are unusual, because the incentives for policy-making do not encourage far-sighted thought and choices.

Democratic governments will inevitably be focussed on pleasing its electorate, and has difficulty looking more than four to five years into the future. The short-term perspective is intensified by a system where media needs to create stories. Furthermore, testing long-term objectives has little opportunity for feedback and could lead to concerns associated with a lack of results.

Genuine sustainable development, and the perspective that would be needed to achieve it, is likely to need changes to the process of decision-making. This is a deeper political question that this book cannot even approach. There are, at least, two issues that can be addressed here in relation to moving the economy onto a sustainable energy path. The first relates to reducing the environmental impact of energy consumption, and especially the effect on climate change. The second considers the use of energy resources in a sustainable way.

The Transition to a Low-Carbon Economy

The process of addressing climate change functions at various levels: for instance, agreements about emission targets and the incentives to encourage the targets to be met. It would be impossible to discuss all the issues and policies that could be proposed in working towards climate stability. A brief discussion of some long-term developments is presented.

Discussed in Chapter 10 was the tendency for environmental legislation to be introduced once solutions were found. Where abatement costs incurred were more than negligible, discretion was given to industry and environmental policies lost out to economic objectives. Despite considerable rhetoric about the need for environmental action, the introduction of policies on the scale necessary to halve the economy's emissions in fifty years would be unprecedented, especially in the context of considerably rising economic growth. Thus, it is questionable how far any British government will actually impose substantial additional costs on the economy to meet environmental standards.

Yet, an ambitious 60 percent reduction in carbon dioxide emissions from the 2000 level by 2050 is becoming a target for the British government. This would require dramatic transformations to the energy system. If the economy was to follow this path, it would be a genuine shift to a low-carbon economy. The economy is likely to grow substantially over the next fifty years. A modest 1 percent growth per year of the economy implies that the carbon-GDP ratio would have to fall four-fold. This target would be equivalent to a 75 percent decline in the carbon intensity of the British economy.

Therefore, in crude terms, an ambitious target implies that three of the four sectors of the economy need to shift completely out of fossil fuels. The transport sector would have to run on a non-carbon fuel. Industry and commercial sectors would have to depend exclusively on electricity. This power would be generated only from renewable energy sources and/or nuclear. Households and businesses would also need to switch away from gas for heating. One of those four sectors of the economy could be allowed to continue to use fossil fuels. For instance, given the efficiency of central-heating systems combined with improvements in building insulation, heating services could still be provided by natural gas. This demands revolutions in the transport and power generation industry.

The transport sector would have to find a solution. The oil companies and the vehicle manufacturers will need to coordinate their efforts. Thinking backwards, this would also involve a complete replacement of the vehicle stock fleet. For a near complete replacement, fifteen to twenty years would be needed. This means that the introduction and successful uptake of non-carbon vehicles would have to begin by 2030.

This leaves around twenty years for vehicle manufacturers to find the solutions, and energy companies to begrudgingly abandon oil for alternative fuels. A few changes need to occur: electric, fuel cell and hydrogen vehicles need to be perfected; oil companies need to genuinely invest in other fuels; legislations in states such as California need to keep imposing ambitious targets. Finally, the marketing companies will need to start convincing the public that these new, no-carbon vehicles are desirable. If these changes occur, a transport revolution will be possible.

Similarly, the electricity generation industry will have to make dramatic changes over the next fifty year to meet the stringent targets. In the last decade, the provision of electricity from wind technology has been growing in many countries, including the United Kingdom. Also, the growing use of biomass is indicating a return to dependence on land to capture energy. Some are pushing for a new generation of nuclear power stations.

Together these have the potential to substantially increase the provision of renewable energy, though it is questionable how much electricity they could produce. It is also probable that this will put downward pressure on the price of traditional electricity sources, making them more attractive, and harder to displace.

The Diffusion of Low-Carbon Technologies

Much of the debate is about developing new technologies to mitigate greenhouse gases. The successful transition to a low-carbon economy depends on the substitution of fossil fuel with energy sources (and the associated technologies) that reduce carbon emissions. While many factors are important, in the analysis of this book, three variables influence the uptake of a new technology. First, a new technology can offer superior characteristics. The chimney represented social status; the steam engine offered a more reliable source of power (compared with water); the car allowed personal control; electric lighting provided exclusivity. For these superior attributes, certain customers were willing to pay more. This allowed a niche market to develop.

Second, the cost of the technology needs to fall. Most technologies start out more expensive than the incumbent technology. As the price of steam engines fell, their adoption grew; the same with cars. The niche market offers the opportunity to achieve certain economies of scale. If they are achieved, the equipment can be sold cheaper and the marketing team can publicise its superior characteristics.

Third, to be successful and dominate the market, the price of energy services provided needs to fall below the price of the service generated by the incumbent technology. In many cases, this will mean that the efficiency of converting energy into the service needs to improve. In some cases, this will involve externalising some of the costs of using energy. Without a lower service price, it is unlikely to be adopted by the majority of the population. Naturally, if the characteristics are far superior or the cost of the equipment is cheaper, than it may become popular, but the price of the service is crucial.

As has been discussed already (in chapters 8 and 10), there are at least three market failures limiting the penetration of low-carbon technologies. First, the reductions in external costs from using low-carbon pollutants are not an incentive for individuals and firms to adopt them. Second, organisations investing in research, development and demonstration projects (R,D&D) may have difficulty capturing the benefits associated with the production of new knowledge. Third, consumers adopting a new low-carbon technology are not rewarded for helping achieve economies of scale in the production of new technologies.

Government should be seeking to address each of these market failures. Clearly, the patent system has been helping capture the benefits of knowledge production for nearly five hundred years. In the last couple of decades, an appreciation of the importance of externalities has enabled government to consider imposing a price on some external costs. While governments are aware of these failures, and are starting to address them, they have not yet coordinated their efforts, either within countries or across nations.

Addressing the Externalisation Process

In Chapter 10, it was proposed that the likelihood of a technology or fuel being used increased the more it externalised the costs of energy service production. So, the government should be aware that any new revolution may cause new environmental problems. Wind power, biomass energy and nuclear power, all candidates for helping reduce carbon dioxide emissions, may be associated with environmental problems of their own. While these may be a worthwhile burden to place on society's shoulders in the face of climate change or in the pursuit of greater service consumption, the government should be aware of the long run risks. Although seeking to internalise costs early in its development may harm a particular technology or fuel's prospects, some awareness and pre-emptive policy might help avoid damages on the scale experienced in nineteenth century Britain associated with coal pollution.

Also, the external effects of a particular environmental damage can change through time – for instance, the damage caused by one tonne of smoke in the 1880s was far greater than an equivalent tonne one century before. Perhaps the government of the time could have encouraged research into ways to minimise the impact, given its inability to discourage the cause. One century later, each tonne of the air pollution caused less damage, partly as cities spread and legislation about industrial zones was imposed. Government can play a role by being aware of potential damage and seek to minimise it.

The experience of external costs associated with coal use in Britain during the nineteenth century highlights the likelihood that, through time, the damage associated with pollution will change. In that case, marginal external costs tended to rise towards the end of the century because population was increasing and, therefore, more people would be victims of the pollution. This damage started to decline with the introduction of suburban railways allowing workers to commute into the city, thus spreading the urban area, the pollution and the location of victims.

Governments introducing policies may want to find mechanisms that allow flexibility in the system. For instance, the authority regulating tradable permits could be allowed to alter the supply of permits according to damage. Permit markets would need to be given advance warning of changes for planning. With the credible incentives in place, like tradable permits, the threat of reducing permits is likely to be effective in altering behaviour.

Another point made in Chapter 10 was about how the nuclear industry was another example of cost externalising. In the 1950s, it was introduced with ambitions of providing cheap electricity. This proved unsuccessful. More recently, it has been proposed as a means of reducing the carbon emissions of power generation. Yet, there are certainly potential problems created by offering nuclear power as a solution.

To be consistent with creating a level playing field for energy technologies, the British government can take one of two approaches in relation to nuclear power, and neither involves subsidies to build new installations. One approach is to accept nuclear power as a low-carbon technology, provide carbon credits to any electricity generated from new nuclear power stations and see whether the market will invest in it.

Another approach is to question its acceptability as a sustainable energy technology. Emissions are the source of concern associated with fossil fuels. They have a long-term impact on the climate. Nuclear power produces radioactive fuel and waste. These create a very long-term legacy. In the same way that fossil fuel emissions ultimately need to be mitigated, nuclear waste does too. Any expansion of nuclear power would simply be solving a problem by creating a new one, and imposing very large external costs on future generations. This would fail to meet most criteria of sustainable development.

A Global Carbon Reserve (GCR)

Individual governments do need to create the incentives to encourage the targets to be met. They also need to work together to agree about emission targets – multilateral agreements are central to working towards climate stability. The Kyoto Protocol was an example of such targets. A series of post-Kyoto targets will have to be developed. If targets are introduced successfully, a more long-term structure could be envisaged.

In time, it is possible that the process of target-formulation would be less politicised. It could take the form of an international agreement to create a Global Carbon Reserve (GCR). In the way that a central bank or federal reserve seeks to control the monetary supply in the economy, the GCR would manage the emissions and concentration of carbon dioxide or greenhouse gases around the globe. The objective would be to ensure climate stabilisation.

Such a GCR would help ensure that climate change was limited. The GCR, perhaps coordinated by the United Nations, would set long-term targets for controlling global carbon emissions, based on anthropogenic and natural releases, and sequestrations. An estimate of the acceptable amount of anthropogenic carbon emission could be made. This would then identify the global supply of tradable carbon (or greenhouse gas) permits, which could be allocated according to (at length) agreed criteria.

4. POLICIES RELATED TO GROWTH

Married to Growth

Some commentators have stressed the need for behavioural changes in tackling
climate stability. Evidence in this book indicates that, in the long run, the
economy expands to consume its resources. The current economic system creates
the incentives to find solutions to our problems of resource scarcity and to
convince consumers to use resources when in abundance. Thus, the economy
could not be considered sustainable, yet it manages to consume within its limits
by expanding them.

Any attempts to move the economy onto a course that uses fewer resources
are likely to be unsuccessful. Heating, power, transport and lighting consumption
are likely to continue increasing, because economic activity will continue to push
up demand and prices of services are likely to fall, partly from energy efficiency
improvements. In the long run, energy efficiency improvements are highly
questionable as a tool for sustainable development.

As a definition of sustainable growth, it could be proposed that the economy
would need to ensure a non-declining energy consumption path in the very long
run. In terms of resource sustainability, the last seven hundred years indicate that
the economy has been successful. It could be stated that the economy has created
incentives to use the resources at an increasing rate.

Others might argue that there are limits to growth. Here, there is no evidence
over the very long run. Any beliefs that we face limits are based on theory and
faith. What are the limits? There is a limited amount of fossil fuels, and of solar
radiation landing on Earth. There is also a finite size of the planet and its core,
number of planets to exploit, and amount of gases in the solar system to convert
into energy.

While the limits are potentially vast, it is presumptuous to assume that the
economy will always find solutions to our latest energy resource constraints. It is
arrogant to believe that these solutions will provide even greater energy
resources. Thus, policy-makers face a conundrum: let growth continue, leaving
future generations to find solutions, or seek some alternative to growth at the
price of deeply unpopular measures. In a sense, it is the same problem that faces
issues of climate change. Policy-makers can propose to invest vast amounts on
research to contain human consumption in a non-harmful way. Or they can
propose measures to reduce growth.

Historically, markets have shown an inherent drive towards growth. Where
prices are low, consumption is encouraged; where prices are high, efforts are
made to reduce these costs. This market tendency is now coupled with
government objectives.

As long as 'material' economic growth is seen as a central government
objective, observers should not be surprised by the market's ability to supply and
consume ever more. Growth policies will tend to encourage an increase in the

demand for services. Furthermore, it is unclear that seeking permanently higher levels of services increase long run well-being.

Changing the Rules and Incentives

Traditional societies, it is often believed, live "in harmony with nature". That is, they consume at rates that allow their natural resources to replenish, possibly following tried-and-tested behavioural rules passed down from generation to generation. Generally, those rules are based on static systems. With limited change to population, society, the economy and technology, the rules that worked relatively well in the past, will continue to ensure successful management of resources (Barbier 2005).

It is, however, uncertain and probably unlikely that those rules manage resources so successfully in the face of change, particularly growth. When faced with the growth of the population, the society, the economy or technology, experience of what is appropriate behaviour or not needs to be learnt, codified and taught to others and future generations. It is possible that, in the face of change, they will not learn to manage their resource constraints successfully. They might live beyond their means, and ultimately fail to survive. In a few lucky cases, they will manage the change successfully.

Only societies that have learnt to manage their resources carefully will survive. The rest will die out. Thus, if we look for examples of resource management in traditional societies, we will mostly see success stories, simply because those that failed to manage their resources adequately disappeared, and they tend to leave little record of their failures.

Some societies managed to grow considerably. Babylon, the Indus Valley, China, Egypt, Greece, Rome, the Aztecs and the Mayans are all examples of civilisations that managed to grow by ensuring their resources met their demands. In the Pacific, the Easter Islanders thrived and expanded for hundreds of years, before they reached their resource limits and failed to adapt (Barbier 2005).

The initial settlement of population prospered, generally due to resource abundance and trade, and grew until they reached the resource limits. Then, signals of resource scarcity occurred – taking the form of economic, social and political pressures. Rather than stagnating or collapsing as other settlements did, these communities found solutions to the problem of resource limits. The solutions included: creating or finding new resources; conquering new land to provide additional resources; increasing efficiency of resource yield; or altering their lifestyle.

Ultimately, all these civilisations collapsed. This was often a combination of internal shocks – such as the poor management of basic resources, social pressures and poor governance – and external shocks – including climate change and disease. This raises the issue of how stable are current civilisations to internal and external shocks?

The key feature of modern societies is the existence of change. In the face of change, modern societies have needed to re-work their understanding of how to manage their resources successfully, codify the lessons and find ways to ensure that their society and economy are living within the resource limits. For many past generations, that has meant expanding the resource limits, either by extracting more from the resources available, expanding the area and volume available, or even by forcing other societies to give up some of their resources.

Because of change, each generation needs to develop new rules. After examining models of the relationship between economic growth and resource limits and pollution, it is probable that it will need to develop new rules or at least incentives for avoiding the collapse of the economy, society and the environment.

If sustainable development is an objective for the economy from the twenty-first century, it probably cannot be achieved using the rules and incentives that existed over the last five hundred years. Ultimately, sustainable development will probably need a deeper change than is currently being prescribed (Daly 1996). Thinkers, academics, policy-makers and other stakeholders need to develop new ideas, rules and incentives to achieve sustainable development. And, this process has only just begun.

Stability and Change

Should policies addressing sustainable development discourage service consumption? Consumer wants, desires and even values would have to change. People would have to lose their expectation of growth – in income, in consumption. Past experience shows that declines in service and even energy consumption have been rare, and never as a consumer choice. This would require large budgets being allocated to repeated public relations and advertising campaigns to discourage consumption.

Yet, striving for lower rates of consumption would feed through into a decline in economic activity, reducing the demand for human input. The consequence would be declining incomes and dissatisfaction, unemployment and idleness, and, ultimately, a loss of sense of identity and possibly social unrest.

At a time in human history when our ability to produce material goods is so efficient and, therefore, the demand for workers is less great, then people are likely to need to redefine their role in society. People's identity would need to be less driven by work.

The problem is that, even if at a national level, greater satisfaction could be achieved with less material possessions, other economies would become wealthier. And, as long as wealth is of value, it will be a source of power, economic and political. So, just like climate change, containment of economic growth requires multilateral agreements. Perhaps there will be a stage in global economic development when countries agree to stabilise economic growth.

Any multilateral agreement to contain growth and, thus, energy service consumption will require developing economies to catch up, to have similar levels of income, consumption and energy services as post-industrialised economies. So, although such a prospect seems highly unrealistic from a political or economic perspective, global policies might be introduced that work towards promoting non-material growth and development in post-industrial economies and allow developing economies to catch up in terms of industrial development.

Naturally, some adjustments need to be made for different countries. The USA is one of the largest, most widely spread countries in the world and greater mobility is required. Similarly, Canada is one of the coldest countries and heating is inevitable. India is warmer and, despite having developed techniques for dealing with the heat for thousands of years, the majority of the population may, as it becomes richer, appreciate energy-intensive cooling systems.

Some might argue for economic stability. Others might say that it is not in human nature to seek stability – material growth is a temptation; individuals armed with the knowledge to generate growth will tend to use it. Yet, this book considered the demand for energy services over very long periods of time, including the medieval period, when numerous people's prime objective was not necessarily material growth. Spiritual growth was seen by many as more important.

Economic growth that seeks greater material possessions is a human construct and belief that organisations and institutions have developed and encouraged. Society and its policy-makers may believe it is still a desirable objective. Alternatively, although it would be difficult to reach a political consensus, society might start to feel that, in post-industrial economies, material growth provided significantly declining marginal benefits and was not improving well-being greatly. If so, government would need to promote other forms of growth.

14. Conclusion

1. OBJECTIVES AND LIMITATIONS

The Oil Shocks of the 1970s forced economists to narrow their perspective on energy markets. They tended to believe that the price hikes had so radically altered markets that the past was no longer relevant to understanding current and future behaviour. Climate change and the pursuit of sustainable development have created a need to look at the longer run.

This book contributes to the literature on long-run trends and offers a framework for anticipating future revolutions in energy markets. It has presented an extensive data collection on energy service prices and consumption, and economic development. The objective was to revisit the past and to observe the transitions from one 'energy system' to the next, identify the major revolutions in mankind's ability to provide heat, power, transport and light, and draw some conclusions about the relationship between key variables and how they evolved in different energy systems.

This book has provided evidence about the variability of energy and energy service prices between decades, as well as the trends over centuries. It investigated the role of energy availability and technical knowledge in the cost of producing energy services, and consumer responsiveness to dramatically cheaper prices and economic development.

The welfare implications from greater consumption were considered. In particular, it dwelled on the external costs of energy service use. It reviewed the government's role and influence on markets for energy and their services. This analysis helped discuss future trends and revolutions, and government development of long run strategies in relation to markets for energy and energy services. This study was also used to consider the 'race' between technological progress and resource scarcity.

Such a wide and complex set of topics over a thousand years will omit many issues and factors. The analysis was limited by the data available and the author's capacities and knowledge. The reader should take account of these omissions and limitations in the graphs and the text.

The data used to present trends was collected from many different sources, of varying degrees of reliability. In spite of a lack of consistency (of geographic boundaries or units of measurement), the various data series were pulled together to form time series. Naturally, considerable effort went into using data from reliable sources and ensuring the units of measurement were comparable. The graphs presented time series that appear to be based on homogeneous, consistent and accurate data, when the evidence is, in some cases, only from qualitative information or assumptions.

Hatcher (1993 p.572) questioned the value of creating a single national price index for energy products in early periods, and his argument was accepted. Here, the purpose was different. Indeed, the reader should not be duped by estimates for individual years or believe they are representative for all of British consumers. They were mostly approximations. The need to present a series was to paint a picture. It sought to give the reader a feel for the cost of heating a home, lifting a tonne of grain, travelling to London or illuminating a room in the past, and to compare these with the equivalent costs at the end of the twentieth century. The reader should focus on trends rather than individual years, appreciating the changes in the orders of magnitude.

The book was an attempt to pull together and present the extensive research completed by economic historians. It would be impossible, in a single volume, to do justice to the richness and complexity of the underlying behaviour and data. Instead, through broad brush strokes, the reader's attention was directed to the revolutions and dramatic trends in energy services that the British economy experienced in its process of development. This has offered an opportunity to draw conclusions about how the market for energy services evolved.

At times, the reader might get the impression that, in the analysis part of the book, points were made on the basis of insufficient data or information. In past publications (Fouquet and Pearson 1998, 2003a, 2006), there was a tendency to restrain from drawing many conclusions. Here, perhaps the opposite was done. This was not done with a claim that fundamental laws of very long run economic behaviour have been identified. Instead, it was, given the scale of the undertaking, an opportunity to propose some economic forces at work in the very long run, which can be a source of debate and become avenues for future research. These insights could be of relevance for anticipating future revolutions in energy services, and possible ways for policy-makers to influence the path taken.

2. PRODUCING CHEAPER AND CONSUMING MORE

Revolutions, Trends and Cycles

Energy markets over the centuries have been defined by a number of revolutions, major trends and recurring features. The revolutions and trends have involved the switch to less expensive fuels, such as fossil fuels, and the supply of increasingly value-added energy products, epitomised by the electrification of the economy. Another trend was the increased capitalisation of energy industries, which achieved economies of scale in production.

Energy markets also appear to follow cycles. One cycle has been associated with market structure and the varying degrees of competition and industrial concentration. Capital-intensive industries, such as those supplying energy, have tended towards horizontal integration, when left in an unregulated environment. As an industry became increasingly concentrated, political forces have worked to fragment the industry. Industrial fragmentation has also resulted from the introduction of new technologies and energy sources, creating a period of competition – until 'the dust settles' again. This cycle has repeatedly altered the relationship between the consumer and supplier, and the positions of power between them.

The economy has also experienced phases of energy abundance and scarcity. Capital-intensive industries have not always reacted immediately to market signals. For instance, developing new stocks of energy have often involved large-scale projects, which have taken time and were probably only worth pursuing above a certain price threshold. A degree of scarcity may have been needed for a supply-side response. Once stocks became accessible, energy was available on a large scale, implying abundance, low prices and rising consumption. This cycle of abundance and scarcity has strongly influenced short-term economic activity and human welfare.

Despite the ebb and flow of abundance and scarcity, three main features associated with the long trend in energy prices were observed. First, the price of successfully adopted fuels tended to fall, and then stabilise. The threat of reaching resource limits tended to either lead to more supply, efficiency improvements or substitute fuels.

Another observation was that the trend in average 'energy' prices, including key agricultural products, mirrored the relationship between economic activity and resource availability. The growing tensions associated with land use in the sixteenth and seventeenth centuries did create a problem for generating power and transport, and to a lesser extent heating and lighting (see Figure 8.3). By the second half of the eighteenth century, institutional and technological innovations enabled fuel prices to remain relatively unchanged, implying that the 'energy' supply industries were managing to meet the demands of an expanding economy. Since the nineteenth century, further technological improvements led to a decline in the average price of 'energy' and indicated energy supply was increasingly able to overcome its resource limitations.

Finally, an upward shift in average energy prices of individual services was noticed, especially for heating and, to a lesser extent, for lighting, power and transport during the second half of the nineteenth century and much of the twentieth century (although the inclusion of the more expensive agricultural products hides the effects – see Figure 8.5). This reflected the switch to more expensive, yet more 'valuable' energy sources, because the consumption technologies they were combined with produced considerably more services per unit of energy. Thus, in support of William Nordhaus' (1997) argument, to focus exclusively on the price of energy and ignore the role of technology would miss one of the important transformations in the market for energy and to underestimate the scale of the welfare improvements that occurred.

Spreading the Knowledge

In spite of the tendency towards declining individual energy prices, periods of scarcity have created incentives to understand and develop technical knowledge about finding new supplies of resources, distributing them more swiftly and using them more effectively to provide energy services. A first major transformation was in the ability to reproduce knowledge. There was a move away from the dependence on human capital to physical capital, from skills about how to stoke a fire, drill a hole or light a room to a machine that can do it for the service-user. Knowledge was costly to pass on if it needed to be transferred from person to person. Any improvements in knowledge were slow to disseminate. Human capital, and the associated labour required, made energy services costly. To employers, industrial consumers of heat and power, the skilled energy service provider also had additional bargaining power in the pursuit of higher wages.

New technologies embodied the knowledge of advanced methods of heating, powering, transporting and lighting. The advances in iron production and in the manufacturing of machinery meant that reproducing knowledge 'in a box' became relatively cheap. While the prices of energy sources fell considerably through time, technology-embodied knowledge has increasingly become the key factor of production of energy services. Thus, the economy produced more energy services with decreasing amounts of energy and increasing amounts of knowledge. The implications of this trend has been that from the mid-eighteenth century, except for a brief period of stagnation in the first half of the nineteenth century for power and transport, Britain experienced consistently declining prices of energy services.

Driving Demand

Cheaper energy services entail more consumption. Although a decline in the price and income elasticities in the twentieth century was discerned, the economy has been consuming ever more energy services and more energy. Engel's Law proposed that individuals should be consuming proportionately less of these relatively basic needs compared with their income. Yet, individual consumption has not stopped growing and is not likely to in the future, without major changes to the energy or economic system.

Much debate surrounds the size of the 'rebound effect', which counteracts energy savings that might result from efficiency improvements. The history of energy services in the United Kingdom suggests that 'rebound effects' have been strong in certain cases, especially for transport and lighting – at times, they seem to have led to an overall increase energy consumption. They often coincide with energy transitions, leading to initially worsening and then improving efficiencies. Other forces may also be at work: for instance, time-saving technological change that increases energy use per unit of service; additional attributes associated with the fuel or the technology improving the value of the service; economically-, socially- or culturally-driven shifts in demand. Thus, dramatic declines in energy service prices certainly lead to rising service consumption and often energy use.

Since before the Industrial Revolution, pressures have been at work encouraging greater consumption of services and energy. These forces appear to have become stronger, which means that despite the process of saturation, service and energy consumption has continued to grow. The greater ability to manufacture goods means that individuals have become owners of more energy-using appliances. The expansion of the economy, in terms of the number of consumers and how much they consume, has enabled the producers of equipment to achieve economies of scale more quickly. Disposable income has also risen rapidly in the last fifty years, and consumers have been able to acquire far more goods, partly out of desire for the service, but also other attributes the goods provide, including the self-perceived status it bestows the owner of the latest technology and the consumer of services.

With rising affluence, the opportunities to part with that income have increased. The retail and marketing revolution reflected the greater incentives to 'capture' upper- and then middle-class income. In the last fifty years, disposable income has increased. Similarly, the economy has evolved in a way that encouraged the acquisition of durable goods and consumption of ephemeral goods and services. It is the role of entrepreneurs and marketing departments to persuade households (and other firms) of the improved lifestyles (and 'workstyles') and well-being from buying better equipment and consuming more.

Either through the advances in science and technology, or from marketing, the consumer today tends to believe technological improvements can avoid lifestyle sacrifices, such as staying less warm or travelling less. That is, when prices rise and resources become scarce, ingenuity will be directed towards discovering more resources and developing ways to use them more efficiently. When resources are abundant, creativity will be aimed at offering ways to use them. The economy is geared increasingly towards producing more knowledge and selling more goods to consumers with rising income. In the long run, without major transformation in the economic structure, institutions and incentives, there is little reason to expect energy consumption to stagnate or fall, until resource limits are reached. To repeat, as Alfred Marshall said (1949, p.186), "The whole history of man shows that his wants expand with the growth of his wealth and knowledge."

The economy of the second half of the twentieth century and now the twenty-first century has been able to avoid sacrifices and seek the pursuit of happiness, through greater consumption (Lebergott 1988). Greater provision of services is being achieved and technological solutions have helped alleviate sacrifices associated with reducing the consumption of heating, power, transport and lighting, as well as of goods and other services. Although undoubtedly the improvements experienced by people in the nineteenth and early twentieth centuries translated into better living conditions, it is ambiguous whether technological progress and dramatically cheaper energy services have achieved significant improvements in levels of happiness over the last fifty years.

The Perpetual Cycle of Growth

Technological developments have often been proposed as a solution to the tension between economic growth and resource scarcity by making the economy more resource-efficient. This belief is tempered by a series of processes, including the 'rebound effect', which imply that the ingenuity of technological innovations can often be seen as ultimately self-defeating.

Until now, this book has only considered the influence of economic and technological development on energy and energy service consumption. The temptation to draw sweeping conclusions about the 'limits to growth' debate is strong. To comment, however, it is necessary to briefly introduce the role of energy scarcity and abundance, as well as the price of energy services, on economic growth and development. This helps to appreciate the feedback loops between economic growth and energy services, and the long run implications for resource availability.

Past experiences have shown that an economy has a tendency to grow unless constrained by institutional, technological or resource constraints. Past experiences suggest that, faced with energy supply constraints, a sector's or economy's growth was likely to falter; inevitably, this implied that energy and related service consumption would stagnate (see Figure 14.1). While solutions do not necessarily appear, the growing tensions (perhaps economic, social or political) from facing limits created increasing incentives to find a fix (North 2005).

The solution may have come from improvements in institutions, technologies or the resource base. Focusing on technological and resource solutions, if one appeared that offered a greater supply or shifts to a new energy source, this removed much of the resource constraint, and growth in the economy and consumption could resume.

If it improved energy efficiency, then it reduced the energy requirements at the existing level of consumption of services. That is, efficiencies reduced the price of energy services, creating an abundance of resources. This implied possible 'rebound effects': directly increasing consumption of energy services; raising the consumption of other goods and, therefore, energy service and energy use; and boosting the economy and, thus, energy service and energy use. If these short-run 'rebound effects' did not push the economy back to the limits, abundance remained. This created incentives to use the energy in other sectors, in new ways or in wasteful ways. This implied that the economy could continue to grow, finding new ways to use the energy (often driven by the creativity of entrepreneurs) and expanding towards the resource limit.

During this period, the energy supply industry may also have found ways to increase the resource base. Thus, energy efficiency improvements could 'buy time' while searching for new supplies. Similarly, more resources could delay the urgency of finding technological solutions.

In other words, technology helps defy scarcity, temporarily. Technology allows us to produce more value with fewer resources. Each technological revolution offers a new period of abundance, a period of new wealth and of growth. In the long run, the modern economy finds ways to use abundant resources and growth continues until hindered, however. This implies the economy moves towards a new phase of scarcity and new search for solutions.

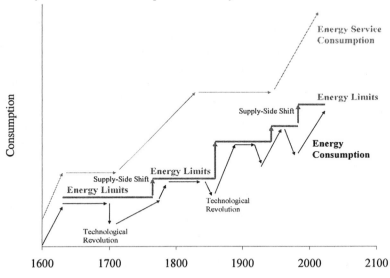

Figure 14.1 The Relationship between Energy Service Consumption, Economic and Technological Development, and Energy Limits

Processes are at work that perpetuate the cycle of technological innovation and diffusion, of market development and expansion, and of resource scarcity. Each cycle creates major economic and social transformations with important consequences for human and nature's well-being.

Technological revolutions can be expected to continue. Mokyr (2004) argues that the scientific knowledge base driving technological revolutions is continually expanding and developing, ensuring that the potential for future technological innovations grows. So, forces are at work driving down the private cost of producing energy services – and they will continue to fall with each technological revolution.

But, the question is: have technological developments improved well-being? While the data cannot provide actual evidence on the question, it does suggest that as each individual uses more heat, power, transport and light, each additional unit of service provides less well-being – this suggests that, say, the shift from tallow candles or oil lamps to gas lighting was far more welfare-enhancing than the move from incandescent to compact fluorescent lighting.

One social implication of the growth of the "knowledge in a box" was the democratisation of energy service provision – each individual has more freedom and control over their heat, power, transport or light. The flip-side of the freedom is, for instance, the growing isolation of individuals in society. When people depended on one another to generate heat, power, transport or light, a stronger bond united them. Weakening bonds reduce trust and identity, which are important for human 'happiness' (Layard 2004, Offer 2006).

Each cycle has beneficial and harmful sides. While each cycle is very different from the previous one, there do appear to be trends in how the economy, society and the environment are affected by each technological-market revolution. Given the inevitable cycles, with questionable benefits, it raises the issue about priorities for the economy, as well as government policy, and whether society's interests are best served by placing resources for the pursuit of certain technological developments in energy services.

Externalising the Costs

While uncertainty remains about the scale of the benefits generated from greater energy services, it seems clear that they were often at the expense of the environment and many people's health. Markets have an incentive to externalise the costs of energy service production. Technologies and fuels that manage to externalise the costs offer lower prices of energy services to the consumer and are more likely to be adopted. They improve the chances that economies of scale can be achieved, and that the technology and fuel will become the dominant means of providing a particular energy service.

Society carries some of the burden for producers and consumers of energy services. This has been one of the prices to pay for cheaper heating, power, transport and light. In particular, at the end of the nineteenth century, the damage to society imposed by industrial heating, as well as power and transport, was huge. In the late nineteenth century, an estimated thirty billion pounds (in 2000 money) in external costs was imposed – at a time when the British economy was worth around four hundred billion. While the damage caused improved significantly during the twentieth century, the growing burden caused by the transport sector at the end of the twentieth century is of concern.

Also, the costs of externalisation are not spread evenly. The poor and the politically weak groups often face a large portion of the costs. Similarly, the benefits of cheap consumption are not shared by all equally. Powerful firms producing energy and technology are able to capture high profits by externalising the costs.

As theory suggests, markets have tended not to respond adequately to the public's demand to reduce external costs. Although governments have frequently sought to lower the costs of pollution associated with energy and energy service production, the political influence of industry and the priorities of government have delayed and limited intervention.

Nevertheless, an evolution towards a declining impact of energy services has been observed in relation to specific services or energy sources. Before the twentieth century, technologies facilitated the use of solid fuel, rather than a liquid one. It has been mostly a coincidence that has shifted the economy's consumption from coal to petroleum and to natural gas, from the polluting towards relatively cleaner fuels.

The market is not necessarily uninterested in environmental improvements, either. The value consumers placed on smokeless fuel showed that, once a certain level of income had been reached, consumers were willing to pay for cleaner fuels. To the entrepreneur, if replacing a polluting fuel with a cleaner energy source adds value and can be converted into profits, then a new market can be created. Thus, the declining environmental impact of energy services does appear to reflect the priorities of the public, first for development, then a cleaner environment.

Policy Influencing Trends

The trends in energy service prices and consumption, as well as the environmental effects, in the United Kingdom over the last few centuries have been directed by a host of factors – from geological and geographical features of the country to the know-how of the people, from the influence of large corporations and their captains of industry, and from the basic needs of human beings to the latest fashions of consumers. Another major influence has been the State. As the single most powerful organisation in the economy, the government has been most likely or able to influence the path of energy services.

The early impact of the British government on trends in energy services was extremely inconsistent. Before the nineteenth century, there was little attempt to promote cheaper energy services. By today's standards, the State was a relatively small organisation with other objectives, such as military security and economic development. If the markets related to energy services were of interest to government, they were simply a means of achieving these more basic objectives. Policies were introduced and repealed with relatively little awareness or interest in their effects.

At the end of the nineteenth century, the government started to appreciate how important energy, and coal specifically, was to the health of industry. This was reflected, to a certain extent, in the closer links that developed between the State and major industries. In particular, it reflected how government objectives related to energy policy started through its interest in the well-being of the industry, rather than of the consumers or the public. The wealth of the nation was governed by the health of its industry.

The decline of the heavy industries, such as iron and coal mining, created an attempt to protect them. The policies were principally to stabilise these industries and ensure employment. Later, as their decline was appreciated as inevitable, when faced with larger international competitors, the protection of such industries was seen as a burden, particularly in the eyes of the government in the 1980s. The privatisation of the British coal industry signalled the end of an era of policies related to energy services.

At the end of the twentieth century, as a reaction to the important role played by the State in the supply of fuel and power, market liberalisation became the main focus of energy policy. This mirrored the new belief that the consumer was central to the market. Competition would create lower prices that would benefit the consumer and the economy.

The most recent objective of government has been to promote 'sustainable' energy. There has been increasing pressure for the government to move the economy on to a path that consumes resources taking account of long-term interests, including minimising its social and environmental impact. In the last two decades, it has started to develop policies that discourage energy use or environmental pollution, although it is questionable whether they are introduced to achieve fiscal or sustainable objectives.

Naturally, the long run influence of government is hard to identify and, even less, measure. Examples of taxing the provision of heating or lighting technologies and fuels in the eighteenth century certainly raised the price of these services, reducing consumption for extended periods. Yet, these distortions have created incentives to develop and adopt new technologies. In some cases, such as the policing of roads in the fifteenth century or the inability to maintain them in the sixteenth century, the price of transport was significantly altered. The latter led to new private organisations, the turnpike trusts, which modified the trajectory of transport services for centuries.

In the last century, government has tried to influence energy markets for their own sake, but not always in consistent ways. A democratically-elected government has to react to demands by powerful individuals and organisations. The post-Second World War experience in the United Kingdom shows that it can nationalise and then liberalise the supply industries in a few decades, dramatically changing the incentives in the market.

In particular, new technologies and fuels, such as nuclear power, can be introduced. Successful uptake depends on providing sufficient support to achieve major economies of scale. In the case of nuclear power, the size of individual power stations and specific features of radioactive fuel imposed high and uncertain costs on electricity production. So, technologies can be introduced by government, but the successful penetration is not always guaranteed.

Nevertheless, the government's decisions, as in the example of nuclear power, clearly directed the energy system down a specific path. The growing capital intensification of the production and supply of energy imply both the need to reach economies of scale and the likelihood of technological lock-ins. Increasingly, only a large player, either a multinational corporation or government, has access to the level of funds necessary to compete or replace an existing incumbent technology or fuel.

Taking a longer-run perspective indicates that there has been a near irresistible force pushing towards cheaper and more energy services. While a government would be unlikely to want to stop this force, if it did, it would find the task near impossible in the long run. So, while government can do little to alter the force of the market, policies can influence the specific path taken. It can create incentives for the technologies and fuels selected. It can also determine who will benefit from cheaper and more energy services. In particular, it has the power to decide the proportion of the costs that will be covered by producers, consumers and the burden placed on society at large.

The Future and its Direction

The existing energy system based on fossil fuels is likely to prevail for many years. It benefits from technological and institutional lock-ins that ensures low costs of providing energy for services. However, we can be confident that future revolutions in energy services will unfold. From past experiences, we can expect that heat, power, transport and light will be provided in new ways. As long as capitalism remains the predominant system for allocating resources, economic incentives will promote creativity, new knowledge and the development of cheaper energy services. Consumption of services and of energy will increase. And, although in the very long run we can anticipate declining prices of energy services and greater consumption, there are likely to be recurring phases of resource abundance and scarcity, and industrial concentration and competition.

These revolutions may include the heating of urban centres, or decentralised electricity generation or interplanetary travel. It may also involve a shift to renewable energy sources. The transition to a low-carbon economy, say, will depend on a number of factors. First, new technologies will generally need to offer superior characteristics, such that consumers will be willing to pay more for them. This will allow niche markets to develop. Second, the cost of the technologies will have to decline. Niche markets enable the costs of production to fall as consumption increases. If economies of scale are achieved, the technologies can be sold more cheaply, allowing advertising teams to promote the superior characteristics.

Third, the price of energy services generated from the new technology will have to drop below the price of the service provided by the incumbent technology. Often, this will involve improvements in the efficiency of converting energy. For some, the costs will be externalised, passing on the burden to society. Together, superior characteristics, lower capital costs and cheaper services will increase the likelihood of any technology penetrating the market and eventually out-competing incumbent technologies.

Market failures limit the penetration of low-carbon technologies. Fewer external costs from using low-carbon pollutants, the difficulty of capturing the benefits associated with the production of new knowledge and the lack of rewards from helping achieve economies of scale in the production of new technologies indicate a role for government intervention. The policies government chooses will reflect its own objectives, the political power of pressure groups and the public's willingness to make changes. Its ability to influence the market and move towards a sustainable path will depend on its vision, political power and ability to develop and use incentives to encourage the market to make the transition.

The very long run path of the economy's energy system can be characterised as a series of 'punctuated equilibriums'. The evolution of the existing energy system is relatively predictable, as if it was in a state of equilibrium. The organisations, their roles and the rules they operate within are relatively clearly defined. Modest improvements in efficiency and energy availability are possible, but large pressures, such as government intervention, may only have minor influences on the trajectory of the energy system.

Then, suddenly, radical change becomes possible. The 'when' and 'why' still need further research, but these phases appear – 'punctuating' the equilibrium. There is great uncertainty about the future of the energy system. This period of transformation exhibits a great deal of instability, when small differences can have dramatic effects.

If government seeks change, it needs to learn to identify when the phase of transformation will begin. Policies need to be timed to coincide with the phase and the unfolding of events. They also need to work in the direction of the transformation, and make 'small differences' in the desired direction. A more adventurous approach would be to understand the forces that generate change and catalyse them. However, the risks of failure and of destabilising more than just the energy system are great.

3. REVOLUTIONS IN ENERGY SERVICES

Over the centuries – despite experiencing cycles of abundance and scarcity, that affected short-term economic activity and human welfare, and of competition and industrial concentration, altering temporary positions of power between consumers and suppliers – the economy has 'progressed' towards cheaper energy services and greater consumption. Mankind's stronger ability and improved know-how to produce and use energy has transformed people's lives. For many today, life is no longer a shivering, weak, geographically-constrained and half-blind experience. Their lives are comfortable, powerful and mobile, as well as independent of the sun's rhythms.

This book sought to convince the reader that dramatic transformations of the energy system, such as hydrogen-fuelled vehicles, climate-controlled cities and interplanetary travel, are not far-fetched ideas. Looking at the past provides many cases of radical innovations transforming the energy system and the economy. The economy, especially since the Industrial Revolution, has been constantly changing and growing, with an eye for the next development.

The development and expansion of markets has created incentives to provide better ways of generating heat, power, transport and light. Sometimes, those new ways appeared or became attractive at times when energy was scarce; in other cases, consumers had to wait long periods for solutions, and the economy suffered as a result. At other times, new ways of providing or using services appeared when energy was abundant. The intensification of incentives to both provide solutions to scarcity and use resources when abundant has led to a series of revolutions in energy services.

These incentives are likely to drive future revolutions. An awareness of these changes can help anticipate them and propose ways to harness them for the continued 'progress' of mankind. At present, scarcity and, therefore, potential hardship exist in relation to three energy service issues. In developing economies, many still lack access to cheap energy supplies. Also, the continued expansion of the global economy will place new pressures on energy reserves, even if, in the long run, efficiency improvements and more resources will be provided. Finally, the expanding economy is placing growing demands on the atmosphere and its capacity to absorb greenhouse gases with potentially dramatic consequences.

The ability to address these scarcity issues will depend on current and future economic forces and political pressures. None of these issues are any longer national problems, and will be determined by economic and political influences at a global level. Unregulated, the global economy will continue to strive for cheaper and more energy services. Its governments need to consider whether the economy is likely to follow a satisfactory path given the incentives it faces. The conclusions they come to and their coordination of objectives will strongly influence the path that the economy follows and the future revolutions that will unfold, possibly affecting the long run survival of the existing economy, society and civilisation.

Data Appendix: Sources and Estimation

1. GENERAL COMMENTS ON THE DATA AND THEIR SOURCES

The trends presented in the text are based on solid empirical evidence. While much of the data is far from accurate, they provide a guide to long-run trends. Nevertheless, the reader that digs into the data appendix will discover that some of the data to produce the trends is based on calculations. When actual data was not available, efforts were made to find indicators that could be built upon to produce estimates. The indicators were then transformed using models, interpolations, extrapolations and/or assumptions. Thus, this appendix plays two crucial roles: to indicate the data sources and to explain what assumptions were made.

The objective was to produce figures, and the reliability of the indicators, models, interpolations, extrapolations and assumptions varied greatly. As much as possible, the assumptions were based on quantitative or qualitative information to guide the process. In some cases, it was necessary to extrapolate estimates from a city, like London, or a region to the country. For many of these types of extrapolations assumptions were made about the share of, say, the London market. While these are likely to be inaccurate, the actual share was probably not more than double or half the assumed share, meaning that the estimates are the correct order of magnitude.

Often, when data was not available for particular years, interpolation was used. A related problem was the decision about how to interpolate prices. Nominal prices were interpolated and then divided by the average price of a basket of goods (Officer 2007b). It was assumed that, although the average basket of goods fluctuated considerably, nominal prices stayed relatively stable, except when markets faced considerable changes in demand or supply. After all, to adjust nominal prices to real price changes required considerable information and it is probable that people in the past had less information about the 'average basket of goods'. A study of nominal prices for goods from, for instance, Rogers (1865–86) or Beveridge (1894) supports the proposition that nominal prices tended to be relatively stable.

For certain estimates, especially ownership of appliances, equipment or machines and improvements in efficiency, evidence was available for certain years, but simple interpolations were not appropriate. Instead, models were created to simulate the growth rates. Calibrations were used to ensure the growth rates and estimates were plausible. Often, the evidence imposed relatively tight boundaries of values for the output of the model. Thus, provided the evidence was a good guide, their outputs were quite accurate – meaning perhaps within a margin of error of five years in the twentieth century, ten years in the nineteenth century, and twenty years before that time.

2. HEATING DATA

Fuel Price Data

As discussed in Chapter 3, records of the costs and prices of heating fuels in Britain have been kept for at least one thousand years. The extensive data collection exercise by Thorold Rogers (1865–86) on agricultural prices in market towns across England provides indicators of the cost of fuels as early as the eleventh century. Thanks to William Beveridge (1894), from around 1500, reliable long run (up to several hundred years) data sets reflecting the price of energy faced by individual institutions are available. They include some of the Oxford and Cambridge colleges, the Eton and Westminster Colleges and the Navy, as well as long-standing hospitals. They have been combined for individual fuels to get an average price estimate for Southern England, since this is where most of the institutions were based.

The weighting of various series tries to balance, as much as possible, the prices in Cambridge and London, two cities for which there is the most information, as well as the beginning of, ending of and gaps in the available series. For charcoal, the index reflects weighted averages of series presented in Rogers (1865–86) and Beveridge (1894). The coal price indexes from 1400 to 1700 combines the series available in Beveridge (1894) and Hatcher (1993). For the final century, the index is based on the authoritative work by Flinn (1984 pp.303–4) and converts his series into pence per tonne.[29]

As mentioned in the text, the concerns raised by Hatcher (1993 p.572) about trying to create a single national coal price index for this period are endorsed here; the same applies to charcoal. There is no claim that the series presented are national indexes; they are for the South-East of England. Nor are they definitive price series for these commodities in this region. They simply try to give the reader a broad comparison of the costs of buying a tonne of woodfuel and a tonne of coal (see Figure 4.1).

From the nineteenth century, data on prices have been available for a large number of institutions across the country, much of it compiled by ministerial bodies. In the twentieth century, especially since the Second World War, statistical information on prices can be considered of high quality, averaging across many consumers, and at times differentiated by types of consumer. The

---

29. Values presented in the text are in tonnes rather than tons (1.016 tonnes = 1 long or statute ton (DTI 2001)). As stated before, much of the historical work relates to the ton. Estimates throughout the text are more likely to be used for analysis where tonnes are the unit of weight.

retail price series used to convert the data into real terms is a series provided by Officer (2007b), which stretches from the thirteenth to the twentieth century.

Fuel Consumption

Statistics on energy consumption in the United Kingdom inevitably become less reliable the further back in time we look. Back to 1960, the latest *Digest of United Kingdom Energy Statistics* (DUKES) provides the necessary information (DTI 2001 and other years). Before that, the Ministry of Power (1961) has statistics back to 1923, which can be extended back to 1913 with the Ministry of Fuel and Power's (1951) data, which marks the end of the direct annual estimates of fuel consumption.

Before 1913, official statistics were produced about the amount of "coal available for home consumption". This was estimated by calculating the level of coal production after subtracting exports and bunkers for steamships; the calculations should also include year-on-year differences in stocks, but these are not available. Between 1873 and 1912, this information can be found in the Mines and Quarries Statistical Tables (BPP 1914), and from 1858 to 1872, official estimates are presented as evidence for a *Select Committee Report on the Scarcity and Dearness of Coal* (BPP 1873). The first official estimates of coal production were in 1854 by Hunt (Church 1987). Church (1989) presents coal production figures back to 1830, explaining that the official estimates prior to 1874 and Pollard's (1980) estimates for 1750–1850 were underestimates, because of omissions of certain regions and collieries. The estimates presented below, therefore, use Church's more reliable production estimates along with the official statistics on exports (back to 1858) and Mitchell's (1988 p.252) figures from 1816 to 1857 and Church's (1987) estimates of coal bunkers back to the 1830s – before then, there were no steamships.

Estimates of coal production before 1830 have not been produced on an annual basis. The two sources of estimates between 1800 and 1830 are from Pollard (1980) and Flinn (1984). Since Church (1989) suggests Pollard's figures are underestimates and Flinn uses Pollard's along with other estimates to present figures for 1800, 1815 and 1830, the latter is considered more reliable and is used for linear interpolations. United Kingdom coal exports in Mitchell (1988) go back to 1816. Flinn (1984) presents figures for most years between 1800 and 1815, which have been used, as well as estimates back to 1700. Hatcher (1993) presents coal production and consumption estimates before 1700 (see Figure 4.2).

Fuelwood consumption appears to have been quite small in the United Kingdom by the mid-nineteenth century; the relatively large institutions whose prices were used to form a part of the early price series stopped buying wood as a fuel in the early 1800s (Beveridge 1894). In the fuel transition period between 1500 and 1800, wood and charcoal may have still provided a significant proportion of the economy's fuel mix, and were thought to be sufficiently important to require estimation.

No historical statistical information exists about woodfuel consumption in Britain. Fouquet and Pearson (2003) show the possible consumption after 1500. The data presented in Chapter 4 builds on the 'back-casting' method used to estimate this series and disaggregates the series into three sectors: the iron industry, other industries and the residential sector. King (2005) presents the latest estimates of English iron production in charcoal and coal furnaces and forges between 1490 and 1840. Estimates of charcoal use per ton of pig and bar iron production are also available between the early sixteenth and late eighteenth century (Hammersley 1973). By multiplying iron production by the charcoal required for each stage of the production process, this detailed research on the iron industry offers an opportunity to present the first estimates of the long-run trends in charcoal use for the iron industry before and at the beginning of the Industrial Revolution (shown in Figure 4.3).

The second set of estimates related to woodfuel consumption is for non-ferrous industries. The core of this series is based on consumption for baking, which starts with Galloway et al.'s (1996) estimates in 1300 and 1400. Peterson (1995) provides an indication of the amount of bread consumed per person in the eighteenth century. Although there was considerable variation in bread consumption over the years, the assumption is that there was a very gradual increase in bread consumption between the fifteenth and the eighteenth centuries (see Chapter 5 for a brief discussion). This per capita consumption provides the basis for estimating the amount of baking needed as population grew through time (see Chapter 3).

Given that in the fifteenth century the economy was focused on feeding its population, baking was assumed to consume 50 percent of all industrial heating fuel requirements in 1500 and 30 percent in 1700, falling substantially in the eighteenth century. Having estimated heating fuel required for baking and made an assumption about the share of baking, it was possible to estimate the amount of heating fuel for all industrial activity. Then, the share of a number of other industries – including brewing, pottery, glass-making, construction (for lime, bricks and tiles), chemicals and non-ferrous metals – was assumed from reviews of their development between the fifteenth and the eighteenth centuries in Musson (1979) and Daunton (1995). Another assumption was about the transition to coal and the percentage of woodfuel consumption in each industry (which is considered in Chapter 4). These percentages multiplied by each industry's heating fuel use determined the size of woodfuel consumption in each industry and, summed, the total industrial woodfuel and heating energy use.

The third sector estimated was the residential sector. A household's demand for heat was modelled as a function of the culturally-desired ambient temperature, average air temperature, income level and the price of heating fuels (see Chapter 4). A growing share of this demand was provided by coal consumption, which was subtracted from the total demand to find a residual – to be met by woodfuel. Hatcher (1993) suggests that in 1650 about half the heating needs were met with coal. This suggests that the coal consumption can be doubled to estimate the amount of heating required in that year. This year acts as an anchor for estimating the total consumption of heating fuels and, therefore, the consumption of woodfuel (see Figure 4.2).

The Efficiency of Heating Equipment

To estimate the evolution of the cost and consumption of effective heating, it was essential to have some idea of the efficiency with which the technology converts the fuel into useful heat. There is little quantitative information about the efficiency of medieval heating technologies. Thus, to estimate past efficiencies, it was necessary to work backwards using the available evidence as clues.

Estimates of gas heaters indicate that efficiencies (combining radiance and convection effects) of about 50 percent were achieved in the early 1900s and of more than 60 percent in the 1950s (Billington 1982 p.172). We can assume that efficiencies were substantially lower in the mid nineteenth century when gas heating was much less widespread.

After the Second World War, coal fireplaces in the UK were reaching efficiencies of up to 30 percent. This was up from about 20 percent efficiencies in the early part of twentieth century (Billington 1982 p.87). During the nineteenth century, the efficiency of the modern fireplace improved – here, assumed to be 4 percent (evidence from efficiencies discussed next suggest this assumption to be appropriate). This implies that the improved Rumford fireplace, which had been introduced in the 1790s, was generating 16 percent heat from the fuel used.

To accommodate for the gradual uptake of Rumford's innovations, his fireplace was considered a separate technology from the basic fireplace (that is, with chimney). Count Rumford, commenting about his innovations, suggested that, between the end of the seventeenth century and the beginning of the nineteenth century, the efficiency of heating from fireplaces had improved by 5 to 10 percent (Roche 2001 p.133). Assuming, therefore, that Rumford's fireplace improved heating by a conservative 6 percent, this suggests that the pre-Rumford fireplace (that is, heat source with chimney) was converting around 10 percent of the fuel's energy into useful heat in 1700. The next assumption made was that the basic fireplace efficiency improved by 0.5 percent every two hundred years, to reflect the very gradual improvement in technology that did not experience any particular innovation. Thus, it is proposed that in 1500, the heating efficiency of the traditional fireplace would have been only 9.5 percent.

Crowley (2004 p.29) suggests that the open hearth (that is, heating source without a chimney) provided more useful heat than the fireplace (with its chimney). The hearth's advantage was that it lost less heat; its disadvantage was that it also kept the smoke. The inevitable tendency of heat to rise, nevertheless, suggests that much of the heat was lost to the ceiling. Thus, it is probable that hearths were not as effective as modern chimneys, and perhaps slightly less efficient than the Rumford fireplace. Using the estimate for his fireplaces of 16 percent efficiency, perhaps the open hearth generated 15 percent efficiency in 1700. Thus, at the time, the open hearth provided about 50 percent more heat than the inefficient traditional fireplace.

Crowley (2004 p.14) also argues that the efficiency of the open hearth did improve in the fourteenth and fifteenth centuries. This might have included hoods to trap the heat, as well as the louvres – although they may in fact have resulted in some loss of heat, given that their main function was to extract the smoke. Thus, perhaps the hearth improved its efficiency by 2 percent between the beginning of the fourteenth century and the end of the seventeenth century, by which time it was disappearing (apart from in a few rural areas) because of the growth of coal use in fireplaces with chimneys.

Table A1 Estimates of Heating Efficiency by Technology, 1300–2000

	Open Hearth	Basic Fireplace	Rumford Fireplace	Gas Heaters	Electric Heaters	Gas Central Heating
1300	13%	9%				
1500	14%	9.5%				
1700	15%	10%				
1750	15%	10.12%				
1800	15%	10.25%	16%			
1850		10.33%	18%	30%		
1900		10.5%	20%	50%	20%	
1950			30%	60%	30%	70%
2000			30%	70%	40%	86%

Source: see text

The Share of Heating Technologies

Estimates of the share of the heating market by different technologies are very approximate (see Table A2). In the early years, virtually all households used biomass fuels in an open hearth. A few castles and nobles might have introduced the chimney. By 1500, the chimney was being used by many wealthier households, with a few urbanites starting to use coal; this means that the large majority were still using open hearths.

In 1700, it was estimated that the basic fireplace provided more than two-thirds of the market share. Hatcher (1993 p.49) suggested that around 1650 coal became the dominant fuel in Britain. Virtually all of that would have needed to be in a chimney due to the toxicity of coal smoke. Plenty of households would still have been using the open hearth, and the growth in chimneys for biomass fuels would have reached its maximum. These trends – of rising coal use and the declining share woodfuels – would have continued for some time.

At the end of the eighteenth century, the designs proposed by Rumford would have been introduced, increasing coal use further. About one-fifth of British households would still have been using woodfuels, as many rural areas did. This share would have continued to decline, both because of the relative decline and the substitution towards coal consumption.

Table A2 Estimates of Share of Market by Heating Technology, 1300–2000

	Open Hearth	Basic Fireplace (Biomass)	Basic Fireplace (Coal)	Rumford Fireplace	Gas Heaters	Electric Heaters	Gas Central Heating
1300	99%	1%					
1500	90%	9%	1%				
1700	25%	15%	60%				
1750	18%	12%	70%				
1800	10%	10%	75%	5%			
1850	2%	3%	55%	40%			
1900		2%	3%	90%	5%		
1950				60%	30%	5%	5%
2000				1%	5%	4%	90%

Source: see text

3. POWER DATA

Animal Power Use

Once again, it is necessary to stress the vague nature of any long run estimates of energy services, and the same applies for power. "Any estimate of the overall power provision in Britain is ... bound to be subject to a wide margin of error and open to criticism as a result of both enumeration difficulties and comparability problems. Provided the limitations of the data are kept constantly in mind it is nonetheless possible to draw some interesting conclusions" (Kanefsky 1979b p.373).

Two main sources provide the central structure to the series reflecting power provided by animals. The first is the Domesday Book. Darby (1984) identify 81,184 plough-teams in 1086. Langdon (1986) calculates the capacity of power associated with the teams. The Domesday Book "strongly suggests" (Langdon 2006) that plough-teams were comprised of eight animals. Thus, there would have been 649 472 oxen or horses – nearly one animal for every two people. Langdon (1986) shows that horses made up 22 percent of ploughing animals on the farm in 1086.

From Langdon (2006), each ox was assumed to provide more than 380 watts. Smil (1994) indicates that a weak horse could provide around 500 watts of power. Combining the percentage of oxen and horses with the strength of each animal, and multiplying by the total number of animals, produced an estimate of the potential capacity of 270 MW.

A more complicated estimation involves calculating the power provided, estimating gigawatts per hour (GWh), which is one thousand million watts (MWh). There is an initial assumption that one MW of capacity can generate one MWh of power in one hour. Then, each figure was multiplied by the number of hours per day the source of power was being used and by the number of days per year. This created an estimate of the power provided in one year. With Langdon's (1986) estimate of capacity, an assumption that each animal worked 300 days per year for six hours per day was made. Thus, the oxen (and horses) of 1086 could generate 400 GWh of power every year at the end of the eleventh century.

The second key reference for animal population is at the beginning of the nineteenth century. Thompson (1976) provides data on the horse population between 1811 and 1924. We use the horse population used on farms and trade; the others were used for draught, which are presented in the next section on transport. Smil (1994) indicates that a weak horse could provide around 500 watts of power. It is assumed that the horses worked 300 days per year, for just 8.5 hours per day at an intensity of 80 percent.

The principle link made between the eleventh and the nineteenth centuries was the number of animals per person. In the eleventh century, there was nearly one animal for every two people. At the beginning of the nineteenth century, the ratio was one to fifteen. This can be explained by the "far more rural society of the eleventh century" (Langdon 2006).

As population grew and land constraints intensified in the later Middle Ages, it is probable that the proportion of animals fell – to perhaps one to eight in 1300 (see Table A3). After the Black Death, the ratio would have fallen, increasing the relative number of animals. Then, the rising population and the increased use of animals for transport, warfare and meat, reflected in the rising price of animals and the cost of caring for them (see Figures 5.3 and 5.4) would have reduced the number of animals per human.

In addition to the Domesday Book and Thompson's (1976) estimate, Edwards (1983) proposes an estimate of 500 000 horses traded in 1714 – or about one horse for every twelve people. This trend would corroborate the nineteenth century estimate.

Table A3 Number of Horses per Inhabitant, 1086–1900

Year	Horses per inhabitant	Year	Horses per inhabitant
1086	2.3	1600	9*
1300	8*	1700	12
1400	4*	1800	15
1500	5*	1900	27

Note
* assumed value.

Source: based on Thompson (1976), Edwards (1983) and Langdon (1986); see text

These figures were multiplied by the human population to calculate a rough estimate of the animal population. Langdon (1986) presented the share of horses on the farm between 1086 and 1600. It increased from 22 percent to 60 percent. It was assumed that the trend continued towards 100 percent of the animals for draught being horses by the nineteenth century.

This share helped calculate the power capacity of the average animal. An ox could generate around 380 watts (Langdon 2006). The weaker horses that ploughed the land before the sixteenth century could manage around 500 watts. Smil (1999 p.115) states that the strongest horses bred at the end of the nineteenth century could generate up to 1 500 watts – note that one 'horsepower' (hp) is 745 watts. Edwards (1983) explains that horses became far stronger from seventeenth century. Thus, it was assumed that the power of the average horse increased to 1 200 watts by 1900. The average animal power capacity was then multiplied by the animal population. In a similar way to the estimates for the eleventh and the nineteenth century, the power provided by animals was calculated, showing the growth from the sixteenth century onwards (see Figure 5.1).

Animal Power Costs

The capital costs or the average price of horses was presented in the appendix of a couple of the Agrarian Histories of England and Wales between 1250 and 1650 (Farmer 1969, Hellen 1988 and Finberg 1967). Ox prices are also available up to 1400. These values were taken and divided by the average power capacity of the animal, creating the horse and ox prices per kW. Only the horse prices were presented, because the two series were quite similar and, therefore, obscure one another (see Figure 5.3).

Regarding the cost of using horses for power, information on the average consumption of fodder and their prices was gathered. There was great variation in the cost of feeding horses. Breeds and size of horses mattered. Even more important was the amount of work provided – plough-horses worked less due to the seasonality of their activity than cart-horses (Turvey 2005).

Langdon (1982) identified the average annual consumption of oats per plough-horse across England around 1300, which was 2 quarters (or about 600 kg). There was considerable regional variation and, especially in the North and the West of the country, oats were not consumed as much. He also found the cost of fodder by food type (principally, oats, hay and peas) for a monastery in York, where they indeed appear to have used far more hay and little oats, in the second-half of the fourteenth century.

It was, therefore, possible to calculate (roughly) the amount of oats, hay and fodder consumed by a horse in the North of England. Assuming that oats provides 15 000 KJ per kg, hay 3 000 KJ per kg and peas 3 200 KJ per kg, this effectively provided an indicator of the energetic consumption of fodder per year – 15 million KJ per year (or 41 000 KJ per day or 10 000 kilocalories per day, about five times the average human's consumption at the time). Given that in the North horses ate few oats, the national average of 600 kg of oats per day was assumed, providing 60 percent of the horse's daily calorific requirements. The rest of the calories were made-up of hay (32 percent) and peas (8 percent). Thus, per year, the average horse in the fourteenth century was estimated to have eaten 600 kg of oats, 1 600 kg of hay and 320 kg of peas.

Clark (2003) presents time-series for the price of oats, hay and peas between 1209 and 1914, and could be combined with the fodder mix to produce a time-series of the fodder expenditure per horse. The additional costs of horse care, such as bedding and shoeing, amounted to about 20 percent of the total cost (Langdon 1982, Turvey 2005) – and this percentage was added to the fodder costs. The provender cost per horse was then increased by growth in power through time (to take account for the fact that bigger horses eat more) and then divided by the power provided by the average horse. This created a series for the running costs of horse power between the thirteenth and twentieth centuries (see Figures 5.2 and 5.4).

The energy consumed by horses for power was calculated by taking account of the calorific content of fodder eaten multiplied by the number of horses. It is assumed that oxen consume the same amount of food per energy output. The horse and oxen energy consumption are added together to provide a total animal energy used (see Figure 9.9).

Human Power

Estimates of the power provided by humans were calculated in a relatively simplistic way. Snooks (1994) provides estimates of the population trend back to 1086 (see Figure 3.1).

They are assumed to work 300 days per year, and twelve hours per day for agricultural labourers and ten hours per day for workers in the industries (Voth 1998). Estimates of manual labour indicate 0.06 kWh can be generated per hour (Smil 1994). This was assumed to be for industrial activities, and 0.04 kWh for agricultural activities; service sector employees were assumed not to exert power – their contribution to output was seen as purely associated with their use of their human capital rather than their muscular power. Given that it might have been hard for manual workers to keep up this rate all day, this figure was reduced – it was assumed to be 60 percent of the maximum intensity for agricultural activities and 80 percent of industrial activities. These provided very rough estimates of the GWh generated by human labour each year (see Figure 5.1).

Wind and Water Power

The costs of water power are not as easily accessible. Often waterwheels were set up by employees of the business and, therefore, less clear information about the full costs remains. Nevertheless, Langdon (2005 p.179) presented some estimates of the cost of constructing a water- and windmill in the fourteenth century. Similarly, Kanefsky (1979a pp.161–7) displayed some useful data about the costs of building a watermill in the nineteenth century for comparison with steam engines.

Starting with the Domesday Book, there is evidence about the number of mills in the eleventh century. Darby identified 6 086 mills. Langdon (2006) proposed that the average mill would have been able to generate 5 horsepower

(3.75 kW). Thus, mills at the end of the eleventh century would have had a total capacity of more than 20 000 kW (or 20 MW). Using the assumption that mills ran for 300 days per year for 8 hours per day, these mills could generate a little more than 40 GWh per year in 1086 (see Figure 5.5).

The assumptions about the rate of use were quite arbitrary. There was, no doubt, much variation across the country in terms of water and wind power. No doubt, there was much variation through time – it is indeed possible that during certain periods, such as during the Mini Ice Age (in the second half of the seventeenth century), there was less evaporation, rainfall and water power. Similar fluctuations could have affected wind power throughout history. Clearly, these factors would affect directly the amount of power provided and, in the long run, the attractiveness of investing in mills to generate power.

Holt (1988) and Langdon (2005) provide the rest of the pre-eighteenth century data for the number of mills. Langdon (2005 pp.26–56) presents detailed estimates of watermills, windmills, horse and hand mills between 1300 and 1540. He identifies the proportion of mills used for gain-crushing, fulling and other industrial activities.

Mill capacity was interpolated between Langdon's (2005) estimate for 1540 and Kanefsky's (1979a p.338) implied values (that is, dividing capacity by the number of mills) for 1760. He implied that the average grain-crushing watermill had a capacity of about 8 kW and the non-fulling mill a capacity of more than 11 kW. He also suggests that windmills had a weaker capacity, assumed to be 6 kW in 1760. Kanefsky's estimates (1979a, also available more accessibly in Crafts 2004), provided the basis for calculating the capacity and generation of power from water and wind mills up to 1907 (see Figures 5.8 and 5.9).

Steam Power

Crafts (2004 p.343) presents evidence on the capital and annualised costs of steam power from the mid-eighteenth century to the early twentieth century in his discussion on its role as a general-purpose technology. He has brought together the main sources of information on costs, such as von Tunzelmann (1978) and Kanefsky (1979a). The capital costs include the expenses associated with materials, the boiler and the installation. The annualised costs include the depreciation of capital deducted, the interest rates to be paid, the labour hired and the fuel used.

Kanefsy (1979a) provides data from 1760 up to 1907 for steam power. Musson (1979 p.353) presents steam-engine capacity for 1930. Afterwards, assumptions were made about the scrapping of steamengines during the Great Depression and the Second World War. The steam engine capacity was multiplied by the number of days worked (assumed to be 300 days – given that Sundays were probably the main days when machines did not work) and by hours running (von Tunzelmann (2003 p. 191) suggests the amount of downtime was around 70 percent in 1760 and 40 percent in 1901). This provided an estimate of the power generated using steam engines between 1760 and 1930 (see Figures 5.8 and 5.9).

Steam engines were powered virtually exclusively with coal. The efficiency of steam engines was based on Smil's (1999 p.145) graph. The efficiency improved, for instance, from 0.67 percent in 1710 to 4 percent in 1850 and 25 percent in 1930. These values represent the most efficient rather than the average engine, so, would underestimate fuel consumption. The efficiency was multiplied by the steam power generated to estimate the slightly understated consumption of coal (see Figure 9.9).

Electricity

The first evidence on the price of electricity is available from the Administrative Council of London (1920 p.49), which presents data for the capital between 1889 and 1913. There was probably considerable variation in prices between towns and cities, but this information acts as an example of the level paid by customers in the early days of electricity use. The rest of the data comes from official sources of national averages across all sectors: from 1924 to 1948 (MoFP 1951); between 1950 and 1960 (MoP 1961); afterwards, various editions of the *Digests of United Kingdom Energy Statistics* (known as DUKES) published annually by the Department of Trade and Industry (DTI) (see Figure 5.10).

Electricity can be used for several energy services, heating and cooling, transport and lighting, as well as powering machines. For Chapter 5, industrial power was sought. DTI (1991, 1997 and 2001) offers data on industrial consumption of electricity from 2000 back to 1950. In the second half of the twentieth century, the industrial sectors were using electricity for non-power activities, including heating, cooling and lighting. Table 4.1 shows that industry demand for 'motors and drivers' was only about 10 percent of the total energy consumed in 2001. Motive power includes pumping, fans (especially in the high temperature industries and chemicals), machinery drives, compressors (for both compressed air supply and for refrigeration) and conveyor systems, not just 'motors and drivers'. So, it was assumed that motive power accounts for the majority of the electricity consumption in the industrial sector.

MoP (1951) presents data on industrial electricity consumption between 1920 and 1950. In that period, the industrial sector's share of total electricity consumption fell from 70 percent to 50 percent. Data on electricity use before 1920 in Mitchell (1988 p.263) does not separate consumption into sectors. The industrial share was probably greatest in the 1920s. Lighting and tramways were the early uses of electricity (Hannah 1979). Thus, an assumption was that in 1895 only 40 percent of electricity consumption was for industrial activities – an interpolation was done between 1895 and 1920. The total final user's electricity consumption was multiplied by industry's share to produce an estimate of motive power use in Britain and then the United Kingdom (see Figure 5.11).

Church (1987 p.19) produces estimates of coal consumption associated with electricity generation between 1895 and 1913. Coal provided more than 95 percent of the fuel required in power stations in the first half of the twentieth century. MoFP (1951) and MoP (1961) indicate fuel consumed for the production of electricity from 1913 to 1960. DTI (1991, 1997 and 2001) presents statistics on the sources of energy for electricity generation between 1960 and 2000 (see Figure 9.9).

4. TRANSPORT DATA

Horse-Drawn Transport

Rogers (1865–86) provides valuable estimates of the cost of carriage across England from the thirteenth century to the beginning of the eighteenth century. Masschaele (1993) focuses on the carriage of wheat for different parts of England in the first half of the fourteenth century and the middle of the eighteenth century (see Figure 6.1).

There is little evidence of the cost of personal transport throughout the Middle Ages. The first indicators appear with the introduction of horse-drawn stagecoaches. The first journey was between London and Chester in 1657 (Hart 1960 p.146). It cost one pound and fifteen shillings (or 420d) to travel the 190 miles in six days. This means it cost 2.2d (that is, old pence) or 55 pence (in 2000 money) per passenger-km for the pleasure of travelling at 2 km per hour. Jackman (1960) collected considerable information on the cost of coach travel between 1750 and 1850. Mitchell (1988) presents data on the total receipts from rail passenger travel between 1843 and 1913. These figures can be divided by estimates of total passenger miles travelled (see below) to suggest the cost per passenger-mile of using railways (see Figure 6.3).

Chartres and Turnbull (1983 p.71) provide estimates of passenger and freight transport services from 1715. This data paints a remarkable picture of the history of transport in the eighteenth and early nineteenth centuries, and it would be futile to try to create estimates of land-based transportation before this date.

Their data was for London and presented in miles per week. This was first converted into kilometres per year. Then, assumptions were made about the proportion of London trade and travel in Britain. These were bold assumptions, and the reader should consider they could be quite misleading. For passengers, it was felt that London was a centre for stagecoach demand, and required 75 percent of transport service in 1715. As the popularity of stagecoaches spread in the eighteenth century, its share was assumed to fall to 50 percent by 1765 and 20 percent by 1800. For freight, London's share was placed at 40 percent, falling to 30 percent by the mid-century and 10 percent in 1800. It was felt that the demand for the transport of goods was more even spread across the country.

Chartres and Turnbull's (1983) estimates went as far 1840. They provide a guide to the levels of transport services. Thompson (1976) offers estimates of the number of horses associated with different activities (stagecoaches, bus and trams, carriage, riding, as well as farm and trade) in 1811 and then 1851 and more estimates afterwards. An interpolation provided estimates for 1840. Then, a ratio of passenger and freight services per horse in 1840 (improving at a rate of 0.5 percent per year afterwards) multiplied by the horse population in each activity provided estimates of horse-drawn activities into the twentieth century (see Figure 6.4).

Energy Used for Horse-Drawn Transport

An awkward problem arose when trying to compare the level of transport services with the number of horses. To calculate, for instance, the fuel consumption used depends on the number of horses pulling and the rate at which they were used. Given that data was limited and inevitably the passenger and freight transport services did not match their respective horse populations, a decision needed to be made about how to calculate energy consumption.

There was only one year before 1851 for which an estimate of the ratio of passenger and freight horse population existed (Thompson 1976). Consequently, it was decided that the variation in energy consumption would be determined by the trends in transport services (Chartres and Turnbull 1983 p.71), but that the total horse population in 1811 would determine the level of energy consumption.

The total transport horse population in 1811 was, therefore, used as the anchor for the level of energy consumption in horse-drawn transport services. In 1811, the first year for which estimates were formally made by Thompson (1976 p.80), 100 000 horses were used for pulling stagecoaches. An impressive 236 000 were privately owned for riding and carriage. A later (1851) estimate of horse population indicates that less than one-fifth were used for riding. Crudely assuming that the same ratio applied forty years earlier, around 28 000 horses were used for riding. In other words, 128 000 horses provided passenger travel in 1811. This means 135 000 horses were used for the private carriage of goods. Another 151 000 were employed in 'trade', which can be assumed to be related to carriage of goods in businesses. This implies that 286 000 were pulling goods. The total horse population for transport appears to have been 487 000.

From this total population, an estimate of the amount of fodder for almost half of one million horses was needed. Fodder consumption was 1.4 tons of oats and 2.4 tons of hay per horse per year for USA town horses (Thompson 1976 p.78). Despite inevitable variation between American and British horses, this was used as the basis of fodder consumption. The energy provided by hay is 1 MJ/kg and by oats is 12 MJ/kg (Smil 1994 p.12), or, 1 000 MJ/tonne and 12 000 MJ/tonne. So, this suggested that one horse consumed about 0.4 tonnes of oil equivalent each year. For 500 000 horses, land-based transport services, excluding human effort (e.g. walking), required 0.2 million tonnes of oil equivalent in 1811.

An estimate of the share of horses for passenger and freight transport was made. An assumption needed to be made about the number of horses used for passenger and freight services in 1811. Here, an assumption had to be made: in terms of the number of horses required, 10 passenger-km were equivalent to one tonne-km. This was based on the amount of effort required to pull one tonne of 'humans' and one tonne of goods. A horse pulling a cart can drag one tonne of goods far more easily than the equivalent weight in passengers; passengers required more space and comfort. The average person in the early nineteenth century weighed no more than 60 kg, and probably less when averaging men and women – perhaps 50 kg. The assumption made was that a human required twice as much horse-power per weight as goods. Given the extra effort required to pull humans in stagecoaches, a human was assumed to weigh the equivalent of 100 kg. In other words, 10 passenger-km were suggested to be equivalent to 1 tonne-km.

In 1811, using the overall estimate of energy consumption and the number of horses required for each service, road passenger transport used 128 000 toe and land freight 91 000 in the form of fodder. It should be remembered that it is believed that much of the carriage of goods at the time was on the waterways. Having estimates of passenger-kilometres and tonne-kilometres back to 1715, it was possible to back-cast the amount of energy used to the early eighteenth century (see Figures 9.9 and 9.10). Due to a lack of information about the nature of changes in breeding to enhance the performance of horses, an assumption was made that the efficiency remained constant. Consumption was also estimated forward through the nineteenth century based on the trend in transport service data.

Railway Prices and Use

Mitchell (1988 p.545) presents data on millions of journeys travelled on the railway in 1838 and then annually from 1842 until 1913. Hawke (1970 p.47) offers data on millions of passenger miles between 1840 and 1870. As well as being useful for directly indicating transport services, the latter can be divided by the former data to calculate average length travelled up to 1870. Munby (1978 pp.106–7) gives estimates of the average length of train journeys between 1920 and 1970. Surprisingly, the calculation of the average length in 1870 and the estimate in 1920 are virtually identical and it was assumed to have remained nearly constant over those fifty years. Mitchell's (1988) passenger journey data was multiplied by the average length of journeys to estimate passenger transport (in bpk). From the 1938, DoT (2002) presents direct estimates of passenger-km (see Figure 6.10).

These can then be used to estimate the price of railway passenger services (see Figure 6.8). Mitchell (1988 p.545) also has railway passenger receipts (in £m) between 1843 and 1980. These were divided by bpk to calculate the price per passenger-km up to 1913. Munby (1978 pp.113–14) has direct estimates of the price (in old pence per km) from 1920 to 1970. Between 1970 and 1980, receipts were again divided by passenger-km. DoT (2002) has estimates of the price between 1991 and 2000. An inability to find values between the 1980s led to interpolation.

Hawke (1970 p.78, p.92) has estimates of railway freight (billion ton miles) between 1840 and 1890 (see Figure 6.11). Similarly, Mitchell (1988 p.545) has data on the millions of miles travelled by freight (from 1856 to 1980) and their receipts (between 1843 and 1926). Munby (1978 pp.86–7, 98–9 and 93–4) provided direct estimates of freight carriage, average length and prices between 1920 and 1970. The same exercise enabled estimates of freight transport use (in billion tonne-km) and price (pence per tonne-km) to be calculated (see Figure 6.9). DoT (2002) presented direct estimates of freight carriage between 1953 and 2000. DoT (1992 and 1996) have estimates of the freight prices between 1969 and 1994. Unable to find data for the second-half of the 1990s, nominal prices were assumed (no doubt, inappropriately) to be constant for this brief period.

To estimate the amount of energy used for railway services, the data is readily available at an aggregate level from Church (1987 p.19) and MOFP (1960) and back copies of DUKES (see Figures 9.9 and 9.10). No evidence existed on how much energy was used by passengers and freight. Following the method developed for fodder consumption, a first attempt was to use estimates of bpk and btk (presented above). However, there was no obvious ratio to use. Efforts were made to find a plausible ratio, starting with 10 bpk using up the same energy as one btk. No ratio seemed to produce realistic estimates. A set ratio ignored the differences in the efficiency changes in passenger and freight services, for instance. In the end, the only long run ratio that was available was for receipts. This was clearly an unreliable indicator of the share of energy used by passenger and freight services, yet it acted as a proxy, producing plausible estimates.

Twentieth Century Road Costs and Use

For twentieth century road travel, DoT (2002) presents data on passenger travel between the early 1952 and 2000, and on freight from 1953. Before the early 1950s, data needed to be pulled together. Mitchell (1988 pp.557–8) had information on the number of cars and of goods vehicles between 1904 and 1980. Car passenger travel per vehicle was calculated for 1952, which seemed relatively high at 16 000 km per car per year. The average distance travelled by a goods vehicle in 1953 was 32 000 km. Before these years, assumption were made about the trend in average travel per vehicle: for cars, an annual 2 percent decrease in the average travel per car ratio each year before 1952 – based on the idea that there were fewer roads and people travelled less per year than they did in the 1950s; for goods vehicles, an annual 1 percent decrease in the ratio for each year before 1953 – because there was less trade for each business, fewer roads and smaller trucks. These assumed trends in average distance per vehicle (back to the beginning of the century) was multiplied by Mitchell's (1988 pp.557–8) numbers of vehicles to produce an estimate of the bpk abd btk back to 1904 (see Figures 6.17 and 6.20).

Passenger road transport 'prices' are more complex than identifying the cost of buying a train ticket, because travellers in the twentieth century tended to own their cars. And, although many (especially in the first half of the century) often used and paid for public transport in the same way they did for railway, the focus here is on the car as the mode of transport. Consequently, at least three costs can be identified: the fuel costs, all marginal costs and the annualized total costs. Table 6.4 shows the breakdown of the annual cost of car travel between 1971 and 1998. Fuel costs accounted for between 20 and 30 percent of the total annual expenses. Few of the other expenses listed are obvious marginal costs – tyre consumption also depends on distance travelled. So, fuel costs were presented as the price (or main private marginal cost) of passenger transport.

The price of driving a car one kilometre was estimated by dividing passenger fuel expenditure (in mtoe) by distance travelled (in bpk). Although freight customers pay a rate, the same method was used to estimate the cost of goods carriage. Two fuels were used by both passengers and freight vehicles. Until the 1930s, motor spirit was the main petroleum product for road vehicles. Then, diesel (that is, 'derv') began to be used by goods vehicles and buses. Cars used exclusively motor spirit until the 1980s, when diesel started to take a small market share. Thus, it was necessary to identify the share of motor spirit and diesel consumed by passengers and freight.

The Ministry of Power (MoP 1961) indicated the share of motor spirit used by both between 1938 and 1960. The share of motor spirit used by commercial vehicles fell from 42 percent to 19 percent in that period – it was assumed that the share of buses was around 10 percent of commercial vehicles in 1938 and 5 percent by 1960, reflecting the relative decline of public transport. The shares enabled motor spirit consumption (found in DTI 1997, 2001, MoP 1961 and King 1952 p.551) to be estimated for passenger and freight travel.

DTI (2006) presents the amount of diesel used by passenger travel back to 1995; in 2000, it was equivalent to 18 percent of the total consumption of diesel. Miller (1993b) indicates the share of diesel vehicles in the passenger vehicle stock into the early 1990s, providing a basis for calculating the small amount of diesel consumed. An interpolation connected 1991 and 1995. The rest of road transport diesel (also found in DTI 1997, 2001, MoP 1961 and King 1952 p.551) was assumed to be for carriage. Thus, consumption of motor spirit and derv for passenger and freight road transport were estimated between 1910 and 2000.

DTI (1997, 2001) presents the price of motor spirit and diesel back to 1954 (see Figure 6.15). The Institute of Petroleum (1994) has data on the price of motor spirit from 1902 to 1953. Lack of price data imposed the assumption that between 1930 and 1953, diesel and motor spirit prices followed the same path – based on post-1953 evidence this was perfectly acceptable. The prices were multiplied to the consumption estimates to calculate the fuel expenditure of both passenger and freight road transport. The procedure for calculating distance travelled (in bpk and btk) was explained above. Dividing fuel expenditure by distance estimated fuel costs of road transport services in pence per passenger-km and per tonne-km (see Figure 6.16).

Carriage along Waterways and at Sea

Because sea trade was such an important part of British economic history, and involved merchants keeping records of deals, considerable evidence remains about the cost of carriage. One of the problems, however, is consistency – different routes were of varying lengths and risks, and different commodities were of varying size and density. The focus in the text was on showing the broad long run trend in price of carriage at sea (rather than providing some definitive average price). Thus, two price series were presented in Figure 6.5. The first series was based on bringing together data on the cost of wine carriage from French, Spanish and Portuguese ports between 1291 and 1783 (Menard 1991) – the cost of carriage by weight was divided by the distance from each port to the Southern coast of England in order to estimate a price in pence per tonne-km. The second series was based on the cost of shipping one ton of coal along Britain's coast between 1740 and 1913 (Harley 1988). It was assumed that the coal was brought from the North-East of England to London, approximately 500 km. This produced an estimate of coal carried per tonne-km. Mohammed and Williamson (2004) offer more data up to 1997. The average index was spliced to the Harley (1988) series to bring the trend to the end of the twentieth century (see Figure 6.13).

From 1846 to 1937 and then from 1965, statistics have been found (in the annual British Parliamentary Papers of the time) on the volume (that is, the weight lifted) of goods that entered and left ports for foreign trade (see Figure 6.12). Between 1848 and 1860, and then after 1965 the same information is also present for goods lifted for coastwise commerce. To give an idea of scale, in 1848, 9.6 million tonnes were lifted for import and export, and 15.5 million tonnes were sent along the coasts. For comparison with land-based transport services, it was desirable to estimate tonne-km. The first year for which tonne-km are available was 1910 (Armstrong 1987); these are for coastwise commerce and for rivers and canal carriage – 33.2 and 1.1 billion tonne-km (btk) respectively.

These values, along with the weight of goods lifted, provided evidence of the km travelled by coastwise commerce and along inland waterways – just over 400 km and a little under 30 km respectively. Naturally, this would vary over time according to the nature of the trade. The next strong assumption was to use the distance travelled by coastwise carriage in 1910 for other years, subtracting a modest 0.1 percent for each year before then.

For international trade, there appeared to be little evidence on distance travelled over the years. DoT (2006) presented information on the main destinations of British freight, and their share of the total weight lifted. From this information, a broad estimate places the average distance for British freight at around 600 km. This was a mix of neighbouring European countries and long-haul freight to Hong Kong and Singapore. Here, the assumption was that each year distance travelled decreased by an arbitrary 0.2 percent. This was used to provide an indicator of the distance travelled in other years and, ultimately, of freighting services.

With this information, and considerable interpolation, indicative estimates of international trade and coastwise carriage is possible between 1846 and 1848, respectively, to the present. On this basis, estimates of international trade and coastwise commerce were 5.6 btk and 6.1 btk in 1850, and 260 btk and 34 btk in 2000 (see Figure 6.14). Clearly, these calculations are to present the magnitude of trade, rather than specific values.

Before 1846, there is no quantitative information on the amount of goods shipped. Back to the mid-sixteenth century, however, there have been estimates of the carrying capacity of vessels (Davis 1962, Hope 1990 and accessible in Mitchell 1988 p.535). They indicate the net tonnage of registered ships in Britain (shown in Figure 6.6).

To paint a broad picture of the magnitude of water-based transport relative to land carriage, estimates of tonne-km can be generated (see Figure 6.7). Here, the assumption is that a particular carrying capacity leads to an amount of goods lifted. Clearly, there are years when the economy is slack and ships sit idle. Also, improvements in organisation and communication reduced this degree of idleness; given the progression over the centuries, earlier vessels tended to sit idle more often and for longer. Based on this crude indicator of goods lifted, estimates of tonne-km can be calculated in the same way as above, post-1846.

In 1760, in Britain, the registered carrying capacity of ships was just under 1 million tonnes, lifting (an estimated) 12.5 million tonnes and freighting them an average (extrapolated) distance of 350 km. As a reference, the British coal production in 1760 was 6.3 million tonnes, and around one-third of it was shipped along the East Coast of England – the distance between Newcastle and London was about 500 kilometres. An estimate of 4 btk for 1760 seems plausible, certainly the correct order of magnitude. In 1830, it was estimated that 8 btk of goods were freighted (see Figures 6.7 and 6.12).

Again, it is crucial to remember that these figures are to illustrate the magnitude of services rather than to estimate actual figures. A number of different estimates of maritime activity before the nineteenth century have been published.

Air Travel

Evidence on the declining cost of travelling by plane was not found. It would have been useful as a comparison with the development of other travel services. For passenger travel, DoT (2002) presents billion passenger-km, as well as the number of travellers (which rose from two million in 1950 to 179 million in 2000). For freight, DoT (2002) presents figures in terms of tonnes loaded and unloaded. The assumption was that cargo flights are on average the same distance as passenger flights (found by dividing bpk by the number of passengers) – clearly this is not correct, but served as a basis for estimating travel in billion tonne-km (see Figure 6.18).

Fuel use from air travel was available from DTI (1997) which offers data on aviation fuel back to 1960, and MoP (1961) between 1947 and 1960. Again, crude assumptions had to be made to separate fuel consumption between passenger and freight transport: it was assumed that one passenger was the equivalent to carrying 200 kg of cargo – naturally, the average person weighs far less but passenger travel is considerably less efficient at carrying a particular weight.

5. LIGHTING DATA

Lighting Fuel Prices

Information about the price of candles can be found from the fourteenth century onwards, partly thanks to Thorold Rogers' considerable efforts in collecting data from market towns across England (Rogers 1865–86). His first figure dates back to 1265, and from 1320 there are data for virtually every year up to 1700. William Beveridge (1894) created a data link between the sixteenth and nineteenth centuries with his volumes that drew on records from old English institutions, including Eton and Westminster Colleges, Greenwich Hospital and the Navy. From the seventeenth century up to 1830, there are thus numerous time series that we have combined to assemble a price series for tallow candles (that is, candles made from moulded animal fat) for England, by weighting each series according to its length, location and likely reliability. While Beveridge (1894) provided series for wax candles, they were a luxury commodity and, therefore, do not reflect the average cost of lighting for the majority of the population. Although the wax series provided insights into the premium paid at a particular period for higher quality light, the time series presented is for tallow candles (see Figure 7.1).

Jackson (1976) is the principal source of information on whale oil prices (and also provides a valuable commentary on the economic history of the British whaling industry). There are data for the price of sperm whale oil. However, because it provided relatively high quality illumination, it was more expensive and exclusive than other whale oils. Consequently, we present here the price series for right whale oil, which provides a basis for assessing the cost of using oil in lamps (see Figure 6.1). Despite attempts, it was impossible to assemble series for fish and vegetable oils, not least because their regional price variations were much greater than those for whale oil. Price series for fish or, say, rapeseed oil ('colza oil') would be valuable because they might help in estimating the value of switching fuel between lamp fuels.

Town gas prices are available from 1823 for different gas companies, mostly in the Sout- East of England, and published in sources in the British Parliamentary Papers (BPP). A time series has been created for an average price of gas for the period up to 1935. After this, the successive ministries (MoFP 1951, MoP 1961, and DTI 1991, 1997 and 2001) associated with energy provide a United Kingdom gas price, although, by then, gas was used less for lighting and increasingly for heating (see Figure 7.3).

From 1857, an average refined petroleum price series can be found in the Parliamentary Papers; this provides an appropriate indicator because lighting and lubrication were the main uses of petroleum until the early twentieth century. From 1903, explicit prices for kerosene (also referred to as paraffin, lamp oil or burning oil) are presented (see Figure 7.3).

The first British statistics on electricity prices date from 1898 and are presented by the Administrative Council of London (1920) – and, therefore, reflect costs to Londoners rather than the whole of the United Kingdom (see Figure 7.7). Following a gap of four years in the series, between 1919 and 1922, national electricity prices have been published from 1923 to date (MoFP 1951, MoP 1961, and DTI 1991, 1997 and 2001) (see Figures 7.8 and 7.9).

Consumption Data

Estimates of tallow candle consumption are available between 1711 and 1830, providing a useful early indicator of light consumption (Mitchell 1988 p. 412) (see Figure 7.2). The figures are based on candles for which tax was paid (see the discussion of the Candle Tax, below). Tax evasion was relatively common in the candle-making industry, since the production process was short and the duty high (Mitchell 1988 p.398). Although the overall production is understated in the series, the degree of understatement is thought to be relatively constant (Fine p. 219 in Mitchell 1988 p.398).

Jackson (1976) provides the basis for data on whale oil consumption. Although there are separate data on the consumption of right whale oil and Sperm whale oil, and only the price series for right whale oil to avoid presenting too much information, the two series have been brought together (having taken account of their different quality of illumination) to produce a single series for 'all whale oil' use (see Figure 7.2). Based on evidence in Jackson (1976), before 1750 sperm whale oil provided only about one-tenth of the total whale oil illumination. This rose to around four-tenths by the end of the eighteenth century, and fell back to one-quarter in the first half of the nineteenth century. Unfortunately, it was impossible to collect any indicators of the consumption of fish and vegetable oils for lighting, as they were used for many other purposes as well, and were often not traded but made within the household. This means that, up to the second half of the nineteenth century, the trends are likely to have underestimated the proportion of oils used for lighting, compared with candles and gas.

For town gas, the British consumption figures start in 1881 (Mitchell 1988 p.269). Before then, estimates of gas consumption for London are available from 1822 (see Figures 7.4 and 7.5). They have been extrapolated to represent the whole country (using the 1881 ratio between London and country consumption as an anchor, which was one-third, and increasing the share of London consumption going back to 1822). Later gas consumption data also come from the British Parliamentary Papers, then MoFP (1951), MoP (1961) and DTI (1991, 1997 and 2001).

There is some statistical evidence about petroleum consumption back to 1842, apparently the first year of imports into the country, in a report for the Select Committee on Petroleum (BPP 1896). Kerosene consumption figures are based initially on estimating the proportion of refined petroleum used as a lighting fuel. From 1910 onwards, actual kerosene data are provided in the statistical digests of the energy ministries. These help provide a basis for estimating the proportion of the total used as a lighting fuel, needed for the period before 1910.

Pre-1920 electricity sales are collected in Mitchell (1988 p. 263), then the usual statistical Digests from the ministries associated with energy. We have estimated the proportion of this consumption used for lighting. MoFP (1951) provides actual electricity figures used for lighting between 1924 and 1949. Estimates of the proportion of lighting consumption between 1900 and 1924 are interpolated, with an assumption that at the turn of the century 60 percent of electricity was for lighting. Mills (2002) indicates that in 1997 14 percent of United Kingdom electricity use was for lighting (see Figures 7.8 and 7.10).

Table A4 Estimates of the Proportion of Fuel Consumption Used for Lighting (percentage shares), 1800–2000

Year	Gas	Petroleum	Electricity	Year	Gas	Petroleum	Electricity
1800	100			1900	91	68	60
1810	100			1910	89	60*	40
1820	100			1920	80	22*	27
1830	99			1930	50	1	32*
1840	98			1940	30		37*
1850	97	90		1950	5		45*
1860	96	88		1960	1		38
1870	95	85	98	1970			28
1880	94	80	91	1980			26
1890	93	75	85	1990			22
				2000			14*

Notes

* based on quantitative information; otherwise, the estimates are based on qualitative evidence.

Source: see text

Table A4 shows the estimates of the proportions of each fuel that was used for lighting purposes for ten-year intervals from 1800 to 2000.

Data on Lighting Efficiency

The conversion of the price and consumption of fuels into their equivalents in light requires estimates of the conversion of energy into light emission by different lighting technologies, be they candles, gas or oil lamps, or light bulbs.

The rate of light emission from a source is the light flux/flow, which can be measured in lumens. A wax candle emits about 13 lumens, a sixty-watt incandescent filament bulb about 700 lumens and a fifteen-watt compact fluorescent bulb about 800 lumens (Nordhaus 1997). Light emission per unit of energy input is one indicator of the efficiency of a lighting appliance, measured in terms of lumen-hours per thousand Btu (British thermal units) or kilo-watt hours or alternatively as lumens per watt. Nordhaus (1997), through experiments of his own and of others, provides estimates of the lumen-hours per 1 000Btu (and lumens per watt) for a particular generation of lighting technology and the year in which it would have been used. Table 7.3 indicates trends in efficiency (in lumen-hours per kWh). A few examples highlight the improvements. An early 'town gas' lamp, circa 1827, would have generated 130 lumen-hours per kWh; by 1916 the innovative 'Welsbach Mantle' gas lamp produced more than six times more light, 870 lumen-hours per kWh. With these estimates (augmented by several additional sources) and the use of a simple diffusion model of generations of lighting technology, four time series of the average lighting efficiency (in lumen-hours per kWh) for each lighting technology were assembled – that is, for tallow candles, gas lamps, kerosene lamps and electric lights.

The figures presented in Nordhaus (1997) were estimates of the lighting efficiency at the time of introduction of a new technology. To generate estimates of the average efficiency between these years, a series of basic epidemic models of the uptake of the new technologies were developed, reflecting an evolving weighting of the proportions of 'old' and 'new' lighting appliances being used. Separate price series were prepared, as well as indices for the cost of illumination from each energy source (tallow, whale oil, kerosene, gas and electricity) and its associated appliance technology.

6. THE DATA

A selection of the data produced for this book is presented below. Estimates are offered every decade between 1300 and 1850. Afterwards the data is on annual basis because the reliability and accuracy of the information improves considerably in the second-half of the nineteenth century. Some might prefer a time series as an index (say, with 1900 = 100). This was not done because the values have meaning, which may help the reader compare them, especially for energy price and consumption.

The data includes estimates of the price and consumption of energy by services (Table A5 and A6)). They incorporate the agricultural products because to ignore them is to omit 80 percent of the energy used for power before the nineteenth century. Table A7 presents rough estimates of average efficiency by service. The transport estimates are for passengers travel on land. The trends for land freight are similar (although the values are clearly different). The major difference is compared with sea freight where until the end of the nineteenth century, sailing ships provided carriage with far less energy requirements. Thus,

Figure 8.9 and Table A7 are quite different. Estimates of energy service prices and consumption are available in Table A8 and A9.

Table A5 Estimates of Energy Prices by Energy Service (£(2000) per tonne of oil equivalent (toe)), 1300–2000

	Average	Heating (Domestic)	Power	Transport (Passenger)	Lighting
1300	-	-	941	675	4 639
1310	-	-	940	671	3 652
1320	-	-	811	506	5 245
1330	-	-	1 061	793	4 294
1340	-	-	1 706	1 201	4 261
1350	-	-	1 107	839	4 723
1360	-	-	1 005	657	4 381
1370	-	-	1 250	477	2 501
1380	-	-	1 088	750	4 949
1390	-	-	1 071	832	4 259
1400	-	-	1 014	743	3 566
1410	-	-	985	639	2 767
1420	-	-	943	772	3 511
1430	-	-	946	741	3 053
1440	-	-	1 002	635	3 284
1450	-	244	1 315	884	3 332
1460	-	294	1 657	1 183	4 062
1470	-	321	1 735	1 114	4 070
1480	-	282	1 148	811	4 204
1490	-	246	1 327	838	3 196
1500	1 153	235	1 217	843	3 178
1510	1 018	221	1 073	849	2 957
1520	1 448	177	1 527	1 118	2 792
1530	1 460	193	1 552	864	2 553
1540	1 267	189	1 339	969	2 773
1550	1 581	212	1 707	1 241	2 677
1560	1 221	190	1 306	1 035	3 344
1570	1 452	202	1 545	1 164	3 578
1580	1 510	214	1 615	1 338	3 599
1590	1 922	195	2 029	1 707	3 562
1600	1 881	159	1 990	1 649	3 739
1610	2 043	199	2 183	1 781	4 142
1620	2 197	204	2 318	1 978	4 146
1630	2 382	170	2 538	2 148	3 438
1640	2 106	235	2 264	1 941	4 097
1650	2 406	173	2 574	2 229	3 000
1660	2 178	192	2 353	1 845	3 863
1670	1 845	245	2 017	1 744	3 897
1680	2 204	232	2 397	2 249	3 784

1690	2 088	291	2 305	2 232	4 309
1700	2 183	246	2 452	2 403	4 547
1710	2 501	248	2 917	1 851	3 968
1720	2 358	265	2 576	2 762	4 518
1730	2 007	281	2 133	2 026	4 937
1740	2 369	233	2 859	3 058	4 148
1750	2 304	267	2 505	2 721	4 698
1760	2 430	301	2 638	2 928	5 234
1770	1 866	223	2 135	2 072	4 016
1780	2 068	222	2 256	2 452	4 073
1790	2 332	182	2 573	2 428	3 708
1800	2 324	119	2 634	2 281	2 676
1810	2 572	144	2 907	2 699	2 780
1820	2 006	159	2 243	2 163	3 215
1830	2 197	163	2 461	2 145	3 426
1840	2 105	119	2 304	2 048	2 644
1850	1 686	107	1 813	1 526	2 626
1851	1 941	105	2 030	1 917	2 605
1852	1 603	107	1 769	1 373	2 426
1853	1 932	117	2 147	1 836	2 097
1854	2 079	118	2 440	1 781	1 710
1855	2 096	110	2 464	1 815	1 562
1856	1 999	96	2 305	1 769	1 506
1857	1 624	99	1 894	1 374	1 606
1858	1 640	109	1 830	1 520	1 638
1859	1 755	110	1 920	1 699	1 706
1860	2 209	111	2 377	2 288	1 695
1861	2 111	110	2 296	2 138	1 527
1862	1 722	103	1 974	1 560	1 385
1863	1 530	110	1 731	1 410	1 458
1864	1 522	121	1 700	1 455	1 411
1865	1 944	120	2 078	2 012	1 497
1866	1 719	111	1 912	1 671	1 315
1867	1 744	108	2 056	1 550	1 159
1868	1 849	105	2 139	1 704	1 278
1869	2 232	113	2 357	2 368	1 304
1870	1 813	113	1 980	1 823	1 291
1871	2 393	111	2 542	2 526	1 205
1872	1 497	134	1 846	1 294	1 141
1873	1 395	162	1 819	1 136	1 145
1874	1 235	141	1 698	878	1 103
1875	1 230	137	1 663	909	1 087
1876	1 914	125	2 070	1 968	1 172

1877	1 924	116	2 154	1 893	1 113
1878	1 728	115	1 907	1 715	1 008
1879	1 629	116	1 821	1 601	1 006
1880	1 653	112	1 830	1 642	981
1881	1 739	117	1 923	1 744	965
1882	2 052	120	2 199	2 137	990
1883	1 527	119	1 721	1 484	967
1884	1 607	119	1 750	1 605	971
1885	1 515	123	1 666	1 490	908
1886	1 665	121	1 795	1 667	850
1887	1 747	124	1 892	1 740	833
1888	2 125	125	2 260	2 182	833
1889	1 852	129	2 007	1 844	791
1890	1 417	141	1 626	1 286	824
1891	1 423	139	1 677	1 243	778
1892	1 826	139	2 018	1 746	806
1893	2 671	148	2 925	2 642	848
1894	2 551	136	2 769	2 534	838
1895	1 689	129	1 849	1 595	1 073
1896	1 614	132	1 777	1 493	1 146
1897	1 693	131	1 873	1 555	1 163
1898	1 643	129	1 839	1 486	1 203
1899	1 516	145	1 707	1 348	1 245
1900	1 555	167	1 792	1 351	1 281
1901	1 828	171	2 034	1 654	1 575
1902	1 975	179	2 187	1 808	1 672
1903	1 694	183	1 872	1 496	1 816
1904	1 576	193	1 766	1 339	1 783
1905	1 552	201	1 743	1 220	1 849
1906	1 468	216	1 665	1 132	1 846
1907	1 431	239	1 685	1 076	1 777
1908	1 315	237	1 566	961	1 686
1909	1 363	240	1 658	998	1 575
1910	1 269	242	1 557	933	1 554
1911	1 535	249	1 881	1 181	1 533
1912	1 636	266	2 079	1 218	1 443
1913	1 492	272	1 909	1 115	1 499
1914	1 141	274	1 451	922	1 420
1915	1 083	273	1 428	848	1 236
1916	1 153	231	1 445	1 021	1 134
1917	1 172	203	1 445	1 044	961
1918	1 136	192	1 434	1 013	838
1919	1 047	206	1 408	827	884

1920	1 123	161	1 434	969	750
1921	1 061	181	1 426	830	691
1922	995	230	1 394	785	801
1923	955	239	1 381	670	826
1924	951	231	1 384	707	821
1925	909	238	1 355	628	831
1926	880	189	1 292	591	934
1927	897	244	1 333	559	944
1928	879	244	1 320	585	977
1929	858	250	1 288	628	1 026
1930	814	269	1 258	565	1 153
1931	836	295	1 236	554	1 287
1932	888	302	1 224	699	1 361
1933	846	309	1 206	633	1 388
1934	841	305	1 207	628	1 394
1935	840	298	1 205	644	1 365
1936	836	306	1 189	656	1 354
1937	786	301	1 126	620	1 300
1938	799	310	1 155	600	1 342
1939	772	308	1 128	578	1 289
1940	784	286	1 080	651	1 193
1941	738	272	1 029	618	1 112
1942	686	265	985	591	1 021
1943	659	267	953	565	1 005
1944	642	278	897	547	1 081
1945	614	288	875	486	1 164
1946	597	287	828	477	1 162
1947	578	282	803	462	1 125
1948	544	279	766	427	1 132
1949	534	280	748	427	1 135
1950	624	279	701	583	1 141
1951	663	274	674	652	1 064
1952	716	282	664	723	1 054
1953	741	294	650	758	1 085
1954	722	292	633	751	1 085
1955	703	295	596	720	1 050
1956	684	313	575	706	1 063
1957	855	322	669	901	1 063
1958	688	333	669	674	1 073
1959	693	335	684	677	1 045
1960	688	330	635	680	1 014
1961	657	322	635	640	1 015
1962	657	307	594	654	998

1963	643	311	580	647	1 004
1964	631	314	583	616	991
1965	598	307	354	661	986
1966	568	307	356	625	979
1967	572	313	334	651	962
1968	553	329	312	634	991
1969	571	333	298	682	924
1970	544	319	294	660	865
1971	513	278	288	625	868
1972	488	259	288	606	853
1973	450	236	278	555	786
1974	490	232	368	574	852
1975	567	237	342	791	945
1976	530	259	326	717	985
1977	514	263	320	647	971
1978	487	270	310	575	992
1979	460	263	332	528	964
1980	636	272	619	675	1 025
1981	516	291	333	663	1 096
1982	554	307	362	735	1 107
1983	541	318	345	737	1 082
1984	631	313	533	770	1 045
1985	578	310	428	748	1 007
1986	521	301	312	725	991
1987	467	282	293	641	936
1988	438	271	275	586	930
1989	422	270	279	549	929
1990	434	257	301	552	873
1991	435	259	288	575	887
1992	427	249	285	576	903
1993	435	240	258	619	896
1994	436	242	211	654	881
1995	445	231	209	673	833
1996	474	198	231	688	769
1997	468	198	191	704	703
1998	486	185	177	749	651
1999	506	163	163	789	614
2000	521	160	186	795	572

Note
* including agricultural products.

Source: see text

Data Appendix

Table A6 Estimates of Energy Consumption by Energy Service (million tonnes of oil equivalent (toe)), 1300–2000

	Total[a] (All Final Users)	Heating (All Final Users)	Heating (Dom.)	Heating (Ind.[b])	Power (Ind.[b])	Transport (All Final Users)	Transport (Pass.)	Transport (Freight)	Lighting
1300	-	-	-	-	1.7	-	-	-	-
1310	-	-	-	-	1.7	-	-	-	-
1320	-	-	-	-	1.7	-	-	-	-
1330	-	-	-	-	1.6	-	-	-	-
1340	-	-	-	-	1.6	-	-	-	-
1350	-	-	-	-	1.6	-	-	-	-
1360	-	-	-	-	1.4	-	-	-	-
1370	-	-	-	-	1.3	-	-	-	-
1380	-	-	-	-	1.2	-	-	-	-
1390	-	-	-	-	1.1	-	-	-	-
1400	-	-	-	-	1.0	-	-	-	-
1410	-	-	-	-	1.0	-	-	-	-
1420	-	-	-	-	1.0	-	-	-	-
1430	-	-	-	-	0.9	-	-	-	-
1440	-	-	-	-	0.9	-	-	-	-
1450	-	-	-	-	0.9	-	-	-	-
1460	-	-	-	-	0.9	-	-	-	-
1470	-	-	-	-	0.9	-	-	-	-
1480	-	-	-	-	0.8	-	-	-	-
1490	-	-	-	-	0.8	-	-	-	-
1500	1.5	0.7	0.4	0.4	0.8	-	-	-	-
1510	1.6	0.7	0.4	0.4	0.8	-	-	-	-
1520	1.6	0.8	0.4	0.4	0.8	-	-	-	-
1530	1.6	0.8	0.4	0.4	0.9	-	-	-	-
1540	1.7	0.8	0.4	0.4	0.9	-	-	-	-
1550	1.8	0.9	0.4	0.4	0.9	-	-	-	-
1560	1.8	0.9	0.4	0.5	0.9	-	-	-	-
1570	1.9	0.9	0.5	0.5	1.0	-	-	-	-
1580	2.1	1.1	0.5	0.6	1.0	-	-	-	-
1590	2.2	1.2	0.5	0.6	1.1	-	-	-	-
1600	2.4	1.3	0.6	0.8	1.1	-	-	-	-
1610	2.5	1.4	0.6	0.8	1.1	-	-	-	-
1620	2.6	1.5	0.6	0.8	1.1	-	-	-	-
1630	2.6	1.5	0.7	0.8	1.2	-	-	-	-
1640	2.6	1.4	0.7	0.8	1.2	-	-	-	-
1650	2.6	1.4	0.7	0.7	1.2	-	-	-	-
1660	2.9	1.6	0.8	0.8	1.3	-	-	-	-
1670	3.1	1.8	1.0	0.9	1.3	-	-	-	-

1680	3.3	1.9	1.1	0.9	1.3	-	-	-	-
1690	3.1	1.7	1.1	0.6	1.4	-	-	-	-
1700	3.6	2.2	1.4	0.8	1.4	-	-	-	-
1710	3.7	2.2	1.3	0.9	1.5	-		-	0.02
1720	4.2	2.6	1.6	1.0	1.6	-	-	-	0.02
1730	4.2	2.5	1.4	1.1	1.6	0.01	-	0.01	0.02
1740	6.3	4.5	3.3	1.2	1.7	0.01	-	0.01	0.02
1750	5.2	3.3	2.0	1.3	1.8	0.01	-	0.01	0.02
1760	6.0	4.0	2.3	1.8	1.9	0.01	-	0.01	0.02
1770	7.7	5.5	3.3	2.2	2.2	0.02	-	0.02	0.03
1780	8.3	5.8	3.1	2.7	2.4	0.04	0.01	0.03	0.03
1790	9.4	6.6	3.3	3.3	2.7	0.07	0.03	0.04	0.04
1800	11.6	8.6	4.2	4.4	2.9	0.13	0.06	0.07	0.04
1810	13.0	9.4	5.6	3.8	3.4	0.20	0.11	0.09	0.06
1820	16.0	11.8	7.1	4.7	3.9	0.21	0.12	0.09	0.08
1830	21.3	15.6	7.7	7.9	5.2	0.4	0.10	0.3	0.11
1840	28.0	20.3	8.7	11.6	6.4	1.2	0.3	0.9	0.17
1850	38.9	28.6	9.4	19.1	7.1	3.0	1.0	2.0	0.21
1851	39.9	29.5	9.5	20.0	7.0	3.2	1.1	2.0	0.22
1852	40.9	30.4	9.5	20.9	7.0	3.3	1.2	2.1	0.22
1853	42.6	31.9	10.1	21.7	6.9	3.6	1.3	2.3	0.24
1854	43.4	32.5	9.9	22.6	6.9	3.8	1.4	2.4	0.23
1855	45.3	34.1	10.7	23.4	6.9	4.0	1.5	2.5	0.25
1856	46.0	34.6	10.4	24.2	6.9	4.2	1.6	2.7	0.27
1857	46.9	35.3	10.2	25.1	6.9	4.4	1.6	2.8	0.29
1858	48.4	36.6	10.8	25.9	6.9	4.6	1.6	3.0	0.30
1859	49.4	37.5	10.8	26.7	6.9	4.7	1.7	3.1	0.30
1860	50.8	38.7	11.2	27.5	6.9	4.9	1.7	3.2	0.34
1861	51.7	39.3	11.0	28.3	6.9	5.1	1.8	3.4	0.34
1862	52.8	40.3	11.2	29.1	6.9	5.3	1.8	3.5	0.34
1863	53.9	41.1	11.2	29.9	6.9	5.5	1.8	3.6	0.37
1864	55.3	42.3	11.6	30.7	7.0	5.6	1.9	3.8	0.37
1865	56.3	43.1	11.6	31.5	7.0	5.8	1.9	3.9	0.40
1866	57.5	44.1	11.8	32.3	7.0	6.0	2.0	4.0	0.41
1867	58.9	45.3	12.2	33.1	7.0	6.2	2.0	4.2	0.40
1868	59.7	45.9	12.0	33.9	7.0	6.3	2.0	4.3	0.42
1869	61.3	47.1	12.4	34.7	7.1	6.7	2.1	4.6	0.43
1870	62.6	47.9	12.7	35.2	7.1	7.1	2.1	5.0	0.47
1871	63.9	48.6	13.0	35.6	7.2	7.6	2.2	5.3	0.51
1872	65.0	49.1	13.1	36.1	7.3	8.1	2.4	5.7	0.48
1873	66.5	50.0	13.5	36.5	7.4	8.6	2.5	6.1	0.52
1874	67.8	50.7	13.8	36.9	7.5	9.1	2.6	6.5	0.53
1875	69.1	51.4	14.0	37.4	7.6	9.6	2.7	6.9	0.53
1876	70.6	52.1	14.3	37.8	7.7	10.1	2.9	7.2	0.61

Data Appendix

1877	72.0	52.9	14.7	38.3	7.8	10.6	3.0	7.6	0.66
1878	73.4	53.7	15.0	38.7	7.9	11.1	3.1	8.0	0.67
1879	75.3	54.9	15.8	39.1	8.0	11.6	3.2	8.3	0.75
1880	76.0	55.1	15.5	39.6	8.1	12.1	3.4	8.7	0.78
1881	77.6	55.9	15.9	40.1	8.2	12.6	3.5	9.1	0.87
1882	78.7	56.5	15.9	40.5	8.2	13.1	3.6	9.5	0.90
1883	80.2	57.3	16.3	41.0	8.3	13.6	3.7	9.9	0.96
1884	81.3	57.9	16.5	41.4	8.3	14.1	3.8	10.3	0.95
1885	83.0	58.9	17.1	41.9	8.4	14.6	3.9	10.7	1.03
1886	84.2	59.7	17.3	42.4	8.4	15.1	4.1	11.0	1.06
1887	85.6	60.6	17.7	42.8	8.5	15.5	4.2	11.3	1.09
1888	86.9	61.3	17.9	43.4	8.5	15.9	4.3	11.7	1.18
1889	88.2	61.8	17.9	44.0	8.6	16.6	4.5	12.0	1.24
1890	89.6	62.5	18.0	44.5	8.6	17.2	4.8	12.4	1.30
1891	91.1	63.3	18.2	45.1	8.6	17.8	5.0	12.8	1.40
1892	92.7	64.1	18.4	45.7	8.7	18.5	5.3	13.2	1.43
1893	93.7	64.5	18.2	46.3	8.7	19.1	5.5	13.6	1.48
1894	95.3	65.4	18.5	46.8	8.7	19.7	5.8	13.9	1.54
1895	97.1	66.3	18.8	47.4	8.8	20.3	6.0	14.3	1.65
1896	98.6	66.9	18.9	48.0	9.0	21.0	6.3	14.7	1.72
1897	100.2	67.6	19.0	48.6	9.3	21.6	6.5	15.1	1.75
1898	101.8	68.2	19.0	49.2	9.5	22.2	6.8	15.4	1.88
1899	103.7	69.1	19.4	49.7	9.8	22.9	7.0	15.8	2.00
1900	105.3	69.7	19.4	50.3	10.0	23.5	7.3	16.2	2.08
1901	106.2	70.1	19.3	50.9	9.8	24.1	7.6	16.6	2.08
1902	107.8	70.9	19.4	51.4	10.0	24.8	7.8	17.0	2.17
1903	109.5	71.5	19.5	52.0	10.3	25.5	8.0	17.5	2.18
1904	111.0	72.1	19.8	52.4	10.4	26.2	8.3	17.9	2.29
1905	112.3	72.7	19.9	52.8	10.6	26.7	8.3	18.4	2.31
1906	113.6	73.3	20.1	53.1	10.8	27.2	8.5	18.8	2.37
1907	115.1	73.9	20.3	53.5	10.9	27.9	8.6	19.3	2.43
1908	116.5	74.5	20.5	54.0	11.0	28.5	8.7	19.7	2.51
1909	117.9	75.2	20.7	54.5	11.1	29.0	8.9	20.2	2.57
1910	119.4	75.9	20.9	55.0	11.1	29.9	9.2	20.7	2.49
1911	120.8	76.6	21.1	55.5	11.2	30.5	9.4	21.2	2.53
1912	122.2	77.3	21.3	56.0	11.1	31.2	9.5	21.7	2.61
1913	123.3	78.0	21.5	56.5	11.1	31.6	9.7	21.8	2.71
1914	113.4	68.0	17.5	50.6	11.0	31.6	9.9	21.7	2.72
1915	111.8	67.0	18.5	48.5	10.9	31.3	9.3	22.0	2.68
1916	111.0	65.9	19.4	46.5	10.7	31.8	9.6	22.2	2.55
1917	110.1	64.8	20.4	44.4	11.1	31.6	9.6	22.0	2.52
1918	108.8	63.7	21.4	42.4	11.0	31.6	9.3	22.2	2.56
1919	107.9	62.7	22.4	40.3	10.8	31.6	9.2	22.4	2.77
1920	107.2	61.7	23.4	38.3	10.5	32.1	9.3	22.8	2.84

1921	88.3	43.8	18.9	24.9	9.8	32.3	10.1	22.2	2.43
1922	103.4	59.7	25.4	34.3	9.8	31.4	8.6	22.8	2.49
1923	108.5	63.7	27.5	36.2	10.0	32.3	9.5	22.8	2.38
1924	112.2	67.3	29.1	38.2	10.1	32.4	10.5	21.9	2.41
1925	100.0	63.8	27.9	35.9	9.9	23.9	10.8	13.2	2.35
1926	85.5	41.0	19.0	22.0	9.6	32.6	10.7	21.9	2.36
1927	111.8	67.5	29.3	38.2	9.7	32.5	9.9	22.6	2.19
1928	106.4	61.2	26.7	34.5	9.5	33.7	11.4	22.3	2.04
1929	110.1	65.7	28.4	37.4	9.5	33.0	11.3	21.7	1.91
1930	104.9	61.6	27.0	34.6	9.1	32.4	11.7	20.7	1.83
1931	99.1	56.7	25.5	31.3	8.6	32.0	11.5	20.4	1.78
1932	97.0	56.0	25.1	30.9	8.2	31.2	11.4	19.8	1.71
1933	97.4	56.4	25.1	31.3	7.9	31.4	11.3	20.2	1.66
1934	101.7	61.0	26.5	34.5	7.9	31.1	11.5	19.6	1.65
1935	104.4	63.5	27.5	36.0	7.9	31.4	12.0	19.4	1.64
1936	108.2	66.7	28.5	38.2	8.0	31.9	12.4	19.5	1.69
1937	110.7	69.3	29.4	39.9	8.1	31.6	12.9	18.7	1.69
1938	106.3	66.1	29.0	37.0	7.6	30.9	13.3	17.6	1.65
1939	108.0	70.8	30.8	40.0	7.8	27.8	12.9	14.9	1.58
1940	109.7	74.6	32.2	42.4	8.4	25.2	12.8	12.4	1.47
1941	109.1	73.7	31.9	41.7	9.0	24.9	13.1	11.8	1.49
1942	108.9	72.4	31.3	41.0	10.0	25.0	13.3	11.8	1.46
1943	103.5	67.4	29.9	37.5	9.9	24.8	13.7	11.1	1.41
1944	100.9	64.1	28.4	35.7	9.5	25.8	13.9	11.9	1.42
1945	100.8	63.7	26.7	37.0	8.1	27.6	14.2	13.5	1.39
1946	99.8	63.0	26.7	36.3	7.9	27.4	14.1	13.3	1.51
1947	102.2	64.6	26.9	37.7	7.6	28.6	14.3	14.3	1.44
1948	102.3	65.8	26.8	39.0	7.5	27.6	13.8	13.8	1.42
1949	103.6	67.3	26.9	40.3	7.5	27.4	14.3	13.1	1.36
1950	117.5	81.7	31.2	50.5	9.4	25.2	15.4	9.8	1.28
1951	119.5	83.3	32.4	50.9	8.5	26.2	15.9	10.3	1.44
1952	118.5	82.2	31.9	50.3	8.6	26.3	16.0	10.3	1.43
1953	120.0	82.8	32.1	50.7	9.2	26.6	16.1	10.5	1.46
1954	123.8	85.8	33.1	52.6	9.4	27.1	16.4	10.7	1.54
1955	126.2	85.9	32.0	53.9	10.6	28.1	17.0	11.1	1.60
1956	125.8	85.1	32.2	52.9	11.1	28.0	16.7	11.2	1.68
1957	120.9	81.1	30.9	50.2	11.4	26.7	16.1	10.5	1.71
1958	119.9	78.1	32.0	46.1	12.1	27.9	16.8	11.1	1.78
1959	116.8	73.6	30.1	43.5	12.4	29.0	17.3	11.7	1.86
1960	123.2	77.8	31.4	46.4	12.1	31.3	18.0	13.3	1.96
1961	123.1	74.6	30.5	44.1	12.2	34.3	20.5	13.8	2.02
1962	124.6	74.1	31.6	42.5	13.4	34.9	21.0	14.0	2.17
1963	127.1	74.0	32.1	41.9	14.6	36.2	21.7	14.6	2.31
1964	126.3	70.6	29.6	41.0	15.6	37.8	22.4	15.3	2.35

Data Appendix

1965	129.2	71.1	30.4	40.7	16.8	38.9	23.0	15.9	2.46
1966	127.8	68.4	30.1	38.3	17.2	39.8	23.3	16.5	2.48
1967	126.6	65.1	29.3	35.7	17.3	41.7	24.4	17.3	2.48
1968	128.0	65.8	29.9	35.9	18.3	41.3	24.2	17.1	2.59
1969	132.8	65.8	30.0	35.8	19.6	44.7	25.9	18.9	2.68
1970	135.7	64.7	29.4	35.2	20.9	47.4	27.4	20.0	2.72
1971	136.8	61.3	28.1	33.2	21.1	51.6	29.8	21.8	2.78
1972	140.2	61.3	28.1	33.2	21.5	54.5	31.4	23.1	2.86
1973	148.6	65.3	28.8	36.5	22.7	57.5	32.9	24.6	3.05
1974	145.0	65.4	29.5	35.9	22.1	54.5	31.0	23.5	2.94
1975	142.5	62.5	28.6	33.9	23.0	54.2	31.3	22.9	2.91
1976	147.8	64.4	28.1	36.3	24.1	56.4	32.4	23.9	2.92
1977	152.1	65.6	29.1	36.6	25.3	58.2	33.5	24.7	2.96
1978	157.0	66.2	29.7	36.5	26.1	61.7	35.5	26.2	3.00
1979	164.9	71.0	32.3	38.7	27.8	62.9	36.0	26.9	3.12
1980	158.7	65.2	31.2	34.0	27.0	63.5	36.2	27.3	2.94
1981	156.9	65.1	31.2	33.9	26.9	62.0	35.5	26.6	2.85
1982	158.2	64.5	30.8	33.7	27.7	63.3	36.2	27.1	2.75
1983	160.3	64.5	30.6	33.9	28.2	64.9	37.3	27.6	2.75
1984	162.3	63.3	29.3	34.0	28.7	67.5	38.8	28.7	2.77
1985	171.0	69.1	33.0	36.2	29.9	69.1	40.0	29.1	2.84
1986	176.1	69.8	34.3	35.5	30.1	73.4	42.8	30.7	2.88
1987	181.5	70.9	34.0	36.9	30.9	76.7	45.0	31.7	3.04
1988	184.3	68.7	32.9	35.8	31.6	80.9	47.6	33.3	3.06
1989	184.5	65.2	31.2	33.9	32.5	83.8	49.5	34.2	3.06
1990	186.7	65.6	31.3	34.3	32.9	85.1	50.1	34.9	3.05
1991	188.6	69.1	34.9	34.2	32.9	83.6	49.2	34.4	3.01
1992	190.8	67.7	33.5	34.2	34.0	86.2	51.0	35.1	2.90
1993	192.0	67.9	34.8	33.1	32.7	88.6	52.8	35.8	2.84
1994	190.7	67.3	33.3	34.0	32.5	88.2	52.7	35.5	2.70
1995	192.1	67.1	32.3	34.8	33.2	89.1	53.5	35.6	2.68
1996	205.6	79.7	37.4	42.3	30.7	92.5	55.9	36.7	2.66
1997	201.8	72.3	34.1	38.2	32.7	94.3	57.2	37.1	2.57
1998	205.8	71.5	34.9	36.6	35.0	96.7	59.0	37.7	2.49
1999	208.6	71.9	34.8	37.2	35.3	98.9	61.0	37.9	2.42
2000	212.7	73.5	35.8	37.6	35.7	101.2	62.9	38.3	2.33

Notes

a: main energy services: heating, power, transport and lighting.

b: industry and all other non-domestic final users.

Source: see text

Table A7 Estimates of Efficiency of Energy Technologies by Energy Service, 1300–2000

Year	Heating (Average) Percentage	Power (Average) Percentage	Land Transport (Passenger) Thousand p-km per toe	Lighting (Average) Thousand lumen-hours per toe
1300	13.0%	12.8%	-	233
1310	13.0%	12.8%	-	236
1320	13.0%	12.8%	-	238
1330	13.1%	12.9%	-	241
1340	13.1%	12.9%	-	243
1350	13.1%	13.1%	-	245
1360	13.1%	13.5%	-	248
1370	13.2%	14.1%	-	250
1380	13.2%	14.3%	-	253
1390	13.2%	14.6%	-	255
1400	13.3%	14.8%	-	258
1410	13.3%	14.8%	-	261
1420	13.3%	14.7%	-	263
1430	13.4%	14.7%	-	266
1440	13.4%	14.7%	-	269
1450	13.4%	14.8%	-	271
1460	13.4%	14.7%	-	274
1470	13.5%	14.6%	-	277
1480	13.5%	14.5%	-	280
1490	13.5%	14.4%	-	282
1500	13.6%	14.4%	-	285
1510	13.5%	14.4%	-	288
1520	13.3%	14.4%	-	291
1530	13.2%	14.6%	-	294
1540	13.1%	14.5%	-	297
1550	13.0%	14.4%	-	300
1560	12.9%	14.1%	-	303
1570	12.8%	13.8%	-	306
1580	12.7%	13.6%	-	309
1590	12.6%	13.4%	-	312
1600	12.5%	13.1%	-	315
1610	12.4%	13.3%	-	318
1620	12.2%	13.4%	-	322
1630	12.1%	13.5%	-	325
1640	12.0%	13.6%	-	328
1650	11.9%	13.6%	-	331

1660	11.8%	13.8%	-	335
1670	11.6%	14.0%	-	338
1680	11.5%	14.2%	-	341
1690	11.4%	14.4%	-	345
1700	11.2%	14.6%	-	348
1710	11.2%	14.9%	-	339
1720	11.1%	15.1%	14.0	341
1730	11.1%	15.3%	14.7	338
1740	11.1%	15.8%	15.4	342
1750	11.0%	16.4%	16.2	338
1760	10.8%	16.3%	17.0	345
1770	10.7%	15.9%	17.9	324
1780	10.5%	15.7%	18.8	347
1790	10.4%	15.2%	19.8	363
1800	11.0%	15.4%	20.8	390
1810	11.4%	14.6%	21.9	418
1820	11.9%	13.8%	27.7	737
1830	12.4%	13.4%	32.2	1 000
1840	12.9%	11.7%	13.8	1 211
1850	13.5%	11.7%	4.4	1 705
1851	13.6%	12.1%	4.4	1 774
1852	13.7%	12.5%	4.1	1 892
1853	13.9%	12.8%	4.1	1 924
1854	14.0%	13.1%	4.0	2 105
1855	14.1%	13.5%	4.0	2 114
1856	14.2%	13.8%	3.9	2 115
1857	14.3%	14.1%	3.9	2 129
1858	14.5%	14.3%	3.9	2 173
1859	14.6%	14.6%	4.0	2 247
1860	14.7%	14.9%	4.0	2 221
1861	14.8%	15.1%	4.0	2 290
1862	15.0%	15.4%	4.1	2 377
1863	15.1%	15.6%	4.1	2 385
1864	15.2%	15.9%	4.2	2 461
1865	15.4%	16.1%	4.3	2 426
1866	15.5%	16.4%	4.4	2 451
1867	15.6%	16.6%	4.4	2 530
1868	15.8%	16.8%	4.2	2 531
1869	15.9%	17.0%	4.5	2 552
1870	16.1%	17.2%	4.5	2 525
1871	16.2%	17.4%	4.6	2 566
1872	16.3%	17.6%	4.6	2 610
1873	16.5%	17.9%	4.7	2 563

1874	16.6%	18.1%	4.7	2 635
1875	16.8%	18.4%	4.7	2 695
1876	16.9%	18.6%	4.7	2 650
1877	17.1%	18.9%	4.7	2 669
1878	17.2%	19.2%	4.6	2 742
1879	17.4%	19.5%	4.6	2 697
1880	17.6%	19.8%	4.7	2 751
1881	17.7%	20.1%	4.6	2 887
1882	17.9%	20.4%	4.6	3 059
1883	18.0%	20.6%	4.6	3 209
1884	18.2%	20.9%	4.5	3 416
1885	18.4%	21.2%	4.4	3 540
1886	18.5%	21.5%	4.4	3 716
1887	18.7%	21.8%	4.3	3 875
1888	18.9%	22.1%	4.2	3 952
1889	19.0%	22.4%	4.1	4 072
1890	19.2%	22.8%	4.1	4 207
1891	19.4%	23.1%	3.9	4 295
1892	19.6%	23.4%	3.9	4 438
1893	19.7%	23.7%	3.8	4 463
1894	19.9%	24.0%	3.8	4 538
1895	20.1%	24.2%	3.7	4 622
1896	20.3%	24.0%	3.8	4 744
1897	20.5%	23.8%	3.8	4 903
1898	20.7%	23.6%	3.8	4 940
1899	20.8%	23.4%	3.8	5 031
1900	21.0%	23.1%	3.9	5 110
1901	21.4%	22.8%	3.9	5 285
1902	21.7%	22.4%	3.9	5 329
1903	22.0%	22.1%	3.7	5 497
1904	22.3%	21.9%	3.6	5 567
1905	22.7%	21.8%	3.4	5 669
1906	23.0%	21.7%	3.6	5 794
1907	23.3%	21.6%	3.8	5 861
1908	23.7%	21.3%	3.9	5 863
1909	24.0%	21.0%	3.9	5 888
1910	24.3%	20.7%	4.3	6 450
1911	24.6%	20.4%	4.9	6 722
1912	25.0%	20.1%	5.0	6 968
1913	25.3%	19.9%	5.4	7 229
1914	25.6%	19.7%	6.0	7 514
1915	26.0%	19.8%	6.2	7 813
1916	26.3%	19.9%	6.6	8 323

Data Appendix

1917	26.6%	18.8%	6.6	8 639
1918	27.0%	18.9%	6.4	8 759
1919	27.3%	18.7%	7.0	8 621
1920	27.6%	17.5%	8.9	8 996
1921	27.9%	18.6%	8.3	9 523
1922	28.3%	18.6%	9.6	9 499
1923	28.6%	18.1%	9.4	10 115
1924	28.9%	17.9%	9.2	10 352
1925	29.3%	17.9%	9.3	10 993
1926	29.6%	18.1%	9.2	11 478
1927	29.9%	18.0%	10.6	12 777
1928	30.3%	18.2%	9.8	14 277
1929	30.6%	18.4%	10.5	16 184
1930	30.9%	18.7%	10.4	17 972
1931	31.2%	19.6%	9.9	19 508
1932	31.6%	20.4%	9.7	21 555
1933	31.9%	21.0%	9.7	23 719
1934	32.2%	21.3%	9.7	26 585
1935	32.6%	21.7%	9.7	30 239
1936	32.9%	21.8%	9.9	33 918
1937	33.2%	22.0%	9.9	38 036
1938	33.5%	23.0%	9.8	42 925
1939	33.9%	22.8%	10.1	45 569
1940	34.2%	21.4%	9.3	49 047
1941	34.5%	20.3%	9.7	52 859
1942	34.9%	19.8%	9.3	53 160
1943	35.2%	19.7%	9.2	55 989
1944	35.5%	19.1%	9.2	63 034
1945	35.9%	19.0%	10.7	70 089
1946	36.2%	18.6%	10.9	79 961
1947	36.5%	18.4%	11.3	86 104
1948	36.8%	18.3%	12.3	98 158
1949	37.2%	17.9%	12.7	105 645
1950	41.0%	16.6%	12.8	116 065
1951	41.6%	17.1%	12.8	117 329
1952	42.3%	17.4%	16.0	119 612
1953	42.9%	17.5%	16.0	123 467
1954	43.6%	18.4%	16.1	126 763
1955	44.3%	18.6%	15.9	131 214
1956	45.0%	19.0%	16.4	134 054
1957	45.7%	19.1%	17.1	136 602
1958	46.4%	19.1%	17.1	138 893
1959	47.1%	19.8%	17.6	141 289

1960	47.8%	20.5%	17.3	143 982
1961	48.6%	20.3%	15.8	148 369
1962	49.3%	20.7%	15.6	151 785
1963	50.1%	21.0%	15.4	154 187
1964	50.9%	21.6%	16.1	156 238
1965	51.7%	22.3%	16.1	158 071
1966	52.5%	23.0%	16.6	159 689
1967	53.3%	23.9%	16.3	161 194
1968	54.1%	24.5%	16.7	162 532
1969	55.0%	24.6%	15.9	163 762
1970	55.8%	24.1%	15.2	164 892
1971	56.7%	24.8%	14.5	165 927
1972	57.6%	25.1%	14.1	166 875
1973	58.5%	25.6%	14.1	167 742
1974	59.4%	26.2%	14.6	168 534
1975	60.3%	26.3%	14.5	169 258
1976	61.2%	27.1%	14.4	169 918
1977	62.1%	27.0%	14.3	170 519
1978	63.1%	27.2%	13.8	171 067
1979	64.0%	26.7%	13.5	171 566
1980	65.0%	27.2%	14.0	172 020
1981	66.0%	28.1%	14.4	172 433
1982	67.0%	28.4%	14.5	172 808
1983	68.0%	29.4%	14.2	173 149
1984	69.0%	30.0%	14.2	173 459
1985	70.0%	30.6%	14.0	173 740
1986	71.1%	31.2%	13.7	173 995
1987	72.1%	32.0%	13.8	174 227
1988	73.2%	33.3%	13.7	174 437
1989	74.2%	34.2%	14.1	174 628
1990	75.3%	33.2%	14.1	174 800
1991	76.4%	34.3%	14.1	174 957
1992	77.5%	34.8%	13.6	175 099
1993	78.6%	37.6%	13.1	175 227
1994	79.8%	38.3%	13.2	175 344
1995	80.9%	38.5%	13.1	176 460
1996	82.1%	39.7%	12.8	198 771
1997	83.2%	35.2%	12.7	219 314
1998	84.4%	37.3%	12.4	237 498
1999	85.6%	36.8%	12.1	253 040
2000	86.8%	38.2%	11.7	311 262

Source: see text

Table A8 Estimates of Energy Service Prices, 1300–2000

	Heating (Domestic) £(2000) per toe of eff. heating	Power (Non-Domestic) p(2000) per kWh	Transport (Pass.) p(2000) per pass-km	Transport (Freight Land) p(2000) per tonne-km	Transport (Freight Sea) p(2000) per tonne-km	Lighting (Domestic) £(2000) per million lumen-hrs
1300	-	138	-	195	10.3	19 868
1310	-	114	-	141	11.9	15 486
1320	-	162	-	166	9.8	22 019
1330	-	152	-	136	11.3	17 846
1340	-	186	-	233	11.0	17 536
1350	-	200	-	132	17.5	19 241
1360	-	173	-	151	18.9	17 672
1370	-	93	-	116	13.4	9 987
1380	-	194	-	186	29.9	19 566
1390	-	188	-	145	19.6	16 669
1400	-	155	-	194	15.6	13 820
1410	-	134	-	162	21.0	10 617
1420	-	169	-	184	11.4	13 339
1430	-	137	-	175	11.0	11 481
1440	-	147	-	188	13.8	12 227
1450	1 081	205	-	183	25.3	12 284
1460	1 302	234	-	159	25.8	14 823
1470	1 418	258	-	146	34.2	14 706
1480	1 246	225	-	157	37.7	15 039
1490	1 087	194	-	140	28.7	11 320
1500	1 036	248	-	130	23.8	11 144
1510	990	237	-	130	20.7	10 267
1520	805	212	-	114	14.7	9 598
1530	887	199	-	103	19.4	8 686
1540	885	220	-	109	21.9	9 343
1550	970	184	-	84	30.5	8 930
1560	874	205	-	114	24.5	11 041
1570	938	269	-	159	27.1	11 697
1580	993	246	-	170	22.6	11 649
1590	909	300	-	182	15.0	11 415
1600	741	241	-	177	11.7	11 863
1610	933	253	-	229	14.8	13 010
1620	968	315	-	254	14.3	12 892
1630	824	232	-	212	11.8	10 585
1640	1 132	250	-	313	12.9	12 488
1650	825	204	-	259	8.4	9 054

1660	936	234	-	310	11.1	11 541
1670	1 211	265	-	315	11.3	11 527
1680	1 154	274	-	324	11.9	11 080
1690	1 492	290	-	339	13.4	12 494
1700	1 263	258	60	296	11.9	13 053
1710	1 282	216	52	240	10.4	11 841
1720	1 366	263	60	306	12.0	13 103
1730	1 460	264	63	341	9.5	14 293
1740	1 219	238	51	297	10.0	12 152
1750	1 396	262	61	305	10.0	13 686
1760	1 594	266	76	339	11.0	15 018
1770	1 181	205	58	250	8.9	11 736
1780	1 189	214	60	235	9.1	11 481
1790	987	209	60	251	9.2	9 496
1800	638	171	41	138	6.8	6 632
1810	763	195	48	173	9.3	7 355
1820	816	197	60	200	7.1	4 403
1830	816	261	77	179	6.6	3 366
1840	577	239	66	123	6.5	2 382
1850	502	239	57	151	5.7	2 298
1851	487	244	55	145	5.5	2 235
1852	491	234	55	126	5.6	2 007
1853	533	219	52	107	6.5	1 718
1854	533	212	52	104	6.4	1 291
1855	489	210	52	101	6.0	1 153
1856	423	208	51	101	5.4	1 097
1857	430	203	52	110	4.7	1 221
1858	469	218	53	105	4.6	1 173
1859	468	217	52	95	5.0	1 209
1860	469	211	51	93	4.9	1 234
1861	454	207	51	93	5.0	983
1862	418	201	51	93	4.6	811
1863	440	204	51	92	4.8	818
1864	482	206	50	90	5.4	750
1865	473	212	50	81	5.2	870
1866	435	201	48	75	4.5	780
1867	421	190	47	48	4.2	651
1868	401	194	47	79	4.1	752
1869	428	209	46	77	4.5	741
1870	422	203	47	73	4.6	740
1871	410	205	45	72	4.1	666
1872	501	190	45	73	4.9	622
1873	607	191	44	76	4.9	629

1874	516	190	44	75	5.5	565
1875	496	178	44	74	4.4	541
1876	444	193	43	72	4.5	610
1877	405	187	43	74	4.5	562
1878	398	184	43	75	4.4	471
1879	396	183	43	69	4.4	467
1880	378	177	42	69	4.7	455
1881	390	178	42	67	4.3	422
1882	398	179	41	67	3.9	430
1883	389	171	40	68	3.9	403
1884	385	173	40	69	3.6	390
1885	396	173	40	69	3.4	327
1886	385	172	39	67	3.4	279
1887	390	173	39	67	3.5	254
1888	392	176	39	66	3.8	263
1889	405	173	38	64	4.1	258
1890	436	170	38	63	3.2	246
1891	427	168	37	61	2.7	233
1892	416	169	37	62	2.5	225
1893	439	177	37	59	2.6	246
1894	394	177	37	58	2.2	240
1895	369	169	37	56	2.2	237
1896	370	168	37	54	2.7	215
1897	368	166	36	53	3.1	186
1898	359	163	36	51	3.1	192
1899	402	164	36	48	3.3	203
1900	461	160	34	48	3.8	216
1901	455	162	33	46	3.0	204
1902	469	161	33	45	2.1	217
1903	470	155	32	44	2.0	192
1904	489	152	31	43	2.0	187
1905	501	149	28	41	2.2	184
1906	531	148	27	40	2.4	198
1907	582	129	26	39	2.3	217
1908	564	126	26	38	2.1	194
1909	563	126	25	37	2.0	195
1910	559	124	29	37	2.1	209
1911	572	128	29	37	2.6	190
1912	613	128	30	34	3.3	179
1913	618	129	31	31	2.8	178
1914	611	124	32	31	3.2	155
1915	608	120	30	30	7.1	143
1916	499	114	34	29	10.6	140

1917	423	117	32	29	13.1	112
1918	400	122	45	30	14.7	103
1919	432	129	30	39	7.1	199
1920	323	120	26	51	5.6	145
1921	357	128	23	52	2.3	94
1922	449	125	22	46	2.3	95
1923	456	119	17	44	2.1	88
1924	426	118	18	44	2.0	93
1925	434	116	16	46	1.8	85
1926	304	117	16	49	2.2	83
1927	420	116	13	53	2.1	78
1928	409	113	13	55	1.9	76
1929	418	111	14	61	2.0	70
1930	446	113	13	66	1.4	70
1931	482	147	11	68	1.5	73
1932	485	149	14	64	1.5	74
1933	487	148	13	73	1.2	73
1934	467	142	12	67	1.4	70
1935	449	136	12	72	1.6	65
1936	456	128	12	75	1.6	61
1937	441	117	11	75	2.8	55
1938	448	117	10	64	2.7	52
1939	436	109	10	57	3.9	50
1940	404	105	13	54	6.6	43
1941	381	91	12	51	8.0	38
1942	366	81	15	51	8.0	36
1943	366	81	15	55	8.1	35
1944	380	84	15	54	7.6	32
1945	395	89	9	54	5.6	29
1946	390	87	8	56	4.5	25
1947	379	89	8	56	3.3	23
1948	376	83	7	52	3.2	19
1949	371	80	6	50	3.1	17
1950	382	80	8	61	3.6	15
1951	371	66	8	50	3.3	11
1952	375	65	9	50	3.0	11
1953	387	64	9	51	3.0	11
1954	374	61	8	48	3.1	10
1955	372	61	7	47	3.0	9
1956	389	59	6	46	3.0	9
1957	395	56	7	42	3.0	9
1958	402	55	5	41	2.7	9
1959	397	52	5	38	2.6	8

Data Appendix

1960	389	48	5	38	2.4	7
1961	379	47	5	37	2.2	7
1962	360	45	5	38	1.9	7
1963	360	43	4	34	1.9	6
1964	356	42	4	29	1.8	6
1965	345	40	4	27	1.8	6
1966	340	40	4	22	1.7	6
1967	350	39	4	21	1.7	6
1968	366	37	4	18	1.7	6
1969	371	35	4	16	1.8	6
1970	364	35	4	15	1.8	5
1971	331	35	4	14	1.7	5
1972	314	36	4	11	1.7	5
1973	287	33	4	10	1.6	5
1974	291	35	4	10	1.4	5
1975	300	36	5	10	1.2	6
1976	326	34	5	10	1.0	6
1977	324	31	4	10	0.9	6
1978	327	32	4	10	0.9	6
1979	319	30	4	10	0.8	6
1980	323	33	5	8	0.7	6
1981	336	34	4	8	0.7	6
1982	341	35	5	7	0.6	6
1983	343	35	5	5	0.6	6
1984	331	33	5	7	0.6	6
1985	322	32	5	6	0.5	6
1986	309	33	5	7	0.5	6
1987	283	29	4	7	0.5	5
1988	267	28	4	7	0.5	5
1989	262	28	3	7	0.5	5
1990	247	27	3	7	0.4	5
1991	244	27	3	7	0.4	5
1992	232	28	3	7	0.4	5
1993	222	27	3	7	0.4	5
1994	218	26	3	7	0.4	5
1995	205	24	3	7	0.4	5
1996	182	22	4	7	0.4	4
1997	175	23	4	7	0.4	3
1998	160	21	4	7	0.4	3
1999	139	21	4	7	0.4	2
2000	132	19	4	7	0.4	2

Source: see text

Table A9 Estimates of Energy Service Consumption, 1300–2000

	Heating (Domestic)	Power (Non-Domestic)	Transport Passenger (Land, Sea & Air)	Transport Freight (Land)	Transport Freight (Sea)	Lighting (Domestic)
	mtoe of effective heating	TWh	Billion pass.-km	Billion tonne-km	Billion tonne-km	Billion lumen hours
1300	-	0.9	-	-	-	-
1310	-	0.9	-	-	-	-
1320	-	0.9	-	-	-	-
1330	-	0.9	-	-	-	-
1340	-	0.9	-	-	-	-
1350	-	0.9	-	-	-	-
1360	-	0.8	-	-	-	-
1370	-	0.8	-	-	-	-
1380	-	0.7	-	-	-	-
1390	-	0.7	-	-	-	-
1400	-	0.6	-	-	-	-
1410	-	0.6	-	-	-	-
1420	-	0.6	-	-	-	-
1430	-	0.6	-	-	-	-
1440	-	0.6	-	-	-	-
1450	-	0.6	-	-	-	-
1460	-	0.5	-	-	-	-
1470	-	0.5	-	-	-	-
1480	-	0.5	-	-	-	-
1490	-	0.5	-	-	-	-
1500	0.1	0.5	-	-	-	-
1510	0.1	0.5	-	-	-	-
1520	0.1	0.5	-	-	-	-
1530	0.1	0.5	-	-	-	-
1540	0.1	0.5	-	-	-	-
1550	0.1	0.5	-	-	-	-
1560	0.1	0.6	-	-	0.3	-
1570	0.1	0.6	-	-	0.3	-
1580	0.1	0.6	-	-	0.3	-
1590	0.1	0.6	-	-	0.4	-
1600	0.1	0.6	-	-	0.4	-
1610	0.1	0.6	-	-	0.5	-
1620	0.1	0.6	-	-	0.6	-
1630	0.1	0.7	-	-	0.6	-
1640	0.1	0.7	-	-	0.9	-
1650	0.1	0.7	-	-	1.1	-

Data Appendix

1660	0.1	0.7	-	-	1.3	-
1670	0.2	0.8	-	-	1.6	-
1680	0.2	0.8	-	-	1.8	-
1690	0.2	0.8	-	-	2.0	-
1700	0.3	0.9	-	-	1.9	-
1710	0.2	0.9	-	-	2.0	-
1720	0.3	1.0	-	-	2.2	7
1730	0.3	1.1	-	-	2.3	7
1740	0.7	1.2	-	-	2.6	7
1750	0.4	1.3	-	-	3.3	8
1760	0.4	1.4	-	-	4.0	9
1770	0.6	1.5	0.1	-	4.5	10
1780	0.6	1.7	0.2	-	4.9	12
1790	0.6	1.9	0.6	0.1	5.4	14
1800	0.8	2.1	1.3	0.1	6.5	18
1810	1.1	2.6	2.5	0.2	8.3	27
1820	1.4	2.9	3.3	0.3	9.0	63
1830	1.6	3.5	3.2	0.3	7.9	111
1840	1.9	4.4	3.6	0.5	9.9	206
1850	2.2	5.2	4.6	1.5	13.0	355
1851	2.2	5.3	4.9	1.6	14.0	393
1852	2.2	5.4	5.0	1.9	14.3	420
1853	2.4	5.5	5.4	2.2	15.3	470
1854	2.4	5.6	5.6	2.6	15.6	481
1855	2.6	5.6	5.9	2.8	15.4	537
1856	2.5	5.7	6.1	3.1	16.6	580
1857	2.5	5.8	6.2	3.3	17.5	619
1858	2.6	5.9	6.3	3.3	17.5	652
1859	2.7	6.0	6.7	3.6	17.8	672
1860	2.8	6.1	6.9	4.1	18.3	752
1861	2.8	6.2	7.0	4.3	19.0	784
1862	2.8	6.3	7.3	4.3	19.7	810
1863	2.9	6.4	7.5	4.8	20.4	886
1864	3.0	6.5	7.9	5.3	21.1	902
1865	3.0	6.5	8.2	5.7	22.4	965
1866	3.1	6.6	8.6	6.3	24.0	1 010
1867	3.2	6.7	8.8	6.8	24.9	1 017
1868	3.2	6.8	8.6	6.8	26.2	1 057
1869	3.3	6.9	9.3	7.2	27.0	1 095
1870	3.4	7.0	9.6	7.8	28.4	1 193
1871	3.5	7.3	10.3	8.8	29.8	1 297
1872	3.6	7.5	10.9	9.3	31.2	1 257
1873	3.7	7.8	11.6	10.0	32.6	1 320

1874	3.8	8.1	12.1	10.1	33.6	1 391
1875	3.9	8.4	12.8	10.7	34.4	1 434
1876	4.0	8.7	13.5	11.1	36.4	1 622
1877	4.1	9.0	14.0	11.4	37.3	1 769
1878	4.3	9.3	14.5	11.3	37.6	1 831
1879	4.5	9.6	14.7	11.7	38.6	2 022
1880	4.5	9.9	15.7	13.2	42.0	2 136
1881	4.6	10.2	16.2	13.8	42.4	2 518
1882	4.7	10.5	16.6	14.5	44.4	2 754
1883	4.8	10.8	17.1	14.9	46.5	3 068
1884	4.9	11.0	17.3	14.8	46.2	3 250
1885	5.1	11.3	17.4	14.8	47.2	3 654
1886	5.2	11.6	17.8	14.8	47.1	3 925
1887	5.4	11.8	18.0	15.8	48.8	4 237
1888	5.5	12.1	18.2	16.5	50.7	4 673
1889	5.5	12.4	18.7	17.5	52.6	5 046
1890	5.6	12.6	19.4	18.4	53.8	5 449
1891	5.7	12.9	19.8	19.2	54.0	6 022
1892	5.8	13.2	20.5	19.6	55.1	6 329
1893	5.8	13.5	21.0	19.0	54.8	6 589
1894	5.9	13.7	21.9	21.4	58.0	6 995
1895	6.1	14.0	22.5	22.4	58.9	7 640
1896	6.1	14.3	23.7	24.3	60.5	8 170
1897	6.2	14.5	24.8	25.9	62.1	8 589
1898	6.3	14.8	25.7	26.7	63.8	9 266
1899	6.4	15.1	26.7	29.6	67.0	10 065
1900	6.5	15.3	28.8	31.0	67.9	10 617
1901	6.5	15.7	29.7	30.9	68.3	10 988
1902	6.6	16.0	30.0	33.0	70.5	11 553
1903	6.7	16.3	30.1	34.0	73.5	11 960
1904	6.8	16.6	30.1	35.1	74.6	12 751
1905	7.0	16.9	28.5	36.6	75.8	13 075
1906	7.1	17.3	30.7	39.4	79.9	13 739
1907	7.2	17.6	32.4	42.1	82.0	14 262
1908	7.4	17.6	33.7	41.1	81.3	14 737
1909	7.5	17.5	34.5	42.4	82.2	15 160
1910	7.6	17.4	39.6	44.4	87.9	16 075
1911	7.8	17.4	45.9	46.0	89.2	17 033
1912	7.9	17.2	48.0	46.5	93.1	18 213
1913	8.1	17.2	52.4	51.3	97.7	19 554
1914	6.6	17.0	59.2	47.0	88.1	20 423
1915	7.1	16.9	58.2	44.1	74.2	20 939
1916	7.5	17.0	63.6	41.0	70.1	21 242

1917	8.0	17.0	63.3	37.5	61.2	21 736
1918	8.4	17.1	60.3	33.7	59.3	22 437
1919	8.9	16.8	64.2	31.3	69.2	23 845
1920	9.4	16.5	83.5	35.4	74.1	25 511
1921	7.7	15.8	84.1	26.4	74.3	23 136
1922	10.4	15.9	82.9	32.5	90.5	23 610
1923	11.4	16.2	89.0	36.5	100.8	24 184
1924	12.2	16.4	96.0	37.3	100.2	25 118
1925	11.8	16.4	100.2	36.4	98.6	25 986
1926	8.2	16.0	98.9	30.1	94.9	27 231
1927	12.7	16.6	105.3	38.4	102.1	28 071
1928	11.7	16.7	112.0	37.1	102.5	29 225
1929	12.6	17.0	118.5	39.5	106.2	31 042
1930	12.1	16.7	121.7	38.2	105.1	32 887
1931	11.5	16.4	114.5	36.2	99.0	34 748
1932	11.4	16.3	111.0	34.2	96.9	36 933
1933	11.5	16.5	108.9	34.8	97.5	39 415
1934	12.3	17.1	112.0	37.5	99.0	43 800
1935	12.8	17.6	116.4	38.5	100.2	49 769
1936	13.4	18.4	122.2	40.9	102.0	57 229
1937	13.9	19.2	127.9	43.2	106.3	64 203
1938	13.9	18.8	130.5	40.3	73.6	70 815
1939	14.8	19.7	130.6	43.6	60.2	72 050
1940	15.5	20.8	118.4	47.5	59.9	72 297
1941	15.5	22.0	127.6	52.8	60.0	78 906
1942	15.4	20.2	123.6	51.9	60.1	77 803
1943	14.9	19.7	126.7	52.8	60.2	78 708
1944	14.3	19.2	128.4	53.0	60.4	89 490
1945	13.6	18.9	152.4	49.9	60.9	97 676
1946	13.7	18.1	154.0	50.4	68.0	120 997
1947	14.0	17.2	161.1	53.2	73.3	124 038
1948	14.0	17.1	169.2	58.8	76.2	139 033
1949	14.2	16.8	181.8	61.9	79.2	143 829
1950	17.3	19.5	196.5	64.0	82.2	155 744
1951	18.1	18.5	203.3	66.8	85.4	169 212
1952	17.8	18.9	255.0	67.2	88.6	171 275
1953	17.9	20.5	258.2	69.0	91.9	179 981
1954	18.5	22.0	263.8	71.0	95.2	195 384
1955	17.8	25.4	271.2	73.0	98.7	210 522
1956	17.9	27.2	274.6	73.0	102.3	225 425
1957	17.2	28.2	274.9	71.0	105.9	233 354
1958	17.8	30.2	287.0	71.0	109.6	247 795
1959	16.8	32.0	305.2	75.0	113.4	262 321

1960	17.5	30.0	311.4	79.0	117.3	282 042
1961	17.0	29.6	323.7	82.0	121.3	300 334
1962	17.7	33.3	327.4	81.0	125.4	329 563
1963	18.1	37.1	333.7	82.0	129.6	355 456
1964	17.0	40.8	362.0	92.0	133.8	366 810
1965	17.8	44.5	369.1	94.0	138.1	388 405
1966	18.2	46.4	387.7	97.0	143.0	395 536
1967	18.3	48.2	398.9	96.0	144.7	399 174
1968	19.2	52.6	404.2	102.0	155.4	420 854
1969	19.9	56.7	411.2	106.0	161.5	439 460
1970	20.2	60.0	416.0	110.0	169.9	449 258
1971	20.3	62.5	431.4	108.0	172.9	461 846
1972	21.3	64.6	444.3	109.0	182.5	477 995
1973	22.3	70.1	463.6	113.0	195.7	510 927
1974	23.8	69.0	454.0	112.0	189.3	494 978
1975	24.5	72.5	452.2	113.0	164.3	491 754
1976	25.0	77.3	468.6	117.0	176.9	496 551
1977	26.4	80.8	477.2	118.0	183.2	505 556
1978	28.2	84.6	490.6	120.0	194.7	513 675
1979	31.5	88.7	486.7	123.0	215.1	534 724
1980	31.6	87.9	509.0	111.0	205.6	506 500
1981	32.4	90.0	512.1	112.0	204.9	491 933
1982	32.4	91.9	523.3	111.0	213.0	475 618
1983	32.8	95.2	529.3	113.0	217.9	476 292
1984	32.4	98.4	551.5	112.9	233.8	480 004
1985	36.0	102.7	561.6	117.9	235.5	493 455
1986	38.0	106.1	584.3	122.4	238.7	501 523
1987	38.7	113.7	619.4	130.3	241.2	529 083
1988	37.8	118.6	652.8	148.2	250.3	533 665
1989	36.5	123.2	698.0	154.8	242.9	535 069
1990	37.4	123.2	704.4	152.2	252.1	533 883
1991	42.0	125.9	695.2	145.0	257.5	527 345
1992	41.2	129.3	692.5	142.0	259.5	508 613
1993	42.8	129.9	689.6	149.0	264.7	497 128
1994	41.5	130.7	697.8	156.7	279.5	474 051
1995	40.9	134.6	702.4	162.6	280.7	472 313
1996	47.4	127.1	713.8	168.9	282.6	528 638
1997	43.7	131.9	726.4	174.4	286.0	563 125
1998	45.1	136.5	733.1	177.3	298.9	591 923
1999	45.5	140.4	735.9	175.7	299.0	611 381
2000	47.2	143.5	737.9	177.4	324.3	724 961

Source: see text

References

Adelman, M.A. (1996) 'Trends in the price and supply of oil' in Simon, J.L. (ed.) *The State of Humanity*. Basil Blackwell. Oxford.

Administrative Council of London (1920) *Electricity Supply 1917–1920*. London County Council. London.

Agrawal, R. and M. Gort (2001) 'First-mover advantage and the speed of competitive entry, 1887–1986.' *Journal of Law and Economics* 4(2) 161–77.

Ahlbrandt, T.S. (2003) 'Hubbert's peak: the impending world oil shortage' (book review). *The Journal of Energy Literature* 8(1) 47–49.

Albert, W. (1972) *The Turnpike Road System in England, 1663–1840*. Cambridge University Press. Cambridge.

Albert, W. (1979) 'Popular opposition to turnpike trusts in early eighteenth century.' *Journal of Transport History* 5(1) 1–17.

Allen, R.C. (1994). 'Agriculture during the industrial revolution' in Floud, M. and D. McCloskey (eds) *The Economic History of Britain since 1700: Vol I (1700–1860)*. Cambridge University Press. Cambridge.

Allen, R.C. (2003) 'Was there a timber crisis in early modern Europe?' in Cavaciocchi, S. (ed.) *Economia e Energia*. Le Monnier. Florence.

Allen, R.C. (2004) 'The Nitrogen Hypothesis and the English Agricultural Revolution: A Biological Analysis.' *Economic History Society Conference*. Royal Holloway. London.

Anderson, D. (1993) 'Energy-efficiency and the economics of pollution abatement.' *Annual Review of Energy and the Environment* 18 291–318.

Anderson, J.L. (1981) 'Climatic change in European economic history.' *Research in Economic History* 6 1–34.

Angerstein, R.R. (2001) *R.R. Angerstein's Illustrated Travel Diary 1753–1755: Industry in England and Wales from a Swedish Perspective*. Science Museum. London.

Appleby, J. (1976) 'Ideology and theory: the tension between political and economic liberalism in seventeenth century England.' *American Historical Review* 81(3) 500–532.

Armstrong, J. (1987) 'The role of coastal shipping in UK Transport.' *Journal of Transport History* 8(2) 164–77.

Arnott, R. (2002) 'Supply side aspects of depletion.' *The Journal of Energy Literature* 8(1) 3–21.

Arthur, W.B. (1989) 'Competing technologies, increasing returns, and lock-in by historical events.' *Economic Journal* 99(394) 116–31.

439

Ashby, E. and M. Anderson (1981) *The Politics of Clean Air*. Oxford. Clarendon Press.

Ashworth, W. (1987). *The History of the British Coal Industry. Vol 5. 1946-1987. The Nationalized Industry*. Clarendon Press. Oxford.

Ayres, R.U. (2005) 'Resources, scarcity, technology and growth' in Simpson, R.D., M.A. Toman and R.U. Ayres (eds) *Scarcity and Growth Revisited: Natural Resources and the Environment in the New Millennium*. Resources for the Future. Washington D.C.

Bagwell, P.S. (1974) *The Transport Revolution from 1770*. B.T. Batsford. London.

Bain, A. (1964) *The Growth of Television Ownership in the UK since the War: A Lognormal Model*. Cambridge University Press. Cambridge.

Baker, P. (1991) *A Model of Household Gas and Electricity Expenditure for the UK: The IFS Simulation Program for Energy Demand (SPEND)*. The Institute for Fiscal Studies. London.

Barbier, E. (2005) *Natural Resources and Economic Development*. Oxford University Press. Oxford.

Barker, T.C. (1989) 'Transport: the survival of the old beside the new' in Mathias, P. and J.A. Davis (eds) *The Industrial Revolutions*. Basil Blackwell. Oxford.

Barker, T. (1995) 'UK energy price elasticities and their implications for long term CO_2 abatement' in Barker, T., P. Ekins. and N. Johnstone. (eds) *Global Warming and Energy Demand*. Routledge. London.

Barnes, D.F. and W.M. Floor (1996) 'Rural energy in developing countries: a challenge for economic development.' *Annual Review of Energy and the Environment* 21 497–530.

Barnett, H. and C. Morse (1963) *Scarcity and Growth*. Resources for the Future. Washington DC.

Barrow, T. (2001) *The Whaling Trade of North-East England 1750–1850*. University of Sunderland Press. Sunderland.

Bastiat, F. (1845) *Sophismes Economiques* (trans. and ed.) A. Goddard. Foundation for Economic Education. Irvington-on-Hudson, N.Y. http://www.econlib.org/library/Bastiat/basSoph.html.

Becker, G.S. (1976) *The Economic Approach to Human Behaviour*. University of Chicago Press. London.

Beenstock, M. and P. Willcocks (1981) 'Energy consumption and economic activity in industrialised countries.' *Energy Economics* 3(4) 225–32.

Berck, P. and M. Roberts (1996) 'Natural resource prices: will they ever turn up?' *Journal of Environmental Economics and Management* 31(1) 65–78.

Berg, M. (1994). 'Factories, workshops and industrial organization' in Floud, M. and D. McCloskey (eds) *The Economic History of Britain since 1700: Vol 1 (1700–1860)*. Cambridge University Press. Cambridge.

Berndt, E.R. and D.O. Wood (1975) 'Technology, prices and the derived demand for energy.' *The Review of Economics and Statistics* 57(3) 259–68.

Beveridge, W. (1894) *Prices and Wages in England: From the Twelfth to the Nineteenth Century.* Longmans, Green and Co. London.

Bikhchandani, S., D. Hirshleifer and I. Welch (1992) 'A theory of fads, fashion, custom, and cultural change as informational cascades.' *Journal of Political Economy* 100(5) 992–1026.

Billington, N.S. (1982) *Building Services Engineering: a Review of its Development.* Pergamon. London.

Binswanger, M. (2001) 'Technological progress and sustainable development: what about the rebound effect?' *Ecological Economics* 36 119–32.

Bogart, D. (2005a) 'Did turnpike trusts increase transportation investment in eighteenth century England?' *Journal of Economic History* 65(2) 439–68.

Bogart, D. (2005b) 'Turnpike trusts and the transportation revolution in 18th century England.' *Explorations in Economic History* 42(4) 479–508.

Boserup, E. (1965) *The Conditions of Agricultural Growth: The Economics of Agrarian Change Under Population Pressure.* London.

Bowers, B. (1969) *R.E.B. Crompton: An Account of his Electrical Work.* HMSO. London.

Bowers, B. (1998) *Lengthening the Day: A History of Lighting Technology.* Oxford University Press. Oxford.

Bowler, C. and P. Brimblecombe (2000) 'Control of air pollution in Manchester prior to the Public Health Act, 1875.' *Environment and History* 6(1) 71–98.

BPP: British Parliamentary Papers (1816) *Reports of the Select Committee Report on the Gas Industry.* Irish University Press. Shannon, Ireland.

BPP: British Parliamentary Papers (1873) *Reports of the Select Committee Report on Dearness and Scarcity of Coal.* Irish University Press. Shannon, Ireland.

BPP: British Parliamentary Papers (1896) *Reports of the Select Committee Report on Petroleum.* Irish University Press. Shannon, Ireland.

BPP: British Parliamentary Papers (1902) *Coal Statistical Tables.* Irish University Press. Shannon, Ireland.

BPP: British Parliamentary Papers (1914) *Mines and Quarries Statistical Tables.* Irish University Press. Shannon, Ireland.

BPP: British Parliamentary Papers (1915) *Statistical Abstract.* Irish University Press. Shannon, Ireland.

BPP: British Parliamentary Papers (1926) *Coal Statistical Tables.* Irish University Press. Shannon, Ireland.

Bright, A.A. (1949) *The Electric Lamp Industry: Technological Change and Economic Development from 1800 to 1947.* Macmillan. London.

Brimblecombe, P. (1987) *The Big Smoke: A History of Air Pollution in London Since Medieval Times.* Methuen. London.

Brookes, L. (1990) 'Energy efficiency and economic fallacies.' *Energy Policy* 20(5) 199–201.

Brown, M.A. (2001) 'Market failures and barriers as a basis for clean energy policies.' *Energy Policy* 29(14) 1197–1207.

Brown, S. (1969) *The Collected Works of Count Rumford, Vol. 2.* Harvard University Press. Harvard, MA.

Buchanan, R.A. (1994) *The Power of the Machine: The Impact of Technology from 1700 to the Present.* Penguin. London.

Buchanan, R.A. (2003) 'Iron shipbuilding on the Thames, 1832–1915: an economic and business history (review)' *Technology and Culture* 44(3) 610–12.

Byatt, I.C.R. (1979) *The British Electrical Industry 1875–1914.* Clarendon Press. Oxford.

Campbell, B.M.S. (2003) 'The uses and exploitation of human power from the thirteenth to the eighteenth century' in Cavaciocchi, S. (ed.) *Economia e Energia.* Le Monnier. Florence.

Carus-Wilson, E.M. (1941) 'An industrial revolution of the thirteenth century.' *Economic History Review* 11 1–18.

Case, R.A.M and J.L. Harley (1958) *Death Rates for Tuberculosis and Selected Respiratory Diseases, 1911–1955.* Institute of Cancer Research. London.

Chartres, J. and G. Turnbull (1983) 'Road transport' in Aldcroft, D. and M. Freeman (eds) *Transport in the Industrial Revolution.* Manchester University Press. Manchester.

Chavas, J.P. and D.W. Bromley (2005) 'Modelling population and resource scarcity in fourteenth century England.' *Journal of Agricultural Economics* 56(2) 217–37.

Chen, X. (1994) 'Substitution of information for energy: conceptual background, realities and limits.' *Energy Policy* 22(1) 15–27.

Chin, A., J. Chinhui and P. Thompson (2004) *Technical Change and the Wage Structure during the Second Industrial Revolution: Evidence from the Merchant Marine, 1865–1912.* Working Paper. University of Houston. Houston, TX.

Church, R. (1987) *The History of the British Coal Industry. Vol 3. 1830–1913.* Clarendon Press. Oxford.

Church, R. (1989) 'Production, employment and labour productivity in the British coalfields, 1830–1913: some reinterpretations.' *Business History* 31 7–27.

Cipolla, C.M. (1962) *The Economic History of World Population.* Pelican Books. London.

Clapp, B.W. (1994). *An Environmental History of Britain since the Industrial Revolution.* Longman Group. London.

Clark, G. (2002) 'Shelter from the storm: housing and the Industrial Revolution, 1550–1909.' *Journal of Economic History* 62(2) 489–511.

Clark, G. (2003) *The Price History of English Agriculture, 1209–1914.* Working Paper. University of California Davis.

Clendinning, A. (2004) *Demons and Domesticity: Women and the English Gas Industry, 1889–1939.* Ashgate. Aldershot.

Coleman, J.S. and A.H. John (1976) *Trade, Government and Economy in Pre-Industrial England.* Weidenfeld and Nicolson. London.

Cowan, R.S. (1983) *More Work for Mother: The Ironies of Household Technology.* Open Basic Books. New York.

Cowan, R. (1990) 'Nuclear power reactors: a study in technological lock in.' *Journal of Economic History* 50 541–67.

Crafts, N.F.R. (2004) 'Steam as a general purpose technology: a growth accounting perspective.' *The Economic Journal* 114(3).

Crompton, G. (2005) 'The tortoise and the economy: inland waterway navigation in international economic history.' *Journal of Transport History* 25(2) 1–21.

Crossley, D.W. (1972) 'The performance of the glass industry in sixteenth-century England.' *Economic History Review* 25(3) 421–33.

Crowley, J.E. (2004) *The Invention of Comfort: Sensibilities and Design in Early Modern Britain and Early America*. John Hopkins University Press. Baltimore & London.

Cullingford, B. (2000) *British Chimney Sweeps: Five Centuries of Chimney Sweeping*. The Book Guild Ltd. Sussex.

Daly, H.E. (1996) *Beyond Growth: The Economics of Sustainable Development*. Beacon Press. Boston MA.

Darby, H.C. (1984) *Domesday England*. Cambridge University Press. Cambridge.

Daunton, M.J (1995) *Progress and Poverty. An Economic and Social History of Britain 1700–1850*. Oxford University Press. Oxford.

Davidson, C. (1986) *A Woman's Work is Never Done: a History of Housework in the British Isles 1650–1950*. Chatto & Windus. London.

Davis, R. (1954) 'English foreign trade 1660–1700.' *Economic History Review* 7 150–166.

Davis, R. (1962) *The Rise of the English Shipping Industry*. Duncan & Charles. Newton Abbot.

DeCanio, S.J. (1993) 'Barriers within firms to energy efficient investments.' *Energy Policy* 21(9) 906–14.

DeCanio, S.J. (1998) 'The "efficiency gap": bureaucratic and organisational barriers to profitable energy savings investments.' *Energy Policy* 26(5) 441–54.

Defoe, D. (1719) *The Life and Strange Surprising Adventures of Robinson Crusoe*. See: http://www.online-literature.com/defoe/crusoe/.

DoT (1992) *GB Transport Statistics (GBTS)*. HMSO. London.

DoT (1996) *GB Transport Statistics (GBTS)*. HMSO. London.

DoT (2002) *GB Transport Statistics (GBTS)*. HMSO. London.

DoT (2003) *GB Transport Statistics (GBTS)*. HMSO. London.

DoT (2006) *GB Transport Statistics (GBTS)*. HMSO. London.

Devine, W. (1983) 'From shaft to wires: historical perspective on electrification.' *Journal of Economic History* 43(2) 347–72.

De Vries, J. (1993) 'Between purchasing power and the world of goods: understanding the household economy in Early Modern Europe' in Brewer, J. and R. Porter (eds) *Consumption and the World of Goods*. Routledge. London.

De Vries, J. (1994) 'The industrial revolution and the Industrious Revolution.' *Journal of Economic History* 54(2) 249–70.

De Vries, J. (2006) 'Industrious Revolution and Economic Growth' in David, P.A. and M. Thomas (eds) *The Economic Future in Historical Perspective.* *Oxford University* Press. Oxford.

Diener, E. and C. Diener (1998) 'The wealth of nations revisited: income and quality of life.' *Social Indicators Research* 36 275–86.

Dingle, A.E. (1982) '"The monster nuisance of all": landowners, alkali manufacturers, and air pollution, 1828–64.' *Economic History Review* 35(4) 529–48.

Dosi, G., C. Freeman, R. Nelson, G. Silverberg and L. Soete (1988) *Technical Change and Economic Theory.* Francis Pinter. London.

Dowell, S. (1965) *History of Taxation and Taxes in England.* Frank Cass. London.

DTI (1991 *Digest of United Kingdom Energy Statistics (DUKES).* HMSO. London.

DTI (1997) *Digest of United Kingdom Energy Statistics (DUKES).* HMSO. London.

DTI (2001) Digest of United Kingdom Energy Statistics (DUKES). HMSO. London.

DTI (2002) *The Energy Report.* HMSO. London.

DTI (2003) *Energy Consumption in the United Kingdom.* HMSO. London.

DTI (2006) *Digest of United Kingdom Energy Statistics (DUKES).* HMSO. London.

Dutton, J.M. and A. Thomas (1984) 'Treating progress functions as a managerial opportunity.' *The Academy of Management Review* 9(1) 235–46.

Dyos, H.J. and D.H. Aldcroft (1969) *British Transport: An Economic Survey from the Seventeenth Century to the Twentieth.* Leicester.

Edwards, P.R. (1983) 'The horse trade in Tudor and Stuart England' in Thompson, F.M.L. (ed.), *Horses in European Economic History.* The British Agricultural History Society. Reading.

Ehrlich, P.R. and A.H. Ehrlich (2004) *One with Nineveh.* Island Press. London.

Electricity Council (1987) *Electricity Supply in the United Kingdom* (4th ed.). The Electricity Council. London.

Epstein, S.R. (1998) 'Craft guilds, apprenticeship, and technological change in pre-industrial Europe.' *Journal of Economic History* 58(3) 684–713.

Epstein, S. (2004) 'Property rights to technical knowledge in pre-modern Europe, 1300–1800.' *American Economic Review* 94(2) 382–7.

Eveleigh, D.J. (2003) *Candle Lighting.* Shire Publications. Princes Risborough.

Eyre, N. (1997) 'Barriers to energy efficiency: more than just market failures.' *Energy and Environment* 8(1) 25–43.

Eyre, N. (2001) 'Carbon reduction in the real world: how the UK will surpass its Kyoto obligations.' *Climate Policy* 1(3) 309–26.

Falkus, M.E. (1967). 'The British gas industry before 1850.' *Economic History Review* 20 494–508.

Falkus, M.E. (1976) 'Lighting in the Dark Ages of English economic history' in D.C. Coleman and A.H. John (eds) *Trade, Government and Economy in Pre-Industrial England*. Weidenfeld and Nicolson. London.

Falkus M.E. (1982) 'The early development of the British Gas Industry, 1790–1815.' *Economic History Review* 35 217–34.

Farmer, D.L. (1969) 'Some livestock price movements in thirteenth-century England.' *Economic History Review* 22 2–3

Farmer, D.L. (1988) 'Prices and wages' in Thirsk, J. (ed.) *The Agrarian History of England and Wales (1042–1250)*. Cambridge University Press. Cambridge.

Finberg, H.P. (1967) *The Agrarian History of England and Wales. Vol. IV (1500–1640)* Cambridge University Press. Cambridge.

Fisher, A.C. (1979) *Resource and Environmental Economics*. Cambridge University Press. Cambridge.

Fitchen, J.F. (1981) 'The problem of ventilation through the ages.' *Technology and Culture* 22(3) 485–511

Flavin, C. and N. Lenssen (1994) *Power Surge: Guide the Coming Energy Revolution*. WW Norton. London and New York.

Flinn, M.W. (1959) 'Timber and the advance of technology.' *Annals of Science* 15 17–29.

Flinn, M.W. (1978) 'Technical change as an escape from resource scarcity: England in the seventeenth and eighteenth century' in Maczak, A. and W.N. Parker (eds) *Natural Resources in European History*. Resources for the Future. Washington, D.C.

Flinn, M.W. (1984) *The History of the British Coal Industry. Vol 2. 1700–1830*. Clarendon Press. Oxford.

Floud, R. and D. McCloskey (2004) *The Economic History of Britain since 1700*. Cambridge University Press. Cambridge.

Flowers, R.J. and R.W. Batterbee (1984) 'Diatom evidence for recent acidification of two Scottish lochs.' *Nature* 305 130–33.

Foreman-Peck, J. (1981) 'The effect of market failure on the British motor industry before 1939.' *Explorations in Economic History* 18(3) 257–89.

Fouquet, R., D. Hawdon, P.J.G. Pearson, C. Robinson and P.G. Stevens (1997) 'The future of UK final user energy demand.' *Energy Policy* 25(2) 231–40.

Fouquet, R. and P.J.G. Pearson (1998) 'A thousand years of energy use in the United Kingdom.' *The Energy Journal* 19(4) 1–41.

Fouquet, R. and P.J.G. Pearson (2003a) 'Five centuries of energy prices.' *World Economics* 4(3) 93–119.

Fouquet, R. and P.J.G Pearson (2003b) *Long-run trends in Energy Services: The Price and Use of Road and Rail Transport in the UK (1300–2000)*. Proceedings of the BIEE Conference. St John's College, Oxford.

Fouquet, R. and P.J.G. Pearson (2006) 'Seven centuries of lighting services in the United Kingdom.' *The Energy Journal* 27(1) 139–77.

Frank, R.H. (2001) *Luxury Fever: Why Money Fails to Satisfy in an Era of Excess*. Free Press. New York.

Freeman, C. and F. Louçã (2001) *As Time Goes by: from the Industrial Revolutions to the Information Revolution.* Oxford University Press. Oxford.

Freeman, M.J. (1980) 'Road transport in the English Industrial Revolution: an interim reassessment.' *Journal of Historical Geography* 6(1) 17–28.

Freudenberger, H. and G. Cummins (1976) 'Health, work and leisure before the Industrial Revolution.' *Explorations in Economic History* 13(1) 1–12.

Fri, R. (2003) 'The role of knowledge: technological innovation in the energy system.' *The Energy Journal* 24(4) 51–74.

Galbraith, J.K. (1970) *The Affluent Society.* Penguin Books. Harmondsworth.

Galloway, J.A., D. Keene and M. Murphy (1996) 'Fuelling the city: production and distribution of firewood in London's region, 1290–1400.' *Economic History Review* 49(3) 447–72.

Geels, F.W. (2002) 'Technological transitions as evolutionary reconfiguration processes: A multi-level perspective and a case-study.' *Research Policy* 31(8/9) 1257–74.

Geels, F.W. (2005a) 'The dynamics of transitions in socio-technical systems: a multi-level analysis of the transition pathway from horse-drawn carriages to automobiles (1860–1930).' *Technology Analysis & Strategic Management* 17(4) 445–76.

Geels, F.W. (2005b) *Technological Transitions and System Innovations.* Edward Elgar. Cheltenham, UK and Northampton, MA, USA.

Geller, H. (2003) *Energy Revolution: Policies for a Sustainable Future.* Island Press. Washington DC.

Gerhold, D. (1993) 'Packhorses and wheeled vehicles in England, 1550–1800.' *Journal of Transport History* 14 1–26.

Gerhold, D. (1996) 'Productivity change in road transport before and after turnpiking, 1690–1840.' *Economic History Review* 49(3) 491–515.

Gledhill, D. (1999). *Gas Lighting.* Shire Publications. Princes Risborough.

Godfrey, E.S. (1975) *The Development of English Glassmaking, 1560–1640.* Clarendon Press. Oxford.

Gould, S.J. (2002) *The Structure of Evolutionary Theory.* Harvard University Press. Cambridge, MA.

Greening, A., D.L. Greene, and C. Difiglio (2000). 'Energy efficiency and consumption – the rebound effect – survey.' *Energy Policy* 28(6/7) 389–401.

Griffin, J.M. (1993) 'Methodological advances in energy modelling: 1970 1990.' *The Energy Journal* 14(1) 111–24.

Griffin, J.M. and P.R. Gregory (1976) 'An inter-country translog model of energy substitution responses.' *American Economic Review* 66(12) 845–57.

Griliches, Z. (1957) 'Hybrid corn: an exploration in the economics of technological change.' *Econometrica* 48 501–22.

Grossman, G.M. and A.B. Krueger (1995) 'Economic growth and the environment.' *Quarterly Journal of Economics* 112 353–378.

Grubb, M. (1990) 'Energy efficiency and economic fallacies.' *Energy Policy* 18(4) 483–5.

Grübler, A. (1998) *Technology and Global Change*. Cambridge University Press. Cambridge.

Grübler, A., N. Nakicenovic and D.G. Victor (1999) 'Dynamics of energy technologies and global change.' *Energy Policy* 27 247–80.

Hamilton, E.J. (1942) 'Sir William Beveridge's price history: prices and wages in England from the twelfth to the nineteenth century, Vol. I.' *The Economic Journal* 52 (205) 54–58.

Hammersley, G. (1973) 'The charcoal industry and its fuel 1540–1750.' *Economic History Review* 26 593–613.

Hannah, L. (1979). *Electricity Before Nationalisation*. Cambridge University Press. Cambridge.

Hannah, L. (1982) *Engineers, Managers and Politicians*. Macmillan. London.

Harley, C.K. (1988) 'Ocean freight rates and productivity, 1740–1913: the primacy of mechanical invention reaffirmed.' *Journal of Economic History* 48(4) 851–76.

Harris, J.R. (1976) 'Skills, coal and British industry in the eighteenth century.' *History* 61(202) 167–82.

Hart, H.W. (1960) 'Some notes on coach travel.' *Journal of Transport History* 4(3) 146–60.

Harvey, A. and P. Marshall (1991) 'Inter-fuel substitution, technical change and the Demand for Energy in the UK Economy.' *Applied Economics* 23 1077–86.

Hassan, J. (1997) *The Powers of Darkness Prevailed: Air Pollution in Nineteenth Century Manchester*. Mimeograph. University of Manchester Metropolitan. Manchester.

Hassett, K.A. and G.E. Metcalf (1993) 'Energy conservation investment: do consumers discount the future correctly?' *Energy Policy* 21(6) 710–6.

Hatcher, J. (1977) *Plagues, Population and the English Economy 1348–1530*. Macmillan. London.

Hatcher, J. (1993) *The History of the British Coal Industry. Volume I*. Oxford: Clarendon Press.

Hatcher, J. (2003) 'The emergence of a mineral-based energy economy in England, c.1550–c.1850' in Cavaciocchi, S. (ed.) *Economia e Energia*. Le Monnier. Florence.

Hausman, W.J. (1996) 'Long-term trends in energy prices' in Simon, J.L. (ed.) *The State of Humanity*. Basil Blackwell. Oxford.

Hawke, G.R. (1970) *Railways and Economic Growth in England and Wales (1840–1870)*. Clarendon Press. Oxford.

Hawke, G.R. and J.P.P. Higgins (1981) 'Transport and social overhead capital' in Floud, R. and D. McCloskey (eds) *The Economic History of Britain since 1700*. Cambridge University Press. Cambridge.

Headrick, D.R. (2000) *When Information Came of Age: Technologies of Knowledge in the Age of Reason and Revolution, 1700–1850*. Oxford University Press. Oxford.

Hellen, H.E. (1988) *The Agrarian History of England and Wales. Vol. II (1042–1350)* Cambridge University Press.

Herring, H. (2000) 'Is energy efficiency environmentally friendly?' *Energy and Environment* 11(3) 313–25.

Hipkins, S. and S.F. Watts (1996) 'Estimates of air pollution in York: 1381–1891.' *Environment and History* 2 337–45.

Hochschild, A. (1998) *King Leopold's Ghost*. Macmillan. London.

Holt, R. (1988) *The Mills of Medieval England*. Basil Blackwell. Oxford.

Hope, R. (1990) *A New History of British Shipping*. John Murray. London.

Horrell, S. (2003) 'The wonderful usefulness of history.' *The Economic Journal* 113(2) F180–F186.

Humphrey, W. and J. Stanislaw (1979). 'Economic growth and energy consumption in the UK, 1700–1975.' *Energy Policy* 7(1) 29–42.

Humphries, J. (2006) 'English apprenticeship: a neglected factor in the First Industrial Revolution' in David, P.A. and M. Thomas (eds) *The Economic Future in Historical Perspective*. Oxford University Press. Oxford.

Hunt, L.C., G. Judge and Y. Ninomiya (2003) 'Modelling underlying energy demand trends' in Hunt, L.C. (ed.) *Energy in a Competitive Market: Essays in Honour of Colin Robinson*. Edward Elgar. Cheltenham, UK and Northampton, MA, USA.

Hunt, L.C. and N. Manning (1989) 'Energy price- and income-elasticities of demand: some estimates for the UK using the cointegration procedure.' *Scottish Journal of Political Economy* 36(2) 183–93.

Hyde, C.K. (1973) 'The adoption of coke-smelting by the British iron industry, 1709–1790.' *Explorations in Economic History* 10 400–407.

Institute of Petroleum (1994) *UK Petrol Prices (1902–1993)*. Library & Information Service. Institute of Petroleum. London.

IEA (2004) *Oil Crises and Climate Challenges: 30 Years of Energy Use in IEA Countries*. International Energy Agency. Paris.

Jackman, W.T. (1960) *The Development of Transportation in Modern England*. Frank Cass. London.

Jackson, G. (1976) *The British Whaling Trade*. A & C Black Ltd. London.

Jaffe, A.B. and R.N. Stavins (1994) 'The energy efficiency gap: what does it mean?' *Energy Policy* 22(1) 804–10.

Jansson, J.O. (2006) *The Economics of Services*. Edward Elgar. Cheltenham, UK and Northampton, MA, USA.

Jenner, M. (1995) 'The politics of London air: John Evelyn's Fumifugium and the Restoration.' *The Historic Journal* 38(3) 535–51.

Jevons, W.S. (1865) *The Coal Question*. Macmillan. London.

Johansson, O., D.W. Pearce and D. Maddison (1996) *Blueprint 5: The True Cost of Transport*. Earthscan. London.

Jones, C.L. (1989) 'Coal, gas and electricity' in R. Pope (ed.) *Atlas of British Economic and Social History since 1700*. Routledge. London.

Jones, E.T. (2000) 'River navigation in Medieval England.' *Journal of Historical Geography* 26(1) 60–82.

Judson, R., R. Schmalensee and T. Stoker (1999) 'Economic development and the structure of the demand for commercial energy.' *The Energy Journal* 20(2) 29–58.

Jupp, P. (2006) *The Governing of Britain, 1688–1848*. Routledge. London.

Kahneman, D. (1999) 'Objective happiness' in Kahneman, D., E. Diener and N. Schwarz (eds) *Wellbeing: the Foundations of Hedonic Psychology*. Russell Sage. New York.

Kander, A. (2005) 'Baumol's disease and dematerialisation of the economy.' *Ecological Economics* 55 119–30.

Kanefsky, J.W. (1979a) *The Diffusion of Power Technology in British Industry, 1760–1870*. PhD Thesis. University of Exeter.

Kanefsky, J.W. (1979b) 'Motive Power in the British Industry and the Accuracy of the 1870 Factory Return.' *Economic History Review* 32(3) 360–75.

Kasser, T. (2002) *The High Price of Materialism*. MIT Press. Cambridge, MA.

Keohane, N.O., R.L. Revesz and R.N. Stavins (1998) 'The choice of regulatory instruments in environmental policy.' *Harvard Environmental Law Review* 22 313–67.

Keynes, J.M. (1931) 'Essays in persuasion' in *Economic Possibilities for Our Grandchildren*. Macmillan. London.

Khazzoom, J.D. (1980) 'Economic implications of mandated efficiency standards for household applicances.' *The Energy Journal* 1(4) 21–39.

Khazzoom, J.D. (1987) 'Energy savings resulting from the adoption of more efficient appliances.' *The Energy Journal* 8(4) 85–9.

King, A.L. (1952) 'Statistics relating to the petroleum industry, with particular reference to the United Kingdom.' *Journal of the Royal Statistical Society* 115(4) 534–65.

King, P. (2005) 'The production and consumption of bar iron in early modern England and Wales.' *Economic History Review* 58(1) 1–33.

Kohn, M. (2001) *The Cost of Transportation Pre-Industrial Europe*. Working Paper 01–02. Dartmouth College. Hannover, NH.

Krausmann, F., H. Schandl and N.B. Schulz (2003) *Long Term Industrial Transformation: A Comparative Study on the Development of Social Metabolism and Land Use in Austria and the United Kingdom 1830–2000*. IFF Social Ecology (Social Ecology Working Paper; 70). Vienna.

Krautkraemer, J.A. (1998) 'Nonrenewable resource scarcity.' *Journal of Economic Literature* 36(3) 2065–107.

Krautkraemer, J.A. (2005) 'Economics of scarcity: the state of the debate' in R.D. Simpson, M.A. Toman and R.U. Ayres (eds) *Scarcity and Growth Revisited: Natural Resources and the Environment in the New Millennium*. Resources for the Future. Washington D.C.

Lancaster, K.J. (1971) *Consumer Demand. A New Approach*. Columbia University Press. New York.

Landers, J. (2003) *The Field and the Forge: Population, Production and Power in the Preindustrial West*. Oxford University Press. Oxford.

Landes, D.S. (1969) *The Unbound Prometheus: Technological Change and Development in Western Europe from 1750 to the Present.* Cambridge University Press. Cambridge.

Langdon, J. (1982) 'The economics of horses and oxen in Medieval England.' *Agricultural History Review* 30(1) 31–40.

Langdon, J. (1986) *Horses, Oxen and Technological Innovation: the Use of Draught Animals in English Farming from 1066 to 1500.* Cambridge University Press. Cambridge.

Langdon, J. (1991) 'Watermills and windmills in the west midlands, 1086–1500.' *Economic History Review* 44 424–44.

Langdon, J. (2003) 'The use of animal power from 1200 to 1800' in Cavaciocchi, S. (ed.) *Economia e Energia.* Le Monnier. Florence.

Langdon, J. (2005) *Mills in the Medieval Economy: England 1300–1540.* Oxford University Press. Oxford.

Langdon, J. (2006) 'Power in the Medieval Economy.' Personal Communication.

Layard, R. (2004) *Happiness: Lesson from a New Science.* Allen Lane. London.

Leach, G. (1992) 'The energy transition.' *Energy Policy* 20(2) 117–23.

Lebergott, S. (1988) *Pursuing Happiness.* Princeton University Press. Hartford, NJ.

Leunig, T. (2006) 'Time is money: a re-assessment of the passenger social savings from Victorian British railways.' *Journal of Economic History* 66(3) 635–73.

Lovins, A.B. (1988) 'Energy saving from more efficient appliances: another view.' *The Energy Journal* 9 155–62.

Lomborg, B. (2001) *The Skeptical Environmentalist: Measuring the Real State of the World.* Cambridge University Press. Cambridge.

Lutzenhiser, L. and E. Shove (1999) 'Contracting knowledge: the organizational limits to interdisciplinary energy research and development in the US and the UK.' *Energy Policy* 27(4) 217–27.

Machin, R. (1977) 'The great rebuilding: a reassessment.' *Past and Present* 77 33–56.

Mackerron, G. (1996) 'What can we learn from the British nuclear power experience' in Mackerron, G. and P.J.G. Pearson (eds) *The UK Energy Experience: a Model or a Warning?* Imperial College Press. London.

MacLeod, C. (1986) *Inventing the Industrial Revolution: The English Patent System, 1660–1800.* Cambridge University Press. Cambridge.

MacNeil, W.H. (1982) *The Pursuit of Power.* Oxford University Press. Oxford.

Maddison, D. and M. Gaarder (2002) 'Quantifying and valuing life expectancy canges due to air pollution in developing countries' in Pearce, D.W., C. Pearce and C. Palmer (eds) *Valuing the Environment in Developing Countries: Case Studies.* Edward Elgar. Cheltenham, UK and Northampton, MA, USA.

Manning, D.N. (1988) 'Household demand for energy in the UK.' *Energy Economics* 10 59–78.

Mansfield, E. (1968) *Industrial Research and Technological Innovation.* Norton. New York.

Marshall, A. (1949) *Principles of Economics*. Ninth Edition. Macmillan. London.

Martin, J.M. (1988) 'L'intensité énergétique de l'activité économique dans les pays industrialisés: les évolutions de trés longues periode livrent-elles des enseignements utiles?' *Economie et Societé*. Cahiers de l'ISMEA.

Mason, R.S. (1981) *Conspicuous Consumption: A Study of Exceptional Consumer Behaviour*. St Martin's Press. New York.

Masschaele, J. (1993) 'Transport costs in medieval England.' *Economic History Review* 46(2) 266–79.

McConnell, K.E. (1997) 'Income and the demand for environmental quality.' *Environment and Developmental Economics* 2(4) 383–99.

McKee, M. (2005) 'Space tourists aim for dark side of the Moon.' *The New Scientist* 11 August.

McKendrick, N., J. Brewer and J.H. Plumb (1982) *The Birth of a Consumer Society: The Commercialization of Eighteenth-Century England*. Europa Publications. London.

Meadows, C.A. (2001) *Discovering Oil Lamps*. Shire Publications. Princes Risborough.

Meadows, D.H. (1992) *Beyond the Limits: Global Collapse or a Sustainable Future*. Earthscan. London.

Medlock III, K.B. and R. Soligo (2001) 'Economic development and end-use energy demand.' *The Energy Journal* 22(2) 77–105.

Menard, R.R. (1991) 'Transport costs and long-range trade, 1300–1800: was there a European "transport revolution" in the early modern era?' in Tracy J.D. (ed.) *The Political Economy of Merchant Empires: State Power and World Trade 1350–1750*. Cambridge University Press. Cambridge.

Met Office (2006) *Monthly Mean Central England Temperatures. 1659–2006.* http://www.metoffice.com/education/about/contact/acadresearch.html.

Micklewright, J. (1989) 'Towards a household model of UK domestic energy demand.' *Energy Policy* 17 264–76.

Mill, J.S. (1909). *Principles of Political Economy with some of their Applications to Social Philosophy. Book V.* Longmans, Green and Co. 7th ed. London.

Miller, K. (1993a) *Domestic Sector Energy Model*. Report for Economics and Statistics Branch. Department of Trade and Industry. London.

Miller, K. (1993b) *Transport Sector Energy Model*. Report for Economics and Statistics Branch. Department of Trade and Industry. London.

Mills, E. (2002) 'The $230-billion global lighting energy bill.' *Proceedings of the Fifth European Conference on Energy-Efficient Lighting*. International Association for Energy-Efficient Lighting. Stockholm.

MoFP: Ministry of Fuel and Power (1951) *Statistical Digest 1950*. HMSO. London.

MoP: Ministry of Power (1961) *Statistical Digest*. HMSO. London.

Mitchell, B.R. (1984) *Economic Development of the British Coal Industry 1800–1914*. Cambridge University Press. Cambridge.

Mitchell, B.R. (1988) *British Historical Statistics*. Cambridge University Press. Cambridge.

Mohammed, S.I.S. and J.G. Williamson (2004) 'Freight rates and productivity gains in British tramp shipping 1869–1950.' *Explorations in Economic History* 41(2) 172–203.

Mokyr, J. (1990) *Levers of Riches: Technological Creativity and Economic Progress.* Oxford University Press. Oxford.

Mokyr, J. (2000) 'Why "more work for mother?" Knowledge and household behavior, 1870–1945.' *Journal of Economic History* 60(1) 1–41.

Mokyr, J. (2004) *Gifts of Athena.* Princeton University Press. Princeton, NJ.

Monier-Williams, R. (1973) *The Tallow Chandlers of London, Vol. 3: The Guild Catholic.* Kaye & Ward. London.

Mosley, S. (2001) *The Chimney of the World: A History of Smoke Pollution in Victorian and Edwardian Manchester.* The White Horse Press. Brighton.

Mott, R.A. (1983) *Henry Cort: The Great Refine.* The Metals Society. London.

Munby, D.L. (1978). *Inland Transport Statistics: Great Britain, 1900–70. Vol. I.* (edited and completed by A.H. Watson). Clarendon Press. Oxford.

Munro, A. (2006) *Luxury and Ultra-Luxury Consumption in Later Medieval and Early Modern European Dress: Relative and 'Real' Values of Woollen Textiles in the Low Countries and England, 1330–1570.* Working Paper 28. Department of Economics, University of Toronto. Toronto.

Musson, A.E. (1976) 'Industrial motive power in Britain 1800–70.' *Economic History Review* 29 415–39.

Musson, A.E. (1979) *The Growth of British Industry.* Homes & Meier. London.

Nef, J.U. (1926) *The Rise of the British Coal Industry. Volume I–II.* London: Routledge and Sons.

Neha, K. and F. Plassmann (2004) 'The demand for environmental quality and the environmental Kuznets Curve hypothesis.' *Ecological Economics* 51(3) 225–36.

Newbery, D.M. (1996) 'The restructuring of UK energy industries: what have we learned?' in MacKerron, G. and P.J.G. Pearson (eds) *The UK Energy Experience: A Model or a Warning?* Imperial College Press. London.

Newell, E. (1997) 'Atmospheric pollution and the British copper industry, 1690–1920.' *Technology and Culture* 38(3) 655–89.

Newell, R.G., A.B. Jaffe and R.N. Stavins (1998) *The Induced Innovation Hypothesis and Energy Saving Technological Change.* NBER Working Paper 6437. Cambridge, MA.

Newman, J. (2003) *A Short History of Price's Patent Candle Company Ltd.* Personal Communication.

Nordhaus, W. D. (1997) 'Do real output and real wage measures capture reality? The history of lighting suggests not' in Breshnahan, T.F. and R. Gordon (eds.) *The Economics of New Goods.* Chicago University Press. Chicago.

North, D.C. (2005) *Understanding the Process of Economic Change.* Princeton University Press. Princeton, NJ and Oxford.

Nye, D.E. (1998) *Consuming Power: A Social History of American Energies.* MIT Press. Cambridge, MA.

O'Dea, W.T. (1958) *The Social History of Lighting*. Routledge & Kegan Paul Ltd. London.

Offer, A. (2006) *The Challenge of Affluence: Self-Control and Well-Being in the United States and Britain since 1950*. Oxford University Press. Oxford.

Officer, L.H. (2007a) *What Was the U.K. GDP Then?* MeasuringWorth.com.

Officer, L.H. (2007b) *Purchasing Power of British Pounds from 1264 to 2006*. MeasuringWorth.com.

ONS: Office of National Statistics (2002a) *Social Trends*. London: HMSO.

ONS: Office of National Statistics (2002b) *Water Freight in the United Kingdom 2001*. HMSO. London.

Oswald, A.J. (1997) 'Happiness and economic performance.' *The Economic Journal* 107 1815–31.

Overton, M. (1996) *The Agricultural Revolution in England*. Cambridge University Press. Cambridge.

Palmer, J. and B. Boardman (1998) *DELight*. Environmental Change Unit. University of Oxford. Oxford.

Panayotou, T. (1997) 'Demystifying the environmental Kuznets curve: turning a black box into policy tool.' *Environment and Development Economic* 2 465–84.

Pawson, E. (1977) *Transport and Economy: The Turnpike Road of Eighteenth Century Britain*. Academic Press. New York.

Pawson, E. (1984) 'Debates in transport history: popular opposition to turnpike trusts?' *Journal of Transport History* 5(2) 57–65.

Pearce, D.W. (2005) 'Environmental policy as a tool for sustainability' in Simpson, R.D., M.A. Toman and R.U. Ayres (eds) *Scarcity and Growth Revisited: Natural Resources and the Environment in the New Millennium*. Resources for the Future. Washington D.C.

Pearce, D.W. and T. Cowards (1995) *Assessing Health Costs of Particulate Air Pollution in the UK*. CSERGE Working Paper GEC 95–27. Centre for Social and Economic Research on the Global Environment. University of East Anglia and University College London.

Pearson, P.J.G. (1988) *Energy Transitions in Less-Developed Countries*. Cambridge University Energy Research Group Discussion Paper. No.40. Cambridge.

Pearson, P.J.G. (1994) 'Energy, externalities and environmental quality: will development cure the ills it creates?' *Energy Studies Review* 6(3) 199–216.

Pearson, P.J.G. and R. Fouquet (2003) 'Long run carbon dioxide emissions and Kuznets curves: pathways to development' in Hunt, L.C. (ed.) *Energy in a Competitive Market*. Edward Elgar. Cheltenham, UK and Northampton, MA, USA.

Petersen, C. (1995) *Bread and the British Economy c.1770–1870*. Scolar Press. Aldershot.

Phelps-Brown, H. and S.V. Hopkins (1956) 'Seven centuries of the prices of consumables, compared with builders' wage-rates.' *Economica* 23 92–110.

Pindyck, R.S. (1979) 'Interfuel substitution and the industrial demand for energy: an international comparison.' *Review of Economics and Statistics* 61(2) 169–79.

Pindyck, R.S. (1999) 'The long run evolution of energy prices.' *The Energy Journal* 20(2) 1–28.

Pollard, S. (1980) 'A new estimate of British coal production, 1750–1850.' *Economic History Review* 33(2) 212–35

Pope, R. (1989) *Atlas of British Economic and Social History since 1700.* Routledge. London.

Rackham, O. (1980). *Ancient Woodlands: Its History, Vegetation and Uses in England.* Edward Arnold. London.

Rappaport, S. (1989) *Worlds Within Worlds: Structure of Life in Sixteenth Century London.* Cambridge University Press. Cambridge.

Ray, G. (1979) 'Energy economics – a random walk in history.' *Energy Economics* 1(3) 139–43.

Ray, G. (1983) 'Energy and the long cycles.' *Energy Economics* 5(1) 3–8.

Reddy A.K.N. (1991) 'Barriers to improvements in energy efficiency.' *Energy Policy* 19(10) 953–61.

Registrar General (1992) *Mortality Statistics: Serial Tables, Review of the Registrar General on Deaths in England and Wales, 1841–1990.* HMSO. London.

Reynolds, T.S. (1983) *Stronger than a Hundred Men: a History of the Vertical Water Wheel.* John Hopkins University Press. London.

Rifkin, J. (2002) *The Hydrogen Economy: The Creation of the Worldwide Energy Web and the Redistribution of Power on Earth.* Polity Press. Cambridge.

Robinson, C. (1991) 'Coal liberalisation: retrospect and prospect' in Pearson, P.J.G. (ed.) *Prospects for British Coal.* Macmillan. London.

Roche, D. (2001) *A History of Everyday Things: The Birth of Consumption in France, 1600–1800.* Cambridge University Press. Cambridge.

Rogers J.E.T. (1865, 1882, 1886) *A History of Agriculture and Prices in England. Vol. I–VI.* Clarendon Press. Oxford.

Rogner, H.H. (1997) 'An assessment and technologies of world hydrocarbon resource.' *Annual Review of Energy and the Environment* 22 217–62.

Romm, J. (2006) 'The car of the future.' *Energy Policy* 34(17) 2609–14.

Rosenberg, N. (1994) *Exploring the Black Box: Technology, Economics and History.* Cambridge University Press. Cambridge.

Rosenberg, N. (1998) 'The role of electricity in industrial development.' *The Energy Journal* 19(2) 7–24.

Rowthorn, R. and K. Coutts (2004) 'De-industrialisation and the balance of payments in advanced economies.' *Cambridge Journal of Economics* 28(5) 767–90.

Sahlins, M. (1972) *Stone-Age Economics.* Atherton. Chicago, Ill.

Sarkar, J. (1998) 'Technological diffusion: alternative theories and historical evidence.' *Journal of Economic Surveys* 12(2) 131–76.

Saunders, H. (1992) 'The Khazzoon-Brookes postulate and neoclassical growth.' *The Energy Journal* 13(4) 131–48.

Schipper, L. and S. Meyers (1992). *Energy Efficiency and Human Activity.* Cambridge University Press. Cambridge.

Schivelbusch, W. (1988) *Disenchanted Night: The Industrialization of Light in the Nineteenth Century.* Berg. Oxford.

Schurr, S. and Netschert, B. (1960) *Energy in the American Economy, 1850 1975.* John Hopkins Press. Baltimore, MD.

Shove, E. (1998) 'Gaps, barriers and conceptual chasms: theories of technology transfer and energy in buildings.' *Energy Policy* 26(15) 1105–112.

Simmons, I.G. (1993) *Environmental History: A Concise Introduction.* Basil Blackwell. Oxford.

Simon, J.L. (1996) *The State of Humanity.* Basil Blackwell. Oxford.

Slade, M.E. (1982) 'Trends in natural resource commodity prices: an analysis of the time domain.' *Journal of Environmental Economics and Management* 9(2) 122–37.

Smil, V. (1994) *Energy in World History.* Westview Press. Boulder, CO.

Smil, V. (1999) *Energies: an Illustrated Guide to the Biosphere and Civilization.* MIT Press. Cambridge, MA.

Smith, A. (1776) *An Inquiry into the Nature and Causes of the Wealth of Nations, Four vols.* Edinburgh. http://www.adamsmith.org/smith/won-intro.htm.

Smith, J.B. (1978) 'Measuring natural resource scarcity.' *Journal of Environmental Economics and Management* 5(2), 150–71.

Snooks, G.B. (1994) *Was The Industrial Revolution Necessary?* Routledge. London.

Stern, D.I. and C.J. Cleveland (2004) *Energy and Economic Growth.* Rensselaer Working Papers in Economics 410. Department of Economics, Rensselaer Polytechnic Institute. Troy, New York.

Stern, P.C. (1992) 'What psychology knows about energy conservation.' *American Psychologist* 47 1224–32.

Stevens, P.E. (1996) 'The economics of science.' *Journal of Economic Literature* 34(3) 297–306.

Stoneman, P. (2002) *Handbook of the Economics of Innovation and Technological Change.* Basil Blackwell. Oxford.

Supple, B. (1987) *The History of the British Coal Industry. Vol. 4. 1914–1945. The Political Economy of Decline.* Clarendon Press. Oxford.

Surrey, J. (1996) *The British Electricity Experiment.* Earthscan. London.

Sutherland, R.J. (1996) 'The economics of energy conservation policy.' *Energy Policy* 24(4) 361–70.

TeBrake, W.H. (1975) 'Air pollution and fuel crises in pre-industrial London, 1250–1650.' *Technology and Culture* 16(3) 337–59.

The Economist (2002) 'A solid future for lighting.' October 3rd.

Thirsk, J. (1978a) *Economic Policy and Projects: The Development of Consumer Society in Early Modern Britain.* Oxford University Press. Oxford.

Thirsk, J. (1978b) *Horses in Early Modern England: for Services, for Pleasure, for Power.* The British Agricultural History Society. Reading.

Thomas, B. (1986) 'Was there an energy crisis in Great Britain in the 17th century?' *Explorations in Economic History* 23 124–52.

Thompson, E.P. (1967) 'Time, work-discipline and industrial capitalism.' *Past and Present* 38 56–97.

Thompson, F.M.L. (1976) 'Nineteenth century horse-sense.' *Economic History Review* 39(1) 60–81.

Thorsheim, P. (2002) 'The paradox of smokeless fuels: gas, coke and the environment in Britain, 1813–1949.' *Environment and History* 8 381–401.

Tinniswood, A. (2003) *By Permission of Heaven: The Story of the Great Fire of London.* Jonathan Cape. London.

Tol, R.S.J. (2002) 'New estimates of the damage costs of climate change, Part I: benchmark estimates' *Environmental and Resource Economics* 21(1) 47–73.

Toman, M.A. and B. Jamelkova (2003) 'Energy and economic development: an assessment of the state of knowledge.' *The Energy Journal* 24(2) 93–112.

Turvey, R. (2005) 'Horse traction in Victorian London.' *Journal of Transport History* 26(2) 38–59.

UK Intellectual Property Office (2006) *The History of Patents.* http://www.ipo.gov.uk/about/about-ourorg/about-history/about-historypatent.

US Department of Energy (2003) *Energy Savings Potential of Solid State Lighting in General Illumination Applications.* Building Technologies Program, Office of Energy Efficiency and Renewable Energy. U.S. Department of Energy.

Vaitheeswaran, V.V. (2005) *Power to the People: How the Coming Energy Revolution will Transform an Industry, Change Our Lives and Maybe Even Save the Planet.* Earthscan Publications. London.

Veenhoven, R. (1995) 'Developments in satisfaction research.' *Social Indicators Research* 37 1–46.

Verdon, J. (2002) *Night in the Middle Ages.* University of Notre Dame Press. Notre Dame, IN.

von Tunzelmann, G.N. (1978) *Steam Power and British Industrialisation until 1860.* Clarendon Press. Oxford.

von Tunzlemann, G.N. (1995) *Technology and Industrial Progress.* Edward Elgar. Aldershot, UK and Brookfield, US.

Voth, H.J. (1998) 'Time, work in eighteenth century London.' *Journal of Economic History* 58(1) 29–58.

Walsh, C. (2000) 'The advertising and marketing of consumer goods in eighteenth-century England' in C. Wischermann and E. Shore (eds) *Advertising and the European City: Historical Perspectives.* Ashgate. Aldershot.

Walton, G.M (1987) 'Obstacles to technical diffusion in ocean shipping.' *Explorations in Economic History* 8(2) 123–40.

Waverman, L. (1992) 'Econometric modelling of energy demand: when are substitutes good substitutes?' in Hawdon, D. (ed.) *Energy Demand: Evidence and Expectations*. Academic Press. London.

White, L. Jr. (1941) *Medieval Technology and Social Change*. Oxford University Press. Oxford.

Willan, T.S. (1937) 'The river navigation and trade of the Severn Valley, 1600–1750.' *Economic History Review* 8(1) 68–79.

Willan, T.S. (1964) *River Navigation in England, 1600–1750*. Frank Cass. London.

Williams, M. (2004) 'Air pollution and policy, 1952–2002.' Science of the Total Environment 334–335 15–20

Williams R. and D. Edge (1996) 'The social shaping of technology.' *Research Policy* 25 865–99.

Williams, T.I. (1981) *A History of the British Gas Industry*. Oxford University Press. Oxford.

Wilms, W. and E. Mills (1995) 'Analysis of price and non-price factors in the adoption of compact fluorescent lamps by households.' *Light and Engineering* 3(1) 33–43.

Witney, K.P. (1990) 'The woodland economy of Kent, 1066–1348.' *Agricultural History Review* 38 20–39.

Wohl, A.S. (1983) *Endangered Lives: Public Health in Victorian Britain*. Harvard University Press. Cambridge, MA.

Woodcock, D (2002) *Lighting the English Home before Gas and Electricity*. London, Science Museum.

Woolgar, C.M., D. Serjeantson and T. Waldron (2006) *Food in Medieval England: Diet and Nutrition*. Oxford University Press. Oxford.

Wrightson, K. (2000) *Earthly Necessities: Economic Lives in Early Modern Britain*. Yale University Press. New Haven, CT.

Wrigley, E.A. (1962) 'The supply of raw materials in the industrial revolution.' *Economic History Review* 15(1) 1–16.

Wrigley, E.A. (1985) 'Urban growth and agricultural change: England and the Continent in the early modern period.' *Journal of Interdisciplinary History* 15(4) 683–728.

Wrigley, E.A. (1988) *Continuity, Chance and Change: The Character of the Industrial Revolution in England*. Cambridge University Press. Cambridge.

Wrigley, E.A. (1993) 'Reflections on the history of energy supply, living standards, and economic growth.' *Australian Economic History Review* 33(1) 3–21.

Wrigley, E.A. (1994) 'The supply of raw materials in the Industrial Revolution' in Hoppit, J. and E.A. Wrigley (eds) *The Industrial Revolution in Britain*. Basil Blackwell. Oxford.

Wrigley, E.A. and R.S. Schofield (1981) *The Population History of England, 1541–1871: A Reconstruction*. Edward Arnold. London.

Yergin, D.H. (1991) *The Prize: The Epic Quest for Oil, Money & Power*. Simon & Schuster. London.

Authors' Index

Adelman, M.A.25
Administrative Council of London 34,
  400, 409
Agrawal, R. 244
Ahlbrandt, T.S. 351
Albert, W. 145–6
Aldcroft, D.H. 151, 171–2
Allen, R.C. 52, 104, 107, 233
Anderson, D. viii, 120
Anderson, J.L. 69, 192
Anderson, M. 327
Angerstein, R.R. 62–3
Appleby, J. 287
Armstrong, J. 406
Arnott, R. 351
Arthur, W.B. 366
Ashby, E. 327
Ashworth, W. 35, 222
Ayres, R.U. viii, 20, 26, 68

Bagwell, P.S. 150, 170–79, 293
Bain, A. 15
Baker, P. 12
Barbier, E. 363, 373
Barker, T. 11
Barker, T.C. 150, 154
Barnes, D.F. 20–21
Barnett, H. 24
Barrow, T. 199
Bastiat, F. 194–5, 340
Becker, G.S. 8, 36
Beenstock, M. 11
Berck, P. 25
Berg, M. 126
Berndt, E.R. 11
Beveridge, W. ix, 31–3, 389–91, 408
Bikhchandani, S. 14
Billington, N.S. 46, 66, 70–71, 81–8,
  103, 393
Binswanger, M. 19, 278
Boardman, B. 211
Bogart, D. 141–7

Boserup, E. 137
Bowers, B. 193, 201, 206–7, 215–16,
  278
Bowler C. 324
BPP (British Parliamentary Papers) 34,
  176–8, 197, 391, 408, 410
Brewer, J. *see* McKendrick
Bright, A.A. 206
Brimblecombe, P. 57, 302, 307, 322–4
Bromley, D.W. 105, 137
Brookes, L. viii, 19
Brown, M.A. 18
Brown, S. 79
Buchanan, R.A. 117, 126, 248
Byatt, I.C.R. 129, 206–7

Campbell, B.M.S. 102–3
Carus-Wilson, E.M. 50, 111–13
Case, R.A.M. 303
Chartres, J. 148–9, 401–2
Chavas, J.P. 105, 137
Chen, X. 237–8
Chin, A. 248
Chinhui, J. *see* Chin
Church, R. 34–5, 123, 165, 222, 391,
  400, 404
Cipolla, C.M. 4, 7
Clapp, B.W. 324
Clark, G. 32, 68, 105, 398
Clendinning, A. 84
Cleveland, C.J. viii, 7
Coleman, J.S. 333
Coutts, K. 284
Cowan, R. 337
Cowan, R.S. 100
Crafts, N.F.R. 7, 120, 124, 137, 246,
  399
Crompton, G. 140, 147–54, 168, 206
Crossley, D.W. 56
Crowley, J.E. 66–7, 71–9, 253, 286,
  301, 393–4
Cullingford, B. 77, 307

Cummins, G. 109

Daly, H.E. 374
Darby, H.C. 15, 62, 244, 395
Daunton, M.J. 51, 61, 392
Davidson, C. 47–8, 76–85, 100
Davis, R. 161, 407
De Vries, J. 109, 246, 286
DeCanio, S.J. 18
Defoe, D. 1982
Devine, W. 128
Diener, C. 294
Diener, E. 294
Difiglio, C. *see* Greening
Dingle, A.E. 323
Dosi, G. 16
DoT (Department of Transport) 183–4,
    403–7
Dowell, S. 195–6
DTI (Department of Trade and Industry)
    34–8, 68, 88, 97–8, 131–2, 391,
    400–407
Dutton, J.M. 16
Dyos, H.J. 151, 171–2

Edge, D. 17
Edwards, P.R. 106–8, 124, 396–7
Ehrlich, A.H. 6, 293
Ehrlich, P.R. 6, 293
Epstein, S.R. 110, 239–41, 292
Eveleigh, D.J. 192, 196–7, 202
Eyre, N. 18

Falkus, M.E. 198–201
Farmer, D.L. 397
Finberg, H.P. 397
Fisher, A.C. 24
Fitchen, J.F. 72, 301
Flavin, C. 4, 356
Flinn, M.W. 33–5, 52–61, 123, 231,
    390–91
Floor, W.M. 20–21
Floud, R. 29
Foreman-Peck, J. 180
Fouquet, R. 4, 11, 21–5, 33, 230–35,
    317, 350, 377, 392
Frank, R.H. 295
Freeman, C. 119
Freeman, M.J. 150–54
Freeman, R. *see* Dosi
Freudenberger, H. 109
Fri, R. 237–8

Gaarder, M. 302–3

Galbraith, J.K. 297
Galloway, J.A. 49–50, 151, 392
Geels, F.W. 14–17, 205, 366
Geller, H. 4, 356
Gerhold, D. 142–7
Gledhill, D. 201–5
Godfrey, E.S. 55–6
Gort, M. 244
Gould, S.J. 214, 349
Greene, D.L. *see* Greening
Greening, A. 20
Gregory, P.R. 11, 58, 322
Griffin, J.M. 11
Griliches, Z. 15
Grossman, G.M. 319
Grubb, M. 19
Grübler, A. xi, 16, 17, 214

Hamilton, E.J. 31
Hammersley, G. 15, 52–3, 60–61, 392
Hannah, L. 207–10, 400
Harley, C.K. 158, 174, 406
Harley, J.L. 303
Harris, J.R. 240
Hart, H.W. 147–8, 164–6, 401
Harvey, A. 13
Hassan, J. 325–7
Hassett, K.A. 18
Hatcher, J. 6, 29–35, 49–60, 71–78,
    222, 336, 377, 390–94
Hausman, W.J. 25
Hawdon, D. *see* Fouquet
Hawke, G.R. 153,163–4, 188, 403–4
Headrick, D.R. 247
Hellen, H.E. 397
Herring, H. 19
Higgins, J.P.P. 153,163–4, 188, 403–4
Hipkins, S. 58, 323
Hirshleifer, D. *see* Bikhchandani
Hochschild, A. 179
Holt, R. 111–3, 399
Hope, R. 161, 407
Hopkins, S.V. 32–3
Horrell, S. 8
Humphrey, W. 22–3
Humphries, J. 110, 239
Hunt, L.C. viii, 11
Hyde, C.K. 62–6, 247, 291

IEA (International Energy Agency) 180
Institute of Petroleum 405

Jackman, W.T. 15–6, 255, 401

Jackson, G. 197–200, 408–9
Jaffe, A.B. 18
Jamelkova, B. 26
Jansson, J.O. 8
Jenner, M. 58, 322–3
Jevons, W.S. 19, 91–2, 222
Johansson, O. 312
John, A.H. 333
Jones, C.L. 129, 208, 222
Jones, E.T. 151–2
Joskow, P.L. viii
Judge, G. *see* Hunt
Judson, R. 11–12, 22–3
Jupp, P. 333

Kahneman, D. 365
Kanefsky, J.W. 115–28, 395–9
Kasser, T. 295
Keene, D. *see* Galloway
Keohane, N.O. 329
Keynes, J.M. 296
Khazzoom, J.D. 19
King, A.L. 405
King, P. xi, 59–64, 287–92, 392
Kohn, M. 141–5, 151–60
Krausmann, F. xi, 20
Krautkraemer, J.A. 4, 24–5, 230–32
Krueger, A.B. 319

Lancaster, K.J. 36
Landers, J. 100
Landes, D.S. 4–7, 16
Langdon, J. xi, 15, 38, 101–15, 143,
    395–9
Layard, R. 294–5, 383
Leach, G. 20
Lebergott, S. viii, 6, 293, 380
Lenssen, N. 4, 356
Leunig, T. 140–43, 164–7, 278
Lomborg, B. 6, 293
Louça, F. 119
Lovins, A.B. 19
Lutzenhiser, L. 18

Machin, R. 53
Mackerron, G. viii, 318, 337
MacLeod, C. 241–2
MacNeil, W.H. 100
Maddison, D. 314–15
Manning, D.N. 13
Mansfield, E. 15
Marshall, A. 8, 299, 380
Marshall, P. 13
Martin, J.M. viii, 22

Mason, R.S. 287
Masschaele, J. 143–5, 401
McCloskey, D. 29
McConnell, K.E. 322
McKee, M. 358
McKendrick, N. 149, 287–8
Meadows, C.A. 191–204
Meadows, D.H. 6
Medlock III, K.B. 33
Menard, R.R. 158–60, 406
Met Office 69–70
Metcalf, G.E. 18
Meyers, S. 297
Micklewright, J. 12
Mill, J.S. 195
Miller, K. 87
Mills, E. 362
Mitchell, B.R. 29–35, 63–6, 132, 161–
    3, 173–8, 195, 261, 391, 400–410
MoFP (Ministry of Fuel and Power),
    130, 400–410
Mohammed, S.I.S., 172–4, 182, 406
Mokyr, J. 16, 100–102, 110–11, 119,
    162, 243–9, 293, 382
Monier-Williams, R. 192, 198–9
MoP (Ministry of Power) 400–410
Morse, C. 24
Mosley, S. 306, 325–6
Mott, R.A. 62–4
Munby, D.L. 403–4
Munro, A. 66–7, 112
Murphy, M. *see* Galloway
Musson, A.E. 89–91, 110, 115, 127–30,
    392–9

Nakicenovic, N. *see* Grübler
Nef, J.U. 35, 52, 231
Neha, K. 322
Nelson, R. *see* Dosi
Netschert, B. 21–22
Newbery, D. 132, 230, 338
Newell, E. 323
Newell, R.G. 19
Newman, J. xi, 197, 202
Ninomiya, Y. *see* Hunt
Nordhaus, W. D. vii, ix, 5, 26, 36, 40,
    192–6, 199, 205, 235, 259, 293,
    298, 378, 411
North, D.C. 381
Nye, D.E. 296

Offer, A. 296
Officer, L.H. 29–32, 40–41, 68, 261,
    389–91

ONS (Office of National Statistics)
180–82
Oswald, A.J. 294
Overton, M. 104

Panayotou, T. 319
Pawson, E. 146, 150
Pearce, D.W. viii, 26, 304
Pearson, P.J.G. vii–xi, 4, 20–25, 33,
230–35, 317, 322, 377, 392
see also Fouquet
Petersen, C. 102
Phelps-Brown, H. 32–3
Pindyck, R.S. viii, 11, 25
Plassmann, F. 322
Plumb, J.H. *see* McKendrick
Pollard, S. 391
Pope, R. 183

Rackham, O. 34, 48, 52
Rappaport, S. 239
Ray, G. viii, 22
Reddy, A.K.N. 18
Registrar General 302–4
Revesz, R.L. *see* Keohane
Reynolds, T.S. 117
Rifkin, J. 4, 356
Roberts, M. 25
Robinson, C. viii, 222
see also Fouquet
Roche, D. 69–80, 298, 393
Rogers J.E.T. ix, 31–3, 151–2, 389–90,
401, 408
Rogner, H.H. 352
Romm, J. 357
Rosenberg, N. 16, 23, 50, 137
Rowthorn, R. 284

Sahlins, M. 363
Sarkar, J. 15
Saunders, H.
Schandl, H. xi
see also Krausmann
Schipper, L. 297
Schivelbusch, W. 163, 278
Schmalensee, R. viii
see also Judson
Schulz, N.B. *see* Krausmann
Schurr, S. 21–2
Shove, E. 18
Silverberg, G. *see* Dosi
Simmons, I.G. 50
Simon, J.L. 6, 293

Slade, M.E. 37
Smil, V. 4, 16, 62–6, 101–3, 111, 140,
395–402
Smith, A. 67, 109, 195, 287
Smith, J.B. 25
Snooks, G.B. 29, 102, 261, 398
Soete, L. *see* Dosi
Soligo, R. 18
Stanislaw, J. 22–3
Stavins, R.N. 18
see also Keohane
see also Newell, R.G.
Stern, D.I. viii, 7
Stern, P.C. 18
Stevens, P.E 238
Stevens, P.G. viii
see also Fouquet
Stoker, T. *see* Judson
Stoneman, P. 14–15
Supple, B. 35
Surrey, J. 230, 338
Sutherland, R.J. 18

TeBrake, W.H. 50, 57, 104–5, 322
The Economist 215
Thirsk, J. 60, 193, 333–4
Thomas, A. 16
Thomas, B. 52–61
Thompson, E.P. 109
Thompson, F.M.L. 125, 150, 396–401
Thompson, P. *see* Chin
Thorsheim, P. 83–6, 307
Tinniswood, A. 201
Tol, R.S.J. viii 316, 328
Toman, M.A. 26
Turnbull, G. 148–9, 401–2
Turvey, R. 107, 169, 397–8

UK Intellectual Property Office 240–41,
250
US Department of Energy 215

Vaitheeswaran, V.V. 4, 356
Veenhoven, R. 294
Verdon, J. 216
Victor, D.G. *see* Grübler
von Tunzelmann, G.N. 16, 119, 126,
237, 399
Voth, H.J. 102, 109, 124, 398

Walsh, C. 149, 289–90
Walton, G.M. 159–60
Watts, F. 58, 323
Waverman, L. 13

Welch, I. *see* Bikhchandani
White, L. Jr. 15
Willan, T.S. 152–3
Willcocks, P. 11
Williams, R. 17
Williams, M. 327–8
Williams, T.I. 202
Williamson, J.G. 172–4, 182, 406
Wilms, W. 216
Witney, K.P. 52
Wohl, A.S. 323
Wood, D.O. 11
Woodcock, D. 192–5

Subject Index

AA (Automobile Association) 176
Abraham Darby 15, 62
acid rain 94, 311–14, 327–8
advertising 14, 289–96
affluence 67, 364, 380
agriculture 4, 12, 29, 49–50, 101–5,
    233, 269
air temperature 69–70, 392
air travel 182–6, 298, 358
Alkali Act 323
Amoco 224, 229
Anglo-Persian 225, 336
animals *see* horses; oxen
appliances/energy equipment
    adoption 12–14, 389
    cars 175–81
    household 98, 100, 351, 358
    lamps 191–208, 358, 362, 408–11
    price 246
Arkwright, Richard 240
attributes *see* characteristics

back-casting 302, 392
baking 47–51, 392
banks 150
BATNEEC 329
beeswax 192, 198
Bessemer, Henry 89
Big Smog 85, 94, 326
biomass *see* charcoal
Boulton, Matthew 119, 201, 335
BP (British Petroleum) vii, 225–9, 336
bread 47–51, 101–5, 111–15
British National Oil Corporation
    (BNOC) 336
Burmah Oil 336
buses 169–86, 235, 405

calories 103–5, 397
canals, 150–54, 163–71, 188–90, 222
candle tax 196–7
candles 33, 40, 191–216, 408–10
capitalism 362, 386, 456

carbon
    carbon dioxide emissions 316–17
    Global Carbon Reserve 371
    transition to a low carbon economy
    4, 367–70, 386–7
cars
    alternative fuels 175, 259, 357
    data sources 404–5
    developing economies 361
    external costs 176–9, 311–13, 361
    fuel costs 176–81, 235
    growth 175–81, 187, 264,
    mobility 16, 179, 292–4
    price 180
    social status 176, 291
CCGT 132, 230, 311–13, 328
central heating 87–8, 96–9, 235, 264,
    273, 295
characteristics 291–3
charcoal
    characteristics 48–51
    consumption 48–55, 287
    crisis 52–4
    data sources 33–5, 390–92
    iron industry 15, 59–64, 333
    price 52–4
    production 219–20, 333
    transition to coal 51–64, 72–3, 232
chemicals 45, 92, 97, 282, 392, 400
chimneys 72–9, 94–6, 251–4, 264, 276,
    287, 292, 307, 340, 393–4
China 359, 360–61, 373
church 145, 192, 255
Churchill, Winston 336
civil war (English) 74–5, 145, 273
civil war (American) 223
climate change
    extreme 362
    Global Common Reserve 371
    greenhouse gas emissions 316–17
    impact and costs 316–17, 328
    Kyoto Protocol 328–9
    long run perspective 5, 376

past 69–70, 373
policies 329, 343, 367–71
see also carbon
clothing, 66, 111, 286 *see also* textile
  industries
coal
  banning use 322–3
  British Coal 338
  chimney 72–7
  coal industry 51–7, 221–2
  Coal Question 90
  coke 60–66, 86, 307–9
  consumption 51–93, 271–3, 418–22
  decline 89–93, 222
  data sources 33–5, 390–400, 406–7
  electiricty 131–2, 400–401
  external costs 301–16
  health damage 302–4
  miners 78, 122, 222, 341–2
  pollution 57–8, 71–2, 83, 94, 324–8
  pollution policies 57–8, 322–8
  prices 53–4, 74–5, 94–9, 221–3,
    413–6
  production 51–7, 219–22
  railway use 166, 272–3
  smoke 57–8, 71–7
  steam engines 271–81
  technology 242–4, 251–3
  transition from charcoal 51– 64, 72–
    3, 231–3
colleges 31, 390
coke 60–66, 86, 307–9
comfort 4, 67–77, 88, 98, 147, 164,
  183, 202, 264, 270–71, 276–94,
  387, 403
conspicuous consumption 290–91
cooking, 33, 45–8, 71–98, 191–2,
copper 86, 90, 154, 286, 323, 452
Cort, Henry 64, 452
cotton 67, 120–26, 247, 288, 326, 336
cycles
  abundance and scarcity 77–8, 257,
    377–87
  business cycles 206, 367
  competition and concentration 230,
    257, 377–8
  of inequality 297
  of perpetual growth 381–3

Dark Ages, the 363, 445
Davy, Humphrey 206
developing economies 34, 316, 359–62,
  374, 388
devices 99, 110, 131–2, 242–8, 325

Domesday Book 29, 38, 101–2, 111,
  133, 395–8
Durno, John 79
dynamo 128

elasticities 11–13, 26, 75, 115, 266,
  299, 350, 351, 379
electricity
  CCGT (Combined Cycle Gas
    Turbines) 132, 230, 311–2, 328
  CEGB 230, 338
  coal 131–2, 400–401
  consumption 93, 129–131, 271–84,
    400, 420–22, 435–7
  effect on production process 128–9,
    292
  electrification of the economy 23,
    128–37, 267, 278–9, 361–2, 377
  electricity generation 400–401
  external costs 313–5, 327–8
  generation 313–5
  hydropower 132
  network 210, 229–30, 337–8
  nuclear 132, 226, 317–18, 336–7
  pollution *see* external costs
  policies 230, 336–8
  power stations 128–30, 252–3, 327
  price 129–30, 231–7, 415–17, 430–
    33
  supply industry 129–33, 229–30
energy *see* charcoal, coal, coke,
  electricity, gas, hydropower,
  hydrogen, nuclear power, petroleum,
  watermills, wind, windmills
energy crisis
  cycles of abundance and scarcity 77–
    8, 257, 377–87
  Oil Shocks vii, 5, 224–7, 263, 268,
    272–6, 336, 376
  Woodfuel Crisis 52–4
energy demand 11–14, 33, 278, 350 *see
  also* energy service demand
energy efficiency
  barriers 18
  future 330–34
  improvements 17–20, 37, 123–6,
    272–8, 283, 330, 381
  long-run benefits 372
  micro v. macro changes 20
  policies 366–72
  rebound effects 19–20, 263, 271,
    276–9, 366, 379–81
  see also technology
energy modelling viii, 11–13

energy policies
    competition 337–8, 365
    environmental 57–8, 322–30
    nuclear power *see* electricity
    security of supply 335–6
    social 341–2
    sustainable policies 367–71
    taxation 340–41
    technological development 333–5
energy service demand
    beyond basic needs 286–8
    characteristics 291–3
    economic development and 21–3,
        281–4, 359, 379–80
    forecasting 349–50
    energy demand and 11–27, 271–81
    lifestyles and workstyles on 285–6
    saturation and 284–5
energy supply industries
    coal 51–7, 219–22
    electricity 129–33, 229–30
    gas 201–2
    petroleum 203–4, 223–9
    policies 335–8
energy transitions
    coal to petroleum 220–22
    declining efficiency after 73–5, 95–
        6, 135–6, 251–3, 276, 379
    fossil fuels to electricity 128, 207
    studies of viii, 21–3
    woodfuel to coal 51– 64, 72–3, 232
engineers 88–92, 162, 179, 206, 238–
    48, 258–9, 355
Environmental Kuznets Curve (EKC)
    319–21
environmental policies 57–8, 322–30
environmental pollution *see* pollution
ESCOs 8
Evelyn, John 57–8, 322–3, 448
external costs
    cars 311–13
    coal use 301–16
    electricity 313–15
    gas lighting 307–9
    historical benefit transfer 302–3
    long-run trends 315–16
    railways 312
    steam engines 309–11
    valuation method 302–4
externalisation process 319–20, 341,
    383
Exxon 225, 229

Faraday, Michael 128

fodder 107, 133–6, 142, 150, 169, 232–
    5, 251, 266, 269, 272, 275, 279,
    397–404
food *see* bread
forecasting viii, 24–5, 350
forests 34–5, 48–61, 104, 219, 315,
    327, 335
Franklin, Benjamin 79

gas
    CCGT 132, 230, 311–12, 328
    data sources 393–5, 408
    discovery of natural gas 87
    external costs of town gas 307–9
    future reserves 351–2
    heating and 84–8, 368
    pollution reductions 316, 327–31
    price 87, 223
    town gas 83–6, 201–16
gas lighting 201–16, 289, 308, 382
George, Lloyd 176
Germany 90, 222, 224, 225
glass-making 46, 56, 99, 392
Global Carbon Reserve 371
government
    evolving objectives 332, 343
    future influence 364–75, 384–5
    influence on trends 343–5
    infrastructure and 338–9
    past policies 332–42
greenhouse gases 316–17
guilds 109–10, 238–40
Great Fire of London 53, 58, 201, 323

happiness 294–300, 380–83
heating *see* central heating; chimney;
    coal; external costs; gas; hearth;
    insulation; iron; stoves
health 302–4, 341–2
hearth 48, 66, 71–7, 251–3
Hearth tax 340
horses
    costs of provender 107–8, 230–35
    data sources 395–403
    improvements in management of
        101–2
    power provision 101–3, 116–17, 125
    price 106–7
    transport provision 147–50, 168–9
hydrogen 3–4, 323, 368, 387
hydropower 132

Ice Age, Mini 69, 154
Industrial Revolution, the

aided by transition to fossil fuels 233
canals during 153–4
coal and 99
features of 31
Industrious Revolution and 108–10
iron industry during 62–5
price of energy during 232–4
road transport during 145–8
shipping during 160–62
skills and 247–8
steam engines 119–27
technology and 251–3
waterwheels and 117–19
Industrious Revolution, the 108–10,
  149, 286
infrastructure
declines in 142–5, 152
energy system and 5, 353–6
future 352–3
heating services to build 353
government in 338–9
investments in canals 152–3
investments in turnpikes 145–6
transport and 139, 187–9
insulation 46, 67–8, 81, 87–8, 96–7,
  368
internal combustion engine *see* cars
Iran 226–7
Iraq 225–7
Ireland 39
iron
charcoal iron industry 59–64
coke 60–66
energy use 64–6
Israel, 225–6

Japan 224–6

kerosene 202–7, 226–42, 374, 421–3
knowledge
apprentices 109, 239–40
costs of producing 256–7
future loss of 362–3
growth of 256–9
guilds 238–40, 291
'knowledge in a box' 242, 257, 382
patents 240–50, 334–5
R&D 13–14
science 249–50
skills 247–8
Kyoto Protocol 361, 371

lamps 191–208, 358, 362, 408–11
Large Combustion Plant Directive 327

Lawson, Nigel 338
liberalisation 132, 211, 230, 338, 365
lighting *see* electricity; external costs;
  gas lighting; lamps; petroleum
living standards 7, 206, 260, 457
lock-ins 5, 11, 17, 189, 214, 229, 257,
  297, 344, 362, 366, 385, 386
LRTAP 327–8

Malthus, Thomas 137
Manchester 153, 190, 288, 306, 326,
  441–7, 452
manufacturing 23, 31, 84, 89, 90–93,
  108–9, 280–88
market failures 18, 309, 366–70
marketing 17, 83–4, 256, 289–99, 368
McAdam, John 146
metals 22, 55, 90, 97–9, 282–6, 315,
  360, 392
Middle East 224–6
mills 111–19
crushing grain 111–12, 114–15
growth in mills 116, 125
ownership of 112–13
use for textiles 111–15
see also watermills; windmills
military power 73, 100, 106, 148, 224,
  247, 269, 333, 340, 344, 356, 384
mortality rates 22, 58, 105, 261, 322

nationalisation 225
Neilson, James Beaumont 65
networks
canals 152–3
pipelines 181, 221, 352
policies related to 337–9
railways 163
turnpikes 145–6
Newcastle 56, 78, 84, 162, 221, 407
nuclear power 132, 226, 317–18, 336–7

oil *see* petroleum
Oil Shocks 5, 224–7, 263, 268, 272–6,
  336, 376
OPEC 179, 225–7
oxen 101–3, 121, 133, 395–8

paraffin *see* kerosene
patents 15, 201–4, 240–43, 334–7
petroleum
available resources 223–4
British-owned 336
car fuel costs 179
external costs 311–13

future reserves 351–2
Oil Shocks vii, 5, 224–7, 263, 268, 272–6, 336, 376
OPEC 225–7
North Sea oil 225–8
resource ownership 224–7
Standard Oil 204, 228
pipelines 181, 221, 352
policies *see* energy policies; *see* environmental policies
pollution
    Big Smog 85, 94, 326
    carbon dioxide emissions 316–17
    cars 311–13
    coal use 301–16
    electricity 313–15
    gas lighting 307–9
    railways 312
    steam engines 309–11
    externalisation process 319–20, 341, 383
population 20–31
pottery 91, 154, 392
power *see* electricity; external costs; horses; mills; oxen; steam engines
power stations 128–30, 252–3, 327–8
privatisation 35, 132, 222, 230, 328, 384
proto-industrialisation 100, 117

R&D (research and development) 13–14, *see also* knowledge
railways
    introduction 162
    coal use 166, 272–3
    external costs 312
    growth of 167–8, 266–76
    network 163
    price of 162–6
rebound effect 19–20, 263, 271, 276–9, 366, 379–81
revolution
    energy services xi, 3–10, 290, 332, 377–87
    effect on happiness 297
    future 355, 368
    Industrial Revolution of the thirteenth century 111
    lighting 214
    medieval power revolution 111
    retail 288–91
    see also Industrial Revolution; Industrious Revolution
Ricardo, David 228

rivers 150–53
Roman Briton 3
Royal Dutch/Shell 225
rubber 179

sailing ship effect, 16
sailing ships 155–62, 171–3, 252, 273–5
saturation of demand 16, 284–5, 299, 354, 366, 380
Saudi Arabia 225–7
Savery, Thomas, 119
science 244–50, *see also* knowledge
Scotland 39, 51, 57, 65, 78
Shell 229, 336
shelter 46–8, 67–70, 269, 285, 294
shipping 155–62, 171–5
    data sources 406–7
    estimates of freight 160–62, 173–5
    piracy 156–7
    price of 158–9, 174
    risk 157–8
    see also sailing ships; steamships
Siemens, William 87, 89
Smeaton, Joseph 118, 337
Smith, R. Angus 324
smoke *see* pollution
soot 58, 74–7, 306–7, 322
stagecoaches 147–50, 163–4, 172, 188–90, 264–6, 401–3
Standard Oil 204, 227–8
steam engine
    capital costs 119–20
    coal mining industry 123, 126
    coal use 271–81
    cotton industry 123–4
    characteristics of the 121–2
    data sources 398–400
    development of the 119
    external costs 309–11
    running costs 120–21
steamships 171–3, 187, 248, 275
steel 31, 89–97, 131, 172, 260, 315, 359–60
stoves 59–79
Sweden 23, 63, 155, 351

tallow candles 192–216
tankers 221, 352
tax
    Candle tax 196–7
    Hearth tax 340
    Window tax 195, 340
technology

diffusion 14–17, 244–7, 369–70
guilds and 239
innovation 13–17, 378–82
'knowledge in a box' 242, 257, 382
patents 240–50, 334–5
price incentives and 241–3
R&D 13–14
science 249–50
social shaping of technology 17
see also energy efficiency; energy
    transitions; knowledge
textile industries 31, 59–67, 110–38
Thatcher, Margaret 336
tolls 141–57, 188, 338–9
transition to low carbon economy 367–
    70, 386
transport *see* air travel; buses; cars;
    external costs; infrastructure;
    railways; shipping; stagecoaches;
    turpikes
Trevithick, Richard 162
Turkish Petroleum Company 225
turnpikes 145–50

USA 3–5, 15, 21–5, 88, 189, 206, 224–
    8, 329, 358, 375

ventilation 72–81, 237, 301

waggons 146–70
war 74–5, 134, 157–8, 176, 182, 194–5,
    223–7
Watermills
    data sources 399
    growth 111–17
    intermittency 122
    price of waterwheel 118
    provision of power 116, 125
    running costs 118
Watt, James 119–20, 201, 241, 335, 337
whaling 199, 335, 408
wind (for sailing) 155, 160–62, 171–2,
    252–3, 399
Windmills
    crushing grain 121–2
    data sources 399
    introduction 111
    provision of power 116, 125
woodfuel *see* charcoal; energy crisis;
    forests
woodland *see* forests
wool 30, 67, 101–15, 123, 134–7, 149,
    197, 286
worsted 67–71, 124

York 58, 223, 229, 323